INTERTEXTUALITY IN PLINY'S *EPISTLES*

Pliny's *Epistles* are full of literary artistry. This volume of essays by an impressive international team of scholars showcases this by exploring the intertextual, interdiscursive and also intermedial character of the collection. It provides a contribution to the recent scholarly interest in Latin prose intertextuality and in the literary and cultural interactions of the Imperial period. Focusing on the whole collection as well as on single books and selected letters, it investigates Pliny's strategies of incorporating literary models and genres into his epistolary oeuvre, thus creating a kind of 'super-genre' himself. In addition to displaying Pliny's literary techniques, the volume also serves as an advanced introduction to Latin prose poetics.

MARGOT NEGER is Assistant Professor of Latin at the University of Cyprus. She has published monographs on Martial and Pliny the Younger as well as articles and chapters on ancient epigram, epistolography and late antique literature.

SPYRIDON TZOUNAKAS is Associate Professor of Latin and Deputy Dean of the Faculty of Letters at the University of Cyprus. His main research and publications focus on Roman satire, Roman epistolography, Roman epic, Roman elegy, Cicero's orations and Roman intertextuality. He is currently working on a monograph on Persius.

INTERTEXTUALITY IN PLINY'S *EPISTLES*

EDITED BY

MARGOT NEGER
University of Cyprus

SPYRIDON TZOUNAKAS
University of Cyprus

Shaftesbury Road, Cambridge CB2 8EA, United Kingdom

One Liberty Plaza, 20th Floor, New York, NY 10006, USA

477 Williamstown Road, Port Melbourne, VIC 3207, Australia

314–321, 3rd Floor, Plot 3, Splendor Forum, Jasola District Centre, New Delhi – 110025, India

103 Penang Road, #05-06/07, Visioncrest Commercial, Singapore 238467

Cambridge University Press is part of Cambridge University Press & Assessment, a department of the University of Cambridge.

We share the University's mission to contribute to society through the pursuit of education, learning and research at the highest international levels of excellence.

www.cambridge.org
Information on this title: www.cambridge.org/9781009294768
DOI: 10.1017/9781009294751

© Cambridge University Press & Assessment 2023

This publication is in copyright. Subject to statutory exception and to the provisions of relevant collective licensing agreements, no reproduction of any part may take place without the written permission of Cambridge University Press & Assessment.

First published 2023

A catalogue record for this publication is available from the British Library.

Library of Congress Cataloging-in-Publication Data
NAMES: Neger, Margot, editor. | Tzounakas, Spyridon, editor.
TITLE: Intertextuality in Pliny's epistles / edited by Margot Neger, Spyridon Tzounakas.
DESCRIPTION: New York : Cambridge University Press, 2023.
IDENTIFIERS: LCCN 2023005988 (print) | LCCN 2023005989 (ebook) | ISBN 9781009294768 (hardback) | ISBN 9781009294799 (paperback) | ISBN 9781009294751 (epub)
SUBJECTS: LCSH: Pliny, the Younger. Correspondence. | Latin letters–History and criticism. | Intertextuality.
CLASSIFICATION: LCC PA6640 .I58 2023 (print) | LCC PA6640 (ebook) | DDC 876/.01–dc23/eng/20230411
LC record available at https://lccn.loc.gov/2023005988
LC ebook record available at https://lccn.loc.gov/2023005989

ISBN 978-1-009-29476-8 Hardback

Cambridge University Press & Assessment has no responsibility for the persistence or accuracy of URLs for external or third-party internet websites referred to in this publication and does not guarantee that any content on such websites is, or will remain, accurate or appropriate.

Contents

List of Contributors	*page* viii	
Acknowledgements	xii	
List of Abbreviations	xiii	
	Introduction	1
	Margot Neger and Spyridon Tzounakas	

PART I INTERTEXTUALITY AND INTERDISCURSIVITY IN PLINY'S LETTERS

1	Pliny, Man of Many Parts (Lucretius, Cicero, Valerius Maximus, Tacitus)	29
	Christopher Whitton	
2	Intertextuality in Pliny, *Epistles* 6	47
	Roy Gibson	
3	Discourses of Authority in Pliny, *Epistles* 10	67
	Alice König	

PART II MODELS AND ANTI-MODELS: PLINY'S INTERACTION WITH ORATORY AND NATURAL HISTORY

4	Oratorical Speeches and the Political Elite in the Regulus Cycle	99
	Matthew Mordue	
5	Again on Corinthian Bronzes and Vases and on the Use of Cicero's *Verrine Orations* in Pliny's Works	116
	Stefano Rocchi	

vi   *Contents*

6   The Elder Pliny as Source of Inspiration: Pliny the Younger's
Reception of the *Naturalis Historia* and His Uncle's
Writing by the Light of a Lamp (*lucubratio*)   129
Judith Hindermann

PART III PLINY AND SENECA: DISCOURSES OF GRIEF AND
POSTHUMOUS REPUTATION

7   Pliny's Seneca and the Intertextuality of Grief   149
Michael Hanaghan

8   Intertextuality and Posthumous Reputation in Pliny's
Letter on the Death of Silius Italicus (Plin. *Ep.* 3.7)   164
Spyridon Tzounakas

PART IV PLINY'S VILLAS AND THEIR POETIC MODELS

9   The Villa and the Monument: Horace in Pliny, *Epistles* 1.3   187
Alberto Canobbio

10   The Villas of Pliny and Statius   200
Christopher Chinn

PART V PLINY TURNS NASTY: SATIRE AND THE
SCOPTIC TRADITION

11   A Busy Day in Rome: Pliny, *Epistles* 1.9 Satirized by
Horace, *Satires* 1.9   219
Ábel Tamás

12   Putting Pallas out of Context: Pliny on the Roman Senate
Voting Honours to a Freedman (Plin. *Ep.* 7.29 and 8.6)   241
Jakub Pigoń

13   *Risus et indignatio*: Scoptic Elements in Pliny's *Letters*   259
Margot Neger

Contents vii

PART VI FINAL THOUGHTS: DISCOURSES OF REPRESENTATION
AND REPRODUCTION

14 Pliny's Calpurnia: Filiation, Imitation, Allusion 281
Ilaria Marchesi

Bibliography 304
General Subject Index 331
Index Locorum 337

Contributors

ALBERTO CANOBBIO is Associate Professor of Latin Language and Literature at the University of Pavia. He studies ancient texts mainly from a philological and intertextual point of view. His research interests focus on Martial (on whom he has published multiple articles and a commentary of *Epigrammaton liber quintus* with critical edition, Naples 2011) and most recently on Pliny the Younger. He has also written about archaic Latin poetry, satire and epic of Imperial age.

CHRISTOPHER CHINN is Professor of Classics at Pomona College, Claremont. His research has focused on vision and visuality in Roman literature, culminating in his book *Visualizing the Poetry of Statius* (Brill 2021). His more recent work engages in ecocriticism and reception studies.

ROY GIBSON is Professor of Classics at Durham University. He is the author most recently of *Man of High Empire: The Life of Pliny the Younger* (Oxford 2020) and co-author, with Ruth Morello, of *Reading the Letters of Pliny the Younger: An Introduction* (Cambridge 2012). He is currently co-director with Andrew Morrison of the Ancient Letter Collections project funded by the Arts and Humanities Research Council UK.

MICHAEL HANAGHAN is Research Fellow at the Australian Catholic University. His research areas include Latin epistolography, historiography, panegyric and philosophy from the Imperial age through into Late Antiquity. He is the author of *Reading Sidonius' Epistles* (Cambridge 2019) and has published numerous article-length studies on the letters of Pliny, Seneca and Sidonius.

JUDITH HINDERMANN is a freelance researcher in Latin Philology at the University of Basel, where she completed her PhD on Apuleius' *Metamorphoses* and Ovid's *Ars amatoria* (2009). Her research interests include ancient letters (especially Pliny the Younger's *Epistulae*), Roman elegy, the ancient novel, animals in ancient literature, Neo-Latin literature, and gender studies in Classics. In 2020, with Henriette Harich-Schwarzbauer, she edited the special issue *The Muses and Leisure in Sidonius Apollinaris* (Journal of Late Antiquity, 13,1). In 2018, she published the collected writings of the sixteenth-century humanist Johannes Atrocianus with Christian Guerra and Henriette Harich-Schwarzbauer. Her *Habilitationsschrift* on Sidonius Apollinaris' second book of letters (text, translation and commentary) was published in 2022 (Edinburgh).

ALICE KÖNIG is a Senior Lecturer in Classics at the University of St Andrews. Founder of the Literary Interactions project, she has published on many different forms of intertextuality, interdiscursivity and interplay of the Roman Empire's Greek and Latin literary culture. With Christopher Whitton, she co-edited *Roman Literature under Nerva, Trajan and Hadrian: Literary Interactions, AD 96–138* (Cambridge 2018) and, with Rebecca Langlands and James Uden, she co-edited *Literature and Culture in the Roman Empire, 96–235: Cross-Cultural Interactions* (Cambridge 2020).

ILARIA MARCHESI is Professor of Classics and Comparative Literature at Hofstra University, where she directs the Classics program. In 2008, she published *The Art of Pliny's Letters: A Poetics of Allusion in the Private Correspondence*, a monograph on the intertextuality in the letters of Pliny the Younger (Cambridge), for which she received a National Endowment for the Humanities Grant. She also edited and contributed to the book *Pliny the Book-Maker: Betting on Posterity in the Epistles* (Oxford 2015). Beside epistolography, her research interests include epigrams, satirical poetry and the ancient novel. She has published articles on Horace, Petronius, Martial, and on the reception of classical authors in Petrarch. In collaboration with Simone Marchesi, she has published *Live in Pompeii*, an essay in narrative form on the cultural value of the archeological past for the young generation (Laterza 2016). She has just completed a manuscript on the semiotics of Martial's women and is working on Virgil's *Aeneid* 6 for a new commentary of the *Aeneid* (Fondazione Lorenzo Valla, Mondadori), curated by Alessandro Barchiesi and Alessandro Schiesaro.

MATTHEW MORDUE received his PhD from the University of Roehampton. His thesis, 'Pliny's Exemplary Society: Crafting Models in Letters', examines Pliny's use of the epistolary form in constructing exemplarity. He has also taught a range of language, literature and history modules at the University of Roehampton. He has recently completed the Classics PGCE at the University of Cambridge and is currently a teacher of Classical Civilisation and Latin in a UK state secondary school.

MARGOT NEGER is Assistant Professor in Latin at the University of Cyprus. Among her main research interests are the literature of the Imperial age, Roman epistolography, ancient epigrammatic poetry, late antique literature and the interaction of genres. Her publications include a book on Martial (*Martials Dichtergedichte. Das Epigramm als Medium der poetischen Selbstreflexion*, Tübingen 2012) and on Pliny the Younger (*Epistolare Narrationen. Studien zur Erzähltechnik des jüngeren Plinius*, Tübingen 2021).

JAKUB PIGOŃ is Associate Professor of Latin literature at the Faculty of Letters, University of Wrocław. Apart from Pliny the Younger, he has published on Tacitus (his main subject), Vergil, Ovid, Martial, Suetonius and Ammianus, contributing to such journals as *Athenaeum, Classical Quarterly, Hermes, Mnemosyne* and *Rheinisches Museum*. He also edited *The Children of Herodotus: Greek and Roman Historiography and Related Genres* (Cambridge Scholars Publishing, 2008). Since 2004, he has been editor-in-chief of *Eos*, Poland's oldest classical journal (est. 1894).

STEFANO ROCCHI has held academic appointments in Munich at the Thesaurus Linguae Latinae and the Monumenta Germaniae Historica, the Ludwig-Maximilians-Universität, where he taught Latin language and literature, and in Berlin at the Corpus Inscriptionum Latinarum. He currently works at the University of Pavia, where he teaches Classical Philology and Reception of Classical Past. His current research interests embrace Latin language and literature, Roman epigraphy, and Renaissance studies. His most recent publications include *P. Annio Floro, Virgilio: oratore o poeta?* (Berlin/Boston 2020) and (with Roberta Marchionni) *Oltre Pompei. Graffiti e altre iscrizioni oscene dall'impero Romano d'Occidente* (Rome 2021). Along with Spyridon Tzounakas, he is a founding editor of the new series *The Seeds of Triptolemus: Studies on the Ancient Mediterranean World*, published by Deinotera Editrice (Rome).

ÁBEL TAMÁS is Senior Lecturer in Latin and Comparative Literature at Eötvös Loránd University (ELTE), Budapest. His research focuses on

Latin Literature from Catullus to Pliny the Younger and beyond. Currently, he is working on a monograph on *Scenes of Curiosity in Latin Literature* (contracted with Bloomsbury) and publishing articles on acrostics, telestichs and other wordplays. He is also interested in literary and cultural theory and the Hungarian reception of classical antiquity.

SPYRIDON TZOUNAKAS is Associate Professor of Latin Literature at the University of Cyprus. His main research and publications focus on Roman satire (especially Persius), Roman epistolography (especially Pliny the Younger), Roman epic (especially Lucan and Valerius Flaccus), Roman elegy (especially Tibullus), Cicero's orations and Roman intertextuality. He has published many articles in international refereed journals and collective volumes, edited a book on praises of Roman leaders and completed a book on Persius' *Satires*. He has also edited a volume on the reception of ancient Cyprus in Western culture (2022, co-edited with Stella Alekou and Stephen Harrison) and is working on a project on the geopoetics of the early Imperial age.

CHRISTOPHER WHITTON is Professor of Latin Literature at the University of Cambridge and a Fellow of Emmanuel College. His publications include a 'green and yellow' commentary on Pliny *Epistles* 2 (Cambridge 2013) and *The Arts of Imitation in Latin Prose: Pliny's Epistles/Quintilian in Brief* (Cambridge 2019).

Acknowledgements

This volume emerged from a conference entitled 'Pliny's Epistolary Intertextuality' which was held in May 2018 by the Department of Classics and Philosophy at the University of Cyprus. We would like to express our gratitude to the University of Cyprus for funding this event which laid the groundwork for this book. Christopher Whitton and Alberto Canobbio, although not able to attend the conference in person, nevertheless agreed to contribute a chapter and enrich our project. Special thanks go to Roy Gibson who supported the preparation of the manuscript with his help and advice, as well as to Michael Sharp and Katie Idle, our editors at Cambridge University Press, for their assistance and patience. Furthermore, we are indebted to Sarah Starkey, Anthony Arthurton, Balamuthukumaran Pasupathy and Nagalakshmi Karunanithi for their support during the production of this book. We also thank the anonymous readers for their critical comments and invaluable suggestions which helped to improve the quality of the volume.

Abbreviations

BNP	H. Cancik and H. Schneider, eds., *Brill's New Pauly: Encyclopedia of the Ancient World*, Leiden 2002– (online).
CEG	P. A. Hansen, *Carmina Epigraphica Graeca*, 2 vols., Berlin 1983–89.
CIL	*Corpus Inscriptionum Latinarum*, Berlin 1863–.
FPL	W. Morel, K. Büchner and J. Blänsdorf, *Fragmenta Poetarum Latinorum epicorum et lyricorum praeter Enni Annales et Ciceronis Germanicique Aratea*, 4th Edition, Berlin/New York 2011.
GVI	W. Peek, *Griechische Vers-Inschriften, I: Grab-Epigramme*, Berlin 1955.
ILS	H. Dessau, *Inscriptiones Latinae Selectae*, Berlin 1892–1916.
LSJ	H. G. Liddell, R. Scott, H. S. Jones and R. McKenzie, *A Greek-English Lexicon*. 9th Edition with Supplement, Oxford 1968.
OCD	S. Hornblower and A. J. S. Spawforth, *The Oxford Classical Dictionary*, 4th Edition, Oxford 2012.
OLD	P. G. W. Glare, *The Oxford Latin Dictionary*, Oxford 1968–82.
PIR²	E. Groag et al., *Prosopographia Imperii Romani saec. I. II. III.*, Berlin 1933–2015.
SVF	H. von Arnim, *Stoicorum Veterum Fragmenta*, Stuttgart 1903–.
TLL	*Thesaurus Linguae Latinae*, Munich 1900–.
VSD	G. Brugnoli and F. Stok, *Vita Suetoniana-Donatiana* (= *Vitae Vergilianae antiquae*, pp. 17–41), Rome 1997.

Introduction

Margot Neger and Spyridon Tzounakas

1 Staging Literary Exchange

Pliny the Younger's letter collection is a polyphonic work of literature. Not at first glance, of course, as Books 1–9 contain only letters written by Pliny himself. It is not until Book 10 that we can finally hear the voice of a correspondent – and a most important one, to be sure: the emperor Trajan himself.[1] But still, there are many other voices to be heard in the letter corpus as a whole – one just has to listen more carefully. Although their letters have not been included in the collection, Pliny's addressees in Books 1–9 are frequently 'allowed' to speak in their capacity as interlocutors, their words, of course, being controlled by Pliny the 'stage director' of these epistolary dialogues. As is well-known, in ancient theory letters were considered one half of a dialogue, and letter writers often supplement the other half by anticipating their addressees' possible comments.[2] Apart from these interlocutors, on an intra-diegetic level we can also hear the words of the acting characters in various epistolary narrations, words which are reproduced by Pliny the narrator both in direct and indirect speech. Finally, there are the voices which Pliny (willingly or unwillingly) 'imported' into his epistolary universe from outside and which, as it were, generate a consistent 'background sound' throughout the oeuvre: the numerous texts, genres and discourses, both on and off the page, which are interacting with the letters. It is the aim of our volume to explore these intertextual 'background noises' and to 'excavate' the additional layers of meaning which are generated through the letters' intertextual dialogues.

As König and Whitton (2018a) have pointed out, Pliny's *Letters* are an especially interactive work of literature:[3] not only because the epistolary

---

[1] For Book 10 see Stadter (2006); Woolf (2006); Noreña (2007); Lavan (2018).
[2] For the letter as the one half of a dialogue see Demetr. *Eloc.* 223; Thraede (1970) 27–38; for the interlocutor in ancient epistolography see e.g. Thorsteinsson (2003) 134–44.
[3] König and Whitton (2018a) 18 with n. 66.

genre per se is based on interactivity through the written exchange between letter writer and addressees, but also because Pliny frequently narrates, describes or imagines various forms of social and cultural interaction in his letters. Literary activity and exchange are an important topic right from the outset of the collection: already the first epistle (1.1) suggests that the genesis of the letter collection results from a conversation (we do not learn whether it was an oral or written one) between Pliny and his friend Septicius Clarus who encouraged Pliny to collect and publish those letters which were written *paulo curatius*. Literary exchange is omnipresent in the so-called Parade Letters 1.1–8;[4] in letter 1.2, Pliny sends a *liber* (probably a speech, though perhaps we should also think of the book of letters?), in which he follows the stylistic ideal of Demosthenes, Calvus and Cicero, to Arrianus Maturus for emendation. In addition to this exchange between the two correspondents as well as between Pliny and his literary models, the letter also envisages a broader public by mentioning the publication of the work (5 *editione*), the circulation of Pliny's *libelli* in public (6 *in manibus*) and on the book market (6 *bibliopolae*). In letter 1.3, Pliny encourages his friend Caninius Rufus to use his free time in his villa in Comum for composing a literary work and gaining immortality (4 *effinge aliquid et excude*).[5] The atmosphere of friendship and mutual encouragement dominating letters 1.1–3 changes conspicuously in letter 1.5 where Pliny quotes from the invectives which Regulus and the members of the Stoic opposition under Domitian hurled against each other both orally and in written form (2 *ut librum recitaret publicaretque*; 3 *ut dixerit ei*; 14 *in epistula quadam*).[6] Quite in contrast, *Ep.* 1.6 advertises Pliny's friendship with Tacitus who is depicted as having a giggle over Pliny's accidental success as a hunter while pursuing studies in the great outdoors. The next letter (1.7) is part of Pliny's correspondence with Octavius Rufus, a written exchange enriched with quotations from Homer and thus 'importing' the heroic world of epic poetry into a conversation over an extortion trial concerning the province of Baetica (4 *cur enim non usquequaque Homericis versibus agam tecum?*).[7] A speech which Pliny had held in his hometown Comum on the occasion of the dedication of a public library financed by Pliny himself is the topic of letter 1.8. The addressee, Pompeius Saturninus, is asked to emend the speech which, according to Pliny, bears

---

[4] A term coined by Ludolph (1997) in reminiscence of Horace's 'Parade Odes'.
[5] See also Canobbio (Chapter 9) in this volume.
[6] Amicable and hostile exchange in the context of the recitation is the focus of Roller (2018); for *Ep.* 1.5 and 1.6 see Neger (Chapter 13) in this volume.
[7] For quotations from epic poetry (especially Homer and Vergil) see Schwerdtner (2015).

Introduction

the risk of appearing as too boastful in advertising Pliny's *munificentia* – thus, he is still hesitating over a publication.[8] As it turns out, Pliny's hometown pops up twice in the opening section of Book 1 as a place where literature is produced, disseminated and read or listened to, be it in the private villa of Pliny's friend Caninius (1.3) or in the public library sponsored by Pliny and made accessible to the community of Novum Comum (1.8).[9] With *Ep.* 1.9 to Fundanus we are back in Rome, witnessing Pliny as he struggles with the various obligations which members of the upper class have to meet day by day. Regarding these social and legal interactions in the metropolis, Pliny opposes the *otium* of his Laurentine villa which enables him both to pursue his studies (Pliny here depicts himself as 'speaking with his books' (5 *cum libellis loquor*)) in peace and enjoy physical recreation.[10]

The list of letters where Pliny discusses various kinds of literary and cultural activities, both in a private and public context, could be continued ad infinitum (i.e. until the end of the collection). Within his oeuvre, Pliny depicts numerous spaces where literary exchange takes place: besides the public library in Comum, already mentioned above (*Ep.* 1.8), Pliny also refers to private libraries such as the one in his Laurentine villa (*Ep.* 2.17.8), the library of Herennius Severus who is planning to decorate it with portraits of Cornelius Nepos and Titus Catius (*Ep.* 4.28),[11] and the library in a building in Prusa which also contains a statue of Trajan (*Ep.* 10.81.7).[12] In letter 4.13 Pliny once more advertises his generosity towards his hometown, this time through his efforts to establish a school in Comum, most probably one for rhetorical education (and which, perhaps, would have met in Pliny's own new library); Tacitus, the addressee of this letter, is asked to recommend a suitable teacher from the crowd of his students (10 *copia studiosorum*).[13] Various other letters refer to recitations, a praxis of literary exchange well-established in Imperial times,[14] as well as private conversations and discussions about literary matters. For instance,

---

[8] For the library in Comum see Dix (1996); for Pliny's reflections on self-praise see Gibson (2003); Neger (2015a).

[9] Comum, in *Ep.* 1.3, is the first location mentioned in Pliny's letters; see Neger (2021) 80.

[10] See also Tamás (Chapter 11) in this volume.

[11] Titus Catius is probably identical with the philosopher Catius mentioned by Quintilian in *Inst.* 10.1.124; Sherwin-White (1966) 307.

[12] For the known libraries in the Roman empire and the libraries existing in Pliny's lifetime see Neudecker (2004); Dix and Houston (2006); König and Whitton (2018a) 1–3; Pliny also mentions portraits and statues in libraries in *Ep.* 1.16.8; 3.7.8; cf. Sen. *Tranq.* 9.9.6–7.

[13] For this letter see e.g. Manuwald (2003); Augoustakis (2005/06).

[14] Cf. *Ep.* 1.5; 1.13; 2.10; 2.19; 3.7.5; 3.10; 3.15; 3.18; 4.7.2; 4.27.1; 5.3; 5.12; 5.17; 5.21.1; 6.6.6; 6.15; 6.17; 7.17; 8.12; 8.21; 9.1.4; 9.27; 9.34; see Binder (1995); Roller (2018).

in *Ep.* 5.3 Pliny summarises the content of a message from Titius Aristo who had written that, in his house, there had been a lively discussion about Pliny's poems (*Ep.* 5.3.1 *fuisse apud te de versiculis meis multum copiosumque sermonem*), probably during a *cena* to which Aristo had invited his friends.[15] A dinner is also the context for the exchange of anecdotes belonging to the realm of paradoxography in *Ep.* 9.33: it was during a symposium (1 *super cenam*) that Pliny had heard the story of the friendly encounter of a dolphin and a boy in Hippo Diarrhytus, Africa, a story which he passes on to his addressee, the poet Caninius Rufus.[16] In Tuscany, where Pliny possesses one of his villas, old men are telling stories from the good old days (5.6.6 *audias fabulas veteres sermonesque maiorum*). Rhetorical tactics too have to be discussed in private conversations, and we find Pliny even interacting with Regulus, his favourite foe, about the question of whether a judicial speech should be extensive or concise (*Ep.* 1.20.14–15). There are several other occasions where Pliny refers to oral conversations regarding literary matters, whether real or fictitious, which he chose to embed into his letters. We have to assume that not only Pliny the epistolary narrator, but also the historical Pliny who wrote, collected and published his letters, was strongly influenced by the oral culture of his times. This aggregate of non-written intertexts which helped to shape his work is difficult, of course, if not almost impossible to track down almost two millennia later.

The better part of literary interaction as depicted in Pliny's letters belongs to the time after Domitian's death in AD 96, a temporal marker which frames the corpus of Books 1–9 (*Ep.* 1.5.1 *post Domitiani mortem*; 9.13.2 *occiso Domitiano*).[17] As Pliny happily observes in *Ep.* 1.10 and 1.13, literature and science are flourishing again in the post-Flavian present of the *Epistles* (1.10.1 *si quando urbs nostra liberalibus studiis floruit, nunc maxime floret*).[18] As an example for this renaissance of the *studia liberalia* in Rome, Pliny picks out the philosopher Euphrates to whom he dedicates a portrait in letter 1.10.[19] Quite in contrast to this positive image, the dark era of Domitian (with the expulsion of the philosophers from Rome) is the

---

[15] For this letter see Auhagen (2003); Morello (2007) 176–7; Power (2014); Neger (2021) 278–9.
[16] See Hindermann (Chapter 6) in this volume.
[17] See Whitton (2013b) 57; Neger (2021) 200–1.
[18] Actually an insult to Statius, Silius Italicus, Martial and Quintilian; what is true is that senators, like Pliny and Tacitus, are now publishing freely for the first time.
[19] See Whitton (2019) 75–8 and 423–4.

topic of conversation in *Ep.* 3.11.[20] Apart from the present and recent past, Pliny from time to time also intersperses anecdotes from earlier ages, often (but not only) concerning rhetorical matters. In *Ep.* 2.3, which praises the Greek orator Isaeus, Pliny narrates the famous anecdote of Aeschines, who read Demosthenes' speech *De Corona* to the Rhodians and praised Demosthenes' oratorical skills.[21] The same letter also contains an anecdote from the time of Augustus about a citizen from Gades, who came all the way to Rome only to see Livy (the historian) and returned home immediately afterwards (8). Pliny's introduction to this anecdote (which is later narrated by Jerome in *Ep.* 53.1) insinuates that it existed in written form and that his addressee, Nepos, could have known it already (8 *numquamne legisti Gaditanum quendam* ...).[22] An anecdote about the emperor Claudius, who unexpectedly visited a lecture by Nonianus on the Palatine, is narrated in letter 1.13.3 and *Ep.* 2.14.10–11 contains an account of Domitius Afer's speech at the Centumviral court, a story which Pliny had heard from his teacher Quintilian and which probably dates from the reign of Nero.[23] In letter 6.20 we encounter the eighteen year old Pliny reading Livy and excerpting passages from his work during the eruption of Vesuvius in the year AD 79.

2 Excavating the Text: Interdiscursivity and Generic Interaction

As the chapters in this volume will demonstrate, literary interaction is not only a recurrent topic within the epistolary collection, but also actively practised on the page of each letter. Considerable work has already been dedicated to Pliny the Younger's intertextual techniques by various scholars. The monographs by Marchesi (2008), Schwerdtner (2015) and Whitton (2019), as well as several articles,[24] have succeeded in showing that, on the one hand, we encounter in Pliny a large number of lexical overlaps, quotations and marked references to various Greek and Latin

---

[20] The banishment of the philosophers is usually dated to AD 93; for a discussion of letter 3.11 see Shelton (1987); Whitton (2015c) 5–9.
[21] Cf. Aeschin. *Or.* 3.167; Cic. *De or.* 3.213; Plin. *Ep.* 4.5; Val. Max. 8.10.*ext.*; Plin. *HN* 7.110; Whitton (2013a) 100; Tzounakas (2015) 210-11; for *Ep.* 2.3 (together with 1.10) see also Pausch (2004) 129–41.
[22] See Whitton (2013a) 98; as the anecdote is not extant in other sources before Jerome, it is also possible that Pliny invented it and the question *numquamne legisti* playfully points to this fact.
[23] See Whitton (2013a) 209: 'this anecdote probably dates from the late 50s'.
[24] See e.g. Hagendahl (1947); Neuhausen (1968); Görler (1979); Cugusi (1983) 91–6; Krasser (1993b); Wenskus (1993); Schenk (1999); Méthy (2004); Whitton (2015b); Mratschek (2018); Whitton (2018).

writers, but on the other, there are also numerous unmarked and indirect allusions in the *Epistles* which are much more difficult to identify. The arrangement of Pliny's *Letters* as well as his art of literary allusion has much in common with the literary strategies we are familiar with from Augustan poetry, and the *Epistles* have aptly been described as a kind of 'prose poetry'.[25] In May 2018, a conference entitled 'Pliny's Epistolary Intertextuality' was held at the University of Cyprus where Pliny's strategies of referring or alluding to various models were discussed. The present volume emerges from the ideas presented at this conference and attempts to focus on an aspect which has not yet been systematically examined in scholarship on Pliny: rather than viewing intertextuality as an end in itself, the volume focuses on the question of how 'generic enrichment'[26] and interdiscursive interaction are established in Pliny's letters and how the letters, as it were, 'absorb' other literary genres and discourses. The interactive potential of the *Epistles* is not limited to literary texts: on several occasions, Pliny also integrates non-literary or sub-literary texts in his work: for example, in *Ep*. 3.18, about the recitation of his *Panegyricus Traiani*, Pliny quotes from the invitation notes he had sent to his friends (4 '*si commodum*' et '*si valde vacaret*').[27] In other letters Pliny either quotes from inscriptions or refers to them, such as in *Ep*. 7.29 (Pallas' prose epitaph),[28] 6.10 and 9.19 (Verginius Rufus' verse epitaph),[29] 3.6.5 (Pliny's name and honorary offices on the base of a Corinthian bronze statue of an aged man)[30] or 8.8.7 (various graffiti on the walls of Clitumnus' sanctuary).[31] The wording of a *senatus consultum* from the year AD 52 is embedded into letter 8.6.[32]

As a writer who constantly experiments with the generic boundaries between his prose letters and other forms of literature, both prosaic and poetic, Pliny the Younger can be compared to his older contemporaries Martial and Statius, whose *Epigrams* and *Silvae* are also distinguished through the art of incorporating elements typical of other literary genres.[33] As it seems, small forms (such as small-scale poetry and epistolography) are

---

[25] E.g. by Stevens (2009) 161.   [26] See Harrison (2007).
[27] For *Ep*. 3.18 see Marchesi (2008) 199–203; one might compare the invitation letter by Claudia Severa written around the same time (AD 100) and found among the Vindolanda tablets (*Tab. Vindol.* 291); see Hallett (2002).
[28] See Pigoń (Chapter 12); Neger (Chapter 13) in this volume.
[29] See König and Whitton (2018a) 16–28.
[30] On this letter and its crucial role in Book 3 see Henderson (2002b).
[31] See Neger (2021) 360–1.   [32] See Pigoń (Chapter 12).
[33] For generic interactions in Martial see, for example, Neger (2012); Mindt (2013); for Statius Newlands (2013); for both poets Baumann (2018).

Introduction 7

particularly susceptible to generic enrichment and, at the same time, show a high degree of literary self-consciousness. The present volume covers a greater range of genres and writers than the monographs mentioned above of Marchesi (2008), Schwerdtner (2015) and Whitton (2019), albeit with a less intense focus than particularly Whitton. Whilst the single chapters offer close readings of Pliny's intertextual dialogue with various writers, the volume in its entirety demonstrates the large scope of genres and discourses which Pliny incorporates into his letters and shows how the epistolographer adapts these pre-texts to the communicative purposes of the respective letters.

The theory of intertextuality, meanwhile, adapted for literary studies by Genette and others[34] and initially applied by classicists to studies on Augustan poetry,[35] has also become an important tool for the interpretation of various prose genres.[36] The volume aims to add to these endeavours and significantly extend them by showing that Pliny, through referring and alluding to a broad range of writers, genres and modes of writing, absorbs various genres in his letters and, at the same time, creates a kind of epistolary 'super-genre'.[37] As Whitton states in his contribution to this volume, 'Pliny's *Epistles* are a work of many intertextual parts', covering both prose and poetry. What Pliny offers to his readers is a blend of genres and discourses within an epistolary framework, including, for example, typical elements of epigram, elegy, satire, lyric and didactic poetry, epic and drama as well as oratory, historiography, philosophy, technical writing, paradoxography and the novel. Rather than narrowing our investigation down to literary genres in the traditional sense, we also explore how discourses which transcend generic boundaries are being absorbed in the *Epistles* and adapted to the epistolary context: government, law, provincial administration, ethical didaxis, gender, reproduction, illness, death, grief and consolation, posthumous reputation, luxury, villas, (control over) nature, literary criticism and so on. In his letters, Pliny repeatedly approaches other literary genres and discourses both through quoting directly from and alluding covertly to various models, thus challenging his readers to read the *Epistles* against the background of a long literary tradition as well as a shared cultural space.

---

[34] Genette (1982); cf. Riffaterre (1978).
[35] See e.g. Conte (1986); Hinds (1998); O'Rourke and Pelttari (forthcoming).
[36] See Joseph (2012); Tischer (2010), (2018) and (2019).
[37] We use the term 'super-genre' in a different sense from Hutchinson (2013) who refers it to large sets of genres with various subsets, for example the hexameter as a super-genre covering subsets such as epic and didactic poetry as well as satire and oracle.

At the same time, he demonstrates the generic mobility of epistolography.[38] The letters become a sort of 'vessel' which can be 'filled' with elements characteristic of other genres, or, to apply the image used by Harrison, the letters resemble a 'host' receiving various 'guests' whose status in the literary hierarchy can be higher, equal or lower than the 'host'.[39] In our volume, we will explore the possible purposes of intertextual allusions: are they drawing the readers' attention to parallels, changed context or differences? Are they supposed to confirm the readers' expectations, to cause amusement, surprise or even irritation? As a study on intertextuality, our volume does not only aim at investigating the phenomenon per se, but also at helping to understand better the cultural profile of the society Pliny was living in and writing for.[40]

When modern scholars attempt to examine the phenomenon of textual relations in ancient writers, terms such as 'intertextuality', 'reference', 'allusion', 'reminiscence' and 'evocation' are often used interchangeably without regard to the semantic differences. As Hinds points out by referring to the *Oxford English Dictionary*, 'a "reference" is "a specific direction of the attention"; an "allusion" ... is "a covert, implied or indirect reference"'.[41] In her chapter on intertextuality in the work of Sidonius Apollinaris, Gualandri emphasises the semantic difference between 'intertextuality' and 'allusion' and argues that 'the concept of "allusion" ... rests precisely on the author's intention', whereas 'intertextuality' does 'not necessarily imply any authorial intentionality'.[42] In this volume, we follow a pragmatic approach: the aspect of intentionality plays an important (although not exclusive) role in this volume's contributions which investigate Pliny's strategies of deliberately incorporating various genres and discourses into the epistolary context or, in some cases, of consciously blending out certain pre-texts. As Marchesi reminds us in her chapter, in addition to the familiar concepts of intra- and inter-textuality which suggest reading one text together with another, we also have to take those cases into account where textual dialogue is either not generated deliberately by the author (but perceived by the reader due to the common background of the texts, not necessarily in written form) or where the author even excludes or tunes out a parallel text. For these forms of textual

---

[38] For the 'generic mobility' of letters in terms of their proximity to autobiography see Gibson (2013).
[39] Harrison (2007) 16.
[40] See Onorato (2020) 38 on intertextuality in the work of Sidonius Apollinaris.
[41] Hinds (1998) 22.
[42] Gualandri (2020) 280; for the question how deliberate imitation can be distinguished from coincidence and commonplace see Whitton (2019) 37–50.

relations Marchesi suggests the concepts of extra- and alter-textuality.[43] König and Whitton (2018a) who focus on literary interaction between contemporaries in the age of Nerva, Trajan and Hadrian, convincingly argue that interaction can be seen 'as a superset of which intertextuality is just a part'.[44] Whereas the majority of chapters collected in our volume will focus on the relation between Pliny's *Letters* and other texts, we will also take into account other forms of literary interaction. In her chapter on Book 10, König explores the large spectrum of interactions from 'allusions' to 'interdiscursivity', i.e. the evocation of whole genres and discourses instead of narrow lexical overlaps. Neither does intertextuality have to be traced only in one direction, i.e. from the older text to the younger. As Tamás demonstrates in his chapter, Pliny's interdiscursive methods can stimulate readers not only to regard Pliny's letters as informed by various source texts, but also to read these sources through the prism of Pliny's adaptation.[45]

One type of intertextual reference which clearly rests on the writer's intention is the quotation, a 'prototype of intertextuality'[46] as it were. Ancient writers use various strategies of marking a quotation as a borrowing from another source:[47] sometimes the name of the model is mentioned explicitly,[48] sometimes a deictic pronoun indicates that a quotation follows (e.g. *illud*),[49] and in other cases readers can identify quotations as borrowings from other sources when poetic lines are integrated in a work of prose or when Greek is used in a Latin text. In addition to these instances, the so-called Alexandrian footnote, i.e. intertextual markers such as *dicitur*, *fertur*, *narratur*, *fama est* etc.,[50] helps to direct the reader's attention to literary models.[51] Whereas in a quotation the original wording of the

---

[43] Langlands (2018) 331 defines extratextuality as 'allusion to a referent that is not in textual form, that reaches beyond intertextuality'.
[44] König and Whitton (2018a) 21.
[45] For the two sides of allusive art in ancient literature see O'Rourke and Pelltari (forthcoming).
[46] Tischer (2010) 93: 'Prototyp intertextueller Beziehungen'; an extreme form of intertextuality where a text only consists of quotations is the Cento, explained e.g. by Ausonius in his preface to the *Cento nuptialis*; see Green (1991) 518–22.
[47] Tischer (2010) 103–6; cf. Schwerdtner (2015) 26–45; Neger (2021) 68–70.
[48] Cf. e.g. Plin. *Ep.* 2.3.10 (*illud Aeschinis*); Martial 3.21; 4.14.5 (*verissimam legem, quam Catullus expresserit*); 4.27 (Sentius Augurinus).
[49] Cf. e.g. Plin. *Ep.* 1.18.4 *egi tamen* λογισάμενος *illud* ('but I carried on, believing that...', introducing a quotation from Hom. *Il.* 12.283); unless indicated otherwise, translations of Pliny the Younger are by Radice (1969).
[50] See Ross (1975) 78; Hinds (1998) 1–5.
[51] In Pliny for example in *Ep.* 7.9.15 *aiunt enim multum legendum esse, non multa* ('for the saying is that a man should be deeply, not widely, read'), recalling Quint. *Inst.* 10.1.59 *et multa magis quam multorum lectione formanda mens* and probably also Sen. *Ep.* 2.2; see Keeline (2013) 120–1.

source is usually maintained to a certain degree – as with *Ep.* 6.33.1 '*Tollite cuncta*', inquit, '*coeptosque auferte labores!*'[52] –, in other forms of intentional allusion only motifs, ideas and contents of a hypotext are evoked, for example, through the use of synonyms. In such cases, the literary knowledge of the reader is challenged to a much higher degree.[53] Apart from the 'Alexandrian footnote', other metaphors and images can serve as intertextual markers, such as memory, recognition, echo, *fama*, the path, footprints, the fountain, *silva/materia*, grafting, the figure of the father/parent, exchange, competitions, hospitality and so on. All these images can be read as symbolic references to various forms of interaction between texts and genres.[54] Closely related to the concept of memory is the idea of renovation, which appears, for example, in Pliny's letter 6.10 on the tomb of Verginius Rufus in Alsium (1 *ipse mihi locus optimi illius et maximi viri desiderium non sine dolore renovavit*)[55] and indicates an intertextual link to Aeneas' famous words at the beginning of *Aeneid* book 2 (3 *infandum, regina, iubes renovare dolorem*).[56] Pliny's visit to the place where Verginius is buried thus resembles Aeneas' emotionally loaded recollection of the *Troiae halosis*. Pliny's memory is also explicitly mentioned in *Ep.* 3.7 on the death of Silius Italicus (10 *quod me recordantem*), a letter which interacts with Seneca's *Dialogi* and other texts (as Tzounakas shows in his chapter). Pliny's intertextual dialogue with Martial, on the other hand, is partially conducted in letters where aspects of the relationship between parents and children are discussed, as Marchesi shows in her contribution.

Although in antiquity a comprehensive theory of intertextuality was never developed, we can find scattered remarks of several writers concerning the art of quotation and literary allusion. One of the most famous passages is certainly Seneca the Elder's anecdote about Ovid who is said to

---

[52] '"Away with everything," he said, "and put aside whatever you have begun!"'; here Pliny quotes from Verg. *Aen.* 8.439; for an interpretation see Schwerdtner (2015) 84–90.
[53] A good example is the first letter of Sidonius Apollinaris which alludes to Pliny's *Ep.* 1.1 by using different vocabulary: *Diu praecipis ... ut, si quae mihi litterae paulo politiores varia occasione fluxerint ... omnes retractatis exemplaribus enucleatisque uno volumine includam* (Sidon. *Ep.* 1.1.1 '... you have this long while been pressing me ... to collect all the letters making any little claim to taste that have flowed from my pen ... and to revise and correct the originals and combine all in a single book'; translation by Anderson 1936) – *Frequenter hortatus es, ut epistulas, si quas paulo curatius scripsissem, colligerem publicaremque* (Plin. *Ep.* 1.1.1 'You have often urged me to collect and publish any letters of mine which were composed with some care'); cf. Köhler (1995) *ad* Sidon. *Ep.* 1.1.
[54] See O'Rourke and Pelttari (forthcoming).
[55] 'The mere sight of the place revived all the grief and longing for that great and noble man'.
[56] See Neger (2021) 256; for further allusions to Vergil in Pliny's letter 6.10 see Gibson (Chapter 2) in this volume.

have justified his borrowings from Vergil (Sen. *Suas.* 3.7).⁵⁷ Prose writers too reflect on their praxis of quoting from poetry, such as Cicero in his *Tusculanae Disputationes*, where he states that he used to cite both Latin and Greek poets (2.26),⁵⁸ and in his *De Oratore*, where he concedes that one also may quote a poetic line only partially or modify it a little bit (2.257).⁵⁹ The art of quoting is also discussed by ancient epistolary theorists such as Demetrius, who recommends the use of proverbs (*Eloc.* 232 παροιμίαι), and the Latin theorist Julius Victor, according to whom Greek passages or poetic lines can be inserted here and there (*Rhet.* 448.14–16 Halm): *Graece aliquid addere litteris suave est, si id neque intempestive neque crebro facias; et proverbio uti non ignoto percommodum est, et versiculo aut parte versus.*⁶⁰

Extensive quotation from, or allusion to passages from other genres might not only serve to embellish the hypertext but also produce a 'blend' of genres. Ancient literary theory and praxis frequently contradict each other when it comes to the definition of genres. From Plato (*Resp.* 3.394b–c) and Aristotle (*Poet.*) onwards, ancient literary critics divided literature into genres and discussed the features which distinguished one from another.⁶¹ In Latin literature too catalogues of genres are provided, among others, by Horace (*Ars P.* 73–98), Ovid (*Tr.* 2.359–468; *Rem. am.* 371–88), Quintilian (*Inst.* 10.1.46–131) and Martial (12.94), and Pliny the Younger offers a list of genres in *Ep.* 7.4 where he presents his own biography as a poet.⁶² In the *Remedia Amoris*, Ovid outlines which features he considers typical of each genre: epic poems recount wars (373 *bella*), sublime topics and anger (375 *grande . . . ira*) are appropriate for tragedy, comedy deals with daily life (376 *usibus e mediis*), iambic poetry is directed against enemies (377 *hostes*) and elegy has an alluring character (379 *blanda*). Epistolography is missing from Ovid's list, but from Martial we learn that in letters (14.11 *chartae epistulares*) everybody is called 'dear', regardless of whether it is only a slight acquaintance or a close friend

---

⁵⁷ For this anecdote and other passages where ancient writers reflect on intertextual references see Hinds (1998) 22–5.
⁵⁸ For quotations in Cicero's philosophical dialogues see Spahlinger (2005), for quotations in Cicero's letters see Behrendt (2013).
⁵⁹ Cf. Quint. *Inst.* 6.3.96–7.
⁶⁰ 'It is pleasant to add a Greek phrase or two in your letter, provided it is not ill-timed or too frequent. And it is very much in form to use a familiar proverb, a line of poetry, or a snatch of verse'; translation by Malherbe (1988) 65.
⁶¹ See the overview in Harrison (2013) 1–6.
⁶² For this letter see Kubiak (2010); Tzounakas (2012); cf. also Plin. *Ep.* 1.16 and 7.9.

(14.11.2 *omnes ista solet charta vocare suos*).[63] Pliny himself was well-aware of the limits and possibilities of the epistolary genre, as becomes clear from his frequent remarks on the art of letter writing throughout the collection.[64] Thus, we can extract an 'immanent' theory of epistolography if we take into account all the passages where Pliny reflects on his letters' function and their position within the cultural and literary landscape.[65]

Although it is evident that ancient writers and readers had a more or less clear concept of each genre's possibilities and limitations, from Hellenistic times onwards the 'crossing of genres' (*Gattungskreuzung*) became an important creative tool, especially for poets.[66] But prose writers too started experimenting with generic boundaries, as Pliny's *Epistles* demonstrate. What is more, these experiments are not only conducted in an implicit way by tacitly incorporating elements characteristic of other *genera*, but on several occasions Pliny explicitly reflects on the relation of his letters to various other genres:[67] already in *Ep.* 1.1 Pliny contends that he 'did not try to write history' (1 *neque enim historiam componebam*), but this statement, which only refers to the non-chronological arrangement of the letters, also invites readers to meditate on similarities between the *Epistles* and historiography.[68] In other passages, Pliny reflects on the proximity between his letters and oratory, especially when his letters are running the risk of exceeding their appropriate length; in this case, one could also compare them with a speech (9.13.26 *habes epistulam, si modum epistulae cogites, libris quos legisti, non minorem*).[69] Furthermore, a letter is also able to transgress generic boundaries with a tone inappropriate for a letter, as for example in *Ep.* 8.6 where Pliny shows an unusual degree of indignation, thus anticipating a satirist in the style of Juvenal.[70]

While single aspects of Pliny's interaction with other genres have already been investigated by scholars, a comprehensive study on Pliny's praxis of absorbing literary *genera* is still a desideratum. The volume aims to begin that study and is designed to be more than the sum of its parts: it demonstrates that the *Epistles* do indeed form a 'super-genre' and thus exhibit a high degree of literary flexibility. Two areas which have been

---

[63] 'This paper calls everyone "dear"'; see Leary (1996) ad loc. [64] See Gamberini (1983) 122–78.
[65] See Neger (2021) 27–36.
[66] Harrison (2013) 4; the term *Gattungskreuzung* was established by Kroll (1924) 202–24.
[67] See Neger (2021) 27–39. [68] Tzounakas (2007) 46–7.
[69] 'Here you have a letter as long as the speeches you have read, if you think what the length of a letter should be'.
[70] *Ep.* 8.6.17 *quamquam indignationem quibusdam in locis fortasse ultra epistulae modum extulerim* ('though in some passages I may have let my indignation carry me beyond the bounds of a letter'); see Pigoń and Neger (Chapter 12 and Chapter 13 respectively) in this volume.

studied comparatively often are Pliny's relation to historiography and oratory,[71] followed by studies on the influence of Catullus and Martial.[72] Some studies have also been devoted to Pliny and biography,[73] the *exempla*-tradition,[74] philosophy,[75] natural science,[76] elegy,[77] Statius' *Silvae*,[78] epic poetry[79] and comedy.[80] This volume aims to build on previous research on intertextuality and generic interaction in Pliny's *Letters* and to extend it significantly. It studies how one increasingly important and influential ancient author has the ambition to absorb a very wide range of other genres and discourses within the hitherto 'humble' genre of epistolography. Do intertextual allusions imply assimilation between the letters and the respective genres or does Pliny distance himself from these texts, even when he seems to absorb them? The examples discussed in this volume suggest that in the case of direct or identified quotations, Pliny tends to present his models as authorities, whereas indirect allusions can also serve to undermine or correct the hypotext. The latter seems to be true especially in the case of writers with whom Pliny competes, such as Cicero and Seneca, who are his epistolary predecessors, or Tacitus, Martial, Statius and Silius Italicus, who are his contemporary rivals in various fields.[81]

3 An Interactive Triptych of Letters: *Ep.* 4.26–28

The series of letters 4.26–28 provides a good example for the combination of various forms of textual (and non-textual) interaction. Let us start with the central piece, *Ep.* 4.27, where Pliny quotes an epigram composed by

---

[71] For Pliny and historiography see e.g. Traub (1955); Cova (1969); Ussani (1971); Cova (1975); Ash (2003); Baier (2003); Tzounakas (2007); Whitton (2012); Woodman (2012); Price (2014); for Pliny and oratory see e.g. Quadlbauer (1958); Ussani (1971); Picone (1978); Armisen-Marchetti (1990); Cugusi (2003); Mayer (2003); Dominik (2007); Mastrorosa (2009); Tzounakas (2015); Whitton (2019).
[72] Adamik (1976); Gunderson (1997); Roller (1998); Pitcher (1999); Auhagen (2003); Marchesi (2013); Tzounakas (2014); Canobbio (2015); Edmunds (2015); Neger (2015b); Fitzgerald (2018); Marchesi (2018).
[73] E.g. Pausch (2004).   [74] Lefèvre (2009) 23–48.
[75] André (1975); Griffin (2007); Tzounakas (2011); Canobbio (2017) and (2019); Blake (2018); Malaspina (2019).
[76] Trinacty (2020).
[77] De Verger (1997–98); Hindermann (2010); Tzounakas (2012); Baeza-Angulo (2015) and (2017).
[78] Fögen (2007); Malamud (2007); Newlands (2010); Pagán (2010).   [79] Schwerdtner (2015).
[80] Fögen (2017).
[81] See the contributions in this volume of Hanaghan and Tzounakas (Chapter 7 and Chapter 8 respectively) on Pliny and Seneca, and Chinn on Pliny and Statius (Chapter 10).

his young contemporary Sentius Augurinus, who had praised Pliny's own qualities as a poet:[82]

C. PLINIUS POMPEIO FALCONI SUO S.

(1) Tertius dies est quod audivi recitantem Sentium Augurinum cum summa mea voluptate, immo etiam admiratione. Poematia appellat. Multa tenuiter multa sublimiter, multa venuste multa tenere, multa dulciter multa cum bile. (2) Aliquot annis puto nihil generis eiusdem absolutius scriptum, nisi forte me fallit aut amor eius aut quod ipsum me laudibus vexit. (3) Nam lemma sibi sumpsit, quod ego interdum versibus ludo. Atque adeo iudicii mei te iudicem faciam, si mihi ex hoc ipso lemmate secundus versus occurrerit; nam ceteros teneo et iam explicui.

> (4) Canto carmina versibus minutis,
> his olim quibus et meus Catullus
> et Calvus veteresque. Sed quid ad me?
> Unus Plinius est mihi priores:
> mavult versiculos foro relicto
> et quaerit quod amet, putatque amari.
> Ille o Plinius, ille quot Catones!
> I nunc, quisquis amas, amare noli.

(5) Vides quam acuta omnia quam apta quam expressa. Ad hunc gustum totum librum repromitto, quem tibi ut primum publicaverit exhibebo. Interim ama iuvenem et temporibus nostris gratulare pro ingenio tali, quod ille moribus adornat. Vivit cum Spurinna, vivit cum Antonino, quorum alteri affinis, utrique contubernalis est. (6) Possis ex hoc facere coniecturam, quam sit emendatus adulescens, qui a gravissimis senibus sic amatur. Est enim illud verissimum:

> γινώσκων ὅτι
> τοιοῦτός ἐστιν, οἷσπερ ἥδεται συνών.

Vale.

To his friend Pompeius Falco

For a third day I have been listening with the utmost pleasure and indeed with admiration to a recitation by Sentius Augurinus. He calls them his short poems. Many are composed with simplicity, many in lofty style; many are elegant, many are tender, many are sweet-tempered, and many are cross. In my view no poetry of this type has been composed more competently for many years, unless perhaps I am beguiled either by my affection for him or by his winning me over with his praises. For he has chosen as one theme the fact that I occasionally make sport with verses. I will go so far as to appoint

---

[82] See Courtney (1993) 365–6; for letter 4.27 see also Dahlmann (1980); Tamás (2020).

Introduction

you arbiter of my judgement, if I can recall the second line of this very epigram, for I remember the rest and have now set the lines down:

> My songs I sing in these shortened verses,
> In which long ago my Catullus sang his,
> As did Calvus and men of old. I don't care!
> Pliny alone is for me all earlier poets.
> He leaves court behind, prefers to write short verses,
> Seeking a love affair. He believes he is loved.
> Ho there, Pliny, worth a thousand Catos!
> All with love affairs, you must stop your loving.

You see how sharp and fitting and polished his writing is. I guarantee that the whole book is redolent of this flavour, and I shall send it to you as soon as he brings it out. Meanwhile show affection to the young man, and be thankful to our times for such talent, which he endows with honest manners. He spends time with Spurinna and with Antoninus; he is a kinsman of one, and a close friend of both. From this you can gather how faultless the young man is, since he wins such affection from most dignified elders. That famous saw is undoubtedly true, that
   'One knows the sort of man he is from those with whom he loves to associate'.
   Farewell.[83]

The opening of the message to Pompeius Falco[84] stresses the oral context of the literary exchange depicted in the letter: Pliny had heard (1 *audivi*) Sentius Augurinus reciting his poems and now picks out one example which he remembers (3 *teneo*) from this lecture. The choice is hardly a coincidence; as in the case of Martial's epigram 10.20(19) embedded into letter 3.21, also here the *lemma* of the poem is Pliny himself, this time not in his role as a reader but as a writer of epigrams. Before quoting Augurinus' lines, Pliny stages (or plays with) the process of remembering and forgetting: as he tells his addressee, he memorised most of the lines (3 *teneo ... explicui*),[85] but he still has yet to recall the second verse (3 *si mihi ... secundus versus occurrerit*), and for the moment he reproduces the rest of the poem which he remembers well. Are we really meant to believe that Pliny, of all things, had forgotten the *secundus versus* (4.27.3)? After

---

[83] Translation by Walsh (2006).
[84] A younger fellow-senator who also receives *Ep.* 1.23 and is known from inscriptions; see Sherwin-White (1966) 138–9.
[85] Cf. *Ep.* 3.21.4 *nisi quosdam tenerem*; Cic. *Tusc.* 5.64 on the verses on Archimedes' tomb: *tenebam enim quosdam senariolos, quos in eius monumento esse inscriptos acceperam*.

all, it is C. Plinius **Secundus** whom Augurinus had chosen as the topic of his poem.[86]

By transferring Augurinus' poem from the oral context of the recitation to the written text of the letter, Pliny provides the poem with a new frame.[87] Oral mobility (i.e. poems disseminated at a reading in a lecture room) is transformed into the mobility of the letter sent to Pliny's friend Pompeius Falco.[88] On the other hand, by including the letter in the book and arranging it at a certain position (as the fourth letter from the end), this mobility is then reduced. What Pliny did during Augurinus' recitation can be compared to the literary theft Pliny warned Octavius Rufus of in *Ep.* 2.10: intellectual property might be stolen unless you publish it in the context of a corpus (3 *enotuerunt quidam tui versus et invito te claustra sua refregerunt. hos nisi retrahis in corpus, quandoque ut errones aliquem, cuius dicantur, invenient*).[89] By 'absorbing' Augurinus' verses in his letter, Pliny takes possession of the poem – albeit by mentioning Augurinus as the author he is not plagiarising his work, unlike with the *quidam* in letter 2.10.[90]

Ep. 3.21 and 4.27 are not the only letters which Pliny embellishes with epigrams. Letter 4.14 quotes from Catullus 16, letters 6.10 and 9.19 contain the epitaph for Verginius Rufus and two instances in Book 7 (7.4, 7.9) give (or try to give) an impression of Pliny's own skills as a poet. With this cycle of epistolary *prosimetra* reaching from Book 3 to 9, Pliny provides an epigrammatic anthology framed by letters; similar to anthologists such as Meleager and Philip, who added their own poems to the epigrams written by their predecessors,[91] Pliny too combines the verses composed by others with his own products and thus acts both as a poet and editor.

In his epigram, Sentius Augurinus claims that he follows the tradition of the *versus minuti* ('short poems') and mentions Catullus and Calvus as his

---

[86] For the pun on Pliny's name see Gibson and Morello (2012) 42 n. 15 who also point to a possible play with the name Augurinus and Pliny's *auguratus* as advertised in letter 4.8.

[87] See Tamás (2020).

[88] We may imagine him outside Italy, as Sherwin-White (1966) 306 suggests.

[89] 'Some of your verses have broken free in spite of you and have become more widely known; unless you recall them to be incorporated in the whole, like runaway slaves they will find someone else to claim them'; for the slave metaphor in this passage see Whitton (2013a) 149–50; a connection between the illegal possession of a slave belonging to someone else (*plagium*) and the theft of intellectual property is also drawn in Mart. 1.52.

[90] Tamás (2020) 38 discovers the acrostic HEU ME or HEU MEI in Augurinus' poem (lines 2–7); depending on which option we prefer, the first one wittily undermines the poem's quality ('Alas!') whereas the second one points to the question of authorship ('Oh no, they are mine!').

[91] See e.g. Cameron (1993); Gutzwiller (1998); Höschele (2010).

predecessors. Yet these models, as he continues, have been replaced by Pliny, who is now the new benchmark (l. 4 'To me, Pliny alone means as much as the former poets' (*unus Plinius est mihi priores*)). Apart from Catullus and Calvus who are mentioned explicitly, another representative of Roman epigram is also present in this poem: by stating that Pliny had already surpassed Catullus and Calvus, Sentius Augurinus (as quoted by Pliny) seems both to evoke and correct an epigram of Martial, where the poet from Bilbilis asks his friend Macer to only prefer Catullus to him (10.78.15–16): *nec multos mihi praeferas **priores**, | **uno** sed **tibi** sim minor Catullo* ('and you may not prefer many of my forerunners to me, but rank me below Catullus only').[92] Through the indirect allusion to Martial, Sentius Augurinus (or rather Pliny, who quotes him) suggests that Pliny the poet has not only equated Catullus and Calvus, but has also surpassed Martial.[93] Maybe we are also invited to compare Pliny with Silius Italicus,[94] whom Martial praises in epigram 7.63.1 as *perpetuus* and his work as *numquam moritura volumina*.[95] After having fulfilled his duties as an advocate and politician in the footsteps of Cicero, Silius in his retirement imitated Vergil by composing poetry (5–10). Martial concludes the poem with the line *proque suo celebrat nunc Helicona foro* (12 'and now he frequents Helicon instead of his Forum') which may be recalled by Augurinus' line *mavult versiculos foro relicto* (l. 5 'After having left the forum he prefers verses').[96] Whereas Silius left the Forum in order to compose an epic poem, Pliny dedicates himself to the composition of light poetry. In a letter which celebrates a promising poet from Pliny's circle of admirers and directly quotes from the young man's work, Pliny indirectly undermines the status of Martial and Silius as (Flavian) literary predecessors.[97]

Not only does Pliny quote Augurinus' poem in his letter, but he also 'imports' the allusions Augurinus made to Martial's epigram on his *aemulatio Catulli*. Whilst the whole letter 4.27 can be read as one half of Pliny's dialogue with Pompeius Falco, the text itself also stages a dialogue between Pliny the letter writer and Augurinus the poet: after the *adulescens*

---

[92] Translations of Martial by Shackleton Bailey (1993).
[93] See the discussion in Neger (2015b) 142–4.
[94] For Pliny and Silus Italicus see Tzounakas (Chapter 8) in this volume.
[95] On this poem cf. Galán Vioque (2002) ad loc.; Neger (2012) 304–6; Mindt (2013) 62–5.
[96] Cf. Martial's poem 10.20(19) on Pliny as quoted by Pliny in *Ep.* 3.21.5.
[97] Cf. also *Ep.* 3.21.6 on Martial (*'at non erunt aeterna, quae scripsit'; non erunt fortasse...*, '"But his writings will not be eternal"; maybe they will not...') and 3.7.5 on Silius (*scribebat carmina maiore cura quam ingenio*, 'He used to write poems with more diligence than talent').

(cf. 4.27.6) had praised Pliny as a literary model in a recent recitation, Pliny answers him, praising his poetic talent with a written *laudatio*. Furthermore, by not only referring to his affection for Sentius Augurinus (2 *amor eius*) but also mentioning that he won the affection of Vestricius Spurinna and Arrius Antoninus, two elder statesmen (6 *qui a gravissimis senibus sic amatur*) who also used to compose poems,[98] Pliny advertises a literary elite of which he too is an important member.

It is probably no coincidence that in close proximity to *Ep.* 4.27, where Pliny is heralded as a new Catullus, letter 4.25 contains a covert allusion to Catullus 22.[99] Moreover, the juxtaposition of *Ep.* 4.27 with letters 4.26 and 4.28 is worth noting. *Ep* 4.26 is addressed to Maecilius Nepos,[100] who had asked Pliny to send his revised *libelli* so he (i.e. Nepos) could take them along to the province he is about to govern (we do not learn any further details). Pliny characterises his *libelli* as 'companions' (3 *comites istos*)[101] which Nepos is going to carry about with him on his journey (2 *scripta nostra circumferre tecum*). Whereas others used to carry about with them the portraits of Epicurus or Corinthian bronzes, as the Elder Pliny states in his *Natural History* (34.48 *ut secum circumferant*; 35.5 *Epicuri voltus ... circumferunt secum*),[102] Maecilius Nepos prefers to have Pliny's books with him. If the Younger Pliny in letter 4.26 is deliberately alluding to his uncle's discussion of people venerating artworks, this would link the letter with *Ep.* 4.28, where we read about Herennius Severus who venerates the portrait of another Epicurean, Titus Catius. In *Ep.* 4.26, Pliny deliberately conceals to which literary genre his *libelli* belong.[103] The *comes*-metaphor recalls Martial's epigram 1.2 where the *libelli* (in the format of the codex) are also advertised as companions on a long journey (1–2 *Qui tecum cupis esse meos ubicumque libellos | et comites longae quaeris habere viae*).[104] As Pliny presents himself as *alter Catullus* in *Ep.* 4.27 and a writer of short poems in several other letters in Book 4 (4.14, 4.18,

---

[98] Vestricius Spurinna wrote *lyrica doctissima* in Greek and Latin (*Ep.* 3.1.7), Arrius Antoninus Greek epigrams in the style of Callimachus (*Ep.* 4.3, 4.18, 5.15).
[99] See Neger (Chapter 13) in this volume.
[100] For him see Sherwin-White (1966) 305 who suggests identifying Nepos with the Metilius Nepos, the recipient of letter 2.3 on Isaeus.
[101] A pun on the usual praxis of Roman governors taking their entourage with them to their provinces; cf. e.g. Curtius Rufus in *Ep.* 7.27.2 *obtinenti Africam comes haeserat*; 8.23.5.
[102] For the discourse on Corinthian bronzes see Rocchi (Chapter 5) in this volume.
[103] Sherwin-White (1966) 305 believes that Pliny is referring to his speeches.
[104] 'You who want my little books to keep you company wherever you may be and desire their companionship on a long journey'; for the codex-format in antiquity see Roberts and Skeat (1983).

Introduction

4.19.4), it is tempting to think of poetic *libelli* in letter 4.26 as well. On the other hand, the *libelli* could also encompass all of Pliny's writings produced so far, and thus Nepos would take his personal 'Companion to the Works of Pliny the Younger' with him to the province.

Another Nepos, better known to modern (and probably also ancient) readers of Pliny appears in *Ep.* 4.28, already mentioned above. In this letter to Vibius Severus, Pliny forwards a request of the scholar (1 *vir doctissimus*) Herennius Severus,[105] who wants to decorate his library with the portraits of Cornelius Nepos and Titus Catius, the addressee's fellow-townsmen (1 *imagines municipum tuorum*).[106] Cornelius Nepos links *Ep.* 4.28 both with the Nepos receiving letter 4.26 and Catullus mentioned in letter 4.27, for it is well-known that it was Cornelius Nepos to whom Catullus dedicated his *libellus* (Catull. 1). Herennius Severus, assuming that images of Nepos and Catius are available in Vibius Severus' hometown, asks for the production of copies of their portraits. This provides Pliny with the opportunity to reflect on the limits of artistic imitation at the end of the letter (3):

> Peto autem, ut pictorem quam diligentissimum assumas. Nam cum est arduum similitudinem effingere ex vero, tum longe difficillima est imitationis imitatio; a qua rogo ut artificem quem elegeris ne in melius quidem sinas aberrare.

> All I ask is that you find as accurate a painter as you can, for it is hard enough to make a likeness from life, but a portrait from a portrait is by far the most difficult of all. Please do not let the artist you choose depart from the original even to improve it.

It has long been noted that in this passage Pliny evokes Plato's theory of art and poetry as imitation of an imitation in the *Republic* (596e–602c) and transfers the philosophical discourse into the reality of epistolary social interaction.[107] But besides Plato's discussion of μίμησις (*mimesis*, 'imitation'), another philosophical discourse might be evoked in *Ep.* 4.28: Titus Catius, the second writer whose portrait Herennius Severus

---

[105] Vibius Severus also receives *Ep.* 3.18 on the recitation of the *Panegyricus*; Herennius Severus might have been the patron of the Greek antiquarian and biographer Philon of Byblos (*FGrHist* 790 (= 1060) whose consulship the *Suda* dates between AD 101 and 104; see Sherwin-White (1966) 307; Radicke (2003) 25 with n. 13.

[106] The praxis of decorating libraries with portrait statues of famous writers is discussed by Pliny the Elder in *HN* 35.9–11; according to Pliny, Asinius Pollio was the *primus inventor* of this praxis in Rome; Martial in 9 *praef.* writes that a certain Stertinius wanted to display his (Martial's) likeness in his library.

[107] Radicke (2003) 29; Marchesi (2008) 204–5.

wants to have in his library, is probably the Epicurean philosopher Catius, to whom Cicero in *Epistulae ad Familiares* 15.16.1 (= 215 SB) refers to as *Insuber* (i.e. from Gallia Cisalpina) and whom Quintilian characterises as 'minor, but not unpleasant writer among the Epicureans' (*Inst.* 10.1.124 *in Epicuriis levis quidem sed non iniucundus tamen auctor*). In his letter to Cassius Longinus, Cicero makes fun of the *spectra Catiana*, Catius' attempt to translate the Epicurean term εἴδωλα (*eidola*, 'images') into Latin, a term which plays a central role in Epicurean theory of perception. Cicero asks Cassius to explain to him how it is possible that these *spectra* not only hit the eyes but also the mind. While reading Pliny's thoughts on the difficulties of creating likeness (*similitudinem effingere*), a reader familiar with the works of Catius (such as Vibius Severus, whose *summus amor studiosorum* is praised in 4.28.2) might not only have recalled Plato, but also the Epicurean explanation of visual perception. According to Lucretius, who in Book 4 of *De Rerum Natura* discusses the *rerum simulacra* (4.30) and uses the term *imago* for the Greek εἴδωλον (4.63–4), every object emits εἴδωλα made of atoms which hit the receptors and thus enable sensation. The εἴδωλα responsible for vision are shed from the surface and thus maintain the object's shape (4.69 *formai servare figuram*). Colour is particularly well-suited to retaining its properties very well as it comes from the object's surface (4.96–7). It is not too daring to assume that, in a letter which discusses the problem of creating the visual likenesses of two Roman writers (one of them being an Epicurean philosopher), the reader is stimulated to recall Epicurean theory on vision as well. Perhaps by concluding the letter with the verb *aberrare*, Pliny even evokes the Epicurean idea of the *declinatio atomorum* as discussed in Lucretius *De Rerum Natura* 2 and Cicero *De Finibus* 1.[108]

Taken together, the triptych of *Ep.* 4.26–8 stages various forms of literary interaction both between Pliny and his contemporaries as well as his predecessors. What is more, it also showcases the letters' intermediality by progressing from the aspect of literary materiality (books personified as companions travelling through the empire) via orality and mnemonic skills (literature as being disseminated orally, perceived acoustically and memorised) to visibility (famous writers are not only read as texts but also looked at as images in libraries).[109]

---

[108] Cf. Lucr. *DRN* 2.221; 250; 253; 259; Cic. *Fin.* 1.19–20; 28.
[109] On intermediality in general see Jensen (2016); in Roman literature see Dinter and Reitz-Joosse (2019).

4 Key to Chapters

One of the questions which will be discussed in this volume is whether we can detect clusters or patterns of references within single books or letters. Roy Gibson, for example, confirms the conclusions drawn by Whitton (2019) by demonstrating in his chapter that Book 6 contains clusters of references to Quintilian and Tacitus, and adds to Whitton's observations by also discovering patterns of references to Vergil. Furthermore, the answer to the question of whether Pliny shows a predilection for old or contemporary writers seems to be that 'contemporary texts play a full part alongside established classics', as Whitton argues in his contribution. Various intertextual allusions and generic interactions within the frame of epistolary communication seem to provide Pliny with the opportunity not only to create stylistic variety but also to demonstrate his literary skills and deep familiarity with the literary tradition. One can also observe that Pliny's strategy of approaching genres is opportunistic, sometimes even inconsistent, depending on the rhetorical aims of the letters in question.

The contributions in this volume examine Plinian intertextuality both over the course of single books (Gibson on Book 6 covers Vergil, Cicero, Catullus, Quintilian, Tacitus and Petronius; König on Book 10 covers technical and specialist discourses by examining Frontinus as a case study) as well as interactions between the letters and specific writers, genres and discourses. We explore Pliny's intertextual dialogue with Ciceronian oratory (Mordue), Pliny the Elder's *Natural History* (Rocchi, Hindermann), Tacitus' *Agricola*, Valerius Maximus and Lucretius (Whitton), Seneca's *Letters* and *Dialogi* (Hanaghan, Tzounakas), Horatian lyric (Canobbio) and Statius' *Silvae* (Chinn), satire and the sceptic tradition (Tamás, Pigoń, Neger) and Martial's poetry for his patrons (Marchesi).

Part I, 'Intertextuality and Interdiscursivity in Pliny's Letters', is dedicated to Pliny's intertextual techniques and starts with a contribution by **Christopher Whitton** who demonstrates that the *Epistles* is a work of many intertextual parts which integrate a broad range of predecessors in prose and poetry, both old and new. Whitton discusses Pliny's method of intertextual eclecticism as well as his strategies of semantic transformations and shifting context by using the examples of Cicero, Lucretius, Valerius Maximus and Tacitus. The chapter illuminates the *Epistles* as an omnigeneric blend, created by a writer who is a virtuoso in exploiting parallels of situation and sequence in the pre-texts. Next, **Roy Gibson** focuses on Book 6 and investigates the range and intensity of intertextual relationships within this book, asking whether particular authors are privileged, clusters of references and patterns of allusions can be detected and if certain types or subjects of letters attract particular instances of intertextual reference. As Gibson observes, Cicero, Catullus and Vergil are especially prominent intertexts in this book, together with Quintilian and Tacitus, all of whom Pliny engages with in his attempts to present himself as the greatest living courtroom orator. **Alice König**, whose contribution also focuses on a single book, examines Pliny's Book 10 and considers how a range of intertextual discourses help to shape both the interiority of *Epistles* 10 and the construction of new kinds of administrative and imperial authority. König in particular looks at the letters' interaction with technical writing, especially Frontinus' work *De Aquis*. She applies a broader definition of intertextuality which not only includes lexical overlaps, discernible allusions, evocative echoes and suggestive re-workings but also wider conceptions of textual interaction such as literary hybridity and heteroglossia, i.e. exploring the multiplicity of voices we encounter in Book 10 as well as Pliny's deliberate channelling of these voices and discourses.

Part II, 'Models and Anti-Models: Pliny's Interaction with Oratory and Natural History', investigates the role of oratory and the *Natural History* in Pliny's *Epistles*. **Matthew Mordue** looks at the Regulus cycle and demonstrates how, by alluding to Demosthenes' *On the Crown* and Cicero's *In Verrem*, the narratives of these oratorical speeches are adapted in the *Epistles*. As Mordue argues, these models highlight Pliny's political pessimism as in both speeches the social elite is criticised for contributing to society's downfall. Thus, Pliny's allusions to these texts suggest that the social elite of his own time is similarly complicit in Rome's moral decline. Mordue's chapter on Pliny's engagement with Cicero's *In Verrem* is complemented by **Stefano Rocchi**'s contribution on the criticism of *luxuria* in the same Ciceronian work, Pliny the Elder's *Natural History* and Pliny the Younger's *Epistles*. Rocchi discovers interdiscursive links between these writers through their comments on Corinthian bronzes and shows how the two Plinii (*HN* 34.6–7 and 48; *Ep.* 3.1.9 and 3.6) allude to Cicero's oratorical discourse (*Verr.* 2.4.98; 2.4.49; 2.5.184), thus incorporating elements of Ciceronian oratory into encyclopaedic and epistolary writing. Rocchi discusses letters (3.1 and 3.6) where social criticism is not expressed directly but evoked implicitly, aiming at contrasting Vestricius Spurinna and Pliny himself with characters such as Verres. In the next chapter, **Judith Hindermann** examines how Pliny the Younger integrates subjects discussed by the Elder's *Naturalis Historia* in his letters on *mirabilia*. Instead of the Elder's scientific completeness and catalogue style, we encounter exemplarity and elaboration in the *Epistles*: geographic inclusiveness gives way to descriptive letters focusing on Italy. As Hindermann observes, the Younger Pliny unites various elements in one letter (e.g. 8.20) which the Elder Pliny distributes over different examples; thus, the Younger intensifies the miracles he narrates or describes, enriching them with more details and shaping them in a more personal way, according to the interest of the addressee. In addition, by demonstrating his capability to compose literature during his *otium* in daytime, Pliny the Younger distances himself from his uncle who used to work during the night (*lucubratio*).

Part III, 'Pliny and Seneca: Discourses of Grief and Posthumous Reputation', examines Pliny's interaction with Seneca. **Michael Hanaghan** focuses on the intertextual dialogue between Pliny's letters 1.12 and 4.2, and Seneca's *Ep.* 98 and 99. In letter 1.12, on Corellius Rufus' suicide, Hanaghan discovers implicit criticism of Seneca's *Ep.* 98 (a conciliatory letter covering the treatment of suicide and pain management) which has not helped Pliny to overcome his grief. Letter 4.2 showcases Pliny's 'mean spirited approach to Regulus' grief' by outlining the problem of *ostentatio doloris* ('ostentation of pain') which Seneca discusses in *Ep.* 99. Pliny's criticism of Regulus is intensified by his use of Seneca. As Hanaghan concludes, Pliny is opportunistic, even hypocritical in applying the Stoic views in Seneca's consolation letters; depending on the communicative aim of his letters, Pliny both agrees and disagrees with his model. Pliny's opportunistic use of Stoic ideas is also discussed in the next chapter by **Spyridon Tzounakas**, who provides an analysis of Pliny's letter 3.7 to Caninius Rufus on the death of Silius Italicus. Genuine grief is surprisingly absent in this letter where, as Tzounakas argues, Pliny tries to undermine Silius' posthumous reputation by alluding to Seneca's *Dialogi* and *Epistles* as well as other models. Pliny evokes several Senecan works and thus virtually creates an epistolary library with a section containing Stoic best sellers. In his obituary letter, Pliny prompts his readers to evaluate Silius' character through the lens of Stoic discourses and to notice an inconsistency between Silius' Stoic death and his un-Stoic way of life. Tzounakas also demonstrates that Cicero's *Epistulae ad Familiares* and Hesiod's didactic poetry play an important role in this letter, serving to distinguish Pliny and his addressee from Silius.

Part IV, 'Pliny's Villas and Their Poetic Models', examines Pliny's interaction with Horace's lyric poetry and Statius' *Silvae* (as well as Lucretius and Vergil). The addressee of Pliny's obituary letter for Silius, Caninius Rufus, reappears in **Alberto Canobbio**'s chapter on *Ep.* 1.3 with its two central motifs, the villa as a *locus amoenus* and literary survival in the memory of posterity. The villa in this letter is imagined as an entity that is not only possessed by its master, but also interacts with him. Canobbio discovers generic echoes of Horace (i.e. not only allusions to specific passages, but also to motifs recurrent in Horace' poetry), such as the ideas expressed in *Carmen* 2.14 and, particularly, the *monumentum*-topos of *Carmen* 3.30. In addition to Horace, Pliny's text also imitates epigraphic language. Whereas Caninius' villa in Comum will be passed on to other owners after Caninius' death, a literary work is a timeless space and will always remain the property of its author. By providing an extensive ekphrasis of his own villas (*Ep.* 2.17 and 5.6), Pliny removes them from their caducity and makes them not only his legal, but also literary possessions. The villa-letters 2.17 and 5.6 are also the subject of **Christopher Chinn**'s contribution. Chinn traces the intertextual history of the didactic discourse which inspired Pliny's own villa-descriptions in Lucretius' *De Rerum Natura* 5.1361–78 via Vergil *Georgics* 1.60–70 until Statius' villa-poems *Silvae* 1.3 and 2.2. Similar to Statius, Pliny too employs a large number of Lucretian echoes in order to describe the physical aspects of the Tuscan landscape against the backdrop of Lucretius' account of the origin of agriculture. The motif of control over nature is integrated into the overall project of praise (Statius) and self-praise (Pliny). As Chinn argues, Pliny acknowledges Statius as an intertextual intermediary and is also aware of the Lucretius-Vergil intertext that he has found in Statius. At the same time, Pliny 'advertises his fuller acknowledgment of the Lucretian pre-text than Statius does'.

Part V, 'Pliny Turns Nasty: Satire and the Scoptic Tradition', explores how satire and invective (both in prose and verse) are absorbed in Pliny' letters. **Ábel Tamás** discusses Pliny's letter 1.9 and argues that it provides an epistolary version of Horace's *Sermones* 1.9 (a text which also can be read as a numerological parallel of this letter). With his critique of the city life, Pliny imports a motif typical of satire into the letters – or rather, he allows the Horatian *sermo* to 'intrude' into the *Epistles*. Pliny reconfigures the satiric space of Horace *Sermones* 1.9 by depicting his life as being separated into urban *negotium* and rustic *otium*. As Tamás argues, in letter 1.9 Pliny is multiplied into different speaking or silent *personae*. Urban interlocutors (among them Pliny himself) represent the noise and buzz which make the urban life intolerable. By re-enacting the atmosphere of urban noise pollution and constant buzzing (probably all too familiar to Pliny's contemporaries) the letter also interacts with the city itself on an intermedial level. Tamás reads letter 1.9 as a metafictional comment on interactions, both social and literary, and the issue of both desiring and trying to avoid interaction.

Whilst Tamás explores the lighter satiric undertones in *Ep.* 1.9, the next two chapters investigate a Pliny who presents himself as more aggressive. **Jakub Pigoń** focuses on the letter pair 7.29 and 8.6, about the once powerful imperial freedman Pallas, whom the Senate under Claudius decided to honour with money and the insignia of a praetor. In this pair of letters, Pliny combines the roles of a paradoxographer, antiquarian and epigraphist with the voice of a satirist. *Risus* and *indignatio* are the reactions which Pliny considers appropriate after reading the 'farce' of Pallas and the Senate. Pallas is remembered not through his monument and his epigraph, but through Pliny's letters which combat the message the freedman wished to transmit to posterity. In his very selective account of the incident, Pliny seems to have deliberately blanked out the historical context in order to present a cautionary tale instead. Pliny's various strategies of integrating the iambic and satiric tradition into his letters are also the topic of **Margot Neger**'s contribution. Iambic *ira* and scoptic laughter are already expressed in the sequence of *Ep.* 1.5–6. In further letter-invectives against certain individuals such as Regulus, Pallas or the anonymous senator criticised in *Ep.* 4.25, Pliny demonstrates a deep familiarity with the conventions of scoptic writing. Apart from epistolary invectives, the scoptic tradition is also evoked within Pliny's correspondence with his friends in a more playful way. For instance, in *Ep.* 2.2 and 5.10 Pliny alludes to scoptic poems by Catullus and Martial and, at the same time, shifts the context by transforming the aggressive or derisive tone of his models into friendly joking with his addressees.

The last part of our volume, Part VI, 'Final Thoughts: Discourses of Representation and Reproduction', consists of a chapter by **Ilaria Marchesi** where the varieties of textual relations investigated throughout the volume are summarised and a perspective for further research is provided: Marchesi distinguishes the concepts of intra-, inter-, extra- and alter-textuality, four modes of textual interference which are often to be co-implicated with one another. As a case study for this shifting of textual relations, Marchesi sheds light on the interaction between Pliny and Martial in those letters where Pliny discusses the issues of reproduction, cross-generational representation and character transmission. As Marchesi observes, Pliny's letter 4.19 with its praise of his wife Calpurnia is not only intratextually connected with previous items in the collection but also evokes a surprising target of distance allusion: Martial's epigram 6.38 praises Regulus, whom we already encountered as Pliny's adversary and target of several letter-invectives in previous chapters. The intertextuality between these two texts transfers to Pliny's wife the charged language which Martial deployed for Regulus' wife and child.

Epistolography is probably the most flexible among ancient literary genres, as the broad range of letter types which are transmitted suggests. On a formal level, ancient letters vary between shorter messages and longer treatises in prose, pure verse epistles, prose letters with embedded poems, prose letters attached to poems and poetic collections; the Latin tradition of epistolography from Cicero to Ennodius especially includes a striking variety of letters and letter collections. In the present volume, Pliny the Younger's letter collection has been chosen as a case study for the literary flexibility of ancient epistolography. In addition to the formal diversity of Pliny's letters, the contributions in this volume focus on the ways in which generic flexibility is mobilised through intertextual and interdiscursive dialogue. By absorbing and channelling various genres and discourses, Pliny invites his readers to draw connections and comparisons, or to detect contrasts and contradictions between the *Epistles* and other types of literary as well as non-literary text and discourse; at the same time, Pliny always seems to be conscious of the limits the epistolary genre imposes upon his literary experiments. By choosing the flexible letter genre, Pliny sets himself to integrate a diversity of other genres and discourses from a large spectrum, including: epic poetry, epigram, oratory, historiography, technical writing and paradoxography. At the same time, Pliny both explicitly and implicitly expresses his literary views and practises literary criticism in an indirect way. Thus, the *Epistles*, which one at first glance might consider a humble and occasional form of writing, reveal themselves as a 'supergenre' with a protean quality, able to compete with canonical and contemporary works. Rather than covering the subject exhaustively, this volume's chapters aim at providing a stimulus for further discussion of the techniques of literary assimilation and implied literary criticism in the letters of Pliny the Younger and in other works of ancient letter writers. We hope to inspire further investigations of ancient epistolography's generic flexibility and interactivity, and to open the field for scholarship which aims to shed light on this phenomenon from a wider perspective.

PART I

Intertextuality and Interdiscursivity in Pliny's Letters

CHAPTER I

Pliny, Man of Many Parts (Lucretius, Cicero, Valerius Maximus, Tacitus)

Christopher Whitton

This chapter has a simple argument: Pliny's *Epistles* is a work of many intertextual parts.[1] Neither beholden to Cicero's *Epistles*, its professed generic forebear, nor privileging 'poetic memory' over prose, it integrates a broad range of predecessors, old and new, verse and prose. In a larger study of Plinian intertextuality, I have argued that Quintilian's *Institutio oratoria* is its unsuspected protagonist, with Tacitus' *Dialogus* tightly caught up in the same weave.[2] I won't rehearse those claims here, and space precludes discussion of the many other underestimated players on this stage: Sallust, for instance, Livy and Seneca the Elder.[3] Instead I have chosen four authors and three letters (*Epistles* 4.3, 5.16, and 7.1). With this handful of examples, I aim to exemplify some modes and norms of Plinian *imitatio*, to demonstrate that Lucretius, Cicero (*rhetorica*), Valerius Maximus and Tacitus (*Agricola*) all have a role in his pages, and to underline, therefore, the breadth of ambition inherent to Pliny's generic self-positioning. We'll also repeatedly see exemplified 'the remarkable Roman capacity for seeing one individual in terms of another'[4] – which

---

[1] I keenly regret that I couldn't accept the kind invitation of Spyridon Tzounakas and Margot Neger to their conference on 'Pliny's epistolary intertextuality', and thank them all the more for inviting this contribution afterwards. I wrote it in June 2018.

[2] See Whitton (2019), to which I refer for substantiation of many claims here, for a survey of the field and for justification of my preferred term 'imitation'. I extend the story elsewhere to Tacitus' *Histories*, another large and unnoticed presence in the *Epistles*, and for that matter the *Panegyricus* (Whitton forthcoming).

[3] Sallust is a frequent presence, above all the proem of *Bellum Catilinae* (as notably in *Ep.* 9.3; see Whitton (2019), index loc.). Livian cameos include *Ep.* 5.21.4 (obsequies for Julius Avitus) ~ Livy 3.12.2 (obsequies for Cincinnatus' son Caeso) and *Ep.* 7.27.5 (the ghost) ~ Livy 2.23.3–4 (the tortured debtor of 495 BC); see also Gibson, p. 52 in this volume. For Seneca the Elder, start with *Ep.* 1.5.1 *non minora commiserat quam ... sed tectiora* (~ *Con.* 1.pr.15 *non minor est quam ... sed occultior*) together with *Ep.* 1.5.12 *nec sum contentus eloquentia saeculi nostri* etc. (~ *Con.* 1.pr.6 *non contenti exemplis saeculi vestri* etc.).

[4] Woodman and Martin (1996) 85.

30   CHRISTOPHER WHITTON

is to say, this is also an occasion to recall the all-encompassing import of exemplarity in the *Epistles* (and thus in Roman culture).[5]

1 *Epistles* 4.3, with Cicero and Lucretius

Epistles 4.3 is the first of three letters complimenting the old senator Arrius Antoninus on his poetry.[6] It starts with his splendid political career, then gets to the point: the peerless quality of his Latin and, above all, his marvellous Greek epigrams and mimiambs. A pair of hyperbolical accolades constitutes the climax:[7]

> Hominemne Romanum tam Graece loqui? **Non** medius fidius **ipsas Athenas** *tam* **Atticas** dixerim. Quid multa? Invideo Graecis quod illorum lingua scribere maluisti. Neque enim coniectura eget quid sermone patrio exprimere possis, cum hoc insiticio et inducto tam praeclara opera perfeceris. Vale. (*Ep.* 4.3.5)

> To think that someone Roman could speak so Greek! I do declare that I wouldn't say Athens herself was so Attic! In a word, I envy the Greeks that you have chosen to write in their tongue: it takes no conjecture what you could express in your native language, when you have produced such splendid works in this grafted and imported one.
> Yours, Pliny

These compliments gain depth from the fragmentary integration of two canonical texts. The first is the *Orator*, Cicero's late treatise on oratorical style. Defending himself against charges of 'Asianist' bombast levelled by self-proclaimed Atticists, he advises his critics to measure their definition of Atticism against the greatest orator of all, Demosthenes:

> Itaque nobis monendi sunt ei quorum sermo imperitus increbruit, qui aut dici se desiderant Atticos aut ipsi Attice volunt dicere, ut mirentur hunc maxime, quo **ne Athenas quidem ipsas** *magis* credo fuisse **Atticas**: quid enim sit Atticum discant eloquentiamque ipsius viribus, non imbecillitate sua metiantur. (Cic. *Orat.* 23)

> And so we must advise those whose naïve talk has been bandied about, who either say they want to be called Attic or want to speak Attic [*i.e.* in the

---
[5] On Plinian exemplarity see first Gazich (2003).
[6] The miniature *Ep.* 4.18 and 5.15 complete this little cycle; he is also mentioned in *Ep.* 4.27.5, another letter on poetry (a major theme introduced in Book 4). *Cos. suff.* 69, II *suff.* 97 (Eck, *BNP* 'Arrius II, 1'), Antoninus was among Pliny's most senior addressees.
[7] Latin texts are cited after Mynors (1963) or relevant Oxford texts, with occasional changes to spelling and punctuation. Translations are mine.

Attic style] themselves, to admire this man [*i.e.* Demosthenes] most of all, a man than whom I believe not even Athens herself was more Attic: let them learn what Attic is and measure their eloquence by his strength, not their own weakness.

Pliny's praise for Antoninus reworks Cicero's for Demosthenes.[8] The imitation is clear formally, with the three key terms (*ipsas, Athenas, Atticas*) reprised in the same case and almost the same order; other elements are varied.[9] It is also clear semantically. Athens 'was no more Attic' than Demosthenes, 'was not so Attic' as Antoninus: each epigram compares a man to a city, and invokes a (mannered) scale of Atticity.[10] Pliny shifts the context and drops a rhetorical technicality: Cicero writes about oratorical style and raises Athens in the specific context of the 'Atticist/Asianist' *querelle*; Pliny writes about a poet and uses Athens more broadly, as the definitive home of good Greek.

As this little encounter exemplifies, Pliny was a far more attentive and productive reader of Cicero's rhetorical treatises than recent scholarship has allowed (he returns several times to this early portion of the *Orator*).[11] The imitation is characteristic in its brevity, in its nonchalance, and in its interpretative potential: readers are welcome to pass over it, but those with eyes to see (or ears to hear) will find that Pliny's praise extends beyond literal hyperbole to encompass implicit comparison with the orator whom he and others uphold as the greatest model of all.[12] I will venture a step further to speculate that he lights upon Cicero by way of an obvious 'associative bridge', as talk of Antoninus' pure Greek prompts and invites recall of Cicero on Demosthenes' pure Attic.[13]

Characteristic too is the speed with which Pliny moves to another model. Look again at how he follows up the 'Athens' line –

---

[8] Seen long ago by Buchner (1644) *notae* p.30. As with most of Pliny's intertextuality, readers relying on twentieth-century commentaries will hear little of it (Trisoglio 1973 ad loc. has a non-committal 'cf.').

[9] P. ∅ ~ C. *quo*; P. *non* ~ C. *ne . . . quidem*; P. *medius fidius* ~ C. *credo* (each an avowal); P. ∅ (*sc. esse*) ~ C. *fuisse*; P. *tam* ~ C. *magis* (making 'Atticity' a scale).

[10] In the idea of 'speaking *more* Attic, in a more Attic *way*' (not quite the same as 'speaking Attic better' or 'sounding more Attic').

[11] Some or all of *Ep.* 1.20.4 (*Orat.* 26), 1.20.19 (~ *Orat.* 29), 1.20.21 (~ *Orat.* 23), 2.14.13 (~ *Orat.* 27), 9.26.9 (~ *Orat.* 26), and 5.20.5 (~ *Orat.* 18): Whitton (2019), index loc. Pliny also looks frequently to *De oratore*, and occasionally to the *Brutus*; he also makes productive use of Cicero's other dialogues, not least *De senectute* (Whitton 2019, index loc.). 'Recent scholarship': summarised by Marchesi (2008) 252–7.

[12] Whitton (2013a) 101.

[13] *Assoziationsbrücke* conventionally denotes an involuntary cognitive process. The crafted *imitatio* of Pliny (and many writers besides), I would say, involves a complex blend of the involuntary (an idea presents itself) and the voluntary (it is worked through with application).

32   CHRISTOPHER WHITTON

> Quid multa? Invideo **Graecis** quod *illorum* **linguā** *scrībĕre*[A] maluisti. *Neque enim coniectura eget* quid **sermone patrio**[B] ex*prim*ĕre possīs,[C] *cum hoc insiticio et inducto tam praeclara opera perfeceris*. (*Ep.* 4.3.5)

– and compare a familiar passage from Lucretius' first book:

> Nunc et Anaxagorae scrutemur homoeomerian
> quam **Grai** memorant nec *nostra dīcĕre* **linguā**[A]
> concedit nobis **patrii sermonis**[B] egestas;
> sed tamen ipsam rem facilest **ex**po*n*ĕre verbīs.[C] (Lucr. *DRN* 1.830–3)
>
> Now let us consider too Anaxagoras' *homoeomeria*, as the Greeks call it and which the destitution of our native language does not allow us to say in our own tongue; but it is easy nonetheless to set out the thing itself in words.

Lucretius is talking about Anaxagoras' theory of 'like parts' and the challenge of translating philosophy into Latin: a far cry from Antoninus and his epigrams. But there can be little doubt that Pliny has imported these lines into his letter. The formal core of the liaison is *patrius sermo*. That isn't rare enough to prove anything on its own[14] (or so you might assume),[15] but the further similarities tell a clear tale.[16] It's an imitative

---

[14] The phrase is extant seven times between Lucretius and Pliny (Cic. *Fin.* 1.4; Verg. *Aen.* 12.834; Hor. *Ars P.* 57; three times in Curt. 6.9–10; Sil. *Pun.* 2.440).

[15] 'Extant seven times' is the truth, but not the whole truth: only three of them refer to Latin, and only one of those at most is independent of Lucretius. (*i*) Hor. *Ars P.* 56–8 *cum lingua Catonis et Enni | sermonem patrium ditaverit et nova rerum | nomina protulerit* is a sure imitation, combining *DRN* 1.830 *patrii sermonis egestas* (~ *sermonem patrium ditaverit*, with *lingua ~ linguā* in the preceding line) with its anticipation at *DRN* 1.139 *propter egestatem linguae et rerum novitatem | (~ et nova rerum |*). (No comment in Brink (1971) ad loc. or Hardie (2009) 41–64, but the latter establishes Lucretius' importance to Horace more broadly.) (*ii*) Despite the silence of Tarrant (2012) and others ad loc., it's a good bet that Vergil (*Aen.* 12.834 '*sermonem Ausonii patrium moresque tenebunt*') does too, given his next line ('*utque est nomen erit: commixto corpore tanto*' ~ *DRN* 1.859 *sive cibos omnis commixto corpore dicent*, less than thirty lines on from *DRN* 1.830; cf. also G. 2.325); again Hardie (2009), though he doesn't mention this passage, firmly establishes Vergil's close and productive reading of Lucretius. That leaves (*iii*) Cic. *Fin.* 1.4 *sermo patrius*, in Cicero's biggest set-piece defence of his practice of writing philosophy in Latin. If he has Lucretius in mind, he takes remarkably little trouble to show it, either here or in *Fin.* 1.10 *Latinam linguam non modo non inopem, ut vulgo putarent, sed locupletiorem etiam esse quam Graecam*; cf. *Caec.* 51 *nostra lingua, quae dicitur esse inops*, antedating *DRN*). All of which is to say: it is rash to take a statement like the one in my previous note at face value when weighing up the probability of imitation.

[16] *Exprimere possis* echoes *exponere verbis* (and turns the hexameter ending into a prose clausula, resolved cretic plus spondee). *Graecis* [second word] ... *nostra dicere lingua* echoes and varies *Grai* [second word] ... *illorum lingua scribere*. The six embolded elements appear in the same sequence. All this is strong reason, too, to privilege these lines of Book 1 over the references to *patrius sermo* at *DRN* 1.136–9 (n. 15) and 3.260 *abstrahit invitum patrii sermonis egestas*. Pliny's *tam praeclara opera* may also have a Lucretian origin: cf. *DRN* 1.729–32 (of Empedocles) *praeclarius ... exponunt praeclara reperta* (likewise a neut. pl. object), nearby in the text, and easily associated with *DRN* 1.833 through *exponere*.

pattern found all over the *Epistles* (and not special to Pliny): a lexical hub (*sermone patrio ~ patrii sermonis*), only moderately distinct as diction, varied, and accompanied by more subtle reflexes.[17] Again, meaning plays no lesser a part. At one level, Pliny and Lucretius are on the same page: both compare Greek and Latin; both stake a claim about the ease of writing Latin. At another, they are talking about two different things altogether. Lucretius tells us that Latin is lexically inadequate for his task, but affirms that this will cause him no difficulty. Pliny writes about poetry, and produces an argument *a fortiori* which leans on the idea of 'native' in *patrius*: if Antoninus can write so marvellously in a foreign language, just think how he'll get on in his native tongue. Again, it's a typical outcome: the idea is in one way the same (making another clear associative bridge), in others thoroughly transformed.[18]

As with Cicero, so with Lucretius: Pliny has been attentive in reading, minute in adapting – and by no means furtive in his *imitatio*. For one thing, it's a fair bet that these lines were as famous in his day as they are in ours.[19] For another, the formal adaptation hardly covers its tracks. For a third, there are the hints of wry self-reflexivity. When Pliny describes Greek with the extremely rare adjective *insiticius* ('grafted on'),[20] he vindicates – *pace* Lucretius – the ability of Latin to innovate lexically. We might also toy with reading the same word as delicate annotation of his own textual act, as he grafts a Lucretian sprig into his prose. Certainly we should recognise the irony when Pliny says, 'it takes no conjecture …'. *Coniectura* is not a Lucretian word, and we naturally take it, in the (faux-)casual context of a letter, to mean 'guess'. But it is also a standard technical term of logic ('conjecture') – strangely familiar from Quintilian's *Institutio*[21] – making, then, a suitable garnish to this briefest of forays into philosophy.

---

[17] Examples in Whitton (2019) ch. 3 and *passim*.
[18] At the risk of trying your patience, I refer again to the examples scattered in Whitton (2019).
[19] Explicit citation and quotation of Lucretius is surprisingly rare between his death and Pliny's day (Butterfield (2013) 47–54; Gatzemeier (2013)), and comments on *patrius sermo* tend to be situated by scholars in a 'poverty topos' (Fögen (2000); Farrell (2001) 28–51). But imitation is a different matter (n. 15; a case in point is Sen. *Ep.* 58.1 *Quanta verborum nobis paupertas, immo egestas sit ~ DRN* 1.132 *concedit nobis patrii sermonis egestas*, surely not just 'topos' but imitation). Lucretius' canonicity is clear from explicit mentions by e.g. Nep. *Att.* 12.4, Vitr. 9.*pr.*17, Ov. *Am.* 1.15.23 and Tr. 2.425, Vell. 2.36.2, Sen. *Tranq.* 2.14 (etc.) and Quint. *Inst.* 10.1.87.
[20] Hence the glossing doublet *inductus*. Far rarer than *insitivus*, it is attested twice in Varro, once in ps.-Sall. *Ad Caes. sen.* (date uncertain) and once in Sen. *Helv.* (conjectural); after Pliny, once each in Apuleius (text uncertain) and Sidonius (probably from Pliny). Details in *TLL* s.v.
[21] Early in his chapter on conjecture, Quintilian writes that facts relating to the present *non egent coniectura, ut si apud Lacedaemonios quaeratur an Athenis muri fiant* ('do not need conjecture, for instance if it is asked in Sparta whether walls are being built at Athens', *Inst.* 7.2.4). The phrasing closely and uniquely matches Pliny's *neque enim coniectura eget*. The technical *Inst.* 7 is not a book

Here, then, is a sure case of Lucretius being imitated in the *Epistles*,[22] significant both for what it says about Pliny's intertexture and as a neglected trace of *De Rerum Natura*.[23] But I also offer it as a characteristic example of Plinian intertextuality: subtle (but not sneaky) in form, extensive in adaptation, and accompanied by more than one sign of wit. Even the choice of target text is typically off-beat: Lucretius, perhaps, makes a more predictable source than Cicero, for this parting touch in a letter to a poet; but neither his argument nor his genre speaks directly to Antoninus' miniatures or Pliny's compliment on them.

Pliny's second letter to Antoninus, by the way, comes later in the same book, and begins like this:

> Quemadmodum magis approbare tibi possum quantopere mirer epigrammata tua Graeca, quam quod quaedam Latine aemulari et exprimere temptavi? In deterius tamen. Accidit hoc primum imbecillitate ingeni mei, deinde inopia ac potius, **ut Lucretius ait, egestate patrii sermonis**. (*Ep.* 4.18.1)

> How can I better prove to you how much I admire your Greek epigrams than by the fact that I have tried to emulate and express some of them in Latin? For the worse, though. This happens first through the weakness of my talent, then through the poverty or rather, as Lucretius says, the destitution of our native language.

This is the only time Pliny quotes Lucretius and the first recorded citation of his line on *patrius sermo* – freely quoted, to be sure (modified for word-order, syntax, and rhythm),[24] but it could hardly be more explicit.[25] As often, he draws our attention to a detail in the original easily passed over, that *egestas* is not just poverty, but severe poverty.[26] It also confirms (if you

---

that features heavily in *Ep.* (I have noticed no other instance; cf. Whitton (2019) 36–7, but I doubt coincidence here, given (*i*) that Pliny imitates Quintilian scores of times in the *Epistles* and (*ii*) that both mention Athens in the same breath.

[22] Some other suggestions in Gigante (1979) 350 and 355–7 (on *Ep.* 6.16 and 6.20; add e.g. *Ep.* 6.16.9 *crassiore caligine* - *DRN* 6.461 *caligine crassa*); Marchesi (2008) 129–31 (*Ep.* 1.6).

[23] Likewise Horace and Vergil in n. 15.

[24] Which consideration came first is hard to say, but the variations integrate the phrase into Pliny's syntax and avoid a heroic clausula. His own rhythm is a rare choice for him, whether we call it a dispondee (the lumpiest of prose clausulae) or a resolved cretic plus molossus. Either way, the four long syllables (-*is* is *brevis in longo*) could constitute a lightly raised eyebrow at Pliny's *non*-versiness. A different thought in Butterfield (2013) 52 ('perhaps ... distancing himself from ... a poet he seemingly did not hold in high esteem'). On Pliny's sensitivity to rhythm see Whitton (2013a) 28–32, with Whitton (2019) 307 on some imitations of Catullan prosody.

[25] Similar phrases with *ut ait* at *Ep.* 4.7.6, 5.8.11 (again freely adapted), 7.32.2.

[26] Hence the 'correction', *inopia ac potius ... egestate*, à la Sen. *Ep.* 58.1 *Quanta verborum nobis paupertas, immo egestas sit.*

needed confirmation) that he knows Lucretius' comment about *patrius sermo*. But more than that: these lines are a clearly signalled sequel to *Epistles* 4.3, picking up the theme of Antoninus' Greek poems[27] and the contrast of Greek and Latin with which that letter ended; it can hardly be accident, then, that Pliny quotes here the passage he imitated there. This looks, in other words, like belated revelation,[28] confirming – for alert readers – that the earlier echoes were planned, not accidental.

I draw three conclusions from that. First, the liaison with Lucretius that I identified in *Epistles* 4.3 is no fantasy, nor the result (if you had been wondering) of sub- or semiconscious repetition. Second, we have confirmation of the self-reflexivity I suggested identifying there. In some measure, at least, this imitation is a game: Pliny is planting trails, and looking over his shoulder to see whether we follow. Third, and arising from both of those: the *Epistles* roves widely as it forages for literary *elegantia* and generic roughage – inviting us to try to keep up with the diverse ingredients being mixed into Pliny's omnigeneric blend.

2 *Epistles* 7.1, with Lucretius and Valerius Maximus

Epistles 7 opens with a brief sermon on *temperantia*.[29] Geminus is suffering a long illness;[30] Pliny urges him to constancy by recalling his own fortitude under duress, demonstrated in two stages. First he reports the standing instruction he gives his slaves: if he is ever ill and demands something the doctors disapprove of, they must refuse it. Second, he provides a specific *exemplum* to crown the letter:

> Quin etiam cum perustus ardentissima febre tandem remissus unctusque acciperem a medico potionem, porrexi manum utque tangeret dixi, admotumque iam labris poculum reddidi. (5) Postea cum vicensimo valetudinis die balineo praepararer mussantesque medicos repente vidissem, causam requisivi. Responderunt posse me tuto lavari, non tamen omnino sine aliqua suspicione. (6) 'Quid,' inquam, 'necesse est?' Atque ita spe balinei, cui iam videbar inferri, placide leniterque dimissa, ad abstinentiam rursus, non secus ac modo ad balineum, animum vultumque composui. (7) Quae

---

[27] Loudly (*Ep.* 4.18.1 *epigrammata tua Graeca* – 4.3.3 *Graeca epigrammata tua*), and discreetly (*Ep.* 4.18.1 *exprimere temptavi* – 4.3.5 *exprimere possis*).

[28] Otherwise called '*e sequentibus praecedentia*', the technique 'whereby a later passage explains an earlier' (Woodman (2014) 77). It is tempting to see *aemulari et exprimere* as intertextual annotation too. Antoninus' third and final letter (*Ep.* 5.15) is again thick with talk of imitation, and precedes one of Pliny's most remarkable epistolary acts of *imitatio* (*Ep.* 5.16, part of which I consider below).

[29] The theme is signalled with a framing repetition: *Ep.* 7.1.1 *temperantissimum* ... 7 *temperantia*.

[30] On Rosianus Geminus, addressed six times, see Sherwin-White (1966) ad loc. and Birley (2000) s.v.

tibi scripsi, primum ut te non sine exemplo monerem, deinde ut in posterum ipse ad eandem temperantiam astringerer, cum me hac epistula quasi pignore obligavissem.[31] *Vale. (Ep.* 7.1.4–7)

Once, in fact, I was racked with a fiercely burning fever. When at last it had abated and I had had a rub-down, the doctor was giving me a drink; I held out my hand and told him to touch it [*i.e.* take my pulse], and I gave back the cup that I had already lifted to my lips. (5) Later, on the twentieth day of my illness, when I was being prepared for the baths, I suddenly saw the doctors muttering, and asked the reason. They replied that I could bathe safely, but not altogether without some concerns. (6) 'What,' I said, 'is it necessary?' And so I calmly and mildly abandoned hope of the baths that I thought I was already being carried into, and I fixed my mind and countenance, as I had a moment before on bathing, back on abstinence. (7) I have written this to you, first so as not to give you advice without an example, and then so that I myself might be obligated to the same temperance, having bound myself over with this letter as if with a surety. Yours, Pliny

A drink and the baths (probably a steam rather than a dip) are the two things a sick man longs for;[32] Pliny sets out his steadfastness in refusing both.

Two very different texts are folded into this exemplary scene, again one prose, one verse. Let me start this time with the verse (Lucretius again). Compare Pliny and his doctors –

Postea cum vicensimo valetudinis die balineo praepararer **mussantesque medicos** *repente vidissem, causam requisivi. (Ep.* 7.1.5)

– with Lucretius' apocalyptic vision of the Athenian plague:

Nec requies erat ulla mali: defessa iacebant
corpora. **Mussabat** *tacito* **medicina** *timore . . . (DRN* 6.1178–9)

And there was no respite from the trouble: their bodies lay exhausted. Medicine muttered with silent fear . . .

---

[31] Guillemin (1953–62) ad loc. reasonably compares Cic. *Fam.* 5.8.12 *Has litteras velim existimes foederis habituras esse vim, non epistulae . . .* and the legal metaphor in *Ep.* 3.1.12 *idque iam nunc apud te subsigno . . .*

[32] *Ep.* 7.26.2 *balinea imaginatur et fontes.* 'Steam': *balineum* is the whole complex of rooms in a Roman bath-house. Here (as e.g. Tac. *Ann.* 14.64.2) the hot and humid *caldarium* is probably in mind.

Pliny's doctors mutter, concerned about the wisdom of taking a bath but nervous of telling him so.³³ Lucretius describes 'medicine' (i.e. doctors) muttering, fearful and impotent in the face of an epidemic. The expression is distinctive, and unparalleled.³⁴ In formal terms, the muttering doctors are more isolated than the liaison with *patrius sermo*, but they too, judging from the further parallels of situation and sequence, aren't isolated or cut free of their context: Lucretius has just described the Athenians plunging their 'burning limbs' (*ardentia ... membra*) into rivers (1172–3), their desperate thirst (1174–7), and Athens' unceasing plight (1178); Pliny has just described his 'fiercely burning fever' (*ardentissima febre*), his impressive refusal of a drink, and an illness lasting three weeks or more. Once again difference and similarity are finely balanced: three elements which are in essence the same, but with very significant *mutata* in the transformation from death-dealing pandemic to individual discomfort.

Strange to tell, Pliny's whole little scene is subtended by Lucretius' plague. Why? One possibility is inadvertence: Lucretius' *mussabat medicina* had lodged in Pliny's mind and now resurfaces – along with its context – without his realising it.³⁵ Such cognitive questions are as fascinating as they are elusive,³⁶ but I am inclined to credit Pliny with very considerable control over his expression, given the minutely attentive detail that attends so much of his *imitatio*.

A second answer concerns aggrandisement, of a particular sort. Taken at face value, this is a quotidian tale of an ordinary (elite) man in his sickroom. But within it resonates one of the great works of poetic therapy. Pliny's handling of his plight acquires grand, we might say epic, dimensions through implicit comparison with the great plague of 430 BC. For unsympathetic readers, that may teeter on the brink of the absurd. Others may identify, rather, an ethical lesson: each struggle with your soul, be it ever so petty, is a tiny part and replica of humanity's greatest trials. A purportedly mundane *exemplum* reveals new ambition and depth.

Third, and not (I think) trivial: the sheer unpredictability of an imitation like this is witty. Readers are tested, challenged, even amused by the

---

[33] *Mussare* describes fearful muttering, as at *Ep.* 3.11.3 *mussantibus ... amicis*, which describes not Pliny's friends, raising eyebrows in disapproval (Sherwin-White (1966) 242), but friends of Artemidorus who evade his requests out of fear (Scheffer (1675) 89).
[34] Missed by Plinian scholarship but registered by Bailey (1947) ad loc.
[35] For the principle see Cook (1901).
[36] And ripe for further study. Lyne (2016) is a bold attempt to bring cognitive studies and (Renaissance) intertextuality together.

unexpected invocation of Lucretius. Speaking of which, is it coincidence that these *mussantes medici* follow hard on Pliny's talk of raising a cup to his lips, or are some other, even more famous lines of Lucretius in mind?

> **cum** ... *acciperem* a **medico** *potionem*, porrexi manum utque tangeret dixi, *admotumque iam* **labris poculum** reddidi. (*Ep.* 7.1.4)

> sed veluti pueris *absinthia taetra* **medentes**
> **cum** *dare* conantur, prius oras **pocula** circum
> contingunt mellis dulci flavoque liquore,
> ut puerorum aetas improvida ludificetur
> **labrorum** *tenus*, interea perpotet amarum
> absinthi laticem deceptaque non capiatur ... (*DRN* 1.936–41 = 4.11–16)

> But as doctors, when they are trying to give foul absinth to boys, first touch the cups around the rim with the sweet and yellow flow of honey, so that the boys' unsuspecting age can be played on as far as their lips, while it drinks deep of the bitter liquid of absinth and is deceived but not taken captive ...

Scenes of doctors giving drink to the sick were presumably not rare, and 'cups' and 'lips' make a natural pair.[37] But we again find similarities both formal and conceptual.[38] Those similarities are less pressing and distinctive than the others we have seen so far, but the possibility of *imitatio* is worth entertaining: this celebrated poetological simile was well known in antiquity too, and surely familiar to Pliny;[39] and we have just seen Lucretius invoked in adjacent lines of his letter. More than that, this is the only other cameo for doctors in *De Rerum Natura*,[40] so that we might legitimately diagnose an 'analytical reading', as Pliny (characteristically) combines two related passages from a pre-text.[41]

---

[37] In fact, *pocula* and *labra* coincide quite rarely in extant Latin: otherwise before Pliny in Verg. *Ecl.* 3.44 and 47 *necdum illis* [i.e. *poculis*] *labra admovi*, Prop. 2.27.10; Mart. 11.11.2–3, 11.26.4; next in Zeno.

[38] Three load-bearing words more or less the same and in sequence; an initial *cum*-clause for the doctors giving their drink; the idea of 'only as far as the lips' (only partly paralleled by Vergil and Propertius (previous n.), both also concerning cups not touching lips).

[39] 'Well known': Quintilian, *Inst.* 3.1.4 is the first to quote it (*DRN* 1.936–8 = 4.11–13), but he writes, *hac, ut est notum, similitudine utitur*; his other quotation of Lucretius also comes from this 'second proem' (*Inst.* 8.6.45, from *DRN* 1.926 = 4.1). 'Familiar to Pliny': (*i*) because he was a student and very close reader of Quintilian; (*ii*) because we have seen him working closely with the nearby *DRN* 1.830–3 (if you suppose, as I do, that the 'second proem' featured in Book 1 from the start; cf. Butterfield (2013) 50 n. 27).

[40] *Medens* only here and *medicus* nowhere; *medicina* also at *DRN* 3.510 and 521, but not personified as in Book 6.

[41] As he often does (Whitton (2019) *passim*). For the principle see Farrell (1991) *passim* on Vergil.

If we agree that this *is* imitation, it produces a fascinating encounter: in the space of a couple of lines, *Epistles* 7.1 swallows up the first and last books of *De Rerum Natura*, its 'second proem' and its finale; alternatively, it tops and tails the second half, from the start of Book 4 to the end of Book 6.[42] You might see the miniaturisation as amusing, aggressive and/or generically pointed, as the emphatically small-scale *Epistles* cuts a classic of the canon down to size. The technique is familiar from other corners of Latin literature, as when Vergil packs the Epic Cycle into Juno's temple at Carthage, or Ovid trims Dido to just four lines,[43] and it isn't foreign to Pliny:[44] his sense of wit, and of generic absorption, is more refined than many readers suspect.

But the 'if' at the start of that paragraph is a big one. I grant that *imitatio* of the 'honeyed cups' is hard to certify, not least because Lucretius isn't the only ingredient in these lines. Here we turn to prose, and to another author rarely mentioned in the same breath as Pliny: Valerius Maximus.

Let me quote Pliny's *exemplum* again –

> Quin etiam **cum**[A] perustus ardentissima febre tandem remissus unctusque **acciperem** a medico **potionem**,[C] porrexi manum utque tangeret dixi, **admotum**que **iam labris poculum**[D] reddidi. (5) Postea cum vicensimo valetudinis die balineo praepararer mussantesque medicos repente vidissem, causam requisivi. Responderunt posse me tuto lavari, non tamen omnino sine aliqua suspicione. (6) **'Quid,'** inquam, **'necésse est?'**[E] Atque ita spe balinei, cui iam videbar inferri, placide leniterque dimissa, ad abstinentiam rursus, non secus ac modo ad balineum, **animum vultumque** *composui*.[B] (*Ep.* 7.1.4–6)

– and compare now the death of Socrates, as recounted in Valerius' *Facta et Dicta Memorabilia*:

> Idem, **cum**[A] Atheniensium scelerata dementia tristem de capite eius sententiam tulisset *fortique* **animo** *et constanti* **vultu**[B] **potionem** veneni e manu carnificis **accepisset**,[C] **admoto iam labris poculo**,[D] uxore Xanthippe inter fletum et lamentationem vociferante innocentem eum periturum, **'Quid** ergo,' inquit, **'nocé**nti mihi mori satius **esse** duxisti?'[E] Immensam illam

---

[42] Cf. n. 39. Either effect would be interesting at the start of Book 7, whether you see it as a prelude to a book Pliny originally planned as his last (Merwald (1964) 132–7), to Books 7–8 (Bodel (2015) 94–5), or (as I would prefer) to his own final triad.
[43] Verg. *Aen.* 1.453–94; Ov. *Met.* 14.78–81.
[44] Some comparable suggestions: *Ep.* 3.5 incorporating Uncle Pliny's massive *Natural History* (Henderson (2002b) 80); *Ep.* 2.5 shrinking Quint. *Inst.* 1 into a letter (Whitton (2015a) 135); *Ep.* 1.21 shrinking *Inst.* 11 into an even shorter one and *Ep.* 1.24.4 topping and tailing the *Odyssey* in the twenty-fourth and final letter of Book 1 (Whitton (2019) 245–8).

> sapientiam, quae ne in ipso quidem vitae excessu oblivisci sui potuit! (Val. Max. *FD* 7.2.*ext.*1)

> Again, when the wicked madness of the Athenians had passed grim sentence on his life, and he had taken, with bold heart and resolved countenance, the poison drink from the executioner's hand, he had already lifted the cup to his lips when his wife, Xanthippe, weeping and wailing, cried out that he was going to die an innocent man. 'What then,' he said, 'did you think it would be better for me to die guilty?' What boundless wisdom, which even at the very moment of leaving life could not forget itself!

Socrates drinking hemlock is a far cry from Pliny on his sickbed, but it would be hard to explain away all the similarities here. Each narrative starts with a long *cum*-clause (A) which ends in 'taking a drink' (C); each features a cup 'already (*iam*) brought to the lips' (D); each climaxes with a brief rhetorical question (E) displaying calmly rational thought, and an echo.[45] That makes four correspondences of lexis, syntax and argument, in order. In that light, the correspondence (B) between Socrates' resolve (*fortique animo et constanti vultu*) and Pliny's understated climax (*animum vultumque composui*) is unlikely to be inadvertent: he controls his mind and expression with – *mutatis mutandis* as ever – the same resolution as the great man himself.[46] Does Valerius even guide Pliny's pen in that first *cum*-clause, so concisely and periodically setting the scene?[47]

As with *patrius sermo* earlier, we find an imitation centred on a hub (*admotumque iam labris poculum ~ admoto iam labris poculo*) which looks unremarkable enough: I have already said that 'cups' and 'lips' are an easy fit.[48] But the liaison is as good as certified by *iam* – a small but distinctive detail – and by the serial correspondences around it. Valerius' Socratic *exemplum* of wise words and deeds has been updated, and given an

---

[45] It is characteristic that Pliny's question (surely as staged as Socrates') is stripped to the severest brevity.

[46] Another possible ripple in Pliny's first piece of wisdom for Geminus: he instructs his slaves not to let him have anything he asks for against his doctors' advice, taking as his premise an implied generalisation, that ill people are prone to do just that (*Ep.* 7.1.3). Valerius' section on Socrates begins with his advice that we let the gods decide what is best for us; *nos autem plerumque id votis expeteremus quod non impetrasse melius fore*. The contexts are quite different (Valerius then inveighs against mortal greed for power and riches), and I see no formal echoes. But there is an essential likeness in the idea, and in the larger sequence of argument.

[47] A single clause establishes the story so far (his long fever), then sets the scene (*tandem remissus unctusque*), then focuses on the telling detail (the cup). Compare Valerius' corresponding *cum*-clause (Socrates' condemnation > his death scene > the cup), and his habit of setting up anecdotes with a densely periodic sentence.

[48] See n. 37, especially Verg. *Ecl.* 3 (surely the other most celebrated cups in Latin poetry besides Lucretius').

everyday twist, in Pliny's tale of personal temperance. How much (metaliterary) weight, then, attends the final verb of this scene, and of the letter 'proper' – *composui*?[49]

This makes another interesting and exemplary transformation. First, it exemplifies once again the boundless Roman capacity for figuring one person in terms of another: as Antoninus was implicitly compared to Demosthenes, so Pliny is to Socrates. Second, here again is exemplary grandeur in imitation. Pliny sets his performance on the loftiest of stages: resisting the simple pleasures of a drink and a steam, he relives the ultimate *exitus*; the quotidian is tinged with the heroic. But the imitation is exemplary too in targeting Valerius Maximus. For one thing, it reaffirms that Pliny's range of resources for imitation extends well beyond verse, and beyond Cicero's letters. (Don't believe the myth that Valerius Maximus wrote only for 'middle-brow' readers: Pliny for one read him,[50] and – since I doubt he intended his filigree to evade all his readers' notice – assumed that others knew their *Facta et Dicta* too.)[51] His choice of antecedent also sits comfortably with the exemplary drive of the *Epistles* itself.

Valerius catalogues exemplary anecdotes, pointedly told, from across Greek and Roman history. Pliny sketches a professedly simpler and more modern suite of portraits, pointed too in their way, featuring the exemplary person, life and circle of one individual: himself. Of course, the *Epistles* won't explicitly claim to be retailing 'memorable deeds and words', but that is precisely, in its way, what it does. If Valerius tends nowadays to

---

[49] A coda follows (*Ep.* 7.1.7 *Quae tibi scripsi*...). Pliny frequently sets the argumentative and imitative climax just before a coda (some instances in Whitton (2019) 189).

[50] Four other traces: (*i*) *Ep.* 4.25.3 *qui ... tam serio tempore tam scurriliter ludat* (outrage at untimely wit in the senate) ~ *FD* 7.8.9 *Hoc ioco quid ... intempestivius? ... scurrili lusu* (outrage at untimely wit by a senator; *scurriliter* and *ludere/lusus* are paired only here). (*ii*) *Ep.* 8.14.4–6 ~ *FD* 2.1.9, two accounts of senatorial apprenticeship in olden times, both emphasising quasi-paternal didaxis and envisaging young men standing at the doors of the senate-house (P. *assistebant curiae foribus* ~ V. *affixi valvis expectabant*) learning the skills (P.)/stamina (V.) they would need as senators. (*iii*) *Ep.* 7.27, centred on the haunted house at Athens, repeatedly grazes *FD* 1.7.7, on the ghost seen by Cassius in Athens (Schwartz 1969: 673–4; Whitton forthcoming). (*iv*) *Ep.* 3.7.10 *Quod me recordantem fragilitatis humanae miseratio subit* seems to echo *FD* 9.12.8 *fragilitatis humanae ratio abstulit* (also ending a sentence, and concerned, like Pliny, with noble deaths), especially given another liaison nearby in both texts: *Ep.* 3.7.13 *oculis obisset, lacrimasse quod* ~ *FD* 9.13.ext.1 *esset obitura, profundere lacrimas* (both on Xerxes; Pliny is also engaged with Herodotus and Seneca, but his *oculis obisset* is unusual and striking). On that rich passage see also Tzounakas (Chapter 8) in this volume.

[51] As well he might have done. Valerius' *Facta et Dicta* is listed among the Elder Pliny's declared sources (*HN* 1.7, 1.33), cited by Plutarch (*Marc.* 30; *Brut.* 53), imitated by Quintilian (e.g. *Inst.* 4.pr.4–5 ~ *FD* 1.pr. with Whitton (2019) 361) and Frontinus, *Strat.* 4.1.31–2 (~ *FD* 2.7.4–5, with Sinclair (1980) 204–5), and cited and imitated by Gellius 12.7–8 (~ *FD* 8.1.amb.1–2, with Holford-Strevens (2001) 489–93); cf. Schanz and Hosius (1935) 591–4.

be sidelined as a lesser creature of the canon, he finds his sure place in Pliny's eclectic generic cocktail. Dare we even suspect a tongue in cheek – or something more serious – when Pliny's seventh book opens by reworking an *exemplum* from early in *Facta et Dicta* 7? A rash thought, perhaps, but let's not forget that Valerius too wrote a work in nine books.[52] If so, here is another hint of the self-awareness, and potentially grand structural stakes, attending Plinian *imitatio*.

In *Epistles* 4.3, we saw Lucretius combined, arbitrarily enough, with Cicero. Here, he is woven together with Valerius Maximus: whether or not we see his honeyed cup in these lines (there's no problem in finding that mixed with Socratic hemlock), the 'muttering doctors' make his part in this little play as clear as Valerius'. We might again call it exemplary of Pliny's eclecticism, as he weaves prose and verse alike into his variegated intertextual fabric. But this particular combination is perhaps less arbitrary. In imitating Valerius and Lucretius, Pliny pairs two texts which look very different but find unity in their common goal of ethical didaxis. In combining Socrates' death with the Athenian plague, he brings together two historical events from the same city and the same age. And in playing Socrates while echoing Lucretius, he evinces the discreet but vaulting philosophical ambitions of the *Epistles*.[53]

Later in the same book, in a partner-letter to *Epistles* 7.1,[54] Pliny is explicit about his ability to say *multum in parvo*:

> Possum ergo quod plurimis verbis, plurimis etiam voluminibus philosophi docere conantur, ipse breviter tibi mihique praecipere, ut tales esse sani perseveremus quales nos futuros profitemur infirmi. (*Ep.* 7.26.4)

> What therefore philosophers try to teach in numerous words and numerous books, I can tell you and myself with a brief precept: when healthy we should persist in being the sort of men we promise to be when ill.

Epistles 7.1, we should recognise, makes the same point, just implicitly: Pliny is our Everyman philosopher, teaching with a soft touch – but passing on lessons from the best.

---

[52] It seems to me beyond question that Pliny wrote the *Epistles* as a nine-book work. Despite recent interventions (see Whitton and Gibson (2016) 45–7), I doubt that he edited the correspondence with Trajan now called *Epistles* 10 (on which see also König, Chapter 3, in this volume), but that is in any case a distinct question. For some claims about his 'grand designs', see Whitton (2015a).

[53] Pliny claims to be no *sapiens* (*Ep.* 5.1.13), but clearly knew his stuff (Griffin (2007)). For some philosophers carefully handled (another matter again), see *Ep.* 1.10 and 1.22 with Hoffer (1999) 109–40 and Whitton (2019) 74–84.

[54] Again thematising the ethics of illness. Sherwin-White (1966) 402 and 435; Bodel (2015) 95.

3 *Epistles* 5.16, with Tacitus

Let me end with a word on consolation, and with one of Pliny's freshest *exempla* and imitative resources: the *Agricola*. *Epistles* 5.16 meditates on the tragic death of a twelve-year-old girl whom we can identify as Minicia Marcella.[55] Discreet pride of place in its imitative texture goes not to Cicero's Tullia, but to Quintilian, whose powerful preface to *Institutio* 6, lamenting the loss of his nine-year-old son, serves as Pliny's running intertext.[56] But let me here pick out a few lines where we glimpse a more contemporary deuteragonist behind the stage.

The letter devotes its first half to a laudatory portrait of little Marcella in life and in death. The second half is given over to her father's grief and to questions of consolation. True to form, Pliny finds that grief exquisitely sad and eminently forgiveable: at times like this, raw emotion trumps philosophy.

> Est quidem ille eruditus et **sapiens**,[A] ut qui se ab ineunte aetate altioribus studiis artibusque dediderit; sed nunc omnia quae audît saepe, quae dixit aspernatur expulsisque virtutibus aliis **pietatis est totus**.[B] (9) Ignosces, laudabis etiam, si cogitaveris quid amiserit: amisit enim **filiam**[C] quae *non minus* **mores**[D] eius *quam* os vultumque referebat,[E] totumque[F] **patrem**[G] mira **similitudine** exscripserat.[H] (*Ep.* 5.16.8–9)

He is a man of learning and wisdom, of course, having devoted himself since his first years to the more profound arts and studies; but now he spurns all the things he has often heard, often said: casting out the other virtues, he is all piety's. (9) You will forgive him, praise him even, if you think about his loss: he has lost a daughter who reflected his character no less than his face and countenance, and had reproduced her whole father with remarkable likeness.

These lines look to the end of the *Agricola*. Having described the death of his laudand, Tacitus closes with the family, and consolation.

---

[55] Recent discussion in Bodel (1995); Carlon (2009) 148–57; Klodt (2012); Shelton (2013) 277–82.
[56] Whitton (2019) 353–80. Tullia, whose death is so large a theme in Cicero's correspondence, would seem an obvious point of reference for this showpiece on the death of a daughter. But she occupies only a tiny place at best, if we recognise in *Ep.* 5.16.8 *expulsisque virtutibus aliis pietatis est totus* the epigram that ends Sulpicius' consolation to Cicero, *Fam.* 4.5.6 *ne ex omnibus virtutibus haec una* (i.e. fortitude) *tibi videatur deesse* (not obvious, but I make the case in Whitton (2019) 373 n. 89); another reflex of the same letter in *Ep.* 3.16.3 *non minus ob alia carus quam quod filius erat* (on a deceased *son*) ~ *Fam.* 4.5.2 *non minus quam liberi cara esse debent* (Whitton forthcoming). It is paradigmatic – and runs counter to the usual assumptions – that Pliny privileges the *Institutio* over Cicero's correspondence as intertextual target.

Si quis piorum manibus locus, si, ut **sapientibus**^A placet, non cum corpore extinguuntur magnae animae, placide quiescas ... (2) Admiratione te potius et immortalibus laudibus et, si natura suppeditat, <u>**similitudine** colamus:</u>^H is verus honos, ea coniunctissimi cuiusque **pietas**.^B (3) Id **filiae**^C quoque uxorique praeceperim, sic **patris**,^G sic mariti memoriam venerari ut <u>omnia facta dictaque eius</u>^F secum revolvant, <u>formamque ac figuram animi *magis quam* corporis complectantur,</u>^E ... forma mentis aeterna, quam tenere et exprimere non per alienam materiam et artem, sed tuis ipse **moribus**^D possis. (4) Quicquid ex Agricola amavimus, ... (Tac. *Agr.* 46.1–4)

If there is any place for the shades of the dutiful, if, as men of wisdom hold, great souls are not extinguished along with the body, may you rest in peace ... (2) Let us honour you rather with admiration and undying praise and, if nature should allow, likeness: that is the true honour, the true piety of everyone who was closest to him. (3) To his daughter and wife too I would give this precept, that they venerate the memory of their father and husband by reflecting on all his words and deeds and embracing the form and shape of his mind rather than that of his body, ... the form of the mind is everlasting, and something you can retain and reproduce not with external substance and art, but by your own character. (4) Whatever we loved in Agricola ...

It is a selective series of little details – philosophy invoked (A), *pietas* underlined (B),[57] a daughter and a father (C, D), talk of *similitudo* (H), and so on – and in lexical terms the imitative hub (E) is the least revealing yet:

<u>non minus</u> *mores eius* **quam** *os vultumque* referebat, (*Ep.* 5.16.9)

formamque ac figuram animi <u>magis</u> **quam** *corporis* complectantur, (*Agr.* 46.3)

But we know how important 'syntactic marking' can be,[58] and the shared idea is distinctive: a filial resemblance which lies more (*or* no less) in character than in physique.[59]

---

[57] As an all-consuming (P.)/climactic (T.) virtue, ending its sentence.
[58] Wills (1996) 20–1 and *passim* amply shows its importance in verse. Prose is no different, as here in *non minus ... quam ~ magis quam* (varied, naturally). Further correspondences are the antithesis of inner character (*mores eius ~ formam ... animi*, each acc. + gen.) and external appearance (*os vultumque ~ corporis*, cases varied) and their order; where Tacitus has a doublet (*formam ... ac figuram*) Pliny has a single word, and *vice versa*.
[59] Contrast Mart. 6.27.3 *est tibi quae patria signatur imagine voltus*, cited in Marchesi's contribution, ch. 14, amid stimulating reflections on physical and intertextual 'dynamics of reproduction'. Pliny's *mores* may find their origin in another little climax, just below in Tacitus (*tuis ipse moribus possis*).

When therefore Pliny continues to the densely mannered phrase *totumque patrem mira similitudine exscripserat*, it is tempting to see an origin both for the taut *totum patrem* in Tacitus' preceding clause (*omnia facta dictaque eius*), and for the phrase-end *similitudine exscripserat* in his phrase-end *similitudine colamus* just above.[60] This and the other similarities, in other words, appear to be not a series of accidents, but ripples around the core of the liaison.[61] The transformations are as thorough as ever, with imitative variation extending from every detail of language to the single difference that it is now the daughter, not the father, who is dead.[62] But that should come by now as no surprise. Pliny knew the *Agricola* intimately,[63] and the situational similarities once again make an easy associative bridge: as he describes a deceased daughter who (he claims) perfectly resembled her father, he has surely not forgotten Tacitus, urging a daughter that she should perfectly resemble her deceased father.[64]

In *Epistles* 4.3, I suggested that imitation is accompanied by self-reflexive 'annotation'. We might suspect the same here, in the striking word *exscripserat*. It's one of those delicate moments of daring that dot Pliny's epistolary prose, as he takes the verb for 'copy out (*sc.* a text)' and applies it to a purely figurative reproduction.[65] But does it also double as a comment on his imitative work in this letter, as he maps Fundanus and his daughter onto Agricola and his daughter?[66] Like all metaliterary readings,

---

[60] This last claim is complicated by corruption in Tacitus' text, where *militum decoramus* is transmitted; I print the usual correction (supported in turn by Pliny's imitation, if you agree).
[61] A couple of elements already perhaps in *Ep.* 5.16.3 *qua etiam constantia ... tulit ~ Agr.* 45.3 *constans ... excepisti* (*etiam* advertises *constantia* as choice) and 5.16.5 *aut spatio valetudinis aut metu mortis ~ Agr.* 45.3 *assidere valetudini, fovere deficientem* (a surprisingly rare double-step).
[62] And the excision of the wife/mother figure, extraneous in Marcella's case (her mother had predeceased her, as we can infer from *Ep.* 5.16.4 *sororem patrem adhortabatur*).
[63] Other significant encounters in *Ep.* 8.14 (Whitton (2010)) and *Ep.* 9.19 (König and Whitton (2018a) 23–5), as well as repeated and productive use in the *Panegyricus* (Mesk (1911) 91–4; Durry (1938) 60–1; Bruère (1954) 162–4; Whitton (2019): 418; Whitton forthcoming), including our passage in *Pan.* 55.11 (with *formam principis figuramque ... exprimat teneatque*; Woodman (2014) ad loc.). *Agr.* 46 also resonates in *Ep.* 2.1.10–12 (Whitton (2013a) ad loc.) and *Ep.* 9.27 (*manet manebit legeturque semper ~ Agr.* 46.4 *manet mansurumque est ... posteritati narratus et traditus superstes erit*) amongst other spots; that last letter concerns the immortality of history, surely Tacitus' (Whitton (2012) 363–4).
[64] Much of the material may be 'topical' in consolations, but is it likely that quite so many details would correspond, and in sequence, by chance?
[65] He has already transferred it from copying text to copying a painting (*Ep.* 4.28.1), itself an innovation. The phrase here is imitated by Sidonius in his *Ep.* 7.13.5 *iucunda similitudine exscripsit*.
[66] I.e. as a form of intertextual annotation. Tacitus ends the *Agricola* with his own role in textualising his honorand (*Agr.* 46.4 *Agricola posteritati narratus et traditus superstes erit*).

it can hardly be proved. But the rarity of the word, and a broader picture of Plinian practice, speak strongly for it.

The liking of the *Epistles* for contemporary *exempla* has been observed before.[67] This little encounter shows that it extends to intertextual *exempla* too – and to the text (and even wife) of his compeer Tacitus:[68] Pliny's page, like Roman life, freely mixes models past and present, dead and alive; contemporary texts mingle proudly with classics.[69] And it underlines once more the generic range of Plinian *imitatio*: however you prefer to label Tacitus' monograph, it joins the works of Cicero, Lucretius, Valerius and many besides on the broad and intensely varied shelf of Pliny's intertextual ingredients. This has been the most selective of tours, but serves, I hope, to make its point: the *Epistles* inscribes, literally, a man of many parts.

---

[67] Whitton (2013a) 9 with references.
[68] Though Pliny makes nothing of it, Agricola's daughter was also Tacitus' wife.
[69] The *Agricola* was presumedly published in AD 98 (*Agr.* 3.1 and 44.5 with Woodman (2014)). Whether or not *Epistles* 5.16 actually dates from *c.* 105–6 (the 'book-date' of Sherwin-White (1966) 34–7; cf. Whitton (2013a) 18), we can safely put it well after 98.

CHAPTER 2

Intertextuality in Pliny, Epistles *6*

Roy Gibson

1 Introduction

Other chapters in this volume focus on Pliny's intertextual relations with particular authors or with a range of specific texts, genres or features of genres.[1] The present chapter, like that of Alice König, deals with a single book of Pliny's *Epistles*. In it, I ask what Plinian intertextuality looks like when considered over the course of a single book in the aggregate, rather than in relation to selected authors over the course of the whole correspondence. It is well known that Pliny produces individual books that, while linguistically homogeneous (Book 10 aside), evince distinctive characters that are the result of artistic investment in issues of selection, arrangement and juxtaposition of subject matter.[2] What do Pliny's *intertextual* investments add to the distinctive texture or character of an individual book?

This chapter looks at Book 6 and makes three interconnected arguments or observations. First, Pliny makes choices about where to invest most deeply. Letter 6.20, the book's second instalment on the eruption of Vesuvius in AD 79, is unusual within the book for the range and sheer intensity of its intertextual activity: readers need to be prepared for the challenge and even oddity of intertextual puzzles with which the text is likely to confront them. Secondly, Cicero, Catullus, Vergil, Quintilian and Tacitus maintain the most persistent intertextual presence across the letters

---

[1] I wish to thank Margot Neger and Spyridon Tzounakas for their kind invitation to the original conference in Cyprus and for editorial improvements of the chapter, as well as members of the audience and the two anonymous readers for their suggestions and contributions. I am grateful also to Chris Whitton for sharing *The Arts of Imitation in Latin Prose* (2019) in advance of publication, and for his characteristically generous supply of new intertexts to consider. Translations of Pliny, Quintilian and Tacitus are taken variously from the Loeb Classical Library or Whitton (2019), and, in Pliny's case, also from Lewis (1879). Translations of other authors are taken from the Loeb Classical Library. All are gratefully acknowledged.
[2] See (e.g.) the various studies of Sherwin-White (1966) 27–52; Ludolph (1997); Hoffer (1999); Henderson (2002b); Gibson and Morello (2012) 26–73; Whitton (2013a), (2015a).

47

of *Epistles* 6, although a wide range of other authors is captured within the intertextual mesh of this unit. The consistency of references to these authors does much to create a sense of artistic unity or continuity within the book. However, and thirdly, the writers for whom Pliny creates either a pattern or coherent purpose for intertextual evocation are a smaller subset of these five authors: Vergil, Quintilian and Tacitus. In particular, there is a special clustering of references to Quintilian and to the *Dialogus* of Tacitus.[3] These allusions can be found in a suite of letters that are designed to mark the death of the orator Regulus and to underline Pliny's pre-eminence in Rome's courts and his role as exemplar to a new generation of young orators. Pliny carries on a dialogue with the great optimist (Quintilian) and the great pessimist (Tacitus) about Rome's courts and oratory as a way of giving substance to his own claims to be the leading courtroom rhetorician of the day. The chapter ends by reflecting briefly on the reasons behind Pliny's confident rebuttal of pessimism regarding the vigour and life-expectancy of public oratory at Rome. From our point of view, Tacitus was (naturally) right: rhetoric was dying on its feet, and as a genre – unlike history or epic – would prove of little or no interest to future generations of readers. But, as we shall see, Pliny had good reason to think he might be right.

A final caveat before we begin: the sounding of the depths of Plinian intertextuality is in its infancy. Much work remains to be done in *Epistles* 6, as elsewhere in the corpus. The findings offered below represent the first results of an initial survey. Further research will deepen and alter our conception of Pliny's intertextual practices in this book (and others).

2 Pliny, *Epistles* 6

The letters of *Epistles* 6 appear to have their dramatic date largely in the period AD 106–7: these are the years of Trajan's final victory in Dacia and subsequent return to Rome in triumph.[4] The unit contains thirty-four letters and addresses twenty-seven different correspondents.[5] All the addressees are male, with the exception of letters 6.4 and 6.7, which are addressed to Pliny's wife. Just under two-thirds of those addressed receive a

---

[3] For a series of engagements, in turn, by the Tacitus of the *Histories* and *Annals* with *Epistles* 6, see Gibson (forthcoming).
[4] See Gibson and Morello (2012) 51–2, with reference to earlier studies.
[5] See Gibson and Morello (2012) 283–5. More generally, Sherwin-White (1966) 65–9 on 'Selection and Distribution of Correspondents' remains essential reading; cf. Birley (2000) 17–21. Over half of the letters in *Epistles* 1–9 are addressed to just 28 correspondents; see Birley (2000) 19.

single letter in *Epistles* 6; one addressee, Tacitus, is privileged with three letters (6.9, 6.16 and 6.20), while five others, including two close relatives, receive two letters apiece.[6] The majority of these favoured addressees are prominent elsewhere in the correspondence, with the exception of Calpurnia, who receives only a single further letter (7.5).[7]

Pliny ensures that *Epistles* 6 is a distinctive epistolary unit in several complementary ways.[8] The book is dominated by letters on senatorial business, the courtroom and associated public affairs; such correspondence, by contrast, slows to a trickle in *Epistles* 7.[9] This dominance is employed to enhance a particular point: Pliny wishes to put himself on display as Rome's greatest living courtroom orator, now that his great rival Regulus is dead.[10] Pliny's record of the recent death of Regulus (6.2), when added to his commemorations of the more distant deaths of Verginius Rufus (6.10) and the Elder Pliny (6.16, 6.20), combine to make the case that it is Pliny who is now an exemplar to younger generations (6.11). The Younger has definitively stepped out of the shadows of his elders. A symmetrical frame to the book, involving the first three and final three letters, emphasises the claim: the death of his old courtroom rival Regulus is deliberately paired with the delivery of Pliny's greatest ever speech in the Centumviral courts (6.2, 6.33).[11]

In this atmosphere of personal optimism and sense of hope for the future, it is appropriate that Domitian should be almost entirely absent from *Epistles* 6. The book belongs instead to Trajan: it represents the highpoint of Pliny's optimism for elite society in the wake of the emperor's

---

[6] The family members are Calpurnius Fabatus (6.12, 6.30), Pliny's grandfather-in-law, and Calpurnia. The other recipients of a pair of letters are the obscure equestrian Cornelius Ursus (6.5, 6.13) and two childhood friends prominent elsewhere in the correspondence: Calestrius Tiro (6.1, 6.22) and Voconius Romanus (6.15, 6.33).

[7] On Pliny and Calpurnia, see Carlon (2009) 157–75; Lefevre (2009) 195–217; Shelton (2013) 93–136; Gibson (2021). The literary aspects of the letters to her are covered later in this chapter.

[8] See Gibson and Morello (2012) 36–73 for a full rehearsal of the evidence.

[9] Cf. *Ep.* 6.2; 6.5; 6.6; 6.9; 6.11; 6.13; 6.18; 6.19; 6.22; 6.23; 6.27; 6.29; 6.31; 6.33; contrast *Ep.* 7.6; 7.10.

[10] Cf. 6.2 (death of Regulus); 6.11 (Pliny in the court of the City Prefect); 6.12 (Pliny to appear on behalf of his grandfather-in-law's associate in the Centumviral court); 6.18 (Pliny's readiness to appear as advocate for the town of Firmum); 6.23 (Pliny accepts a private case in the Centumviral court); 6.29 (a review of Pliny's most important senatorial cases to date); and 6.33 (Pliny's 'greatest ever' speech in the Centumviral court).

[11] See Gibson and Morello (2012) 39–45: 6.1–3 vs. 6.32–4 sets a pair of strong Ciceronian motifs (6.1: longing for Tiro and 6.34: African beasts needed for gladiatorial games) and a pair of gifts to women (6.3 and 6.32) in relation to one another so as to highlight a third symmetrical relationship involving Regulus (6.2) and Pliny's Centumviral triumph (6.32).

triumphal return to Rome.¹² (In the years thereafter, during the most prolonged residence of Trajan in Italy during his reign, Pliny's pessimism grows markedly.¹³) Pliny also contrives to give geographical and topographical distinctiveness to *Epistles* 6 by omitting mention of the 'Tuscan' villa so prominent in *Epistles* 5 (5.6), referencing Comum only once (6.25),¹⁴ and filling the book instead with venues in central and southern Italy.¹⁵ Campania, which has little visibility elsewhere in the *Epistles*, makes several prominent appearances. Pliny is arguably creating a suitable home for the two great Vesuvius letters contained in the book, whose action, of course, takes place on the bay of Naples. Finally, Pliny gives some formal unity to *Epistles* 6 by including a noticeably large number of internal sequels or pairs.¹⁶

3 The Vesuvius Letters

Pliny makes choices about where to invest his intertextual riches. In *Epistles* 1, he lavishes particular care on the question of the proper style and length of a courtroom speech (1.20); in *Epistles* 7, Pliny expends notable energy in crafting a reply to a question about suitable literary

---

[12] Trajan intervenes *in absentia* to resolve senatorial disputes (6.5; 6.13; 6.19), before turning up in Italy to deal with a trial in person (6.22). Pliny next advises a correspondent on what subject he should include in a speech to the emperor as consul designate (6.27), where 'the recent achievements of our illustrious emperor', i.e. his new military successes, are highlighted as a felicitous subject (6.27.5). The sequence is crowned with a celebration of the splendour of the new regime and a sustained sojourn in the presence of Trajan himself in 6.31. The emperor's *humanitas* is emphasised (6.31.14–15), and the letter ends with a detailed description of the imperial harbour at Centum Cellae where, as Saylor (1972) suggests, the harbour is a metaphor for the bulwark of Trajan himself. For the re-emergence of Domitian in *Epistles* 7, cf. 7.19; 7.27; 7.33; Gibson and Morello (2012) 50.

[13] See Gibson (2015).

[14] On the geographical distinctiveness of *Epistles* 6 by comparison with Books 5 and 7, see Gibson and Morello (2012) 49.

[15] In 6.4 Calpurnia is found recuperating in Campania (and again at 6.7); in 6.10 and 6.31 Pliny is on the coast not far north of Rome at Alsium and Centum Cellae respectively; in 6.14, Pliny arranges a visit to Formiae in Latium; letters 6.16 and 6.20 revisit the scenes on the Campanian coast of AD 79; in 6.18, Pliny agrees to act as advocate for the Picenum town of Firmum; in 6.25, Pliny is asked to intervene in the case of someone who has gone missing in Umbria not far from Rome; 6.28 relates the visit of Pliny to a friend's villa in Campania; and 6.30 deals with the management of an estate in Campania.

[16] Cf. 6.4 and 6.7 (to the absent Calpurnia); 6.5 and 6.13 (senatorial skirmishes over the Bithynian prosecution of Varenus Rufus: both addressed to Cornelius Ursus); 6.6 and 6.9 (the candidature of Iulius Naso); 6.11 and 6.26 (the first appearance of Fuscus Salinator followed by the report of his betrothal); and 6.16 and 6.20 (the two Plinii at Vesuvius: both addressed to Tacitus). Other, less strongly realised pairs include letters addressed to the same addressee on different subjects, i.e. those to Calestrius Tiro (6.1; 6.22), Calpurnius Fabatus (6.12; 6.30), and Voconius Romanus (6.15, 6.33).

Intertextuality in Pliny Epistles *6*   51

exercises for improving one's style (7.9).[17] In *Epistles* 6, Pliny invests most deeply in a letter devoted to demonstrating his own literary prowess as an historian.

As is well known, there is a clear stylistic difference between the two Vesuvius letters of *Epistles* 6: the first is relatively sparing in allusions to earlier literature (6.16),[18] while the second exhibits references to earlier epics and histories in abundant supply (6.20).[19] In the words of Ilaria Marchesi,[20] the more stylistically elaborate 6.20 'embodies Pliny's version of the work of the historian. The epistle not only pointedly alludes to a work of history (Livy's); it also reproduces in miniature the close dialogue that writers of Roman history establish with their epic counterparts'. This feature comes bathed in irony: Pliny designates the first letter as fit for incorporation into history (6.16.22), while the second is said to be fit only for discarding (6.20.20).

The intertextual riches of *Ep.* 6.20 are signaled to the reader by the explicit quotation from the second book of Vergil's *Aeneid* which opens the letter: *quamquam animus meminisse horret . . . incipiam* ('Though my mind shrinks from remembering . . . I will begin') (6.20.1).[21] The choice of *Aeneid* 2 and its narrative of the fall of Troy as a major intertext for 6.20 is pertinent: the letter narrates the fate of an entire *populus*, i.e. the inhabitants of Misenum.[22] *Ep.* 6.16, by contrast, had focused on the fate of a single individual, Pliny the Elder. More generally, the insistent allusion to Vergil throughout 6.20 is appropriate in view of the fact that much of the action of the letter takes place at the cape Misenum. This is a site with strong Vergilian associations of its own: in *Aeneid* 6.149–235, it is

---

[17] See the index locorum for 1.20 and 7.9 in Whitton (2019) 536–7, 539–40.
[18] Even so, a series of references to Vergil, Lucretius, the *Agricola* of Tacitus, and to the proem of Sallust's *Bellum Catilinae* can be detected: e.g. *Ep.* 6.16.1 ~ Tac. *Agr.* 1.1 (Whitton (2019) 110 n.6); 6.16.2 ~ Verg. *Aen.* 2.361–2 (Gigante (1989) 50); 6.16.3 ~ Sall. *Cat.* 3.2 (Ussani (1970) 285–7, 300–1, Marchesi (2008) 151–3, Whitton (2019) 114 n.21); 6.16.4 ~ Verg. *Aen.* 6.851 (Gigante (1989) 29); 6.16.11 ~ Verg. *Aen.* 10.284 (Gigante (1989) 32). For Lucretian *color* in *Ep.* 6.16, see Gigante (1989) 50, 52, 55–6.
[19] See Gigante (1989), Marchesi (2008) 175 ff.   [20] Marchesi (2008) 188.
[21] Cf. *Aen.* 2.12–13 *quamquam animus meminisse horret luctuque refugit | incipiam* ('though my mind shudders to remember and has recoiled in pain, I will begin'). The first sentence of *Ep.* 6.20 (*ais te . . . cupere cognoscere, quos ego . . . non solum metus verum etiam casus pertulerim* ('You say you . . . are eager to hear about . . . the terrors and also the hazards I had to face')) also clearly alludes to *Aen.* 2.10 *sed si tantus amor casus cognoscere nostros* ('yet if such is your desire to learn of our disasters') – and so on throughout the letter; cf. e.g. *Ep.* 6.20.7 ~ *Aen.* 2.450, 796–8 (Marchesi (2008) 178); 6.20.10 ~ *Aen.* 3.310–12, 338–43 (Marchesi (2008) 180–2); 6.20.11 ~ *Aen.* 2.378, 382 (Gigante (1989) 42); 6.20.11 ~ *Aen.* 5.204 (Gigante (1989) 42); 6.20.12 ~ *Aen.* 2.287, 638–40 (Lillge (1918) 289–90, Görler (1979) 427, Cova (2001) 56), and see Gibson (forthcoming).
[22] Gigante (1989) 39, 49.

52 ROY GIBSON

the site of the burial of Aeneas' comrade Misenus, whose funeral rites must be completed before entry is allowed to the underworld at nearby Avernus. Livy also figures as an important intertext in the letter:[23] a fitting choice given that this is the very historian whose work Pliny has been asked by the Elder to 'excerpt' as part of his 'homework' prior to the eruption (6.20.5). The scientific and 'rational' poet Lucretius likewise features prominently in 6.20 at various points: he seems a natural choice for writers in search of descriptions of existential terror.[24] A reference at *Ep.* 6.20.17 to Seneca's *Natural Questions* takes inspiration from a similar taste for catastrophe in the Neronian writer.[25] More generally important is Ovid's *Tristia* 1.3, where the poet had shown how both *Aeneid* 2 and Livy (himself alluding to Vergil) might be incorporated into a text so as to describe a personal catastrophe.[26] This was Ovid's last night in Rome prior to exile.

There are further references in *Ep.* 6.20 to Horace's *Epistles*, Ovid's *Metamorphoses*, Lucan and Tacitus' *Agricola*.[27] But if proof were needed that this letter is an intertextual treasure house, the closing paragraphs of the letter offer a somewhat puzzling (and potentially alarming) interaction with the *Satyricon* of Petronius. Pliny records the anxious night spent by his mother and himself after they had endured the terrors of the terrible black cloud emanating from Vesuvius (6.20.19):

> Regressi Misenum curatis utcumque corporibus suspensam dubiamque noctem spe ac metu exegimus. Metus praevalebat; nam et tremor terrae perseverabat, et plerique lymphati terrificis vaticinationibus et sua et aliena mala ludificabantur.
>
> We returned to Misenum where we attended to our physical needs as best we could, and then spent an anxious night alternating between hope and

---

[23] *Ep.* 6.20.5 *posco librum Titi Liui, et quasi per otium lego atque etiam ut coeperam excerpo* ('I called for a volume of Livy and went on reading as if I had nothing else to do') includes a Livian turn of phrase (Livy 27.2.10 *spolia per otium legere* ('gathered spoils at their leisure')) at the very moment Pliny asks for a copy of Livy; see Marchesi (2008) 188. Cf. also (e.g.) *Ep.* 6.20.12 ~ Livy 26.9.5 (Gigante (1989) 43); 6.20.15 ~ Livy 3.42.6 (Gigante (1989) 47); 6.20.20 ~ Livy 38.29.3 (Berry (2008) 300 n.14); and see Gibson (forthcoming).

[24] For the allusion of *Ep.* 6.20.14 to Lucr. 3.79–82, see later in this chapter. Cf. also (e.g.) *Ep.* 6.20.9 ~ Lucr. 6.694–5 (Gigante (1989) 54–5); 6.20.15 ~ Lucr. 6.1276–7 (Gigante (1989) 46–7); 6.20.19 ~ Lucr. 1.102–3 (Gigante (1989) 48); and see Gibson (forthcoming).

[25] *Ep.* 6.20.17 *nisi me cum omnibus, omnia mecum perire misero, magno tamen mortalitatis solacio credidissem* ('had I not derived some poor consolation in my mortal lot from the belief that the whole world was dying with me and I with it') is a version of a sentiment expressed by Seneca, albeit adapted by Pliny to the prospect of imminent death rather than used, as by Seneca, of the general mortality of mankind; cf. *NQ* 6.2.6, 6.2.9, also *Tro.* 1009–55.

[26] See Marchesi (2008) 185–88.

[27] *Ep.* 6.20.18 ~ Ov. *Met.* 15.85–6; 6.20.19 ~ Hor. *Epist.* 1.4.12 (Gigante (1989) 48 n.7); 6.20.10 ~ Lucan 1.496–8 (Marchesi (2008) 179–80); 6.20.20 ~ Tac. *Agr.* 1.2.

fear. Fear predominated, for the earthquakes went on, and several hysterical individuals made their own and other people's calamities seem ludicrous in comparison with their frightful predictions.

A parallel with an incident in Petronius was spotted in 1958 by Luigi Pepe.[28] Encolpius, at *Sat.* 115.6, narrates the aftermath of a shipwreck: *hoc opere tandem elaborato casam piscatoriam subimus maerentes, cibisque naufragio corruptis utcunque curati tristissimam exegimus noctem* ('When this business was at last completed, we came sadly to a fisherman's cottage, refreshed ourselves more or less with food spoilt by sea-water, and passed a very miserable night'). Alongside strong verbal similarities, a contextual closeness is clear: a night time disaster survived, the resort to the relative safety of a settlement, the enjoyment of such refreshment as was possible, and the passing of an anxious night. This was enough for Pepe to conclude that Petronius, now re-dated to a post–Neronian age, was the imitator of Pliny rather than the reverse.[29]

The contextual relationship is even stronger than Pepe realised. In his next sentence, Pliny reveals the purpose of the return to Misenum: *nobis tamen ne tunc quidem, quamquam et expertis periculum et exspectantibus, abeundi consilium, donec de avunculo nuntius* ('Even then, however, we ourselves did not plan to leave, in spite of our experience and expectation of the dangers, until the message came about my uncle') (6.20.20). In his next sentence, the Petronian Enclopius relates the discovery of a corpse on the seashore: *postero die, cum poneremus consilium, cui nos regioni crederemus, repente video corpus humanum circumactum levi vertice ad litus deferri* ('Next morning, as we were trying to decide into what part of the country we should venture, I suddenly saw a man's body caught in a gentle eddy and carried ashore') (*Sat.* 115.6). Of course, at the time of the Younger Pliny's return to Misenum, the corpse of the Elder Pliny was lying on the seashore, across the bay of Naples at Stabiae: the time is precisely marked at *Ep.* 6.16.18–21.

That these two passages are intertextually related is abundantly clear. But who is the imitator? To re-date Petronius on the basis of this passage alone would be to allow the tail to wag the dog. To refuse to contemplate Pliny as the imitator might perhaps say more about our aesthetics and the sense of literary decorum that we wish to impose on the *Epistles*. This

---

[28] Pepe (1958). Many thanks to Chris Whitton for drawing my attention to this intertext and its bibliography; cf. Whitton (2019) 42 n.118.
[29] Pepe (1958) 292–3; cf. Ratti (2015). Roth (2016) argues that Petronius imitates Pliny on the basis of other and unrelated parallels in *Ep.* 10.

choice would say rather less about the abilities of Pliny as a literary artist able to recuperate meaning even from the most challenging of texts. The engagement with Petronius might be polemical: whereas, in the *Satyricon*, the participants take thought only for their own well being, in the *Epistles*, Pliny's thoughts remain fixed on another (who is now dead). The context of wild prophecy in Pliny's letter (*terrificis vaticinationibus*) might even contain a hint that the allusion to Petronius contains its own premonition of the arrival of the news of discovery of the body of the Elder Pliny on the beach at Stabiae. Pliny's eye might well have been caught also by an allusion in the Petronius passage to the first book of the *Aeneid*.[30] Pliny takes up the challenge to incorporate Vergil into his own account.

4 Intertextual Range and Intensity in *Epistles* 6

Ep. 6.20 is untypical of the unit as a whole for its combination of range *and* intensity of intertextual reference. Like Vesuvius itself on the bay of Naples, this letter rather looms over the rest of the book. Some authors who are the subject of prominent allusion in 6.20 are more thinly in evidence elsewhere. Further references to Livy in *Epistles* 6 await detection; Sallust and Lucretius make at least one more prominent appearance each, in letters 6.8 and 6.21 respectively, although more may yet be uncovered.[31] References to Seneca elsewhere in the book, unsurprisingly, tend to privilege the *Epistulae Morales* rather than the *Natural Questions*.[32] Perhaps the only letters to approach *Ep.* 6.20 for intertextual intensity are the pair of epistles addressed to Calpurnia (6.4, 6.7). These letters, as is well known, make extensive reference to the terms and concepts of Latin love poetry.[33] However, they restrict the *range* of their reference largely to Catullus and the love elegists, particularly Ovid.[34] Other letters, as we

---

[30] Schmeling (2011) 440 notes the reference in *cibisque naufragio corruptis* to Verg. *Aen.* 1.177 *Cererem corruptam undis*.
[31] *Ep.* 6.8.5 ~ Sall. *Cat.* 5.4; 6.21.1 ~ Lucr. 2.1149–51.
[32] Cf. e.g. *Ep.* 6.6.9 ~ Sen. *Ep.* 22.3 (Whitton (2013a) 139–40); 6.10.1 ~ Sen. *Ep.* 49.1; 6.14.1 ~ Sen. *Ep.* 13.1, 74.1; 6.18.1 ~ Sen. *Ben.* 5.23.1; 6.24.4 ~ Sen. *Ep.* 77.10; 6.25.1 ~ Sen. *Dial.* 11.99; see further Whitton (2019) 41 n.110, Gibson (forthcoming).
[33] On literary aspects of the Calpurnia cycle of letters, see Guillemin (1929) 138–41; de Verger (1997–98); de Pretis (2003); Carlon (2009) 166–79; Hindermann (2010); Gibson and Morello (2012) 55–61, 99–101; Baeza-Angulo (2016), (2017).
[34] In *Ep.* 6.4 e.g.: concern for health of beloved (*Ep.* 6.4.2–3; cf. Prop. 2.28, Tib. 1.5, Ov. *Am.* 2.13); anxiety caused by the absence of the beloved (*Ep.* 6.4.3; cf. Prop. 1.11–12); the lover's tendency to entertain baseless fears (*Ep.* 6.4.4; cf. Ov. *Her.* 1.11–12, *Met.* 7.719 *sed cuncta timemus amantes*); and the elegist's typical oscillation between hope and fear (*Ep.* 6.4.5; cf. Ov. *Am.* 2.19.5, *Ars* 3.471–8, *Tr.* 4.3.11–14). For elegiac and Ovidian tropes in *Ep.* 6.7: cf. e.g. emotional solace (*Ep.* 6.7.1; cf.

shall see later, offer sustained engagement with Quintilian and Tacitus. Evidently, the subject matter of *Ep.* 6.20 – the experience at Misenum of the effects of the eruption – inspired Pliny to scale new intertextual heights in terms of scope and concentration. Like letters 1.20 and 7.9, with their deep investment in matters of specifically literary interest, letter 6.20 invests in the idea of being the sort of literary historian that contemporary readers so greatly valued.

5 Cicero, Catullus and Vergil in *Epistles* 6

Some authors who do not feature strongly or at all in *Ep.* 6.20 are prominent elsewhere throughout Book 6, particularly Cicero and Catullus. Together with Vergil, Tacitus and Quintilian, these five authors maintain the strongest and most consistent intertextual presence across *Epistles* 6 as a whole.[35] There appears to be no clear pattern or coherence in the references to Cicero, other than the fact that Pliny seems particularly drawn to the letters of what now makes up our *Ad Familiares*.[36] Likewise, there is no obvious coherence in the Catullus references: this may well be a heterogeneous group of intertexts.[37] Yet, the simple fact of Pliny's sustained intertextual investment in these authors does much to provide *Epistles* 6 with a consistent literary texture – against which oddities like the reference to Petronius stand out all the more sharply.

By contrast, there appears to be a consistent pattern to the usage that Pliny makes of Vergil at heightened moments in Book 6. Pliny, as the *Epistles* make abundantly clear, has a strong attachment to water, from lake Como in the Transpadana to the river Clitumnus in Umbria, to lake Vadimon in central Italy and the seascapes of his Laurentine villa and on to

---

Catull. 2.7, Ov. *Rem. am.* 241, de Verger (1997–98) 116); emotional investment in *tabellae* (*Ep.* 6.7.1; cf. Prop. 3.24.23, Ov. *Am.* 1.11–12); the *vestigium* of the beloved (*Ep.* 6.7.1; cf. Ov. *Her.* 10.53–4, *Ars* 3.721–2); erotic *desiderium* (*Ep.* 6.7.3; cf. Catull 2.8, 96.3, Prop. 4.3.28, de Verger (1997–98) 114); *accendor* of love (*Ep.* 6.7.3; cf. Ov. *Am.* 1.2.9); request for the pleasure that brings pain (*Ep.* 6.7.3; cf. Ov. *Am.* 2.19, *Ars* 3.577–610); *torqueat* of love (*Ep.* 6.7.3; cf. Prop. 3.6.39, 3.17.11, Ov. *Am.* 1.4.46, 2.5.53, 2.19.34). See Gibson (forthcoming) for further evocations of Ovid in *Ep.* 6.9, 24.

[35] The intertextual favour shown to this group of five authors is typical of *Epistles* 1–9 as a whole; see Whitton (2019) 38–43 for a useful survey of the range of Plinian intertexts across his entire corpus.

[36] Ciceronian references in *Ep.* 6: *Ep.* 6.1 ~ Cic. *Fam.* 16.1.1 9 (etc.); *Ep.* 6.4 ~ Cic. *Fam.* 14.2–3; *Ep.* 6.7 ~ Cic. *Fam.* 4.6.2; *Ep.* 6.8 ~ Cic. *Fam.* 5.12.1; *Ep.* 6.10 ~ Cic. *p. Red. ad Quir.* 8, *Cato* 37; *Ep.* 6.12 ~ Cic. *Amic.* 97; *Ep.* 6.13 ~ Cic. *Fam.* 8.15.1; *Ep.* 6.29 ~ Cic. *De or.* 1.150, *Off.* 1.2; *Ep.* 6.32 ~ Cic. *Brut.* 290; *Ep.* 6.34 ~ Cic. *Fam.* 2.11.2, 8.8.10, 8.9.3.

[37] Catullan references in *Ep.* 6: *Ep.* 6.1 ~ Catull. 50; *Ep.* 6.6 ~ Catull. 101; *Ep.* 6.7 ~ Catull. 2.7, 42; *Ep.* 6.8 ~ 72.3–4, 16.7; *Ep.* 6.19 ~ Catull. 63.53–5.

the vistas of the bay of Naples.[38] In *Epistles* 6, scenes by sea and lake are regularly accompanied by detailed engagements with Vergil. We have already witnessed such references in *Ep.* 6.20. Its companion on the bay of Naples, *Ep.* 6.16, likewise features instances of Vergilian language and associations.[39] In *Ep.* 6.10, the unfinished tomb of Verginius Rufus at his old seaside villa in Alsium, just north of Rome, is equipped with a reference to the fall of Vergil's Priam on the Trojan shore.[40] The wife who takes the lead in an exemplary suicide with her husband on lake Como is hailed as *dux immo et exemplum* ('in fact his example and leader') (*Ep.* 6.24.4): an echo, arguably, of Dido *dux femina facti* ('the leader of the enterprise a woman') (*Aen.* 1.364). She would herself commit suicide for love within sight of the Carthaginian shore. And the description of Trajan's great harbour at Centum Cellae in *Ep.* 6.31, as Anne-Marie Guillemin demonstrated over nine decades ago, draws heavily on Vergil's description of the north African coastline in the first book of the *Aeneid*.[41] Italy's western coast from Misenum, Cumae and Caieta in the south to the mouth of the Tiber was already saturated for men of Pliny's generation with the atmosphere and events of the *Aeneid* – including the *ager Laurens* on which Pliny's Laurentine villa stood. Pliny extends the effect north of the Tiber to Alsium and Centum Cellae.

Not every reference to Vergil in *Epistles* 6, of course, is associated with a seaside location.[42] All the same, when describing such waterside locales, Pliny is clearly drawn to engaging with the great Augustan poet. Perhaps this says more about water than it does about Vergil (or Pliny): bodies of water call for evocations for grandeur, and Vergil is the obvious port of call here, much as Lucretius is the obvious place to find existential dread. There may also be a hint of polemic. In the *Aeneid*, the sea is routinely associated with exile and alienation. Pliny's Vergilian seascapes are redeployed in service of the praise of great men, and a lake in praise of one

---

[38] See Gibson (2020) 34–6.
[39] Cf. *Ep.* 6.16.2 ~ Verg. *Aen.* 2.361–2 (with Gigante (1989) 50); 6.16.4 ~ Verg. *Aen.* 6.851 (with Gigante (1989) 29); 6.16.11~ Verg. *Aen.* 10.284 (with Gigante (1989) 32).
[40] *Ep.* 6.10.3 *cinerem . . . sine nomine iacere* ('ash lying without a name') contains an echo not only of inscriptions for the nameless dead (e.g. *CE* 403.8), but includes a reference to Priam's makeshift resting place beside the shore: Verg. *Aen.* 2.556–7 *iacet ingens litore truncus |. . . sine nomine corpus* ('he lies, a huge trunk upon the shore . . . a corpse without a name'); see Gibson (forthcoming).
[41] For the references in *Ep.* 6.31.15–17 to Verg. *Aen.* 1.159–61 etc., see Guillemin (1929) 118. The rock in the sea as symbol for a ruler's authority, implicit within Pliny's description of Trajan's mole, also draws in part on Vergil's famous simile for King Latinus at *Aen.* 7.586–90; see Saylor (1972) 48.
[42] Most conspicuously, Pliny's announcement of his greatest ever speech in the Centumviral courts at *Ep.* 6.33.1 quotes directly from Verg. *Aen.* 8.439; see later in this chapter.

woman. More such configurations may emerge in *Epistles* 6 and elsewhere in the correspondence to strengthen the suggestion that there are meaningful patterns and clusters within the practice of Plinian intertextuality.

6 Pliny, Tacitus and Quintilian in *Epistles* 6: Letters 6.2, 6.11, 6.21, 6.29, 6.33

We now come to the most sustained and most significant of intertextual conversations in *Epistles* 6: Pliny's engagement with the *Institutio Oratoria* of Quintilian and the *Dialogus de Oratoribus* of Tacitus. Here I draw on the massive achievement of Chris Whitton's *The Arts of Imitation in Latin Prose: Pliny's Epistles / Quintilian in Brief*. Putting this work alongside the results of my own more modest study of Tacitus within *Epistles* 6 (derived from my forthcoming commentary), I aim to make the argument that the intertextual dialogue with Quintilian and the *Dialogus* has particular meaning in Pliny's sixth book. This is the unit, as suggested earlier, in which – amidst a great deal of reporting on Pliny's activities in the senate and courtroom – he marks the death of Regulus (*Ep.* 6.2). Pliny twins that death with the production of his greatest ever speech in the Centumviral courts (*Ep.* 6.33), and announces his own emergence as an exemplar to Rome's rising generation of orators (*Ep.* 6.11). It is in this context that Pliny engages pointedly with the writings of his own teacher, Quintilian, and locks horns with the great pessimist about the future of Roman oratory, Tacitus.

The death of Regulus is lamented by Pliny in *Ep.* 6.2 within the context of a complaint about the tendency of modern courts to limit the length of time given to the orator: '*At quaedam supervacua dicuntur.*' *Etiam; sed satius est et haec dici quam non dici necessaria* ('"But," you'll say, "some things are said which are superfluous." Certainly, but it is preferable for these to be said too than for things which are necessary not to be') (*Ep.* 6.2.8). These words perceptibly echo the formulation of Quintilian on the same matter (*Inst.* 4.2.44):

> Non minus autem cavenda erit, quae nimium corripientes omnia sequitur, obscuritas, satiusque aliquid narrationi superesse quam deesse: nam supervacua cum taedio dicuntur, necessaria cum periculo subtrahuntur.

> But we must equally avoid what follows if we contract everything unduly – namely obscurity; and it is better for the narrative to contain too much than too little: it is tedious when superfluous things are said, but dangerous when essential things are removed.

Here, in the analysis of Whitton, 'Quintilian and Pliny make the same point (better too much than too little); the subject is broadly identical (length in oratory), but not the same (*narratio* for Quintilian, speeches for Pliny); there are intricate similarities of diction and syntax: all the indications point to precise and minute reworking'.[43] This is the 'poetics' of intertextuality in prose: similarity of content or theme, allied to complex, small-scale similarities or re-elaborations and variations in syntax and diction.[44]

The same letter demonstrates an engagement with the protagonists of the *Dialogus*. In a passage that we have already had occasion to glance at, Pliny remarks on the undue lack of respect for oratory in contemporary society (*Ep.* 6.2.5–6):

> tanta neglegentia, tanta desidia, tanta denique irreverentia studiorum periculorumque est. An nos sapientiores maioribus nostris, nos legibus ipsis iustiores, quae tot horas tot dies tot comperendinationes largiuntur?
>
> There is so much negligence, so much laziness, in short so much *irreverence* for oratory and for clients in danger. Are we wiser than our ancestors, juster than the laws themselves, which bestow so many hours, so many days, so many adjournments?

Through a combination of shared vocabulary and rephrasing, Pliny signals agreement with the Messalla of the *Dialogus* on the same subject (Tac. *Dial.* 28.2):

> Quis enim ignorat et eloquentiam et ceteras artis descivisse ab illa vetere gloria non inopia hominum sed desidia iuventutis et neglegentia parentum et inscientia praecipientium et oblivione moris antiqui?
>
> Who is unaware that eloquence, and the other arts too, have declined from that glory of former times not through a lack of people but through the laziness of the youth, the negligence of parents, the ignorance of teachers and the forgetting of ancient custom?

Pliny combines this echo of Messalla's position with a second reference in *Ep.* 6.2.5–6 to sentiments expressed by Maternus in the same Tacitean work (*Dial.* 38.1):

> Transeo ad formam et consuetudinem veterum iudiciorum, quae etsi nunc aptior est <veritati>, eloquentiam tamen illud forum magis exercebat in quo nemo intra paucissimas horas perorare cogebatur et liberae

---

[43] Whitton (2019) 116. [44] See the full analysis of Whitton (2019) 115–18.

> comperendinationes erant et modum in dicendo sibi quisque sumebat et numerus neque dierum neque patronorum finiebatur.

> I pass to the form and custom of ancient courts, which, even if it is now better suited <to truth,> still that forum better exercised eloquence in which no one was obliged to complete his plea within just a few hours, when adjournments were unrestricted, each man chose his own bounds when he spoke, and there was no limit to the number of days or of advocates.

Using common subject matter and shared vocabulary (including the rare *comperendinatio*), Pliny registers a partial protest against Maternus, who thinks modern courts are 'better suited to truth', despite the curtailment of speaking time. There is broad agreement on the superiority of unrestricted time; but Pliny takes issue with Maternus' complacent acceptance of the relegation of unlimited time for speaking to the past.[45]

In sum, this set of engagements with the stated positions of both Messalla and Maternus in the *Dialogus*, registering both assent and disavowal, is allied to emphatic agreement with sentiments of Quintilian on the use of time in modern courts. Through subtle engagements with two authorities on Roman oratory, Pliny outlines his position at the outset of a book that is designed to mark a watershed moment in his own career as an orator.

Around a third of the way through *Epistles* 6, as suggested earlier, Pliny marks his emergence from the shadow of Regulus (and of his own exemplary elders), by hailing two young aristocratic orators who have chosen *him* as their model (*Ep.* 6.11.1–4):

> O diem laetum! ... audivi ex diverso agentes summae spei summae indolis iuvenes, Fuscum Salinatorem et Vmmidium Quadratum, egregium par nec modo temporibus nostris sed litteris ipsis ornamento futurum ... quae singula mihi voluptati fuerunt, atque inter haec illud, quod et ipsi me ut rectorem, ut magistrum intuebantur, et iis qui audiebant me aemulari, meis instare vestigiis videbantur. O diem (repetam enim) laetum notandumque mihi candidissimo calculo! Quid enim aut publice laetius quam clarissimos iuvenes nomen et famam ex studiis petere, aut mihi optatius quam me ad recta tendentibus quasi exemplar esse propositum?

> Happy day! ... I heard two young men of the highest prospects and the highest character pleading on different sides: Fuscus Salinator and Ummidius Quadratus, a splendid pair destined to decorate not just the age, but letters themselves. ... I took delight in each of those details, but

---

[45] For a full analysis, see Gibson (forthcoming); cf. Whitton (2019) 451–2.

especially in the fact that they themselves looked on me as a guide and teacher, and that they appeared, to those who heard them, to be emulating me and treading in my footsteps. Happy day (let me say it again), to be marked with the whitest of pebbles! For what could be happier the state than that young men of the highest rank are seeking a name and repute through *studia*, what more desirable for me personally than to stand as an exemplar, so to speak, for those striving in the right direction?

These heady sentiments re-echo, in part, Quintilian's vigorously optimistic view of the health of modern courtroom oratory (*Inst.* 10.1.122):

> Habebunt qui post nos de oratoribus scribent magnam eos qui nunc vigent materiam vere laudandi: sunt enim summa hodie quibus illustratur forum ingenia. Namque et consummati iam patroni veteribus aemulantur et eos iuvenum ad optima tendentium imitatur ac sequitur industria.

> Those who write about orators after us will have abundant scope for genuine praise of those who are currently at their peak: the talents by which the courts are illuminated today are of the highest order. For mature advocates rival the ancients, and are imitated and followed by the efforts of the young men striving in the best direction.

The expert speakers of contemporary Rome, in Quintilian's estimate, rival their classical predecessors and, in turn, are emulated by the modern young men of the city. Pliny signs himself up, albeit with necessary indirection, for this Quintilianic role of contemporary classic and exemplar. The language of high achievement (*summa spei summae indolis ~ summa ... ingenia*) is echoed. Plus, in the analysis of Whitton, 'Quintilian's *ad optima tendentium* is varied to *ad recta tendentibus*, with a displaced reflex (a false etymology, even?) in *optatius*'.[46] In addition, Pliny's observation that the young orators are 'treading in my footsteps' (*meis instare vestigiis*, 6.11.2) draws on a nearby passage from Quintilian on the necessary task of following in the oratorical footsteps of others: *eum vero nemo potest aequare cuius vestigiis sibi utique insistendum putat: necesse est enim semper sit posterior qui sequitur* ('But no one can level with the man whose footsteps he thinks he must tread in at all times: someone who follows must always come after') (*Inst.* 10.2.10). We are invited to understand that Pliny is the man whom the young of today must strive to surpass.[47]

---

[46] Whitton (2019) 326; cf. Henderson (2011) 151–2 on the play on *optare* and *optimus/Optimus* in *Ep.* 10.1, 10.4 and *Pan.* 10, 45.
[47] See Whitton (2019) 326–7.

To reminiscences of Quintilian, Pliny adds allusions in *Ep.* 6.11 to some of the most optimistic sentiments about oratory expressed in the *Dialogus*, by Aper. The latter asks of the orators of his day (Tac. *Dial.* 7.3):

> qui illustriores sunt in Vrbe non solum apud negotiosos et rebus intentos sed etiam apud <u>iuvenes et adulescentis</u>, quibus modo <u>recta indoles</u> est et <u>bona spes sui</u>?

> Which men are more illustrious in Rome, not just among those at work and fixed on their business, but even among young men and teenagers, at least those of proper character and with good hopes for themselves?

With precise echoes of vocabulary (e.g. *iuvenes, spes, indoles*), Pliny insinuates the young Fuscus and Ummidius into the role of Aper's admiring protégés.[48] Pliny also adds an allusion to Aper's immediately prior reflection on the happiest days of his life. The opening exclamation of the letter (*O diem laetum*, ('Happy day!') (*Ep.* 6.11.1)) makes reference to Aper's insistence that his ascent of the *cursus honorum* gave him pleasure fully equal to those occasions on which he argued successfully before the Centumviral court: <u>*non eum diem laetiorem egi* quo mihi latus clavus oblatus est ... *quam eos quibus mihi ... apud centumviros causam aliquam feliciter orare ... datur*</u> ('the day when I received my broad stripe ... was no happier than those on which I am permitted ... to plead a case with happy outcome before the Hundred Men') (Tac. *Dial.* 7.1).[49]

Pliny means to use Quintilian and Aper as weapons against the broad pessimism about oratory expressed by other interlocutors in the *Dialogus*.[50] The aim is to establish that this is the new golden age of oratory – in which Pliny, of course, has a leading role. The references have a precise, polemical point, designed to bolster Quintilian's enthusiastic sentiments and to combat the apparent negativity of the *Dialogus* as a whole towards contemporary rhetoric. Such allusions have particular point in *Epistles* 6 by giving value to Pliny's performances in the courtroom and senate.

In *Ep.* 6.21, Pliny declares: *sum ex <u>iis qui mirer antiquos</u>, non tamen (ut quidam) <u>temporum nostrorum ingenia despicio</u>* ('I am one of those who admire the ancients, not that (like some) I despise the talents of our own times') (*Ep.* 6.21.1). This is a clear echo, as the great eighteenth century Plinian commentator Johannes Gierig realised,[51] of Aper's criticisms of

---

[48] See Gibson (forthcoming); cf. Whitton (2019) 456. [49] See Whitton (2019) 456–7.
[50] Cf. Whitton (2019) 457, 'Pliny combines upbeat Aper with upbeat Quintilian ...: he too, it would seem, saw in him some distinctly Quintilianic qualities'.
[51] See Gierig (1800–2) ad loc.; cf. Gibson (forthcoming).

Messalla in the *Dialogus*: *non desinis, Messalla, vetera tantum et antiqua mirari, nostrorum autem temporum studia irridere atque contemnere* ('Messalla, you persist in admiring only what is old and ancient, while you mock and condemn the literary culture of our own times') (*Dial.* 15.1). The closeness of Pliny in language and thought to the Tacitean passage prompts the question of who he means by *ut quidam*. Whitton glosses the phrase as 'one of the clearest allusive flags of the collection, as Pliny professes to join Messalla in his cultivation of antiquity, but Aper in admiring modernity too (a typically genial resolution)'.[52] Tacitus, author of the positions of both Aper and Messalla, is perhaps the ultimate target of the phrase. Whatever the disagreements of the *Dialogus*, Pliny maintains a determined faith in today's writers and orators.

Echoes of both Quintilian and Tacitus can be found in *Ep.* 6.29, where Pliny writes to Ummidius Quadratus, one of the young aristocratic orators encountered in 6.11, to give advice on which kinds of cases the addressee ought to take up in court.[53] More significant, however, is the joint engagement with Quintilian and particularly Tacitus that can be detected in the penultimate letter of *Epistles* 6. Pliny here celebrates the publication of his speech *Pro Attia Viriola*, recently delivered in the Centumviral courts. In the course of the letter, Pliny describes the content and style of the speech for the benefit of his addressee: *sunt multa (non auderem nisi tibi dicere) elata, multa pugnacia, multa subtilia: intervenit enim acribus illis et erectis frequens necessitas computandi ac paene calculos tabulamque poscendi, ut repente in privati iudicii formam centumvirale vertatur* ('There are many elevated moments (I wouldn't dare call them such in front of anyone but you), many combative, many matter-of-fact: for those fierce and grander parts are frequently interrupted by the need for doing sums and virtually calling for pebbles and counting-board, so that a hearing in the Court of a Hundred suddenly takes on the look of a private one') (*Ep.* 6.33.8–9). Pliny here echoes in some detail Quintilian's strictures on the appropriate use of stylistic ornament.[54]

---

[52] Whitton (2019) 436.

[53] Compare *Ep.* 6.29.5 *commode agendo factum est ut saepe agerem, saepe agendo ut minus commode*, 'pleading well led me to plead often, pleading often to plead less well', with Quint. *Inst.* 10.2.10 *cito scribendo non fit ut bene scribatur, bene scribendo fit ut cito*, 'Writing quickly does not make you write well, but writing well does make you write quickly'. For the relationship between 6.27.4 and Aper's speech at *Dial.* 19.2, see Whitton (2019) 450 n.205. The more important intertextual relationship in this letter (which reviews some of Pliny's most prominent cases, from the prosecution of Baebius Massa to the defence of Varenus Rufus), is with chapters 1.149–50 of Cicero's *De Oratore*; see Whitton (2019) 328–37.

[54] Quint. *Inst.* 8.3.14. Whitton (2019) 98 observes that 'Each of Quintilian and Pliny ... (*i*) distinguishes more elaborate styles from a plain one, (*ii*) associates the latter with a "private"

Rather more significant, however, is Pliny's use of *Ep.* 6.33 as a launch pad to take on derogatory sentiments expressed in the *Dialogus* specifically on the subject of the oratory of the Centumviral courts. He opens the letter in dramatic fashion, with quotation from Vergil's *Aeneid* – a privilege accorded elsewhere only to the second Vesuvius letter (*Ep.* 6.33.1–2):[55]

> 'Tollite cuncta' inquit 'coeptosque auferte labores!' Seu scribis aliquid seu legis, tolli auferri iube et accipe orationem meam ut illa arma divinam (num superbius potui?), re vera ut inter meas pulchram; nam mihi satis est certare mecum. Est haec pro Attia Viriola, et dignitate <u>personae</u> et exempli <u>raritate</u> et iudicii <u>magnitudine insignis</u>

> 'Put all away,' he said, 'discard the work begun.' Whether you are writing something, or reading, bid it be shifted and set aside; take up like those famous arms this godlike speech (could I possibly be more arrogant?). This is the really handsome one among my speeches, for I am content to compete with myself. This one is on behalf of Attia Viriola, and is notable for the distinction of her character, the unusual precedent set, and the importance of the judgement.

Pliny's emphasis on the distinction of the case has a twofold purpose. First, it reverses his own earlier pessimism, expressed in *Epistles* 2 on the decline of the reputation of the cases of the Centumviral courts. There Pliny had lamented that: *sunt enim pleraeque parvae et exiles; raro incidit vel <u>personarum claritate</u> vel negotii <u>magnitudine insignis</u>* ('For most of the cases are small and insignificant; rarely does one occur that is noticeable from the position of the parties or the importance of the issue') (*Ep.* 2.14.1). Echoing his own vocabulary, Pliny celebrates the confounding of earlier sentiments: the modern Centumviral courts *do* provide cases worthy of notice.[56] More broadly, Pliny means to reject the position of Maternus in the *Dialogus* (Tac. *Dial.* 38.2):

> causae centumvirales, quae nunc primum obtinent locum, adeo splendore aliorum iudiciorum obruebantur, ut neque Ciceronis neque Caesaris neque Bruti neque Caelii neque Calvi, non denique ullius magni oratoris liber apud centumviros dictus legatur, exceptis orationibus Asinii, quae pro heredibus Vrbiniae inscribuntur.

> The actions before the Centumviral court, which are now considered to outrank all others, used to be so much overshadowed by the prestige of

---

context and money matters, (*iii*) introduces ornamental pebbles, and (*iv*) finds ironic humour in a mismatch of style and setting'.
[55] Verg. *Aen.* 8.439; cf. the quotation from *Aen.* 2.12–13 at *Ep.* 6.20.1.
[56] See Gibson (forthcoming); cf. Whitton (2013a) 203.

other tribunals that there is not a single speech, delivered before that court, that is read today, either by Cicero, or by Caesar, or by Brutus, or by Caelius, or by Calvus, or in fact by any orator of rank. The only exceptions are speeches of Asinius Pollio entitled 'For Urbinia's Heirs'.

Pliny, with proper modesty (to be sure), may be 'content to compete with [him]self'; but his ultimate purpose is surely to counter the pessimistic view of Maternus that the modern Centumviral courts are incapable of producing a published speech worth preserving for the instruction of future generations.

7 Conclusion

Pliny engages most consistently with five authors in *Epistles* 6: Cicero, Catullus, Vergil, Quintilian and Tacitus. Consistency of engagement engenders consistency of literary texture. However, each book normally features one or more letters that significantly extend the palette of intertextual reference and offer new challenges to the reader. In *Epistles* 6, there is an observable pattern to Pliny's references to Vergil (connected to water), and a clear and coherent purpose to Pliny's engagements with Quintilian and Tacitus. Pliny consistently highlights Quintilian's optimistic belief in the potency of contemporary courtroom oratory by way of combatting the pessimistic sentiments espoused by Maternus and Messalla in the *Dialogus*. Often he does so by using Aper – the enemy within the gates of Tacitus' dialogue (on a pessimistic view of that work, at least). By supporting some speakers in the *Dialogus* and questioning the views of others, Pliny actively intervenes in Tacitus' work, and insistently asks: where are we to find the voice of that eponymously silent author? He strongly resists the contemporary decline in respect for oratory, adopting the stance that Trajanic Rome represents a new golden age for oratory (where contemporary figures can act as role models for the young, quite as much as exemplars of the classical past), and he strongly insists that the Centumviral courts are capable of producing published speeches likely to be read well beyond their own generation. All this takes place within the confines of a book, one of whose purposes is to celebrate the definitive establishment of Pliny as the leading orator of the Centumviral court and exemplar to Rome's young orators.

From our point of view, this may seem like wasted effort on Pliny's part. Why did he nail his colours to the mast of a genre that Tacitus had so clearly seen was already doomed? In the early AD 90s, Quintilian put together a programme of Greek and Latin authors that the budding orator should read (*Inst.* 10.1.38–131). The list includes nearly sixty Latin authors, featuring poets, historians and philosophers as well as orators. Of this particular group of Latin authors, we possess over a third either whole or in whole parts, and substantial fragments of many of the rest: a remarkable rate of survival, given that as little as 1–2 per cent of classical Latin literature survives today in simple terms of quantity. The rate of survival is spread unevenly across Quintilian's authors and genres: we possess whole parts (i.e. one book or more) of two-fifths of his poets and historians, and one-third of his philosophers. Of Quintilian's fourteen named orators, however, we possess only one: Cicero. The Christians who copied classical literature into codex in the fourth and fifth centuries, and recopied it onto parchment in the ninth and tenth centuries, showed consistent enthusiasm for the historians and poets on Quintilian's list; but they found little to interest them in Quintilian's roll call of Roman rhetorical giants: Asinius Pollio, Messalla, Caelius, Calvus and Servius Sulpicius. In fact, only one piece of Roman public oratory would survive whole from the age between Cicero and the dawn of late antiquity: Pliny's *Panegyricus*. (Pliny of course is not named by Quintilian in his list of his greats, since he is Quintilian's living contemporary.) Yet Pliny's bullish confidence in the future and longevity of rhetoric was not a simple matter of egoistic investment in the self: from the viewpoint of his own day, such confidence must have seemed well placed. In the Greek world, as Reviel Netz has shown, the canon of the most widely circulated authors had stayed remarkably stable for hundreds of years: Homer, Menander, Euripides and Hesiod, plus the great poets of the Hellenistic era (Callimachus, Apollonius and Theocritus). What determined popularity was, it seems, 'vividly present performativity', i.e. texts that responded well to oral dramatisation. Change would come to the Greek canon in the Roman era, when three classical authors finally reached levels of circulation high enough to challenge tragedy for popularity: Demosthenes, Isocrates, Aeschines.[57] What these authors share with the others in the upper echelons of the canon is (again) *performativity*. All three masters of Greek rhetoric are mentioned by Pliny.[58] Given the currently high reputation of five-hundred-year old orators in the Greek world and the

---

[57] Netz (2020) 93–5, 113–14.
[58] Cf. e.g. 1.2.2; 1.20.4; 6.29.6; see Whitton (2019) 13–14 on the importance of Demosthenes to Pliny.

enduring and even increasing appeal of the performativity of their texts, Pliny had every reason to believe that future generations would value the dramatic speeches that he and the oratorical predecessors listed by Quintilian had laboured so hard to perfect. The question then becomes: why did Byzantine copyists largely replicate the interests of their pagan predecessors in such performativity, where western copyists evidently did not?

CHAPTER 3

Discourses of Authority in Pliny, Epistles *10*[1]

Alice König

Although scholarship on Pliny's tenth book of letters has not kept pace with the research being done on Books 1–9, it has not been entirely left behind. Since a trio of publications in 2006–7 (Stadter 2006; Woolf 2006; Noreña 2007), new conversations have begun about the book's literary, rhetorical, and ideological features. Long gone is the notion that its contents are purely administrative, that it constitutes a simple archive of unadulterated correspondence between a provincial governor and his emperor.[2] In its place have come suggestions (inspired by the ways that we now read Pliny's self-fashioning in Books 1–9) that *Epistles* 10 is 'not a raw dossier, but a sophisticated exercise in imperial self-representation'; that it is 'an artfully constructed image of the good aristocrat in his province, and of the best of emperors in Rome'; that it 'could even contribute to Trajan's positive public image and favourable judgement in the eyes of posterity', framing the emperor 'not just as a good ruler but also as the embodiment of the senatorial ideal of the *civilis princeps*'.[3]

In stressing its rhetorical and not (merely) documentary features, these contributions have invited us to begin analysing *Epistles* 10 as one might

---

[1] I extend warm thanks to Spyridon Tzounakas and Margot Neger not only for hosting such an enjoyable and stimulating conference on Plinian intertextuality in Cyprus in 2018, but also for their support and patience during the production of this volume.
[2] Sherwin-White (1966) and Williams (1990) popularised this viewpoint; see also Coleman (2012).
[3] In order of citation: Stadter (2006) 69; Woolf (2006) 105; and Noreña (2007) 239, who stresses that: 'The letters exchanged between Pliny and Trajan belong to the world of imperial communications and administration … [but] also belong to the world of aristocratic competition and public self-representation and should be seen at least in part as the currency of an elaborate symbolic exchange carried out through the textual interaction of two carefully constructed epistolary *personae*' (ibid. 254 and 271–2). See also Woolf (2006) 98: *Epistles* 10 'models the proper relationship between "the ideal emperor and the ideal senator" … portraying a partnership that works in the interest of the provincials and the empire … [and] contributing like all imperial panegyric to a blue-print for good government as the senate saw it'. For an illuminating tour of *Epistles* 10 and Pliny's time in Pontus-Bithynia, see esp. Gibson (2020) 190–237.

Martial's *Epigrams* or Tacitus' *Agricola*.[4] At the same time, the striking differences in substance and style between *Epistles* 1–9 and 10 continue – rightly – to be stressed.[5] For all its rhetorical dimensions, Book 10 reads very differently from the rest of Pliny's *Letters* and other more conspicuously 'literary' texts. As a result, it remains on the margins of – and usually outside – studies of Plinian epistolarity. In fact, with its political agenda now on our radar but its literary merits still widely doubted, it occupies something of a scholarly limbo. Neither simply 'administrative' nor able to shake off that tag: Book 10 defies straightforward categorisation.[6] Above all, it defies one-track scholarship, requiring us instead to look at it from multiple angles and to read it through a mix of lenses.

That is what makes it a particularly stimulating laboratory for exploring ancient reading and writing habits. Indeed, analysis of *Epistles* 10 has an important role to play in this volume's wider project, both in illuminating Pliny's ability to cross between different genres even as he perfects one particular generic form ('Imperial Correspondence') and in prompting us to think about different manifestations of 'intertextuality'. In the last decade or so, Pliny's more 'literary' *Letters* have played an important role in the advancement of intertextuality studies within Classics, thanks especially to the work of Ilaria Marchesi and Christopher Whitton.[7] This chapter – inspired by them and other members of the 'Literary Interactions' research network (including those field-changing Plinian scholars, Roy Gibson and Ruth Morello) – will explore a whole spectrum of interactions in *Epistles* 10, from 'allusion' to 'interdiscursivity',[8] and in the process aims to stimulate further reflection on how, why, and where we study intertextuality.[9]

---

[4] In fact, Woolf (2015) 137 suggested that 'these three contributions, which began by rejecting the notion that Book 10 is essentially a documentary archive or dossier, have not done enough to take it seriously as literature.' See also Whitton's contribution (Chapter 1) in this volume.
[5] Gamberini (1983); Woolf (2006) 96; (2015) 132–3, 135; Noreña (2007) 266–7.
[6] See e.g. Noreña (2007) 245–50 on its blending of 'personal' and 'official', 'public' and 'private'.
[7] Marchesi (2008); (2013); (2015a); (2018); Whitton (2010); (2012); (2018); (2019).
[8] I.e. the evocation of whole discourses as opposed to individual texts.
[9] The 'Literary Interactions' project (https://arts.st-andrews.ac.uk/literaryinteractions/) has produced two volumes – König and Whitton (2018b), and König, Langlands, and Uden (2020) – which have promoted new approaches to the study of prose intertextuality, interactions in less 'literary' texts (like technical writing), 'extratextuality' (Langlands 2018), and interaction as omission/occlusion (Geue 2018), among other phenomena. On the project's conception of 'literary interactions' and its road map for future intertextuality studies, see esp. König and Whitton (2018a) 9–13.

1 Heteroglossia in *Epistles* 10

2018 saw the publication of two ground-breaking essays by Myles Lavan and Jill Harries, which suggested new ways of looking at *Epistles* 10 via its connections to and interactions with other forms of epistolary writing. Taking issue with claims made by Greg Woolf, Philip Stadter, and Carlos Noreña, that the letters of Book 10 were unusual (even artificial) forms of imperial correspondence,[10] Myles Lavan underlined the striking similarities between Pliny's letters from Bithynia and what we can excavate of other correspondence between emperors and administrators across the Roman Empire. The comparison makes Pliny's letters look like the real thing, individually at least.[11] However, while re-asserting the overwhelmingly administrative/documentary nature of the intertextual space in which the letters of *Epistles* 10 were originally compiled and consumed, Myles Lavan also recognised that the book as a whole ended up circulating in other intertextual contexts, asking: 'What happens when ordinary letters are selected, arranged and published as a unit in a reading culture in which the letter-book was well established as a literary form?'[12] Even 'unliterary' texts may take on 'literary' forms/attributes (raising questions about what we classify as 'literature' in the process), and they may enter into intertextual dialogues with works of quite a different category or status.[13]

Jill Harries's essay wrestled with the same phenomenon, the forging of intertextual connections across different genres which can transform expectations, interpretations, and even established reading habits. She drew attention to the publication of successive collections of legal letters (the earliest dating from some time before Pliny published any of his letter-collections), which ended up circulating in a format – as carefully curated books of *Epistulae* – that had strong literary associations even before Pliny had got to grips with the genre. She suggested that some of these legal letter-collections may then have accrued additional cultural capital through association with Pliny's epistolary corpus, which elevated letter-writing and

---

[10] Handily summarised in Woolf (2015) 133–4.
[11] Cf. Gibson (2020) 209, who underlines the 'illusory' nature of Pliny and Trajan's epistolary exchanges: given the timescales involved in the transmission of letters 'the scenario of request submitted and resolution received must have seemed pure artifice to the first readers of Book 10 of the *Letters*. If Pliny did in fact wait for Trajan's replies before acting, then his reputation as an energetic problem solver appears severely compromised. In either case, Book 10 takes on the appearance of propaganda for governor, or emperor, or both'.
[12] Lavan (2018) 282.
[13] As Lavan (2018) 281–2 puts it, 'Book 10 problematises the very distinction between the literary and the non-literary'.

letter-collections to new literary heights. She argued further that Pliny himself may have been engaging in some competitive dialogue with these lawyers' letters in turn when he penned his own version of administrative and legal questions and answers in *Epistles* 10, 'show[ing] the lawyers how exchanges of "question and answer" should be conducted'.[14] In other words, we should read Pliny's tenth book of letters as just one iteration in a longer set of intertextual experiments/rivalries, which crossed back and forth between a range of 'literary' and less-'literary' genres, adjusting their form and identity in the process.

Myles Lavan and Jill Harries both remind us, then, that 'literary interactions' are not the preserve only of obviously 'literary' texts. In exploring connections between whole letter-collections or whole epistolary genres, they also remind us that intertextuality can play out just as effectively at the macro-level – in the structure, register, overall aesthetics, and generic resemblances of texts – as through minute lexical echoes or narrowly focused allusions. Many of the chapters in this volume examine instances of the latter, intertextual activity at the micro-level. However, through its interest in Pliny's absorption of whole genres like epigram and invective, this volume also recognises the role that 'macro interactions' play in the texture and interpretation of Plinian epistolography. In the chapter to come, I will discuss a number of micro level echoes or allusions, where an individual letter in *Epistles* 10 triggers thought of a particular passage in another text; but I will also build on Myles Lavan and Jill Harries's important work to look more broadly at the different generic 'voices' and discourses which Pliny channels over the course of his 'administrative' letter-collection, which affect how we might read the whole book and not just individual components of it.[15]

A single chapter cannot cover all the different voices or intertexts present in this multifaceted text. Rather than offering a comprehensive survey, I here present a carefully selected sample, focussed on Pliny's use of technical discourses and intertexts (especially Frontinus' *De Aquis*) to construct aspects of expertise which contribute to the wider establishment of his administrative authority.[16] That said, my aim beyond this narrow

---

[14] Harries (2018) 278.
[15] In so doing, I follow Stadter (2006); Woolf (2006); (2015) and Noreña (2007) in viewing Pliny as the careful curator/editor and not just the author of the letters in *Epistles* 10; cf. Lavan (2018) 283 who disagrees.
[16] I draw here on important work in König and Woolf (2017) as well as modern theorising about the social construction of expertise such as Collins and Evans (2007); Collins and Evans (2018); Hartelius (2011); Summerson Carr (2010).

focus is to invite further investigation of Book 10's 'heteroglossia':[17] the multiplicity of voices we find in it. Greg Woolf has analysed *Epistles* 10 as an 'unfolding narrative';[18] but for the most part scholars have tended to treat the book as an internally consistent, homogeneous whole (with the exception of letters 1–14, which are often treated as something of an anomaly[19]). Discussions sometimes note the variety of themes in Pliny's correspondence with Trajan,[20] but other kinds of variegation (of voice, generic register, authorial identity, and authority) remain underexplored.[21] In what follows, I want to draw more attention to the book's internal hybridity and, in particular, to the range of intertextual resonances that accumulate as the text goes on, connecting *Epistles* 10 to a variety of genres and prompting the reader to put on different sets of reading glasses and thinking caps as they make sense of the whole.

There is an important reason for this: in exploring the gradual build-up of different voices and different 'discourses of authority' across *Epistles* 10, we can get valuable insights into how intertextuality and interdiscursivity function in society, not just in literature. In Pliny's correspondence with Trajan (this archive of real, if carefully curated letters), we can glimpse the nexus of ideas, discourses, linguistic registers, and tropes which helped people like Pliny to negotiate their authority in an evolving political world. Intertextuality and other forms of narrative interaction not only *leverage* recurring ideas (about e.g. leadership, technical expertise, or good governance); they also help to *perpetuate* or *canonise* them. Sometimes intertextuality can be deployed to tweak, shift, or nuance shared assumptions; but allusions to common reference points and the re-use of well-known tropes and voices can also reinforce established viewpoints and construct a body of 'tacit' knowledge, which elevates some while marginalising others.[22] In other words, in looking at the network of interactions across Pliny's letter-collection, we have opportunities to learn more about intertextuality itself and its social, cultural, and political impacts, as well as better understanding Pliny's intertextual writing.

---

[17] A concept first articulated by Bakhtin (1934).
[18] Woolf (2015) 143 (see also 133: 'a form of narrative, a dialogue that moves forward').
[19] E.g. Williams (1990); see also below, n. 23. [20] E.g. Stadter (2006) 66; Woolf (2015) 146.
[21] See e.g. Coleman (2012), whose detailed analysis of Pliny's use of language in *Epistles* 10 is firmly focused on proving how consistently 'bureaucratic' it sounds.
[22] On 'tacit knowledge', see esp. Cuomo (2016).

2 *Epistles* 10.1–3b

I begin at the beginning, with the set of letters at the start of *Epistles* 10 that have sometimes been side-lined in studies of Pliny's Bithynia-based correspondence.[23] The dramatic date of *Epistles* 10.1–14 is around AD 98–103, taking us back chronologically to the time of *Epistles* 1. This invites us to chart the course of *Epistles* 10 in parallel to the rest of Pliny's letter-collection, or even to re-read those years afresh, with Trajan now front and centre.[24] *Epistles* 10.1–14 are arranged roughly chronologically, beginning with Trajan's accession and building up to a victory in the first Dacian war. Compressed within these letters is a snapshot of Trajan's early years as emperor, with Pliny reminding us that he has known Trajan well – and been a loyal and energetic subject (and letter-writer) – all this time. With the rest of *Epistles* 10 dating roughly to AD 110–12, when Pliny was posted to Bithynia-Pontus as governor and his relationship with Trajan shifted into a different gear, the bulk of the book then captures a slice of Trajan's principate about a decade later, differing significantly in geographic and thematic terms as well as chronologically. For all their differences, these two sets of letters now sit alongside each other in one volume, with 10.1–14 representing a beginning from which the rest of *Epistles* 10 then flows – or to which the rest of *Epistles* 10 responds intratextually.

In what follows, I will argue that letters 1–14 (and 1–3b in particular) engage intertextually with some other change-of-regime literature and discourse that accompanied Domitian's downfall and the accession of Nerva and Trajan. I will then suggest that, in sitting alongside and following directly on from those change-of-regime letters, the rest of *Epistles* 10 might be read as responding to all the accessional literature and reflection that emerged around AD 98, as a sequel of sorts, revealing 'what happened next' after the initial reactions to the start of Trajan's principate. If Greg Woolf is right, that we should read the whole of *Epistles* 10 as a self-conscious sequel to *Epistles* 1–9, Pliny's correspondence from Bithynia might provide a counter-balance to (or at least prompt further reflection on) the progressive pessimism that Roy Gibson has identified in *Epistles* 6–9, when Pliny's enthusiasm for regime-change seemed to

---

[23] On their relative neglect, see e.g. Noreña (2007) 241, citing Millar (2004) 32–4; on their connectedness to the rest of *Epistles* 10, see esp. Stadter (2006) 67 and Woolf (2006) 97; (2015) 140–6.

[24] Woolf (2006) 99; Woolf (2015) 139–40; see also Gibson and Morello (2012) 252 on the way that *Epistles* 10 '"restarts the clock" on the collection'.

falter.[25] As we will see, however, it also dialogues with – and acquires meaning from – a range of other texts and genres outside the Plinian corpus that were themselves shaping discourse and ideals about imperial administration and Trajanic rule at the same time.

The first four letters of *Epistles* 10 work particularly closely together, evoking some key strands of discourse that accompanied the supposedly watershed political changes of AD 96–8. *Ep.* 10.1 offers accessional panegyric to Trajan:[26]

> Tua quidem pietas, imperator sanctissime, optaverat, ut quam tardissime succederes patri; sed di immortales festinaverunt virtutes tuas ad gubernacula rei publicae quam susceperas admovere. Precor ergo ut tibi et per te generi humano prospera omnia, id est digna saeculo tuo contingant. Fortem te et hilarem, imperator optime, et privatim et publice opto.

> Holiest of emperors, your love for your father made you wish to succeed him as late as possible; but the immortal gods were impatient to see you at the helm of government, a challenge you had already embraced. Therefore I pray that you and, through you, the whole human race be granted every prosperity, as befits your reign. As a private citizen as much as a public servant, I wish you health and happiness, best of emperors.

Indeed, as Stanley Hoffer has shown, it captures in miniature some of the accessional panegyric of Pliny's *Panegyricus*, not only through shared themes but also through some tangible intertextual echoes.[27] For example, Trajan's *pietas* and *sanctitas*, amongst the first qualities highlighted at the start of the *Panegyricus* (1–2), are both flagged at the beginning of 10.1.[28] So too is the suggestion at *Panegyricus* 1 and 10 that good rulers are bestowed on men by the gods, and that Trajan was in no hurry to succeed Nerva (*Pan.* 9–10).[29] So far so generic, one might argue: imperial praise is full of such tropes; it might be reasonable to put these overlapping features between 10.1 and the later *Panegyricus* down to rhetorical conventions or contemporary political discourse rather than to any more specific

---

[25] See Woolf (2015) esp. 132 where he references Gibson (2015). Gibson and Morello (2012) 257–8 toy with reading *Epistles* 10 as 'the crowning book of the collection', which consigns Domitian to the past and celebrates the advent of a new era more fervently/explicitly than *Epistles* 1–9 had done.
[26] Woolf (2015) 140 reads Trajan's appearance in 10.1 as an epiphany, noting how Pliny's language is 'suffused with the sacred'.
[27] Hoffer (2006) focuses more on overlaps (and 'intersecting axes of ideology', 87) rather than arguing for intertexts as such.
[28] The first epithets ascribed to Trajan at *Pan.* 1 are *castus et sanctus et diis simillimus*; after a digression on changed times/changed forms of praise, Pliny next mentions Trajan's *pietas, abstinentia*, and *mansuetudo* (*Pan.* 2).
[29] Hoffer (2006) particularly homes in on this last point.

interaction. Other features tighten the intertextual (not just the interdiscursive) links between the two texts, however.

For instance, Pliny's ship of state metaphor in 10.1 ('the immortal gods hastened to entrust the steering of the state (*ad gubernacula rei publicae*) to your virtues') is reminiscent of the lines at *Panegyricus* 6, where Pliny laments recent unrest and the plots against Nerva, and then says 'but if this were the only way to place you at the helm (*quae te publicae salutis gubernaculis admoveret*), I will willingly declare it was worth it'.[30] The brevity of 10.1 and its mid-way shift from praise to prayer also chimes with the comments made at *Panegyricus* 2–3, about the modesty and moderation (and indeed, the change) of speech which Trajan's principate calls for.[31] Pliny's closing words (*et privatim et publice opto*) may even anticipate or allude to some of Pliny's public speeches of praise, even as *privatim* preserves some epistolary intimacy.[32]

Of course, the dramatic dates of this letter and the *Panegyricus* would suggest that 10.1 was written first. The compilation and circulation of *Epistles* 10 post-dates both the delivery and subsequent publication of Pliny's *Panegyricus*, however; furthermore, *Ep*. 3.13 and 3.18 suggest that Pliny expected his readership to be at least broadly familiar with it. It is thus reasonable to assume that anyone opening a scroll of *Epistles* 10 might recognise overlaps and be inclined to make comparisons. While I would not go as far as suggesting that 10.1 was written afterwards, an epigrammatic distillation of the *Panegyricus* penned to launch Pliny's collection of Trajanic correspondence, it might have been edited to bring certain overlaps out and, even if it was not, the decision to place a letter replete with *Panegyrical* echoes at the start of the book invites us to bring the texts into dialogue with each other. In other words, we are encouraged to read *Epistles* 10 in the light of what Pliny said in the *Panegyricus* and, perhaps, also to revisit the aspirational rhetoric of the *Panegyricus* in the light of how things in *Epistles* 10 then pan out.

If 10.1 evokes the start of Pliny's *Panegyricus* (among other examples of accessional panegyric), 10.2 evokes some other contemporary responses to

---

[30] As Hoffer (2006) 76 and n. 12–13 notes, the 'piloting the ship of state' metaphor goes back to Plato (*Resp*. 342E, 488) and was taken up by Cicero (*Off*. 1.87, *Rep*. 1.51.1) among others. Even so, Pliny's re-use of the same language in both *Ep*. 10.1 and the *Panegyricus* might prompt readers of one to think of the other.

[31] An idea also captured by Martial 10.72 in the book he revised and re-published to reflect the change of times; cf. Pliny, *Ep*. 6.27.

[32] Pliny's reference to his public persona here also helps bind the personal and administrative parts of *Epistles* 10 together, looking ahead to the role we will see Pliny playing in much of the book. On the mix of public and private in *Epistles* 10, see esp. Noreña (2007) 245–50.

the change of regimes: in particular, the contrast of good/bad *saecula* (Domitianic and Nervan-Trajanic) which we find (for example) in Tacitus' *Agricola* and some of Martial's *Epigrams*. 10.2 begins personally ('thank you for granting me the privileges normally granted to parents of three children'[33]), but this opening becomes an opportunity for Pliny to look back at the *tristissimum saeculum* just passed and to express optimism for the incipient Trajanic age, in which he feels safe and happy (*et securus et felix*) and all the keener to start a family.[34]

> Exprimere, domine, verbis non possum, quantum mihi gaudium attuleris, quod me dignum putasti iure trium liberorum. Quamvis enim Iuli Serviani, optimi viri tuique amantissimi, precibus indulseris, tamen etiam ex rescripto intellego libentius hoc ei te praestitisse, quia pro me rogabat. Videor ergo summam voti mei consecutus, cum inter initia felicissimi principatus tui probaveris me ad peculiarem indulgentiam tuam pertinere; eoque magis liberos concupisco, quos habere etiam illo tristissimo saeculo volui, sicut potes duobus matrimoniis meis credere. Sed di melius, qui omnia integra bonitati tuae reservarunt; malui hoc potius tempore me patrem fieri, quo futurus essem et securus et felix.

> Sir, I cannot express in words how much joy you have given me, in thinking me deserving of the privileges granted to parents of three children. For although it was the prayers of Julius Servianus that swayed you, that best and most devoted of men, I understand from the correspondence that you were all the more willing to grant his request since he was asking on my behalf. I feel that I have achieved my greatest wish because you judged me deserving of this special favour at the very start of your auspicious reign. Though I longed for children before, during that most oppressive of ages, as you can tell from my having married twice, I now desire them all the more. The gods knew better than me, when they postponed all good things until your benevolent reign. For I would far rather become a father now, when I am able to look forward to being happy and secure.

In fact, Pliny here inverts the rhetoric of *Agricola* 44–5, where Agricola's children lament their father/father-in-law's untimely death as having prevented him from enjoying the fortunes of Trajan's reign, as well as having protected him from the worst excesses of Domitian's reign.[35] More like Tacitus' return-to-life metaphors at *Agricola* 3, Pliny-the-prospective-father

---

[33] Cf. *Ep.* 2.13, where Pliny also celebrates winning this privilege for Voconius Romanus, the subject of more imperial petitioning in 10.4, and 10.94, where Pliny requests the same favour on behalf of Suetonius.

[34] See Hoffer (2006) 77–8 on Pliny's expressions of joy.

[35] For another paradigmatic death, used to thematise this regime-change as a move from bad to good times, see Corellius Rufus on his deathbed in Pliny, *Ep.* 1.12.8.

anticipates new life under Trajan in 10.2 as a way of reflecting on the dramatic change of atmosphere that this *felicissimus principatus* brings with it. In other words, Pliny's response to Trajan's accession at the start of Book 10 gains another strand: namely the stock-in-trade contrast with the Domitianic past that was a marked feature of imperial and literary rhetoric in the years around AD 98–100.[36]

Letter 10.3a then adds a third strand:

> Ut primum me, domine, indulgentia vestra promovit ad praefecturam aerarii Saturni, omnibus advocationibus, quibus alioqui numquam eram promiscue functus, renuntiavi, ut toto animo delegato mihi officio vacarem. Qua ex causa, cum patronum me provinciales optassent contra Marium Priscum, et petii veniam huius muneris et impetravi. Sed cum postea consul designatus censuisset agendum nobiscum, quorum erat excusatio recepta, ut essemus in senatus potestate pateremurque nomina nostra in urnam conici, convenientissimum esse tranquillitati saeculi tui putavi praesertim tam moderatae voluntati amplissimi ordinis non repugnare. Cui obsequio meo opto, ut existimes constare rationem, cum omnia facta dictaque mea probare sanctissimis moribus tuis cupiam.

> Sir, when your generous patronage elevated me to the position in charge of the Treasury of Saturn, I stepped back from my legal practice (though I had never been one to take on cases indiscriminately) so that I could concentrate all my attention on my new duties. It was for this reason that, when the province of Africa appealed to me to act in their case against Marius Priscus, I asked and was granted permission to turn the request down. Later, however, when the consul-elect had recommended that those who had been granted an exemption should be persuaded to remain at the Senate's disposal and agree to have our names thrown into the ballot, I decided that it would be most in keeping with the harmonious nature of your reign not to reject the wishes of that noble order, especially given how moderately they were expressed. I hope that you will judge my obedience appropriate, since I want all my deeds and words to find approval with your most venerable character.

Again it starts personally, with grateful mention of an appointment Pliny received from Nerva and Trajan: a post in charge of the Treasury of Saturn.[37] The aim of the letter is not to express thanks, however, but (ostensibly at least) for Pliny to seek Trajan's approval for some subsequent decision-making. In other words, another 'private' letter that anticipates some of the more official correspondence later in *Epistles* 10. In fact, through a series of intertexts, 10.3a becomes a discussion of good

---

[36] See also e.g. *Pan.* 34, 38–9, 47.   [37] See also *Ep.* 5.14, 10.8, and *Pan.* 91.1.

statesmanship under Trajan and of the wider political conditions in which Pliny and his peers were operating. Pliny begins by stressing how seriously he took his new post, deciding to give up other commitments – particularly his advocacy work – in order to devote his full attention to the role (*ut toto animo delegato mihi officio vacarem*). He explains that this prompted him to excuse himself initially from involvement in the trial of Marius Priscus, which forms the subject of one of Pliny's longest and best-known letters, 2.11. Had his resolve not been broken, he would never have written that extraordinary account of a trial – which took place in the presence of the emperor – that lasted days; this event did great credit not only to Pliny and his fellow advocates but also to the Senate where it took place, whose dignity and integrity could once more be seen flourishing.[38]

The triumph of Trajanic over Domitianic Rome is a fundamental subtext in 2.11, brought out not least when Regulus shows up on the side of the losers (2.11.22). In his account of the same trial in the *Panegyricus*, Pliny is more explicit: Trajan's exemplary behaviour as consul in charge is compared with how badly Domitian would have behaved in a similar situation, introducing a wider panegyric on Trajan's modesty and respect for the Senate (*Pan.* 76–7). In other parts of his corpus, the trial of Marius Priscus becomes an opportunity for Pliny to reflect on how Roman law, administration and government functions under Trajan in comparison with the Domitianic past. 10.3a is no exception. It is difficult to imagine that Pliny really resisted getting involved in Marius Priscus' trial for long; but as 10.3a develops, he explains that it was his sense of obligation to the consul-elect and Senate that persuaded him to be signed up as an advocate in the case: 'I then thought I would best accord with the peaceful atmosphere of your reign (*tranquillitati saeculi tui*) if I did not oppose that distinguished body, especially since they were so reasonable in their request (*tam moderatae voluntati*).' Pliny here models the behaviour of a senator who not only has a strong personal sense of public duty but is now able to please his emperor *and* answer the call of the Senate at one and the same time.

The letter closes with Pliny expressing his hope that Trajan will judge his decision to have been the right one; but this is hardly something he can have been in doubt about. Nor are we left on tenterhooks ourselves. Trajan immediately responds in the affirmative in 10.3b, echoing Pliny's language

---

[38] On 2.11's pivotal place in Book 2 and its representation of the Senate as 'once again the arbiter of justice', see Whitton (2010) 120.

and giving his full backing to both Pliny and the 'most distinguished' Senate, who were 'fully justified' in demanding Pliny's involvement:

> Et civis et senatoris boni partibus functus es obsequium amplissimi ordinis quod iustissime exigebat, praestando. Quas partes impleturum te secundum susceptam fidem confido.

> I am happy to say that you have done your duty both as a citizen and as a member of the Senate in obeying the request which that noble body rightly made of you. I have confidence that you will fulfil your role in accordance with the trust that has been placed in you.

This is the first time we hear Trajan's voice in *Epistles* 10 and, reassuringly, he sounds just as Pliny has led us to expect he might: civic-minded, pro-Senate, and full of confidence in Pliny.[39] It is a brief missive, but its message and tone chime perfectly with the wider narrative that *Epistles* 10 has begun to tell; Trajan's final word (*confido*) prepares us for the rest of the book by highlighting the emperor's faith in Pliny's decision-making. In short, arranged as they are now in the wider letter-collection, 10.3a–b are no longer (simply) about acquiring Trajan's approval but an exercise in establishing some important principles (to which Pliny proves himself fully supportive) underpinning his reign. In particular, this pair of letters interacts with the popular contemporary theme of 'The Senate Revived', which Pliny had treated at length in *Ep.* 8.14 and in the *Panegyricus*, whilst also dialoguing with Tacitus' *Agricola* in the process.[40]

As Christopher Whitton puts it, *Ep.* 8.14 'both proclaims the return to life of the Senate after its Flavian stagnation and leads the way in the continuation of that revival'.[41] Similarly, Tacitus' *Agricola*, Pliny's *Panegyricus*, and the start (if not the whole) of *Epistles* 10 also seek to embed and enact some of the political changes that they begin by celebrating. Parallels between Tacitus' *Agricola* and *Epistles* 10 have long been noted, in particular by Philip Stadter and Greg Woolf, who read the two texts in loose dialogue as contemporary reflections on models of statesmanship and senator-emperor relations.[42] However, to date little attention has been paid to the significant parallels between *Epistles* 10 and another near-contemporary 'administrative' text – Frontinus' *De Aquis* – which

---

[39] The presence of Trajan's voice and sense of co-authorship in *Epistles* 10 lends it a degree of authority on the subject of regime-change that no other text of the period could muster. On the knotty issue of whether Trajan's replies were authored by Trajan himself, see esp. Sherwin-White (1962) and Noreña (2007) 240, 251–2.

[40] For a masterly reading of *Ep.* 8.14 and its intertextual activation of the *Agricola*, among other texts, see Whitton (2010).

[41] Whitton (2010) 138. [42] Stadter (2006) 61; Woolf (1998) 69; Woolf (2006) 106.

also reflects upon and seeks to embed emerging ideals about senator-emperor relations and statesmanship under Trajan.

Written around AD 97/98, Frontinus' treatise on the management of Rome's aqueduct network begins by thanking Nerva for his new appointment as *curator aquarum* and stressing his absolute devotion to and focus on the role (*Aq.* 1):

> cum omnis res ab imperatore delegata intentiorem exigat curam, et me seu naturalis sollicitudo seu fides sedula non ad diligentiam modo verum ad amorem quoque commissae rei instigent sitque nunc mihi ab Nerva Augusto, nescio diligentiore an amantiore rei publicae imperatore, aquarum iniunctum officium ad usum ... primum ac potissimum existimo, sicut in ceteris negotiis institueram, nosse quod suscepi.
>
> Since every assignment commissioned by the emperor demands particularly close attention, and since both my natural concern and my industrious loyalty prompt me to show not only diligence but also devotion in this matter, and since the office of *Curator Aquarum* has been conferred on me by Nerva Augustus (it is hard to say whether he is more diligent or more devoted in his service to the state), an office which is concerned not only with the health but even with the safety of the city, and which has always been held by Rome's foremost men, I think that the first and most important thing to be done (a practice I have established in all previous posts) is to find out about what I have undertaken.

The verbal overlaps between Frontinus' preface and Pliny's explanation for giving up his advocacy work in 10.3a (*ut toto animo delegato mihi officio vacarem*) are not significant enough to be suggestive. There is a strong semantic overlap, however, between what Pliny wrote there (shortly after the *De Aquis* was published) and the more extended philosophy outlined at the start of the *De Aquis* by a senior statesman (a triple consul, no less) who was part of Nerva and Trajan's inner circle, one of Pliny's patrons, and clearly viewed as a role model with whom other public figures could be compared (*Ep.* 4.8, 9.19).[43] Frontinus' *De Aquis* promotes a rigorous new approach to public office and imperial administration thoroughly in keeping with Nervan and Trajanic ideals (thematising transparency, accountability, an end to corruption, and recourse to the law), proving the regime right to entrust such positions of responsibility to the senatorial class.[44] Pliny might have gained a great deal, in other words, by triggering thought of Frontinus and the *De Aquis* towards the start of 10.3a.

---

[43] On 9.19, see König and Whitton (2018a) 16–28; on Frontinus as a potent contemporary role model, see König (2013).
[44] On the *De Aquis*' politics, see esp. DeLaine (1995); Peachin (2004); König (2007).

I will argue in what follows that this faint echo of Frontinus' treatise at the start of *Epistles* 10 is just a prelude to more extended engagement across the rest of the book, which helps to characterise and contextualise Pliny's own (somewhat different) approach to imperial administration. In fact, Pliny's engagement with Frontinus and other kinds of technical and administrative writing in the rest of *Epistles* 10 gains added meaning from the intertextual and interdiscursive dynamics at the opening of *Epistles* 10, which put the whole book in dialogue with a range of texts and ideas that accompanied the start of Trajan's reign. In moving rapidly from accessional panegyric to elite angst and aspirations about change and a newly empowered Senate, this opening set of letters invite critical reflection on the very aspirations and ideals that texts like Frontinus' *De Aquis* articulated. In following 10.1–14 up with a detailed snapshot of how things turned out on the ground/in 'reality' a decade later, the rest of *Epistles* 10 thus responds not only to the picture of regime-change that letters 1–3b (and indeed 1–14) paint but also to the wider contemporary discourses and texts with which those letters engage. In a nutshell, 10.1–3b set up further interactions that will continue throughout the book, encouraging comparison between visualisations of Trajan's reign in AD 98–100 and how it panned out, relative to early expectations.

3 Reading On

As Greg Woolf noted, the first fourteen letters of *Epistles* 10 not only take us back to the chronological starting point of Pliny's previous nine books but also contain multiple intertextual allusions to them.[45] In sending us burrowing back into earlier volumes, Pliny positively invites us to begin reading *Epistles* 10 in much the same way as *Epistles* 1–9, channelling familiar aspects of his epistolary voice as he works through a series of petitions and expressions of thanks, with Trajan's occasional affirmations turning narrative into dialogue. For all their dotting about between different issues, the trajectory of this small selection of letters is carefully managed. Picking up on the end of 10.1 (*et privatim et publice opto*), 10.13 again collapses distinctions between Pliny's private and public personas (*publice ... pietate privata*), but with reference this time to Pliny's career progression and increasing profile (or potential) under Trajan ('in my role as priest [if you were to make me one] I could offer

---

[45] Woolf (2015) 143; see also Stadter (2006) 63 and Woolf (2006) 98 on the likelihood that Pliny was addressing the same audience in Book 10 as in 1–9.

public prayers to the gods on your behalf, in addition to the prayers I already make out of private loyalty'). In recalling 10.1, 10.13 generates a sense of internal coherence, even ring composition; but it also hints that over the course of this small cycle of letters subtle evolutions of identity and voice have already begun taking place, with Pliny anticipating new promotions.[46] 10.14 then bookends this opening cluster of letters from near the start of Trajan's reign with a fresh burst of panegyric, taking us back to 10.1 (and to Pliny's public voice) once more, while also moving us forward in time, charting progress from Trajan's accession to his first major military victory as emperor:

> Victoriae tuae, optime imperator, maximae, pulcherrimae, antiquissimae et tuo nomine et rei publicae gratulor, deosque immortales precor, ut omnes cogitationes tuas tam laetus sequatur eventus, cum virtutibus tantis gloria imperii et novetur et augeatur.

> For your victory, noble emperor, so great, glorious and worthy of our ancestors, I offer congratulations both to you and to our nation, and I pray that the immortal gods grant that all your campaigns have the same happy outcome, with the glory of our empire renewed and increased through your merits.

By 10.14, the realisation of the hope expressed in 10.1 is well under way. *Epistles* 10.15–18 then fast-forward to around AD 110, when Pliny embarks on his mission to Bithynia-Pontus. We learn details of his journey, with 10.15 and 10.17 evoking other travel writing (and painful literary journeys) as they move us across space as well as time.[47] But within a sentence or two on his arrival, Pliny switches registers (genres even), writing mid-way through 10.17a:

> **nunc** rei publicae Prusensium impendia, reditus, debitores excutio.

> NOW [in an emphatic position, catapulting Pliny into action after the slow build-up of his arrival] I am investigating Prusa's public finances: its outgoings, income and what is owed.

The flurry of financial terms (*impendia, reditus, debitores*) directs our attention to Pliny's new focus, with *excutio* performing a metatextual role, shaking the book out as well as capturing Pliny's no-nonsense, new-broom-in-the-broom-cupboard persona. From this point on, his language takes on an official, administrative, technical tone (alongside

---

[46] Pliny's reference to the post of augur here intersects with *Ep.* 4.8, where we discover that it was Frontinus who put Pliny's name forward to succeed him in the role.
[47] See Gibson and Morello (2012) 259–63 and Woolf (2015) 144 on parallels with Ovid's *Tristia*.

ongoing panegyric and petitioning) as he embraces the role he was given: to put Bithynia-Pontus in order.[48]

There has been some valuable discussion of Pliny's bureaucratic language in *Epistles* 10,[49] but much less debate on how its echoes of and interactions with other forms of speech and writing help to build Pliny's identity and authority across the course of the book. Kathleen Coleman discusses overlaps between some of Pliny's phrases and common formulae used (for example) in despatches to the Senate, senatorial resolutions, and legal consultations. In passing, she also compares one aspect of Trajan's language in 10.91 with 'professionals in the medical field, veterinarians as well as doctors'.[50] This is her only acknowledgement that *Epistles* 10 sometimes evokes the technical or scientific discourse of experts, however; she does not attribute any real agency to him in this, seeing his language merely as an inevitable consequence of his subject-matter and context:

> 'The Pliny of the first nine books is supremely competent in the legal and administrative sphere, the sole audible voice ... and a consummate stylist. In Book 10, on the other hand, Pliny controls neither administrative affairs, nor the discourse, nor the stylistic register: much of the time he is writing because he does not know what to do, nearly half the letters are from Trajan, and the language is the bureaucratic tool of officials whose job it was to put problems and their solutions in writing.'[51]

My view is different: I suggest that, as well as employing and evoking bureaucratic and administrative registers (to set the right tone and signal good governance), Pliny knowingly borrows from a range of specialist and technical discourses, dipping into the worlds of land surveying (10.17b and 10.61), hydraulics (10.37, as I discuss further below) and architecture (e.g. 10.39) as well as law (tentatively at 10.29, 10.31, 10.56, and more confidently thereon, e.g. at 10.108–15). While he maintains his focus on financial mismanagement, he shows a passing knowledge of (for example)

---

[48] See also 10.18, where Trajan spells out that mission, and also mirrors Pliny's business-like approach, moving swiftly from journey to the technicalities of provincial administration part-way through the letter.

[49] Esp. Coleman (2012), with further references at n. 10–14.   [50] Coleman (2012) 218.

[51] Coleman (2012) 233; she goes on: 'The survival of Book 10 accidentally lets us glimpse the public official toiling in private for his absent manager. The correspondence between Pliny and Trajan lets us overhear two bureaucrats running the empire at an absolutely nuts-and-bolts level. To do so, they employ the bureaucratic register that was recognized and understood across the Roman world, characterized by a lack of variety in diction, the repetition of standard formulae, and, above all, self-conscious observance – on both sides – of the proper codes inflecting the relationship between a civil servant and his imperial master. This is not the image of the suave, urbane Pliny that he was so careful to project in Books 1–9. This is the fussy bureaucrat, trying to do things properly and not put a foot wrong. He seems to have died in the attempt!'

building materials, the weight-bearing capacity of walls (10.39) and the engineering involved in lake-draining/canal-building (10.61), which testifies to a basic grasp of new specialisms that accumulate to enhance his authority overall. Far from having no control over register, style, or discourse, Pliny interacts with and adopts different specialist discourses to develop the picture that is emerging of a governor who really knows what he is talking about.

In other words, interdiscursivity proves an important tool in the evolution of Pliny's administrative expertise, authority, and identity over the course of Book 10. As new registers are borrowed and new layers of expertise are added, Pliny's language and self-presentation become more confident. He is diffident when first dipping his toe into a new area, but as the book goes on, verbs of hesitation, fearing, and thinking give way to verbs of discovering, knowing, and recommending as Pliny grows his knowledge and refines the extent (and limits) of his expertise and responsibilities. There is a strong sense of development over the course of *Epistles* 10. This is not surprising, of course, and some of it simply comes from the chronological arrangement of letters (it was inevitable that over time Pliny would acquire or at least seek to display increasing competence as his relations with Trajan subtly shifted). Our sense of Pliny's evolution and growth as an administrator comes not just from the passage of time, however, but from the book's conscious heteroglossia, through Pliny's deliberate channelling of different (and differently authoritative) discourses and voices.

The run of letters from 10.17a–37 illustrates this well.[52] 10.17b carries over some of the panegyrical register of 10.1–14, before appealing to Trajan for advice: 'Please consider (*dispice*), Sir (*Domine*), whether or not you think it necessary (*an necessarium putes*) to send a land surveyor out here'. *Domine* defers to Trajan's political status,[53] while *dispice ... an necessarium putes* defers to his administrative expertise. Pliny has a hunch ('It looks as if significant sums of money could be recovered, if reliable surveys were carried out') confidently based on his 'reckoning' of Prusa's accounts, with which he's wrestling as he writes (*Ita certe prospicio ex ratione Prusensium, quam cum maxime tracto*). The phrase 'I am dealing with it right now' (*cum maxime tracto*) ends the letter, leaving us with a picture of Pliny hard at work, *handling* things. Mention of Prusa's

---

[52] Here I can only gesture towards the wider pattern; an extended treatment would deliver much more evidence.
[53] On Pliny's use of the term *dominus*, see esp. Noreña (2007) 247–50 and Lavan (2018) 291–3.

accounts naturally recalls the previous letter, inviting us to read the book as an ongoing narrative; but it also helps to establish an area of growing expertise, with Pliny emerging as a tenacious accountant. He is not just investigating or beginning to 'shake out' (*excutio*) Prusa's finances, as in 10.17a: he is now getting to grips with them.[54] Trajan's reply (10.18) immediately establishes his superior know-how, and his refusal to send Pliny any surveyors might be read as a rebuff ('Trustworthy surveyors can be found in every province, and you won't be short of them yourself if only you look carefully' (*modo velis **diligenter excutere***)). Significantly, though, while teaching Pliny a thing or two about provincial administration, Trajan's recommendation that he looks for local surveyors embraces some of Pliny's own administrative rhetoric; he guides but also affirms Pliny's tentative first steps.

In 10.19–22 we again see Trajan teaching Pliny how to proceed. These four letters (two pairs of question-and-answer between Pliny and Trajan) are loosely connected, revolving around the appropriate employment of soldiers; but they also show Pliny hesitantly, but conscientiously, delving into other administrative areas – prison staffing and the management of other officials – with Trajan correcting his decisions and dispensing wise generic advice (10.20: 'let us stick with custom'; 10.22: 'our greatest concern should be the public good') while adjudicating also on points of detail. The following pair of letters sees Pliny on firmer ground. In 10.23 he returns again to Prusa's accounts (which he is well on the way to sorting by now), this time with a strong recommendation for Trajan, that a new bathhouse be built;[55] in 10.24 Trajan agrees, echoing Pliny's carefully considered language back to him.[56] 10.27–30 then follow up 10.19–22, by returning to questions of the employment of soldiers and slaves. Although Pliny repeatedly defers to Trajan's advice, and Trajan's replies (particularly in 10.30) continue to take a didactic tone (instructing Pliny on important legal and administrative processes and principles), Pliny himself displays greater confidence and some new expertise (in military law as well as provincial staffing), paving the way for 10.31–2 where we see him

---

[54] The phrase *ex **ratione** Prusensium* ('from my calculation of Prusa's accounts') supplants the *Prusenium impendia, reditus, debitores* of 10.17a, showing that Pliny is imposing **order** already.

[55] While *quod videris mihi desiderio eorum indulgere posse* ... (10.23.1, 'It seems to me that you could grant them this wish ...') is not exactly assertive, it is a step up from *rogo, domine, consilio me regas haesitantem* ... (10.19, 'I beg you, Sir, to guide my hesitant thoughts ...'); Pliny's closure of the letter with a rhetorical statement about the benefits of the scheme, as befitting 'the dignity of the city and the splendour of your era' (*quod alioqui et dignitas civitatis et saeculi tui nitor postulat*), channels imperial ideology/the voice of the regime.

[56] *possumus desiderio eorum indulgere* ...: 'we can grant them this wish ...'.

beginning to shine. For, in 10.31, Pliny reasons like an experienced lawyer and reveals himself to be the tenacious and reflective investigator (on yet more tricky employment issues), which Trajan's reply in 10.30 had implied he must become. In 10.32, Trajan then famously endorses Pliny's investigative activities in Bithynia, reminding us how badly managed it has been in the past ('Let us remember that you have been sent to that province since a great many things seem to need correcting there'), while displaying further legal and administrative expertise himself. Over the course of this small and interconnected set of letters, in other words, Pliny's authority grows not only because he shows himself to be the apt pupil of his imperial instructor but also because his (and Trajan's) language and the texture of this letter-collection manifests a growing range of specialist discourses (especially financial and legal), steadily adding new layers to Pliny's administrative expertise in the process.

4 *Epistles* 10.37

Fast-forward to 10.37 and we see some intertextuality (not just interdiscursivity) enhancing both the book's heteroglossia and Pliny's administrative authority. This letter comes immediately after a pair that signals the start of a new year: 10.35–6 give us a moment to draw our breath, pause, and reflect after a flurry of busy administrative exchanges. Pliny's mention of prayers for the emperor and state takes us back to the opening of *Epistles* 10, giving us a brief chance to look beyond all the provincial minutiae (and beyond our view of Trajan-as-micro-manager) to see the bigger imperial picture. It also charts progress over time (as 10.13–14 did): Pliny prays this now not as an individual but as provincial governor, with the first person plurals *suscepimus* and *solvimus* making it clear that he has discharged vows and offered prayers on behalf of all loyal subjects in Bithynia-Pontus.[57]

10.37 then plunges us back into the administrative fray by discussing the rights and wrongs of aqueduct-building:

> In aquae ductum, domine, Nicomedenses impenderunt HS XXX CCCXVIII, qui imperfectus adhuc omissus, destructus etiam est; rursus in alium ductum erogata sunt CC. Hoc quoque relicto novo impendio est opus, ut aquam habeant, qui tantam pecuniam male perdiderunt. Ipse perveni ad fontem purissimum, ex quo videtur aqua debere perduci, sicut initio

---

[57] See also 10.52 and 10.102 for successive accession-day celebrations; also Hoffer (2006) 75, on the way that they also mark the passage of time.

temptatum erat, arcuato opere, ne tantum ad plana civitatis et humilia perveniat. Manent adhuc paucissimi arcus: possunt et erigi quidam lapide quadrato, qui ex superiore opere detractus est; aliqua pars, ut mihi videtur, testaceo opere agenda erit, id enim et facilius et vilius. Sed in primis necessarium est mitti a te vel aquilegem vel architectum, ne rursus eveniat quod accidit. Ego illud unum affirmo, et utilitatem operis et pulchritudinem saeculo tuo esse dignissimam.

Sir, the citizens of Nicomedia have spent 3,318,000 sesterces on the construction of an aqueduct which they abandoned, unfinished, and it has since been destroyed. Later a further 200,000 sesterces were earmarked to build another; but this too was abandoned. Now, despite having squandered so much money in this wasteful way, they will need new funds if they are to have a supply of water. I have myself visited the excellent spring which looks the most likely to supply a clean source of water via an aqueduct, as per the original plan, to ensure that water is not only channelled to the lower parts of the city. Only a few arches remain; some more could be built using what is left of the stone that was cut for the earlier construction; and I think that other sections could be built with brick, which would be easier and cheaper. But first it is vital that you send out a water-engineer or architect, to avoid history repeating itself. To this I will just add that the usefulness and splendour of the new aqueduct will be most worthy of your reign.

From the start, Pliny's language evokes his (now well-established) financial knowhow and adds further evidence that he is busily addressing financial mismanagement. Other aspects of his language conjure a new area of expertise, however, bringing Pliny and *Epistles* 10 into dialogue once again with that other renowned Trajanic-era administrator, Frontinus, and his aqueduct treatise. For example, Pliny's emphasis on autopsy (***ipse** perveni ad fontem purissimum* ...) recalls the emphasis that Frontinus put on looking into things for himself in the *De Aquis* (1–2) – a fundamental aspect of his own expertise and something that he suggests every (ideal) Trajanic-era official ought to do:

primum ac potissimum existimo, sicut in ceteris negotiis institueram, nosse quod suscepi. Neque enim ullum omnis actus certius fundamentum crediderim, aut aliter quae facienda quaeque vitanda sint posse decerni, aliudve tam indecorum tolerabili viro, quam delegatum officium ex adiutorum agere praeceptis, quod fieri necesse est, quotiens imperitia praepositi ad illorum decurrit usum; quorum etsi necessariae partes sunt ad ministerium, tamen ut manus quaedam et instrumentum agentis.

I think that the first and most important thing to be done (a practice I have established in all previous posts) is to find out about what I have undertaken. For in my view, there is no surer foundation for any business; how otherwise can one work out what needs to be done and what must be avoided? For a resourceful man, there is nothing so shameful than to carry out the duties he has been assigned according to his subordinates' instructions; and yet this is the only thing he can do when, through lack of expertise, he has to rely on their experience. They do play an important role in offering assistance, but should be thought of as the hands and tools of the man in charge.

In other words, there is a political subtext to this insistence on finding out for oneself, which Pliny's letter may be drawing on to parallel (or perhaps even surpass) Frontinus' blue-print of the ideal, Trajanic-era administrator. Pliny steps beyond his area of expertise in going to look for himself at a spring that might supply pure water were an aqueduct to be constructed (*ex quo videtur aqua debere perduci*), channelling Frontinus' voice as he does so.[58] By taking on this persona, however briefly, Pliny figures himself as an administrator in the Frontinian style. Indeed, he becomes the autodidact that Trajan (and not just Frontinus' text) has recently been urging him to become, a capable researcher with a new aura of authority that may even adjust how we read verbs of discovering, knowing, and thinking (and claims to uncertainty) in the rest of *Epistles* 10.

Pliny's brief outline of which arches are still standing and the materials they are made from may also recall Frontinus' interest in the monumentality and upkeep of the aqueduct structures and, indeed, a long section in which he details lengths of overground arches as well as underground tunnels (*Aq.* 4–22). It reinforces both parallels and differences, however: while Frontinus' expertise on this is exhaustive, Pliny's is limited and focused on the case in hand. 10.37 then ends with a faint evocation of perhaps the most famous passage of Frontinus' *De Aquis* (*Aq.* 16), where Frontinus compares Rome's 'indispensable' aqueducts with the 'idle' pyramids and 'useless though famous' works of the Greeks (*Tot aquarum tam multis necessariis molibus pyramidas videlicet otiosas compares aut cetera inertia sed fama celebrata opera Graecorum*). If Trajan sends an engineer to Pliny, the latter promises, the result will be a structure that combines usefulness (*utilitas*) and beauty (*pulchritudo*), in keeping with Trajan's *saeculum*. Here again, Pliny appropriates some of the language and themes of Frontinus' text (and wider imperial rhetoric too, of course) not only to correspond persuasively with Trajan but to refine and adjust his own

---

[58] Frontinus makes much of first-person research; e.g. *Aq.* 64, 74; see also *Aq.* 17, where Frontinus had detailed maps made.

identity as an imperial administrator/adviser, in oblique comparison with Frontinus.

Contrast is as important in these intertextual interactions as overlaps or parallels. Anyone familiar with Frontinus' treatise might be struck by the fact that as soon as aqueducts are mentioned, Pliny starts quoting numbers (having done little of this up to now, despite the book's emphasis on financial auditing). Frontinus spends much of the *De Aquis* bombarding the reader with complex sums to underline the scale of waste and corruption that has beleaguered Rome's aqueduct network in the past (especially *Aq.* 64–86) and Pliny's brief turn to the numerical register might be read as a (subconscious?) response to that, as if he knows that when one talks about aqueducts one ought to start comparing big numbers. He stops almost as soon as he has started, however; for while Frontinus' sums relate primarily to pipe lengths, their capacity, and the volume of water they deliver, Pliny's relate to wasteful expenditure, *his* area of expertise. Even as the start of his letter evokes the *De Aquis*, Pliny establishes different areas of expertise; a trend which continues as 10.37 goes on. Indeed, when he asks Trajan to send him a water-engineer or architect at the end of the letter, Pliny signals the limits of his own expertise (as often in the book). While Frontinus, as *curator aquarum*, felt (or claimed) that he had to master every aspect of aqueduct-related know-how (*Aq.* 1–2), Pliny draws the line. He toys with hydraulic expertise, briefly playing at being Frontinus and even borrowing his voice. Yet his interactions with Frontinus' treatise also help him to differentiate himself from that model administrator, who had outlined his ideal vision of a senator-emperor partnership a good decade before Pliny and Trajan began their dialogue over Bithynia.[59]

Frontinus' voice is thus deployed (as one amongst many) in *Epistles* 10 to add a new layer to Pliny's administrative expertise (some general hydraulic knowledge, fleshing out the evolving picture of Pliny's identity and authority). Through contrasts as well as parallels, however, Pliny subtly adjusts and rewrites Frontinus' vision of what the ideal senator-cum-administrator should look like and how the senator-emperor partnership really works, updating it not just for a different administrative context (a provincial governorship, with its wide-ranging responsibilities as opposed to a more narrowly focused post, like the role of *curator aquarum*), but also for a subtly different time: not the transitional, aspirational period

---

[59] See below, n. 61, on the limited – or 'interactional' – expertise which Pliny displays, whereby he knows *about* things, but he does not know enough to *do* things.

between Nerva and Trajan (when senior senators could perhaps imagine being supremely authoritative) but Trajan's reign 'proper' – or at least that is how Pliny wants us to see it panning out.

5 'Interactional' Expertise

Trajan's response to Pliny at 10.38 is both firm and affirming. It opens with a gerundive ('Steps must be taken to ensure that water is provided' (*curandum est ut aqua ... perducatur*)), which appropriates the language of Frontinus' *curator aquarum* in turn; it then declares the emperor's faith in Pliny's 'diligence'. As we saw above, *diligentia* is a hallmark of Frontinus' self-portrait at the start of the *De Aquis*, where he explains that it is a trait he shares with the Emperor Nerva – a claim that generates a sense of close partnership between emperor and senator/administrator, providing Frontinus with a launchpad from which to assert his own administrative authority (*Aq.* 1). At the very least, Trajan's repetition of *diligentia* (he adjures Pliny to be diligent in finding those responsible for wasting money as well as in supplying Nicomedia with water) shows him to be in tune with the administrative rhetoric of the age in general. As with some of Pliny's phrasing in 10.37, however, the language used in 10.38 may trigger a more focused comparison with Frontinus' *De Aquis*, on one hand, inviting readers to see a continuity of approach from Nerva-Frontinus to Trajan-Pliny, but on the other, also prompting scrutiny of the exact (changed?) nature of the emperor-administrator relationship in Trajan and Pliny's case. For while the *De Aquis* foregrounds the assiduous administrator, working energetically on behalf of a concerned – but largely distant – emperor, Pliny and Trajan's epistolary duet promotes a slightly different model, with Trajan (for all Pliny's growing experience and expertise) exercising ongoing diligence at a micro-level, calling most of the shots himself.[60] Pliny and Trajan's administrative ethics and the power dynamics that emerge between them are made visible in all sorts of other ways across *Epistles* 10, of course; but, I suggest, they are brought into sharper relief in this pair of letters via intertextual engagement with Frontinus' change-of-regime text, which provides a co-ordinate for

---

[60] Following *Aq.* 1, Frontinus again celebrates the emperor's 'care' and 'diligence' at 64 and 87–9; most of the care and diligence shown throughout the text is Frontinus', however, with the emperor given credit for strategic decisions which Frontinus himself works hard to implement. Trajan in *Epistles* 10 is both the embodiment and a refinement of the 'diligent' emperor(s) we see lauded in the *De Aquis*, getting involved in the nitty gritty of many different areas of administration, not just the macro-level policy-setting.

comparison (ten–fifteen years on) as well as bolstering the general rhetoric in *Epistles* 10 of assiduous statesmanship.

Pliny returns to hydraulic issues in three further letters (10.41, 10.61, and 10.90) and, as he does so, he not only continues to engage obliquely with Frontinus' treatise but also absorbs other specialist discourse/voices into his letter-collection. At 10.41 he tentatively suggests a project to link a lake to the sea, recommending the idea to Trajan as something that will again be characterised both by usefulness (*utilitas*) and beauty (*pulchritudo*), words which evoke the close of 10.37 and invite us to read them in dialogue. His on-the-spot research (autopsy again: *ego per eadem loca invenio fossam*: 'In my own investigations at the site, I have come across a ditch') gets him talking of heights, cubits, and ancient canals – a mix of history, surveying, hydraulic engineering, and past and future marvels – but he again identifies the limits of his own knowledge and requests a surveyor or architect to assess what can be done next. As in 10.37, Pliny does not present himself as a hydraulic expert and Trajan's reply at 10.38 confirms this, promising him a surveyor and someone 'skilled in this kind of work', whose job it will be to research the lake's water sources and capacity 'diligently' (*diligenter*).

At 10.61, Pliny returns to the subject, hinting that the emperor had been making inquiries of his own ('Sir, you are very wisely concerned that . . .' (*tu quidem, domine, providentissime vereris* . . .)) and revealing that Pliny has also researched the matter further ('through being on site, I think I have discovered . . .' (*ego in re praesenti invenisse videor* . . .)). Some detailed discussion of various engineering options testifies to Pliny's 'diligent' acquisition of more expertise (something that Trajan then remarks on in 10.62); but as in 10.41, Pliny ends by deferring some of the detailed decision-making to specialists, and Trajan renews his promise of a surveyor and the availability of provincial *artifices* to help. Pliny briefly writes and reads like an engineer or a surveyor himself, then, introducing technical discourses into his administrative letter; but he and Trajan ultimately veer away from the Frontinian model of administrators needing to know as much as their subordinates (*Aq.* 2), happy to delegate to specialists on the nitty-gritty.[61]

---

[61] Pliny's expertise here might be defined as functional or 'interactive'/'interactional': see e.g. Collins and Evans (2015) and (2016), who define 'interactional' expertise as knowing *about* things, but not knowing enough to *do* things. The title of this section is a deliberate pun, alluding to the 'literary interactions' which draw attention to how 'interactional' Pliny's technical expertise is. Cf. Woolf (2006) 107 on *Epistles* 10 reflecting 'an ideology of provincial rule as the application of general virtues, rather than the work of knowledgeable specialists'.

Discourses of Authority in Pliny, Epistles 10

By 10.90, Pliny's voice is increasingly authoritative, thanks in part to his heteroglossia: he has continued to absorb other discourses and specialisms, from architecture to religious lore, as the letter-collection goes on. While we see him just moving into Frontinus' area of expertise in 10.37, we see him in full possession in 10.90, as he confidently states Sinope's need for an aqueduct, notes that he has identified a good source sixteen miles away, reveals that he has already commissioned a (cheap) survey, and promises Trajan that sufficient funds can be (carefully) earmarked for so important a project: 'With me overseeing the project, the allocated funds will not run out, if only you, Sir, grant permission for a project that will enhance the health and amenities of a thirsty town' (*pecunia curantibus nobis contracta non deerit, si tu, domine, hoc genus operis et salubritati et amoenitati valde sitientis coloniae indulseris*). 10.90 is a powerful follow-up to the tentative suggestions of 10.37 and 10.41, a testament to Pliny's mastery of multiple provinces of knowledge. It may even follow up – and trigger thought of – an important passage in Frontinus' *De Aquis*, where Frontinus breaks off from aqueduct inventories to celebrate the effects that an increase in water volume has had on the city (*Aq.* 88). This celebration goes on for several chapters (to the end of *Aq.* 93), enumerating the different ways in which the city and its waters are now healthier, all thanks to the emperor's diligent attention.[62] Of all the parts of the *De Aquis* that Pliny's readers may have been familiar with, this extended panegyric of the emperor's role in improving the city's water supply is likely to have been the best-known. Pliny's mention at the end of 10.90 of the *salubritas* ('health benefits') and *amoenitas* ('pleasures'), which his proposed aqueduct in Sinope might bring to that 'thirsty' colony, may thus tap into ideas that the *de Aquis* had recently underlined about the advantages (and reflected glory) of imperial patronage of aqueduct schemes. Channelling Frontinus' voice first on the technical side of things, as he identifies a good spring and sets the wheels in motion for a new construction, Pliny then closes the letter with a nudge to Trajan about the project's wider benefits, which not only engages with general discourse about imperial benefaction, but may also invite the emperor to live up to the specific model established by the *De Aquis*. All that is left for Trajan to do in 10.91 is to echo Pliny's words back to him in agreement (as he duly does: 'look into this carefully ... it will contribute a very great deal to the town's health and

---

[62] The city's improved *salubritas* flows from an increased volume of drinking water as well as its increased purity, thanks to a range of administrative and engineering solutions. At *Aq.* 1, Frontinus elevated the importance of the role of *curator aquarum* as a post concerned with 'the health and security of the city' (*ad salubritatem atque etiam securitatem urbis pertinens*).

happiness' (*explora diligenter . . . cum plurimum ea res et salubritati et voluptati eius collatura sit*)), using the language of *diligentia* and *salubritas* again which Pliny shares with or has absorbed into his administrative voice from Frontinus.[63]

6 Conclusions

A critic might argue that I have pounced on – and perhaps talked up – these possible interactions with the *De Aquis* because Frontinus has been a key focus of my research for the past couple of decades, an obsession that gets me seeing things when I read other texts. That point plunges us into the dynamics of intertextuality itself, however, and the role played by readers in recognising and activating transformative interactions, even in/ with texts that are not traditionally subject to intense intertextual scrutiny. As Myles Lavan put it in relation to *Epistles* 10, '[t]he "literary" is an effect produced as much by the reader as by the text . . . When Book 10 was edited and published as a supplement or appendix to Books 1–9, it circulated in a reading culture whose expectations had been shaped by those earlier collections. The question to ask is how a *doctus lector* – one with an eye for "the frames, sequences, juxtapositions, symmetries" created within a book and a taste for "the *delectatio* of discovery (and of foiled expectations)" – would read Book 10.'[64] Myles Lavan is making a point about reading at the macro-level, exploring how readers' experiences and expectations of the letter-book as a literary phenomenon enable or encourage them/us to take the entirety of *Epistles* 10 'seriously as literature'.[65] The same principle applies when we drill down into the details of *Epistles* 10, however: readers' (variable) experiences and expectations of other forms of writing enable and encourage us to draw connections, apply particular reading frames, and explore new layers of meaning in Pliny's 'administrative' correspondence. Just as Jill Harries – with her expertise in Roman law – foregrounded Pliny's interactions with legal texts and authority figures,[66] so I – with my interest in technical and scientific writing – have homed in on moments where Pliny's voice sounds particularly specialist or channels some recognisably scientific discourse.

---

[63] At 10.98, Pliny returns briefly to a connected issue, confidently recommending a solution to the open sewer which is threatening the health (*salubritas*) and pleasant appearance (*decor*) of Amastris; Trajan's reply (10.99) again endorses Pliny's recommendation.
[64] Lavan (2018) 301, citing Whitton (2013a) 12; cf. Woolf (2006) 98 on the probability that Pliny's intended readership in *Epistles* 10 is the same as for *Epistles* 1–9.
[65] Lavan op. cit, citing Woolf (2015) 136–7.   [66] Harries (2018).

Neither of us has done so uninvited. As this volume shows, Pliny's epistolary corpus repeatedly encourages readers to apply different generic lenses to their reading of individual letters, so that, by the time we get to *Epistles* 10, we have become adept at following up all sorts of intertextual and interdiscursive triggers and at processing subtle changes in authorial voice, register, and genre. Despite its obvious differences from *Epistles* 1–9, Pliny's tenth book continues in the same vein. In fact, I have foregrounded the ways in which Pliny appears to channel Frontinus' voice not to prove that the *De Aquis* itself is a particularly stand-out intertext for *Epistles* 10, but rather as a case-study to illustrate a wider trend.

In some ways, Pliny's administrative correspondence with Trajan is remarkably repetitive, even formulaic; as we read through, we become used to recurring requests for the same kind of advice, lots of talk of finances and previous mismanagement, interspersed with occasional panegyric and petitions. There is a point to this: as well as painting a picture of Pliny and Trajan's consistently careful, unimpeachable administration of Bithynia-Pontus, *Epistles* 10 conjures the ongoing routine of (outstanding) empire-wide imperial government, modelling an interior world of provincial administration that is applicable anywhere.[67] Pliny's correspondence with Trajan works rhetorically not just by hammering home recurring methods, attitudes, and values, however, but also by becoming gradually encyclopaedic via its increasing heteroglossia. A read-through of *Epistles* 10 in search of conventional markers of allusion and intertextuality will yield very little; but, working with a broader understanding of 'textual interaction', which incorporates interdiscursivity and generic ventriloquism, reveals how rich the texture of Pliny's tenth book of letters is. My analysis here has only scratched the surface, focusing particularly on the technical voices that bubble up and their role in constructing Pliny's administrative expertise and authority. There is a significant build-up of other kinds of intertexts within this epistolary 'archive' which I have not had time to dive into: Pliny gives us glimpses of other people's letters (e.g. 10.58, 10.63-4), edicts (e.g. 10.50, 10.58, 10.65), *senatus consulta* (10.72–3), wills (10.70, 10.75, 10.104), and even libelous pamphlets (10.96–7) – texts within texts, which call for more investigation in future analyses of intertextuality within *Epistles* 10. As I have argued, Pliny also evokes, draws on, and interacts with wide range of discourses – from panegyric to scientific – using interdiscursivity as well as intertextuality to add new layers to his administrative authority.

---

[67] Woolf (2006) 98.

Some of these interactions invite reflection on Trajanic (not just Plinian) models of government, in particular in comparison with previous times. One final example will serve to bring together the different threads of this chapter. In 10.56, Pliny channels his legal persona to ask Trajan's advice on a couple of cases concerning men sentenced to exile whose sentences may or may not have later been annulled. In good lawyerly style, Pliny establishes the legal issues that are at stake, identifying in each case the question that Trajan (as legal authority) must answer and setting out what evidence he has been able to find. Indeed, he appends to the letter the relevant documentation: copies of the original sentences and, in one case, an edict of reversal. 10.56 thus cites external texts as well as adopting legal discourse and evoking the kinds of legal question-and-answer correspondence dealt with by Jill Harries (2018).

In addition, it is just possible that there is another kind of 'literary interaction' in the form of an allusion to Pliny the Elder's epistolary preface to the *Natural History*, also addressed to an emperor (Titus).[68] At the end of that preface, the elder Pliny cites government business as a reason why Titus may not have had time to read his encyclopaedia:

> Quia occupationibus tuis publico bono parcendum erat, quid singulis contineretur libris, huic epistulae subiunxi summaque cura, ne legendos eos haberes, operam dedi. tu per hoc et aliis praestabis ne perlegant, sed, ut quisque desiderabit aliquid, id tantum quaerat et sciat quo loco inveniat. (*HN praef.* 33)

> Given how busy you are and how much in the public interest it is to spare you extra trouble, I have attached to this letter a list of the contents of each individual book and have taken great pains with this so that you are not obliged to read them yourself. In fact, you can set an example for others in not reading the whole text through; the idea is that each reader may look up only the specific thing he wants to learn and may know where in the book to find it.

At 10.56, the younger Pliny also refers to the imperial workload, thanking Trajan for answering all his inquiries in the midst of his other occupations ('Sir, I am grateful that in the midst of your important work, you have deigned to guide me on everything I have consulted you about' (*summas, domine, gratias ago, quod inter maximas occupationes in iis, de quibus te consului, me quoque regere dignatus es*)). However, rather than offering him the opportunity to read no further or to read only selectively, as the elder

---

[68] On the elder Pliny's address to Titus, see esp. Morello (2011).

Pliny does (slightly tongue-in-cheek), the younger Pliny turns this metatextual moment into an appeal for Trajan to keep reading and responding: to keep *Epistles* 10 going, no less (*quod nunc quoque facias rogo*: 'Now I ask that you do so again').[69] This is one of many moments in the book where a letter draws explicit attention to the text's dialogic nature. Here Pliny clearly refers to *previous* exchanges, not just the present correspondence (i.e. to the collection as a whole, not just its constituent parts), and in doing so he underlines the joint nature of their ongoing administrative *and* literary endeavour. Indeed, through its possible evocation of the elder Pliny's 'letter' to Titus, 10.56 tells us that, far from being a distraction from government, all this letter-writing (*Epistles* 10) *is* government, Pliny-and-Trajan-style. This is just one of the many ways in which the book poses the question: where does literature start and stop?

If there is any interaction with the elder Pliny's *Natural History*, in other words, it is a contrastive one, highlighting shifts in the relationship between loyal subject/letter-writer and emperor/recipient. The elder Pliny's 'no need to read' message maintains his control over the specialist knowledge in his text and admits Titus, at best, to only partial understanding. The younger Pliny's 'please reply again' establishes Trajan as the ultimate expert (perhaps even inviting us to view the emperor's knowledge/authorship/authority as encyclopaedic) and as co-author of a different kind of government. Through oblique contrast with his uncle's writing – as with Frontinus' *De Aquis* – Pliny thus illuminates how Trajan's administration is unfolding in contrast to earlier times/ideals: there is no great gulf between experts and emperors, as in the *Natural History*, nor such an intense partnership of 'equals', as Frontinus suggests in the *De Aquis*. Rather, Trajan models a form of functional expertise that Pliny himself also gradually acquires (following the emperor's lead), as different discourses of authority build up across (and thanks to) *Epistles* 10. To return to where I started, *Epistles* 10 looks, feels, and reads very differently from *Epistles* 1–9; but it is equally 'intertextual', albeit in less obvious ways. Indeed, even as it weaves different 'genres' of letter-writing (administrative, legal, and literary) into a new epistolary text, it leverages other generic registers, discourses, and voices to give us the 'inside scoop' not just on Pliny's actions in Bithynia-Pontus, but on the style of imperial government that Pliny had optimistically visualised in the *Panegyricus*.

---

[69] Cf. König (2020) on Aelianus Tacticus' different engagement with the elder Pliny's offer to Titus at *HN praef.* 33.

PART II

Models and Anti-Models: Pliny's Interaction with Oratory and Natural History

CHAPTER 4

*Oratorical Speeches and the Political Elite in the Regulus Cycle**

Matthew Mordue

The traditional view of Pliny as an optimist, confident about the new age of Trajan, is not as widely accepted as it once was. Instead, scholars have started to examine his increasing disillusionment with political life in the capital; within this context, Strunk has drawn attention to *Ep.* 2.20 as particularly representative of Pliny's pessimism.[1] In this letter, Pliny reveals that his political rival Marcus Regulus has been legacy hunting in Rome and informs us that his nemesis was successful in writing himself into the will of the sick and vulnerable Verania.[2] Yet, despite Pliny's exposure of Regulus' shocking moral transgressions, he makes it clear throughout the letter that Regulus is not solely responsible for his actions. The *civitas* (political elite community of Rome), Pliny complains, often rewards wickedness and so are complicit in his rival's crimes.[3] Thus, as Strunk argues, Regulus is presented as only one manifestation of the community's general support of *nequitia* (wickedness) and its consequences in society.[4]

In this chapter, I will argue that *Ep.* 2.20 contains intertextual allusions to Cicero's *In Verrem* and Demosthenes' *De Corona*, which highlight Pliny's political pessimism. By investigating these references, we will see

---

* I am indebted to Kathryn Tempest for commenting on several drafts of this chapter. I am also thankful to Marta Garcia-Morcillo for her advice, which has improved my understanding of Pliny's cultural backdrop, as well as the audience at the International Pliny Conference held at the University of Cyprus in 2018, whose questions helped me shape my argument.
[1] Strunk (2012); a view endorsed in Gibson (2015).
[2] Regulus has become a popular topic in scholarship and has numerous studies dedicated to him. For Pliny's portrait of Regulus as a dark reflection of himself and a 'bad senator', see Hoffer (1999) 55–92. For Pliny's rivalry with Regulus more generally, see Méthy (2007) 142–51; Lefèvre (2009) 50–60; 106–9; Gibson and Morello (2012) 68–73. For a linear reading of the Regulus cycle and an analysis of Pliny's invective against Regulus, see Ash (2013).
[3] Plin. *Ep.* 2.20.12. The word *civitas* was often used in early imperial Rome to refer to the political community of an *urbs*, see Ando (2015) 7–28. As Whitton (2013a) 279 argues, the *civitas* consists of Pliny's fellow members of the elite Roman community.
[4] Strunk (2012) 179.

that Pliny's concern for Rome's future is given further emphasis, strengthening Strunk's argument that *Ep.* 2.20 is a particularly dark point of the correspondence. However, I also believe that this passage provides additional insight into the craft of the *Epistles* because, as Marchesi has argued more generally, Pliny creates his own artistic project and a kind of semiotic web through his engagement with other literary genres.[5] In other words, the hints in *Ep.* 2.20 to Cicero and Demosthenes position Pliny's criticisms of his community alongside the similar complaints made in the *In Verrem* and *De Corona*, and they provide a key to how he conveys his political sentiments.

To demonstrate this point, I shall begin by explaining the context of Pliny's criticism, before going on to demonstrate how, and to what effect, he evokes his oratorical predecessors. I will then outline how Pliny's allusions reinforce the central themes of *Ep.* 2.20. To conclude, I will argue that Pliny's criticism of his community in *Ep.* 2.20 is a turning point, prefiguring more explicit political pessimism in the later letters of the Regulus cycle. Hence, Pliny's uncertainty for Rome's future in *Ep.* 2.20 stems from his own community, which could suggest that the darkening of his private correspondence in the latter books may also originate from an unease with the political institutions of the principate more generally.

1 Intertextuality and Generic Enrichment

Yet before I can examine the allusions in *Ep.* 2.20, I first need to outline my approach to intertextuality. After all, whether we approach the interactions between the texts as by authorial design or a product of reader-response could impact our view of Pliny's self-identification with Demosthenes and Cicero as well as his messages about his *civitas*. I am personally sympathetic to Whitton's view that we can treat many of the *Epistles*' intertextualities, such as the ones in this chapter, as intentional on Pliny's part.[6] However, authorial intention is always a difficult matter, especially when examining very subtle references.[7] Therefore, although I am tempted to read *Ep.* 2.20's allusions as carefully crafted by Pliny himself, it is also valid and equally possible to privilege the text over the

---

[5] Marchesi (2008) 10–11.   [6] Whitton (2019) 45.
[7] For the challenges of authorial intention, see Lyne (1994). As Lyne states, 'allusion' is somewhat problematic because it implies design on part of the author. Throughout this paper, I use allusion strictly to describe the *Epistles*' links to other texts, and with no presumption of intent on Pliny's part.

author and consider how the 'allusions' of the letter augment its themes and complement the narrative of the complete collection.[8] To accomplish this, I will look at the 'generic enrichment' of *Ep.* 2.20; that is, the ways in which the letter's hints to oratory give it added depth.[9] Consequently, I will argue that the themes of *Ep.* 2.20 are amplified through the narrative parallels between the letter and the speeches to which it alludes. The *Epistles'* engagement with rhetoric has been well studied, yet I hope to show that *Ep.* 2.20's links to oratory can provide us with further insight into Pliny's construction of his 'epistolary super-genre'.[10]

2 *Epistles* 2.20

When we reach the end of Book 2, it is not surprising to encounter Regulus' criminal legacy hunting, as Pliny has already made his villainous nature abundantly clear in the opening book of the collection.[11] What is most unexpected is *Ep.* 2.20.12, where Pliny reveals that his community supports Regulus' actions; the crucial line is:

> Ἀλλὰ τί διατείνομαι in ea civitate, in qua iam pridem non minora praemia, immo maiora nequitia et improbitas quam pudor et virtus habent?

> But why do I exert myself over this community, where, for a long time, wickedness and dishonesty have no less rewards, or on the contrary greater ones, than honour and virtue?[12]

Admittedly, Pliny has already suggested that his rival is supported by powerful men before now. In the first letter of the Regulus cycle, Pliny had complained that Regulus was δυσκαθαίρετος ('hard to knock down', *Ep.* 1.5.15) because of his influential friends. Moreover, at *Ep.* 2.11.22, Pliny had also revealed that several senators supported Regulus' attempt to give the corrupt governor, Marius Priscus, a lighter sentence than was being proposed in court. But despite these minor incidents, this is the first

---

[8] My analysis is thus in the vein of Marchesi (2008) 5.
[9] For a key analysis of 'generic enrichment', see Harrison (2007).
[10] The primary goal of this volume. For studies on the *Epistles'* engagement with oratory, see Marchesi (2008) 207–40; Whitton (2019).
[11] Regulus slanders the Stoic opposition so aggressively that even their prosecutors were taken off guard: Plin. *Ep.* 1.5.2–3. Later (*Ep.* 1.20.13), Pliny contrasts Regulus' violent oratory with his own more classical approach. Pliny depicts his rival here as a typical villainous *delator* (informant). On the perceived threat of *delatores* and their style of oratory, see Rutledge (2001) 10–16.
[12] All translations of Latin and Greek are my own. I have used the Loeb editions of the Latin text (Radice) and Greek text throughout. In difficult passages I have consulted the Loeb translations for help, I have also used John Delaware's excellent translation for assistance.

time Pliny has held the elite accountable for their complicity, and so it represents a significant shift in political sentiment within the Regulus cycle. To make the point more poignant still, Pliny appears to embed two intertextual allusions into his expression of frustration.

Thus, if we look back at the quotation above, τί διατείνομαι picks up on and self-consciously alludes to Demosthenes' rhetorical question in *De Corona*: τί οὖν ταῦτ' ἐπήραμαι καὶ **διετεινάμην** οὑτωσὶ σφοδρῶς ('but why have I called down this curse and exerted myself so vehemently in this way?', *De cor.* 142).[13] Additionally, Pliny's complaint that there are greater prizes for ***nequitia et** improbitas **quam** pudor et **virtus*** seems to echo Cicero's criticism in the *In Verrem* that the friendship of Hortensius (Verres' defendant) is more readily available to men like Verres, who are guilty of ***nequitia** et audacia* ('recklessness and daring'), than to virtuous and honest men like Cicero: ***quam** cuiusquam nostrum **virtus** et integritas* ('than for any of us that are virtuous and honest', *Verr.* 2.3.7).[14] As Whitton has argued, Pliny's pairing of *pudor* and *virtus*, and *nequitia* and *improbitas*, is Ciceronian in style, making the reference more pronounced.[15] What is more, the coupling of Demosthenes and Cicero was natural in Pliny's time and used by writers such as Quintilian, Plutarch and Juvenal.[16] Pliny was also not the first writer to link *De Corona* to *In Verrem*, as Quintilian directly compared the two speeches' use of transitions.[17] But as we shall see in the next section, Pliny's line does not simply serve to align him with Demosthenes and Cicero; it emphasises that men like Regulus cannot operate in society without the complicity of Rome's political elite. That is: the intertextual allusions here serve to reinforce the central message of *Ep.* 2.20 and so conclude Book 2 on a remarkably pessimistic note.

3 The *Epistles* and *De Corona*

Tzounakas has shown in a recent study that Pliny often links himself to Demosthenes in his *Epistles*.[18] But what is particularly striking about

---

[13] As Trisoglio (1973) 339 shows, Pliny's allusion is an adaption and simplification of *De Corona*; cf. Whitton (2013a) 279; Tzounakas (2015) 213; Carlon (2017) 46.

[14] As discovered by Whitton (2013a) 279. A similar mentality can be seen in Cicero's other texts, for example, *Off.* 2.69.

[15] Whitton (2013a) 279. Also of note is Pliny's use of Greek quotations, which, as Schwerdtner (2015) 29–30 argues, is a Ciceronian epistolographic technique.

[16] Quint. *Inst.* 2.4.16; 3.8.5; 4.1.66; 8.5.33; 9.4.36; 10.1.105–9. Quintilian pairs them as the greatest orators of all time at *Inst.* 6.3.2; cf. Juv. 10.114–7. Plutarch pairs the two orators in his *Parallel Lives*.

[17] Quint. *Inst.* 9.2.61–2.   [18] Tzounakas (2015).

Tzounakas's findings is that Pliny becomes more confident in linking his oratorical abilities to Demosthenes as the *Epistles* progress. Pliny is initially cautious when first connecting himself to Demosthenes in *Ep.* 1.2, citing a number of Attic influences upon his style to show that he possesses *varietas* (oratorical variety) rather than claiming a specific rhetorical lineage to Demosthenes.[19] Tzounakas argues that it is not until after Book 3, a unit which celebrates Pliny's success as consul, that Pliny indirectly compares himself to Demosthenes in particular.[20] As we will see, the allusion of *Ep.* 2.20 is a key moment in Pliny's acceptance of his role as the 'Roman Demosthenes', as it offers his first substantial self-identification with the great Greek orator.[21]

De Corona is one of Demosthenes' most celebrated speeches and *Ep.* 2.20's reference to it doubtlessly aligns Pliny with Demosthenes' oratorical genius.[22] In this way, the letter prefigures Pliny's confidence in later books of the *Epistles*, where he indirectly compares his speech *De Helvidi Ultione* to that of Demosthenes' *Against Meidias* and one of his friends compares another of his particularly successful speeches to *De Corona*.[23] But it is also possible that the allusion highlights the parallel between Pliny's rivalry with Regulus and that of Demosthenes and Aeschines. For, although Demosthenes argues his right to receive a crown in honour of his services to Athens in *De Corona*, the speech also functions to condemn Aeschines, specifically for betraying Greece and assisting Philip of Macedon's conquests.[24] In this context, Demosthenes' prayer to the gods, the section which is partially quoted, serves to express his fear that Aeschines might corrupt the minds of his jurors into believing him innocent: and so Aeschines' audience would support him over Demosthenes. The letter's reference to this section of the *De Corona* does more than align Pliny's own oratorical genius with that of Demosthenes; it functions to establish Regulus as a rival, a counterpart to Demosthenes' Aeschines.[25]

However, while Pliny's allusion indirectly compares Regulus and Aeschines, it also draws a parallel between the corruption of the political

---

[19] Tzounakas (2015) 208.   [20] Tzounakas (2015) 211–13.
[21] 'Pliny as the Roman Demosthenes' is the title of Tzounakas's 2015 study.
[22] Whitton (2013a) 279.   [23] Plin. *Ep.* 7.30.5; 6.33.11; also see 1.2 and 9.23.
[24] Kochin (2002) 80.
[25] See Tzounakas (2015) 212, who has shown that Pliny draws a similar comparison between Aeschines and Regulus in *Ep.* 4.7. We should also not assume that Pliny is criticising Aeschines' moral character. Pliny preferred Demosthenes to Aeschines, see *Ep.* 2.3.9–10; 9.26.10–11. However, he also praises Aeschines' ability as an orator at various points and clearly respects him, see *Ep.* 2.3.9.10–11; 4.5.1–2; 1.20.4. Similar sentiments can be seen in Cic. *De or.* 3.28; *Orat.* 9.29; Quint. *Inst.* 2.17.12; 7.1.12.

elite in Pliny and Demosthenes' respective societies. For, although Demosthenes had claimed that those involved in Greek political affairs were bribed and corrupted by Philip, he also excused the citizens who were simply unaware of the encroaching danger of Macedon.[26] Thus, by emphasising that most of Greece's citizens were largely ignorant as to what was going on, Demosthenes emphasises that it was the political elite who were specifically to blame for Greece's downfall. Aeschines, he claims, was simply one among many of these corrupt Greek politicians:

> μὴ τοίνυν λέγετ', ὦ ἄνδρες Ἀθηναῖοι, περιιόντες ὡς ὑφ' ἑνὸς τοιαῦτα πέπονθεν ἡ Ἑλλὰς ἀνθρώπου. οὐχ ὑφ' ἑνός, ἀλλ' ὑπὸ πολλῶν καὶ πονηρῶν τῶν παρ' ἑκάστοις, ὦ γῆ καὶ θεοί· ὧν εἷς οὑτοσί, ὅν, εἰ μηδὲν εὐλαβηθέντα τἀληθὲς εἰπεῖν δέοι, οὐκ ἂν ὀκνήσαιμ' ἔγωγε κοινὸν ἀλειτήριον τῶν μετὰ ταῦτ' ἀπολωλότων ἁπάντων εἰπεῖν, ἀνθρώπων, τόπων, πόλεων·

> Don't say now, O men of Athens, that this suffering which befell Greece was the result of one man. It was not the result of one person, but the result of many wicked men in each state, O earth and the gods be my witness: this man Aeschines was one of them, and if I am to speak the truth with no restraint, I for one would not hesitate to say that he was guilty of the pollution of all the men, districts and cities. (*De cor.* 158–9)

On one level, Demosthenes is defending his own conduct in this passage. His use of ἀλειτήριος ('plague' or 'pollution') is a response to Aeschines' depiction of him as a curse which pollutes Athens and causes its misfortunes in *Against Ctesiphon*, and so he instead insists that it is Aeschines who is complicit in Greece's troubles.[27] However, Demosthenes is also clear that his rival is not solely responsible for the downfall of Greece, as it is ultimately the fault of the political elite's corruption as a whole.[28] When we look back at Pliny's criticism of Regulus in *Ep.* 2.20, we can draw a parallel in the ways each 'orator' has depicted his opponent as just one manifestation of the general degradation of his *civitas*.[29]

---

[26] Dem. *De cor.* 45. The contrast of the *dēmos* (common people) and the political elite was a standard feature of democratic political discourse; see Yunis (2001) 135.
[27] Martin (2009) 89–91; 103.
[28] MacDowell (2009) 391 claims that Demosthenes sees Aeschines as 'the ultimate cause of all trouble', but Demosthenes is clear here that the Greek political elite as a whole are complicit. For more on Demosthenes' critical portrait of the Greek elite in his speeches, see Wooten (1979), who argues that Demosthenes presents himself as a doctor who must heal the disease of corruption which has seized Greek politicians.
[29] Pliny often assumes the role of orator in presenting the cases in his *Epistles*, see Williams (2006).

But the pessimism of *Ep.* 2.20 is not only reflected in its narrative parallels with Demosthenes; it also appears in the differences between the two texts. Demosthenes stresses that most Athenians were patriotic and agreed with his policy of resistance against Philip:[30]

> λοιπὸν τοίνυν ἦν καὶ ἀναγκαῖον ἅμα πᾶσιν οἷς ἐκεῖνος ἔπραττεν ἀδικῶν ὑμᾶς ἐναντιοῦσθαι δικαίως. τοῦτ' ἐποιεῖτε μὲν ὑμεῖς ἐξ ἀρχῆς εἰκότως καὶ προσηκόντως, ἔγραφον δὲ καὶ συνεβούλευον καὶ ἐγὼ καθ' οὓς ἐπολιτευόμην χρόνους.

> Well the only remaining policy, and the necessary one, was to oppose all of the injustices he did to us with righteousness. You did this from the beginning in a reasonable and suitable manner, and I decreed and argued for this from the start of my political career. (*De cor.* 69)

Demosthenes' direct address to the Athenian audience, and his self-association with them through the μὲν ... δὲ structure, emphasises their unity in the face of Macedonian hegemony.[31] Demosthenes claims at various other points of the speech that Athens was more resistant to Philip than the other Greek city states, especially in their heroic stand with the Thebans against Macedon at the battle of Chaeronea.[32] It is implied that only a minority of Athenians, such as Aeschines, were complicit in Greece's fall to Macedonian control. Demosthenes' praise of his fellow Athenians is in stark contrast to Pliny's sentiment in *Ep.* 2.20, where he claims that the majority of his *civitas* support immorality. Unlike Demosthenes' patriotic speech, Pliny's letter is more pessimistic in political outlook and draws attention to the falling moral standards of Rome.

The reference to Demosthenes then, draws attention to Pliny's criticism of his *civitas* for indulging *nequitia* and darkens the already pessimistic note on which *Ep.* 2.20 ends. I suggest that the gloom implied by the letter's links with Demosthenes is a prelude to the even more intense pessimism which can be detected in the hint to Cicero that follows. As Hoffer observes, difficult Greek words and epithets in the *Epistles* are typically glossed with more straightforward Latin.[33] I believe this principle also applies to *Ep.* 2.20, because, as we shall see, the political messages surrounding Pliny's allusion to Demosthenes are developed upon and clarified in the subsequent one to Cicero. While the hint to Demosthenes in *Ep.*

---

[30] Kochin (2002) 85.
[31] Wolpert (2003) 543 shows that Demosthenes often used direct address to the jury in a similar manner, to convince them that they are acting in the city's interests.
[32] Dem. *De cor.* 79; 88; 93, 96–100; 203; 297; Worthington (2013) 303.   [33] Hoffer (1999) 88–9.

2.20 compares Pliny's contemporary community with the distant Greek past, the implications of its links to Cicero draw more specific attention to the failings of the Roman political elite.

4 The *Epistles* and *In Verrem*

In *Ep.* 2.20, when Pliny goes on to ask his correspondent why he exerts himself for a community which rewards wickedness and dishonesty more than it does honour and virtue, his question takes a new turn by recalling Cicero's frustration that the 'recklessness and daring' of Verres was rewarded more than his own virtue and integrity. In bringing to mind the struggles Cicero faced in his prosecution of Verres, whom he brought before the extortion court in 70 BC, Pliny may have had another great rivalry in mind; after all, as he admitted later in life, the trial offered him the opportunity to enter into an oratorical contest with Hortensius.[34] However, as it soon becomes apparent, the allusion draws a more significant parallel between Regulus and Verres.

Both Regulus and Verres have notably similar personalities; they are prone to violent threats and outbursts, become afraid when they feel threatened, are somewhat feminine and have corrupted their sons through their own vices.[35] Regulus and Verres are also compared to tyrants: a classic symbol of villainy and lack of self-control in Greek and Roman ideology.[36] Most significantly for our purposes, Verres was charged by Cicero with the pillaging of Sicily's riches and with hunting the legacies of both Heraclius and Epicrates.[37] Verres' greed for money is a key theme of the speeches – a further link between Regulus and Verres.[38] Hence, while Regulus and Verres are comparable generally, they are strikingly similar within this letter's context of Regulus' legacy hunting. *Ep.* 2.20's allusion to Cicero implicitly likens Regulus with Verres and so depicts him not only as a rival, but as a criminal.[39]

---

[34] Cic. *Brut.* 319.
[35] On violence: Cic. *Verr.* 2.2.73; 74; 101; Plin. *Ep.* 1.5. On fear: Cic. *Verr.* 2.3.160-1; 2.5.30; 2.5.109; Plin. *Ep.* 4.2; 4.7. On Verres and Regulus' femininity: Cic. *Verr.* 2.4.100-3; 2.5.81-2; Plin. *Ep.* 2.20.10-1. On their sons: Cic. *Verr.* 2.4.100-3; 2.5.81-2; Plin. *Ep.* 2.20.10-11.
[36] Henderson (2002b) 31 shows that Pliny has Regulus acting like a king. This would be especially notable because of his name's etymological link with *rex*. Verres is called a tyrant by Cicero, see Steel (2001) 30-1; Frazel (2009) 164-73; Hammar (2013) 165-7. For the role of the Greek tyrant in Roman invective, see Dunkle (1967).
[37] Cic. *Verr.* 2.1.9; 47; 2.2.45-6; 53-61.
[38] Frazel (2005); (2009) 132-6; Hammar (2013) 145-53.
[39] Verres was seen by Juvenal as an obvious *exemplum* of a Roman criminal, see Juv. 2.26; 3.53. Steel (2001) 24 notes that Verres was perceived as the quintessential corrupt governor after Cicero's time.

Yet, when we look back at the larger context of Cicero's argument – that Hortensius was more likely to support a man like Verres than those who are virtuous – we can see an added layer to the letter's message: just as Cicero was the sole opponent of Verres, Pliny is the only challenger of Regulus.[40] Of course, Cicero was a major influence on Pliny, who clearly wished to emulate him in his *Epistles*.[41] However, the allusion also draws attention to the similarities between the political elite's support of men like Regulus and Verres. In fact, Cicero regularly criticises the senatorial order for assisting Verres throughout the *In Verrem*, claiming that his supporters in the senate helped him embezzle funds in Sicily, protected him in court and that even quaestors and praetors threatened anyone who went to Rome to give evidence against him. Cicero can be particularly explicit when he accuses Hortensius and others of complicity:[42]

> Quo quidem tempore, iudices, iste spem maximam reliquorum quoque peccatorum nactus est; vidit enim eos qui iudiciorum dominos se dici volebant harum cupiditatum esse servos.

> Indeed, it was at that time, judges, that Verres received his greatest hope for future crimes, for he saw that the men who wanted to be called the masters of the courts were the slaves of desire for these wrongdoings. (*Verr.* 2.1.58)

However, Cicero's line of attack is also closely linked to the historical context of the speech, in which he could build on existing prejudices surrounding the corruption of the senate.[43] In this way, Cicero suggests that if the senate do not prosecute Verres, whose guilt he claims is obvious, then it will be clear that they will never prosecute a powerful member of their own order: in other words, there would be no choice but to implement the *Lex Aurelia* and deprive the senatorial order of their monopoly over the law courts.[44] There were, of course, a number of reasons why Cicero took the prosecution against Verres, such as proving that his talent as an orator was a match for the famous Hortensius, as well as securing the

---

This reception may be the result of Cicero's presentation of Verres as a uniquely wicked man throughout the *In Verrem*, see Hammar (2013) 143.

[40] Cic. *Verr.* 2.3.7; Whitton (2013a) 279.   [41] Riggsby (1995); Gibson and Morello (2012).

[42] Cic. *Verr.* 1.17; 40. On quaestors and praetors, see 2.2.12. As May (1988) 32 highlights, Cicero tells us Verres was not only protected by Hortensius, but the *nobiles* at large. Of course, Cicero was no stranger to criticising the political elite of society, as he had previously criticised Sulla and Chrysogonus in his *Pro Sexto Roscio Amerino*, see Tempest (2011) 32–7. Later in his career, Cicero would even argue that treacherous Romans were Rome's greatest threat, see Gildenhard (2011) 200–2.

[43] Hawthorn (1962) esp. 56; Steel (2014) 330.

[44] Cic. *Verr.* 1.1–3, with discussion by Manuwald (2015) 29; Vasaly (2009).

political support of the Sicilians, whom Verres stood accused of oppressing.[45] However, Cicero also used the case to present himself as a virtuous member of the senate fighting against the corruption of the order, in a manner that reminds us of Pliny's own criticisms of the imperial senate.

In this way, *Ep.* 2.20's allusion to *In Verrem* further identifies Pliny with Cicero's struggles against the Roman elite through their shared status as *homines novi* (new men); that is, as outsiders who must restore the integrity of the senate by fighting the corruption within it.[46] In fact, the very lines to which the letter alludes reference Cicero's *homo novus* status and the struggle he faced in reaching a senatorial position.[47] Pliny too was from an equestrian background, was the first in his family to reach the consulship and repeatedly self-identifies as a *homo novus* throughout his *Epistles*.[48] Even Calvisius Rufus, this letter's addressee, was not a member of the Roman nobility, as he was an equestrian and a provincial town councillor (*decurio*) in Comum.[49] Both Pliny and Calvisius look at and bemoan the rewarding of wickedness by Rome's elite in a Ciceronian manner. The reference to *In Verrem* thus draws a parallel between Pliny's and Cicero's criticism of the Roman political elite for supporting men such as Verres and Regulus.

However, what, precisely, is Pliny's criticism of the Roman elite and how does an intertextual approach enable us to interpret it? While the allusion is a partial quotation of Cicero, the line is also reworked and certain virtues and vices have been changed. I suggest that the substitution of these words offers us a key insight into Pliny's attitude to his *civitas*. For example, Cicero's *audacia* is swapped out for *improbitas*.[50] While this is the sole use of *improbitas* in the correspondence, Pliny uses its related adjectival form, *improbus*, frequently after this letter. Perhaps most notably, Pliny later uses *improbus* in Book 8 to describe the shamelessness of those who legacy hunt.[51] Upon a re-reading of the *Epistles*, Pliny's criticism of his *civitas* for supporting *improbitas* is a further reference to their support

---

[45] Tempest (2011) 50–1.
[46] Tempest (2011) 57; Cicero emphasises the difficulty the *novi homines* face in attaining high rank at *Verr.* 2.5.181.
[47] May (1988) 42.
[48] Winsbury (2014) 23; for more on Pliny's family and career, see Birley (2000) 1–17.
[49] Whitton (2013a) 270.
[50] *Audacia* would have worked within its new context, but Pliny's choice of *improbitas* more clearly highlights Regulus' dishonesty.
[51] Plin. *Ep.* 8.18.3; see Whitton (2013a) 279.

of Regulus' legacy hunting, which is, as he calls it, *improbissimum genus falsi* ('the most dishonest kind of fraud', *Ep.* 2.20.14).[52]

Yet, Pliny also uses *improbus* frequently after Book 2 to refer to moral shamelessness more generally. For example, Pliny claims that he accepted all of the gifts from one of his friends, but found doing so *improbum*; elsewhere, he notes that he is not so *improbus* as to hope that his speech *De Helvidi Ultione* would achieve the quality of Demosthenes' *Against Meidias*, and worries that another of his friends thinks his speeches can sometimes be more *improbus* than bold.[53] In all of these cases, *improbus* refers to a kind of character flaw which Pliny depicts himself as checking and keeping under control. By establishing that his *civitas* actively rewards *improbi* in Book 2, Pliny's own efforts to live an honest life are undermined. While Pliny has enough *pudor* (modesty) to check his *improbitas*, those who are unapologetically shameless are supported by the community.

Pliny's criticism of his community's incentivising of *improbitas* is further developed by the replacement of Cicero's *integritas* with *pudor*. While Pliny notes that his *civitas* neglect those who possess *virtus*, his claim that they also disregard *pudor* has significant implications within the Regulus cycle.[54] First, it is a frequent complaint of Pliny's that Regulus lacks that very quality.[55] In *Ep.* 1.5.12, Pliny reveals that Regulus does not blush when confronted about his misdeeds, but instead becomes pale; in other words, he does not feel shame or remorse for his crimes but fears the threat of exposure.[56] 'Shame' was a theoretically transparent virtue, because it was strongly associated with a reddening of the cheeks, unlike *integritas* which prevented a person from committing immoral behaviour.[57] Consequently, the possession of *pudor* is obviously visible and a communitarian virtue which encourages social harmony.[58] Conversely, *integritas* is a much more passive and quiet virtue.[59] Pliny's substitution of *integritas* for *pudor* thus emphasises that the community does not support men who are

---

[52] Gibson and Morello (2012) have shown that re-reading the *Epistles* is essential in appreciating the collection's literary art.
[53] Plin. *Ep.* 6.28.1; 7.30.5; 9.26.
[54] Pliny's use of *virtus* is a reference to moral excellence and is in clear alignment with Cicero's definition of the word. Cicero was the first to use *virtus* in this sense. Before then, *virtus* was often associated with military accomplishments. Cicero was not a skilled military commander and so formed this new meaning of *virtus*, see McDonnell (2006) 330. For more on Cicero's reinterpretation of *virtus* as a social good, see Balmaceda (2017).
[55] Plin. *Ep.* 2.20.2; 13; 4.7.1–5; Kaster (1997) 15–16. [56] Kaster (1997) 7; Hoffer (1999) 62.
[57] Kaster (1997) 11; 142. Sen. *Ep.* 11.7 claims that actors cannot blush on demand and so are unable to 'fake' *pudor*.
[58] Kaster (1997) 11. [59] Kaster (2005) 147–8.

transparently doing good for society. This reworking of Cicero serves to clarify Pliny's criticism of his *civitas* by showing his disappointment that they reward shameless men such as Regulus rather than those who possess modesty such as himself.

To sum up: as *Ep.* 2.20's reference to Demosthenes suggested a growing pessimism, so does its allusion to Cicero's *In Verrem*. However, the latter allusion goes further still in emphasising Pliny's dissatisfaction with his *civitas*, because Cicero composed the *In Verrem* at a time when real change could be made to help re-establish the reputation of the senate. Cicero warns the senate that they are perceived as corrupt by the populace and urges the jurors to convict Verres and establish their body as an *exemplum* for future court rulings.[60] Consequently, the senatorial jury to whom Cicero appeals is presented as occupying a hypothetical turning point in its history and the judges are described as particularly virtuous.[61] Conversely for Pliny, Regulus has become emblematic of the worst elements of the senate of his own day and, more bleakly, the majority of the political elite support him and *nequitia* itself. This contrast accentuates Pliny's pessimistic outlook on Rome's future.

5 Pliny's Intertextual Allusions and *Epistles* 2.20

While these allusions draw parallels between Pliny's community and those of Demosthenes' and Cicero's time, they also serve to highlight the key themes of *Ep.* 2.20 itself. As we have seen, Demosthenes counters Aeschines' allegation that he curses Athens with religious language and prayers. By evoking Demosthenes' expression of religious integrity, *Ep.* 2.20 highlights its contrary theme of Regulus' use of superstitious practices to satisfy his *nequitia*. When Regulus visits Verania, he performs gestures akin to those of an astrologer and claims that she has reached a *climactericum tempus*: an astrological term which referred to a critical moment in someone's life.[62] Pliny is not necessarily passing judgement on astrological practices here, but is rather suggesting that Regulus appropriates them to

---

[60] Van der Blom (2010) 79.
[61] Cic. *Verr.* 2.1.18. As May (1988) 39 argues, Cicero appeals to the jury as 'virtuous' members of the senatorial order. Cicero praises the senatorial jury partially for his own purposes, as he can only prosecute Verres with their support.
[62] Plin. *Ep.* 2.20.3; Whitton (2013a) 273.

frighten Verania into writing him into her will, and so to serve his own wicked agenda.[63]

Yet Regulus is not only prepared to use astrology inappropriately, he also consults *haruspices* (soothsayers) to scare Verania into believing she is about to die.[64] That Regulus is prepared to work with these men so he can force himself into Verania's will emphasises his superstitious character, and also underlines his *nequitia*, something which Verania herself exclaims on her deathbed: *clamat moriens hominem nequam perfidum ac plus etiam quam periurum* ('she cries out as she dies on the man's wickedness and treachery, and his character was even worse than perjurious', *Ep.* 2.20.5). The letter's allusion to Demosthenes therefore draws attention both to Regulus' superstitious behaviour, and more specifically to his misuse of religious practices in service of his *nequitia*.

Perhaps more remarkable still is that, unlike Demosthenes who expresses religious devotion through his prayer, Regulus displays no respect for the gods. Pliny tells us that Regulus was able to steal Verania's inheritance because he had falsely claimed an oath to her on his son's life.[65] Pliny claims that Regulus often does this, and only escapes the *ira deorum* ('anger of the gods') because it falls *in caput infelicis pueri* ('onto the head of his unfortunate boy', *Ep.* 2.20.6). Pliny's claim that divine anger follows perjury was a trope in antiquity.[66] However, the evocation of Demosthenes' prayer highlights Regulus' disregard for, and aggravation of, the gods.

Yet while *Ep.* 2.20's reference to Demosthenes emphasises the letter's theme of Regulus' *nequitia*, the hint to Cicero highlights the failings of Pliny's community. By twisting Cicero's words, and claiming that the *civitas* actively supports *improbitas*, the allusion emphasises a key theme of the letter: that Regulus' legacy hunting, the very activity Pliny calls the *improbissimum genus falsi*, has largely remained unchecked.[67] In fact, Regulus' attempts to steal inheritances are narrated in three independent

---

[63] Astrology was popular throughout Rome, see the *OCD*. Green (2014) 97–108 states that even rulers who used astrology to promote their political careers, such as Augustus, often outlawed personal astrology because it could potentially disrupt their own image and public ideology. There was thus a rocky relationship between the popularity of astrology and its subversive qualities.
[64] The *haruspices* Regulus addresses are presumably unaffiliated with the Etruscan college or another official local custom, which makes them inherently untrustworthy, see Haack (2002) 112; Whitton (2013a) 273. Pliny later concedes in *Ep.* 6.2.2 that Regulus' consultation of *haruspices* evidenced his devotion to oratory, but condemns it as *nimia superstitio* (an excessive superstition).
[65] Plin. *Ep.* 2.20.5.   [66] Whitton (2013a) 275.
[67] Pliny tells us that only Velleius Blaesus, a wealthy ex-consul, was able to keep his inheritance safe from Regulus. As Scarcia (1985) 293 has pointed out, it is noteworthy that the only individual who completely foils Regulus' legacy hunting is a man.

stories in this letter, a detail which highlights the scale of his dishonest conduct: one attempt has been successful, and another remains in the balance.[68] Pliny even claims that *est unde fiat* ('there is more material available', *Ep.* 2.20.9), hinting that there may be further untold stories of Regulus' fraudulent activities. Most notable is the conclusion of Pliny's letter, where he claims that Regulus was hoping to make one hundred and twenty million sesterces, and laments that he will manage to do so if Regulus continues writing himself into other people's wills.[69]

6 Pessimism and the Later Regulus Cycle Letters

The intertextual references at *Ep.* 2.20.12 thus encourage us to look in more detail at Pliny's wider criticism of his *civitas* for supporting men like Regulus. For, leaving aside such questions as Pliny's actual intention, when we focus on the contents of the letter we can begin to appreciate the fuller significance of Pliny's allusions to Demosthenes and Cicero. In fact, I argue, this letter acts as a turning point in the collection – one which foreshadows a pattern of increasing political pessimism in the later letters of the Regulus cycle. In *Ep.* 4.2 and 4.7, for example, Pliny complains of his rival's audacity in hoping to profit from the death of his own son (*Ep.* 4.2.1), as well as his hypocrisy in putting on a show of excessive grief (*Ep.* 4.2.2–3); yet Pliny also attaches blame to the town councillors, the *decuriones*, who indulge Regulus' behaviour by providing their best speakers to recite the biography he wrote of his son (*Ep.* 4.7.1–2).

In *Ep.* 6.2, Pliny reveals that Regulus has died and, although admitting that he misses his rival's dedication to oratory, he draws a parallel between the dangerous consequences (*pericula*) of the new generation's lackadaisical approach to oratory (*Ep.* 6.2.5) and the danger (*periculum*) Regulus had earlier posed to the Stoic opposition (*Ep.* 1.5.2).[70] Pliny thus compares Regulus and his oratorical colleagues' detrimental effect on society, and so his point is politically charged. While Pliny claims in *Ep.* 6.2 that men such as Regulus would not be able to operate as *delatores* (informants) under Trajan, he nevertheless concedes that the Trajanic governmental

---

[68] As Whitton (2013a) 270 points out, Aurelia's inheritance is pending because she is still alive; that Regulus has already fooled Verania leaves Aurelia in a worrying position. Furthermore, as Whitton notes at 277, threes recur as a motif throughout the *Epistles* itself.

[69] Plin. *Ep.* 2.20.13–14.

[70] See also Plin. *Ep.* 2.20.5, where Verania may not only be in the *periculum* of her illness, but of Regulus himself.

institutions are as corrupt as before, a point which is repeated later in the correspondence.[71]

The pessimism of these later Regulus letters seem to contrast with the general optimism of Books 4 and 6. Book 4 features a number of optimistic episodes, such as the introduction of Pliny's marriage to Calpurnia, the political success of Pliny's friends, the flourishing of literature in Rome and Pliny's own successful literary pursuits.[72] However, Pliny's pessimism over his community's support of Regulus is not an anomaly in Book 4; in fact, it complements darker letters, such as *Ep.* 4.25, where Pliny reveals that his fellow senators are unprofessional and abuse the practice of anonymous voting by vandalising their papers. We can therefore see that Pliny's anxieties about his community in *Ep.* 2.20 mar Book 4. Likewise, Book 6 is generally regarded as a particularly optimistic unit because of Trajan's presence throughout as a virtuous emperor.[73] Moreover, Pliny emphasises throughout Book 6 that his legal career has entered a golden age.[74] But what is most interesting for our purposes is the link Pliny establishes between his own successful career and the demise of his great rival. Regulus' death is recorded in *Ep.* 6.2, and Pliny reveals that he has delivered his greatest speech in the book's penultimate letter (*Ep.* 6.33). The structural parallel between the two letters invites us to link them.[75] However, despite this optimism over Regulus' death we can see that Pliny's anxieties over Rome's future have not vanished, and he continues to accuse his community of disregarding the good of society in *Ep.* 6.2. Even within bright units such as Book 6, the pessimistic undertones established in *Ep.* 2.20 can persist.

7 Conclusion

This chapter has aimed to show that the intertextual allusions of *Ep.* 2.20 give additional emphasis to Pliny's anxieties about Rome's future. The hints to *De Corona* and *In Verrem* thereby serve to draw parallels between

---

[71] As Hoffer (1999) 56 argues, Pliny implies Regulus could do no harm specifically as a *delator*. For a good example of the political pessimism later in the *Epistles*, see 8.14. Whitton (2010) has pointed out the significance of this letter in the collection. As Gibson (2015) 219 argues, Pliny's virtuous actions in the senate in *Ep.* 8.14 are presented as atypical, even under Trajan.
[72] Pliny's marriage to Calpurnia: *Ep.* 4.1; 4.19; success of Pliny's friends: 4.4; 4.8; flourishing of literature in Rome: 4.20; Pliny's successful literary pursuits: 4.5; 4.16; cf. 4.14 and 4.27 on poetry.
[73] Plin. *Ep.* 6.13; 6.19; 6.22; Gibson (2015) 204. As Gibson's forthcoming commentary shows, Book 6 is largely optimistic. I am thankful to Roy Gibson for providing me with an early copy of his commentary.
[74] Gibson (2015) 203. [75] Gibson and Morello (2012) 40.

the corruption of Pliny's *civitas* and the respective societies of Demosthenes and Cicero. Moreover, these references connect to the main themes of *Ep.* 2.20, intensifying Pliny's condemnation of Regulus' inappropriate religious conduct and emphasising the community's support of *improbitas* and their neglect of *pudor*. Yet Pliny's concerns about his *civitas* are not exclusive to *Ep.* 2.20, since they permeate the later letters of the Regulus cycle. Consequently, even optimistic units such as Book 6 are affected by the pessimistic undertones established in *Ep.* 2.20. I therefore argue that *Ep.* 2.20 serves as a turning point in the Regulus cycle, and that Pliny's intertextual allusions are a key feature of the cycle's shift to a darker tone.

However, that Pliny uses intertextual allusions to express his political sentiments has consequences for our understanding of his allusive strategies more generally in the *Epistles*. Recently, scholars have shown that Pliny engaged with a wider range of contemporary texts than has usually been presupposed, and they have also pointed to a wider culture of literary interaction among Trajanic writers.[76] Pliny was an individual within this cultural movement, and so expressed a variety of ideas through engagement with other literary genres. By examining Pliny's allusions as an expression of his shifting optimism and pessimism, we can not only gain a greater appreciation for his literary abilities, but also better understand his political views and thus his historical context. I hope this chapter can provide a starting point for such approaches in the much-studied field of intertextuality in Pliny's *Epistles*.[77]

Finally, *Ep.* 2.20's allusions can provide us with further insight into Pliny's political pessimism. Of course, Pliny can often be optimistic and is not nihilistic throughout his correspondence.[78] In fact, Book 3's focus on Pliny's success as a consul somewhat alleviates the pessimism of Book 2.[79] Nevertheless, that Pliny's criticism of his community persists in later letters of the Regulus cycle demonstrates that his concerns about his *civitas* do not

---

[76] See the collection of essays in König and Whitton (2018b), especially the introduction (which outlines the interaction between various writers under the reigns of Nerva to Hadrian). Also see Whitton (2019) for Pliny's engagement with Quintilian.

[77] Leading monographs on intertextuality in Pliny's *Epistles* have been written by Marchesi (2008) and Schwerdtner (2015). As discussed in the introduction, Marchesi's work shows that Pliny uses allusions to engage with contemporary literary genres and place his semiotic project within the Graeco-Roman literary canon. Schwerdtner offers a more focused look on Pliny's engagement with Homer and Vergil, while also detailing his citation techniques, esp. see 7–10.

[78] As Strunk (2012) 190 concedes. Nor is Pliny only optimistic in the *Epistles*, his *Panegyricus* was contemporary to Book 2 and is largely optimistic.

[79] Gibson (2015) 213.

dissipate upon his consular career. *Ep.* 2.20 thus shows us that Pliny's unease with the future of Rome stems from his own community, which could have significant implications for the *Epistles*' second half. Perhaps the encroaching darkness of the private correspondence's final books is not only rooted in a gradual discomfort with Trajan, as Gibson has suggested,[80] but also from a similar dissatisfaction with Rome's political elite as expressed in *Ep.* 2.20.

---

[80] Gibson (2015) 213.

CHAPTER 5

Again on Corinthian Bronzes and Vases and on the Use of Cicero's Verrine Orations *in Pliny's Works*

Stefano Rocchi

In the first half of the second century BC, Cato the Censor lamented in his oration against Q. Sulpicius (*orat.* fr. 181 Sbl.): *quotiens vidi trull<e>os, nassiternas pertusos, aqualis matellas sine ansis!* ('How many times have I seen wash basins and pots with holes in, water pots without handles!'). The fragment is usually interpreted as a moralistic eulogy of the old virtue of *parsimonia* – probably also on display in the houses of the upper class which were not ashamed of showing vases used for practical purposes, even if they were in bad condition – and as a tirade against luxury items possibly owned and displayed by Q. Sulpicius.[1]

The degeneration in traditional values induced by imported *luxuria* was already in progress, according to the moralising periodisation of Roman history proposed by Pliny the Elder in the section on silver in Book 33 of his *Natural History*.[2] 148 *Asia primum devicta luxuriam misit in Italiam* (189 BC) ('It was the conquest of Asia that first introduced luxury into Italy'; see also *HN* 34.34); 148 *at eadem Asia donata multo etiam gravius adflixit mores* (133 BC) ('but receiving Asia also as a gift dealt a much more serious blow to our morals'); 149–50 *inmenso et Achaicae victoriae momento ad inpellendos mores; ... ne quid deesset, pariter quoque luxuria nata est et Carthago sublata* (146 BC) ('An impetus having also been given to manners by the enormous shock of the conquest of Achaia; ... so that nothing might be lacking, luxury came into being simultaneously, with the downfall of Carthage').[3] Afterwards, no Roman aristocrat would have paraded the old simplicity

---

[1] See Sblendorio Cugusi (1982) ad loc. and (2001) 384–5, with a different translation: 'tutte le volte che vedo ...' ('every time I see ...'). For my interpretation of *quotiens vidi* cf. Long (1901) 25. See also a fragment concerning Cato's own *parsimonia* (*orat.* fr. 218a Sbl.): *neque mihi aedificatio neque vasum ... est manupretiosum* ('I neither possess any luxurious building nor any precious vase').

[2] The theme goes back at least to Polybius (31.25.3 ff.) and L. Calpurnius Piso Frugi (Calp. *hist.* 36 and 40 Cornell), but has its most famous codifications in Sall. *Cat.* 10–11 and Liv. 39.6.7–9.

[3] Transl. Rackham. On Pliny's periodisation, see Citroni Marchetti (1991) esp. 185–7; Isager (1998) 70–3.

probably longed for by Cato. However, the public discourse on luxury had certainly not come to an end, as is shown, for example, by a fragment on everyday vases from Varro's *De vita populi Romani*, where the author, clearly assuming the typical role of the *laudator temporis acti*, compares the strict modesty of passed ages with contemporary *luxuria* (Varro *De vita populi Romani* fr. 41 P. = Non. p. 547.5): *itaque ea sibi modo ponere ac suspendere, quae utilitas postularet – trulleum, matellionem, pelvim, nassiternam –, non quae luxuriae causa esse<nt> parata* ('... and therefore to place and hang for their personal use only what utility demanded – a wash basin, a bowl, a basin, a water pot –, not what had been acquired for luxury').[4]

More than two centuries later than Cato and a good century after Varro, Pliny the Younger described Vestricius Spurinna's table in these terms (*Ep.* 3.1.9): *adponitur cena non minus nitida quam frugi, in argento puro et antiquo; sunt in usu et Corinthia, quibus **delectatur nec adficitur*** ('Dinner is served in antique plain silver, a meal that was no less elegant than simple; Corinthian vases are also in use, by which he is delighted, not obsessed'). The old general and *consularis* Spurinna is one of Pliny's models and in the idealised portrait offered by the epistolographer he is characterised as a living testimony of the past (3.1.6 *quam pulchrum illud ... quantum ibi antiquitatis!* ('there is a special sort of pleasure in being ... given the entry into a bygone age', transl. Radice)).[5] Spurinna owns a silver plate, which is *purum*, meaning 'not chiseled',[6] and *antiquum* because probably inherited

---

[4] I modify the traditional interpunction of the fragment as given in Müller's, Lindsay's, and Gatti's editions, which is misleading (*quae utilitas postularet: trulleum, ... nassiternam, non quae luxuriae causa esse<nt> parata*), in order to present with greater graphical evidence the list of vases as a parenthesis, which makes the content of *ea ... quae utilitas postularet* more explicit. On the moralistic tones in the *de vita populi Romani* and in the fragment itself, see the thorough commentary by Pittà (2015) 11–12, 192–5.

[5] This *antiquitas* is of course to be interpreted according to an axiological, not a chronological dimension: the 'good old times' represented by Spurinna, whose chronological frame is blurred and undefined, are obviously not the same as the ones regretted by Cato; Pliny is simply alluding to the positive value of the past, which was widely recognised among the Romans. In other words, one might also say that the 'good old times' Pliny is referring to never really existed (on the chronological and axiological dimension of the 'antiquity' see Rocchi and Mussini 2017, 6–9). On Spurinna as a living testimony to the *vetustas*, see also Lefèvre (2009) 45–6. On the letter 3.1 in general, cf. Pausch (2004) 114–29.

[6] Cf. Cic. *Verr.* 2.4.49, where the *argentum ... purum* is set against *pocula ... cum emblemate*: (Verres) *cenabat apud eum*, scil. Eupolemum Calactinum; *argentum ille ceterum purum adposuerat, ne purus ipse relinqueretur, duo pocula non magna, verum tamen cum emblemate. Hic*, scil. Verres, ... *emblemata evellenda curavit* ('He was dining at this man's house: most of the silver put on table was bare of embossed work, since Eupolemus did not wish to be stripped bare himself; but there were two cups, of no great size, but with embossed work upon them. Our friend here ... had the embossed work torn off', transl. Greenwood). That Cicero's passage could possibly have caught the attention of the readers is demonstrated also by an intertextual reference in the first of the two

from his ancestors.[7] Spurinna also possesses vases of Corinthian bronze,[8] but Pliny immediately specifies that he is delighted by them, though *nec adficitur*: in other words, he has no immoderate passion for his precious tableware – which would be unsuitable for the moral 'portrait' Pliny is sketching of him.[9] The apparently unnecessary remark on the pleasure Spurinna derives from his Corinthian vases can be better understood if we consider the place that Corinthian bronzes held in the late-republican and contemporary discourse on luxury, as reflected in two well-known passages by Pliny the Elder (*HN* 34.6–7 and 48 respectively):

> Ex illa autem antiqua gloria Corinthium maxime laudatur. Hoc casus miscuit Corintho, cum caperetur, incensa, mireque circa id multorum *adfectatio furit*, quippe cum tradatur non alia de causa Verrem, quem M. Cicero damnaverat, proscriptum cum eo ab Antonio, quoniam Corinthiis cessurum se ei negavisset. Ac mihi maior pars eorum simulare eam scientiam videtur ad segregandos sese a ceteris magis quam intellegere aliquid ibi suptilius; et hoc paucis docebo. 7 Corinthus capta est olympiadis CLVIII anno tertio, nostrae urbis DCVIII, cum ante haec saecula fictores nobiles esse desissent, quorum *isti* omnia signa hodie Corinthia appellant. Quapropter ad coarguendos eos ponemus artificum aetates; nam urbis nostrae annos ex supra dicta comparatione olympiadum colligere facile erit. *Sunt ergo vasa tantum Corinthia, quae isti elegantiores modo ad esculenta transferunt, modo in lucernas aut trulleos nullo munditiarum dispectu.*

> Of the bronze which was renowned in early days, the Corinthian bronze is the most highly praised. This is a compound that was produced by accident, when Corinth was burned down at the time of its capture; and there has been a wonderful mania among many people for possessing this metal — in fact it is recorded that Verres, whose conviction Marcus Cicero had procured, was together with Cicero, proscribed by Antony for no other

---

ekphrastic epigrams *de scutellis* by Ennodius (*carm.* 2.101 (232 Vogel), 2–3 *argenti pretium est facinus retinere vetustum, | ne purum superet, quod furtis Iuppiter egit*).

[7] T. Vestricius Spurinna could have also boasted of Etruscan forefathers, as his onomastics clearly betray (on the *Vestricii* and on the *Spurinnae* see Torelli (2017) 704 ff., esp. 707).

[8] The history of what is known as Corinthian bronze could be taken as a subject for an independent contribution and it is impossible to review the entire topic comprehensively here (for an overview, see Giumlia-Mair and Craddock 1993), also because the fascination for the purported *aition*, which was the origin of the wondrous alloy – the fire which destroyed Corinth after the sacking by Mummius –, was not confined to Antiquity, but was still recalled in Late Antiquity (for instance, Oros. 5.3.7 and Isid. *Etym.* 16.20.4) and through its texts in the Middle Ages (see Frechulfus, *Historiae*, I 6.3; Rabanus Maurus, *De universo*, XVII 14; Landolfus Sagax, *Historia Romana*, IV 14; Frutolfus, *Chronica*, 628^C).

[9] And thus in the Flavian period the possession of luxury items, an object of moral rebuke from the republican authors down to Seneca the Younger and Pliny the Elder, begins to be regarded as a sign of distinction and good taste – a phenomenon we can observe in Martial, Statius, and Pliny the Younger himself.

reason than because he had refused to give up to Antony some pieces of Corinthian ware; and to me the majority of these collectors seem only to make a pretence of being connoisseurs, so as to separate themselves from the multitude, rather than to have any exceptionally refined insight in this matter; and this I will briefly show. Corinth was taken in the third year of the 158th Olympiad, which was the 608th year of our city, when for ages there had no longer been any famous artists in metalwork; yet these persons designate all the specimens of their work as Corinthian bronzes. In order therefore to refute them we will state the periods to which these artists belong; of course it will be easy to turn the Olympiads into the years since the foundation of our city by referring to the two corresponding dates given above [transl. Rackham]. *Therefore (genuine) Corinthian (bronzes) are only the vases, which these connoisseurs sometimes convert into dishes for food and sometimes into lamps or washing basins, with no regard for cleanliness* [my own transl.].[10]

Signis, quae vocant Corinthia, plerique in tantum capiuntur, ut secum circumferant, sicut Hortensius orator sphingem Verri reo ablatam, propter quam Cicero illo iudicio in altercatione neganti ei, aenigmata se intellegere, respondit debere, quoniam sphingem domi haberet. Circumtulit et Nero princeps Amazonem, de qua dicemus, et paulo ante C. Cestius consularis signum, quod secum etiam in proelio habuit. Alexandri quoque Magni tabernaculum sustinere traduntur solitae statuae, ex quibus duae ante Martis Ultoris aedem dicatae sunt, totidem ante regiam.

Owners of the signa *called Corinthian are usually so enamoured of them that they carry them with them* [my own transl.]; for instance the orator Hortensius was never parted from the sphinx which he had got out of Verres when on trial; this explains Cicero's retort when Hortensius in the course of an altercation at the trial in question said he was not good at riddles. 'You ought to be,' said Cicero, 'as you keep a sphinx in your pocket.' The Emperor Nero also used to carry about with him an Amazon which we shall describe later, and a little before Nero, the ex-consul Gaius Cestius used to go about with a figurine, which he had with him even on the battlefield. It is also said that the tent of Alexander the Great was regularly erected with four statues as tent-poles, two of which have now been dedicated to stand in front of the temple of Mars the Avenger and two in front of the Royal Palace [transl. Rackham].

For the purpose of this paper it is useful to point out the moral/ideological criticism attached in both passages to the precious Corinthian bronze: this

---

[10] For this new interpretation of the passage, see Rocchi (2021) 217 and 220; Darab (2012) 155–7; Ead. (2015) 3–4.

finds a close parallel, with its moralising tone, in the section on the use of silver at the end of Book 33. Pliny condemns the immoderate and sick passion of these purported connoisseurs for goods made of that material, which they desperately look for (34.6 *circa id multorum adfectatio furit*),[11] and from which they cannot part (34.48 *in tantum capiuntur ut secum circumferant*).[12] The naturalist also condemns the affectation (*simulare*) of a knowledge (*scientia*), that moreover – as he states – turns out to be false, as demonstrated by inaccuracy of language (34.7 *omnia signa hodie Corinthia appellant*; 34.48 *signis, quae vocant Corinthia*, etc.) and ignorance of chronology (34.6–7). Furthermore, Pliny indicates the possibility of a sort of 'redemption' of private luxury by its destination or restitution to public use. The so-called *signa Corinthia* are collected and hoarded by private individuals from Alexander to Verres, Antony, Cestius, and Nero, but in Pliny's time some of them are accessible to everyone, for example the tent-poles of Alexander the Great, which had been displayed by Augustus outside the *regia* and the temple of Mars Ultor (34.48). In the same way Vespasian, who had succeeded Cestius in the conduct of the Jewish War, is said by Pliny to have newly dedicated in the Temple of Peace and other buildings many famous statues raided by Nero in Greece and first displayed in the *domus aurea* (34.84).[13]

I would now like to propose a passage from Cicero's fourth oration (*De signis*) of the second pleading against Verres (Cic. *Verr*. 2.4.97–8), which I think both Pliny the Elder and Younger may have had in mind when they were discussing Corinthian bronzes.[14] Cicero speaks of the Corinthian bronzes raided by Verres from the temple of the *Magna Mater* at *Engyum*, where they had been dedicated by no one less than Scipio Africanus (4.97 *idem ille Scipio ... posuerat et suum nomen inscripserat*; ('the great Scipio ... placed there, with an inscription containing his own name', transl. Greenwood)) (*Verr*. 2.4.98):

> tu videlicet solus *vasis Corinthiis delectaris*, tu illius aeris temperationem, tu operum liniamenta sollertissime perspicis! Haec Scipio ille non intellegebat, homo doctissimus atque humanissimus, tu sine ulla bona arte, sine

---

[11] The increase in demand for Corinthian bronzes in the early empire made prices rise to such a point that Tiberius proposed to place a limit on household furniture (Suet. *Tib*. 34.1), most probably without particular success (see also Sen. *Brev*. 12.2 *Corinthia paucorum furore pretiosa* ('Corinthian bronzes, that the mania of a few makes costly', transl. Basore)).

[12] On this topic, see in particular Citroni Marchetti (1991) 234 and n. 51.

[13] Cf. Gros (1978) 302–3 on Vespasian's restitution of the statues to public display. The Emperor Titus displayed Polycletus' *astragalizontes* in the atrium of his *domus* (Plin. *HN* 34.55) – also a public place, since it was accessible to callers from the *salutatio* onwards.

[14] Cf. also Darab (2015) 5 and 6–7.

humanitate, sine ingenio, sine litteris, intellegis et iudicas! Vide ne ille non solum temperantia, sed etiam intellegentia te atque *istos qui se elegantis dici volunt* vicerit. Nam quia quam pulchra essent intellegebat, idcirco existimabat ea *non ad hominum luxuriem, sed ad ornatum fanorum atque oppidorum esse facta,* †ut posteris nostris monumenta religiosa esse videantur†.

It would appear that you are the one person to whom Corinthian bronzes can appeal, and who has an expert's appreciation of the fine temper of the metal and the craftsmanship of the design; that an educated and cultivated man like Scipio had no understanding of such things, whereas an utter savage like yourself, uncivilised and stupid and illiterate, can understand and appreciate them. Ask yourself if Scipio was not superior, in understanding as well as in temper, to you and to those friends of yours who aspire to be considered men of taste. He did understand how beautiful those things were, and for that very reason regarded them as meant not for the luxurious enjoyment of individuals, but for the adornment of temples and cities, and to be hallowed memorials in the sight of future generations [transl. Greenwood].

It seems possible that Pliny the Elder took inspiration from the Ciceronian phrase *istos qui se elegantis dici volunt* for his expression *isti elegantiores*. However, even if Pliny did not have Cicero's passage in mind when he wrote his own account of Corinthian bronzes, it is nevertheless certain that in both authors the tone of *elegantis* and *elegantiores* has to be taken as scornful and sarcastic.[15]

In the light of Cicero's and Pliny the Elder's passages we may perhaps read Pliny the Younger's letter on Spurinna from a new perspective. Spurinna is not an *elegans* like Cicero's Verres, because he is not a fanatical collector, nor is he one of Pliny's *elegantiores*, because his Corinthian bronzes are only for the table and not misused as lamps or washing basins. Moreover, we notice an interesting shift in the concept of the delight that one can derive from works of art: whilst the sick, fetishistic delight of Verres is sarcastically attacked by Cicero (*tu videlicet solus vasis Cortinthiis delectaris*), Pliny re-uses the Ciceronian phrase, but purifies it of the moral rebuke contained in the original context, since Spurinna has no immoderate attachment to his tableware. Furthermore, the Ciceronian passage from the Verrinian oration *De signis* provides an interpretative key to (re-)reading some passages of Pliny's famous letter on the Corinthian figurine he had purchased thanks to a legacy (3.6).

---

[15] On Cicero's irony in the passage quoted see Baldo (2004) ad loc. and Lazzeretti (2006) ad loc.

After affecting a lack of expertise in recognising craftsmanship in works of art, Pliny nonetheless affirms that the figurine is such as to keep the attention of experts and delight amateurs. He furthermore states that he has not bought the bronze to keep it in his house – he points out that he has not yet allowed himself such a luxury for private use – but in order to dedicate it as an ornament to his home town, Comum, and to its temple of Jupiter, on a base inscribed with his name (3.6.1 and 3–5):[16]

> Ex hereditate quae mihi obvenit, emi proxime Corinthium signum, modicum quidem sed festivum et expressum, *quantum ego sapio, qui* fortasse in omni re, *in hac certe perquam exiguum sapio*: hoc tamen signum ego quoque intellego. ... Aes ipsum, quantum verus color indicat, vetus et antiquum; talia denique omnia, ut possint artificum oculos tenere, *delectare* imperitorum. Quod me *quamquam tirunculum* sollicitavit ad emendum. Emi autem non ut haberem domi (neque enim ullum adhuc Corinthium domi habeo), verum ut *in patria nostra celebri loco* ponerem, ac potissimum *in Iovis templo*; *videtur enim dignum templo, dignum deo donum*. Tu ergo ... *iube basim fieri*, ex quo voles marmore, *quae nomen meum honoresque capiat*, si hos quoque putabis addendos.

> Out of a sum of money I have inherited I have just bought a Corinthian bronze statue, only a small one, but an attractive and finished piece of work as far as I can judge – though in general maybe my judgement is limited, and certainly very much here. But this is a statue that I feel even I can appreciate ... The bronze appears to have the true colour of a genuine antique; in fact every detail is such as hold the attention of an artist as well as delight the amateur, and that is what persuaded me to buy it, novice though I am. However, my intention was not to keep it in my house (I have no Corinthian bronzes there yet) but to place it in some public position in my native town, preferably in the temple of Jupiter; it is clearly a gift well

---

[16] On the letter in general see Lehmann-Hartleben (1936) ad loc.; Becatti (1951) 256–8; Sherwin-White (1966) ad loc.; Henderson (2002b), esp. chapter 3; Carlon (2018) 64–5; Neger (2021) 306. This epistle constitutes a prime example of both intertextuality and intermediality – a concept developed to define the relationship between means of communication conventionally perceived as different (word, image, sound) and now applied by classical scholars too (see Dinter and Reitz-Joosse 2019; cf. also the discussion of intermediality in the Introduction to the present volume). In fact *Ep.* 3.6 implies a constellation of different media (texts, plastic art, voice) and materials (wooden tablets/papyrus, bronze, marble) potentially interacting in several ways after the publication of the epistolary corpus, too. Thanks to a detailed ekphrasis, an image of the bronze figurine bought by Pliny is conjured up in the minds of the recipient and future readers, and possibly also in that of a more immediate audience, since letters could of course be read aloud, shown, or handed round by the recipients to further people. But the epistolary text immediately envisages future interactions between the real bronze figurine and the epigraphical text inscribed on its marble base after display in a temple. It is not just a matter of pure speculation to suggest that the inscription in its turn could have been read aloud not only at the official dedication of the monument but also occasionally later by worshippers and passers-by. For further considerations on the letter, see below p. 127–8.

Corinthian Bronzes & Vases

worthy of a temple and a god. Will you ... give immediate orders for a pedestal to be made? Choose what marble you like, and have it inscribed with my name and official titles if you think they should appear too. [transl. Radice].

Pliny follows the reading of Scipio's dedications as suggested by Cicero (*Verr.* 2.4.98): that works of art should be made *non ad hominum luxuriem, sed ad ornatum fanorum atque oppidorum*. Whilst a further possible echo from Cicero's *Actio Secunda* had already been detected in the letter,[17] Pliny's insisted lack of expertise in works of art seems furthermore to recall the similarly affected ignorance displayed by Cicero in the *Verrine orations*.[18]

As far as the structure of the book is concerned, we can first observe that, for the reader of the third book-roll of the letters, the exemplary representation which Pliny offers of himself has a *pendant* in the contrasting attitude of Silius Italicus, a voracious collector, in the letter immediately following (3.7.8): *erat φιλόκαλος usque ad emacitatis reprehensionem* ... ('He was a great connoisseur; indeed he was critized for buying too much', transl. Radice).[19] Secondly, we can point out that the encomium of the exemplary Spurinna at the beginning of the volume (3.1) has a parallel in the praise of Pliny himself as a second Cicero in Martial's wording at the very end of the scroll (3.21.5 = Mart. 10.20[19].16–17).[20]

---

[17] Gesner (1770) 95 considered Pliny's passage ... *in Iovis templo; videtur ... dignum templo, dignum deo donum* as a reminiscence of Cic. *Verr.* 2.5.184 *nunc te, Iuppiter optime maxime, cuius iste **donum regale, dignum** tuo pulcherrimo **templo, dignum** Capitolio ..., **dignum regio munere*** ('Hear me now, O almighty and most gracious Father Jove; thou whose royal offering, so worthy of thy glorious temple, of thy Capitoline hill ... so worthy to be the gift of princes', transl. Greenwood); cf. also *Verr.* 2.4.65.

[18] See, for instance, at the very beginning of the speech *De signis* (Cic. *Verr.* 2.4.4): *erat apud Heium sacrarium ... in aedibus ... in quo signa pulcherrima quattuor ... **quae non modo istum hominem ingeniosum** et intellegentem, **verum etiam quemvis nostrum**, quos iste idiotas appellat, **delectare possent**, unum Cupidinis marmoreum Praxiteli; **nimirum didici etiam**, dum in istum inquiro, **artificum nomina*** ('There was in this house of Heius a stately chapel ..., in which stood four statues; ... capable of giving pleasure not only to so highly gifted an expert as Verres, but also to any of us "outsiders", as he calls us. One was a marble Cupid by Praxiteles – I learnt the artist's names, you will understand, in the course of my investigations as prosecutor', transl. Greenwood). Perhaps even more interesting is Cic. *Verr.* 2.2.87 *capella quaedam est, ea quidem mire, **ut etiam nos qui rudes harum rerum sumus intellegere possumus**, scite facta et venuste. Haec et alia Scipio non neglegenter abiecerat, ut homo intellegens Verres auferre posset, sed ...* ('There is ... the figure of a she-goat, and this certainly is, as even we who know little of such things can tell, a wonderfully clever and charming bit of work. These and other such objects Scipio had not thrown carelessly aside for a connoisseur like Verres to appropriate, but ...', transl. Greenwood. Cf. also *Verr.* 2.4.13, 4.94, and *infra* p. 124.

[19] On this letter see Tzounakas' (Chapter 8) contribution in this volume.

[20] In addition to this, Pliny lets us know elsewhere in the same book that Silius Proculus also compared him to Cicero, though in a less directly flattering manner (3.15.1): *petis ut libellos tuos ... legam examinem, an editione sint digni; adhibes preces, adlegas exemplum: ... adicis M. Tullium mira benignitate poetarum ingenia fovisse* ('You want me to read through some of your poems ... to see if they are worth publishing, and, in begging me ... you can cite a precedent

In order to anticipate a possible objection, it seems convenient to address very briefly another issue, namely Pliny's actual knowledge of the *Verrinae*. In the *Dialogus*, Aper makes fun of the excessive length of the *Verrinae*, while asking (*Dial.* 20.1): *quis quinque in Verrem libros expectabit?* ('Would anyone sit out the five orations against Verres?', transl. Peterson and Winterbottom). The character refers only to the *Actio Secunda*, apparently or deliberately ignoring that it had never been really delivered at the court. But did Pliny, who was certainly not scared of lengthy texts,[21] bother himself with the study or reading of the *Verrinae*? Did the work belong to 'the literary canon which he shared with his first readers'?[22] Of course it did, since the *Verrine orations* were a milestone of Roman oratory and, despite their length, one of Cicero's most read and quoted works. Educated Romans should have known (or studied at least) some passages by heart, otherwise such references as *nolo inridere ... 'ius verrinum'* ('I don't want to make fun of ... his "Boar's Sauce"', transl. Peterson and Winterbottom,) in the *Dialogus* – a phrase from the *Actio Secunda* (2.1.121) mocked by Aper in *Dial.* 2 –, would have been impossible.[23] More importantly further references to those speeches – in form of quotation, allusion or imitation – have been detected in Pliny's letters:

a) In *Ep.* 1.20.10 Pliny introduces one direct quotation from the book *De signis* as a good example of an apparently spontaneous rhetorical figure (*Verr.* 2.4.5): *ideo in optima quaque*, scil. oratione, *mille figuras extemporales invenimus, in iis etiam quas tantum editas scimus, ut in Verrem: 'artificem quem? quemnam? recte admones; Polyclitum esse dicebant'* ('That is why we find so many rhetorical figures, apparently spontaneous, in any good written speech, even in those which we know were published without being delivered; for

---

to support your plea; Cicero, you say, was wonderfully generous about encouraging the talent of poets', transl. Radice). In a similar way, *Arrianus Maturus* drew a parallel to Cicero, while congratulating Pliny on being appointed augur (4.8.4): *te ..., ut scribis, ob hoc maxime delectat auguratus meus, quod M. Tullius augur fuit* ('And you, as you say in your letter, are particularly pleased to see me an augur because Cicero held the same priesthood', transl. Radice).

[21] See for instance what he says in *Ep.* 1.20.4 most probably referring to the speech *Pro Cluentio*: *ego ... Gracchis et Catoni Pollionem, Caesarem, Caelium, in primis M. Tullium oppono, cuius oratio optima fertur esse quae maxima* ('I counter ... the Gracchi and Cato with Pollio, Caesar, Caelius, and above all Cicero, whose longest speech is generally considered his best', transl. Radice).

[22] Cf. Marchesi (2008) 243.

[23] On the *Verrine orations* as one of Cicero's most read and quoted works in the West as well in the East of the empire, see Seider (1979) 104, 113–14; Rouse and Reeve (1983) 55; Pecere (1990) 372 and 374; De Paolis (2000) 40 n. 9–10, 43 n. 18, 44, 46–7, 60–1, 63 n. 73, 64; La Bua (2019) 87, 89–90, 93, 151, 154 n. 369, 155 n. 378, 156, 157 n. 398, 158, 174 n. 465, 205–7, 325.

example, in Cicero's speech against Verres: "an artist—now who was he? thank you for telling me; people said it was Polyclitus'", transl. Radice).

b) Reporting to a friend the trial of Caecilius Classicus in epistle 3.9, Pliny tells of a joke made by the *Baetici* in a similar way as Cicero presents a witticism on Verres by the Sicilians: *Ep.* 3.9.3 *inde dictum Baeticorum, ut plerumque dolor etiam venustos facit, non inlepidum ferebatur:* ... ('hence the neat joke current among the Baetici – for exasperation often breaks out into wit – ...', transl. Radice); *Verr.* 2.4.95 *Numquam tam male est Siculis quin aliquid facete et commode dicant, velut* ... ('Sicilians are always ready with some appropriate jest, even under the most trying circumstances; thus ...', transl. Greenwood).[24]

c) In the same epistle (3.9.9) *verebamur ne nos dies, ne vox, ne latera deficerent* ('It looked as though we should run short of time and lose our breath and voice', transl. Radice) is a 'particularly clear allusion' to *Verr.* 2.2.52 *me dies vox latera deficiant* ('time, voice, and lung would fail me', transl. Greenwood).[25]

d) At the letter 6.8.8, the description of Atilius Crescens' character – *non feret magnum et liberum ingenium cum contumelia damnum* ('his bold spirit of independence will not submit to loss coupled with insult', transl. Radice) – seems to owe something to, or could be an amalgamation of *Verr.* 2.3.60 (*damna* ... *nulla tanta sunt quae non viri fortes ac magno et libero animo adfecti ferenda arbitrentur;* ('as for material injuries ... none are so serious that a brave man, a man of high and generous disposition, finds them unendurable', transl. Greenwood))[26] and *Verr.* 2.3.228 (*etiamne haec tot* ... *damna cum maximis iniuriis contumeliisque perferre?* ('and must they even submit to having all these forms of ... loss accompanied by the most unjust and insulting treatment?', transl. Greenwood)).[27]

Of course, if we had the speeches composed for the trials *de repetundis* and delivered against Baebius Massa (7.33; trial: AD 93), Caecilius Classicus

---

[24] As far as I know, Gesner (1770) ad loc. was the first to notice the parallel. See also Mayor (1880) 139; Pflips (1973) 198–9; Neger (2021) 159–60 n. 179.
[25] Cf. Whitton (2013a) 175.
[26] This is the only other passage in the Latin corpus where the two adjectives *magn* et liber** occur together.
[27] Minos (1598) II 109 has already brought to attention the latter passage.

(3.4; 3.9; trial: AD 99), Marius Priscus (2.11; trial: AD 100),[28] and in defence of Iulius Bassus (4.9; trial: AD 103), we could learn more on Pliny's possible sources of inspiration and on his use of the *Verrinae*. However, if we also take into account the *Panegyricus* there is at least one passage, in which a phrase originally intended to describe the rapacity of *Verres* is re-used by Pliny to set the good and honest management of the *aerarium* under Trajan against Domitian's rapacious enrichment of it in complicity with *delatores*.[29]

---

[28] See esp. *Ep.* 2.11.15, where, according to Whitton (2013a) 175, *voci laterique* ('voice and lungs') could come from *Verr.* 2.4.67 (***quae vox quae latera***, *quae vires huius unius criminis querimoniam possunt sustinere?* ('Can any man's voice, or lungs, or bodily strength avail adequately to describe the heinousness of this single deed?', transl. Greenwood)).

[29] See *Verr.* 2.5.59 *illud tibi oppidum* ***receptaculum praedae*** *fuit, illi homines testes custodesque furtorum* ('this town was the receiving-station of your booty, this town's inhabitants were the witnesses and custodians of your thefts', transl. Greenwood); *Pan.* 36.1 *quam iuvat cernere aerarium silens et quietum, et quale ante delatores erat! Nunc templum illud nunc vere dei <sedes>, non spoliarum civium cruentarumque* ***praedarum*** *saevum* ***receptaculum*** ('It is a pleasure to see peace and quiet restored to the treasury, to see it as it was before the days of informers. Now it is a real temple and sanctuary of a god, not a mortuary of citizens and a grim depository for blood-soaked spoils', transl. Radice). The phrase *receptaculum praedae/arum*, which occurs only in these two passages in the Latin corpus, has been identified as a possible intertextual connection by Schuster (1958) ad loc. (see also the phrase *praedarum . . . receptrix* in *Verr.* 2.4.17, 4.150).

Appendix

As a last point I would like to add a few remarks on the *Corinthium signum* described in *Ep.* 3.6 as well as on the lost inscription commissioned as its plinth.[30] Pliny wanted to dedicate the work of art in a public place of his home town (*celebri loco*),[31] preferably as a gift for Jupiter in his temple.[32] Since he clearly states that the *signum* is *modicum*, also the base of the inscription must have been correspondingly small. Likewise the plinth erected by *L. Acilius Clodianus* – an *eques* who dedicated a now lost *signum* ... *Corinthiu(m)* to Jupiter – is 73 × 31 × 31 cm, which furthermore means that his Corinthian bronze was relatively small too (*CIL* VI 36787).[33] The same seems to be true for the *imaginem Corintheam Traiani* ('a Corinthian bronze bust of Trajan') dedicated by Trajan's freedman *M. Ulpius Aeglus*, whose plinth is only 50 × 32 cm (*CIL* VI 8686).[34] Albeit

---

[30] For some considerations on the intermediality and intermateriality of this letter see also above p. 122.
[31] The expression *celebri loco* has an official, epigraphical sound: it is a variation of the epigraphical formula *loco celeberrimo* ('in a public place'; cf. also Plin. *Ep.* 2.7.7 *in celeberrimo loco*).
[32] According to Pliny's desire, the statue must have been exhibited in that temple, because it is not mentioned among the *beneficia* for the town and for its citizens recorded in the famous inscription erected in Comum after Pliny's death (see *CIL* V 5262 and Eck 2001 with further bibliography). See also *CIL* X 6, in which the heirs of *Ti. Bervenus Sabinus* recorded the long list of works of art, which *Sabinus* had left by testament to the citizens of *Regium Iulium*: they were displayed partly in the Prytaneion – among these a *pelbem aeream Corintheam* ('a Corinthian bronze basin') – and partly in the temple of Apollo.
[33] *CIL* VI 36787 (= *ILS* 9514) *L. Acilius Clodianus | eques roman(us) | decurialis pro reditu | ... | ... vo| to suscepto signum | Iovi Olumpio | Corinthiu(m) | consecravit cum fili(i)s.*
[34] *CIL* VI 8686 (= *ILS* 1577) *M. Ulpius | Aug(usti) l(ibertus) Aeglus | proc(urator) Mausol{a}ei | imaginem |Corintheam | Traiani Caesaris | ... | d(onum) d(edit).* It could be also interesting to observe that by so doing the freedman tries to get around the emperor's refusal of statues in precious materials like silver and gold, which aimed to stress the difference from Domitian's tyrannical excesses: see Plin. *Pan.* 52.3 *tuam statuam in vestibulo Iovis optimi maximi unam alteramve et hanc aeream cernimus. At paulo ante aditus omnes omnes gradus totaque area hinc auro hinc argento relucebat* ('of your statues, only one or two are to be seen in the vestibule of the temple of Jupiter Best and Highest, and these are made of bronze; whereas only recently every approach and step, every inch of the precinct was gleaming with silver and gold', transl. Radice) (cf. also *Pan.* 55.6, 55.11); Suet. *Dom.* 13.2 *statuas sibi in Capitolio nonnisi aureas et argenteas poni permisit ac ponderis certi* ('He suffered no statues to

small the fine stone, which Annius Severus had to choose to have the pedestal made (*iube basim fieri, ex quo voles marmore*), must have offered enough space to accommodate not only Pliny's name, but also his titles, which the orator and politician certainly wanted on it despite his affectation of modesty (*basim ... quae nomen meum honoresque capiat, si hos quoque putabis addendos*).[35] It has been observed that Pliny must have given advice to his agent about the size of the figurine as well as of the desired dimension of the pedestal; the omission of this technical information can be taken as a sign of reworking of the letter in view of publication.[36] The same could be assumed even for the text of the inscription. It is reasonable to think that Pliny would have not left the formulation of the *titulus* to his agent. He probably sent it to Annius Severus attached to the letter.[37] While adapting the epistle for a literary edition he later revised the passage in order to display exemplary modesty and to grant his correspondent more responsibility.

---

be set up in his honour in the Capitol, except of gold and silver and of a fixed weight', transl. Rolfe) (on statues in honour of Trajan and other emperors, see Cordes 2017 52–3 and Audano 2018 *passim*). As Corinthian bronze was considered more valuable than silver and quite as precious as gold (Plin. *HN* 34.1), we could regard this act of honouring the emperor with such a special bronze alloy as a cunning kind of obsequiousness.

[35] According to Sherwin-White (1966) 226 'Pliny reveals his true motive. He wants to make sure that his recent distinctions are publicly recorded at Comum. ... This points to a date after his consulship when he entered the top class of the Senate' (see also Gibson 2020, 30 'a statue gifted by Pliny on the occasion of his consulship', 107, 155 n. 62, 179).

[36] Van Buren (1905) 446–7; Lehmann-Hartleben (1936) 70.

[37] It has been suggested that *CIL* v 5262, though displayed in a public place after Pliny's death, was actually composed by him himself (see Eck 2001, 231–2). For Pliny's interest in inscriptions, cf. also Pigoń's (Chapter 12) contribution in this volume.

CHAPTER 6

The Elder Pliny as Source of Inspiration: Pliny the Younger's Reception of the Naturalis Historia and His Uncle's Writing by the Light of a Lamp (lucubratio)

Judith Hindermann

1 Introduction

Pliny the Younger's letters have very often been studied as a source for the life and work of the Elder Pliny, the most important ones being the famous letters about the eruption of Mt. Vesuvius and Pliny the Elder's death (*Ep.* 6.16 and 6.20) as well as the letter about his numerous literary works (*Ep.* 3.5).[1] While in earlier times studies concentrated on how the Younger depicts the Elder Pliny, recent research has raised the question of how the Elder influences the work of the Younger Pliny and his self-portrayal in the *Epistles*.[2]

I will look into the relation between the two Plinies by showing how the Younger integrates subjects known from the Elder's *Naturalis Historia* in his *Epistulae* and adapts them to the genre, i.e. the miraculous stories of a volcanic eruption, dolphins, lakes and fountains (*Ep.* 4.30; 6.16; 6.20; 8.20; 9.33).[3] By presenting the miracles of Italy and repeatedly highlighting his close relationship with his hometown of Comum, Pliny the Younger shows alternatives to the wondrous phenomena of the world described in the *Naturalis Historia* and thereby distinguishes himself from his uncle. Pliny also deviates from his uncle's habit of writing at night (*lucubratio*) and serving the emperor by day. I will show that the Younger

---

[1] Copony (1987); Lefèvre (1989); Schönberger (1990); Eco (1990); Lefèvre (1996a); Jones (2001); Henderson (2002b); Carey (2003) 5–11; Berry (2008); Doody (2010) 1–2; 20–1; Beck (2013a); Keeline (2018); Neger (2021) 310–42; Foss (2022). I'm omitting the purely volcanological research on letters 6.16 and 6.20.
[2] Cova (2001); Hindermann (2011a); Gibson (2011b) 193–5; Henderson (2011); Gibson and Morello (2012) 108–15.
[3] For further parallels cf. the sub-chapter *Writing About Men and Miracles: Como versus the Cosmos* below; Beagon (1992) 82–91; Henderson (2002b) 90–7; Gibson (2011b) 189–95 on Plin. *Ep.* 1.16 and Plin. *HN praef.* 1; Plin. *Ep.* 5.3 and the function of learned lists in the *Natural History*; *Ep.* 5.6.10 and *HN* 18.181.

Pliny finds his own time of day to write literature and unite the claims of leisure and work (*otium* and *negotium*), which have a different importance for the two Plinii. In doing so, the Younger Pliny also underlines the differences that arise from his senatorial career and his uncle's military success. There are other subjects where a comparison between the two Plinii would be worthwhile, such as the treatment of medicine and physicians[4] or statues and commemoration.[5] In order not to exceed the format of this article, I will write about these elsewhere.

2 A Volcanic Eruption and the Importance of *studia*

Pliny the Elder is one of the most influential reference figures in the life and writings of the Younger Pliny. The special importance of the Elder for the Younger Pliny stems naturally from their family connection: the uncle was an important person during his youth and even adopted him after the death of his father.[6] The idea that Pliny wanted to imitate and succeed his uncle was derived from these facts,[7] but also the opposite notion, that the Younger shows an ambivalence toward his adoptive father. He has been accused of criticizing and presenting the Elder in an unflattering light and looking for other role models, about whom he writes about with more warmth.[8] Pliny's uncle may be a model for his work ethic and tenacity, but he was not a senator, which makes him unsuitable to serve as the sole or even a prominent model for his nephew.[9]

Nevertheless, there can be no doubt that his uncle had great influence on Pliny's development. Illuminating for the Younger Pliny's self-portrayal is the moment when he first mentions the value of *studia* in his life.[10] While his uncle is on his way to observe the eruption of Mt. Vesuvius and

---

[4] Cf. Plin. *Ep.* 1.22; 2.2; 2.20; 3.7; 5.6.1; 5.6.46; 5.19; 5.21; 6.4.1; 6.24; 7.1; 7.19; 7.21; 7.24; 7.26; 7.30; 8.1; 8.10; 8.11; 8.18; 8.23; 8.24.5; 10.5; 10.11; 10.17a; Plin. *HN* 22–32, esp. 29.1–28, cf. Weilbach (2020).

[5] Cf. Plin. *Ep.* 2.7; 3.6; 3.7.8; 3.10; 4.7.1–2; 4.28; 6.10.4; 7.29.2; 8.6; 8.18.11; 9.19.1; 10.8; 10.9; 10.60; 10.81.7; Plin. *HN* 33–7, esp. 34.15–93, cf. Henderson (2002a).

[6] Plin. *Ep.* 5.8.5. Pliny's legal guardian though was Verginius Rufus, cf. Plin. *Ep.* 2.1.8; Sherwin-White (1966) 334. The adoption probably was formalized only after the Elder's death, but he still appears more prominently in the letters and inscriptions than Pliny's father; cf. Gibson and Morello (2012) 106–10.

[7] E.g. Lefèvre (1996a); Jones (2001); Berry (2008). Keeline (2018) 173–74 n. 1 contains an overview of the other representatives of this research opinion.

[8] Cova (2001); Beck (2013a) 22; Keeline (2018) 174; 198–9.

[9] Thanks to the anonymous reviewer for this thought.

[10] Schönberger (1990) 534–6; Lefèvre (1996a) 207; Keeline (2018) 193–5; Gibson and Morello (2012) 112–15 refer to the important and parallel role of the *studia* in the daily routine of the two Plinii. In *Ep.* 7.4.2, Pliny mentions that he wrote a Greek tragedy at the age of fourteen.

rescue a friend,[11] the Younger Pliny, then seventeen or eighteen years old, decides to stay at home and study. His homework, Livy, was assigned to him by his uncle and Pliny prefers it to the real events around him; even though he has his uncle's permission to accompany him on the ship he remains behind:

> Magnum propiusque noscendum ut eruditissimo viro visum. Iubet Liburnicam aptari; mihi si venire una vellem facit copiam; respondi studere me malle, et forte ipse quod scriberem, dederat. (Plin. *Ep.* 6.16.7)[12]

> As a man with a scientific interest, the matter seemed to him to be significant and worthy of closer observation. He ordered to make a boat available; he gave me the opportunity to come with him if I wanted to; I replied that I would rather study, and by chance he had given me the homework himself.

Twice more, in *Ep.* 6.20, the Younger Pliny emphasizes the importance of the studies for him during the natural disaster and how he found comfort in them.[13]

The circumstances that led to his uncle's death were told to the Younger Pliny after the catastrophe. He noted them down and, twenty-seven years later, published his elaborate account of his uncle's death.[14] What supposedly is Pliny's memory of a terrible experience as a young man is, in truth, a carefully written, poeticized narrative of his uncle's most extreme scientific experience. Pliny portrays his uncle as brave by putting the proverbial words *fortes fortuna iuvat* ('fortune helps the brave')[15] in his mouth and as concerned about others,[16] but at the same time interested in science: under terrifying circumstances, his uncle dictates his observations of the eruption to his secretary.[17] Pliny represents his uncle as not only a

---

[11] Plin. *Ep.* 6.16.8–9.
[12] Here and below the Latin text is quoted after Mynors (1963), translated by me.
[13] Plin. *Ep.* 6.20.2; 6.20.5. For the allusion to Livy cf. Marchesi (2008) 188; Neger (2021) 331–2.
[14] Plin. *Ep.* 6.16.22. Pliny the Younger was born in AD 61 or 62, Mt. Vesuvius had erupted on 24 August or 24 October AD 79; cf. footnote 96 below. The sixth book of Pliny's letters has been published around AD 106 or 107, but we don't know when Pliny wrote his letter 6.16; cf. Sherwin-White (1966) 36–7; Beck (2013a) 18–20.
[15] Plin. *Ep.* 6.16.11; cf. for this citation and its intertextuality Bütler (1970) 81; Görler (1979) 431; Lefèvre (1996a) 198–9; Copony (1987); Berry (2008) 305.
[16] Plin. *Ep.* 6.16.12–13; Cova (2001) 58.
[17] Plin. *Ep.* 6.16.10. In *HN* 3.62 Pliny mentions Mt. Vesuvius without knowing that it is still an active volcano. *HN* 2.236–8 contains a section on various volcanoes, so the Elder Pliny was familiar with the phenomenon; cf. Sherwin-White (1966) 372–3; Eco (1990) 127–8; Gibson (2011b) 203.

scientific hero,[18] but also as Stoic sage, an example of tranquillity.[19] In the evening, the Elder sleeps calmly and deeply like other great commanders before him. He even snores,[20] and when dead he looks as peaceful as if he were sleeping.[21]

The Younger Pliny wrote his account of the events very carefully, making use of the aforementioned literary topoi, possibly to hide the inconsistencies in his uncle's behaviour and to defend him against accusations.[22] Even so, the Younger Pliny pretends to provide only notes from which his addressee, the historian Tacitus, could draw upon for his own writings.[23] In fact, however, the Younger Pliny adopts the position of an observer who transforms his uncle's experiences into an artistically condensed form, marked by the genres of historiography[24] and epistolography, and personalized by his own feelings and thoughts. This pattern of appropriation can also be observed in Pliny's dealings with the *Natural History*. This work, the only one of his uncle's numerous writings that has survived whole to this day, is an important source of inspiration for the Younger who also wrote on various topics. The Younger Pliny attaches great value to his uncle's monumental *Natural History*, which he recommends in his letter 3.5 as his uncle's most important work, signalling through his allusions that he also expects the readers of his letters to be familiar with it.[25]

---

[18] Eco (1990) 124; Cova (2001) 55–7. Keeline (2018) 185–93 instead reads Pliny's portrait of his uncle in completely negative terms, cf. p. 193: 'a damning portrait of the Elder's inadequacies'.
[19] Copony (1987) 215–17; Schönberger (1990) 531; 538; Lefèvre (1996a) 200–3.
[20] Plin. *Ep.* 6.16.13; cf. Görler (1979) 432 who refers to Alexander the Great, Cato the Younger and the Emperor Otho. Keeline (2018) 190 instead thinks this entire portrait of the snoring and overweight uncle to be 'unflattering in the extreme' and that all of it could have been omitted. Neger (2021) 325 interprets the description as a retarding element before the action approaches the end.
[21] Plin. *Ep.* 6.16.20; Lefèvre (1996a) 194–6; 203–6.
[22] For the inconsistencies in his uncle's behaviour in Pliny's account cf. Haywood (1952); Copony (1987). Beck (2013a) offers a comprehensive overview of the previous research with its various assumptions on the events and clinical pictures that led to the death of the Elder Pliny.
[23] Plin. *Ep.* 6.16.22 *Tu potissima excerpes* ('You'll pick out the essential'); cf. Schönberger (1990) 530–1; Lefèvre (1996a) 195; 214.
[24] Schönberger (1990) 530–4; Beutel (2000) 165–73; Ash (2003); Augoustakis (2005); Tzounakas (2007) 49–52; Marchesi (2008) 144–206.
[25] Gibson (2011b) 187: 'the Younger was ... a close and careful reader of the *Natural History*, and – more importantly for the history of the reception of Pliny's great work – expected his best readers to be similarly inclined.' Beck (2016) 70 is decidedly against this attitude: in his opinion, it is out of the question that a contemporary reader should have thought of the Elder Pliny as a kind of literary competitor, compared him with the Younger and even recognized similarities or differences in their works, especially as the *Naturalis Historia* is not a canonical text like which one had to have in mind as a normally educated member of the Roman upper class. Shannon (2013) 9 sees the Elder Pliny in

3 The Dolphin-Letter 9.33

The dolphin-letter (9.33) is, to cite the title of Stevens's article (2009), 'A Story About Storytelling', or, more precisely, about Pliny the Younger's way of transforming a traditional story and inserting it into his self-portrait.[26] The dolphin-letter has a special position among Pliny's letters because it is the only one with an animal as the main subject.[27] The dolphin is a worthy topic because in antiquity it was considered to be an intelligent and musical animal, associated with the mythical poet Arion and the god Apollo,[28] thus corresponding with Pliny's interest in literature and art and his self-representation as an inspired poet.[29] His dolphin-letter serves him as a didactic example of how to describe a subject poetically. Fittingly, he addresses this letter to his friend and alter ego Caninius, whom he helps to develop into an author in the course of the seven letters he writes to him. As the last in the series, the letter occupies a special position.[30] Pliny's version is a mixture of various dolphin-stories; its core, though, is the second dolphin-story of the Elder Pliny (Plin. *HN* 9.26). Both authors write about a certain dolphin in Hippo Diarrhytus (modern-day Bizerte or Bizerta in Tunisia) that is fed by men and swims with them. After the Proconsul of Africa orders the animal to be smeared with an ointment, it first withdraws, but then reappears off the coast. The inhabitants of Hippo finally kill the dolphin.

Pliny the Elder dedicates a large part of his *Natural History* to animals, nine of the thirty-seven books.[31] The dolphin is described as the fastest of

---

the background of the Younger's description of the natural wonder in *Ep.* 4.30 and 8.20. Keeline (2018) 176 thinks that Pliny criticizes the *Naturalis Historia* with his description as *diffusum* and *varium*: 'Is the *Natural History* a loose, baggy monster?'. Ash (2018) 139 contests in her article on *Ep.* 8.20, that Pliny is surely engaging with his uncle's work. Cf. also n. 39 below with the discussion of the dolphin-stories.

[26] Cf. Beck (2016) 78–9.

[27] Cf. Hindermann (2011a) 346–7. In other letters of his collection animals are only briefly mentioned, mostly in the context of hunting (*Ep.* 1.6; 2.8; 5.6.7; 5.18; 9.10), as food and animal husbandry (*Ep.* 2.11.25; 2.17.3; 2.17.28; 5.2; 8.17.4) or entertainment (*Ep.* 6.34.3; 9.6.2).

[28] Cf. Stebbins (1929) 66–70; 77–9; Rabinovitch (1947); Hünemörder (1997).

[29] Hindermann (2009) 227–8.

[30] Cf. Plin. *Ep.* 1.3; 2.8; 3.7; 6.21; 7.18; 8.4; 9.33 to Caninius; Ludolph (1997) 121; Henderson (2002b) 107; Hindermann (2011a) 348–9; Gibson (2015) 190–1; Carlon (2018) 58; 61; 63; Canobbio (Chapter 9) in this volume. Against Beck (2016) 64, who postulates that there is no connection between addressee and content and that Pliny writes for the general reader. Beck (2016) 82–6 sees the reason why Pliny reproduces the history of dolphins in his interest in historiography and in the fact that Pliny wants to extend his collection to nine books and therefore searches for additional material in the ninth book.

[31] Book 8: land animals; Book 9: aquatic animals; Book 10: birds; Book 11: insects; Books 28–32: the importance of animals in pharmacology.

all animals and appears in the catalogue of the aquatic creatures after the whale. With a scientific approach, the Elder Pliny starts his account of the dolphin with its description and only later adds, with some skepticism, the various stories about its behaviour. First, he recounts three stories about friendship between humans and dolphins.[32] Subsequently, he adds three love stories about boys and dolphins.[33] For the Elder, other authors (whom he refers to by name) who tell the same stories prove the truth of the incredible dolphin-stories and this confirmation is the reason why he even bothers to retell them.[34]

There are many differences in how the Younger and the Elder Pliny present the story.[35] Pliny the Younger adds the description of a lagoon where the story takes place[36] and concentrates on one particular boy who connects with the dolphin instead of the large crowd which appears in the Elder's account.[37] He adds the theme of a friendship between dolphins – mentioned by the Elder Pliny in another story – by introducing a second dolphin. At the end of his dolphin-story the Younger Pliny also gives us more details than his uncle did: he writes about the various reasons for killing the dolphin and the name of the deputy who did it.[38]

The Younger Pliny writes his dolphin-letter as if he doesn't know the literary tradition of dolphin-stories[39] and he neither mentions his uncle

---

[32] In the first story, which takes place during the reign of Emperor Augustus, a dolphin takes a poor boy from Baiae on his back to school in Pozzuoli and back home. After long years of friendship, the boy dies of an illness and the dolphin also dies out of longing (Plin. *HN* 9.25). For the second story see above in the text. In the third story, the love of a dolphin for a boy in Iasus is interpreted as a divine sign and the boy is appointed by Alexander the Great as the high priest of Poseidon (Plin. *HN* 9.27).

[33] Hegesidemus tells a story about a boy in Iasus called Hermias, for whom a dolphin commits suicide out of love by throwing himself on the shore. Theophrastus reports that this also happened in Naupactus, and the inhabitants of Amphilochus and Taranto tell the same story about boys and dolphins (Plin. *HN* 9.27–8). For love between dolphins and boys cf. Hindermann (2011b); Williams (2013) 204–12.

[34] Cf. Plin. *HN* 9.25; 9.27; 9.28 *nec modus exemplorum* ('and there are many more examples').

[35] For a comparison of the two stories, cf. Cova (2001) 62–3; Stevens (2009); Hindermann (2011a) 349–52.

[36] Plin. *Ep.* 9.33.2–3.   [37] Plin. *Ep.* 9.33.6–7; Plin. *HN* 9.26.   [38] Cf. Plin. *Ep.* 9.33.9–10.

[39] In the older secondary literature it is concluded that the Younger Pliny had not known the work of his uncle or didn't read all the books; cf. McAlindon (1956) 166; Higham (1960) 85; Sherwin-White (1966) 514. Montgomery (1966) 312 supposes that Pliny the Younger 'was of course familiar with much of the material collected by his elder namesake', but he doesn't compare the two accounts of the story. In the more recent literature, however, the Younger Pliny's concealment of his uncle's dolphin-stories is interpreted as intentional to create suspension and invite the reader to compare the two versions; cf. Stevens (2009) 161–4; 169–70; Hindermann (2011a) 348; Keeline (2018) 197–8. Ash (2003) 222 suspects 'some gentle literary rivalry' between the nephew and his dead uncle and reads the letter 9.33 in context with other *exitus*-letters of Pliny dedicated to the death of great men and women. Beck (2016) 66–71; 81 on the other hand takes the view that in the presentation of the Younger Pliny there is no reference to the dolphin-story of the Elder Pliny and

nor other authors as his source. His reference is an anonymous acquaintance who told the story during dinner and then disappears behind Pliny's role as narrator. Pliny claims to have heard about the story only by chance, which he underlines with a double *incidi* and by embedding his dolphin-story in a series of stories allegedly told during a dinner, which is a popular setting for exciting tales in the Roman novel and other literary genres:[40]

> Incidi in materiam veram sed simillimam fictae … incidi autem, dum super cenam varia miracula hinc inde referuntur. (Plin. *Ep.* 9.33.1)

> I came across a true story, which certainly looks as if it had been invented. … I came across it recently when all sorts of miraculous stories were told from here and there during dinner.

While his uncle presents his stories in a scientific context and claims to narrate the miraculous stories about men and dolphins only reluctantly,[41] the Younger Pliny is eager to do so.[42] Just as in his account of the eruption of Mt. Vesuvius and his uncle's death, Pliny again claims to simply present some unordered raw material available for the addressee's own literary use. And, as with the story about the uncle's death, it provides a closed, unified story that cannot be excerpted, shortened or rewritten.[43]

While the list is a typical element of the Elder's encyclopaedia, the Younger chooses one example with which he can demonstrate how a poetic revision works. Only through the comparison with the dolphin-stories in the *Naturalis Historia* does the reader understand the achievement of the Younger Pliny. While the Elder seeks credibility through his scientific treatment of animal behaviour and through a multitude of examples mentioned in various sources, the Younger creates an appealing

---

that he did not want a reader to compare the two versions, otherwise he would have referred to his uncle. That the underlying history is also testified in the *Naturalis Historia* might be more or less coincidence. Nevertheless, Beck (2016) 70 thinks that the Younger Pliny had well-known the version of the Elder Pliny, since the *Naturalis Historia* had a completely different meaning for him as nephew and eyewitness than for the 'normal' Roman reader. Neger (2021) 378–9 argues that the Younger Pliny evokes the *Natural History* indirectly. Cf. also n. 25 above for the Younger's use of the *Naturalis Historia* in general.

[40] Cf. Apul. *Met.* 2.18–31, Petron. *Sat.* 61–3; Görgemanns (2001); Beck (2016) 71. For discussions about *mirabilia* at dinner cf. Neger (2021) 384–5 who refers to Plutarch's *Quaestiones Convivales* and the *Convivium Septem Sapientium*.

[41] Plin. *HN* 9.25.

[42] Cf. Stevens (2009) 165–6 about the frequent use of words starting with *mir-* in Pliny's letters Books 1–9.

[43] Stevens (2009) 162; Beck (2013a) 12. Beck (2013a) 22 proposes an interesting thesis, that Pliny merely edited a confirming doublet of Tacitus' desirable positive representation of his uncle, just as he recorded important texts of others in his letters as testimonies for posterity (Plin. *Ep.* 3.21 with Martial; *Ep.* 4.27 with Sentius Augurinus).

and exemplary story, authorized by himself. By claiming that *Ep.* 9.33 features only notes, Pliny also underlines his literary talent as he did in *Ep.* 6.16, regarding the death of the Elder Pliny. He signals to the reader that even his alleged notes are of high literary quality.

4 Fountains and Lakes

Pliny uses the same strategy, i.e. to formulate one gripping example instead of writing down a complete list of phenomena, in his letter about a special fountain near Lake Como (*Lacus Larius*) (*Ep.* 4.30) and the floating islands on the Lago di Bassano (*Lacus Vadimonis*) (*Ep.* 8.20).[44] From all the miracles of the wide world contained in the *Naturalis Historia*, Pliny the Younger chooses an example from his homeland and gives it a prominent place at the end of Book 4, which is topographically framed by Pliny's home, Comum.[45] The other example, the Lago di Bassano (close to Ameria, about seventy-three kilometers north of Rome) is located in the eighth book that has travel as a main theme. The wonder also has personal relevance, because it is near an estate of Pliny's grandfather-in-law.[46]

The Elder Pliny mentions the spring near Lake Como briefly in connection with rivers, lakes and springs that have special characteristics in the second book of his *Natural History*, but without noting any closer personal relation or experience. Chapters 227–33 of the second book are dedicated to sources that are worth mentioning because of a special trait, such as temperature, water quality, colour, taste, effect or quantity and timing of water flow. The characteristic feature of the spring on Lake Como is that it rises and then disappears again within a certain period of time.[47] The floating islands on the Lago di Bassano are mentioned by the Elder Pliny briefly in connection with a list of moving islands.[48] In Pliny's

---

[44] Saylor (1982); Lefèvre (1988); Shannon (2013) 9–11; Ash (2018) 133–40; Neger (2021) 305–10; 368–76.
[45] Cf. Neger (2021) 305–7. Letter 4.1 is addressed to Calpurnius Fabatus, the grandfather of Pliny's wife Calpurnia, and announces an upcoming visit to Fabatus in Comum. In *Ep.* 4.13.3, the middle of Book 4, Pliny mentions his recent visit in Comum and the closing letter 4.30 presupposes that Pliny was at home, since he brings the story of the miracle of nature back as a gift to his friend.
[46] Neger (2021) 369–70.
[47] Plin. *HN* 2.232 *In Comensi iuxta Larium lacum fons largus horis singulis semper intumescit ac residit* ('In the area of Comum on Lake Larius there is a strong spring that grows and falls for one hour each').
[48] Plin. *HN* 2.209 *Quaedam insulae semper fluctuantur, sicut in agro Caecubo et eodem Reatino, Mutinensi, Statoniensi; in Vadimonis lacu* ... ('Some islands float constantly back and forth, as in the area of Caecubum and the already mentioned Reate, furthermore of Mutina and Statonia, on the Vadimonic Lake ...').

enumeration of natural wonders in chapter 2.209 they are followed by other islands that can be moved by hand, move to music or take on different forms.

In both epistles the Younger Pliny emphasizes first and foremost that he had experienced the wonders himself.[49] While in the dolphin-letter he names an anonymous third person as his source, in these two letters he states that he himself saw the marvels,[50] investigated them and now describes them in such a way that they become worthy of being the subject of a whole letter. When describing Lago di Bassano in letter 8.20, Pliny emphasizes his personal experience by writing the letter in the first-person and giving us the reason for the visit: he has to inspect his grandfather-in-law's estate near Ameria. After he hears stories about Lago di Bassano, he wants to check the lake for himself and describes it in detail.[51] The lake has a circular shape, a light colour, a smell of sulphur and healing power. The most striking feature are islands floating on the lake, which are inadvertently used by cattle to cross the water as if they were on boats. A river flows out of the lake, disappears into a cave and runs on invisibly. As with the dolphin-story, Pliny's description of the lake unites various individual elements which the Elder Pliny attributes to multiple bodies of water and through this he intensifies the miracle.

In his description of the intermittent source in letter 4.30, Pliny emphasizes his personal experience by describing it as a beautiful resting place where you can have a picnic. He also describes an experiment he conducted with a finger ring that is gradually washed over by the spring water.[52] In both cases we have a short reference by the Elder Pliny in the context of similar phenomena, to which the Younger Pliny adds descriptions of the surrounding nature and animals or people, but without

---

[49] Plin. *Ep.* 8.20.3 *audivi pariter et vidi* ('I heard and saw at the same time'). In *Ep.* 4.30.3–4 Pliny does not use the first person, but three verbs of seeing directed to the addressee: *cernitur, observes, videas.*

[50] Cf. Ash (2018) 127 on the common feature of *mirabilia* that they are triggered through the visual sphere; Shannon (2013) 6; 10–11. On the subject of miracles in Pliny the Younger cf. Neger (2018).

[51] Plin. *Ep.* 8.20.3–4 *Simul quaedam incredibilia narrantur. Perveni ad ipsum* ('At the same time, all kinds of incredible things were related. I went there myself').

[52] Plin. *Ep.* 4.30.1 *Attuli tibi ex patria mea* ('I brought you from my homeland'); 4.30.2 *Excipitur cenatiuncula manu facta* ('it is caught in an artificial grotto'); 4.30.3 *Iuxta recumbis et vesceris, atque etiam ex ipso fonte – nam est frigidissimus – potas* ('you lie down beside it, eat and also take a sip from the spring every now and then – because it is nice and cool'); 4.30.4 *Anulum seu quid aliud ponis in sicco* ('If you put a ring or something on the dry part').

reference to the *Naturalis Historia*.[53] The Younger Pliny enriches the letters with those narrative elements which, according to the Elder Pliny, have no place in his encyclopaedic work which belongs to a different literary genre.[54] Pliny the Younger adds more details to increase their credibility[55] and links the wonder stories with emotions and personal experience. In his letters, nature and human reaction alternate and are closely related.[56]

5 Writing About Men and Miracles: Como versus the Cosmos

The letters I have discussed about natural phenomena should not give the impression that they predominate thematically in Pliny's letter collection.[57] The Younger Pliny is far more interested in humans than in animals and nature. In his letters, he presents a range of predominantly outstanding men and women who shaped him, and a few bad examples from which one must distinguish oneself.[58] The Elder Pliny, on the other hand, dedicates only one book out of thirty-seven specifically to mankind, the seventh book of *Naturalis Historia*. Still, there are many thematic parallels between the two authors' discussion of men: both write about the importance of Cicero,[59] about their compatriot (*conterraneus meus*) Catullus and his style (*duriusculus*),[60] about exemplary decent women,[61] about examples of love between children and their parents,[62] about mourning the dead,[63] about dreams and apparitions,[64] about luck and fate.[65] Moreover, the Elder and Younger share an interest in artificial

---

[53] Shannon (2013) 22 states the same for phenomena of the *Naturalis Historia* described by Tacitus and Suetonius without referring to the Elder Pliny.
[54] Plin. *HN praef.* 12; cf. Neger (2021) 341–2 for the narrative elements in *Ep.* 6.16 and 6.20.
[55] Cf. Hindermann (2011a) 352–4; Lefèvre (1988) 244.
[56] The same narrative can also be found in letter 6.20 about the experiences of the Younger Pliny during the volcanic eruption; cf. Lefèvre (1996a) 212.
[57] Cf. also *Ep.* 7.27 about a ghost and 8.8 about the *fons Clitumnus*.   [58] Bütler (1970) 85–93.
[59] Plin. *HN* 7.116–17; Plin. *Ep.* 1.2.4; 1.5.12; 3.15.1; 4.8.4–6; 7.4.3–6; 9.2.2–3; 9.26.8; Lefèvre (1996b).
[60] Plin. *HN praef.* 1; Plin. *Ep.* 1.16.5; 4.27.4; Howe (1985) 567–70; Gibson (2011b) 189–93; Morello (2011) 152.
[61] Plin. *HN* 7.120; Plin. *Ep.* 5.16.1–2; 7.19.4; 8.5.1.
[62] Plin. *HN* 7.121; Plin. *Ep.* 5.16.7–9; 6.25.5; 9.9.2.
[63] Plin. *HN* 7.5; 7.145–6; 7.187–90; e.g. Plin. *Ep.* 1.12; 2.1; 4.2; 4.7; 5.16; Hindermann (2014).
[64] Plin. *HN* 2.21; 7.109; 7.138; 7.166; 10.211–12; 22.44; 25.17; 28.116; 34.58; 35.71; 36.64; 36.97; 37.160; 37.167; Plin. *Ep.* 1.18; 3.5.4; 7.27; Önnerfors (1976).
[65] Plin. *HN* 7.130–46; 7.165; e.g. Plin. *Ep.* 3.19.4; 4.8.2; 4.11; 4.24; 5.20.2; 7.29.2; cf. Bütler (1970) 15–17.

gardens and nature imitating art.[66] Both authors also deal with the relationship between Romans and Greeks and their respective merits. The Younger Pliny frequently cites Greek authors, likes to compare himself with Demosthenes[67] and is especially proud that he is being read by the Greeks.[68] The Elder Pliny in contrast shows an overall critical attitude towards the Greeks, especially their vanity (*Graeca vanitas*), and combines this aversion with his traditionalist love of his homeland.[69]

These various thematic parallels can be explained by the fact that Pliny's letter collection also has an encyclopaedic character with striking variety[70] and, like the *Naturalis Historia*, covers wonderous phenomena as well as historical bits, which were of interest for his contemporaries and not restricted to a certain literary genre like paradoxography or history.[71]

The Elder Pliny collects in his *Naturalis Historia* various *mirabilia* of the known world. He presents them not only out of interest for the spectacular, but also because they refer back to Rome, which stands at the centre of the *oikoumene*. Interesting facts from all over the world are listed in order to demonstrate the greatness of the Roman empire and to explain phenomena of the city.[72] The Younger Pliny, instead, concentrates on the exemplary moral power of Comum. He represents the Upper Italian region of the Transpadana as an area that preserves the spirit of ancient *Romanitas*, strength and modesty, and praises the outstanding deeds and character of its inhabitants.[73] Pliny proves his personal attachment to Comum by addressing his important role models like Vestricius Spurinna, Corellius Rufus and Verginius Rufus.[74] He also marries a woman born and brought up there, Calpurnia, whose family Pliny greatly appreciates and links to the natural wonder described in *Ep.* 8.20.[75] Pliny's

---

[66] Cf. Plin. *HN* 4.29; 12.9–10; 12.22; 14.11; Plin. *Ep.* 5.6.22–3; 5.6.35–6; 5.6.39–40; Beagon (1992) 82–91; Harich-Schwarzbauer and Hindermann (2010) 62–6.

[67] Plin. *Ep.* 1.2.2; 1.20.4–5; 2.3.9–10; 4.5; 6.33.10–11; 7.30; 8.24; 9.23; 9.26; cf. Bütler (1970) 109; 135; Tzounakas (2015).

[68] Plin. *Ep.* 7.4.9; cf. 4.18.

[69] Plin. *HN praef.* 24–6; *HN* 3.42; 3.122; 7.110–20; 37.31; 37.195; cf. Carey (2003) 25–6; 32–40; Howe (1985) 570.

[70] Cf. Goetzl (1952); Gibson (2014a).   [71] Cf. Shannon (2013) 22–3.

[72] Murphy (2004) 19; 23; Beagon (2005) 19; 21–6; Naas (2011) 62–3.

[73] E.g. Plin. *Ep.* 1.14; 6.24; 7.22; Bütler (1970) 85–93; Gasser (1999) 212–13; Mratschek (2003) 226–33.

[74] Corellius Rufus: 1.12; 4.17; 7.11.3; 7.31.4; 9.13.6; Verginius Rufus: 2.1; 5.3.5; 6.10; 9.19; Vestricius Spurinna: 1.5.8–10; 3.1; 3.10; 4.27.5–6; 5.17; cf. Cova (2001) 65–6; Gibson and Morello (2012) 106; Keeline (2018) 182–3; Neger (2021) 255–67; Keeline (2018) 199 shows though, that ultimately Pliny embraces no one from the older generation uncritically as a model.

[75] Plin. *Ep.* 4.19; cf. Carlon (2009) 157–75. The connection of Calpurnia's grandfather, Calpurnius Fabatus, to Comum is evident in *Ep.* 5.11; 6.12; 6.30; 7.11; 7.16; 7.23; 7.32; 8.10. Gibson (2021)

love of his homeland is a central leitmotif throughout his letter collection: although Pliny owns two estates in other places and describes them in two extensive letters,[76] the praise of his birthplace dominates. Pliny reveals his manifold contacts to Comum[77] and mentions in several letters his possessions and estates in the region, which are of great economic and emotional importance to him.[78] In order to secure the flourishing area for future generations, Pliny also provides the community with generous charity, be it the foundation of public buildings or scholarships and financial support for needy fellow citizens.[79]

Pliny the Elder also mentions Comum, but without special distinction.[80] His focus is on the catalogue of phenomena from the regions dominated by the Roman empire. His preface to the description of Italy, the core of the empire, is a proper eulogy[81] and the addressee and recipient of the entire work is the future Emperor Titus, who watches over everything, and – as the Elder Pliny hopes in his preface – should precede his citizens in reading his work.[82] The Elder's gift to the emperor, an encyclopaedia full of interesting items, is put on public display.[83] His inventory of nature reflects the perspective of the conqueror who sees the material world filled with objects to be catalogued. In this interpretation, the encyclopaedia not only becomes an image of Roman military power, but also serves as an instrument for the moral education of Roman citizens.[84] The transmission of knowledge is therefore not objective and neutral, but takes place from the point of view of Roman rule at the height of its power.[85]

---

interprets Calpurnia as representing Pliny's (north) Italian future and the antique values of the Transpadana.

[76] Cf. Plin. *Ep.* 2.17 about his estate Laurentinum near Ostia; *Ep.* 5.6 about his estate near Tifernum Tiberinum; cf. Gasser (1999) 196–7; Gibson and Morello (2012) 200–33.

[77] Cf. Plin. *Ep.* 1.3.1; 2.5.3; 2.8.1; 3.6.4; 4.13.9; 5.7; 5.11.2; 5.14; 6.24; 7.22.2; 7.32.1; 9.7; Bütler (1970) 129–47; Gasser (1999) 193–8; Krieckhaus (2006) 31–50; Carlon (2018).

[78] Plin. *Ep.* 2.15.2; 3.19; 6.3; 7.11.5; 7.14.1; 9.7; Krieckhaus (2006) 36–7; Gibson and Morello (2012) 203–11; Page (2015) 319–25.

[79] Plin. *Ep.* 1.8; 1.19; 4.13; 5.7; cf. Gasser (1999) 201–9; Krieckhaus (2006) 44–50; Hartmann (2012) 121–5; Germerodt (2015) 95–7; 190–207; Page (2015) 326–41; Carlon (2018) 64–5.

[80] Cf. about Como: Plin. *HN* 2.232; 3.124; 3.132; 34.144; 36.159; about the Transpadana: 3.123.

[81] Plin. *HN* 3.39–42; cf. Carey (2003) 33.

[82] Plin. *HN praef.* 33; cf. Murphy (2004) 197–215; Morello (2011) 165.

[83] Cf. Ash (2018) 126 about the custom of exhibiting exotic gifts to the emperors in public, e.g. Suet. *Aug.* 43.4.

[84] Cf. Howe (1985) 561; 571 who calls the *Naturalis Historia* a 'didactic work' and a 'nationalistic encyclopedia'; Nikitinski (1998) 345; Naas (2002) 418–21; Naas (2011) 61–5; 426–32; Fear (2011).

[85] Fear (2011) 25.

The Younger Pliny, on the other hand, explicitly rejects the wonders of the world and reminds us that there is also something impressive to see nearby. He combines his inspection of a property belonging to his grandfather-in-law with a visit to a natural wonder, thus demonstrating at once a sense of family, economic interest, scientific curiosity and literary activity:

> Ad quae noscenda iter ingredi, transmittere mare solemus, ea sub oculis posita neglegimus, seu quia ita natura comparatum, ut proximorum incuriosi longinqua sectemur, seu quod omnium rerum cupido languescit, cum facilis occasio, seu quod differimus tamquam saepe visuri, quod datur videre quotiens velis cernere. 2 Quacumque de causa, permulta in urbe nostra iuxtaque urbem non oculis modo sed ne auribus quidem novimus, quae si tulisset Achaea Aegyptos Asia aliave quaelibet miraculorum ferax commendatrixque terra, audita perlecta lustrata haberemus. (Plin. *Ep.* 8.20.1–2)[86]

> We tend to undertake journeys, to cross the sea in order to get to know things that we are not interested in when we have them before our very eyes, either because it is natural for us to wander far away, indifferent to the immediate surroundings, or because the desire for everything that is easy to reach cools down or because we postpone it as if we could look at any time at that, what is presented to the eyes, as often as you want to see it. 2 Either way, there are a lot of things in our city and its surroundings we have never seen or even heard of, that we would have heard, read and visited long ago, if it had been in Achaea, Egypt, Asia or any other country rich in natural wonders that know how to advertize for them.

With the mention of the foreign lands Achaea, Egypt and Asia the Younger Pliny evokes the thrilling miracles of the *Naturalis Historia*[87] but he suggests to his readers an alternative program through the miracle of a lake near the estate of his revered grandfather-in-law in Umbria. Instead of the wonders of the world, he seeks the wonders near him and proves them with his examination. The message and values which he delivers do not differ from his uncle's, but the Younger Pliny chooses a different approach to convince his readers that both he and his work are trustworthy.

---

[86] Here and below the Latin text is quoted after König (1973), translated by me.
[87] Saylor (1982) reads this passage as a rejection of tourism. Neger (2021) 369 thinks that the juxtaposition of native and foreign wonders is inspired by Vergil (*G.* 2.136–76) and Propertius (3.22.17–18). Ash (2018) 137 refers to Hdt. 3.106, who argues that the most beautiful regions of the world are the furthest away, and Shannon (2013) 10 to Hdt. 1.8 about Candaules' statement that ears are less trustworthy than eyes.

6 *lucubratio*: Writing at Night

For Pliny the Younger, the diligence and great productivity of his uncle is a problem, but also his own goal.[88] Pliny ends *Ep.* 3.5, the famous catalogue of works written by the Elder, with the remark that he himself could be called industrious (*studiosus*), but only if one does not compare him with his uncle. By comparison with his uncle, however, he is very lazy (*desidiosissimus*).[89] This superlative corresponds to the two superlatives with which Pliny describes his uncle elsewhere: in *Ep.* 6.16.7, the Elder is praised as *eruditissimus*, the same adjective Pliny used in *Ep.* 3.5.6 when describing the *Naturalis Historia*;[90] in *Ep.* 6.16.3, he is immortalized as very blessed (*beatissimus*) because he succeeded in both doing great deeds and describing them, regardless of whether Tacitus includes the Younger's literary descriptions in his history or not.[91]

One of the reasons why Pliny the Elder managed to write so many works is that he wrote at night.[92] Night work as an ideal is based on rural frugality,[93] it allowed one to use time that would otherwise be lost. People worked at night in addition to their day work, not instead of it.[94] Moving the literary activity into the night meant that one could fulfil one's regular duties as a Roman citizen during the day. The Elder Pliny announces in the famous preface to his *Naturalis Historia* that he would work during the day and study at night in order to fulfil his commitment to science and public service equally:

> Nec dubitamus multa esse quae et nos praeterierint. homines enim sumus et occupati officiis subsicivisque temporibus[95] ista curamus, id est nocturnis, ne quis vestrum putet his cessatum horis. dies vobis impendimus, cum

---

[88] Hindermann (2009) 224. For a different view, see Lefèvre (1989) 118, who takes the humility gesture of the Younger Pliny at face value. He argues that the Younger wants to work as much as the Elder, but is not in a position to do so and that the large workload causes him stress ('intellectual paralysis'). Keeline (2018) 195–8 compares the careers and lifestyles of the two Plinii and states: 'The Younger Pliny departs from his uncle in all these ways, but he never explicitly mentions them. The implications are left for the reader to notice. Pliny's forging his own path is perhaps most visible in the literary realm.'

[89] Plin. *Ep.* 3.5.19.   [90] Cf. Gibson (2011b) 203.

[91] Cf. Schönberger (1990) 533; Lefèvre (1996a) 195–6; Beck (2013a) 23; Neger (2021) 314.

[92] Ker (2004) 232–6.   [93] Ker (2004) 217–19; 221–7.

[94] Plin. *Ep.* 9.40.2; Colum. *Rust.* 1 *praef.* 15–17. People who party through the night or use the secrecy of the night for crime, on the other hand, are severely criticized, cf. e.g. Sen. *Ep.* 122; Ker (2004) 219–21.

[95] The Younger Pliny uses the same formulation to denote his free time, cf. *Ep.* 3.15.1 *Rogas enim, ut aliquid subsicivi temporis studiis meis subtraham, impertiam tuis* ('you demand indeed that I withdraw part of my spare time from my studies and use it for yours'). The adjective is also similarly used by Cicero, cf. Cic. *Leg.* 1.3.9; Lefèvre (1996b) 341–2.

> somno valetudinem computamus, vel hoc solo praemio contenti, quod, dum ista, ut ait M. Varro, musinamur, pluribus horis vivimus. profecto enim vita vigilia est. (Plin. *HN praef.* 18)

> However, I am well aware that I have overlooked many things. We are only human beings and are taken up by our daily business; only in our spare time, i.e. in the nights we deal with it, and none of you should believe that these hours go at the expense of my obligations. We dedicate the day to you, we calculate the sleep according to our well-being, satisfied only with the profit, that we are, as Marcus Varro says, more hours alive, if we consecrate them so to the muses: for only being awake means life.

In *Ep.* 3.5.8–9, Pliny confirms the statement of his uncle and notes with admiration that he studied during the festival of the Vulcanalia, i.e. on August 23,[96] well into the night by lamplight:

> Lucubrare Vulcanalibus incipiebat non auspicandi causa sed studendi statim a nocte multa, hieme vero ab hora septima vel cum tardissime octava, saepe sexta. Erat sane somni paratissimi, non numquam etiam inter ipsa studia instantis et deserentis. 9 Ante lucem ibat ad Vespasianum imperatorem (nam ille quoque noctibus utebatur), inde ad delegatum sibi officium. (Plin. *Ep.* 3.5.8–9)

> From the Vulcanalia on he began to work deep in the night by the light of a lamp, not for the sake of a good omen, but to study, in winter around the seventh or at the latest the eighth, often even around the sixth hour of the night; sleep, of course, was at his command at all times, afflicted him and sometimes even left him while studying. 9 Before dawn he used to go to Emperor Vespasian, for he too was a night worker, and from there to the service assigned to him.

For himself though, the Younger Pliny rejects the topos of *lucubratio* ('writing by the light of a lamp'). Instead he chooses, in *Ep.* 3.1, Vestricius Spurinna, and not the Elder Pliny, as model for lifestyle and daily routine despite the Plinii's common love for the *studia*.[97] As I stated for the dolphin-letter, Pliny defies his uncle and goes his own way, but he never explicitly says so. Pliny's distancing of himself is both sophisticated

---

[96] Because of the rare dating in Pliny's letters, Gibson and Morello (2012) 111–12 propose a reference to letter 6.16 on the eruption of Mt. Vesuvius, which took place on August 24. But cf. Stefani (2011) who suggests 24 October AD 79; the date in August is defended by Foss (2022). The Elder Pliny adheres strictly to his daily routine, despite the unusual natural spectacle. Beck (2013a) 21–2 writes that the Younger Pliny, despite mentioning the festival of the Vulcanalia, concealed the end of his uncle in *Ep.* 3.5, because he did not want to remember his careless urge to investigate which led to his death.

[97] Cf. Beck (2013a) 22; Keeline (2018) 183–5.

and indirect.[98] The inference, nevertheless, can be drawn because of the Younger's conspicuous omission of *lucubratio* in his daily routine. As Keeline (2018) correctly states, Pliny is always crafting his *own* literary monument: Pliny's letters are about Pliny himself, even if he writes about his uncle.[99]

In his letters, Pliny shows other persons besides his uncle, but not himself, writing poems or other literary works at night. He is awake for other reasons: because he misses his wife or dines with the emperor,[100] but he writes literature only during the day. At the same time, the Younger Pliny often presents himself as busy with boring office work or problems with his subordinates that he has to solve.[101] So how does he manage to work and write at the same time during the day? Pliny often mentions that, like his uncle, he uses every free second to write. His aim is to publish as much as possible and he proudly lists his many works from different literary genres.[102] Thanks to his talent for multitasking, Pliny also writes in situations where other people do nothing. Like his uncle[103] he writes during the bath, while travelling and eating and even uses his sleepy minutes in bed shortly after waking up for thoughts that he later dictates to his secretary.[104] Using all the small breaks during the day, he is able to write literary works efficiently while still fulfilling his professional duties.

But why does he present himself as not writing at night?[105] By rejecting night work, Pliny underlines the importance of his literary work. One could assume that Pliny does not have to work at night because he has less to do in his public offices and in the service of the emperor than his uncle.[106] However, Pliny rejects this idea in a prominent place: the last letter of the ninth book. It is the only letter in which he shows himself working at night, but not writing poems; he is revising a speech for court that he has to give the next day. While the Elder had given up legal

---

[98] Cf. Keeline (2018) 197–8.   [99] Keeline (2018) 175.
[100] Plin. *Ep.* 5.5.5–7: night work of C. Fannius and complaint about transience and mortality; *Ep.* 6.31.13: after working at the court Pliny spends leisure time with the emperor till late; *Ep.* 7.2: Iustus is so busy that he has to work late into the night; *Ep.* 7.5.1: Pliny stays awake in the night because his wife Calpurnia is away.
[101] Plin. *Ep.* 1.10.9–10; 1.16.7; 5.14.8; 7.30.2–3; 9.15.
[102] Plin. *Ep.* 2.5.6–8; 4.14.1–3; 7.4; 8.21.1–4; 9.29; Hindermann (2009).
[103] Plin. *Ep.* 3.5.9–18.   [104] Plin. *Ep.* 4.14.2; 7.4.8; 9.10.2; 9.36.1–2.
[105] In a poem Martial wrote about him (10.20), Pliny is shown reading easy literature at night, while during the day he works strictly and hard, cf. *Ep.* 3.21.5 *Seras tutior ibis ad lucernas:* . . . *Tunc me vel rigidi legant Catones* ('you will have more success if you go by the late lamplight . . . let then even stiff Catos read me').
[106] Plin. *Ep.* 3.5.7; 3.5.9; 3.20.10–12.

advocacy,[107] the Younger prides himself on being a case pleader and uses night work for preparation:

> Nihil, nisi quod meridianus somnus eximitur multumque de nocte vel ante vel post diem sumitur, et, si agendi necessitas instat, quae frequens hieme, non iam comoedo vel lyristae post cenam locus, sed illa, quae dictavi, identidem retractantur ac simul memoriae frequenti emendatione proficitur. (Plin. *Ep.* 9.40.2)

> Nothing but a nap is taken away and a large part of the night is added either before dawn or after sunset; and when an inevitable process is imminent, which often happens in winter, there is no place for an actor or lute player after dinner, but I rework again and again what I have dictated; and this frequent improvement also benefits my memory.

This last letter in the collection of nine books of letters emphasizes darkness and the dimming of light, a common literary device for closing a poem or a collection of poems.[108] It also can be read as the Younger's response to the preface of the *Naturalis Historia*. There the Elder explains that he works at night so that he is not accused of neglecting his duties. The Younger Pliny, on the other hand, prepares his work in court during the night, if necessary because of the great amount of work involved, and writes literary works during the day. In doing so, he attaches greater importance to literature in the context of creating his self-image in the *Epistles*.

Interestingly, a later admirer did not believe Pliny's own self-representation. Writing in the fifth century, Sidonius Apollinaris shows the Younger Pliny as the middle of five examples in which men write at night while their wives hold lamps for them and inspire and support them in their literary activities. The topos of the *lucubratio* seems to be a stronger and more long-lasting image than the filled working day that Pliny sketches as an alternative in his letters.[109]

7 Conclusion

As I have shown, the Younger Pliny tries to distinguish himself subtly from the Elder Pliny by developing some of his uncle's topics. By using material from his uncle's *Naturalis Historia*, Pliny shows the worth of his own work, which consists of the poeticized and literary transformation of scientific

---

[107] Plin. *Ep.* 3.5.7; Sherwin-White (1966) 219; Keeline (2018) 196.
[108] Cf. Marchesi (2008) 248–50; Gibson (2015) 189–91.　　[109] Sidon. *Ep.* 2.10.5.

material. As we have seen in the letters on natural phenomena discussed above, one elaborate example replaces scientific completeness and remains in the readers' mind because of its emotional value for Pliny and the addressee. While the *Naturalis Historia* offers a wide range of themes in thematic order, Pliny chooses individual topics for his letters. He enriches them with more details, adds personal experience as proof of the miracles, and shapes the letters according to the interest of the addressees. Whilst the Elder Pliny focuses on the wonders of the world, Pliny the Younger is particularly interested in the examples from Transpadana and his hometown of Comum with its traditional values. The Elder Pliny, a strict and conscientious man, is difficult to surpass as a role model. Both Plinii show a great work ethic and define themselves by the number of their writings. The Younger Pliny, however, develops his own attitude toward the relationship between *otium* and *negotium*, rejecting the topos of *lucubratio*. He shows himself writing literature and studying in daylight rather than at night like his uncle, thus giving his writings additional meaning as an honourable day's work.

PART III

Pliny and Seneca: Discourses of Grief and Posthumous Reputation

CHAPTER 7

Pliny's Seneca and the Intertextuality of Grief

Michael Hanaghan

1 Introduction

When Pliny came to write, organise and circulate his letters two major Latin literary predecessors loomed: Cicero, whose letters detail the political machinations of the last days of the Roman Republic and its aftermath, and Seneca, whose corpus is almost an exact antithesis of the former, with its apolitical and almost timeless content, and single, possibly imaginary, addressee, Lucilius.[1] Pliny understandably turned to Cicero's life and letters as his model when he looked to fashion himself as a successful politician, either by explicitly invoking the great Republican statesman or alluding to his work with varying degrees of subtlety.[2] Seneca's political career was problematic, to say the least, and so he is presented more exclusively as a philosophical model, as a thinker who had found the time and space to ruminate on the fundamental challenges of life. All three Latin letter writers expressed Stoic beliefs in their works, with varying degrees of frequency.[3]

At times Pliny appears to be Stoic, but at others Pliny distances himself from Stoic thought, rejecting its utility in the face of acute personal

---

[1] For Pliny's use of Cicero as a model in the letters see Gibson and Morello (2012) 74–103, who also note (75–6) the extreme paucity of references to Seneca and the total absence of any explicit reference to him as a letter writer in Pliny's collection. The apolitical tenor of Seneca's letters has been interpreted as a political survival strategy aimed at stressing his distance from the day-to-day intrigue of the Neronian court, for which see Murray (1965) 50 and Edwards (1997) 23–4, and for its near lack of temporality Hanaghan (2017c) 203–6. Poetic epistolary collections such as Ovid's exile poetry also exerted some influence on Pliny, for which see Gibson and Morello (2012) 259–63.
[2] See for example Morello (2003).
[3] The label Stoic is used for the authors in this study who may be considered more precisely as 'Roman Stoics' rather than strict adherents to the teachings of the Stoa. Seneca is most comfortably thought of as Stoic. Cicero's philosophy eludes any single label, but certainly exhibits Stoic features, for a detailed study of which see Colish (1990) 61–158, who earlier (4) notes the challenge of distinguishing between 'a Roman Stoic who wrote in Latin and a Latin author who was influenced by Stoicism.' Pliny's 'Stoicism' is opportunistic, as argued here.

suffering.[4] This chapter analyses how Pliny used the consolatory philosophy of Seneca by examining his allusions to two of Seneca's epistles (98 and 99) that treat death. It extends Tzounakas's analysis of the intertextual link between Pliny's *Ep.* 1.12 and Seneca's *Ep.* 85 by arguing that *Ep.* 98 also looms behind Corellius' decision to die.[5] Then it examines how Pliny's criticism of Regulus' display of grief following the death of his son (4.2) echoes Seneca's condemnation of improper mourning practice in *Ep.* 99. Regulus' portrayal in this epistle is set against Pliny's subsequent descriptions of Regulus in the collection, especially in *Ep.* 4.7. These allusions to Seneca's consolation letters show that Pliny knew and could use philosophical concepts to express his own grief or criticise others', but struggled to apply Stoic beliefs when he found this incompatible with the profound emotional upheaval of losing a close friend to suicide.

2 Corellius Rufus' Suicide

In AD 97 or 98 Corellius Rufus committed suicide. He had suffered from gout for decades, a disease which had no effective treatment in the ancient world and was consequently known for the chronic agony it inflicted on its sufferers.[6] His death hit Pliny hard.[7] They had been close friends; Pliny had trusted and valued his older friend's advice, but try as he might, Pliny had been unable to dissuade his friend from taking his final, fatal decision. Scholars have long noted the abundance of Stoic terms that Pliny uses in letter 1.12.[8] More recently, attention has turned to specific allusions, such as Tzounakas's convincing analysis of how Pliny alludes to Seneca's *Ep.* 85 in this letter, and Hindermann's comparison of Plinian and Ciceronian thought.[9]

At the end of the letter Pliny clearly indicates that he has tried to use consolation philosophy to overcome his grief (Plin. *Ep.* 1.12.12–13):

---

[4] Pliny's uncle, Pliny the Elder, held some Stoic beliefs, for mention of which see Wallace-Hadrill (1990) 84. Colish (1990) 334–5 outlines the limitations that must be taken into account in trying to label Pliny the Elder as a Stoic.

[5] Tzounakas (2011).

[6] For a general study of gout in antiquity see Porter and Rousseau (1998) 13–21, who note that the ancient diagnosis of gout embraced a range of modern ailments including arthritis and joint pain.

[7] This was due not only to their long standing friendship, but also Pliny's consideration of Corellius Rufus as an important mentor, for discussion of which see Fögen (2015) 26.

[8] Griffin (1986a) 66–7 noted 'philosophical overtones' in Pliny's description of Corellius Rufus' suicide and drew comparison between the circumstances of his death and Seneca's own; similar general engagement was perceived by Lefèvre (1989) 119, Hoffer (1999) 145 ff. and Méthy (2007) 200–3.

[9] Tzounakas (2011); Hindermann (2014).

> In summa dicam, quod recenti dolore contubernali meo Calvisio dixi: 'Vereor ne neglegentius vivam.' Proinde adhibe solacia mihi, non haec: '*Senex erat*, infirmus erat' – haec enim novi –, sed nova aliqua, sed magna, quae audierim numquam, legerim numquam. Nam quae audivi quae legi sponte succurrunt, sed tanto dolore superantur. Vale.

> In all I will say, what I said to my close fried Calvisius when my grief was fresh 'I'm afraid that I will live more indifferently now.' So send me some remarks to comfort me, but not that 'He was an old man, he was weak' — send me something new, something great, which I haven't already heard, which I haven't already read. Farewell.

Tzounakas is surely right to take this as an Alexandrian footnote of sorts, which gestures towards Cicero and Seneca. Two wordplays on Seneca's name promote him as the key source of Pliny's intertextual engagement in this letter.[10] The first is Pliny's decision to address the next epistle in the collection to Sosius Senecio which, as Gibson argues elsewhere in this volume, is typical of how Pliny highlights allusive play in a preceding epistle (Senecio standing in as almost Seneca). The second is Pliny's description to his addressee, Calestrius Tiro, of what he does not want to hear: *Senex erat* is nearly homonymic with *Seneca erat*, especially given the final 'a' in *Seneca* could be elided in spoken Latin.[11] Calestrius Tiro's imagined dialogue reads like a forensic indictment: 'It was Seneca.' The implication is that Corellius Rufus' Stoicism, derived from Seneca, empowered him to commit suicide, and so establishes an antagonistic relationship between Pliny's experience as described in the letter and Senecan philosophy. This antagonism is further evident in Pliny's request for Calestrius Tiro to send him new reading material, which amounts to a direct criticism of the consolation philosophy that Pliny already had access to – including Seneca's letters which he has liberally alluded to throughout the epistle – for its failure to alleviate Pliny's grief.[12] Reading has not

---

[10] In a circular way, both of these interpretations are supported by Pliny's sustained use of Seneca in this epistle.
[11] This reading is substantiated by the fact that the two reasons that Pliny cites as coming from Roman consolatory philosophy, age and physical weakness, are not used by Seneca to defend suicide. Tzounakas (2011) 353 argues that Calestrius Tiro's name is reminiscent of Cicero's secretary, Marcus Tullius Tiro, and so likely functions to highlight the Ciceronian allusions in this letter, for which see Hindermann (2014) 291–3.
[12] Pliny's detailed use of Seneca in this letter resonates with Seneca's suicidal exemplum. For the description of Seneca' death see Tacitus *Ann.* 15.60–4, and for a recent analysis Fögen (2015) 40–4.

helped him come to terms with his loss, nor did it help Corellius Rufus to live; all this philosophical reading has got them where they are.[13]

Pliny's critique of Stoic consolatory philosophy fundamentally rejects the Stoic premise that reading and understanding the principal tenets of Stoicism can prepare the Stoic practitioner for times of intense emotional stress and hardship. His knowledge of Stoicism (prior to Corellius Rufus' suicide) was likely derived from reading Stoic thought and his personal interaction with leading Roman Stoics, such as Musonius Rufus.[14] Thus Pliny's critique may be broadened to encompass not just Stoicism's failure to assist him in recovering from the suicide of a close friend, but its failure more broadly to act as the peremptory guard to suffering which its teachers regularly claimed it to be.

Corellius Rufus' suicide is a political act of sorts (Plin. *Ep.* 1.12.8):[15]

> Circumtulit oculos et 'Cur' inquit 'me putas hos tantos dolores tam diu sustinere? – ut scilicet isti latroni vel uno die supersim.' Dedisses huic *animo par corpus*, fecisset quod optabat. *Adfuit tamen* deus voto, cuius ille compos ut iam *securus liberque moriturus*, multa illa vitae sed minora retinacula abrupit.
>
> He [Corellius Rufus] looked around and said 'Why do you think I continue to put up with all this pain? – it's so I might outlive that robber [Domitian] if only by a single day.' If you could have given him a body equal to his mind, he would have achieved what he wanted. But a god attended to his wish and granted that he could now die untroubled and free, and so he broke off the many small bonds of life.

Stoicism held two criteria for suicide to take place: a valid reason and the right moment.[16] The former is Corellius Rufus' crippling gout;[17] the death of Domitian is the latter.[18] The direct speech implies that Corellius Rufus

---

[13] Pliny's description of Corellius Rufus' decision to die has broad parallels with the locus classicus of philosophical defences of suicide, Plato's *Phaedo*. Pl. *Phaed.* 62c states μὴ πρότερον αὑτὸν ἀποκτεινύναι δεῖν, πρὶν ἀνάγκην τινὰ θεὸς ἐπιπέμψῃ ('that a man must not kill himself until some god sends a necessity'). Pliny describes Corellius Rufus as being driven by *necessitas* and references the presence of a *deus* who enables him to act. A similar sentiment is expressed by Cicero *Tusc.* 1.74. Pliny further likens Corellius Rufus' death to the breaking of chains which resonates with Plato's earlier claim at *Phaed.* 62b ὡς ἔν τινι φρουρᾷ ἐσμεν οἱ ἄνθρωποι καὶ οὐ δεῖ δὴ ἑαυτὸν ἐκ ταύτης λύειν οὐδ' ἀποδιδράσκειν ('that we men are in a kind of prison and must not set ourselves free or run away'). For discussion of the Platonic and Ciceronian passages see respectively Griffin (1986a) 70–2 and Griffin (1986b) 195.

[14] Plin. *Ep.* 3.11.5.   [15] Borg (2014) 85–8; Fögen (2015) 26–7.

[16] *SVF* 3.757–68. For the two criteria see Griffin (1986a) 72.

[17] At *Dig.* 28.3.6.7, Ulpian is listed as allowing *valetudinis adversae impatientia* ('intolerance of ill health') as an acceptable reason for suicide.

[18] Hindermann (2014) 291 analyses Corellius Rufus' claim regarding the timing of his death.

died very shortly after Domitian, whom he was known (to a certain select few) to dislike, but Corellius was alive until at least the middle of AD 97.[19] It is difficult to ascertain whether this animosity stemmed from personal enmity between the former suffect consul (AD 78) and governor of Germania Superior, or from the possible curtailing of his career by Domitian. After his governorship, it seems that Corellius Rufus effected a Seneca-like withdrawal from politics, but the decision may not have been his to make.[20]

Pliny implies a contrast between the sentiments expressed by *adfuit tamen* and his hypothetical wish that Corellius continue to live; but Corellius' *corpus* was not equal to his *animus*. A god of some sorts allows him to die. The phrase *securus liberque moriturus* ('die untroubled and free') alludes to Seneca's letter 98 (Sen. *Ep.* 98.15–16):

> Sed *securus* de illo sum: de nostro damno agitur, quibus senex egregius eripitur. Nam ipse vitae plenus est, cui adici nihil desiderat sua causa sed eorum quibus *utilis* est. Liberaliter facit quod vivit. Alius iam hos cruciatus finisset: hic tam turpe putat mortem fugere quam ad mortem confugere. 'Quid ergo? non si suadebit res exibit?' Quidni exeat, si nemo iam uti eo poterit, si nihil aliud quam dolori operam dabit?
>
> But I am untroubled for him; the issue is our loss; an outstanding old man has been taken from us. For he was full of life; he desired nothing to be added to it for his own sake but for those to whom he was useful. By living he acted generously. Someone else might have already ended their suffering; but he thought it as bad to flee from death as to flee towards it. 'What does that mean? If the situation demands it, will he not depart?' Of course he should go, if no-one is able to make use of him, if he devotes all his effort to nothing but pain.

The precise context of this extract must be inferred as there is a lacuna in the text immediately prior; Seneca has clearly turned from discussing his general theme to the death of an old man. According to Seneca, pain should only be a factor in the decision to die if the patient is of no use (*utilis, uti*). His claim that he is unconcerned for his friend who has passed

---

[19] Plin. *Ep.* 7.31.4 and 9.13.6.
[20] Corellius Rufus is referred to as the governor of Germania Superior in *CIL* XVI 28 (*ILS* 1995). This inscription dates to 20 September AD 82. It is likely, as Eck (1982) 303 n. 83 notes, that this appointment followed shortly after Corellius Rufus' consulship. The next attested governor of the province was L. Antonius Saturninus, whom Eck (1982) 314 first lists as governor in 87. It is possible that someone else served between Corellius Rufus and Saturninus, or that Saturninus took over the post shortly after his suffect consulship in 82 or 83. An estimate of Corellius Rufus' term ending ca. 84 seems reasonable given terms of more than five years, such as Agricola's governorship of Britain from 77 to 85, were relatively rare.

away uses the same adjective (*securus*) as Pliny when he describes the circumstances of his friend's death. This on its own is hardly convincing (a single word would need to be very unusual to sustain an intertextual connection) even if the context encourages the intertext as *securus* is relatively common.[21] The end of Seneca's letter provides further evidence for reading Pliny's *securus liberque moriturus* as signposting this letter (Sen. *Ep.* 98.18):

> Quid opus est verbis? in rem praesentem eamus: nec mors illum contra dolorem facit fortiorem nec dolor contra mortem. Contra utrumque sibi fidit nec spe mortis patienter dolet nec taedio doloris *libenter moritur*: hunc fert, illam expectat. Vale.
>
> What's the use of words? Let's get to the point: death does not make us braver towards pain nor does pain towards death. He who trusts himself against both, neither suffers patiently in hope of death nor freely dies worn out by pain; he puts up with the pain, he awaits death. Farewell.

Seneca's description of the relationship between pain and the advent of death uses the phrase *libenter moritur*, which is closely paralleled by Pliny's *liberque moriturus*.[22] In Pliny's epistle, the phrase *securus liberque moriturus* is focalised through Corellius Rufus; it is his wish to die, his words or at least his sentiment. Such a desire is explicitly frowned upon by Seneca unless it is motivated by the avoidance of severe and chronic pain, and the sufferer is otherwise of no use to anyone. There is no doubt that Corellius was in chronic and severe pain – he had suffered from gout for some thirty-four years – but it seems Pliny disagreed with Corellius Rufus regarding his utility.[23] Once his higher purpose had passed, seeing out the end of a tyrant's rule, he had no reason to keep going. Pliny's allusion to Seneca's *Ep.* 98 speaks to the philosophical disagreement he had with Corellius Rufus over his decision to commit suicide despite the usefulness that he still offered to those dear to him. Pliny may well have come into contact with this philosophical argument through his interaction with Musonius Rufus, a prominent Stoic in Rome whom Pliny knew and admired despite

---

[21] Hinds (1998) 25 allows that the rarity of a word may offset the risk of accidental confluence. For the methodological challenges of reading allusions that rely on only one or two words see Hanaghan (2017b) 250–2.

[22] The adverb *libenter* explicitly encapsulates the notion of *libertas*. Cf. Sen. *Tro.* 49–50, where the death of Priam is described in Stoic terms for which see Boyle (1994) 141.

[23] Plin. *Ep.* 1.12.4 states that Corellius Rufus began to suffer from gout when he was thirty-three and 1.12.11 indicates that he was sixty-seven when he died.

their considerable age difference.[24] In a fragment of his extant work, Musonius Rufus states (fr. 29):

> Οὐκ ἔστιν ἐπὶ πολλῶν συμφέροντι ζῶντα καθηκόντως ἀποθανεῖν, μὴ ἐπὶ πλειόνων ἀποθνήσκοντα συμφέροντι.
>
> One who by living is of use to many has not the right to choose to die unless by dying he may be of use to more.[25]

Pliny makes no mention of any one person who found Corellius Rufus' death of use to them. This represents a higher standard than Seneca, who merely argued that the sufferer needed to be useless, not of more use dead than he was alive.[26] For Pliny, the fact that he had a wife, daughter and friends should have been enough. There were people who could have still made use of him.

3 Regulus the Bereaved

Seven epistles relate to Regulus, a *delator* of the worst kind.[27] In Book 2 of the collection, Pliny describes how Regulus tried to worm his way into the inheritance of three individuals. His antics include swearing on his son's life while trying to trick the elderly widow Verania into bequeathing her estate to him (Plin. *Ep.* 2.20.5–6):[28]

> Mox ingravescit, clamat moriens hominem nequam perfidum ac plus etiam quam periurum, qui sibi per salutem filii peierasset. Facit hoc Regulus non

---

[24] Plin. *Ep.* 3.11. For their relationship see Lutz (1947) 19.
[25] This fragment is Musonius' only statement on suicide. Two other fragments and a discourse on suicide were preserved by Stobaeus, but their authenticity has been disproven, for which see Lutz (1947) 6 n. 11. Musonius' most prominent student, Epictetus, claimed that he would rather die than follow Musonius' path and end up as an exile in Gyara (Arr. *Epict. diss.* 1.25.20–1): 'ἐν Γυάροις οἴκει.' οἰκῶ. ἀλλὰ πολύς μοι καπνὸς φαίνεται τὸ ἐν Γυάροις οἰκεῖν. ἀποχωρῶ, ὅπου μ' οὐδεὶς κωλύσει οἰκεῖν· ἐκείνη γὰρ ἡ οἴκησις παντὶ ἤνοικται. ('"Live on Gyara." Ok. But living in Gyara seems to me to be a load of smoke. I'm going to where no-one can stop me living, for that place lies open to all').
[26] Von Baumhauer (1842) 218 n. 5 notes some similarity between Senecan and Musonian thought, which is perhaps unsurprising given their other similarities (as prominent Stoic philosophers who were active under Nero), notwithstanding the generational gap between them as noted by Grilli (1992) 177. Laurenti (1989) 2121 specifically links the presence and relevancy of the theme of death in Musonius to the 'political-social reality' (*realtà politicosociale*) of the first-century AD and its philosophical tradition.
[27] Plin. *Ep.* 1.5; 1.20; 2.11; 2.20; 4.2; 4.7; 6.2; for a detailed analysis of which see Ash (2013). For Regulus' career see Sherwin-White (1966) 93–4. Martial presents a far more positive portrayal of Regulus in his epigrams (1.12; 1.82; 6.38), for which see Hoffer (1999) 59; Henderson (2001) 56–87; Marchesi (2013) 101–18, (2018) 351–63 and in this volume (Chapter 14).
[28] Verania was the wife of Lucius Calpurnius Piso Licinianus, who was killed in AD 69 on the same day as his adopted father Galba (for which see Tac. *Hist.* 1.43). For her family see Rogers (1931) 172–7.

> minus scelerate quam frequenter, quod iram deorum, quos ipse cotidie fallit, in caput infelicis pueri detestatur.

> Subsequently she grows worse and exclaims as she dies, 'What a rascal, what a lying and worse than perjured wretch, thus to have sworn falsely on the head of his son!' That is Regulus' trick, and he has recourse to the scandalous device constantly, for he calls down the anger of the gods, whom he daily outrages, upon the head of his luckless son.

These comments take on renewed significance for Regulus' portrayal after his son passes away. His actions are excessive, in keeping with how someone might react who felt responsible or partly culpable for their own son's passing. A key criticism of the epistle is how publicly Regulus mourns the passing of his son. This includes collecting all of his animals and immolating them on a pyre (Plin. *Ep.* 4.2.3–4):

> Amissum tamen luget insane. Habebat puer mannulos multos et iunctos et solutos, habebat canes maiores minoresque, habebat luscinias psittacos merulas: omnes Regulus circa rogum trucidavit. Nec dolor erat ille, sed *ostentatio doloris*.

> But now that his son has died, he has gone mad in his mourning. The boy used to have quite a few ponies, both broken in and not, dogs, both big and small, nightingales, parrots and blackbirds; Regulus slaughtered them all around the pyre. That wasn't grief, but the display of grief.

Pliny is unconvinced.[29] The phrase *ostentatio doloris* only occurs in prior extant texts in one of Seneca's letters (Sen. *Ep.* 99.16):[30]

> Nihil vero maerori adiciamus nec illum ad alienum augeamus exemplum. Plus *ostentatio doloris* exigit quam dolor: quotus quisque sibi tristis est? Clarius cum audiuntur gemunt, et taciti quietique dum secretum est, cum aliquos videre, in fletus novos excitantur; tunc capiti suo manus ingerunt (quod potuerant facere nullo prohibente liberius), tunc mortem comprecantur sibi, tunc lectulo devolvuntur: sine spectatore cessat dolor.

> Let us, indeed, add nothing to natural grief, nor augment it by following the example of others. The display of grief makes more demands than grief itself: how few men are sad in their own company! They lament the louder for being heard; persons who are reserved and silent when alone are stirred to new paroxysms of tears when they behold others near them! At such times they lay violent hands upon their own persons, – though they might

---

[29] Hindermann (2014) 295–300 offers a detailed analysis of Pliny's attitude towards Regulus' mourning.
[30] Hindermann (2014) 297 notes this specific verbal connection and links it to Seneca's negative use of *ostentatio* elsewhere in his corpus.

have done this more easily if no one were present to check them; at such times they pray for death; at such times they toss themselves from their couches. But their grief slackens with the departure of onlookers.

Seneca includes within his own letter an epistle he wrote to a friend whose son died. In that embedded epistle, he distinguishes between real grief and the display of grief (*ostentatio doloris*). The allusion is substantiated by the exact phrase and the shared experience of a father trying to overcome his grief at the passing of his son. Pliny uses the allusion to co-opt Seneca's philosophical condemnation of incorrect mourning to attack Regulus' bizarre behaviour as described in *Ep.* 4.2. Both texts characterise excessive grief as insane.[31] In Seneca, this point is directly used to criticise those who mourn excessively but fail to recall the deceased.

In *Ep.* 4.2, Pliny implies that Regulus has taken the opportunity of being attended to by society to put out feelers for a new wife (Plin. *Ep.* 4.2.6–7): *Dicit se velle ducere uxorem, hoc quoque sicut alia perverse. Audies brevi nuptias lugentis nuptias senis.* ('He says that he wants to take a wife, this, like his other behaviour, is totally bizarre. Soon you will hear about the nuptials of the bereaved, the nuptials of an old man.') The odd *iunctura* of *nuptias* and *lugentis* creates an awkward tone that is accentuated by the repetition of *nuptias*.

Seneca would not have approved of Regulus' behaviour at all. In *Ep.* 99, he quotes and then carefully rejects the argument of Epicurean philosopher Metrodorus that there is pleasure to be had in grief (Sen. *Ep.* 99.26):

> *Quid enim est turpius quam captare in ipso luctu voluptatem, immo per luctum, et inter lacrimas quoque quod iuvet quaerere?*
>
> For what is more distasteful than to search for pleasure in grief, even during the grieving process, and search through tears for some sort of pleasure.

Neither Seneca nor even Metrodorus envisaged that the source of pleasure might be anything more than fond memories of the deceased, and certainly not a new bride; but the sentiment nevertheless resonates with Regulus' perverse and opportunistic grieving for his son and the social event it has become.[32]

---

[31] Plin. *Ep.* 4.2.3 *insane*; Sen. *Ep.* 99.5 *furor*, 24 [*amor est*] *paene rabidus*. Graver (2007) 109–32 analyses this rhetoric in detail, at 111 she summarises: 'In Stoic usage ... the general-insanity claim has particular reference to the ordinary person's susceptibility to emotion.'

[32] For Seneca' rejection of Metrodorus' argument see Graver (2009) 248–9. Cf. Arr. *Epict. diss.* 1.11.31, where the cause of Achilles' grief over Patroclus' death is determined to be his desire to grieve. Plin. *Ep.* 8.16 notes the *dolendi voluptas* (joy of grieving) that presents when a friend offers solace during a bereavement, for which see Tzounakas (2011) 356.

By introducing Regulus' potential nuptials into an epistle that is otherwise devoted to a funeral, Pliny creates a grotesque inverse of the situation in *Ep.* 5.16, which laments the death of a young girl prior to her wedding.[33] In *Ep.* 4.2, the dead child is a boy, and it is the parent instead who blurs a funeral with the potential for a new spouse. In both epistles the conceit is jarring – tragically in *Ep.* 5.16 and bizarrely, irritatingly, offensively in *Ep.* 4.2.[34] Pliny's differing attitude to the death of the two children is highlighted by an allusion in *Ep.* 5.16 to the death of Corellius Rufus.[35] The young girl's fight to live ((*Ep.* 5.16.4) *destitutam corporis viribus vigore animi sustinebat* ('sapped of bodily strength, she kept herself alive by the vigour of her mind')), echoes Corellius' defiance in the face of acute pain ((1.12), *viribus animi sustinebat* ('he kept himself alive by the strength of his mind')). This intratextual allusion shows that Pliny admires those who put up a fight even as illness hampers them; but his admiration for Corellius is tempered through comparison to the girl; the former chose to die, whereas the latter died against her will.

The allusion to Seneca's arguments in *Ep.* 99 creates a link between them and Pliny's condemnation of Regulus' grief in *Ep.* 4.2. According to Seneca, the correct way of responding to a bereavement is to (Sen. *Ep.* 99.24) *meminisse perseveret, lugere desinat* ('continue to remember, cease to mourn'). Yet Regulus fails to heed Seneca's advice. The next letter which features Regulus puts his antics on full display (Plin. *Ep.* 4.7.1–2):

> Placuit ei lugere filium: luget ut nemo. Placuit statuas eius et imagines quam plurimas facere: hoc omnibus officinis agit, illum coloribus illum cera illum aere illum argento illum auro ebore marmore effingit. Ipse vero nuper adhibito ingenti auditorio librum de vita eius recitavit; de vita pueri, recitavit tamen. Eundem in exemplaria mille transcriptum per totam Italiam provinciasque dimisit.

---

[33] Plin. *Ep.* 5.16.4, 6 *Medicis obsequebatur, sororem patrem adhortabatur ipsamque se destitutam corporis viribus vigore animi sustinebat.* ... *O morte ipsa mortis tempus indignius! iam destinata erat egregio iuveni, iam electus nuptiarum dies, iam nos vocati.* ('She obeyed her doctor's orders, she cheered her sister and father, and when her body had lost all its strength, she kept herself alive by the vigour of her mind. ... Oh how the moment of her death was more unfair than death itself! For she had just been betrothed to a youth of splendid character; the day of the wedding had been decided upon, and we had already been invited.') The girl was Minicia Marcella. For discussion of this letter see Carlon (2009) 147–57.

[34] Gibson and Morello (2012) 41 note Pliny's 'lavish disgust' at Regulus' plans to remarry as an old man.

[35] Carlon (2009) 155 notes that the qualities of Minicia Marcella as she battles her illness, *temperantia, patientia* and *constantia*, recur in similar situations in other letters, including Corellius Rufus' battle with gout in *Ep.* 1.12.

Pliny's Seneca and the Intertextuality of Grief 159

It pleased him to mourn for his son – and no-one mourns like him; it pleased him to erect a number of statues and busts to his memory, and the result is that he is keeping all the workshops busy; he is having his boy represented in colours, in wax, in bronze, in silver, in gold, ivory and marble – always his boy. He himself just lately got together a large audience and read a memoir of his life – of the boy's life; he read it aloud, and still had a thousand copies written out which he has distributed to be broadcast all over Italy and the provinces.

Another jarring *iunctura* involving *lugere* is deployed as Pliny describes the unprecedented pleasure Regulus has in the process.[36] Regulus' attempts at memory-making are intricate; they include creating artwork and a poem, which was performed and distributed through the empire.[37] This could be considered broadly consistent with Seneca's assertion that the deceased should not be forgotten, but is clearly inconsistent with Seneca's claim that grieving should be done in private. Pliny stresses the size of the audience that attended the reading of the poem (*adhibito ingenti auditorio*).[38] Regulus' gathering of such a group directly contradicts Seneca's advice that mourning be done *sine spectatore* ('without observers').[39] Failure to do so risks only prolonging the mourning process. His advice not to grieve publicly is at least partially motivated by the compassionate desire to save the mourner from the inconsistent criticism of the mob.[40]

Spectators to the grieving process could prompt genuine sorrow, as the sight of other family members and close friends in mourning prompt an outpouring of emotion, or insincere grief, as the mourner plays up to the audience that has gathered. Seneca is only concerned with the latter eventuality. He details the kind of behaviour that invariably follows, including praying for death, beating chests and throwing oneself out of bed,[41] but also stipulates that that consolation is of little use in the initial stage of mourning when the force of nature can prompt tears to flow.[42]

---

[36] The first use of *placere* makes it clear to the reader that Pliny is using it to denote that Regulus gets some joy out of the process, and not simply to indicate that Regulus 'decided' to act the way he did.
[37] Ash (2013) 237–8.   [38] E.g *Ep.* 6.33, for which see Hanaghan (2018) 150–4.
[39] Sen. *Ep.* 99.16. As Graver (2009) 239 notes Seneca's criticism is reserved for grieving responses that are 'additions to the natural response' of crying and feeling inner pain.
[40] Sen. *Ep.* 99.17 [*populus*] *videt aliquem fortem in luctu suo, impium vocat et efferatum; videt aliquem conlabentem et corpori adfusum, effeminatum ait et enervem* ('The people see someone bravely grieving: they call him impious and savage; they see someone collapse and cling to the body: they call him effeminate and weak').
[41] Sen. *Ep.* 99.16.
[42] Seneca similarly stresses the difficulty in consoling someone when their grief is new in *Consolatio ad Helviam* 1.2 *dolori tuo, dum recens saeviret, sciebam occurrendum non esse ne illum ipsa solacia inritarent et accenderent* ('your pain, when it was violently fresh, I knew it could not be met lest the very attempts to console you irritated it and made it burn').

Comparison between Pliny's description of Fundanus' mourning of his daughter's death in *Ep.* 5.16 and Regulus' mourning of his son, highlights Pliny's mean-spirited approach to Regulus' grief. In both cases the mourner has lost a child and in both cases their mourning accentuates their grief. In *Ep.* 5.16, Pliny is highly sympathetic towards Fundanus' heartache, but is also, as Klodt has argued, somewhat critical, especially in the comparison that he draws between Fundanus' daughter stoically comforting her family and her father's subsequent grief.[43] So when Fundanus publicly redirects the funds for the wedding to the funerary costs, Pliny subtly acknowledges the Senecan principle that grieving leads to further pain, even as he asserts that such expressions of grief are warranted.[44] This gnomic ideal segues directly into Pliny's praise of Fundanus' education and knowledge of philosophy, which are completely powerless to assuage his grief given the severity of his loss.[45] Pliny's only sympathy for Regulus is reserved for the final letter in the cycle, *Ep.* 6.2, where there is no explicit mention of Regulus' bereavement.

Pliny's criticism of Regulus' grieving draws on his surprise at the large audience that he has attracted for what should be a private process; normally the big audiences in his epistolary collection are reserved for his court cases or important speeches.[46] Pliny claims to be concerned that Regulus may well set an example (*Ep.* 4.2.4):

> Convenitur ad eum mira celebritate. Cuncti detestantur oderunt, et quasi probent quasi diligant, cursant frequentant, utque breviter quod sentio enuntiem, in Regulo demerendo Regulum imitantur. ... in summa infamia gloriosus.

> It is strange how people are flocking to call upon him. Everyone detests and hates him, yet they run to visit him in shoals as though they both admired and loved him. To put in a nutshell what I mean, people who are paying court to Regulus are copying the example he set ... he is boastful towards even his greatest outrages.

The relationship between *imitatio* and *exemplum* is of direct concern to Seneca in *Ep.* 99, where he is at pains to point out that following the wrong examples may augment grief. Pliny's description, informed by his

---

[43] Klodt (2012) 23–61.
[44] Plin. *Ep.* 5.16.7 *ut multa luctuosa dolor invenit* ('grief leads to abundant sorrows'). Gnilka (1973) 110–12.
[45] Plin. *Ep.* 5.16.8.
[46] Johnson (2010) 48 contrasts Pliny's description of Regulus' large recital audience with Pliny's description at *Ep.* 5.3.10 of the intimate group of friends who gathered to hear Pliny recite his poetry.

use of that letter by Seneca, implies that the crowd which flocks to see Regulus is fuelling his display of grief. Pliny's frustration at Regulus' status as an exemplum is borne out by his concern that Regulus should really be an anti-exemplum, or at least, an exemplum of perverse actions inspired by his unflinching audacity; this sentiment he expressly indicates in *Ep.* 4.7.3–4 *perversa confirmat audacia. Exemplo est Regulus* ('audacity strengthens wrongs. Take Regulus as an example').[47] Regulus' *audacia* enhances his status as an anti-exemplum of correct Stoic behaviour.[48] Early practitioners of Stoicism maintained that no glory on earth should ever be coveted; by Pliny's period (and arguably earlier) Stoics had moved away from this kind of absolutist approach, but still registered concern as to how one might speak to achievements without coming across in such a self-aggrandising way.[49]

Pliny's criticism of Regulus is made all the harsher by his use of Seneca.[50] He refuses to give credit to Regulus' attempt to recall his son, which is, according to Seneca, the kind of action that is appropriate. In *Ep.* 4.2, he does this by suggesting that Regulus is trying to find a new wife; in 4.7, he specifically refutes the suitability of the artwork and poem. Regulus' excessive grief may well have been a product of the tremendous guilt he felt at swearing falsely on his son's life (as Pliny claims he did in *Ep.* 2.20). Pliny may not have been aware that he might come across as being harsh to Regulus when he wrote and circulated the epistles in Book 4. He may, however, have come upon this realisation prior to the composition and inclusion of the last epistle in the cycle, *Ep.* 6.2, by which time Regulus was dead. That letter is a lot kinder in tone towards Regulus, an outlier which softens the entire Regulus cycle, and in so doing goes some way towards softening Pliny's lack of compassion for Regulus' bereavement.[51] This is not to undo Regulus' role in the letters; his antics put Pliny's positive exemplum in stark relief.

---

[47] Plin. *Ep.* 4.7.3–4. For an overview of exemplarity in Pliny's *Letters* see Bradley (2010) 391–7.
[48] A more proper mode of grieving a child may be found in Tac. *Agr.* 29, where Agricola avoids displaying his grief with the kind of ostentation that is so common for brave men.
[49] This rhetoric included acts of suicide as Griffin (1986a) 68 notes 'charges of ostentation and glory-chasing ... were common ones levelled by the unsympathetic at Stoic adherents. Suicide was one occasion when these qualities would be particularly apparent.'
[50] Ash (2013) 208 examines why Pliny may have not published the letters in Book 4 until after Regulus' death (ca. AD 105), despite Pliny's stringent criticism of him in that book.
[51] For discussion of the relationship of *Ep.* 6.2 to the remainder of the Regulus cycle see Ash (2013) 229–30.

4 Conclusion

Pliny's understanding of the correct way to mourn is influenced by his knowledge of Stoic thought, conveyed through his reading of Seneca, and his interaction with leading Roman Stoic philosophers of the mid to late first-century AD, including Musonius Rufus. This understanding did not make it easier for Pliny to come to terms with the suicide of his close friend, Corellius Rufus, but it did help Pliny sharpen his criticism of Regulus' ostentatious grieving over his own son's death.

Both Seneca and Musonius Rufus considered the utility of the sufferer an important factor in determining the suitability of suicide. Seneca's standard was lower than Musonius'; if the sufferer of chronic and debilitating pain was of no-use to anyone, then he was better off dead. Musonius' argument is difficult to assess in its totality, given that only a single extant fragment discusses suicide, but this fragment at least clearly stipulates that the sufferer must be of *more* use to others when dead than he was when alive. Utility is central to the philosophical disagreement Pliny had with Corellius Rufus; according to Pliny, Corellius' own benefit from death – being free from the earthly prison of pain – was outweighed by his ongoing usefulness to those around him, including his family and friends.

Regulus' mourning egregiously contravened established Stoic modes of grief, but it is difficult to divorce Pliny's philosophical condemnation of Regulus from their intense political rivalry; the former is certainly reflected in the latter, given that both Nero and Domitian viewed Stoics as a political threat, it makes sense that a *delator* like Regulus would have avoided Stoic thought. Still, one would expect Regulus not to have been completely ignorant of the right way of doing things, including mourning his own son. Conversely, Pliny's use of Stoic thought to criticise Regulus' mourning may also be read politically, as a way of identifying himself with the Stoic political opposition, and so go some way towards covering up the career successes Pliny enjoyed under Domitian.

Pliny's approach to the genre of consolation is informed by his quotidian interaction with friends and adversaries. His contribution to consolation literature is therefore directly tied into the reality of experience; polished ideals may still be found, either when Pliny criticises Regulus, or when he reminds his readers that grief can overwhelm even those who are well versed in Stoicism. Consequently, Pliny is not religious about his use and application of Stoic principles, adhering to them strictly in *Ep.* 4.7, but sidelining them in *Ep.* 1.12 and 5.16. Such a hypocritical application of Stoic views prompts the question as to whether his rejection of consolatory philosophy in *Ep.* 1.12 should be taken as a temporary rejection of Stoic thought, as the recent passing of his friend has left Pliny in Seneca's raw period of grief (where nature forces emotional pain and inhibits the rational process), or as an example that speaks to his complete rejection of the Stoic claim that Stoicism equips the sufferer with the tools to manage periods of intense person suffering. This dichotomy arises from the expectation that Pliny needed to be consistent in his application of Stoic beliefs, but where one might be notionally Stoic, the real test was pragmatic. According to Epictetus the perfect Stoic did not exist (Arr. *Epict. diss.* 2.19.24–5):

> δείξατέ μοί τινα νοσοῦντα καὶ εὐτυχοῦντα, κινδυνεύοντα καὶ εὐτυχοῦντα ... δείξατ' ἐπιθυμῶ τινα νὴ τοὺς θεοὺς ἰδεῖν Στωικόν. ἀλλ' οὐκ ἔχετε τὸν τετυπωμένον δεῖξαι· τόν γε τυπούμενον δείξατε, τὸν ἐπὶ ταῦτα κεκλικότα.

> Show me someone who is sick and happy, who is in danger and happy ... show this man to me, by the gods I would love to see a Stoic. But you cannot show me a man so formed, so show me someone being moulded, someone inclining towards it.

Epictetus' repetition of τυπόω builds on the analogy of a statue which introduces these remarks.[52] The statue is considered Pheidian as it is fashioned κατὰ τὴν τέχνην (*kata ten technen*, 'according to the skill') of Pheidias just as the philosopher is termed Stoic if they are fashioned κατὰ τὰ δόγματα (*kata ta dogmata*, 'according to the teaching') of Stoicism. Pliny may therefore be considered a Stoic; though under the limitations outlined by Epictetus: no-one can be a Stoic all the time, but they can try.

---

[52] Arr. *Epict. diss.* 2.19.24–5.

CHAPTER 8

Intertextuality and Posthumous Reputation in Pliny's Letter on the Death of Silius Italicus (Plin. Ep. 3.7)*

Spyridon Tzounakas

1 Introduction

Pliny's obituary of the epic poet Silius Italicus (Plin. *Ep.* 3.7) is one of his most famous letters in his epistolary corpus and has affected Silius' reputation for many centuries.[1] This is a peculiar letter, consisting of two distinct parts, which, at first glance, are not related to each other.[2] Such an arrangement is contrary to Pliny's usual practice.[3] In the first part, Pliny refers to Silius' illness, his manner of death, his damaged reputation stemming from political connections to Nero, and his writings and everyday life. The second part of the letter is devoted to the shortness of human life and the need for prolonging our passing moments by writing works of literature. This chapter argues that the two parts of the letter work harmoniously together, purposefully creating a depiction of Silius which is far from positive. Pliny artfully achieves this result by using a series of apposite intertextual allusions drawn from a variety of sources,[4] including from Seneca's *Dialogi* and *Epistles*. He thus absorbs elements of their philosophical discourses and adroitly incorporates them into his epistolary

---

* I am grateful to Roy Gibson, Jakub Pigoń, Margot Neger and Michael Hanaghan for their invaluable comments and suggestions on a previous version of this chapter.
[1] Cf. e.g. Matier (1981); Matier (1988); Matier (1989); Dominik (2010). For Pliny's critical stance towards Silius and the latter as a negative exemplar in Book 3, see Johnson (2010) 40–1; Gibson and Morello (2012) 123–6; cf. also Cova (1966) 67; Trisoglio (1972) 102–3; Aubrion (1975) 107; Gagliardi (1990); Ludolph (1997) 78–9 with n. 249; Wolff (2003) 86; Méthy (2007) 384; Strunk (2012) 187–90; Winsbury (2014) 179.
[2] Cf. Lefèvre (2009) 142.
[3] On Pliny's tendency to confine his letters to a single topic, see e.g. Sherwin-White (1966) 3–4, with a list of exceptions, and Gibson and Morello (2012) 1–2, who note that 'the truth of this observation can be overplayed' (1).
[4] As is natural, allusions to Silius Italicus' *Punica* are expected in a letter that is written on the occasion of his death and therefore they are out of the scope of my study. For cases of intertextual connections between Plin. *Ep.* 3.7 and Silius' *Punica*, see Henderson (2002b) 109–13 and more recently Stoffel (2017).

corpus. At the same time, Pliny's aim is further supported by intratextual links with other letters in the collection.

In *Ep.* 3.7, Pliny deals with discourses that frequently appear in philosophical treatises, such as: the theme of death; the power of literature to bestow immortality; the shortness of human life; the correct use of time. It is thus no surprise that philosophical elements dominate the second part of this letter. As is well known and as is re-affirmed in this volume, in Books 1–9 of his *Epistles*, Pliny follows the principle of *varietas* and demonstrates his ability to flirt with various literary genres without violating the *lex* of his own genre. The case of philosophy is not an exception. In this chapter, I show that Pliny exhibits a deep knowledge of philosophical texts, but that he utilises it for his ulterior literary and communicative purposes in an opportunistic manner.[5] In *Ep.* 3.7, which is an indicative case of the way in which Pliny engages with philosophical topics, he evokes philosophy in order to urge his readers to judge Silius against the background of philosophical criteria and see him in a negative light; but at the same time Pliny does not fully identify himself with the philosophical traditions he evokes. Consequently, the aim of this chapter is not to suggest that Pliny is philosophising in *Ep.* 3.7, rather it argues that Pliny mines Seneca's *Dialogi* and other relevant texts in order to pass negative comments about Silius and reflect on the dubious nature of posthumous reputation (itself a prominent and recurrent theme throughout the *Epistles*).

Elsewhere, I have argued that 'in his work Pliny often appears to be familiar with philosophical matters or arguments, which was of course the norm amongst educated Romans of his day, without, however, having to adopt a particular philosophical school. Many times the philosophical tone of an epistle should be connected to literary aims and be attributed either to the addressee, or to the person who is the subject of the epistle and the matter in question'.[6] All these parameters seem to justify Pliny's philosophical tone in *Ep.* 3.7. Moreover, it should not be forgotten that, along with Cicero, Seneca is one of Pliny's most significant predecessors in prose epistolography. Consequently, since Seneca's *Epistulae ad Lucilium* focuses on philosophical matters, intertextual dialogue with Seneca will inevitably include engagement with the philosophical themes that he treated. Additionally, it is worth noting that, as Whitton has remarked, Pliny

---

[5] Cf. Hanaghan's contribution, Chapter 7, in this volume.
[6] Tzounakas (2011) 347. On the influence of philosophy on Pliny's *Epistles*, see also André (1975); André (1979); Krasser (1993c); Hoffer (1999) 119–59; Griffin (2007); Guérin (2012–13); Blake (2018); Malaspina (2019); cf. also the bibliography regarding Seneca's influence on Pliny cited in n. 17.

'presents at every turn a model life in the fragmentary self-portrait that is the *Epistles*. This may be no Senecan course in Stoicism; but as an exemplary guide to ethics, a practical demonstration of life lived, these letters too could aspire to the title *Epistulae morales*'.[7] Given the particular character of Pliny's *Epistles*, in many cases a philosophical tone and allusions to other philosophical texts are to be expected.

In this chapter, building upon Henderson's suggestion, who argues persuasively for a Senecan influence on Plin. *Ep.* 3.7,[8] I investigate further allusions to Seneca's *Dialogi* (and especially to his *De Brevitate Vitae*) in this letter. These allusions allow Pliny to enter into a philosophical dialogue and implicitly facilitate his intention to besmirch Silius' posthumous reputation. As we shall see in due course, the letter writer has good reasons to do so, since Silius was Pliny's rival for the title of Cicero's heir. In this framework, apart from associating Silius with the Neronian period and implying suspect political connections, Pliny urges his readers to judge Silius' personality through the lens of Stoicism: they are asked to realise an inconsistency between Silius' un-Stoic way of life and the Stoic tone of his epic or his decision to starve himself to death (which implies commitment to Stoicism).[9] However, though Pliny frequently alludes to Seneca's *Dialogi* and employs terms that point to almost all the titles of the essays in that particular collection (thus absorbing Seneca's Stoicism within his letter), at the same time Pliny differentiates himself from the Stoic philosopher by rejecting some of his central ideas, e.g. his idea that human life is not short. An intertextual allusion to Cicero's *Epistulae ad Familiares* through the use of the Greek word φιλόκαλος (*philokalos*, 'loving the beautiful') indicates Pliny's intention to go further, since it implicitly associates Silius with Epicureanism and connects him with the *sectores* ('purchasers at a public sale of confiscated goods') during the Sullan proscriptions. Apart from philosophy, in this letter Pliny also absorbs elements from Greek didactic poetry. The citation of Hesiod's famous phrase ἀγαθὴ δ' ἔρις (*agathe d' eris*, 'rivalry is good') could be seen as another apposite choice, since it helps Pliny to protect himself from possible accusations of mistreating Silius' image. Finally, valuable

---

[7] Whitton (2013a) 9–10.   [8] Henderson (2002b) 118–22.
[9] Of course, the Stoics did not have a 'monopoly' here. For example, Atticus the Epicurean also starved himself to death (for Nepos' description of his death, see recently Schubert 2015). For various philosophical schools' attitudes towards suicide, see Van Hooff (1990) esp. 181–97. On Silius' commitment to Stoicism and the Stoic colour of his *Punica*, see e.g. D'Agostino (1962) 71; Sherwin-White (1966) 227; Vessey (1974) 109, 115; Billerbeck (1985); Danesi Marioni (1989); Matier (1990); Rocca-Serra (1990); Lefèvre (2009) 143; Dominik (2010) 429–30; Fögen (2015) 31.

conclusions could be drawn if we consider *Ep.* 3.7, addressed to Caninius Rufus, alongside other letters addressed to the same person (*Ep.* 1.3 and 2.8, see also Canobbio, Chapter 9, in this volume). By composing *Ep.* 3.7 in a way that recalls the content and the diction of these earlier letters to Caninius (which also contain allusions to Seneca's *Dialogi*), Pliny ensures that, while reading the obituary of Silius, both Caninius and the general reader will remember these letters. This intratextual link accentuates the negative insinuations against Silius.

2 Seneca's Presence in *Ep.* 3.7

Pliny delivers the news of Silius Italicus' death rather coldly, revealing nothing concerning his own emotional connection to the event: *Modo nuntiatus est Silius Italicus in Neapolitano suo inedia finisse vitam. Causa mortis valetudo*, 'It has recently been announced that Silius Italicus has committed suicide by starvation in his villa at Naples. His reason for dying was his illness' (Plin. *Ep.* 3.7.1–2).[10] At this point it is worth juxtaposing this delivery with the manner in which Martial's death is announced (*Audio Valerium Martialem decessisse et moleste fero*, 'I hear that Valerius Martial has died, and I find it sad news' (Plin. *Ep.* 3.21.1)), where, despite any implicit comments against the epigrammatist that underlie the epistle,[11] Pliny nevertheless still expresses his sorrow at the news of Martial's death.[12] Silius' decision to commit suicide by refusing to eat as a result of his incurable disease[13] (combined with Pliny's choice of vocabulary, which points to the Stoic school of thought, e.g. the phrase *inrevocabili constantia*, 'resolute determination')[14] has, with good reason, been interpreted by many scholars as suggestive of Silius' adoption of the Stoic

[10] For the Latin text and the translation of Pliny's *Epistles*, I follow Mynors (1963) and Walsh (2006) respectively; for the translation of Seneca's *De Tranquillitate Animi*, *De Brevitate Vitae* and *Epistulae ad Lucilium*, I follow Fantham (2014), Williams (2014) and Gummere (1917–25) respectively.
[11] Tzounakas (2014); cf. Marchesi (2013) and Neger (2015b).
[12] Cf. D'Agostino (1962) 70, who also compares the announcement of Silius' death to that of Corellius Rufus' in *Ep.* 1.12; Fögen (2015) 30–2. According to Strunk (2012) 187–90, *Ep.* 3.7 indicates Pliny's pessimism towards contemporary society, and especially towards contemporary political life.
[13] On Pliny's stance towards the particular way of death, see e.g. Galimberti Biffino (2015) 180; Stucchi (2015) 183–4; cf. also the similar way in which Corellius Rufus is presented as having ended his life at Plin. *Ep.* 1.12.9 *Iam dies alter tertius quartus: abstinebat cibo*, 'A second and a third and a fourth day came while he declined to eat'. For Corellius Rufus' Stoic orientation, see Tzounakas (2011) 346–7.
[14] Cf. Vessey (1974) 109; McDermott and Orentzel (1977) 26; Griffin (2007) 462; Lefèvre (2009) 143. However, the term *constantia* also appears in the description of Atticus' suicide at Nep. *Att.* 22.1 *tanta constantia vocis atque vultus*, 'with such steadiness of voice and expression'.

dogma.[15] Many facts relating to Silius' life as described in the epistle, however, imply that, even if Silius had in theory espoused Stoicism at the point of death, he did not espouse its deeper principles in life. This contradiction is artfully highlighted by Pliny. Thus he composes the epistle using elements drawn from Stoicism so that his readers may judge the epic poet within a Stoic context; Pliny achieves this by including allusions to the philosophical work of Seneca, the emblematic figure of Roman Stoicism. At the same time, Seneca's presence in this letter creates a parallel between Silius and the Stoic philosopher, who was also accused of inconsistency between the Stoic principles he espoused and his way of life. This analogy is further reinforced by broader parallels between Seneca and Silius: both writers were wealthy, withdrew from politics, were connected to Nero and put an end to their lives by committing suicide.[16]

That Seneca is one of the Latin writers with whom Pliny is frequently in intertextual dialogue has already been noted by a number of scholars.[17] In fact, elements pointing to Seneca's presence in Pliny's *Ep.* 3.7 have already been noted by Henderson (2002b: 118–22): inter alia, he offers a political interpretation arguing for Pliny's intention to reinforce the connection between Silius and Nero[18] through allusions to the principal writer of the Neronian period. In particular, Henderson underlines that '"Seneca" is the name we should be hearing, between every last line. I am sure that Pliny studied Seneca's great *oeuvre* more than dutifully. Specifically, these stand-out *Letters* of Book 3 whisper "Seneca" in our ears rather loudly' (118). Through this framework, he demonstrates links between Pliny's portraits in Book 3 (that of Spurinna in *Ep.* 3.1, Pliny the Elder in *Ep.* 3.5 and Silius Italicus in *Ep.* 3.7) with Seneca's moral essays *De Vita Beata, De Otio, De Tranquillitate Animi* and *De Brevitate Vitae*.

With specific regard to *Ep.* 3.7, Henderson mentions several interesting cases: the story of Xerxes' tears – due to the loss of many thousands of soldiers in so short a time (Plin. *Ep.* 3.7.13) – is inspired by Sen. *Brev.* 17.2.[19] Pliny's reference to the shortness of the longest of human lives –

---

[15] See above, n. 9.
[16] For Seneca' suicide at Tac. *Ann.* 15.60–4, see Fögen (2015) 40–4; cf. also Hanaghan, Chapter 7, in this volume, who notes that Seneca's presence in Pliny's description of Corellius Rufus' suicide (*Ep.* 1.12) 'resonates with Seneca's suicidal exemplum'.
[17] See e.g. Cova (1997); Griffin (2000); Marchesi (2008) 14–20, 234–6; Tzounakas (2011); Gibson and Morello (2012) esp. 101–3, 170–80, 303; Canobbio (2017); Trinacty (2020); see also Hanaghan, Chapter 7, in this volume.
[18] For the evocation of Nero in this letter, see also Devillers (2015b) 67–8.
[19] Henderson (2002b) 117–18, 121. The example of Xerxes' tears that dominates in the second part of Pliny's letter is first told by Herodotus (7.45) and also occurs in Valerius Maximus (9.13.*ext*.1);

(*Quid enim tam circumcisum tam **breve** quam hominis **vita** longissima?*, 'What is so confined and short as even the longest life of man?' (Plin. *Ep.* 3.7.11); see also *Tam angustis terminis tantae multitudinis vivacitas ipsa concluditur*, 'Within such narrow limits is the lifespan of such a huge number confined' (Plin. *Ep.* 3.7.13)) – points to Seneca's essay *De Brevitate Vitae*.[20] Pliny's reference to the calmness of Silius' life at Plin. *Ep.* 3.7.9 – *In hac **tranquillitate** annum quintum et septuagensimum excessit*, 'He enjoyed this peaceful existence beyond his seventy-fifth year' – points to Seneca's essay *De Tranquillitate Animi*.[21] The reference to Campania at Plin. *Ep.* 3.7.6 – *Novissime ita suadentibus annis ab urbe secessit, seque in **Campania** tenuit*, 'Most recently, at the prompting of his years, he retired from Rome and settled in Campania' – corresponds to Sen. *Tranq.* 2.13 '*Nunc **Campaniam** petamus.' Iam delicata fastidio sunt,* '"Let's make for Campania now." Soon they are sated with fancy resorts'.[22] Finally, he links Plin. *Ep.* 3.7 to Sen. *Tranq.* 9.4–7, *Brev.* 10.1 and 12.1–2.[23]

I suggest that indications of Pliny's attempt to link this letter with Seneca's *Dialogi* go further. The title of Seneca's essay *De Constantia Sapientis* is recalled by Pliny's words at *Ep.* 3.7.2 *ad mortem inrevocabili **constantia** decucurrit*, 'caused him to hasten his death with resolute determination' and *Ep.* 3.7.3 *in Vitelli amicitia **sapienter** se et comiter gesserat*, 'after becoming a friend of Vitellius he had conducted himself in a prudent and genial way'. The title of Seneca's essay *De Otio*, it can be reasonably suggested, is recalled by *Ep.* 3.7.3 *maculam veteris industriae laudabili **otio** abluerat*, 'He had erased the stain of his former busy activity in praiseworthy leisure'. The phrase *usque ad supremum diem **beatus** et felix*, 'Until the day of his death his life was happy and successful' at *Ep.* 3.7.2 reminds us of the title of Seneca's essay *De Vita Beata*. Pliny's focus on the fact that Silius lost the younger of his two sons brings to mind the case of Seneca's *Consolationes*, especially his *Consolatio ad Marciam*. Similarly, Pliny's reference at *Ep.* 3.7.12 to L. Calpurnius Piso, consul in AD 27, which does not seem to be easily integrated in its context, can be understood as a reference to Seneca's *De Ira*, since in that essay (*De Ira*

---

see also Whitton, Chapter 1, in this volume. For the history of this motif, see Borzsák (1966), who thinks that Pliny may have followed a rhetorical text and cites Sen. *Suas.* 2.3, the latter sharing with Pliny the notion of *fragilitas humana*, also in connection with Xerxes. On the example of Xerxes in relation with other examples of historical figures of the past in Pliny's *Epistles*, see Méthy (2003); cf. also Méthy (2007) 218–20.

[20] Henderson (2002b) 118, 119.   [21] Henderson (2002b) 119.   [22] Henderson (2002b) 119.
[23] Henderson (2002b) 119–21.

1.18.3–6) the philosopher cites the example of that Piso's father (Gnaeus Calpurnius Piso). Thus, almost all the essays that constitute Seneca's *Dialogi* are skilfully recalled in Pliny's letter.

In my view, this is not just a cluster of references but a principle followed by Pliny since this is not the only instance in which he refers allusively to the titles of the works of others.[24] Moreover, by evoking Senecan titles, the letter seems to have the character of an epistolary library containing a section on philosophical literature; see also similar virtual libraries in Martial 14.183–96 or Book 10 of Quintilian's *Institutio Oratoria*. Maybe here one should think of the books in Silius' library (cf. *Ep.* 3.7.8 *multum ubique librorum*, 'in every place he had many books'); although Silius possessed copies of Seneca's essays, he did not manage to live up to the instructions of Stoicism – the books served rather as decoration. One might also think of Sen. *Ep.* 2.3–4 *Distringit* **librorum multitudo**. *Itaque cum legere non possis quantum habueris, satis est habere quantum legas*, 'And in reading of many books is distraction. Accordingly, since you cannot read all the books which you may possess, it is enough to possess only as many books as you can read'. This connection amounts to an additional negative insinuation against Silius.

Further verbal echoes reinforce even more the intertextual relation between the two writers. Pliny's reference to human frailty at *Ep.* 3.7.10 – *Quod me* **recordantem fragilitatis** *humanae miseratio subit*, 'As I recall this, I am struck with pity for the frailty of the human condition' – suggests that he has taken into account Seneca's observation at *Brev.* 3.4 *numquam vobis* **fragilitas** *vestra succurrit*, 'your own human frailty never enters your head' (cf. also Sen. *Brev.* 10.2 *Hoc amittunt occupati; nec enim illis vacat praeterita respicere, et si vacet, iniucunda est paenitendae rei* **recordatio**, 'Preoccupied people lose this part; for they have no leisure to look back at the past, and even if they had it, there's no pleasure in recalling something regrettable', where Seneca's *recordatio* corresponds to Pliny's choice of the word *recordantem*).[25] It is tempting to suggest that

---

[24] Cf. e.g. the allusion to Horace's *Satires* or *Sermones* through the word *sermonibus* at *Ep.* 1.9.5 (see Tamás, Chapter 11, in this volume) or the allusion to Lucretius' *De Rerum Natura* through the phrase *rerum natura* at *Ep.* 5.6.7 (see Chinn, Chapter 10, in this volume).
[25] Another passage of Seneca that is close to Pliny is Sen. *Ep.* 15.11 *oblitus fragilitatis humanae congeram?*, 'Shall I heap up my winnings, and forget that man's lot is unsubstantial?'. Interestingly, *fragilitas humana* is more often coupled with a verbal form relating to memory/oblivion. On the other hand, Pliny's *Ep.* 3.7.10 may be inspired by his uncle's lament on *fragilitas humana* at *HN* 7.44.

recordantem could also serve as a metaliterary comment on Pliny's intertextual engagement with Seneca.

Pliny's *Ep.* 3.7.13 (*Tam **angustis** terminis tantae multitudinis vivacitas ipsa concluditur*, 'Within such narrow limits is the lifespan of such a huge number confined') recalls Seneca's *Brev.* 14.1 (*si magnitudine animi egredi humanae inbecillitatis **angustias** libet, multum per quod spatiemur temporis est*, 'if we want to transcend the narrow limitations of human weakness by our expansiveness of mind, there is a great span of time for us to range over'). Both passages underline the narrow limits of human life and weakness; it is worth noting that in both cases the words *angustis* and *angustias* are contrasted with the words *multitudinis* and *magnitudine* respectively. At the same time, it would be reasonable to assume that *tam angustis terminis* also implies the brevity of the letter which, through intertextual allusions, manages to encompass and condense the larger work of Senecan philosophy.[26]

Another interesting case is that of Plin. *Ep.* 3.7.14 *Sed tanto magis hoc, quidquid est **temporis** futilis et **caduci**, si non datur factis ... certe studiis proferamus*, 'But if it is not granted to us to expend our fragile and fleeting days on famous deeds ... let us all the more devote it at least to writing'. Here the phrase *temporis futilis et caduci* corresponds to the phrase *exiguo et caduco temporis transitu* at Sen. *Brev.* 14.2 (*Cum rerum natura in consortium omnis aevi patiatur incedere, quidni ab hoc exiguo et **caduco temporis** transitu in illa toto nos demus animo quae inmensa, quae aeterna sunt, quae cum melioribus communia?*, 'Since nature allows us shared possession of any age, why not turn from this short and fleeting passage of time and give ourselves over completely to the past, which is measureless and eternal and shared with our betters?'). Both passages mention the fleeting time of the present and imply the notion of the timelessness of studies. Furthermore, the implicit contrast between 'really' living (*vixit*) and merely existing (*fuit*) that immediately follows in Pliny's text (*quatenus nobis denegatur diu vivere, relinquamus aliquid, quo nos vixisse testemur*, 'in so far as a long life is denied to us, let us bequeath something to attest that we have lived') corresponds to what is explicitly stated at Sen. *Brev.* 7.10 *Non est itaque quod quemquam propter canos aut rugas putes diu vixisse: non ille diu vixit sed diu fuit*, 'So there's no reason to believe that someone has lived long

---

[26] Cf. a similar metapoetic strategy in Mart. 14.190 on Livy: *Pellibus exiguis artatur Livius ingens | quem mea non totum bibliotheca capit*, 'Vast Livy, for whom complete my library does not have room, is compressed in tiny skins' (trans. Shackleton Bailey, Loeb).

because he has gray hair and wrinkles: he's not lived long but long existed'.[27] This is arguably Pliny's source of inspiration here.

3 Silius the Fake Stoic?

Having enriched his letter with multiple allusions to Seneca's *Dialogi* and especially to *De Brevitate Vitae*,[28] Pliny implicitly urges his readers to interpret Silius' life within a Senecan framework. In this way, the epistolographer passes on negative comments about the epic poet without having to assume direct responsibility for them. Thus, while he gives the impression that he presents a fair depiction of him, in fact, details of Silius' life, as presented in this letter, appear to be compatible with the traits of a person who could be the target of a Stoic philosopher's attack (according to Seneca's work). As a result, Silius' commitment to Stoicism is undermined and he appears as a man who spends his time in a manner inconsistent with Stoic principles. Let us examine some characteristic examples.

By establishing a strong intertextual link with Seneca's *De Brevitate Vitae*, Pliny's comment that Silius' body was delicate rather than feeble (**delicato** *magis corpore quam infirmo*, 'being frail rather than feeble in body' (*Ep.* 3.7.9)) allows the reader to connect Silius to the *delicati* described in Seneca's essay, especially at *Brev.* 12.6–7; here it is stated that they could not be considered as leisured (*Ne illos quidem inter otiosos numeraverim qui **sella** se et **lectica** huc et illuc ferunt*, 'Nor would I count among the leisured those who have themselves carried around in a sedan chair and litter' (*Brev.* 12.6)) and their excessive sloth is highlighted (*usque eo nimio **delicati** animi languore solvuntur ut per se scire non possint an esuriant*, 'they are so enervated by the excessive sloth of a pampered mind that they can't tell by themselves if they are hungry' (*Brev.* 12.6)). Given that in Seneca's description special emphasis is placed on the fact that the *delicati* liked to be set down in a sedan chair and be carried on a litter, Pliny's statement that Silius used to spend many hours on his couch in his room acquires greater importance and proves to be less innocuous than it may first appear (*multumque in **lectulo** iacens*, 'for much of the time he lay on his couch' (Plin. *Ep.* 3.7.4)). Thus, it is implied that this habit of Silius must be attributed not to his weak body, but to his desire for *deliciae* and

---

[27] On this contrast at Sen. *Brev.* 7.10, see Williams (2003) 164. For the same view, cf. also *Brev.* 2.2 '*exigua pars est vitae qua vivimus.' Ceterum quidem omne spatium non vita sed tempus est*, '"Scant is the part of life in which we live." All the rest of existence is not living but merely time'.

[28] On prose intertextuality and the textual small hints on which it depends, see Whitton (2018) and Whitton (2019).

that, according to Seneca's criteria, he cannot therefore be included in the circle of the *otiosi*: Silius seems *vitam et consuetudinem humanam dediscere*, 'to have unlearned life and normal human practice' (*Brev.* 12.7), to use Seneca's own words.

Similar comments could be made about Pliny's references (*Ep.* 3.7.8) to Silius' interest in collecting works of art, purchasing numerous country residences[29] and owning many books, statues and portraits:

> Erat φιλόκαλος usque ad emacitatis reprehensionem. Plures isdem in locis villas possidebat, adamatisque novis priores neglegebat. Multum ubique librorum, multum statuarum, multum imaginum, quas non habebat modo, verum etiam venerabatur, Vergili ante omnes, cuius natalem religiosius quam suum celebrabat, Neapoli maxime, ubi monimentum eius adire ut templum solebat.[30]

> He was *un connaisseur*, to the point of being criticised for his mania for buying. He owned a number of villas in the same region; he would fall in love with his new purchases, and neglect the former ones. In every place he had many books, many statues, and many busts. He not merely possessed but also revered them, especially those of Vergil, whose birthday he would celebrate with greater devotion than his own, and above all at Naples, where he used to visit Vergil's tomb as if it were a shrine.

Apart from Sen. *Tranq.* 9.4–7, where the collection of books, works of art and portraits is eloquently criticised as a vain display of wealth, such practices are also negatively remarked upon in various passages of *De Brevitate Vitae*, where they are presented as examples of the poor management of free time: see also e.g. *Brev.* 10.4, where, amongst others, avarice and the squandering of money are criticised; 12.2, where it is stated that country retreat and withdrawal do not ensure leisure (*otium*), while the collection of highly prized vessels and statues is called *furor* and is regarded as *desidiosa occupatio*, 'idle preoccupation';[31] or 13, where the preoccupation with pointless literary problems is reproached. Thus, the Senecan parallels skilfully overturn any positive impressions concerning Silius one

---

[29] Thus Silius shows a lack of *constantia*, which is in contrast to the manner of his death. Besides, in Silius' stance towards the works of art there may be an implied contrast with Pliny: cf. the letter immediately preceding, featuring a statue which Pliny bought *non ut haberem domi ... verum ut in patria nostra celebri loco ponerem*, 'not to keep it at home ... but to have it set in some populous place in my native region' (*Ep.* 3.6.4). For Pliny's views towards collection of works of arts and his criticism of *luxuria*, see also Rocchi, Chapter 5, in this volume.

[30] For Silius as an enthusiastic collector, cf. also Mart. 6.64.10 *perpetui ... scrinia Sili*, 'the boxes of the immortal Silius' and see Vessey (1974) 115.

[31] For Seneca's hostility to collections of antiques in this passage, see Williams (2003) 189, who also cites Sen. *Tranq.* 9.6 and *Helv.* 11.3.

could have obtained from Pliny's references to the epic poet's interest in works of art: they imply that the latter represents an example of how one can fail to achieve *otium* according to Stoic thought.

Negative implications are also evident if we read Pliny's comment at *Ep.* 3.7.4 *salutabatur **colebatur***, 'People paid early morning visits to him, and cultivated him' in connection with Seneca's essay. The fact that Silius spent his time with many guests in his room is something Seneca would have frowned upon, especially if we take into account his words at *Brev.* 7.2 *Omnia istorum tempora excute, aspice ... quam diu colant, quam diu **colantur***, 'Scrutinise every moment of such people's lives, and note how much time they spend on ... cultivating others or being cultivated by others'. Here the visits we receive are considered to be a form of time wasting. Compare also *Brev.* 2.4 and 7.6, where the hordes of the clients are seen to be wasting our time and note the possible allusion to the particular institution of *clientela* through the use of the word *salutabatur* in Pliny's epistle.

4 Silius' and Pliny's Personae

Though Pliny appears to be exploiting Seneca's *Dialogi* and especially the essay *De Brevitate Vitae* to convey negative implications for Silius' image (i.e. to present him as representing an erroneous life model and to highlight the inconsistency between the Stoic manner of his death and the rest of his life), this does not mean that Pliny attempts to identify with Seneca. This Pliny makes clear at *Ep.* 3.7.10–11:

> Quod me recordantem fragilitatis humanae miseratio subit. Quid enim tam circumcisum tam breve quam hominis vita longissima?
>
> As I recall this, I am struck with pity for the frailty of the human condition. What is so confined and short as even the longest life of man?

Here Pliny appears to be overcome by sorrow at the thought of the *fragilitas humana* and to believe that even a long life is brief – a stance contrary to Seneca's central idea, namely that our life is not short, but lengthy.[32] One reason why Pliny might want to differentiate himself from Seneca is his intention to safeguard for himself the image of *humanus*

---

[32] Cf. e.g. ***Satis longa vita*** *et in maximarum rerum consummationem large data est, si tota bene conlocaretur*, 'Life is long enough, and it's been given to us in generous measure for accomplishing the greatest things, if the whole of it is well invested' (*Brev.* 1.3); ***non accipimus brevem vitam*** *sed facimus nec inopes eius sed prodigi sumus*, 'the life we are given isn't short but we make it so; we're not ill provided but we are wasteful of life' (*Brev.* 1.4); ***vita, si uti scias, longa est***, 'life, if you know how to use it, is long' (*Brev.* 2.1).

Intertextuality & Posthumous Reputation 175

which he carefully constructs across the entirety of his work.[33] This image would be jeopardised if he fully adopted a strictly Stoic philosophical approach. Another reason might have something to do with the promotion of his own image with the help of intertextual allusions again to the work of Seneca himself. The Stoic philosopher has taken care to highlight that the view that life is brief is shared not only by the ignorant masses, but also by *clari viri*[34] and learned thinkers, such as Hippocrates,[35] Aristotle[36] and the *maximus poetarum*,[37] as we can read at *Brev.* 1.1–2 and 2.2. By adopting the view that life is brief and having made it clear that he does not belong to the foolish masses, Pliny implicitly urges his readers to make the connection between him and the *clari viri* who hold the same view, thus claiming for himself the adjective *clarus*.

Pliny's intention to convey negative intimations concerning Silius' image in a seemly and discreet manner seems to be facilitated by the possibility of an intertextual dialogue with a letter from C. Cassius Longinus to Cicero (Cic. *Fam.* 15.19). The Greek[38] word φιλόκαλος (*philokalos*, 'loving the beautiful') chosen by Pliny to describe Silius' interest in collecting works of art (*Ep.* 3.7.8 *Erat* φιλόκαλος *usque ad emacitatis reprehensionem*, 'He was *un connaisseur*, to the point of being criticised for his mania for buying') is only found once before in earlier Latin literature[39] in a letter of Cassius. Here elements of Epicurean philosophy are discussed (Cic. *Fam.* 15.19.2–3): Epicurean ἡδονή (*hedone*, 'pleasure') is strictly associated with living καλῶς καὶ δικαίως (*kalos kai dikaios*, 'rightly and justly') as well as with the notion of virtue. Moreover, in the same passage, P. Sulla is criticised for acting as a purchaser at auctions of confiscated

---

[33] More generally for Pliny's attempt to associate himself with the notion of *humanitas* in his *Epistles*, see e.g. Rieks (1967) 225–53; Bütler (1970) 107–18; Cova (1978) 107–13; Aubrion (1989) 345–52; Méthy (2007) passim; Tzounakas (2011) 354–6; Malaspina (2019) 136–7.
[34] *Nec huic publico, ut opinantur, malo turba tantum et inprudens vulgus ingemuit: clarorum quoque virorum hic adfectus querellas evocavit*, 'And it's not just the masses and the unthinking crowd that complain at what they perceive as this universal evil; the same feeling draws complaints even from men of distinction' (Sen. *Brev.* 1.1–2).
[35] For this view (ὁ βίος βραχύς, ἡ δὲ τέχνη μακρή, 'life is short, art is long' (4.458 Littré)) of Hippocrates of Cos, the *maximus medicorum* according to Seneca, see Williams (2003) 119–20.
[36] In all probability, Seneca attributes to Aristotle a saying that belongs to Theophrastus. For possible reasons behind this 'mistake', see Williams (2003) 120 with the relevant bibliography.
[37] For the much-disputed identity of the poet mentioned here and the various suggestions, see Williams (2003) 125–6 and more recently Setaioli (2016).
[38] For the use of Greek in Pliny's *Epistles*, see Deane (1918); Venini (1952).
[39] Cf. the use of the antonym ἀφιλόκαλον at Plin. *Ep.* 2.3.8 Ἀφιλόκαλον *inlitteratum iners ac paene etiam turpe est, non putare tanti cognitionem qua nulla est iucundior, nulla pulchrior, nulla denique humanior*, 'To fail to regard as worthwhile an acquaintance which is as pleasant, charming, and civilised as can be, is an attitude which is *malappris*, uneducated, sluggish, and virtually degrading', a word first here and in Plut. *Quaest. Conu.* 672e, according to Whitton (2013a) 99.

goods (*sector*), while his indifference to the philosophical good (*bonum*) is underlined. Since Pliny undoubtedly knew Cicero's correspondence and the word φιλόκαλος is found nowhere else, the possibility of an intentional allusion to the particular passage is very strong. In this way, Pliny attributes to Silius Epicurean characteristics[40] and slyly casts a negative light on the latter's mania of buying works of arts.

Although at Cic. *Fam.* 15.19.3:

> itaque et Pansa, qui ἡδονὴν sequitur, virtutem retinet et **ii qui a vobis φιλήδονοι vocantur sunt φιλόκαλοι** et φιλοδίκαιοι omnisque virtutes et colunt et retinent

> Thus it is that Pansa, whose goal is Pleasure, retains Virtue; and those whom you and your friends call Pleasure-lovers are Good-lovers and Justice-lovers, practising and retaining all the virtues (trans. Shackleton Bailey, Loeb)

the word φιλόκαλοι has positive overtones, its identification with the word φιλήδονοι (*philedonoi*, 'fond of pleasure') could be artfully exploited by Pliny in the framework of his general intention to besmirch Silius' image. Thus he associates him with the notion of ἡδονή, which is compatible with other traits of Silius' image illuminated by Pliny (cf. e.g. the references to the fact that for much of the time Silius lay on his couch at *Ep.* 3.7.4, to his enthusiasm for new villas and works of art at *Ep.* 3.7.8, or to his delicate body at *Ep.* 3.7.9). Moreover, what is more interesting here are the words that immediately follow in Cassius' letter:

> itaque Sulla, cuius iudicium probare debemus, cum dissentire philosophos videret, non quaesiit quid bonum esset <s>ed omnia bona **coemit**

> And so Sulla (whose judgement we must respect) saw that the philosophers were at loggerheads: instead of trying to discover *what* was good, he went and bought up all the goods he could find! (trans. Shackleton Bailey, Loeb)

In this passage P. Sulla is castigated for his stance towards the philosophers, as he '"did not seek for what was the highest good, but bought up all goods" – a sharp hit at Sulla's disgracefully expensive purchase of the goods of proscribed Pompeians', according to Tyrrell and Purser (1918) 553, who also underline 'the ill-fame which attached to the purchasers of

---

[40] In my view, Pliny's aim to attribute Silius Epicurean characteristics is also facilitated by the phrase *usque ad supremum diem beatus et felix*, 'Until the day of his death his life was happy and successful' (*Ep.* 3.7.2). As Dupraz (2020) demonstrated, this phrase constitutes an allusion to Epicurus (cf. Cic. *Fin.* 2.96; Diog. Laert. 10.22).

confiscated goods (*sectores*) during the Sullan proscriptions'. By alluding to this passage through the Greek word φιλόκαλος, Pliny implicitly links Silius' *emacitas* (cf. *coemit* at Cic. *Fam.* 15.19.3) and his interest in works of art with the *sectores* of the past and once again reminds his readers of Silius' role under Nero's reign.

The second instance of the use of Greek in the epistle is when Pliny, at the end of the text (*Ep.* 3.7.15), urges the recipient to dedicate himself to *studia* and create, through them, something that will survive the ravages of time:

> Scio te stimulis non egere: me tamen tui caritas evocat, ut currentem quoque instigem, sicut tu soles me. Ἀγαθὴ δ' ἔρις cum invicem se mutuis exhortationibus amici ad amorem immortalitatis exacuunt.[41]

> I know that you do not lack the spur, but none the less my regard for you summons me to urge on even a galloping horse, as you likewise often urge me. *La lutte, c'est bonne*, when friends spur on each other by mutual exhortation to embrace the love of immortality.

The Greek phrase Ἀγαθὴ δ' ἔρις (*agathe d'eris*, 'rivalry is good') is taken from Hesiod (*Op.* 24),[42] specifically the famous passage in which the Greek didactic poet refers to the emulation and envy which develops between those practising the same craft (20–6) and considers this competition to be a positive factor for social progress:

> ἥ τε καὶ ἀπάλαμόν περ ὁμῶς ἐπὶ ἔργον ἔγειρεν·
> εἰς ἕτερον γάρ τίς τε ἴδεν ἔργοιο χατίζων
> πλούσιον, ὃς σπεύδει μὲν ἀρόμεναι ἠδὲ φυτεύειν
> οἶκόν τ' εὖ θέσθαι, ζηλοῖ δέ τε γείτονα γείτων
> εἰς ἄφενος σπεύδοντ'· ἀγαθὴ δ' Ἔρις ἥδε βροτοῖσιν.
> καὶ κεραμεὺς κεραμεῖ κοτέει καὶ τέκτονι τέκτων,
> καὶ πτωχὸς πτωχῷ φθονέει καὶ ἀοιδὸς ἀοιδῷ.

> She stirs up even the shiftless to toil; for a man grows eager to work when he considers his neighbour, a rich man who hastens to plough and plant and put his house in good order; and neighbour vies with his neighbour as he hurries after wealth. This Strife is wholesome for men. And potter is angry with potter, and craftsman with craftsman, and beggar is jealous of beggar, and minstrel of minstrel. (trans. Evelyn-White)

---

[41] On Pliny's melancholic tone at the end of this letter, see Guillemin (1929) 15.
[42] Maybe by quoting from a Greek source at the end of the letter Pliny imitates a Senecan strategy: in *Ep.* 1–30, Seneca often quotes from Epicurus, although in Latin. For a general comprehensive treatment of the citations in Pliny's *Epistles*, see Méthy (2004) and more recently Schwerdtner (2015).

Recalling Hesiod's relevant passage, Pliny succeeds in placing the mutual encouragement for *amor immortalitatis* between himself and Caninius Rufus (the addressee of the letter) within the greater framework of good sportsmanship between fellow artists. Thus he implies that he is inspired by this very principle, which according to Hesiod (*Op.* 11–13) is the kind of competition which deserves praise:

> Οὐκ ἄρα μοῦνον ἔην Ἐρίδων γένος, ἀλλ' ἐπὶ γαῖαν
> εἰσὶ δύω· τὴν μέν κεν **ἐπαινήσειε** νοήσας,
> ἡ δ' ἐπιμωμητή· διὰ δ' ἄνδιχα θυμὸν ἔχουσιν.

> So, after all, there was not one kind of Strife alone, but all over the earth there are two. As for the one, a man would praise her when he came to understand her; but the other is blameworthy: and they are wholly different in nature. (trans. Evelyn-White).

The intertextual allusion to Hesiod has additional implications. By endorsing Hesiod's view that a certain degree of competition between fellow artists is innocent and praiseworthy, Pliny facilitates not only the better reception of his encouragement by Caninius Rufus, but also the more positive interpretation of his own stance towards Silius Italicus. In other words, he implicitly urges the reader to read his remarks about the epic poet through the prism of healthy competition between fellow artists and not as a spiteful act through which Pliny would undermine his own positive image. Such criticism is presented as predictable and constructive in similar instances and thus Pliny should not be criticised for it.

There are good reasons for Pliny to treat Silius as a fellow artist and to feel he is in competition with him. As is well known, Pliny invests heavily in his own image as an orator, and in his *Epistles* he often promotes his victories in court.[43] It is worth noting that in the last letter of his third book, which functions as a *sphragis*, he cites the second half of an epigram concerning himself by Martial (3.21.5), in which, amongst others, the writer compares Pliny with Cicero:[44]

> Totos dat tetricae dies Minervae,
> dum centum studet auribus virorum
> hoc, quod saecula posterique possint
> Arpinis quoque comparare chartis.

> He devotes all his days to stern Minerva,
> While for the ears of the court of Centumviri

---

[43] See e.g. Tzounakas (2015) 207 with n. 1.
[44] For a rich bibliography on Pliny and Cicero, see Tzounakas (2015) 207 n. 2.

> He works away at what men of later ages
> Can compare even with Arpinum's pages.

A similar comment, however, is made by Martial concerning Silius in epigram 11.48, where he draws a connection between Silius and Cicero as well as Vergil:

> Silius haec magni celebrat monimenta Maronis,
>   Iugera facundi qui Ciceronis habet.
> Heredem dominumque sui tumulive larisve
>   Non alium mallet nec Maro nec Cicero.[45]

> Silius, who possesses the acres of eloquent Cicero, honours this monument of great Maro. No other heir and proprietor of his tomb or dwelling would either Maro or Cicero choose. (trans. Shackleton Bailey, Loeb)

As both Pliny and Silius are competing for the part of *alter Cicero* for their rhetorical activity,[46] the former appears to be discrediting the latter's image, hoping, perhaps, to claim the part exclusively for himself. Thus, it is probably no coincidence that in his obituary Pliny makes no reference whatsoever to Silius' rhetorical prowess; the only explicit remark he makes to the latter's literary activity is exclusively in connection to his poetic work: *Scribebat carmina maiore cura quam ingenio*, 'He composed poetry with greater diligence than genius' (*Ep.* 3.7.5).[47] The emphasis Pliny lays on connecting Silius exclusively to poetry is also evident, albeit less explicitly, later on in the epistle, when at *Ep.* 3.7.8 Silius' adoration of Vergil is highlighted – including the fact that Silius celebrated Vergil's birthday with greater reverence than his own and would visit his grave as though it were a temple:

---

[45] Cf. also *Sacra coturnati non attigit ante Maronis, | Implevit magni quam Ciceronis opus: | Hunc miratur adhuc centum gravis hasta virorum, | Hunc loquitur grato plurimus ore cliens*, 'He did not put his hand to buskined Maro's mysteries before he filled the measure of great Cicero's work. The solemn spear of the Hundred Men still wonders at him, and a host of clients speak of him with gratitude' (Mart. 7.63.5–8) (trans. Shackleton Bailey, Loeb). On Martial's identification of Silius as a new Cicero and a new Vergil, see e.g. Vessey (1974) esp. 111–14. For the social dimension of such gestures of epigonality, see Pausch (2004) 62–3.

[46] Cf. McDermott and Orentzel (1977) 32; Henderson (2002b) 117; Gibson and Morello (2012) 124 n. 67.

[47] In fact, negative criticism is not wholly absent from his brief reference to Silius here, as he notes that the latter's poetry is marked more by *cura* than *ingenium*. It is a statement which implies lack of talent and should be linked to Pliny's remarks about both Martial, who is called *ingeniosus* (*Ep.* 3.21.1), and Pliny the Elder, who is thought to combine *cura* and *ingenium* skilfully (*Ep.* 3.5.3), while it could also be linked to the programmatic statement made by Pliny himself with regard to his epistles, referred to as *paulo curatius*, 'composed with some care' at *Ep.* 1.1.1; see Tzounakas (2007) 44; Gibson and Morello (2012) 125–6; cf. Lefèvre (2009) 142.

> Multum ubique librorum, multum statuarum, multum imaginum, quas non habebat modo, verum etiam venerabatur, Vergili ante omnes, cuius natalem religiosius quam suum celebrabat, Neapoli maxime, ubi monimentum eius adire ut templum solebat.
>
> In every place he had many books, many statues, and many busts. He not merely possessed but also revered them, especially those of Vergil, whose birthday he would celebrate with greater devotion than his own, and above all at Naples, where he used to visit Vergil's tomb as if it were a shrine.

The particular reference throws Silius' literary interest of Vergilian epic into sharp relief and reinforces the insinuation as to the absence of *ingenium* and presence of excessive *cura*, as well as highlighting Silius' extreme devotion to Vergil. Pliny, however, refrains from mentioning the fact that Silius also owned Cicero's estate, as disclosed by Martial, so as to avoid linking him with Rome's leading orator. This interesting exclusion of Silius' role as a new Cicero, as praised by Martial in epigrams 7.63 and 11.48, could be interpreted according to the concept of 'alter-textuality' as suggested in Marchesi's contribution in this volume: parallel texts that are mutually exclusive and mutually indifferent. Pliny probably knew Martial's epigrams on Silius, but he tries to make us forget about Silius' *imitatio Ciceronis*.

Pliny's attempt to mar Silius' image as an orator could also be implied in Pliny's mention of the fact that Silius damaged his reputation during Nero's time, as it was believed that he acted as an informer, at *Ep.* 3.7.3 *Laeserat famam suam* **sub Nerone** *(credebatur sponte* **accusasse***)*, 'Silius had besmirched his reputation under Nero (for it was believed that he voluntarily turned informer)'. This comment not only casts aspersions on Silius' morals and reputation, but connects him to the *delatores* and their rhetoric, whose typical representative in Pliny's work is Regulus. The very phrase which is used to describe the latter (*quos ille* **sub Nerone accusaverat**, 'Regulus had laid accusations against them in Nero's day' (Plin. *Ep.* 1.5.3)) is strongly reminiscent of the words Pliny uses here in connection to Silius. This rhetoric is very different from that found in the time of *res publica*, which Pliny is yearning for and with which he is attempting to associate himself. Thus, it is skilfully implied that Silius could not be rightfully considered to be Cicero's heir. The particular aim seems to be further facilitated by Pliny's statement that Silius did not incur odium at *Ep.* 3.7.4 *Fuit inter principes civitatis sine potentia, sine invidia*, 'He became one of the most prominent figures in the state, but without exercising power or incurring odium'. Since *invidia* was a prominent motif in Cicero's works, where it appears as an inevitable part of public life,[48] Pliny's remark at *Ep.* 3.7.4 could be interpreted as another implicit attempt to dissociate Silius from Cicero.

Finally, useful conclusions can also be drawn from the dialogue which seems to develop between this letter and other epistles which are also addressed to Caninius Rufus[49] – a practice favoured by Pliny, skilfully connecting epistles addressed to the same recipient.[50] Just as in *Ep.* 3.7, so in *Ep.* 1.3 and 2.8 – to keep within the boundaries of the preceding texts – the topic of *studia* enjoys a central position.[51] Furthermore, in both these epistles, as in the case of the one referring to Silius' death, we find the themes of the retreat into the country and the correct use of *otium*; Seneca's presence is again strong.[52] In this way Pliny has ensured that he presents his views effectively so that both Caninius and his readers will judge Silius accordingly.

Let us focus on an indicative example. At *Ep.* 1.3.2 (*Si possident*, **felix beatusque** *es; si minus, 'unus ex multis'*, 'If they are claiming you, what a lucky and blessed soul you are! If not, you are "one of a crowd"') Pliny states that the amenities of Comum can make Caninius Rufus lucky and blessed, as they can facilitate his devotion to *studia* and contribute to the creation of a work that will be timeless. The only other instance in the entirety of Pliny's epistolary corpus in which these two adjectives occur in conjunction with one another is at *Ep.* 3.7.2:

> Erat illi natus insanabilis clavus, cuius taedio ad mortem irrevocabili constantia decucurrit usque ad supremum diem **beatus et felix**, nisi quod

---

[48] See Morello (2007) 179–80, who notes (179) that *invidia* 'is a prominent motif in Cicero's letters; indeed the negotiation of *inuidia* was one of the principal challenges of Cicero's public life as we see it represented in his letters (and even in his philosophical and oratorical works)'. For a good examination of the occurrences of *invidia* in Pliny's collection, see Morello (2007) 179–89, who builds on Hoffer (1999) 137.

[49] According to Henderson (2002b) 105, Caninius Rufus, the addressee of *Ep.* 1.3, 2.8, 3.7, 6.21, 7.18, 8.4, 9.33 and perhaps 7.25, appears as 'an *alter ego* who will make the perfect reader for *all* the *Letters*'. For an excellent consideration of Pliny's relationship with Caninius Rufus, see recently Carlon (2018). For his important role in the whole collection, see further Whitton (2013a) 137–8, who also notes that *Ep.* 1.3 is a 'partner' letter to *Ep.* 2.8, and cf. Stevens (2009) 173–8. For the connection between *Ep.* 1.3 and *Ep.* 3.7, cf. Méthy (2007) 405–6. For the cycle of letters addressed to Caninius Rufus, see also Egelhaaf-Gaiser (2002) 130 ff.; Pausch (2004) 69 with n. 102, 123 with n. 410; Canobbio, Chapter 9, in this volume.

[50] On this practice in Pliny's *Epistles*, see Pausch (2004) 69; Marchesi (2008) 16–27; cf. also Gibson and Morello (2012) 136–68.

[51] For the programmatic role of *Ep.* 1.3, which deals with the importance of *studia*, see e.g. Ludolph (1997) esp. 91–8, 121–32; Hoffer (1999) 29–44.

[52] See Gibson and Morello (2012) 181–2, 184–5, who read *Ep.* 1.3 and 2.8 in relation with the Senecan tradition of *otium*; Whitton (2013a) 140, who meticulously investigates cases of Seneca's influence (especially from his *De Tranquillitate Animi*) on Plin. *Ep.* 2.8.

> minorem ex liberis duobus amisit, sed maiorem melioremque florentem atque etiam consularem reliquit.

> He had developed an incurable tumour, and the weariness it induced caused him to hasten his death with resolute determination. Until the day of his death his life was happy and successful, except that he lost the younger of his two children. However, his elder son, the better of the two, is doing well and has in fact attained the consulship.

Reading this passage, however, in the light of the earlier use of the adjectives *felix beatusque*, the image of Silius' happiness is subtly undermined. Pliny connects real happiness with *otium* and *secessus*, 'away from the demands of life, with peaceful time for studies'.[53] Although Silius had the opportunity to follow this scheme and achieve real happiness (cf. *maculam veteris industriae laudabili **otio** abluerat*, 'He had erased the stain of his former busy activity in praiseworthy leisure' (*Ep.* 3.7.3); *Novissime ita suadentibus annis ab urbe **secessit**, seque in Campania tenuit*, 'Most recently, at the prompting of his years, he retired from Rome and settled in Campania' (*Ep.* 3.7.6)), it is implied that he did not use his *otium* in the correct way that Pliny wishes Caninius to adopt. The comparison of the two men, Silius and Caninius, prompts the reader to consider who is truly *felix beatusque*. Furthermore, Silius' *otium* in Campania, as mentioned in Pliny's obituary, can be read against the background of a passage in Silius' own work, the *Punica*. In Book 11, we read that Hannibal and his army, after their victory in the Battle of Cannae, spent the winter in Capua where they indulged in the amenities of the place. As a consequence of their *otium*, they lost their energy and strength and thus enabled the Romans to prevail during the rest of the war.[54] For the reader familiar with Silius' epos (and the historical tradition), the *otium* in Campania mentioned in Pliny's letter might arouse suspicions regarding the debilitating effects which this *otium* could have had on Silius Italicus.[55]

Moreover, there could be a possible connection between Silius and Servilius Vatia who is mentioned in Seneca's letter 55. Here, like Silius, Seneca is carried in a litter when he visits sights in Campania, but the philosopher believes that such luxuries are unnatural and have condemned people to weakness (*Ep.* 55.1–2). (See especially § 3 regarding Vatia's villa:

---

[53] Carlon (2018) 58.   [54] Cf. Liv. 23.18.10–16; Sen. *Ep.* 51.7.
[55] See Stoffel (2017) 379 who points to the parallel between Hannibal's and Silius' physical condition (*languentia* | *membra* (*Pun.* 11.418–19); *delicato magis corpore quam infirmo* (*Ep.* 3.7.9)); also Martial in epigram 4.14 to Silius plays with the background of *Punica* 11; see Neger (2012) 301–4; Neger (2019) 93–7. Campania, especially Baiae, was notorious for its luxury and dangerous effects on people's morals; see Stärk (1995).

In hac ille praetorius dives, nulla alia re quam otio notus, **consenuit** *et ob hoc unum* **felix** *habebatur*, 'So this was the place where that famous praetorian millionaire passed his old age! He was famed for nothing else than his life of leisure, and he was regarded as lucky only for that reason'.) The letter is also playing with the language of epitaphs (§ 4): *Vatia hic situs est*, 'Here lies Vatia!'. The second part of the letter contains a description of Vatia's villa which is reminiscent of Plin. *Ep.* 1.3 (cf. Sen. *Ep.* 55.6 *platanona ... euripi modo*, 'a grove of plane trees ... like a canal' and *quid platanon opacissimus, quid euripus*, 'that grove of plane trees with their abundant shade, that watercourse' (Plin. *Ep.* 1.3.1)). See also § 9 about the physical meeting with friends (in Campania): *praesentia enim nos* **delicatos** *facit*, 'For the presence of friends makes us fastidious'.

5 Conclusion

The main theme of *Ep.* 3.7 is *amor immortalitatis*. Pliny and Caninius are spurred on by it and they may reasonably hope to achieve *immortalitas*. As is implied, however, this is not the case for Silius, whose death ends everything. Significantly, when Pliny speaks about Silius' *fama* or *gloria*, he connects these concepts with episodes from his life, not his literary activity. But under an emperor, it is impossible to prolong one's life in this way.

Evaluating this obituary letter, we could conclude that it is an elaborate text, full of allusions that help Pliny incorporate other genres and achieve his purposes at multiple levels. Thus he appears as a well read person, dedicated to *studia*, and capable of making sound judgements of other men of letters.[56] At the same time, through intertextuality Pliny implicitly besmirches Silius' image and artfully facilitates his self-promotion in a way that protects him from the risk of appearing malignant and arrogant.

Of course, *Ep.* 3.7 is not the only letter in which Pliny evokes philosophical discourses. In many other cases (cf. e.g. *Ep.* 1.12, 7.26, 8.9, 8.19) it is evident that he had some philosophical education; moreover, he picks out single philosophers whom he favours (e.g. Euphrates, Artemidorus,

---

[56] It is interesting that after the allusions to Seneca, letter 3.8 is addressed to Tranquillus, i.e. Suetonius; thus, a letter to Suetonius is juxtaposed with an obituary which, in its first part, contains elements of a biography of a poet. As Pliny might have been familiar with Suetonius' work *De Viris Illustribus* (see Neger, Chapter 13, in this volume), we have the juxtaposition of a letter to a poet and about a poet (3.7) with a letter to a biographer of poets, although 3.8 deals with another subject matter than poetry.

Musonius Rufus or the so-called Stoic opposition).[57] He was friends with Minicius Fundanus and Sosius Senecio (the Roman patrons of Plutarch), but Pliny does not share their interest in Plutarch's middle Platonism; besides, it should not be forgotten that on the divide between rhetoric and philosophy, Pliny (the pupil of Quintilian) is firmly on the side of rhetoric.[58] Apart from Seneca (see also Hanaghan, Chapter 7, in this volume), there are also some other philosophers Pliny frequently employs, such as Lucretius (see Whitton, Chapter 1, Gibson, Chapter 2, and Chinn, Chapter 10, in this volume) and Cicero (with special emphasis on his *De Officiis*[59]). When his literary expediency demands it, Pliny adroitly absorbs a philosophical text in order to engage in a dialogue with an author; but, as a rule, while he exploits the philosophical intertext, at the same time he attempts to differentiate himself from the philosopher or the author he is alluding to. In some cases, as for example in his obituary letters, Pliny seems to absorb philosophical ideas and then to nullify them,[60] while in some other cases Pliny's engagement in a philosophical dialogue aims to 'correct' a view, to besmirch implicitly the image of a person (e.g. Silius Italicus or Regulus) or to safeguard his own image. Since Pliny's morality appears more humane compared to that of the philosophers,[61] the philosophical intrusion in his *Epistles* is opportunistic and could be interpreted as a skilful literary device that facilitates his self-fashioning. Thus, in Pliny's epistolary corpus, his flirtation with philosophy appears to be a strategy rather than a literary end in itself.

---

[57] See e.g. Griffin (2007) esp. 452–6.   [58] See Gibson (2018) 421.
[59] For cases of Pliny's intertextual allusions to Cicero's *De Officiis*, as e.g. *Ep.* 1.23 and 5.8.5, see Griffin (2007) esp. 458–60.
[60] Cf. Tzounakas (2011).   [61] Cf. Griffin (2007) 475; Blake (2018) 339.

PART IV

Pliny's Villas and Their Poetic Models

CHAPTER 9

The Villa and the Monument: Horace in Pliny, Epistles 1.3*

Alberto Canobbio

The *Letters* of Pliny the Younger begin with three texts that can be considered a kind of proemial sequence, its unifying theme being literary activity.[1] Pliny first speaks to us about the publication of his letters (1.1); next, he puts forward a request to revise one of his speeches (1.2); the sequence ends with a bipartite text, in which Pliny first asks for news from his friend Caninius Rufus about the latter's villa, located on Lake Como, and thereafter urges him not to worry about the estate but instead take advantage of the *secessus* ('retreat') that his suburban villa guarantees, enabling him to cultivate his literary studies (1.3).

The 1-2-3 sequence retraces the phases of the birth of a text in inverse order (publication, correction, conception) and, with its last part, suggests a strong link to the literary discourse about the villa, which Hoffer rightly termed a 'factory of literature'.[2] Indeed, in the Roman society of Pliny's time, it was the residences outside urban areas – and not the increasingly chaotic *Urbs* ('the City'), the place of *negotia* ('tasks') – that offered members of the upper class the ideal conditions (i.e. tranquillity, comfort, beauty) to produce, in moments of *otium* ('leisure'), a worthy text that would be able to survive its author.

As we shall see, in letter 1.3 the literary discourse is enhanced by an intertextual gesture: Pliny, since he is predicting the immortality of his friend Caninius' works, conveniently evokes Horace, the poet who in *Carm.* 3.30.1 said of himself *Exegi monumentum aere perennius* ('I have finished a monument more lasting than bronze'). The presence of Horace in Pliny has been acknowledged by many scholars;[3] however, the

---

* I thank Erin Brady for helping me with the English translation of this paper.
[1] On Plin. *Ep.* 1.1–3 see Marchesi (2015b) 226–7.
[2] See Hoffer (1999) 29–44, with a detailed analysis of Plin. *Ep.* 1.3; on this text see also Ludolph (1997) 121–32; Marchesi (2008) 30–6; Lefèvre (2009) 237–39; Marchesi (2015b) 227–30.
[3] See Guillemin (1929) 119–22 and, more recently, Marchesi (2008) 8 ('Pliny learned from Horace and Ovid to pay the same attention as they did to the arrangement of the book and the deployment

importance of Horace's poetry for Plinian intertextuality still appears underestimated: as Whitton wrote in 2014, the doors of 'Pliny's Horatianism' are barely opened;[4] by this paper I aim to offer my contribution to this promising line of research.[5]

This is the text of Plin. *Ep.* 1.3 according to Mynors:[6]

> (1) Quid agit Comum, tuae meaeque deliciae? quid suburbanum amoenissimum, quid illa porticus verna semper, quid platanon opacissimus, quid euripus viridis et gemmeus, quid subiectus et serviens lacus, quid illa mollis et tamen solida gestatio, quid balineum illud quod plurimus sol implet et circumit, quid triclinia illa popularia illa paucorum, quid cubicula diurna nocturna? Possident te et per vices partiuntur? (2) an, ut solebas, intentione rei familiaris obeundae crebris excursionibus avocaris? Si possident, felix beatusque es; si minus, 'unus ex multis'. (3) Quin tu (tempus enim) humiles et sordidas curas aliis mandas, et ipse te in alto isto pinguique secessu studiis adseris? Hoc sit negotium tuum hoc otium; hic labor haec quies; in his vigilia, in his etiam somnus reponatur. (4) Effinge aliquid et excude, quod sit perpetuo tuum. Nam reliqua rerum tuarum post te alium atque alium dominum sortientur, hoc numquam tuum desinet esse si semel coeperit. (5) Scio quem animum, quod horter ingenium; tu modo enitere ut tibi ipse sis tanti, quanti videberis aliis si tibi fueris. Vale.

> (1) How is Comum, your delight and mine? What of your pleasant suburban villa? What of that portico, where it is forever spring? What of the shady plane tree? What of the canal, with its green and crystalline waters? What of the lake that lies below and is at his service? What of that path, soft and yet firm? What of that bath, filled and surrounded by so much sun? What of the dining rooms, those for many and those for few? What of the bedrooms for day and night? Do they enjoy your presence and share it amongst themselves? (2) Or, as usual, are you frequently summoned away in order to manage your estates? If they enjoy your presence, you are a lucky and happy man; if not, you are 'one of many'. (3) Why do you (it is certainly time) not delegate these humble and wretched tasks to others and dedicate yourself to literary studies in that secluded and comfortable retreat?

---

of a peculiar poetic allusive art'); Whitton (2013a) 3–4; Whitton (2014) esp. 151 ff.; Gibson (2020) 159 n. 105 – summarizing Whitton (2014) – writes that Pliny and Horace 'share an unresolved tension between city and country life, with extensive overlaps between texts connected to that theme'. A further reason why Plin. *Ep.* 1.3 contains Horatian echoes could be the fact that Horace too considers the suburban area the perfect place to create literature, cf. e.g. Hor. *Epist.* 2.2.77 *scriptorum chorus omnis amat nemus et fugit urbem* ('the entire chorus of writers loves the woods and flees the city'); Lefèvre (2009) 239.

[4] See Whitton (2014) 154.
[5] For another interesting instance of intertextual relationship between Pliny and Horace see Tamás (Chapter 11 in this volume) on Plin. *Ep.* 1.9 and Hor. *Sat.* 1.9.
[6] See Mynors (1963).

Let this be your task, this your leisure; this your labour, this your rest; to these activities let your waking and sleeping self be dedicated. (4) Fashion and forge something that will be forever yours. All your other possessions will receive another master and then yet another; but this will never cease to be yours, once it has started to be. (5) I know what spirit, what talent I urge on; only force yourself to think of yourself as highly as others will value you if you have first esteemed yourself. Be well.

The letter begins with a phrase belonging to the colloquial register (*Quid agit Comum*). This gives way to a series of questions introduced by *quid*, all predicate ellipses which articulate a text characterized in §§ 1–2 by the figure of speech of personification.

The insistence on personification – first applied to the sender and the recipient's native city,[7] and therefore to the suburban villa and finally its individual parts – is a way of insisting that the villa is not only a *locus amoenus* ('a pleasant place'), but also an entity that interacts with the master and, in particular, influences his mood: when Caninius is in the villa he is *felix beatusque* (§ 2). There is a genuine relationship between master and villa; it is no coincidence that Pliny, in an attempt to create an effect of wonder, confers life on the individual sections of the villa, which are animated and, in a surprising reversal of roles, own their master (*possident te*). The figure of Caninius is thereby divided into parts (*per vices partiuntur*) corresponding to the different activities that might occur in that same villa: enjoying the shade (*porticus, platanon*) or the water (*euripus, lacus*), taking a walk (*gestatio*), bathing (*balineum*), dining (*triclinia*), or resting (*cubicula*). If he manages to do all this, Caninius should be considered a happy man; but if the administration of his estates keeps him away from the villa, he is *unus ex multis*, i.e. a man like many others.[8]

---

[7] The city of Comum has the appellative *deliciae* ('delight'), often used to refer to a beloved person, cf. e.g. Cic. *Att.* 1.5.8 (his daughter Tullia); Verg. *Ecl.* 2.1–2 (the slave Alexis). Fondness for one's town of origin is a sentiment shared by both Caninius and Pliny (§ 1 *Quid agit Comum, tuae meaeque deliciae?*); this suggests an equivalence between the two: therefore we should not forget that Pliny, in urging his friend to life in the villa and to literary studies, is implicitly encouraging himself to do the same. Not by chance Henderson (2002b) 105 calls Caninius an *alter ego* of the author. More recently Carlon (2018) studied Pliny's relationship with both his hometown (esp. 56, 65) and his friend Caninius; the important role of this friend within Pliny's correspondence is also mentioned in the conclusions drawn by Tzounakas (Chapter 8 in this volume) about the connection between letters 1.3, 2.8 and 3.7, all addressed to Caninius. On Pliny and Comum see also Gibson (2020) 162–89 and *General Index* s.v. *Como (Comum)*; Hindermann (Chapter 6 in this volume) about the contrast between the personal attachment to Comum that Pliny proves many times in his letters and the oecumenical outlook of his uncle Pliny the Elder, who in his encyclopaedic work mentions his hometown without special distinction.

[8] The expression *unus ex multis* indicates a common person, who does not distinguish himself for particular reasons or merits, cf. Cic. *Tusc.* 1.17; *Fin.* 2.66; *Brut.* 274; *Off.* 1.109; Sen. *Ep.* 93.5. In

In the letter we are examining, in fact, Pliny depicts the villa, according to Hoffer, 'as an island of trascendent value above the ordinary life of upper-class moneymaking';[9] and this transcendent value, as Hoffer emphasizes (and as we shall soon see), 'comes from literature'.

The call to literary activity in the second part of the letter also draws strength from rhetoric. Pliny builds a sequence consisting of three pairs of antonyms which are given rhythm by the polyptotic anaphora of the deictic pronoun that indicates proximity (§ 3): *hoc sit negotium tuum hoc otium; hic labor haec quies; in his vigilia, in his etiam somnus reponatur*. The sequence aims to present literature as an all-absorbing activity, to which Caninius would do well to dedicate every moment of his day. Additionally – precisely when he urges Caninius to *studia* – Pliny stimulates the literary expertise both of his friend and of the reader by adding a Vergilian tag to the text.

The syntagm *hic labor* conjures the memory of the expression *hoc opus, hic labor est*, from the Sibyl's speech to Aeneas before his catabasis. The Sibyl, as we know, calls the descent to the underworld easy, but says of the return to the living (*Aen.* 6.129–31): *hoc opus, hic labor est. Pauci, quos aequus amavit | Iuppiter aut ardens evexit ad aethera virtus, | dis geniti potuere* ('this is the task, this the labour. Few, whom the just Jupiter loved or whom a blazing virtue lifted towards heaven, born of gods, have managed to do it'). Pliny's intention to allude to this, first noted by Marchesi, seems supported by the existence of an intratextual link: the second part of line 129 is in fact cited in the former letter (*Ep.* 1.2.2): *temptavi enim imitari Demosthenen semper tuum, Calvum nuper meum, dumtaxat figuris orationis; nam vim tantorum virorum, 'pauci quos aequus …' adsequi possunt* ('I have indeed tried to imitate Demosthenes, always yours, and Calvus, lately mine, at least when it comes to figures of speech; in fact, "few whom the just …" may reach the value of men so great').[10] Marchesi additionally points out 'an audible allusion'[11] between Verg. *Aen.* 6.129 *hoc opus, hic labor* and Plin. *Ep.* 1.3.3, where we read *hoc otium* and immediately after *hic labor*; the allusion is nonetheless complicated by the fact that the two Plinian syntagms in question belong to two distinct polar pairs (*hoc sit negotium tuum hoc otium; hic labor haec quies*).[12]

Horace we find a variation of this expression, cf. Hor. *Sat.* 1.9.71–2 *sum paulo infirmior, unus | multorum* ('I am a little weaker, one of many').

[9] See Hoffer (1999) 39.   [10] See Marchesi (2008) 27–36, esp. 28–9 (*Ep.* 1.2), 32–3 (*Ep.* 1.3).
[11] See Marchesi (2008) 32.
[12] Lefèvre (2009) 18 n. 46 and Schwerdtner (2015) 81 n. 51 express doubts about Marchesi's intertextual analysis, which, besides Vergil, also brings Horace into play (cf. below n. 15). I argue

After Vergil the expression *hoc opus, hic labor est* is found quoted with a view to emphasize a task, this time of a terrestrial nature, considered to be very difficult and require great effort. Ovid, in a parodic revival, repeats the words from the *Aeneid* to say that it is not easy to seduce a girl without first having given her a gift (*Ars am.* 1.453): *hoc opus, hic labor est, primo sine munere iungi* ('this is the task, this the labour, being joined without a first gift'); in Quintilian *opus* and *labor* is the appeal to pathos, a real test of an orator's abilities (6.2.7): *an cum ille qui plerisque perorationibus petitur fletus erupit, non palam dicta sententia est? Huc igitur incumbat orator: hoc opus eius, hic labor est* ('when those tears, sought after during most perorations, are drawn out, has the sentence not already been clearly pronounced? It is to this, therefore, that the orator devotes himself: this is his task, this his labour'). Pliny, however, seizes on and emphasizes the applicability of Vergil's expression within the literary sphere; in fact, in the letter we are examining, the word *labor* refers to the effort required for the composition of a literary *opus*. The word *opus* does not appear in Pliny's text but can nonetheless be easily linked to the syntagm *hic labor* by readers mindful of Vergil.

A second possible intertext for Plin. *Ep.* 1.3.3 highlighted by scholars is a hexameter from Horace's third letter in which the poet, by now committed to philosophical writing, urges his friend Julius Florus to dedicate himself to *sapientia* ('wisdom') (*Ep.* 1.3.28): *hoc opus, hoc studium parvi properemus et ampli* ('let us, both small and great, hasten to this work, to this study'). Horace's text is an exhortation to study and, if compared to Pliny's text, certainly presents some similarities, already noted by Guillemin;[13] the fact that both letters have the same serial number (1.3) – as observed by Marchesi and Lefèvre[14] – focuses attention. In Pliny, however, we find neither of the two words that Horace places in an anaphoric relationship.[15]

The vocabulary used by Pliny in his exhortation to study gives us an essay on the power that literature has to transform ordinary words and situations into significant elements. When they enter the literary universe, words, even the most common ones, take on a different and greater weight: in fact, they can take on a kind of metaliterary meaning. I refer in particular to the lexemes *labor, vigilia, somnus* ('labour', 'vigil', 'sleep'), gathered together in § 3 of the letter we are examining, and all three of

---

that Pliny's revival of the Vergilian syntagm *hic labor* is enough to activate an allusive gesture that seems contextually justified.

[13] See Guillemin (1929) 119–20.   [14] See Marchesi (2008) 36; Lefèvre (2009) 240 n. 55.
[15] The relationship between Hor. *Epist.* 1.3.28 and Plin. *Ep.* 1.3.3 was addressed thoroughly by Marchesi (2008) 33–6, who also extended the analysis to Horace's other letter to Florus (2.2).

them traceable to Callimachean poetics, first adopted in Rome by the *poetae novi* ('new poets') and afterwards by Horace.[16]

The concurrence of these words – which I believe to be no coincidence – together with the revival of the Vergilian tag *hic labor* could be the first clue in favour of the argument, as we shall see in due course, that the most appropriate medium for Caninius, with whose *animum* and *ingenium* Pliny claims he is well acquainted,[17] would be not prose but poetry. Pliny therefore appears to urge his friend in this direction, offering him examples of writing techniques usually perceived as characteristic of poetry: intertextuality and metaliterarity.

After an opening invigorated by repeated questions and personifications (§§ 1–2), a rhetorical effort that combines anaphora and antonymy (§ 3), and before an ending that is somewhere between moral precept and psychological nuance (§ 5),[18] we find the paragraph that alludes to the already recalled Horatian *monumentum aere perennius*. Like the three preceding paragraphs, it also appears to be ruled by a figure of speech, in this case metaphor (§ 4): *effinge aliquid et excude, quod sit perpetuo tuum. Nam reliqua rerum tuarum post te alium atque alium dominum sortientur, hoc numquam tuum desinet esse si semel coeperit.*

In these lines Pliny, extending the jussive movement that has already occurred in § 3 (*sit ... reponatur*), urges Caninius to take up the literary arts with two verbs (*effinge ... excude*) that suggest the act of extracting (*ex-*) an artistic object, usually a statue, from an inert material.[19] This linguistic choice activates the metaphor whereby the literary work takes on the three-dimensional concreteness of a sculpture or commemorative

---

[16] Cf. Call. *Epigr.* 27.4 Pf. ἀγρυπνίη ('vigil'); Cinna *FPL* fr. 11.1–2 Bl. *invigilata* ... | *carmina* ('verses elaborated in night vigils'); Hor. *Ars P.* 291 *limae labor et mora* ('the labour of the file and delay'); for a *somnus* ('sleep') that produces literature we might cite the prologue of the *Aetia* ('Causes'), where it is precisely during the dream that Callimachus imagines being transported to Mount Helicon (cf. Anon. *AP* 7.42). This is obviously not the only instance; think of the proem of Ennius' *Annales*, of *The Dream of Scipio* or of Plin. *Ep.* 3.5.4: the uncle of the author begins to write the *Bella Germaniae* ('The War in Germany') after seeing the shade of Drusus in a dream. Nonetheless, the co-presence in that same Plinian context of two lexemes (*labor* and *vigilia*) used in what is essentially a unique way from a poetological point of view leads me to 'read' this third 'literary' word as Callimachean as well.

[17] Cf. Plin. *Ep.* 1.3.5 *scio quem animum, quod horter ingenium* ('I know what spirit, what talent I urge on').

[18] Pliny ends the letter with an elaborate turn of phrase that highlights, with that same circularity, the importance of self-confidence for a man of letters (*Ep.* 1.3.5): *tu modo enitere ut tibi ipse sis tanti, quanti videberis aliis si tibi fueris* ('only force yourself to think of yourself as highly as others will value you if you have first esteemed yourself').

[19] Cf. Verg. *Aen.* 6.847 *excudent alii spirantia mollius aera* ('others will forge, with greater delicacy, bronze statues that seem to breathe'); Prop. 3.9.9 *gloria Lysippo est animosa effingere signa* ('it is Lysippus' glory to give shape to statues full of life'); for *effingo* cf. also Plin. *Ep.* 4.7.1; 7.9.11 v. 4; for *excudo* Apul. *Flor.* 7; Ambr. *Hex.* 2.5.21.

artefact. This occurs already in Cicero's letters,[20] in Petronius,[21] and especially in Horace, which is undoubtedly the baseline intertext for this paragraph: at this point of the letter, in fact, Pliny introduces the theme of the posthumous permanence of the literary work (*aliquid ... quod sit perpetuo tuum*), in other words, Horace's *non omnis moriar* ('I will not die entirely').

Ludolph[22] has identified a second – but less direct – allusion to Horace in the first part of the next line (*nam reliqua rerum tuarum post te alium atque alium dominum sortientur*). Horace, just like Pliny, speaks of material goods that are handed down after the death of their owners at the end of the ode addressed to Postumus (*Carm.* 2.14.21–8):

> Linquenda tellus et domus et placens
> uxor, neque harum quas colis arborum
>   te praeter invisas cupressos
>   ulla brevem dominum sequetur;
>
> absumet heres Caecuba dignior
> servata centum clavibus et mero
>   tinguet pavimentum superbo
>   pontificum potiore cenis.
>
> You must leave the earth, your house, and your beloved wife; and none of the plants that you grow, except the hateful cypresses, shall be passed on to you, ephemeral master: a worthier heir will waste the Caecuban wine you have kept under a hundred keys and bathe the pavement with superb, pure wine, better than that of pontifices' dinners.

This is not an example of a specific allusion, but rather of a generic echo of Horace, who also expresses the very same concept elsewhere: given that men are destined to die, about the goods that they own we cannot speak of personal property but rather of usufruct.[23]

---

[20] Cf. Cic. *Att.* 15.27.2 *excudam aliquid* Ἡρακλείδειον *quod lateat in thesauris tuis* ('I will make something in the manner of Heraclides that may stay hidden in your archives'); the verb *excudo* ('I forge') – more 'technical' than *effingo* ('I form'), which in Pliny's letter comes first (*climax*) – is found in reference to a literary text again in Tac. *Dial.* 9.3; Auson. *Cento nupt.* 132.1–2 G.

[21] Cf. Petr. 4.5 *quod sentio et ipse carmine effingam* ('I will also give shape to what I think in verse').

[22] See Ludolph (1997) 131.

[23] Cf. Hor. *Sat.* 2.2.129–32; *Epist.* 2.2.171–7 *tamquam | sit proprium quicquam, puncto quod mobilis horae | nunc prece, nunc pretio, nunc vi, nunc morte suprema | permutet dominos et cedat in altera iura. | Sic quia perpetuus nulli datur usus et heres | heredem alterius velut unda supervenit undam, | quid vici prosunt aut horrea?* ('as if it were really ours that which, in an instant of the moving hour, either with prayers or money or force or finally death, will change master and pass, by law, under the control of another. So, given that no one is granted perpetual use and a new heir comes after another heir as a wave does a wave, what use are estates or granaries?'); Nisbet and Hubbard (1978) 236.

The text to which Pliny stays closest is instead Hor. *Carm.* 3.30. The Plinian definition of the literary work as an inalienable good (§ 4 *hoc numquam tuum desinet esse*) is perfectly suited to a funerary monument: according to the Roman law, indeed, *hoc monumentum heredem non sequitur* ('this monument is not passed on to the heir'), a formula commonly abbreviated to H. M. H. N. S. in epigraphic documentation.[24] Pliny, paraphrasing this formula in his letter, shows that he has grasped the key element of the Horatian ode, namely the reuse of the lexeme *monumentum* – already attested in literature as an indication of a text that preserves and transmits the memory of its author – with the more specific meaning of sepulchral monument.[25] This leads to a metaphor that is also a paradox: the object that confirms the death of the author (the book-tomb) is also the one that guarantees his survival among posterity.

Pliny, through double allusion to Hor. *Carm.* 3.30 (generated first by the metaphorical verbs *effingo* and *excudo*, then by paraphrasing the formula H. M. H. N. S.), inserts in this letter an echo of Horace's existential thought (*nam reliqua rerum tuarum post te alium atque alium dominum sortientur*). In doing so, he emphasizes to Caninius that, while the material goods that his friend now possesses – including his splendid villa – will be inherited (and are therefore in the hands of fate), intellectual property instead always belongs to its author as *dominus* ('master') in perpetuity of the works produced by his intellect: such is the not inconsiderable added value that literary objects have compared to real things.

The object of the imperatives *effinge* and *excude* is an intentionally generic circumlocution (*aliquid ... quod sit perpetuo tuum*): in this way actually Pliny leads both Caninius and the reader to wonder what the *aliquid* that the letter's recipient must produce is. For those who recognize the allusion to Hor. *Carm.* 3.30 in Pliny's words, the answer is certainly not difficult: through literature Caninius must begin to erect his *monumentum*,[26] inalienable and destined to last throughout time, just like Horace's. The solution to the problem is a literary object that Pliny's

---

[24] See Nisbet and Hubbard (1978) 237; Trimalchio also requests that this declaration of perpetual ownership appear, clearly visible, on his funerary *monumentum* (Petron. *Sat.* 71.7): *ante omnia adici volo 'hoc monumentum heredem non sequatur'* ('above everything I want there to be added "this monument shall not be passed onto the heir"').

[25] See Nisbet and Rudd (2004) 368: '*monumentum* is commonly used of works of literature that preserve an author's memory; cf. Lucil. 1084M, Catull. 95.9 [...] Horace has given new life to the word by describing his poetry as a sepulchral monument'.

[26] The phrase that highlights the singularity of the *monumentum* (*hoc numquam tuum desinet esse*) is followed by a clarification (*si semel coeperit*) that leads one to think that Caninius has not yet written anything of importance.

friend is urged first to identify and then realize. The lexeme *monumentum* – much like the aforementioned *labor, vigilia, somnus* – is another common word, now 'literarized' and associated with a text so famous that it generates an intertextual link even *in absentia* of the specific term.

The word *monumentum* appears instead in letter 2.10, which also has a literary theme: in this text Pliny calls on the *loci classici* concerned with poetic immortality, one after another.[27] The context is very similar to that of letter 1.3: in the text we are examining, Pliny encourages Caninius to start writing; the recipient of letter 2.10 is encouraged to publish his verses[28] (§§ 2–4):

> (2) Sine per ora hominum ferantur isdemque quibus lingua Romana spatiis pervagentur. Magna et iam longa exspectatio est, quam frustrari adhuc et differre non debes. (3) Enotuerunt quidam tui versus, et invito te claustra sua refregerunt. Hos nisi retrahis in corpus, quandoque ut errones aliquem cuius dicantur invenient. (4) Habe ante oculos mortalitatem, a qua adserere te hoc uno monimento potes; nam cetera fragilia et caduca non minus quam ipsi homines occidunt desinuntque.

> (2) Let your verses be transported on the mouths of men and spread through the same spaces where the tongue of Rome is spoken! Expectation of them is great and by now protracted, and you must no longer disappoint or prolong it. (3) Some of your verses have been released and broken free against your will. If you do not lead them back to the group, sooner or later – runaways that they are – they will find someone to whom it will be said they belong. (4) Keep in mind your mortal condition, from which you can free yourself only with a monument of this kind; all other things are fragile and fleeting, not unlike men themselves who die and cease to exist.

In the first sentence of § 2 it is easy to recognize the echo both of Ennius' famous self-epitaph[29] and of the end of Ovid's *Metamorphoses*,[30] though Horace also plays an important part in this intertextual inlay.

In fact, the first phrase of § 4 (*habe ante oculos mortalitatem, a qua adserere te hoc uno monimento*[31] *potes*) alludes very clearly to the last ode of Book 3. The apt clarification *hoc uno* suggests two things: (1) different types of *monumentum* exist; (2) the only *monumentum* capable of allowing

---

[27] See Whitton (2013a) 147 ff. (esp. 147, 149, 151).
[28] Letter 2.10 is addressed to Octavius Rufus, whom Pliny has already asked if he can read his verses in *Ep.* 1.7.5; Octavius Rufus is not further mentioned in the rest of the *Letters*.
[29] Cf. Enn. *Var.* 18 V. *volito vivos per ora virum* 'I continue to fly, alive, on the mouths of men'.
[30] Cf. Ov. *Met.* 15.877–8 *quaque patet domitis Romana potentia terris, | ore legar populi*, 'and wherever the power of Rome is extended over conquered lands, I will be read by the mouths of the people'.
[31] The form *monimentum* is interchangeable with *monumentum*.

man to free himself from mortal condition is the kind of *monumentum* erected by Horace (*Carm.* 3.30.6–7 *non omnis moriar multaque pars mei | vitabit Libitinam* 'I will not die entirely and a great part of me will avoid Libitina'). The allusion to Hor. *Carm.* 3.30, moreover, not only appears in the final – and rhetorically strongest – position but seems to be prepared and reinforced also by the possible revival in §§ 2–3 of a second text by Horace.

The piece in question is *Ep.* 1.20, another closing composition that also pertains to its author's posthumous survival, in this case entrusted to the personified book.[32] In fact, the image of the literary text as a *fugitivus* ('runaway slave') who leaves the house of his master (i.e. the author) without permission might come from this very letter: *quidam tui versus ... invito te claustra sua refregerunt ... ut errones*.[33] The image of a slave without a master is used by Pliny to warn his friend about the risk that his verses are attributed to others: as is already the case in the letter to Caninius (*Ep.* 1.3.4) *effinge aliquid et excude, quod sit perpetuo tuum*), in this text, too, his friend's literary production is introduced through metaphorical language[34] and in terms of a right to property.

Appearing not far from letter 2.10 is the second letter addressed to Caninius Rufus (*Ep.* 2.8), whom the author imagines spending his *otium* ('leisure') in the pleasant villa of Comum, involved in studies, hunting, and fishing while Pliny, a slave to increasingly numerous *negotia* ('tasks'), is instead held 'chained' to Rome.[35] The life lived by Caninius corresponds to the life that Pliny desires himself (§ 2).[36]

---

[32] Cf. Hor. *Epist.* 1.20.19 ff., where the book sketches out a condensed biographical profile of Horace, now dead, for whoever gathers around. Ferri (1993) 131–7 likens the end of letter 1.20 to a funerary epigraph; with regard to the relationship between these lines and the posthumous memory of Horace good observations in Oliensis (1995) 222–4.

[33] See Whitton (2013a) 150 s.v., with further instances of the metaphor of the *liber fugitivus* ('runaway book').

[34] In Plin. *Ep.* 2.10.3, in addition to the metaphor of the *liber fugitivus* (cf. above note), we should also highlight the one that originates from the word *corpus* ('body'), see Whitton (2013a) 150 s.v., which, in a context such as this, can be understood as a reference both to a literary work and to the body of slaves in the service of a master. Additionally, in § 4, the expression *adserere te ... potes* 'keeps live the imagery of manumission' (Whitton (2013a) 151); the verb *adserere* ('to declare one to be free') – pertaining to the legal sphere and similar to Seneca's *vindicare* ('to claim as one's property') – appears also in letter 1.3, where Pliny invites Caninius to free himself from the *curae* ('worries') of his estate and to devote himself to what is truly important and lasting (§ 3 *Quin ... ipse te ... studiis adseris?*).

[35] On Plin. *Ep.* 2.8 see Whitton (2013a) 137 ff., esp. 140 for the metaphor of the slave that Pliny applies, this time, to himself (§§ 2–3).

[36] On Caninius as an *alter ego* of Pliny cf. above n. 7.

The Villa and the Monument: Horace in Plin. Ep. 1.3

In Pliny's correspondence Caninius is the recipient of another five letters: 7.18 concerns an economic matter;[37] all the others (3.7; 6.21; 8.4; 9.33) have to do with literature, just like two other letters (7.25; 9.38) which address or mention a Rufus who, at least in the second case, should in all probability be identified as Caninius.[38] From these texts we learn with certainty what we had already suspected from letter 1.3: Caninius Rufus has a talent for poetry. One of his projects – we do not know if it was completed – consists of a historical epic poem dedicated to the victory of Trajan over the Dacians, an initiative that Pliny particularly admires (*Ep.* 8.4.1): *Optime facis, quod bellum Dacicum scribere paras* ('You do very well to ready yourself to write of the war against the Dacians'); a second topic for a work in verse is suggested to him by Pliny himself (*Ep.* 9.33.1):

> Incidi in materiam veram sed simillimam fictae, dignamque isto laetissimo altissimo planeque poetico ingenio; incidi autem, dum super cenam varia miracula hinc inde referuntur. Magna auctori fides: tametsi quid poetae cum fide? Is tamen auctor, cui bene vel historiam scripturus credidisses.
>
> I came across a matter that is true but entirely like one that has been invented, and worthy of your delightful, elevated, and truly poetic talent; I came across it during a dinner, as wonders of various kinds were being reported on all sides. The reliability of the author is great. But what does reliability matter to a poet? Nonetheless, this is an author whom you could undoubtedly believe even if you were intending to write a historical work.

In this paragraph, where we find the word *miracula* ('wonders') and a laudative mention of a highly reliable nameless author, Pliny evokes indirectly the figure of Pliny the Elder, who in his *Naturalis historia* ('Natural history') often reports natural *mirabilia* ('marvels') and, in particular, tells a story similar to the one contained in his nephew's letter:[39] a dolphin makes a habit of playing with a boy and his friends. This unusual spectacle is repeated several times, attracting more than a few curious

---

[37] Pliny suggests to his friend a device to guarantee that a donation made to their native city lasts over time.

[38] See Sherwin-White (1966) 522; Whitton (2013a) 138; Gibson (2015) 190–1, who observes that in that case the third letter of the collection (1.3), in which Pliny encourages Caninius Rufus to write, and the third from last (9.38), where he instead praises a *librum omnibus numeris absolutum* ('book perfect in all its elements') composed by *Rufus noster* ('our friend Rufus'), would refer to the same person; this structural element would confirm the importance of the figure of Caninius Rufus for Pliny (cf. above n. 7).

[39] Cf. Plin. *HN* 9.26; about the relationship with Plin. *Ep.* 9.33 see Hindermann (Chapter 6) in this volume. According to an older bibliography, the Younger Pliny does not have in mind the work of his uncle; but recently several scholars have argued (and I agree) that Pliny intentionally invites the reader to make a connection and a comparison between his letter and the uncle's text.

bystanders; at this point the decision is made to kill the dolphin to protect the tranquillity of the locale. In the final paragraph, Pliny says that it is certain that Caninius will obtain a worthy text from this sad event, probably an epicedium.[40]

Caninius' flair for poetry is also substantiated by the fact that Pliny writes to him to tell him of other poets: living, like the otherwise unknown Vergilius Romanus (a comic poet whom Pliny valued as much as Plautus and Terence),[41] or recently deceased, like the epic poet Silius Italicus, about whom Pliny writes a famous commemorative letter (*Ep.* 3.7).[42]

In this last text we once again find the word *monimentum*, now in reference to Vergil's tomb, which Silius approached as a temple (*Ep.* 3.7.8);[43] in this letter it is possible to recognize Pliny's intention of evoking two important authors who placed the theme of time at the centre of their poetics: certainly (and widely) Seneca, as Tzounakas has shown in detail,[44] but also Horace.

In the penultimate paragraph Pliny compares himself and his friend Caninius, in a joint exhortation to leave a trace of their own existence after death (*Ep.* 3.7.14):

> Hoc, quidquid est temporis futilis et caduci, si non datur factis (nam horum materia in aliena manu), certe studiis proferamus, et quatenus nobis denegatur diu vivere, relinquamus aliquid, quo nos vixisse testemur.
>
> This fleeting and transient time, whatever it is, if it is not granted to us through our actions (the opportunity for those, after all, lies with others), let us at least extend it through our literary studies and, from the moment that living longer is denied us, let us leave something by means of which we can give evidence that we have lived.

The call to leave *aliquid, quo nos vixisse testemur* may recall (this time on an intratextual level) the earlier invitation that Pliny gives to Caninius to

---

[40] Cf. Plin. *Ep.* 9.33.11 *haec tu qua miseratione, qua copia deflebis ornabis attolles!* ('with what compassion, with what eloquence you will wield, adorn, elevate these facts!'); the text hoped for by Pliny and worthy of Caninius' poetic talent (§ 1) should probably be identified as something similar to Statius' *Psittacus* ('The Parrot', *Silv.* 2.4) or *Leo mansuetus* ('The tame Lion', *Silv.* 2.5).

[41] Cf. Plin. *Ep.* 6.21; this letter begins with an important defence of contemporary authors (§ 1): *Sum ex iis qui mirer antiquos, non tamen (ut quidam) temporum nostrorum ingenia despicio. Neque enim quasi lassa et effeta natura nihil iam laudabile parit* ('I am one of those who admire the ancients, all the same I do not disdain, like some, the talent of our times. It is not in fact true that nature, as if weary and barren, no longer generates anything worthy of praise').

[42] On this letter see Gibson and Morello (2012) 123–6; Tzounakas (Chapter 8 in this volume).

[43] On the cult of Silius Italicus for Vergil cf. also Mart. 11.48 and 50; 12.67.

[44] See Tzounakas (Chapter 8 in this volume); the scholar notes allusion to almost all the Seneca's dialogues and especially to his *De brevitate vitae* ('On the Shortness of Life').

create (*Ep.* 1.3.4) *aliquid . . . quod sit perpetuo tuum*, an expression behind which we have already glimpsed Horace's *monumentum*. Pliny's two phrases, both deliberately vague, have the very same jussive movement. Moreover – just as in *Ep.* 1.3 – in *Ep.* 3.7.14, quoted above, we also find lexemes traceable to epigraphic customs (*vixisse* makes one think of the formula *vixit* ('he/she lived')) as well as legal language (*testemur*).

Thus, in the circumlocution *aliquid, quo nos vixisse testemur* it is possible to find another allusion to the cultural *monumentum* that a man of letters may erect for himself in hopes of conquering immortality, a word which – not coincidentally – ends the letter that concerns Silius Italicus (*Ep.* 3.7.15): ἀγαθὴ δ' ἔρις[45] *cum invicem se mutuis exhortationibus amici ad amorem immortalitatis exacuunt. Vale* ('good emulation is when friends encourage each other, with mutual exhortations, to wish for immortality. Be well').

To return, in conclusion, to letter 1.3, in this text Pliny exalts the villa but also reveals its limitations: a villa is destined to pass on to other masters, a literary *monumentum* is not.[46] Considered from this perspective, the famous letters wherein Pliny describes his suburban residences in great detail[47] take on additional meaning. Using the literary process of *ekphrasis*, transferred from poetry – its original setting – to prose,[48] the author 'reconstructs' his villas *per verba* ('by words') within a timeless space that he has generated himself: the literary space. In this way, he removes the villas from the destructive action of years and assumes full and perpetual control of his residences, as the holder of a property that is no longer legal, but literary.

---

[45] Quotation from Hes. *Op.* 24.
[46] Over the course of the letter Caninius' suburban villa progressively loses prominence: at first the surprising owner of its master (§§ 1–2 *possident te . . . possident*) it then becomes a place – inanimate – suited for studies (§ 3 *in alto isto pinguique secessu*) and finally (§ 4) ends up implicitly included among Caninius' material possessions (*reliqua rerum tuarum*), which passively endure the unpredictable action of luck (*sortientur*).
[47] Cf. Plin. *Ep.* 2.17; 5.6; 9.7; among the most recent studies on these letters – many times examined by scholars – see Gibson and Morello (2012) 200–33 and 306–7 (bibliography); Canobbio (2020); on *Ep.* 2.17 and 5.6 see Marchesi (2015b) 230–8; Gibson (2020) 132 ff.; on *Ep.* 2.17 see Whitton (2013a) 218–55; on *Ep.* 5.6 see Jacquier (2019); Chinn (Chapter 10 in this volume).
[48] As terms of comparison in the description of his Tuscan villa, Plin. *Ep.* 5.6.43 cites the lines that Homer and Vergil have dedicated to Achilles' (*Il.* 18.468 ff.) and Aeneas' weapons (*Aen.* 8.617 ff.), as well as Aratus' astronomical poem. On the way in which the rhetorical genre of *ekphrasis* is interpreted by Pliny in letter 5.6 see Chinn (2007).

CHAPTER 10

The Villas of Pliny and Statius

Christopher Chinn

Scholars have long noticed similarities between Pliny's two ekphrastic villa letters (*Ep.* 2.17, on a villa near Laurentum, and *Ep.* 5.6, on a mountain villa in Tuscany) and Statius' two long villa poems (*Silv.* 1.3, on Vopiscus' villa near Tibur, and *Silv.* 2.2, on Pollius' villa on the Bay of Naples).[1] Both authors describe the beauty of the estates,[2] the peace and quiet they offer,[3] the views from the buildings,[4] the retention of light in various rooms,[5] and how the villas manage to stay cool in summer and warm in winter.[6] In addition, both authors locate, in apparently tongue-in-cheek fashion, the literary pedigree of their respective works within the epic tradition. For example, Statius compares his description of Vopiscus' villa to Homer's description of Alcinous' palace in the *Odyssey* (*Silv.* 1.3.81–2).[7] Additionally, Stephen Hinds notes that Statius' description of the views from the bedroom in the estate of Pollius Felix (*Silv.* 2.2.72–82) constitutes an intertextual trip through Vergilian literary history.[8] Pliny, in a famous digression (*Ep.* 5.6.41–4), humorously excuses the length of the

---

[1] Bibliography on Pliny's villa letters: Gibson and Morello (2012) 306–7, Marchesi (2015b) 230–8, esp. 231 n. 4. Bibliography on Statius' villa poems: Newlands (2011) 120–1 (on *Silv.* 2.2); Newlands (2002) 119–53, Marshall (2009), Martelli (2009) 154–6 (on *Silv.* 1.3); Delarue (2014) (on both). Bibliography on the relationship between the villas of Pliny and Statius: Myers (2005) 122 n. 77, Gibson and Morello (2012) 211–12. Other connections between Pliny and Statius: Fögen (2007) 267–70 and Pagán (2010). Sherwin-White (1966) 186–7 commented on the overall similarities between the villas of Pliny and Statius, though he is skeptical of any specific use of Statius by Pliny. Zerbini (2006) 12 notes some specific verbal echoes.
[2] E.g., *Silv.* 1.3.13–17; 2.2.36–42; *Ep.* 2.17.1; 5.6.7, 13. Cf. Newlands (2002) 132 with n. 60.
[3] E.g., *Silv.* 1.3.20–3, 29–30, 39–42; 2.2.25–9, 50–1; *Ep.* 2.17.7, 13, 33; 5.6.21. Cf. Myers (2000) 119 with n. 72.
[4] E.g., *Silv.* 1.3.39–40; 2.2.72–82; *Ep.* 2.17.4–5, 20–2; 5.6.19, 22–4. Cf. Newlands (2011) 139 and Morzadec (2009) 55–6.
[5] E.g., *Silv.* 2.2.45–9; *Ep.* 2.17.6, 8. Cf. Newlands (2002) 164 on Statius. Cf. Hoffer (1999) 35 on Pliny.
[6] E.g., *Silv.* 1.3.5–8; 2.2.26–9; *Ep.* 2.17.17–18; 5.6.24, 26, 30. On Statius cf. Myers (2000) 119. On Pliny cf. Rossiter (2003) 359–60 and Hoffer (1999) 43.
[7] For an extended discussion of this intertext see Marshall (2009). Cf. Morzadec (2009) 232–3.
[8] Hinds (2001) 237–55.

description of his Tuscan villa by invoking the shields of Achilles and Aeneas in Homer and Vergil respectively.[9] Finally, both writers appear to employ the villa ekphrases as a kind of figure of praise for the homeowner. In Statius, the houses are like their owners and hence praise of the estate equals praise of the man.[10] For example, the calm winds and water around Pollius' maritime estate are said to 'imitate the character of the owner' (*dominique imitantia mores*, *Silv*. 2.2.29) while the smooth-running Anio river that flows through Vopiscus' estate at Tibur reflects the owner's 'placid' character: *ceu placidi veritus turbare Vopisci | Pieriosque dies et habentes carmina somnos* ('as though loath to disturb peaceful Vopiscus' Pierian days and song-filled slumbers', *Silv*. 1.3.22–3, trans. Shackleton Bailey, modified).[11] Scholars have pointed out that Pliny's villa descriptions may constitute a kind of elite self-fashioning and hence a form of self-praise.[12] Pliny, for his part, claims that he is at his best when he is at his Tuscan villa: *ibi animo, ibi corpore maxime valeo* ('I am strong in mind and body there', *Ep*. 5.6.46).[13] A consequence of these numerous parallels is that we are invited to explore the extent of Pliny's intertextual debt to Statius. I propose to look at one potential intertext between the two authors – the issue of human control over nature – in order to address this question.

1 Control Over Nature in Statius and Pliny

Lise Bek has shown that control over nature is thematic in the villa descriptions of both Statius and Pliny.[14] In this chapter, I examine this theme in Statius' description of Pollius' Surrentine villa (*Silv*. 2.2) and in Pliny's description of his Tuscan villa (*Ep*. 5.6), paying close attention to the intertextual relationship between the two ekphraseis. I first argue that Statius alludes to Lucretius and Vergil (in the *Georgics*) in order to conceptualize nature in his villa poems. Then I show that Pliny appropriates this intertext in his own villa letters. Let us first examine in detail how Pliny and Statius

---

[9] On this passage see Chinn (2007) 276–8, Gibson and Morello (2012) 214–16, Marchesi (2015b) 233–5. On Pliny and poetry generally see Gamberini (1983) 82–121.
[10] See Delarue (2014) 91–2; Van Dam (1984) 6–7 and 188; Hardie (1983) 128–36.
[11] Myers (2005) 108–9.
[12] For bibliography on this issue see Chinn (2007) 266 n. 5, Gibson and Morello (2012) 216–17.
[13] Gamberini (1983) 103–10 understands this as a celebration of leisure devoted to informal poetic composition. This suggests a metonymic equivalency between the villa, poetry, and hence (a part of) Pliny's identity.
[14] Bek (1976) 161–3. Cf. Morzadec (2009) 260–70 (*ars* and *natura* in the *Silvae* generally), Newlands (2002) 156–8, 164–74 (domination of nature in *Silv*. 2.2) and Hoffer (1999) 33–5 (control of nature in Pliny).

address the issue of control over nature and come to some preliminary conclusions about the relationship between the two writers.

In *Silv.* 2.2, the theme of control over nature stands out clearly in Statius' description of the manipulation of the landscape surrounding Pollius' villa:[15]

> his favit natura locis, hic victa colenti
> cessit et ignotos docilis mansuevit in usus.
> mons erat hic ubi plana vides, et lustra fuerunt
> quae nunc tecta subis; ubi nunc nemora ardua cernis
> hic nec terra fuit: domuit possessor, et illum
> formantem rupes expugnantemque secuta
> gaudet humus. nunc cerne iugum discentia saxa
> intrantemque domos iussumque recedere montem.
> iam Methymnaei vatis manus et chelys una
> Thebais et Getici cedat tibi gloria plectri;
> et tu saxa moves, et te nemora alta sequuntur.
>
> (Stat. *Silv.* 2.2.52–61)

Some spots Nature has favoured, in others she has been overcome and yielded to the developer, letting herself be taught new and gentler ways. Where you see level ground, there used to be a hill; the building you now enter was wilderness; where now you see lofty woods, there was not even land. The occupant has tamed it all; the soil rejoices as he shapes rocks or expels them, following his lead. Now behold the cliffs as they learn the yoke, and the dwellings as they enter, and the mountain bidden to withdraw. Let the hand of Methymna's bard and therewith the Theban lyre and the glory of Getic quill give you best: you too move rocks and lofty forests follow you.

(trans. Shackleton Bailey)

Although some aspects of the site are naturally amenable to human activity, we learn that nature has been conquered (*victa*) and taught (*docilis*) by Pollius to conform to his needs. Moreover, as a way to demonstrate the extent of Pollius' control over the landscape, Statius employs a commonplace hyperbole in which mountains are leveled and seas filled in as a result of construction activity.[16] Throughout this passage we find the language of warfare (*victa, expugnantem*) and of taming animals (*domuit, formantem, iugum*).[17] One way to understand all this is as a

---

[15] Basile (2014) 84; Morzadec (2009) 273–5.
[16] Cf. Sall. *Cat.* 13.1; Hor. *Epist.* 1.10; *Carm.* 2.16; Tib. 1.1; Sen. *Ep.* 55 and 86. On the issue of buildings and morality in Rome see Edwards (1993) 137–72.
[17] Newlands (2002) 180; Goguey (1982) 610. Cf. *Silv.* 4.3.50–6 and 78.

response to Roman moralizing, whereby writers such as Horace and Seneca condemn such hyperbolic manipulation of the landscape (often in the form of the mountain-leveling and sea-filling topos) as exemplifying decadent luxury.[18] According to this view, Statius is polemically partaking in a new aesthetics of luxury that reflects on both the objects of praise (the villas and their owner) and the poetry that praises them.

Pliny too touches on the issue of control of nature in his long description of the landscape surrounding his Tuscan villa:

> Regionis forma pulcherrima. Imaginare amphitheatrum aliquod immensum, et quale sola rerum natura possit effingere. Lata et diffusa planities montibus cingitur, montes summa sui parte procera nemora et antiqua habent. Frequens ibi et varia venatio. Inde caeduae silvae cum ipso monte descendunt. Has inter pingues terrenique colles (neque enim facile usquam saxum etiam si quaeratur occurrit) planissimis campis fertilitate non cedunt, opimamque messem serius tantum, sed non minus percoquunt. Sub his per latus omne vineae porriguntur, unamque faciem longe lateque contexunt; quarum a fine imoque quasi margine arbusta nascuntur. Prata inde campique, campi quos non nisi ingentes boves et fortissima aratra perfringunt: tantis glaebis tenacissimum solum cum primum prosecatur adsurgit, ut nono demum sulco perdometur. Prata florida et gemmea trifolium aliasque herbas teneras semper et molles et quasi novas alunt. ... magnam capies voluptatem, si hunc regionis situm ex monte prospexeris. (Plin. *Ep.* 5.6.7–11, 13)

> The countryside is very beautiful. Picture to yourself a vast amphitheatre such as could only be a work of nature; the great spreading plain is ringed round by mountains, their summits crowned by ancient woods of tall trees, where there is a good deal of mixed hunting to be had. Down the mountain slopes are timber woods interspersed with small hills of soil so rich that there is scarcely a rocky outcrop to be found; these hills are fully as fertile as the level plain and yield quite as rich a harvest, though it ripens rather later in the season. Below them the vineyards spreading down every slope weave their uniform pattern far and wide, their lower limit bordered by a plantation of trees. Then come the meadows and cornfields, where the land can be broken up only by heavy oxen and the strongest ploughs, for the soil is so stiff that it is thrown up in great clods at the first ploughing and is not thoroughly broken until it has been gone over nine times. The meadows are bright with flowers, covered with trefoil and other delicate plants which always seem soft and fresh ... It is a great pleasure to look down on the countryside from the mountain ... (trans. Radice)

---

[18] See Pavlovskis (1973) 6–7 with note 22; Newlands (1988) 403–4; Edwards (1993) 142; Myers (2000) 112–13; Myers (2005) 107–8; Hinds (2001) 240; Zeiner (2005) 75–7.

Pliny here seems to echo Statius on several points. Pliny's 'high groves' (*procera nemora*) point to similar ideas in Statius (*nemora ardua*, *Silv.* 2.2.55 and *nemora alta*, *Silv.* 1.3.61). The lack of stones in the soil (*neque . . . facile usquam saxum . . . occurrit*) perhaps resembles Pollius' musically translocated stones (*tu saxa moves*, *Silv.* 2.2.61). Like Statius, Pliny also uses violent language (*perfringunt*, cf. *expugnantem*, *Silv.* 2.2.57) and the language of animal training (*perdometur*, cf. *domuit*, *Silv.* 2.2.56) in describing the plowing of the land. Pliny could be thinking of Statius in all these instances, or he could be employing a lexicon of landscape description common to both writers.[19] Pliny does seem to celebrate his wealth through his presentation of the villa,[20] but it is not clear that he is engaging with the Roman moralizing tradition of ostentatious houses in the same way that Statius has (allegedly) done. In other words, even though Pliny and Statius both employ imagery of the violent control of nature in their villa descriptions, it may be that each author has a different set of conceptual assumptions in mind.[21]

I think, however, we can bolster the case that Pliny has Statius in mind in his villa description by looking at a larger intertext involving the presentation of nature in each writer. As mentioned above, I am thinking in particular of an intertext involving Lucretius and Vergil's *Georgics*. My argument proceeds by examining (1) the intertext between Lucretius and the *Georgics* on nature, (2) Statius' engagement with this intertext, and (3) Pliny's engagement with Statius' version of the intertext. At the end, I draw some conclusions about Pliny's intertextuality in *Ep.* 5.6.

2 Lucretius and Vergil on Nature

Both Lucretius and Vergil provide characterizations of nature in their respective accounts of the origin of agriculture. In his account of the development of human life in *DRN* 5, Lucretius offers a history of farming:

>   at specimen sationis et insitionis origo
>   ipsa fuit rerum primum natura creatrix
>   . . .
>   inde aliam atque aliam culturam dulcis agelli
>   temptabant fructusque feros mansuescere terra
>   cernebant indulgendo blandeque colendo.
>   inque dies magis in montem succedere silvas

---

[19] Myers (2000) argues that many of the features common to both writers are conventional.
[20] Myers (2005) 103–4.
[21] On some general differences between the villa descriptions of the two authors see Van Dam (1984) 188–9; Gibson and Morello (2012) 212; Hoffer (1999) 35 n. 19.

cogebant infraque locum concedere cultis,
prata lacus rivos segetes vinetaque laeta
collibus et campis ut haberent, atque olearum
caerula distinguens inter plaga currere posset
per tumulos et convallis camposque profusa;
ut nunc esse vides vario distincta lepore
omnia, quae pomis intersita dulcibus ornant
arbustisque tenent felicibus obsita circum.

(*DRN* 5.1361–2, 1367–78)

But the pattern of sowing and the beginning of grafting first came from nature herself the maker of all things ... Next one after another they tried ways of cultivating the little plot they loved, and saw wild fruits grow tame in the ground with kind treatment and friendly tillage. Day by day they made the forests climb higher up the mountains and yield the place below to their tilth, that they might have meadows, pools and streams, crops and luxuriant vineyards on hill and plain, and that a grey-green belt of olives might run between to mark the boundaries, stretching forth over hills and dales and plains; just as now you see the whole place mapped out with charming variety, laid out and intersected with sweet fruit-trees and set about with fertile plantations.

(trans. Rouse and Smith)

Here Lucretius begins by portraying nature as a kind of divinity who provides the model for humans to imitate in their agricultural endeavors. The poet then proceeds to a picturesque description of the developed rural landscape, complete with various forms of cultivation. Similarly, near the beginning of the *Georgics*, Vergil provides his own account of the origins of agriculture, but in fairly conventional mythological terms:

continuo has leges aeternaque foedera certis
imposuit natura locis, quo tempore primum
Deucalion vacuum lapides iactavit in orbem,
unde homines nati, durum genus. ergo age, terrae
pingue solum primis extemplo a mensibus anni
fortes invertant tauri, glaebasque iacentis
pulverulenta coquat maturis solibus aestas;
at si non fuerit tellus fecunda, sub ipsum
Arcturum tenui sat erit suspendere sulco:
illic, officiant laetis ne frugibus herbae,
hic, sterilem exiguus ne deserat umor harenam.

(*G.* 1.60–70)

From the first, Nature laid these laws and eternal covenants on certain lands, even from the day when Deucalion threw stones into the empty world, whence sprang men, a stony race. Come then, and where the earth's soil is rich, let your stout oxen upturn it straightway, in the year's first months, and let the clods lie for dusty summer to bake with her ripening suns; but should the land not be fruitful, it will suffice, on the eve of Arcturus' rising, to raise it lightly with shallow furrow – in the one case, that weeds may not choke the gladsome corn; in the other, that the scant moisture may not desert the barren sand.

(trans. Fairclough and Goold)

Like Lucretius, Vergil begins with general statements about nature, then proceeds to show how humans learned to become farmers within these natural conditions. Scholars have pointed out that Vergil employs Lucretian language in his account.[22] Vergil's 'dusty summer' (*pulverulenta ... aestas*) is a compression of Lucretius' 'dry heat and dusty Ceres' (*calor aridus et ... | pulverulenta Ceres*).[23] Vergil's description of the men born after the Flood as a 'hardy race' (*durum genus*) looks like Lucretius' early humans: 'but the [early] human race was much hardier regarding agricultural work ... a race that the hard earth had created' (*at genus humanum multo fuit illud in arvis | durius ... tellus quod dura creasset*, DRN 5.925–6).[24] It seems clear, therefore, that Vergil is thinking of Lucretius in this passage. Moreover, Monica Gale has argued that Vergil 'corrects' Lucretius by removing nature as the model for human agricultural practice, and returns to the old Hesiodic conception of agricultural toil as a kind of moral punishment.[25] This sentiment appears in our passage with the reference to the immutable laws of nature and toil stemming from the time of Deucalion, and to the 'original sin' story implied by the Flood (*G.* 1.60–3). In what follows, I argue that Statius and Pliny pick up on these various aspects of the Lucretius-Vergil intertext.

3 Statius and Lucretius

In *Silv.* 2.2, Statius makes a point of emphasizing Pollius' Epicureanism.[26] This provides the most obvious basis for a Lucretian intertext within his villa description. Pollius, according to Statius, is able to see 'the truth of things since darkness has been dispersed' (*at nunc discussa rerum caligine verum | aspicis*, *Silv.* 2.2.138–9). The imagery of light and darkness here, as

---

[22] See Gale (2000) 60–3.   [23] Thomas (1988) 79.   [24] Mynors (1990) 14; Thomas (1988) 78.
[25] Gale (2000) 65–6.
[26] For discussion and bibliography on this issue see Myers (2000) 122–3, Basile (2014) 84–5, Newlands (2002) 170–4. On Statius and Lucretius generally see Kenney (1970) and Laguna (1996) 257–8.

well as the jingle *rerum . . . verum*, points to the beginning of Book 2 of *De Rerum Natura*, where Lucretius says that knowledge of nature (*naturae species ratioque*, *DRN* 2.61), not the actual light of the sun, may disperse the 'shadows of the mind' (*animi tenebras*, *DRN* 2.59).[27] Let us return to the landscape description in *Silv.* 2.2, quoted above, in which Statius deploys the theme of the control of nature. In this passage, we see that Statius' opening phrase points directly to Lucretius' statement on the origin of agriculture.[28] Statius says that the site of Pollius' villa is in places naturally amenable, but in other places has had to be cultivated: *his favit natura locis, hic victa colenti | cessit et ignotos docilis mansuevit in usus* ('Some spots nature has favoured, in others she has been overcome and yielded to the developer, letting herself be taught new and gentler ways', *Silv.* 2.2.52–3). The collocation of *natura, colenti,* and *mansuevit* echoes Lucretius' description of the early stages of agriculture: *natura* is the model (*at specimen sationis et insitionis origo | ipsa fuit rerum primum natura creatrix*, *DRN* 5.1361–2), but farmers make wild plants accustomed (*mansuescere*, *DRN* 5.1368) to cultivation (*colendo*, *DRN* 5.1369).[29] It is clear that the underlying thought of each writer is slightly different. Lucretius is literally talking about farming, while Statius is talking about creative landscaping. Nevertheless, Statius at some level implies the origins of agriculture here. The term 'cultivator' (*colenti*, *Silv.* 2.2.52) obviously implies farming, and the idea that the cultivator changes nature into 'unknown uses' (*ignotos . . . in usus*, *Silv.* 2.2.53) suggests a contrast between pre- and postagricultural worlds. Moreover, we find further details in Statius' account of Pollius' transformation of the landscape that seem to echo Lucretius' description of the progress of agriculture. Early farmers, according to Lucretius, forced the forests to recede towards the mountains (*in montem succedere silvas | cogebant*, *DRN* 5.1370–1), and the land to yield to cultivation (*concedere cultis*, *DRN* 5.1372). Statius inverts the first idea when he describes the mountains themselves receding as a result of Pollius' landscaping (*recedere montem*, *Silv.* 2.2.58). The second idea, that of yielding to cultivation, we have already seen in Statius' phrase *colenti | cessit* (*Silv.* 2.2.52–3). The aggregate of all these parallels suggests that Statius is appropriating Lucretius' description of the origin of agriculture as a means to compare Pollius to an innovative Lucretian farmer and, by extension, to an Epicurean sage.

---

[27] Newlands (2011) 154.   [28] Newlands (2011) 143; Van Dam (1984) 227–8.
[29] Van Dam (1984) 228.

4 Statius and Vergil

Statius' landscape description in *Silv.* 2.2 also alludes heavily to Vergil's *Georgics*.[30] Recall how Vergil had corrected Lucretius' quasiscientific conception of agriculture with the traditional Hesiodic moral one (see Section 2 above). Statius seems to borrow Vergil's moral theme of a struggle against nature. We have already noted Statius' terminology of military conquest and of animal taming in our passage. In this connection, Van Dam points out that Statius' ideas of teaching nature new 'uses' (*ignotos docilis mansuevit in usus, Silv.* 2.2.53), of 'forming' the landscape (*formantem rupes, Silv.* 2.2.57), and of 'taming' the earth (*domuit, Silv.* 2.2.56) echo a passage from Vergil's precepts on caring for cattle: *tu quos ad studium atque usum formabis agrestem | iam vitulos hortare viamque insiste domandi* ('as to the calves that you shape to agricultural uses, enter the path of taming,' *G.* 3.163–4).[31] Statius' language also points specifically to Vergil's own (Lucretian) description of the origins of agriculture quoted above (Section 2). His phrase 'nature favours these places' (*his favit natura locis, Silv.* 2.2.52) echoes Vergil's description of the laws of nature and their demand for toil in certain places (*leges . . . certis | imposuit natura locis, G.* 1.60–1). Additionally, Statius' personification of the earth rejoicing under the leadership of Pollius (*gaudet humus, Silv.* 2.2.57) recalls the happiness of well-tended Vergilian crops (*laetis . . . frugibus, G.* 1.69). Indeed, scholars have noted that Statius at times tries to create a symbiosis between nature and human activity.[32] At first sight, this seems to be at odds with those passages in which Statius seems to celebrate the pure domination of nature. However, the happy coexistence of natural features of the environment and human domination of these features makes better sense against the backdrop of the *Georgics* and its celebration of agricultural toil. The didactic tradition expects nature to be tamed and does not, like the moralizing tradition, condemn such activity.

5 Statius on Lucretius and Vergil

We can now see that the first lines of Statius' landscape description combine Lucretian and Vergilian allusions. The collocation of nature

---

[30] Van Dam (1984) 227 points out that the notion that the struggle against nature is a kind of warfare seems to emanate from the *Georgics*. Cf. Myers (2000) 113–14.
[31] Van Dam (1984) 227.
[32] Myers (2000) 114–15 and (2005) 107–8; Wray (2007) 137–8; Newlands (2002) 132 and 136; Cancik (1965) 53.

and place (*natura locis*, *Silv.* 2.2.52) recalls Vergil's natural laws of toil (*natura locis*, *G.* 1.61), while the ideas of nature yielding to cultivation (*colenti | cessit*, *Silv.* 2.2.52–3) and of nature growing accustomed to human needs (*mansuevit*, *Silv.* 2.2.53) echo Lucretius' account of the origin of agriculture (*mansuescere ... | ... colendo*, *DRN* 5.1368–9 and *concedere cultis*, *DRN* 5.1371). Statius, in other words, has intertextually juxtaposed the Lucretian cultivator and Vergilian laws of nature, understood as the preconditions of human labor. Statius thereby inserts Pollius' villa into the natural history of both writers. Through this intertextual association, Pollius' villa gains a kind of historical and cosmic significance, which amplifies the poem's panegyrical tone. Simultaneously, moreover, Statius establishes his descriptive poem within the literary history activated by the Lucretian-Vergilian intertext. In other words, while the establishment of Pollius' villa is equated to the invention of agriculture in both of Statius' models, the poem that describes the villa situates itself within these models' didactic tradition. The main Statian innovation in the genre of natural history is that nature itself has (or has not) been transformed according to both the principles of personal comfort (i.e. is the landscape conducive to human happiness?) and of aesthetic criteria (i.e. does the landscape look beautiful?). Obviously, the landscape of Pollius' villa has been radically transformed into an object for visual contemplation. Since, however, this visual contemplation takes place within the Lucretian-Vergilian intertext, his landscape ekphrasis becomes a didactic topos. Recall that the traditional interpretation of Statius' villa poems identifies ekphrasis as a figure of praise within the context of a polemical response to the Roman moralizing tradition (see Section 1 above). According to the interpretation offered here, we may also see Statian villa descriptions against the backdrop of the history of agriculture and its (overall) praise of human enterprise and activity.

6 Pliny and Lucretius

Pliny's description of the landscape surrounding his Tuscan villa also contains a concentration of lexical echoes of Lucretius and Vergil. Pliny alludes directly to Lucretius when he says that the valley in which his estate is located (which he compares to a gigantic amphitheater) is like a work of art that only 'the nature of things' could create: *regionis forma pulcherrima. imaginare amphitheatrum aliquod immensum, et quale sola rerum natura possit effingere* (*Ep.* 5.6.7). Here the name-dropping of the title of Lucretius' poem (*rerum natura*) suggests a generic affinity between

Lucretian science and the Tuscan landscape. Moreover, the phrase *rerum natura* could also point to the beginning of Lucretius' agricultural history that we have been examining (*rerum ... natura creatrix*, *DRN* 5.1362). Indeed, in the rest of Pliny's landscape description we see numerous resonances of Lucretius' history of agriculture. When Pliny says that 'forests descend along with the mountain' (*silvae cum ipso monte descendunt*, *Ep.* 5.6.7) his words have some affinity with Lucretius' notion that the development of agriculture involved 'the forests retreating to the mountains' (*in montem succedere silvas*, *DRN* 5.1370). Pliny's description lists hills, plains, meadows, vineyards, and groves of fruit trees (*pingues ... colles; planissimis campis; prata inde campique, campi; vineae; arbusta*, *Ep.* 5.6.8–9), all of which occur in the Lucretian passage (*prata lacus rivos segetes vinetaque laeta | collibus et campis ...*, *DRN* 5.1372–3). Aspects of Lucretius' phrase about the land yielding to cultivation (*concedere cultis*, *DRN* 5.1371) are echoed in Pliny's notion that the hills are no less fertile than the plains (*colles ... campis fertilitate non cedunt*, *Ep.* 5.6.8, where Pliny redoubles Lucretius' alliteration). Moreover, both writers refer to fruit trees segmenting the landscape (*margine*, *Ep.* 5.6.9; *plaga*, *DRN* 5.1374). Finally, both Lucretius and Pliny refer to the visual pleasure received when viewing the countryside in panorama. Pliny says 'you will take great pleasure in looking at the place from the mountain' (*capies voluptatem si hunc regionis situm ex monte prospexeris*, *Ep.* 5.6.13); Lucretius says 'now you see that everything is set out with various pleasures' (*nunc esse vides vario distincta lepore | omnia*, *DRN* 5.1376–7). As in Statius, Pliny appears to employ a large number of Lucretian echoes in order to imbue the Tuscan landscape with aspects of Lucretian natural history.

7 Pliny and Vergil

Let us turn to the intertextual connections between Pliny's landscape description and the account of the origins of agriculture in the *Georgics*. Vergil, as we recall, claims that the laws of nature have determined the necessity of agricultural toil, and that human toil has shaped the landscape (see Section 2 above). Therefore, when Pliny says that nature has fashioned (*effingere*, *Ep.* 5.6.7) the landscape, he is compressing these Vergilian notions. Nature, in Pliny's formulation, acts as a kind of sculptor, that is to say like a human artisan, in establishing both the wild and cultivated lands of Tuscany. Pliny also refers to the relevant times of year when crops ripen (*opimamque messem serius tantum, sed non minus percoquunt*, *Ep.* 5.6.8) in language that echoes Vergil's description of the sun's role in 'cooking' the clods (*glaebasque...* | *pulverulenta coquat maturis solibus aestas*, *G.* 1.65–6). Pliny's assertion that the Tuscan soil is so hard that it takes nine passes of the plow to break up the earth contains several words and phrases that point to Vergil: *ingentes boves* (*Ep.* 5.6.10) ~ *fortes... tauri* (*G.* 1.65); *glaebis* (*Ep.* 5.6.10) ~ *glaebas* (*G.* 1.65); *sulco* (*Ep.* 5.6.10) ~ *sulco* (*G.* 1.68). Notice that Pliny, in his description of oxen, replaces the prosaic Vergilian verb *invertant* (*G.* 1.65) with two more descriptive verbs. The oxen in Pliny 'break' (*perfringunt*) the soil, which must be 'tamed' (*perdometur*) into furrows (*Ep.* 5.6.10). This language of violence and taming, as we have seen, appears to derive from Statius and could constitute an acknowledgment by Pliny of Statius's position as an intertextual intermediary (see Section 9 below). Finally, Pliny refers to the beauty of grasses in meadows (*prata... herbas teneras... et molles... alunt*, *Ep.* 5.6.10), grasses that Vergil condemns as weeds (*officiant laetis ne frugibus herbae*, *G.* 1.69). This modification is a very Statianesque correction, provided that we understand Statius as polemically valorizing luxurious aesthetics over the traditional Roman idea of the simple rustic life.

8 Pliny on Lucretius and Vergil

Overall, it seems that Pliny alludes to Lucretius in his visual presentation of physical features of the landscape (hills, plains, meadows, groves, vineyards), while he alludes to Vergil when he dwells on the agricultural labor that goes on there (clods, furrows, farm animals). Although Pliny in general is uninterested in the labor that goes into the construction and maintenance of his estates,[33] here he takes particular care to 'cap' Vergil by multiplying the toil of plowing nine times; but the main point here is that Pliny acknowledges the Lucretius-Vergil intertext that he has found in Statius, his evident model for villa description.[34] For Statius, the Vergilian-Lucretian intertext gives a slightly different version of the control over nature topos than is found in the Roman moralizing tradition. The didactic background allows Statius to portray the domination of nature as a perfectly normal activity for humans and the hyperbolic transformation of the landscape as a legitimate figure of praise (legitimate in the sense of being attested to in a Roman literary tradition). Pliny seems to acknowledge this in his villa letter through his digression on the history of ekphrasis (famously at *Ep.* 5.6.41–4). There he compares his letter to the descriptions of the shields of Achilles and Aeneas: *vides quot versibus Homerus,*

---

[33] Myers (2005) 114.   [34] Myers (2005) 111. See also Section 1 above.

quot Vergilius arma hic Aeneae Achillis ille describat ('you see how many verses it takes Homer and Vergil to describe, respectively, the arms of Achilles and Aeneas,' *Ep.* 5.6.43). But in addition, Pliny adduces the example of Aratus as well, and emphasizes that the entire *Phaenomena* is a kind of gigantic ekphrasis: *vides ut Aratus minutissima etiam sidera consectetur et colligat* ('you see how Aratus traces and lists even the tiniest stars', *Ep.* 5.6.43). Thus, Pliny overtly evokes the heroic epic tradition (the shields of Achilles and Aeneas), which is already present in Statius' villa poems through various intertextual gestures (Alcinous' palace; Bay of Naples as setting of the *Aeneid*), alongside the didactic tradition (Aratus), which is implicit in Statius' allusions to Lucretius and Vergil's *Georgics*.

9 Pliny and Statius

Scholars have noted that Pliny repeatedly compares natural and artistic beauty in his villa letters.[35] In *Epistle* 5.6, we saw how Pliny combines the two ideas in his overt allusion to Lucretius. There, Pliny says that the nature of things (*rerum natura*) can artistically fashion (*effingere*) the landscape (see Section 7 above). The end of Pliny's landscape description also implies the art-nature contrast: 'you will see a painted scene of unusual beauty rather than a real landscape' (*neque enim terras tibi sed formam aliquam ad eximiam pulchritudinem pictam videberis cernere, Ep.* 5.6.13). Later on, Pliny compares a manicured garden with the wild meadow while overtly using the art-nature contrast: 'outside is a meadow, as well worth seeing for its natural beauty as the formal garden I have described' (*pratum inde non minus natura quam superiora illa arte visendum, Ep.* 5.6.18).[36] These art-nature antitheses recall Statius' villa poems. We have noted that some parts of Pollius' estates are naturally beautiful while others have been transformed by human effort:

> his favit natura locis, hic victa colenti
> cessit et ignotos docilis mansuevit in usus.
>
> (*Silv.* 2.2.52–3)
>
> Some spots Nature has favoured, in others she has been overcome and yielded to the developer, letting herself be taught new and gentler ways.
> (trans. Shackleton Bailey)

---

[35] Bek (1976) 163–4. For the contrast in Statius see Myers (2005) 105. For Pliny see Hoffer (1999) 33–4 (with comparison to Statius).
[36] Bek (1976) 163.

The Villas of Pliny and Statius

Recall that in Statius, cultivation has an aesthetic dimension, in so far as he is predominantly describing landscaping as opposed to pure agriculture. Hence the nature-cultivation contrast here implies the art-nature. Indeed, in Statius' other villa poem (*Silv.* 1.3), the poet makes the same distinction, overtly contrasting *natura* and *ars*:

> ingenium quam mite solo, quae forma beatis
> ante manus artemque locis! non largius usquam
> indulsit natura sibi.
>
> (*Silv.* 1.3.15–17).

> How gentle the nature of the ground! What beauty in the blessed spot before art's handiwork! Nowhere has Nature indulged herself more lavishly.
>
> (trans. Shackleton Bailey)

This praise of the natural state of the villa's site is surrounded by statements valorizing the results of human activity. As in *Silv.* 2.2, Statius here employs violent language: the introductory lines of the poem tell us that the coolness of the place 'breaks' (*frangunt*) the heat (*Silv.* 1.3.7–8). Moreover, Statius describes the villa as having the Anio inserted in the middle (*inserto... Aniene, Silv* 1.3.2), implying the primacy of the buildings over the river. Finally, immediately after his statement about art and nature, Statius claims that the river miraculously becomes less noisy as it enters the villa's grounds (*Silv.* 1.3.20–2). Thus Statius, in both his villa poems, anticipates Pliny's juxtaposition of art and nature within the context of landscape description. Notice, furthermore, that both of Statius' villa poems allude generally to Epicureanism,[37] and that the pairing of these two passages constitutes a sort of quotation of Lucretius. Let us return once again to Lucretius' agricultural history:

> at specimen sationis et insitionis origo
> ipsa fuit rerum primum natura creatrix
> ...
> inde aliam atque aliam culturam dulcis agelli
> temptabant fructusque feros mansuescere terra
> cernebant indulgendo blandeque colendo.
>
> (*DRN* 5.1361–2, 1367–9)

> But the pattern of sowing and the beginning of grafting first came from nature herself the maker of all things ... Next one after another they tried ways of cultivating the little plot they loved, and saw wild fruits grow tame in the ground with kind treatment and friendly tillage.
>
> (trans. Rouse and Smith)

---

[37] The Lucretian elements of the landscape description in *Silv.* 2.2 have been noted above (Section 3). On the Epicurean content of *Silv.* 1.3 see Cancik (1978).

Lucretius' characterization of agricultural labor as a combination of indulgence and cultivation is picked up in the characterization of nature in Statius' villa poems: *indulsit natura* (*Silv.* 1.3.17) and *natura ... colenti* (*Silv.* 2.2.52). This pairing is also present in Pliny, and provides the key to his understanding of the overall intertext. Returning to Pliny's theoretical digression (*Ep.* 5.6.41–4), we find Pliny characterizing his act of description in the following way: *praeterea indulsi amori meo; amo enim, quae maxima ex parte ipse incohavi aut incohata percolui* ('moreover I have indulged in my love; for I love the things I have for the most part begun myself, or the things begun already that I have cultivated', *Ep.* 5.6.41). Here we see the Lucretian pairing of indulgence and cultivation that we found (separately) in Statius' two villa poems. As in Statius, cultivation in Pliny is not literally agricultural toil, but a kind of aesthetic stewardship. In this way, his conceptions of cultivation and indulgence have a Statian inflection. Pliny, in other words, both demonstrates his awareness of the Lucretius-Vergil intertext within his Statian model and at the same time advertises his fuller acknowledgment of the Lucretian pretext than Statius does.

10 Conclusion

We are now in a position to draw conclusions about the intertextuality of Pliny's villa descriptions. First, Pliny has followed Statius in establishing a partial literary history in which the 'genre' of villa description is situated within the didactic tradition. Second, the presentation of nature and its domination in Pliny and Statius is the means by which this didactic intertext is activated. That is to say, Statius' (and hence Pliny's) presentation of control over nature is not entirely a response to the moral critique of luxury found in Horace and Seneca, but is also informed by the history of agriculture and toil found in Lucretius and Vergil. Finally, Statius and Pliny employ the didactic intertext as an innovative way to configure ekphrasis as a figure of praise. Statius uses Lucretian language to portray Pollius in the role of the early Lucretian farmer who cultivates and ultimately controls nature. Statius also appropriates the language of violence and animal taming that Vergil used in his presentation of the farmer's toil. Statius applies this language, however, to the Lucretian farmer, and hence changes its force: instead of struggling against nature like a soldier or animal tamer, Pollius easily controls nature and manipulates the landscape like a general or even a god.[38] For his part, Pliny allusively 'corrects' Statius by providing a complete and coherent version of the Lucretian quotation. Pliny combines Pollius' Lucretian cultivation and Vopiscus' Lucretian indulgence into his own relationship to the villa. Pliny both affirms his reading of Statius as privileging the Lucretian farmer of ancient times, and places himself in that role. Pliny thus affords himself the same praise that Statius lavishes upon Vopiscus and Pollius, and therein lies the intertextual relationship between the ekphrastic praise of the two writers.

[38] Cf. Newlands (2002) 156.

PART V

Pliny Turns Nasty: Satire and the Scoptic Tradition

CHAPTER 11

A Busy Day in Rome: Pliny, Epistles *1.9 Satirized by* Horace, Satires *1.9*[*]

Ábel Tamás

1 Introduction: A 'Self-Sufficient' Letter?

Insisting on the chronology or the date of certain texts is something truly far from my method of research. However, as we know from the now classic book by Roy Gibson and Ruth Morello on Pliny the Younger, the first book of Pliny's epistles is one where dates actually matter.[1] The letter to be discussed in this chapter, *Ep.* 1.9, is a text which shows us a Pliny who seems to be free from regular public duties.[2] He can choose between being in the city (where he gives himself up to the disturbing effects of urban life) and being in his Laurentine villa (where he can enjoy his rural *otium*). We could say that it is not necessary to historicize the situation depicted here: this letter, lacking any concrete hint of biographical events and devoting itself to a fancied literary topos, might be taken as a literary tour de force on the topic of *urbs* versus *rus* and *negotium* versus *otium*, since it is totally independent of any historical context or Pliny's own biography. The problem is that the emphatic 'literariness' and 'independence' – or rather 'self-sufficiency' – of the epistle is part of a strategy followed throughout the whole of his first book. Here, as Gibson and

---

[*] This chapter was supported by the János Bolyai Research Scholarship of the Hungarian Academy of Sciences. I'm highly grateful to the participants of the conference on 'Pliny's Epistolary Intertextuality' for their very helpful suggestions. Special thanks are due to the editors of this volume, Margot Neger and Spyridon Tzounakas, and also to Roy Gibson for their perceptive comments and bibliographical help. The constructive criticism of the anonymous readers is particularly appreciated. For their readiness in polishing my English, I'm highly grateful to Janka Kovács and Rebecca Tamás. Pliny, Horace, and Terence are quoted in the editions by Mynors (1963), Gowers (2012), and Barsby (1999); translations of Pliny and Horace are taken from Walsh (2006) and Davie and Cowan (2011), respectively.

[1] On Pliny's Book 1, see Gibson and Morello (2012) 20–35.

[2] Sherwin-White (1966) 106: 'Pliny's freedom from public business in this account of his life dates the letter before his appointment to the prefecture of Saturn.' Cf. Hoffer (1999) 111–12; Gibson and Morello (2012) 34–5.

Morello convincingly argue, there are some historical or biographical circumstances which he does not want to emphasize.[3]

Pliny does not feel that it is obligatory to give an account of the fundamental historical events of the time covered by the epistles (probably the period between AD 96 and 98).[4] Although he mentions that Domitian is dead (*Ep.* 1.5.1), there is no account of the assassination of Domitian or the accessions of Nerva and Trajan, nor does he recount how he personally went through this politically difficult period.[5] Some facts and events – or some letters testifying to these facts or events – will be included in later books, while others remain entirely unmentioned. The latter category includes his position under Domitian as *praefectus aerarii militaris* (known to us only through the great Comum inscription),[6] or the fact that his position as *praefectus aerarii Saturni* (AD 98 and probably AD 99) is not independent of his action against Publicius Certus, which is narrated much later in Book 9, but without any hint at this correlation.[7] Pliny's self-representation in Book 1 is largely built on reticence and omission, and this is also true of the fact that for a short period of time – which roughly coincides with Nerva's reign from September 96 until January AD 98 – he held no public position apart, of course, from his membership in the Senate.

Pliny's letter 1.9, addressing the writer's preference for countryside *otium* over urban *negotium*, is followed by another letter, 1.10, where Pliny complains of his public duties (probably due to his position as *praefectus aerarii Saturni*, but this is unmentioned as well), which do not allow him to have leisure and live an intellectual form of life.[8] The 'diptych' consisting of

---

[3] Cf. Gibson and Morello (2012) 23–35. On Pliny's epistles as a kind of autobiography, see Gibson and Morello (2012) 14–19. For the implicit presence of historiographical ambitions in Pliny's epistolographic program as outlined in *Ep.* 1.1, see Tzounakas (2007); for Pliny's connection with historiography in general, see Ash (2003).

[4] For a highly useful chronology of Pliny's life, see Gibson and Morello (2012) 266–9. In this chapter, I'm not dealing with the dates of publication of Pliny's letters; for these, see Bodel (2015) in detail. On the different views, see his very useful appendix on pp. 106–8. He dates Books 1 and 2 to late AD 100.

[5] Cf. Gibson and Morello (2012) 24–7.   [6] Cf. Gibson and Morello (2012) 34–5.

[7] Cf. Gibson and Morello (2012) 28–32. In more detail, with emphasis on Pliny's 'revisionist agenda' in Book 9 encouraging us to re-read and re-evaluate Book 1, see Gibson (2015) 194–9.

[8] See *Ep.* 1.10.9 *Nam distringor officio, ut maximo sic molestissimo: sedeo pro tribunali, subnoto libellos, conficio tabulas, scribo plurimas sed illitteratissimas litteras.* ('For I am torn away by my official duties, which though most important are also most troublesome. I take my seat on the bench, sign petitions, present accounts, write countless letters of a most unliterary kind.') Cf. Sherwin-White (1966) 108 on the date of *Ep.* 1.10: 'After the accession of Nerva and the return of the philosophers, and almost certainly after Pliny's appointment to the *aerarium Saturni* at the beginning of 98 .... Hence after January 98 and probably the latest letter in the book.' Additionally, see Gibson and Morello (2012) 21.

letters 1.9 and 1.10 shows us a Pliny who, on the one hand, has a free choice between urban occupations and countryside leisure and, on the other hand, has no other option but to perform his duties as, probably, prefect of Saturn's treasury, which, unmentioned again, guarantees his future consulship.[9] The two situations, as scholars argue, cannot be true at the same time. Consequently, it is assumed, with good reason, that *Ep.* 1.9 had been written in the period when Pliny had no public position (96/7) whilst *Ep.* 1.10, as mentioned, represents his new life in an eminent position under Trajan's reign (98/9).[10] The first book of Pliny's epistles tries to represent its author as both being more or less independent of the dense political events following Domitian's assassination and free from their consequences (namely the atmosphere of fear and uncertainty), and letter 1.9 seems to participate in this strategy of 'de-concretization'.[11]

The 'self-sufficiency' of Pliny and his letter, however, is vulnerable in a manifold sense of the word. First of all, the letter's independence of any historical or autobiographical context is vulnerable because, as mentioned, it can be read as a testimony to Pliny's everyday life in the somewhat difficult, post-Domitianic period when his political future was not yet guaranteed. Secondly, Pliny's *otium* is vulnerable because of the urban interactions which are inevitable while the author lingers in Rome. Thirdly, the letter – as this chapter will show – involves its author in an intertextual play, where interactions between different times, persons, texts, and genres are inevitable. *Ep.* 1.9, when read against the background of Horace's *Sat.* 1.9, establishes interactions which contribute to the 'satirization' of both the letter and the letter-writer. Consequently, the generic (epistolographic) 'independence' of this letter is strongly threatened. Due to interactions which threaten their autobiographical, urban, and literary 'self-sufficiency', *Ep.* 1.9 and its author are being systematically satirized.[12]

2 *Otium* and Self-Satirization

At first glance, it would be unproblematic to read letter 1.9 as reinforcing the spatial opposition between *otium* and *negotium*: you can only have

---

[9] Cf. Gibson and Morello (2012) 22. [10] Gibson and Morello (2012) 22.
[11] On the 'great uncertainty and fear of further chaos' after Domitian's death, see Gibson and Morello (2012) 25. On *Ep.* 1.9's participation in the strategy followed by Pliny in Book 1, see Gibson and Morello (2012) 34–5, with emphasis on Pliny's 'potentially awkward immediate past' which is successfully obscured by letter 1.9.
[12] For 'generic variety' (*Gattungsvielfalt*) in Pliny's letters in general, see Fögen (2017).

negotium in the city and *otium* in the countryside.[13] I think, however, that whilst this opposition is evident in the letter, it is challenged as well. The problem lies, obviously, with the different forms of *otium*. It is true that Pliny is suggesting that the real, intellectual, valuable form of *otium* is available only in your countryside villa, and it is a privilege[14] of the elite figures implicit in the letter (the letter's 'I', 'you' or 'he'). This form of *otium* is almost inaccessible in the city. But there is another form of *otium* which you can 'enjoy' (if there is anything positive in it at all) in the city: *otium* as 'free time', i.e. when you have simply nothing to do and, therefore, are bothered by requests coming from people who automatically suppose that having free time means being available for others. This is supported by the whole social system of Imperial Rome, where the members of the senatorial aristocracy had been expected to make themselves useful in various senses of the word. This seems to be the risky form of *otium* that *Ep.* 1.9's Pliny – senator and advocate, but, for the time being, without any other political position – has chosen for himself, with all its consequences.

In *Ep.* 1.10, Pliny presents himself as so busy that the option of intellectual *otium* is entirely impossible. Furthermore, whilst he is in the miserable situation of being deprived of the company of Euphrates, the philosopher, by his office, it is similarly unimaginable for him to attend events described in *Ep.* 1.9.2, such as toga ceremonies, betrothals, weddings, or to help people with his legal expertise. Consequently, *Ep* 1.10's Pliny is deprived both of the freedom implied in real *otium*, but also of the *otium* of 'free time in the city,' which seems to encourage others to take advantage of his availability. In sum, letter 1.10's Pliny is available only as *praefectus*; whereas *Ep.* 1.9's Pliny is available for everyone when he is in the city, simply because he is in the city. But why is he there?[15]

I think the answer lies in the consequences depicted in *Ep.* 1.10: he achieved the appointment at which he was aiming. During Nerva's very short reign, Pliny was in a somewhat uncertain situation. His first (or second) wife had died; his political career was temporarily suspended. Presumably, this is the time when he started to write letters for publication, which proved to be suitable for de-concretizing these circumstances.

---

[13] For the problem of *otium* in this letter, see Leach (2003) 157–8; Méthy (2007) 373–8; Gibson and Morello (2012) 172–6; Neger (2016) 135–7.
[14] For the interconnection of *otium* and *luxuria* in Pliny, see Leach (2003).
[15] Cf. Hoffer (1999) 112: 'indeed, the letter does not really tell us why Pliny and this friends spend any time at Rome at all'.

As mentioned, Pliny does not inform us about the process which led to his appointment as *praefectus* under Trajan; but as *Ep.* 1.9 and 1.10 are juxtaposed, we are encouraged to speculate on what happened in between. *Ep.* 1.9 shows us a Pliny who has a lot of opportunities to attend various events in Rome and voluntarily help others, he also has the option of going to his Laurentinum whenever he wants; yet, *Ep.* 1.10 shows us a Pliny who is so busy that he has no time for anything but his official work. I believe we are encouraged to speculate on the correlation between the two letters, and one of the many possibilities is to conclude that Pliny got this appointment *because* he has stayed in Rome for an extended period of time (not only for single days, but often for many days in a sequence, see *Ep.* 1.9.1) – more than would have been necessary. Pliny might suggest that it is even his frequent presence in the city (under Nerva) which helped him to restart his political career (under Trajan): 'I had to be quite often in Rome. I had no position, but, you know, I had to be there'.[16]

But lingering in the city just for the sake of lingering has its own risks, not only in life, but also in literature. A situation of this kind – i.e. that you have to waste your time in the city just because you feel like you have to be there, while you have a comfortable *villa rustica* in Laurentum – can be easily *depicted* in a way which makes you an object of parody or self-parody. This is due to the fact that such behaviour has been variously described by literary texts as an emphatically non-elite one: when you are lingering in the city, you will be dangerously similar to comic figures, such as Peniculus (Plautus' parasite from the *Menaechmi*), who performs his *otium* particularly in the forum (see *Men.* 453), and thus prepares the ground for, say, the *otiosus* 'Catullus' figure of Catullus 10.[17] Those 'parasitic' figures are, to be sure, inherent parts of the usual description of city life from Theophrastus' *Characters* onwards. This is not far away from the urban experience of the Imperial Age established in the poetic works of Juvenal and Martial, whose 'satiric criticism of city life'[18] was acknowledged by Nicole Méthy – on different grounds – as an important context of Pliny *Ep.* 1.9.[19] According to Méthy, 'la tradition satirique' is present in Pliny's presentation of the urban *discursus*, *strepitus*, and *labor* in

---

[16] Cf. Hoffer (1999) 112: 'Pliny pursues literary and moral ideals at his villa, not indolence and luxury, whereas his hopes at Rome for patronage to launch him further up the senatorial *cursus* are disguised as selfless performance of minor duties among equals.'

[17] For '*otium* in *foro*' in Catullus 10, see Culpepper Stroup (2010) 44–5. Catullus 10 has much in common with Horace's *Sat.* 1.9 (which will feature as an intertextual precedent of Pliny's 1.9 in this chapter), see e.g. Gowers (2012) 280.

[18] Gibson and Morello (2012) 172 n. 15.   [19] Méthy (2007) 330–3.

Ep. 1.9;[20] but, I think, Rome's parasitic *otiosi*, potentially present in the letter, form an inherent part of this picture as well. Accordingly, Pliny *Ep.* 1.9 becomes associated with a kind of 'satiric criticism of city life', where the satirist complains about the city life without which he would not have material for his satires, not to mention that he can be easily depicted as an annoying figure who is part of the urban bustle he is complaining about.[21]

In this chapter, I will interpret Pliny's letter 1.9 in terms of Roman satire with my specific proposal of regarding the letter's connection with its Horatian 'numerological parallel', *Sat.* 1.9.[22] The question remains, however, whether the topic (lingering in the city without specific reasons) automatically gives itself up to satirical representation, or whether it is Pliny's specific literary tactics in this letter which turn our thinking in this direction. By all means, there is something in the 'autobiographical background' of this letter – that is, of course, a background which is artificially constructed by the letter itself and especially its place in the collection – which has something to do with satire, and Pliny, for his part, does not resist this temptation. He avoids the risk of describing the 'real' history of his everyday life under Nerva. Instead, he takes the risk of being intertextually satirized.

This 'satirization' goes hand in hand with an aspect of *Ep.* 1.9 (a highly dialogic letter) which has generally been ignored: the vastly complex process where Pliny is multiplied into different – speaking or silent – personae.[23] To be sure, *Ep.* 1.9 radicalizes Demetrius' well-known view according to which an epistle is 'one half of a dialogue' (Demetr. *Eloc.* 223): it seems to supplement 'the other half' as well, while generating situations where the reader cannot clearly separate his or her role from that of the letter-writer. This strategy, on the one hand, assimilates the situation of the addressee to that of the epistolographer – involving him (and thus every reader) in his ambivalent position –, and, on the other hand, changes the epistle into a vivid 'urban satire', with the following characters present:

---

[20] I'm highly grateful to Alice König, Margot Neger, and Spyridon Tzounakas for having directed my attention towards Juvenal's (esp. *Sat.* 3), Persius', and Martial's representation of Roman everyday life. Mart. 10.58, suggested to me by Alice König as a potential parallel of Pliny's letter, is in my view, an especially striking example, where the oppositions of city vs country, *negotium* vs *otium* and the everyday experience of city life are so acutely presented, that it could be rightly interpreted as an epigrammatic 'precedent' of Pliny's 1.9. Actually, Méthy (2007) 331 n. 37 refers to this epigram as one of many examples as well. For this poem, see also Rimell (2008) 205. Another possible parallel is Mart. 10.70, referred to by Hoffer (1999) 114.
[21] The standard rhetorical topic of 'attacks on life in the city and praise for life in the country' is closely associated with the genre of satire, see Edwards (1996) 126; cf. Braund (1989).
[22] For other examples of numerological parallelism in Pliny's epistles, see n. 29 below.
[23] See, however, Hoffer (1999) 111–18, where this trait of *Ep.* 1.9 is mentioned repeatedly.

1) There is Pliny the epistolographic self, who writes his letter evidently in his Laurentine villa, where he enjoys the leisure which he desired when in Rome. This is not (or not necessarily) a biographical fact, but a way of setting the scene in this letter: at the end of a busy day in the city, Pliny, already in Laurentum, writes his *castigatio urbis* and *laudatio ruris* to his friend Minicius Fundanus. This letter's 'Pliny' is the Pliny we know from the letter collection in general, but also the 'de-concretizing Pliny' of Book 1, and also a 'de-concretized (or de-autobiographized) Pliny' as produced by the poetical processes of this very letter.

2) The addressee is Minicius Fundanus, a fellow senator interested in philosophy and closely associated with Plutarch.[24] He was *praetor* under Nerva in AD 97, so the proposal for leaving the city and enjoying the *otium* (see *Ep.* 1.9.7) can be read as an ironic hint at his important position: 'while I'm free to choose what I want, city life or countryside *otium*, you are in the prison of your political career'. Through this rhetorical strategy, Pliny rearranges the configuration: his relative freedom seems to compensate for the temporary uncertainty of his political future. This is the first letter in the collection addressed to Minicius Fundanus, though not the only one. As further letters – either addressed to him (*Ep.* 4.15, 6.6, and 7.12) or mentioning him (*Ep.* 5.16) – show, he is a trusted friend of Pliny. The two men remain connected both politically (*Ep.* 4.15, 6.6) and personally (*Ep.* 5.16), and, as we learn from letter 7.12, Fundanus is a friend whom Pliny likes to joke with. As with many of Pliny's addressees in the first nine books in general, he remains silent as well. Yet in this letter, Pliny (if we want) manages to make him speak as a literary figure of the text. The verbs in second person singular in *Ep.* 1.9.2–3 (*interroges, feceris, reputes, secesseris*), namely, can be read either as referring to a 'generic you' or to Fundanus himself. Either way, this 'you' of the text – identifiable with the general reader as well – is involved in imaginary urban interactions in the subjunctive (*interroges* etc.): it is emphatically Pliny the letter-writer, who makes him (a current *praetor* perhaps) act as an urban interactor. Through the transition *Quod evenit mihi* in *Ep.* 1.9.4, however, this 'you' will be, so to speak, identified with 'Pliny' himself, while this kind of identification will be also true of the 'somebody', *(ali)quis*, i.e. the anonymous urban interlocutor no. 1. For him, see below.

---

[24] On Minicius Fundanus, see Gibson (2018) 407.

3) As an interlocutor of the letter's 'you' (Fundanus or generic you), in *Ep.* 1.9.2, Pliny presents to us a 'somebody', an *(ali)quis* (cf. *si quem interroges*), who answers the question posed by 'you' (*'Hodie quid egisti?'*) as follows: *'Officio togae virilis interfui, sponsalia aut nuptias frequentavi, ille me ad signandum testamentum, ille in advocationem, ille in consilium rogavit.'* This answer characterizes the 'somebody' as an average (elite) figure of Imperial Rome who devotes his day to the urban occupations constituting the 'Roman everyday'. The next two sentences, in turn, present these occupations as characteristic of the day of the letter's 'you': *Haec quo die feceris, necessaria, eadem, si cotidie fecisse te reputes, inania videntur, multo magis cum secesseris. Tunc enim subit recordatio: 'Quot dies quam frigidis rebus absumpsi!'* (*Ep.* 1.9.3). This means that 'you' and 'somebody' become more or less identical, and if this is not enough, letter 1.9.4 (*Quod evenit mihi...*) identifies both of them with the 'epistolographic self'. Consequently, in the letter's rhetoric, the 'you' (Minicius Fundanus / generic you / the general reader), the 'he' ('somebody'), and the 'I' (the epistolographic self) – i.e. the letter's second, third, and first person singular – seem to play interchangeable roles. He, you, and I – we're all playing the same role: the urban and elite one. And at the end, we all have the same complaint: *'Quot dies quam frigidis rebus absumpsi!'* (*Ep.* 1.9.3).

4) Finally, there are further anonymous interlocutors as well, namely the ones included in the line: '... *ille me ad signandum testamentum, ille in advocationem, ille in consilium rogavit'* (*Ep.* 1.9.2). At the first glance, these *illi* seem to be interlocutors of the 'somebody', 'somebody no. 2, 3, and 4', yet, considering the process of identification detailed just now, '2, 3, and 4' are interlocutors of everybody else as well: he, you, and I, as the letter explicitly suggests, will have the same experience and thus very similar interlocutors (in *Ep.* 1.9.3, this will belong to 'you', and in *Ep.* 1.9.4, to 'me'). Considering the anonymity and exemplarity of these urban interlocutors, and the fact that they are characterized only by their short requests, what they represent, is primarily the *strepitus, discursus*, and *inepti labores* (*Ep.* 1.9.7) which make the urban life intolerable.

This cast of characters suggests that, in the city, everybody plays the same role. You interrupt others (for example, with your annoying questions and requests) and you are interrupted by them at the same time. The city has a strong uniformizing effect: we are all being changed into figures who, criss-crossing the crowded streets of Rome, bother each other with ridiculously unimportant things. The city makes even members of the senatorial aristocracy behave like average *illi* lingering in the middle of the city, searching out occasions which could guarantee them a better future: a scene which Pliny wants to simultaneously hide and emphasize. This effect is, I think, very close to the poetics of satire itself. Satire, especially in its Horatian form, is a highly urban genre which is based on the satirization of the satirist himself,[25] and for that, I can find no better example than Horace's *Sat.* 1.9.

3   *Ep.* 1.9 Meets *Sat.* 1.9: 'Horatian' *curiosi* in Pliny's Letter

The intertextual background of Pliny *Ep.* 1.9 is eminently manifold. Nicole Méthy, as mentioned above, has recognized the importance of the satirical tradition. Roy Gibson and Ruth Morello have emphasized the Senecan background and Margot Neger the Ciceronian,[26] which could be enriched with allusions to Tacitus' *Dialogus*.[27] Christopher Whitton has directed the attention to *Sat.* 2.6 as a Horatian model for Pliny's letter.[28] However, in the following pages, I will read the letter as an intertextual recycling of Horace's *Sat.* 1.9. My proposal regarding the intertextual relation is enhanced by the numbering: *Sat.* 1.9 as a 'numerological parallel' of Pliny's *Ep.* 1.9 has been left out of consideration so far. I owe this term to Ilaria Marchesi who has found fascinating examples of this phenomenon.[29] However, the numerological parallel between Horace's *Sat.* 1.9 and Pliny's *Ep.* 1.9 is a special one where it is pre-eminently the numbering itself which offers us the possibility of an intertextual reading. Horace's *Sat.* 2.6 may be a thematically stronger parallel, featuring Horace as a proud owner of his Sabine farm, who, from this new countryside perspective, satirizes his own urban way of life. At any rate, numerology

---

[25]   See Schlegel (2005) 7–8.   [26]   Gibson and Morello (2012) 175; Neger (2016) 136–7.
[27]   See Tac. *Dial.* 12 (Maternus' speech, repeating phrases of Aper's speech, cf. *Dial.* 9): *Nemora vero et luci* (famously alluded to by Plin. *Ep.* 9.10.2 *inter nemora et lucos*) *et secretum* (cf. *secretumque* μουσεῖον, 1.9.6) *ipsum, quod Aper increpabat, tantam mihi adferunt voluptatem, ut inter praecipuos carminum fructus numerem, quod non in strepitu* (cf. *strepitum*, 1.9.7) *nec sedente ante ostium litigatore nec inter sordes ac lacrimas reorum componuntur, sed secedit animus* (cf. *secesseris*, 1.9.3, *animus*, 1.9.4) *in loca pura atque innocentia fruiturque sedibus sacris. Haec eloquentiae primordia, haec penetralia* (cf., again, *secretumque* μουσεῖον, 1.9.6); *hoc primum habitu cultuque commoda mortalibus in illa casta et nullis contacta vitiis pectora influxit: sic oracula loquebantur.*
[28]   Whitton (2014) 151–4. Also, Hoffer (1999) 118 and Méthy (2007) 331 hint at Hor. *Sat.* 2.6.
[29]   Cf. Marchesi (2008) 36, 89 on the connections between Plin. *Ep.* 1.3 and Hor. *Epist.* 1.3, and Plin. *Ep.* 2.2 and Hor. *Epist.* 2.2. See also Hanaghan (2017a) on Sidonius Apollinaris' epistle 1.5 alluding to Hor. *Sat.* 1.5. Many thanks to Michael Hanaghan for having directed my attention to this parallelism. For the internal arrangement of Pliny's Book 1, based on the numbering of the letters, see Bodel (2015) 54–7.

encouraged me to compare Pliny's 1.9 with Horace's 1.9, and I found that the two texts have some interplay with each other. I can imagine Pliny as ordering his first book of epistles (as it is famously depicted in *Ep.* 1.1) and saying: 'A letter on the turbulences of the city with a praise of the rustic *otium*? Wait a minute, it's a perfect candidate for being my... 1.9!'[30] This choice is especially interesting if one considers Matthias Ludolph's interpretation of *Ep.* 1.1–8 as Pliny's 'parade epistles' arranged along the model of Horace's 'parade odes' (*Carm.* 1.1–8). Since Pliny places *Ep.* 1.9 – with its numerological parallel Hor. *Sat.* 1.9 – directly after his 'parade epistles', it might be interpreted as a continuation of the structural allusion to Horace present in the arrangement of the first eight letters.[31]

As is the case with intertextuality in general, in the moment the connection between two texts is 'recognized' (in my above scenario, it is Pliny the editor who 'recognizes' the connection and marks it, paratextually, through the numbering), some features of both texts are immediately strengthened, while others fade. In this special case, Pliny's letter becomes more 'dramatic' in the light of Horaces' satire, the latter being a posteriorly and auto-diegetically narrated dialogue between Horace the satirist and his interlocutor, defamed in Horatian criticism as the *Schwätzer*, the Pest, or the Bore.[32] Pliny's letter contains dialogue as well, but, without the effect of Horatian intertextuality, we would easily attribute it to the loquacious nature of the epistolary genre (Pliny is talking here to Minicius Fundanus *per litteras*) or to the fact that Pliny is fond of quasi-dialogic scenarios as rhetorical devices. However, if we scrutinize *Ep.* 1.9 in the light of *Sat.* 1.9, this dialogism seems to be something more significant. This is how this letter begins (*Ep.* 1.9.1–3):

> Mirum est quam singulis diebus in urbe ratio aut constet aut constare videatur, pluribus iunctisque non constet. Nam si quem interroges 'Hodie quid egisti?', respondeat: 'Officio togae virilis interfui, sponsalia aut nuptias frequentavi, ille me ad signandum testamentum, ille in advocationem, ille

---

[30] On the questionable sincerity of Pliny's claim in *Ep.* 1.1 about the 'random ordering' of his letters, see Gibson (2015) 191–2 and Bodel (2015) 51–2, the latter in the broader context of the arrangement and publication of Pliny's letters.

[31] I'm very grateful to Margot Neger for this amazing suggestion. For the concept of 'parade epistles', see Ludolph (1997) 92–8.

[32] *Schwätzer* is justified by *garrulus* in Plin. *Ep.* 1.9.33, while the 'Bore' or the 'Pest', as Schlegel (2005) 119 rightly emphasizes, 'presupposes a reading of the poem that fails to consider its consequences'. However, instead of using more neutral nicknames such as Schlegel's 'interlocutor' or others' *quidam* or *ille*, I will use 'Bore' for the sake of clarity and, particularly, because I believe that it does not differ much from the way this satire was read in Pliny's time. As we will see, it does not exclude keeping the interpretation open.

in consilium rogavit.' Haec quo die feceris, necessaria, eadem, si cotidie fecisse te reputes, inania videntur, multo magis cum secesseris. Tunc enim subit recordatio: 'Quot dies quam frigidis rebus absumpsi!'

It is remarkable how we account, or seem to account, for each individual day in Rome, but not for a number of days combined. If you were to pose to anyone the question, 'What did you do today?', the answer would be: 'I attended an investiture of the adult toga, or I was present at a betrothal or a wedding; one person asked me to witness his will, a second to plead for him in court, a third to act as assessor on the Bench.' These duties seem necessary on the day you perform them, but once you reflect that you have spent every day doing the same things, they seem pointless, and much more so when you retire from Rome, for it is then that you recollect: 'How many days I have wasted, on what tedious pursuits!'

At a first glance, *'Hodie quid egisti?'* ('"What did you today?"') seems to be an entirely neutral question. However, in the light of the Horatian satire, this question can be understood as a variation of *quid agis* ('how do you do'), which opens the way for the Bore to disturb Horace's urban tranquillity on the *Via Sacra*. Horace, namely, had been meditating on poetic trifles when he was put off from his meditations by the Bore, which can be read as a dramatic illustration of the impossibility of enjoying literary *otium* in the city. At the time when the letter's 'you' poses the question *'Hodie quid egisti?'*, this question inscribes itself into a series of urban questions which constitute the urban *strepitus*, *discursus*, and *inepti labores*, condemned with a great emphasis at the end of the letter. This question is, consequently, very far from being a neutral one: it proves that if you are in the city, you are not only being disturbed by others, you are continuously disturbing others as well. If the 'you' is Fundanus himself, he is changed into someone who has a lot of time for lingering in the city, with the consequence that, to some extent, he will be assimilated into Horace's Bore. But, in some sense, as detailed above, the 'you' and Pliny are identical, which redirects the joke to Pliny: he himself is suspected of being 'everybody's bore' in Rome.

There is another reason why this question is far from neutral. If you ask someone in the city 'What did you do today?' and this happens in a literary landscape not far from satire and, hence, not far from comedy (guaranteed by the contextual and intertextual relations), you characterize yourself as a *curiosus*, a 'busybody' in the sense of *curiositas* as *polypragmosyne* or *periergia*.[33] One of the *loci classici* of this kind of curiosity is Terence's *Eunuchus*, where Chaerea, in his special situation, desires the presence of one of those

---

[33] For a thorough investigation of these concepts, see Leigh (2013).

curiosi who, in Plautus' words, 'concern themselves with the utmost zeal for the affairs of others' (*curiosi ... alienas res qui curant studio maxumo*);[34] Antipho is happy to play the role (*Eunuchus* 553–61, transl. Leigh):

> CH. sed neminemne curiosum intervenire nunc mihi
> qui me sequatur quoquo eam, rogitando obtundat enicet
> quid gestiam aut quid laetu' sim, quo pergam, unde emergam, ubi siem
> vestitum hunc nanctu', quid mi quaeram, sanus sim anne insaniam!
> AN. adibo atque ab eo gratiam hanc quam video velle inibo.
> Chaerea, quid est quod sic gestis? quid sibi hic vestitus quaerit?
> quid est quod laetus es? quid tibi vis? satine sanu's? quid me aspectas?
> quid taces? CH. o festus dies! amice salve. hominum omnium
> nemost quem ego nunciam magis cuperem videre quam te.

> CH. To think that there is no busybody to bump into me now, follow me whenever I go, and belabour me half to death with questions about what I'm excited about, why happy, where I'm off to, where I'm coming from, where I got these clothes, what I'm aiming at, whether I'm sane or mad. AN. I'll go up and I'll do him the favour that I can see that he wants. Chaerea, why are you so excited? What does this clothing mean? Why are you happy? What are you aiming at? Are you quite sane? Why are you looking at me? Why are you silent? CH. O you one-man festival! Greetings, friend: there is no man I would sooner see now than you.

Although Chaerea is delighted to have found Antipho as his *curiosus*, it is true that this text can be understood as a precedent for Horace's *Sat.* 1.9.[35] This Terentian passage shows us that Horace's interlocutor, represented as a typical character of the metropolitan life, represents not only the Theophrastean category of *lalos* ('the talker', *Char.* 7) or *alazon* ('the boastful man', *Char.* 23), but *areskos* ('the obsequious man', *Char.* 5) and *periergos* ('the overzealous man', *Char.* 13) as well. Horace's satiric Bore is a figure not only from Rome of the 30s BC, but also from the literary landscape of urban life: he is a parasitic figure from New Comedy or *palliata*, significantly contributing to the feeling that being in the city means being disturbed all the time.

It is important that the literary *curiosus* is, typically, a man of *otium* in the primary sense of 'having nothing to do'. This is not only how Horace's Bore characterizes himself: 'I've nothing to do and plenty of energy: I'll accompany you the whole way' (*'nil habeo quod agam et non sum piger: usque sequar te', Sat.* 1.9.19), but this is true for Horace as well, who, in

---

[34] *Stichus* 198–9 (above: transl. Leigh).
[35] Leigh (2013) 63. According to Gowers (2012) 283, Ter. *Eun.* 335–42 is a model of Hor. *Sat.* 1.9.

spite of his otherwise comfortable position as *scriba quaestorius*,[36] would like to practice an intellectual, elite form of doing nothing (labelled by Cicero as *otium honestum*;[37] cf. Plin. 1.9.6 *o dulce otium honestumque*) and is prevented from doing it even by the intervention of this busybody. Paradoxically, it is an *otiosus* person who tries to push him to *negotium*. He resists strongly, although their walk in the direction of the Trastevere is anything but literary *otium*; it is a forced tour based on Horace's forced lie about the sick friend whom he has to visit right at that very moment. Considering Pliny's sentence quoted from Atilius in *Ep.* 1.9.7 which identifies useless *negotium* (i.e. the negative consequence of urban *otium*) with *nihil agere*,[38] the philosophically correct answer to the question '*Hodie quid egisti?*' would be ultimately: *nihil*, i.e. 'I did nothing today.' Since *nihil agere* is how Horace's Bore characterizes himself (*nil habeo quod agam*), and this is, or will be, true of Horace in the progress of the satiric plot as well (initially, he is really free; later, he is forced to 'do nothing' in the sense of useless *negotium*), it is not only the question but also the potential answer which brings the two texts together.

That the urban life changes the letters' 'you' – and, because of the identifications, 'me' and 'him' as well – into a kind of *curiosus*, is confirmed by the next passage where the letter-writer contemplates the city's bustle from the safe position of his countryside villa (*Ep.* 1.9.5):

> Nihil audio quod audisse, nihil dico quod dixisse paeniteat; nemo apud me quemquam sinistris sermonibus carpit, neminem ipse reprehendo, nisi tamen me cum parum commode scribo; nulla spe nullo timore sollicitor, nullis rumoribus inquietor: mecum tantum et cum libellis loquor.

> I hear or say nothing which I regret having heard or spoken; no one in my presence criticizes another with unkind insinuations, and I have no harsh words for anyone – except myself, when my writing falls below standard.

---

[36] On the duties of Horace as *scriba quaestorius*, see Fraenkel (1957) 14–15.
[37] See Culpepper Stroup (2010) 49.
[38] **Satius est** enim, ut Atilius noster eruditissime simul et facetissime dixit, **otiosum esse quam nihil agere** (*Ep.* 1.9.8). See its counterpart in *Ep.* 1.10.10–11, where Euphrates the philosopher interprets Pliny's *officia* as part of his *negotium publicum*, but does not entirely convince the author: *Ille me consolatur, adfirmat etiam esse hanc philosophiae et quidem pulcherrimam partem, agere negotium publicum, cognoscere, iudicare, promere et exercere iustitiam, quaeque ipsi doceant in usu habere. Mihi tamen hoc unum non persuadet,* **satius esse ista facere** *quam cum illo dies totos audiendo discendoque consumere* ('who consoles me, and also maintains that it is not merely a part but in fact the most noble part of philosophy to conduct public affairs, to investigate and to pass judgements, to promote and to wield justice, and to put into practice what the philosophers preach. However, he does not persuade me of this one thing: that it is better to conduct these public affairs rather than to spend whole days with him in listening and learning').

> No hope, no fear agitates me; no gossip disturbs my mind. Conversation is confined to myself and my books.

Pliny's 'honest' words suggest that the idea that he is changed into a kind of busybody in the city is very far from being an absurd assumption. At least we are invited to think of him as somebody who, when remaining in the city for a long time, becomes *curiosus*, being eager to *curare res alienas*. Temporarily metamorphosed into an urban busybody by the city itself, Pliny significantly contributes to Rome's urban *strepitus* (cf. *Ep.* 1.9.7). This din may be understood not only as the physical noise of the city,[39] but also as a continuous buzzing in the figurative sense of the word, constituted by the permanent streaming of various urban rumours, created, changed, and disseminated by Rome's *curiosi*, potentially changing anyone into ridiculous – comic or satiric – characters. This implies a massive danger for the members of Rome's elite circles, especially for a person who is so proud of his intellectual autonomy, taste, and elegance. This is reinforced by the historical context described above: Pliny, in the hope of restarting his political career, must waste his time in the city without specific reasons, just to 'be present' and to 'show himself' in the hope of a political renewal. In this uncertain situation, it is not surprising that, while being in Rome, he cannot separate himself from his own uncomfortable feelings, such as regretting others' and his own words, unkind insinuations, hope, fear, gossip[40] – all this being the hotbed of curiosity and the *curiosi*.[41] In *Ep.* 1.9.5, Pliny describes his anxiety in a way which is profoundly interesting: similarly to Horace's Bore with his literary and social ambitions, Pliny performs urban tactics in the hope of a – in his case, a political – breakthrough. From a Horatian point of view, the *sermones sinistri* ('unkind insinuations') through which Pliny and his acquaintances criticize persons who are not present – are particularly

---

[39] For an excessive discussion of noise (both internal and external) and its damages on the human soul, see Sen. *Ep.* 56. On noise pollution in Rome, see Mart. *Ep.* 12.57.24–7. However, while for the 'poor' Martial it is the literal noise of the city itself, which does not let him sleep (cf. Rimell 2008: 25), in Pliny's case nothing similar is possible. When he cannot sleep during the night in his elegant urban villa on the Esquiline (cf. *Ep.* 3.21 quoting Mart. *Ep.* 10.20(19), more on that later in Section 5), this is hardly due to the literal noise of the *urbs*. The noise comes from his soul which cannot rest because of uncomfortable thoughts detailed in *Ep.* 1.9.5. Figuratively, this is Pliny's Roman 'noise pollution'.

[40] The best illustration of this atmosphere is *Ep.* 9.13, see esp. 10–11 with the 'private and anxious words' (*secreto curatoque sermone*) of a friend, an intriguing parallel of the *sinistris sermonibus* in *Ep.* 1.9.5. For 'the fear and paranoia that must have characterized much of the reign of Nerva' as manifested in *Ep.* 9.13, see Gibson (2015) 198.

[41] On the other hand, as *Ep.* 9.32 testifies, 'real *otium*' can serve as the hotbed of curiosity as well (*nihil est ... curiosius otiosis*).

relevant: this might be read as a hint at the intrusion of the genre of Horatian *sermo* (i.e. satire) into Pliny's urban experience and epistolography.[42]

Retroactively, this can be read as an unpleasant interpretation of Horace *Sat.* 1.9, whereby he desperately tries to separate himself from the Bore both spatially and discursively, representing himself as an insider member of Maecenas' circle, while his Bore appears as an outsider in every sense of the word. Interpreters have astutely reminded us how this opposition can be deconstructed by the poetics of Horace *Sat.* 1.9, and how easily the roles can be reversed: Horace as a satirist needs the city as his subject, but this situation can assimilate him into the persons he satirically depicts in his satires.[43] Pliny *Ep.* 1.9, if read as alluding to Horace *Sat.* 1.9, relentlessly radicalizes (and, at the same time, banalizes) this scenario. In Pliny, there is no difference between the various interlocutors: in the *urbs*, everybody is everybody's Bore. It is as if Pliny's letter would rewrite Horace's satire, posing the question: 'Flaccus, don't you think that you have been a bore for the Bore?'

4 Talking and Walking

The further anonymous interlocutors in Pliny – i.e. *ille*, *ille* and *ille* – have their antecedent in Horace's Bore as well. In spite of the satirist's desperate efforts to make himself free, the Bore follows him in his walk through the city. When they enter the Forum Romanum, his legal duties come to the Bore's mind, and so he tries to draw in the satirist as well, temporarily without success (*Sat.* 1.9.35–43):

> ventum erat ad Vestae, quarta iam parte diei
> praeterita, et casu tum respondere vadato
> debebat, quod ni fecisset, perdere litem.
> 'si me amas' inquit 'paulum hic ades.' 'interam si
> aut valeo stare aut novi civilia iura;
> et propero quo scis.' 'dubius sum quid faciam' inquit,
> 'tene relinquam an rem.' 'me, sodes.' 'non faciam' ille,
> et praecedere coepit; ego, ut contendere durum
> cum victore, sequor.

---

[42] Many thanks to Spyridon Tzounakas for this brilliant suggestion. As he suggests to me, *satius est* (*Ep.* 1.9.8) might be recognized as a further generic marker alluding to Horace's recurrent etymological play with *satis* and *satura* throughout the *Satires*, for which see Dufallo (2000).
[43] Above all, see Welch (2001) 181–2.

> Vesta's temple had been reached, with a quarter of the day already gone, and at that time by chance he had to give answer to a plaintiff; failure to do this would mean forfeiting his case. 'Just oblige me,' he says, 'and lend me your support here for a while.' 'Damn me if I have the strength to stand, or know the laws of the land,' say I, 'and I'm hurrying off to that place you know about.' 'I just don't know what to do,' comes his reply, 'whether to lose your company or my case.' 'Oh, my company, please!' 'I won't,' he replies, and starts forging ahead. As for yours truly, I follow on, since it's hard to do battle with one who's stronger.

As Tadeusz Mazurek convincingly argued, Horace has not been in the position of being allowed to resist such inquiries: after he has been asked, he had to help his 'somebody' (*quidam, Ep.* 1.9.3), in other words the Bore.[44] Similarly, Pliny's 'he', the 'somebody', who answers the question posed by 'you' in *Ep.* 1.9.2, has no opportunity to refuse the various requests coming from the numerous interlocutors: 'one person asked me to witness his will (*ille me ad signandum testamentum*), a second to plead for him in court (*ille in advocationem*), a third to act as assessor on the Bench (*ille in consilium rogavit*).' Perhaps he could have repudiated the participation in toga ceremonies, betrothals, weddings – though he obviously didn't, seemingly following the Plinian imperative of 'be present' –, but it would have been hard to refuse these various forms of legal help, which are widely described as time-wasting activities by Horace, Juvenal, Martial and Seneca.[45] These activities, exaggerated by Pliny's anaphoric enumeration (*ille, ille*, and *ille*), suggest a day which is not far from being satirical: a hyperbolized Roman weekday, full of all the possible time-wasting activities. The requests coming from the *illi* can be read as a kind of commentary on Horace's legal issue: the three legal scenarios implied by the requests of the Plinian interlocutors may serve as intertextual amplifications of Horace's single issue which is being 'multiplied' by Pliny's letter. To help the interlocutors, however, is what Pliny characterizes as *nihil agere* ('to do nothing') and contrasts with real, countryside *otiosum esse* ('to seek relaxation', both 1.9.7).[46] *Nihil agere*: this is what Pliny cannot or does not want to avoid when he lingers in the city, and this is what is being generalized in this letter: everybody, suggests *Ep.* 1.9, has the same fate.

---

[44] Cf. Mazurek (1997), based on the legal context (furthermore, see Gowers 2012: 292 *ad* v. 36 and 301 *ad* vv. 74–8). According to Mazurek's interpretation, *sic me servavit Apollo* at the end of *Sat.* 1.9 is an ironic statement, implying that Horace had to follow the Bore and his *adversarius* to the court.

[45] See Sherwin-White (1966) 107 with both the legal background and literary parallels. For the case of Horace, see *Sat.* 1.9 itself, unmentioned by the commentary.

[46] For the Ciceronian background of the words of *Ep.* 1.9's 'Atilius', see Neger (2016) 136–7.

Horace, when writing *Sat.* 1.9, probably did not possess a countryside villa, which he announces only in *Sat.* 2.6 (*Hoc erat in votis*), the other Horatian model of Pliny's letter.[47] Pliny did possess his Laurentinum, as this letter eloquently testifies, but when he was in the city, he was the slave of his agenda. While for Horace, it is pre-eminently the genre of satire – *Musa pedestris*, the 'walking Muse'[48] – which detains him in the city and satirizes his own behaviour,[49] Pliny must be here because of the imperatives he follows, but it goes hand in hand with his potential satirization. Simultaneously, this satirization is generalized, suggesting that this is the fate of anybody – 'me', 'you' or 'he' – who risks lingering in the city. As the intertextual reading of Pliny's 1.9 suggests, all of us – *ego*, *tu* and *ille* (or more precisely, *illi*) – are potential Horatian 'bores', and it is the city itself which may turn this potential into reality.

Reading Pliny's 1.9 with eyes trained on Horace's 1.9, we are tempted to ask how the anonymous *illi* formulated their requests. Maybe during various walks? This is of course an almost illegitimate question, because this detail remains a *Leerstelle* in the text, to be filled up variously in the various acts of reading. But it is certainly one of the effects of intertextuality that it is able to influence the reader's mental activity in filling up the 'blank spaces' in a literary text. This time, Horace's satire might direct us towards imagining Pliny as walking in Rome and being addressed by different interlocutors during his various walks. In *Ep.* 3.5.15–16, Pliny informs us about the transport preferences of his uncle, Pliny the Elder:

> In itinere quasi solutus ceteris curis, huic uni vacabat: ad latus notarius cum libro et pugillaribus, cuius manus hieme manicis muniebantur, ut ne caeli quidem asperitas ullum studii tempus eriperet; qua ex causa Romae quoque sella vehebatur. Repeto me correptum ab eo, cur ambularem: 'poteras' inquit 'has horas non perdere'; nam perire omne tempus arbitrabatur, quod studiis non impenderetur.

> When on a journey, as though freed from other preoccupations he devoted himself solely to study. His secretary sat by him with a book and writing-tablets; in winter his hands were shielded with gauntlets so that not even the harsh temperature should deprive him of any time for study. For this reason even when in Rome he was conveyed in a chair. I recall his rebuke to me for

---

[47] Cf. Fraenkel (1957) 15: 'The poet's economic circumstances changed completely when, at some time before 31 B.C., presumably not long after the publication of the first book of his *Satires*, Maecenas presented him with the Sabine farm which was to mean so much to him. It is likely that, in consequence of this change, he resigned his post as *scriba*, or at any rate ceased to spend much trouble on it; he could now be expected to attend a meeting of the corporation only when some extraordinary matter was under discussion.'
[48] Cf. Freudenburg (1993).   [49] See Welch (2001) 181–2, hinting at Henderson (1993) 69.

walking: 'You could', he said, 'have avoided wasting those hours.' For he believed that any time not devoted to study was wasted.

Although this is of course a young Pliny who is warned by his uncle, and not a serious senator, this letter allows us to imagine the Younger as walking in Rome and being disturbed by the requests of his interlocutors. In his eyes, *otium* in the city has been an absurd thing (except in exceptional situations such as when the whole city was attending the circus and he could dedicate himself to his intellectual work, see *Ep.* 9.6), and in contrast to the Elder, he represents himself as a person who, when in the city, gives himself up consciously to the disturbing effects of urban life. In *Ep.* 7.3.3, he creates a perfect ideology for this, based on variety and balance between rural and urban forms of being: *terere in hac turba, ut te solitudo delectet* ('[e]xperience the crush of this Roman crowd, so as to take full delight in solitude').[50] But is this a real opportunity for Pliny and his friends? *Teri in hac turba*, like Horace, Juvenal or Martial, or the everyday people of Pliny's time? I think these images are rather the products of Pliny's literary representation of Rome. As Timothy O'Sullivan pointed out, the elite forms of urban walk were significantly different from that of ordinary people: as a VIP, you could either use litter-bearers (as the Elder suggested) or walk with servants on your side, who cleared your way in the middle of the crowd.[51] (NB. Horace had his *puer* as well, as we know from v. 10![52]) This does not mean that a member of the imperial elite, especially when holding a magistracy, was not approachable for *ille, ille* and *ille*. Quite the contrary: as O'Sullivan points out, there was a strong tradition of a 'mobile version of office hours' in Rome, with leading citizens 'promenading' in the forum and waiting for people to ask their advice on matters.[53] I only suggest that the intertextual suggestions of Pliny's 1.9 directing our mind towards imagining a walking 'he' (and, thus, Pliny), who is being continuously disturbed by his anonymous interlocutors are rather misleading – but this image is at the heart of Pliny's intertextually loaded representation of being in the city.

5 Where is Your Mouseion?

It's time to investigate the scene where Pliny depicts his way of life in the countryside (*Ep.* 1.9.6):

---

[50] Cf., again, Mart. 10.58.6 *nunc nos maxima Roma terit*.   [51] Cf. O'Sullivan (2011) 51–76.
[52] On the absent presence of the *puer* in *Sat.* 1.9, see Fitzgerald (2021) 239–42.
[53] O'Sullivan (2011) 70.

> O rectam sinceramque vitam! O dulce otium honestumque ac paene omni negotio pulchrius! O mare, o litus, verum secretumque μουσεῖον, quam multa invenitis, quam multa dictatis!
>
> What straightforward, unblemished living this is! What delightful and what honourable leisure, nobler than virtually any active occupation! The sea and shore, my true and private *maison des Muses*, how many thoughts do you inspire, and how many do you dictate!

In *Ep.* 1.9, Pliny reconfigures the satiric space of Hor. *Sat.* 1.9. In contrast to *Sat.* 2.6 featuring Horace the villa-owner, which may have primarily influenced Pliny's laudation of *otium*,[54] Horace's 1.9 does not imply the possibility of having a villa in the countryside: the place of his *otium* is, on the one hand, the city centre of Rome (this is what seems to be a bad idea), and, on the other hand, Maecenas' house. This urban place of *otium* is absolutely undisturbed as he characterizes it for the Bore (*Sat.* 1.9.48–52):

> 'non isto vivitur illic,
> quo tu rere, modo; domus hac nec purior ulla est
> nec magis his aliena malis; nil mi officit, inquam,
> ditior hic aut est quia doctior; est locus uni
> cuique suus.'
>
> 'The relations we live under there are not as you suppose them to be: no household is as unsullied as that one, or less accustomed to distasteful behaviour such as that; it is no disadvantage to me whatever that someone is richer than I or has more literary talent; each one of us has his own position.'

This characterization of Maecenas' circle, as Tara Welch points out, is focused on the configuration of space.[55] There is a place in the city, namely Maecenas' house on the Esquiline Hill, which lacks urban bustle entirely: the battle of positions, which is, both literally and figuratively, so typical of urban life, is completely absent from the *horti Maecenatis*. In Maecenas' house, as Horace says, 'everybody has his own place'; consequently, the people around Maecenas do not need to participate in the urban *discursus* and *strepitus*. As Horace in *Sat.* 1.6 tells us, after he entered Maecenas' house and attained a position there, that position remained fixed and unchangeable. These hints direct us toward thinking of *horti Maecenatis* as a non-*urbs* in the *urbs* itself: the physical and the social space is free from the urban bustle which destroys your life in the city. In

---

[54] Hor. *Sat.* 2.6.60 ff. *o rus* ... *o quando* ... *o noctes*; Plin. *Ep.* 1.9.6 *O rectam* ... *o dulce* ... *o mare, o litus*. Cf. Whitton (2014) 152. On Plin. *Ep.* 1.9 in the context of Pliny's concept of *otium*, see Gibson and Morello (2012) 172–6.

[55] See Welch (2001), also for the following argument on Maecenas' house (169–71).

Horace's eyes, at least in the framework of *Sat.* 1.9, to be in Maecenas' house means both to be present (physically) in and absent (symbolically) from Rome. This cannot be guaranteed for a public personality such as Pliny the Younger: while he is in the city, even if in a luxurious *villa urbana* with gardens and other 'non-urban' features, he could not free himself of *sinistri sermones, rumores,* and other annoying things. To gain real *otium* and an 'unblemished' life,[56] he had to leave Rome and go to his Laurentinum, which is characterized in *Ep.* 1.9.6 as his own Mouseion. This metaphor can redirect us to the *horti Maecenatis* themselves. Welch recapitulates Chrystina Häuber's assumption, suggesting that the *Diaeta Apollonis* in the *horti Maecenatis*, close to Maecenas' house itself, was modelled after the Alexandrian Mouseion and represented the worship of Apollo and the Muses as an inherent part of his life, making him similar to the Ptolemaic kings.[57] If we read Pliny's passage against this background, we can argue that Pliny intertextually relocates Horace's place of *otium*, as he would say: 'Flaccus, you may have enjoyed your literary *otium* in and around the Mouseion of your great friend, but I'm sorry, I need my own Mouseion – outside the city, if you don't mind! In contrast to your urban temple of Muses, which is in fact not yours, this is my *verum secretumque* μουσεῖον!'

Pliny's letter on Martial's death (*Ep.* 3.21) which, partially, quotes Martial's epigram addressed to Pliny himself (10.20(19)),[58] enriches this picture with a further important aspect. We are informed that Pliny's Roman house stood on the Esquiline itself, and this house, especially in the evenings, served as a house where the Muses – pre-eminently Thalia, who delivers Martial's poetry book to Pliny – are very welcome. Although it is Martial's epigram through which this is suggested, Pliny does not confute this state of affairs, but rather he closes Book 3 with this letter, preparing the reader to welcome him as a poet in Book 4, where we find his first reports on his own poetic activity.[59] This means that (even if *Ep.* 3.21 is the only letter in the whole collection which hints in this direction) it seems to be not altogether impossible that, for Pliny, his Roman house on

---

[56] *Ep.* 1.9.6 *sinceramque vitam*! Cf. Horace's words on Maecenas' *domus pura* in *Sat.* 1.9.49.

[57] See Welch (2001) 169 n. 18: 'Häuber 1990: 65 with note 184 gathers literary indicia of the poets' residence in the Esquiline estate. She places the poets' houses and Maecenas' in proximity to the *Diaeta Apollonis* (100), a building evocative, she argues (92–3), of the famous Mouseion, by which Maecenas styled his gardens as the Roman Alexandria.'

[58] On Pliny's letter on Martial's death (3.21) and its partial quotation of Mart. 10.20(19), see Marchesi (2013); Tzounakas (2014); Neger (2015b) 132–8.

[59] See Neger (2015b) 134.

the Esquiline Hill could occasionally serve as a place of literary *otium*. Moreover, in letter 3.21, Pliny is explicit about his role as a 'patron' in Martial's life: 'When he was retiring from Rome, I presented him with his travelling expenses as a gesture of friendship and acknowledgement of the verses he composed about me' (*Prosecutus eram viatico secedentem; dederam hoc amicitiae, dederam etiam versiculis quos de me composuit*). If we read *Ep.* 1.9 with that in mind, we can say that, on the one hand, Maecenas' house on the Esquiline – Horace's 'non-*urbs*' in Rome – is mirrored not only by Pliny's Laurentinum (the true place of *otium*), but, to a smaller extent, by Pliny's own Roman house on the Esquiline Hill itself. On the other hand, in contrast to the Horace of *Satire* 1.9 who is Maecenas' protégé, the Pliny of *Ep.* 1.9 is a 'patron of his own':[60] after a busy day in the city, he can return to his *own* – Laurentine or even Roman – 'horti Maecenatis'.

6 A Metafictional Conclusion

I cannot resist using the term 'literary interaction', which has recently become the keyword for the relations between authors and texts in the post–Domitianic period, with good reason.[61] While Pliny is a key figure of the literary interactions of this era, his first book, due to the strategy outlined in my introduction to this chapter, is rather cautious with interactions. Pliny's *Ep.* 1.9, as I have argued, participates in Book 1's strategy of biographical de-concretization. This epistle, in the framework of a highly subtle and complex literary play, presents both the author and his text as desiring to protect themselves against real and fictional encounters which they cannot, or are unwilling to, avoid. Specifically, it establishes a kind of 'indirect' literary interaction, which is not only an 'indirect' intertextual play with another literary text (Horace's *Sat.* 1.9), but is also a metafictional play addressing the topic of 'interaction' itself. Accordingly, the fundamental topic of the epistle and its Horatian intertextuality is nothing but the question of 'how to avoid urban interactions with other (literary) texts or people?' *Ep.* 1.9's Pliny, while hopelessly desiring his countryside *otium* and solitude, does, for whatever reason, still linger in the city and perform 'unnecessary' encounters. Simultaneously, while letter 1.9 itself seems to be hopelessly desiring a kind of self-sufficiency – an independence of any autobiographical context and subversive intertextual/ generic connections – it is contextually (cf. the juxtaposition between *Ep.* 1.9 and 1.10) inscribed into a specific period of Pliny's life and,

---

[60] Many thanks to Meike Rühl for this brilliant suggestion.   [61] See König and Whitton (2018b).

paratextually (cf. the numbering of the letter), into an 'annoying interaction' with a Horatian satire.

The interaction between Pliny's letter and Horace's satire 1.9 might make us meditate on the metafictional level of this intertextual encounter. Since both texts concern the possibility of urban tranquillity and its disruption by the city's effects, especially the various interlocutors, we can see the meeting of 'Horace' and 'Pliny' as generating intertextual intrusions into each other's urban or rustic tranquillity. If we read Horace *Sat.* 1.9 from the perspective of Pliny's *Ep.* 1.9, we can argue that Pliny retroactively intruded upon Horace's satire when he, through problematizing the cast of characters, suggested that Horace himself can be considered as a 'bore', and questioned the possibility of enjoying real literary *otium* in Maecenas' gardens. As a highly urban *curiosus*, Pliny intertextually met 'Horace' in the literary landscape of Rome and disturbed his urban tranquillity. If we, however, read Pliny's *Ep.* 1.9 from the perspective of Horace's *Sat.* 1.9, we can argue as follows: when Pliny walks in Rome, he cannot dissociate himself from Horace's walk, and when he depicts his busy day(s) in Rome, he, or his letter, is being intertextually influenced by Horace and his *sermones sinistri*. From this perspective, it is Pliny whose rustic tranquillity is being disturbed in this urban epistle. Rome's *inanis discursus* is taking place in the epistle itself.

Consequently, this annoying literary interaction disturbed Pliny's and his letter's self-sufficiency: due to the encounter with Horace and his satire, both the epistle and its epistolographer have been – in some sense – satirized. Their literary and non-literary encounters, all of them connected to the city, involved them in a situation where their epistolary self-sufficiency has been significantly damaged: intertextually, the epistle, and its Pliny have entered a realm where everything's and everybody's position is being continuously challenged. This is the realm of the *urbs* and, simultaneously, satire. In the framework of this volume, which documents how Pliny's epistles interact with various literary genres, my chapter aimed to point out the potential risks of the interaction with the genre of satire. As my intertextual reading of epistle 1.9 showed, in Pliny's intertextual poetics, the genre of satire is like the city of Rome: both of them generate interactions that the letter-writer simultaneously desires for himself and wants to avoid.

CHAPTER 12

Putting Pallas out of Context: Pliny on the Roman Senate Voting Honours to a Freedman (Plin. Ep. 7.29 and 8.6) *

Jakub Pigoń

If we are searching the corpus of Pliny's correspondence for those rare examples of outrage and indignation,[1] so distinctly standing out from the mild, tranquil and benevolent voice which we usually associate with his epistolographic persona, the two so-called Pallas letters (7.29 and 8.6) will, next to the Regulus cycle,[2] offer the most profitable examples, even on the level of vocabulary. Out of eight instances of Pliny's use of the noun *indignatio* ('indignation') or the verb *indignari* ('to be indignant') in his *Epistles*, three are found here.[3] Admittedly, there is a difference between the two texts in Pliny's treatment of indignation and the object of that indignation. But in spite of this difference, the letters, addressed to the same person (Montanus),[4] belong closely together and should be included in the well-known category of Pliny's epistolographic diptychs (epistles grouped in pairs), a category most famously represented by the Vesuvius letters addressed to Tacitus (6.16 and 6.20).[5]

---

* My thanks are due to Margot Neger and Spyridon Tzounakas in their double capacity as organisers of the Cyprus conference and editors of the present volume – for their hospitality, insightful comments and patience, as well as for sharing with me their unpublished studies. Rhiannon Ash and Christopher Whitton also kindly provided me with copies of their works. Some research on this chapter was conducted during my stay in Oxford in the summer of 2018. I am grateful to the Lanckoroński de Brzezie Foundation for granting me a scholarship which made my stay in Oxford possible.

[1] 'Indignant Pliny' was the title of the panel session during which this chapter was originally presented.
[2] On these five letters (1.5, 2.20, 4.2, 4.7, 6.2), see Ash (2013) and, on 2.20 in particular, the chapter by Mordue (Chapter 4) in the present volume.
[3] 7.29.1, 7.29.4, 8.6.17. Other instances are 4.25.2, 6.10.3, 6.17.1 (*indignatiuncula*, a diminutive attested to only in Pliny), 6.17.6, 6.33.10. See also *Pan.* 16.5, 73.6.
[4] According to Sherwin-White (1966) 438, the addressee is probably T. Junius Montanus, *cos. suff.* 81 (and thus some twenty years older than Pliny). But see Birley (2000) 73: perhaps it refers to L. Venuleius Montanus Apronianus, *cos. suff.* 91 (and see n. 58 below). Anyway, it should be assumed that Pliny's correspondent was a senator. No other letters are addressed to him.
[5] For other examples, see e.g. 2.11 and 2.12; 7.7 and 7.8; 8.10 and 8.11 (see Morello 2015: 145); 9.36 and 9.40. But a pair of letters may be divided, as in our case, between two separate books; see e.g. 3.20 and 4.25; 6.10 and 9.16 (for this pair and its connection with the Pallas letters, see Leach

It was probably during his journey to or from Tibur sometime around AD 107[6] that Pliny came across the sepulchral monument of the once powerful imperial freedman Marcus Antonius Pallas (d. AD 62).[7] Pliny's first Pallas letter appears to have been written while this discovery was fresh in his mind, *proxime adnotavi* ('I noticed the other day', 7.29.2).[8] It opens with a curious sentence which, if we disregard pronouns and particles, consists solely of verbs: *Ridebis, deinde indignaberis, deinde ridebis, si legeris, quod nisi legeris non potes credere* ('You will first laugh, then feel annoyed, and then laugh again, if ever you read something which you will think almost incredible, unless you see it with your own eyes', 7.29.1). This is one of the 43 letters (out of 247, from Books 1–9)[9] in which Pliny begins with a verb in the second person singular, referring to one addressee. But there is no other instance of an opening in which there is such an accumulation of verbs.

Moreover, Pliny's choice of verbs in this sentence is in itself significant. Let us take, firstly, the second part of the sentence: *quod nisi legeris non potes credere*. Pliny presents himself, in a sense, as a paradoxographer whose reliability as an author lends credence to information that is otherwise difficult to accept as true. Another example of paradoxography from the Plinian corpus is the dolphin letter which begins with a statement that *incidi in materiam veram sed simillimam fictae* ('I have come upon a true story – though it sounds very like a fable', 9.33.1), followed by an assurance that *magna auctori fides* ('the author is a man you can implicitly credit', 9.33.1). In our case, however, differently than in the dolphin letter, the credibility of the information rests not just on the *fides* of the source, but on one's own first-hand experience:[10] it was Pliny himself who saw the monument, not heard about it (of course, in the dolphin letter the

---

2013); 1.6 and 9.10 (for other links between the first and the last book of the collection, see Whitton (2013a) 17).

[6] For the date, see Sherwin-White (1966) 37–8.

[7] For his life and career, see *PIR*² A 858; Oost (1958).

[8] The Latin text here used is that by Mynors (1963, OCT). The English translation of Pliny is that by Firth (1900), occasionally modified.

[9] The average ratio is thus 17.4 per cent. In Book 7 it is slightly higher at 21.2 per cent. But, apart from 7.29, there is only one instance of a letter beginning with a verb in the future tense, and thus pointing to the expected reaction of its recipient to what Pliny has written, namely *ridebis, et licet rideas* ('You will laugh, and I give you leave to', *Ep.* 1.6.1.). This is the same verb as at 7.29.1, and it may be relevant that the recipient is Tacitus (see below).

[10] And note that Pliny corroborates his evidence by indicating the location of the monument (*est via Tiburtina intra primum lapidem* – 'just before you come to the first milestone on the Tiburtine Road', 2). This may be seen as a piece of *Beglaubigungsapparat*, a regular device in paradoxographical texts. For Pliny's paradoxographical interests, see Ash (2018) 133–40, focusing on *Ep.* 8.20.

insistence on the truthfulness of the story is not quite serious and the fact that the letter is addressed to a poet is relevant: *quid poetae cum fide?*, 'what has a poet to do with faithfulness?', 9.33.1, as Pliny rhetorically asks).[11] Secondly, looking at the first part of the sentence we may come to the conclusion that Pliny defines his subject matter in terms of yet another literary genre (apart from epistle and paradoxographical writing), namely satire.[12] Moreover, this definition seems to have taken into account both the Horatian model of satirical writing (cf. **ridentem** *dicere verum*, 'to say the truth while laughing', Hor. *Sat.* 1.1.24) and its more bitter variety, which we usually associate with Juvenal (cf. *si natura negat, facit* **indignatio** *versum*, 'when talent is lacking, indignation will write the verse', Juv. 1.79; of course, there is no need to assume that Juvenal's *Satires* 1 antedates Pliny's Book 7[13]). Laughter coupled with indignation (or laughter versus indignation) is the motif on which the ring composition in this letter is hinged; the opening sentence being picked up towards the end by these two sentences: *Sed quid indignor? Ridere satius,*[14] *ne se magnum aliquid adeptos putent, qui huc felicitate perveniunt ut rideantur* ('Why should I lose my temper? It is better to laugh at it, lest those who have by sheer good fortune arrived at such a pinnacle as to become laughing-stocks should think that they had reached a dignified position', 7.29.4).[15] Pliny seems to suggest that to be indignant with Pallas would be to give him too much credit; he does not deserve our indignation, only our ridicule.

---

[11] On the dolphin letter, see Stevens (2009); also Hindermann (2011a), as well as her contribution (chapter 6) in the present volume. As is well-known, in this letter Pliny does not mention his uncle's treatment of what is almost the same story (Plin. *HN* 9.26).

[12] We should note that there are some points of contact between satire and paradoxography. Cf. e.g. Juv. 15 (cannibalism in Egypt; note esp. 13–6 and 27–8), recently discussed by Ash (2018) 140–4.

[13] It is commonly assumed that Juvenal's first book (comprising *Sat.* 1–5) was written during the second decade of the second-century AD, thus a few years later than Plin. *Ep.* 7.29. For the closeness of this letter to satire, see Neger (2021) 248, who also quotes Hor. *Sat.* 1.1.24 and Juv. 1.79.

[14] Perhaps another word evoking satire; for *satis* ('enough') as a generic marker, with reference to Hor. *Sat.* 1.1, see Dufallo (2000). He shows that '[r]ather than producing a balance, *satis* and *satura* perpetually undermine each other' (580). A fine example of this 'unstable relation' between the two terms is provided in *Sat.* 1.10.7–8 *ergo non* **satis** *est risu diducere rictum | auditoris; et est quaedam tamen hoc quoque virtus* ('Therefore it is not enough to make the smiling listener burst out laughing – and yet there is a certain merit here, too', trans. in Dufallo 2000, 589). In the case of Pallas, on the other hand (Pliny assures us), laughing is perfectly enough.

[15] *Ep.* 7.29 is the only letter in the Plinian corpus which begins and ends with the same word (*ridebis – rideantur*). For ring composition within individual letters as a structural device in Pliny, see Winniczuk (1975). It may be argued that the introductory sentence, with its anticipation of the addressee's three stage reaction to the Pallas monument, is mirrored in the description of Pliny's own reaction in the second part of the letter (3–4): first laughing (*equidem numquam ... mimica et inepta*), then indignation (*quae interdum ... posteris prodere*) and finally laughing once again.

Thus far, we have not considered what actually sparked Pliny's emotional reaction. It was not the monument itself, but an inscription incised on it (*monimentum Pallantis ita inscriptum*, 'a monument to Pallas bearing this inscription', 7.29.2). And now we encounter, coming after Pliny the satirist and Pliny the paradoxographer, Pliny the epigraphist or, rather, the antiquarian. He takes care to write down, verbatim, the text of the inscription[16] – and in this respect he is not very different from such antiquarian writers as Varro or his contemporary and friend Suetonius:[17]

> Huic senatus ob fidem pietatemque erga patronos ornamenta praetoria decrevit et sestertium centies quinquagies, cuius honore contentus fuit.
>
> To him, because of his loyal services to his patrons, the senate decreed the honourable distinctions of praetorian rank together with fifteen million sesterces, but he was content to take the distinctions alone. (7.29.2)

Pliny likes to associate himself with Cicero, but his discovery of the tomb of Pallas is a far cry from Cicero's discovery of the tomb of Archimedes in Syracuse (see Cic. *Tusc.* 5.64–6).[18] The differences are much greater than the similarities, most notably the fact that Pliny spotted the monument of Pallas incidentally, whereas Cicero organised and headed a team, which included some leading citizens of Syracuse, to search for it. A common feature of both discoveries is a tomb inscription, but even here there is a difference: Cicero knew the text of the inscription beforehand, and in fact the information contained in it helped him track down the grave. Consequently, he only briefly mentions the inscription without quoting it – in contrast to Pliny, for whom the *titulus* is the most important part of his discovery.

---

[16] Since the *text* of the letter is focused on the *text* of the inscription, it is not quite clear whether the initial *legeris* refers to the former or to the latter. Both texts may serve as proofs in paradoxographical discourse, Pliny's letter attesting that Pallas' monument is not fictitious, and the inscription showing that Pallas was in fact so incredibly arrogant. From the times of Herodotus, epigraphy played an important role in accounts of *mirabilia*.

[17] Or, for that matter, his uncle, Pliny the Elder who, in his lost history, resorted to epigraphical evidence to determine the birth place of Caligula (wrongly, as argued by Suetonius, *Calig.* 8). For a good discussion of antiquarian writers (including Varro) in the late Republic, see Rawson (1985) 233–49. For Suetonius as an antiquarian scholar, see Wallace-Hadrill (1983). See also *Ep.* 8.8.7 for Pliny's epigraphical interests (graffiti in the temple of Clitumnus, in this case).

[18] See Jaeger (2002) for a discussion of this passage. For Pliny's Ciceronian contexts, see the contributions of Matthew Mordue (Chapter 4), Stefano Rocchi (Chapter 5) and Christopher Whitton (Chapter 1) in the present volume.

Pliny's comment on the Pallas inscription is truly indignant:

> ... maxime tamen hic me titulus admonuit,[19] quam essent mimica et inepta, quae interdum in hoc caenum, in has sordes abicerentur, quae denique ille furcifer et recipere ausus est et recusare, atque etiam ut moderationis exemplum posteris prodere.

> ... but this inscription, more than anything else, reminded me of how unreal and empty are the distinctions which are sometimes thrown away on such vile and disreputable rascals as Pallas. Yet the scoundrel had the audacity to accept the one, refuse the other, and then parade it before posterity as a proof of his moderation! (7.29.3)

Two terms of abuse, *caenum* (lit. 'dirt, filth, mud') and *furcifer* (lit. 'a yoke-bearer'), are found only here in Pliny. *Furcifer* is particularly interesting, because it undoubtedly alludes to Pallas' servile origins: the noun means primarily someone bearing the *furca* ('yoke') and is commonly applied to slaves (since as an instrument of punishment the *furca* was associated with slaves and condemned criminals). The word appears three times in Cicero,[20] although Pliny's literary debt here is most probably not to him, but to Plautus and Terence – because it is in these two authors that *furcifer* is most frequently attested (fifteen times in Plautus, four times in Terence).[21] Thus the Roman *palliata* may be singled out as yet another literary genre evoked in this short letter, with Pallas playing the role of a successful *servus callidus*.[22] It is worth mentioning in this context that several years later Pliny's friend Tacitus will represent (in Books 11 and 12 of his *Annals*) the situation at the court of Claudius in terms reminiscent of Plautine comedy, featuring the emperor as a *senex* duped by his cunning *servi*, Pallas among them.[23]

Posteris prodere, on the other hand, reminds us of commemorative literature, especially historiography and biography. In view of the fact that the phrase *posteris prodere* (or *tradere*) is so frequently attested, it would be

---

[19] Pliny uses this verb on purpose, because *admonere* is in fact what honorary or sepulchral inscriptions were set up for. Here, however, what the inscription reminded Pliny of contrasts sharply with its intended message. See Neger (2021) 248–9.

[20] *Vat.* 15, *Pis.* 14, *Deiot.* 26. In the first two instances Cicero uses the word in reference to non-slaves (Vatinius and Piso, respectively).

[21] And of course it is used there in reference to slaves (but also by slaves themselves, e.g. to a *leno*). See Dickey (2002) 171.

[22] Theatrical associations are further evoked by *mimica* (lit. 'relating to mimes, farcical'; in Pliny only here and at *Pan.* 16.3). As for the combination of *mimica* and *inepta*, compare Sen. *Tranq.* 11.8 *mimicas ineptias et verba ad summam caveam spectantia* ('farcical absurdities and words spoken with the most debased audience in mind'; in the context of stage performances, with reference to Publilius Syrus).

[23] See Vessey (1971); Dickison (1977).

rather unwise to posit Pliny's intertextual reference to the opening words of Tacitus' *Agricola* (published some ten years earlier): *clarorum virorum facta moresque **posteris tradere*** ('to hand down to posterity the deeds and moral standards of distinguished men', Tac. *Agr.* 1.1).[24] But the combination of *posteris prodere/tradere* and *exemplum/exempla* (as something which is transmitted to posterity) occurs very seldom[25] and it seems quite possible that Pliny is alluding here to this famous sentence from Augustus' autobiography[26] (and, if so, it may be relevant that this autobiography was made public as an epigraphic document):

> Legibus novis me auctore latis multa exempla maiorum exolescentia iam ex nostro saeculo reduxi et ipse multarum rerum **exempla** imitanda **posteris tradidi**.
>
> By new laws passed on my proposal I brought back into use many exemplary practices of our ancestors which were disappearing in our time, and in many ways I myself transmitted exemplary practices to posterity for their imitation. (RGDA 8.5, trans. Brunt and Moore)

Thus we would have an imperial freedman, a secretary and a *rationibus* at the court of Claudius, who is posing as a latter-day Augustus, the founder of the principate (and the husband of Livia, Claudius' grandmother). Moreover, *moderatio* is one of the imperial virtues, and also *recusare* is used in reference to imperial power and its trappings.[27] Pliny's intertextual reference (if we are right to regard it as such) serves to emphasise that he has every reason to be indignant with Pallas.[28] But, as we already know, he

---

[24] The *Agricola* passage is evoked by Pliny at 6.16.1 (addressed to Tacitus!): *petis ut tibi avunculi mei exitum scribam, quo verius **tradere posteris** possis* ('You ask me to send you an account of my uncle's death, so that you may be able to give posterity an accurate description of it'); 'a courtesy nod', according to Whitton (2010) 123 n. 30.

[25] Apart from the passage quoted below, it is found prior to Pliny only in Caes. *BGall.* 7.77.13 and Quint. *Inst.* 3.7.21.

[26] Scholars have noted references to *RGDA* in such writers as Velleius Paterculus, Seneca, Tacitus and Suetonius; see Cooley (2009) 48–50. For Suetonius' use of *RGDA* in the *Life of Augustus*, see Gascou (1984) 522–32; for Tacitus' use, see Urban (1979), who, among other similar passages, notes an echo of *RGDA* 8.5 at Tac. *Ann.* 3.55.5 (*nec omnia apud priores meliora, sed nostra quoque aetas multa laudis et artium **imitanda posteris** tulit* – 'nor was everything better in the past, but our own age too has produced many specimens of excellence and culture for posterity to imitate', trans. Church and Brodribb).

[27] *Moderatio*: see e.g. Levick (1975). Of course, *moderatio* is not restricted to emperors (see Tac. *Ann.* 12.54.1 for *moderatio* used, with bitter irony, in reference to Pallas). *Recusare*: e.g. Tac. *Hist.* 1.52.4, *Ann.* 1.3.2, Suet. *Tib.* 24.1, *Claud.* 12.1, *Ner.* 8.1. A classic discussion is Béranger (1953) 137–69.

[28] But even if there is no allusion to Augustus, Pliny's *ut moderationis exemplum posteris prodere* is sarcastic. See Roller (2001) 271: 'thus Pallas seeks to install himself as one of the *maiores*, an aristocratic ancestor notable for the honors conferred upon him, and hence a model for future generations to emulate.' It should be stressed that, contrary to what is maintained by Lefèvre (2009) 82, the object of Pliny's indignation in this letter is Pallas, not the senate. But, as the use of *furcifer*

Putting Pallas out of Context

eventually comes to realise that derision, not indignation, is the proper attitude to assume towards the freedman and his arrogant inscription. Pallas will be immortalised – not through his *monumentum* in stone and his epigraph – through Pliny's literary work, and the message for posterity will be the exact opposite of what the freedman wished for.[29] The reader may feel that this observation finishes the matter[30] and that there will be no further reasons to come back to Pallas; there is no open ending which may suggest a continuation of the story.[31]

But the story *is* continued. Pliny's second Pallas letter, 8.6, is in fact conspicuous because of its length. Numbering 781 words, it is the second longest letter in this book, and it closely resembles the longest one (8.14; 1,131 words),[32] with which it shares its general subject matter – a reflection on the senatorial slavery of earlier times.[33] Although the second letter to Montanus is placed in the next book, Pliny suggests that not much time has elapsed since he wrote the first one (and since he found the monument of Pallas): the *proxime* of 7.29.2 is now *nuper* (8.6.1);[34] the opening paragraph cross-references to the former letter and the text of the inscription is repeated.[35]

Immediately after quoting once again the inscription, Pliny explains his reasons for coming back to Pallas:

---

and *mimica* suggests, this indignation is diluted with ridicule, even before the last paragraph of the letter.

[29] See n. 19 above (*admonuit*). Contrast Tac. *Agr.* 46.5: *Agricola posteritati narratus et traditus superstes erit* ('Agricola will survive, since his biography was written and handed down to posterity'); earlier in that chapter, a reference is made to the transience of images *quae marmore et aere finguntur* ('which are moulded in marble or bronze', 46.3). The topos of the superiority of literary texts over sculptural or pictorial images goes back at least as far as Pindar (*Nem.* 5.1–5).

[30] For a different view, see Lefèvre (2009) 82: 'Daher ist es klar, daß Plinius von vornherein eine Fortsetzung des Pasquills plant.'

[31] As, for example, at the end of 7.6; the subject matter of this letter is continued in 7.10 (addressed to the same person).

[32] Pliny's longest letter is 5.6 (1,520 words). See Whitton (2013a) 13 n. 71. Following Whitton, I have not counted letter headings and closing formula (e.g. *vale*).

[33] See Whitton (2010) 138: 'Taken together, 8.6 and 8.14 make a stimulating pair of meditations on senatorial *servitus*. The kowtowing of the Claudian Senate prefigures the Domitianic slavery that the later letter will decry.' We will come back to the connection between these two letters later on.

[34] But the fact that the second Pallas letter is divided from the first by being placed in another book (and separated by four letters of Book 7 plus five letters of Book 8) suggests that some time *did* elapse after the writing of 7.29 – namely the time needed to consult the archives (see below). For such a 'reality effect' as one of Pliny's principles of arranging his letters, see Gibson and Morello (2012) 60.

[35] In a similar fashion, the text of Verginius Rufus' epitaph, quoted in 6.10, is repeated in 9.19. See n. 5 above for the connection between the Verginius pair and the Pallas one.

> Postea mihi visum est pretium operae ipsum senatus consultum quaerere. Inveni tam copiosum et effusum, ut ille superbissimus titulus modicus atque etiam demissus videretur.
>
> Subsequently I thought it worthwhile to look up the actual text of the decree, and I found it couched in such exaggerated and fulsome language as to make even that pompous inscription on the monument look modest and humble by comparison. (8.6.2)

We can now see that the Pallas inscription, succinct as it was, contained the crucial information that the honours to the freedman were voted by the senate (*huic senatus* [...] *decrevit*, 'to him the senate ... decreed', 7.29.2).[36] Pliny the senator might have been interested in learning the circumstances of, and background to, this peculiar decree. Yet in the previous letter his attention was focused on Pallas alone and the freedman, not the *patres conscripti*, was the object of Pliny's indignation (or ridicule). The shift from 7.29 to 8.6 is remarkable.

At first sight we may think that Pliny has turned historian – even if we do not accept Eleanor Leach's suggestion that he is alluding to the famous opening words of Livy's history: *facturusne operae pretium sim* ... ('whether it will be worthwhile ...') (I regard her suggestion as somewhat farfetched, given the frequent attestation of the phrase).[37] Moreover, Pliny appears to have become a historian who is accustomed to working with primary sources and does not recoil from archival searches. For, despite Anthony Woodman's claim,[38] it seems improbable that *quaerere* and *inveni* refer to his quest around the city of Rome for a publicly displayed official inscription containing the text of the senatorial decree. Rather, it

---

[36] For various functions of Pliny's references to *senatus consulta* in his letters, see recently Haake (2019). His treatment of 7.29 and 8.6 is rather brief, and he thinks that Pliny's principal aim here was to stress the happiness of his own times and to indirectly praise Trajan.

[37] Livy, *praef.* 1. See Leach (2013) 131. Also Neger (2021) 250 (who notes (242) Pliny's reference to Livy, *praef.* 9 at 3.20.8).

[38] In his devastating criticism of a book by Potter (1999), Woodman (1998) 312 discusses Potter's use of Plin. *Ep.* 8.6 to support his claim that Tacitus used the *acta senatus*: 'P. assumes that in that letter Pliny is referring to a consultation of the *acta senatus*; but there seems nothing to justify that assumption: on the contrary, section 14 of the letter strongly implies that Pliny consulted a bronze inscription on public display in the middle of Rome.' But Pliny, when he learnt (thanks to his coming across the monument of Pallas) about the existence of the senatorial decree concerning the freedman, did not yet know that it had been put on public display – and it is highly likely that it was no longer on display by Pliny's times, more than fifty years after the event. And even if it still were to be seen in the early second-century AD, should we imagine Pliny going to and fro across the city, looking hard to find a decree which he could inspect, with much less fatigue, in the archives? (But probably not the *acta senatus*; see next note.)

must refer to his consulting the public records, most probably the *aerarium Saturni* in which the *senatus consulta* were deposited.[39]

But it soon turns out that Pliny has not become a historian. For one thing, in this letter he quotes long passages from the decree in its original wording, thus disregarding Greek and Roman historians' standard practice of avoiding verbatim quotations of documents, letters or speeches. Instead, Pliny follows antiquarians[40] – as he did when he paid attention to the inscription on the tomb of Pallas. Additionally, and more importantly, Pliny focuses solely on the text of the decree and is entirely indifferent to its historical context and background.

The main body of the letter (paragraphs 4–16, 586 words) consists of the following:

(a) three direct quotations from the *senatus consultum*[41] (totalling 107 words or 18.3 per cent; paragraphs 6, 7 and 13),
(b) four indirect quotations preserving (so it seems) most of the original wording of the document (totalling 134 words or 22.9 per cent; paragraphs 4, 5, 8 and 10),
(c) six introductory statements, announcing a quotation which follows (totalling 50 words or 8.5 per cent),
(d) six authorial comments (totalling 295 words or 50.3 per cent).[42]

This part of the letter is in fact a running commentary on the decree, but a commentary which serves not to elucidate its historical background and meaning, but to stimulate the reader's emotions of disbelief, disgust or indignation. Pliny's omission of the historical context is striking: we are not told when the decree was voted, what the reason for honouring Pallas was, who was active in promoting the awards or how the debate in the

---

[39] See Talbert (1984) 315, who notes that Pliny did not consult the *acta senatus* 'which might have been expected to give an account fuller in some degree than the decrees alone'. For another view, see Sherwin-White (1966) 453: 'He would find it [the decree] [...] in the senatorial archives kept by the *curator actorum senatus* or *ab actis* and consulted by historians...' See also Storchi Marino (1995) 194–5 (Pliny looked for *senatus consulta*, not for *acta senatus*).
[40] Or grammarians or, more generally, scholars; see e.g. Wallace-Hadrill (1983) 21. Thus Suetonius quotes verbatim the text of the *S.C. de philosophis et rhetoribus* of 161 BC (Suet. *Gramm.* 25.1), as does another scholar, Aulus Gellius (15.1.1).
[41] Or rather *senatus consulta*, since there were two decrees, the first voted on 23 January AD 52 (and quoted or paraphrased by Pliny in paragraphs 4–9) and the second on the following meeting of the senate (paragraphs 9 and 13). But, for the sake of simplicity, I will speak of them as a single decree.
[42] The division between (c) and (d) is somewhat arbitrary, because introductory formulas may also contain evaluative elements which are typical for Pliny's commentary passages. Here, the formal distinguishing feature (a statement introducing, and not following, a direct or indirect quotation of the decree) was decisive.

senate proceeded. Perhaps most curiously, we are not even told the identity of the 'Caesar', although he is mentioned four times in the text.[43] Admittedly, Roman readers of Pliny were likely to be able to connect the imperial freedman Pallas with the reign of Claudius, an emperor notorious for his obsequiousness (real or alleged) to his powerful *liberti* – but the suppression of the name 'Claudius' is nevertheless remarkable.[44] The conclusion suggests that Pliny's lack of interest in the historical context of the *senatus consultum* results from his willingness to present the story as, in a sense, a cautionary tale which happened 'once upon a time' but which need not, or even should not, be dated to a specific period of time. The question remains whether the story in fact belongs to the past or whether it is still relevant to the present – and we will come back to this issue towards the conclusion of this chapter.

What seems clear so far is that Pliny inspected the *senatus consultum* alone (as it was stored in the *aerarium Saturni*), and not the *acta senatus*, which would have given him some insight into the circumstances of the senatorial debate. His comments are those of an angry senator who looks upon the Pallas affair from the safe vantage point of Trajanic Rome and makes no attempt to understand the specific position and possible motivation of the Claudian senators – despite his rhetoric at 8.6.3, where he singles out three alternative motives for their action only to reject them one by one.[45] Of course, we should not be surprised by the fact that Pliny did not consult the *acta senatus* to obtain additional information. What is

---

[43] In paragraphs 5, 9, 12 and 15; with the exception of the first passage, all these mentions come from Pliny's commentary (so 'Caesar' was his own choice). It was probably Pliny's suppression of the historical context and the identity of the 'Caesar' which led Morello (2015) to wrongly regard Pallas as 'Tiberius' freedman' (158) and to summarise the Plinian account as 'the miseries of the Tiberian period' (157). In her more recent treatment of 8.6, Morello (2018) 323–8 assigns the senatorial proceedings, rightly, to the times of Claudius

[44] Cf. 1.13.3 (*Claudium Caesarem*), 3.16.7 and 9 (*contra Claudium, apud Claudium*) and 10.70.2 (*Claudio Caesari*). Pliny is usually specific when mentioning an emperor (e.g. 3.5.9) and 'Caesar' alone is regularly used in a contemporary context, referring to Trajan (or Nerva); see Whitton (2013a) 7. (But sometimes it is left unspecified, for various reasons; thus e.g. 1.18.3 and 7.16.2 where Domitian is implied.)

[45] One of them is *urbanitas*, namely (we may add, because Pliny does not develop the point) the senate's artful method of ridiculing the freedman by heaping fulsome praise on him. For the classic treatment of this (not only) senatorial 'doublespeak' in early imperial Rome, see Bartsch (1994); her discussion of Plin. *Ep.* 8.6 is brief (174–5). Some modern scholars assume that the Claudian senate in fact wanted to ridicule Pallas, and in particular to humble him by offering a financial reward (which, on this interpretation, was proposed by the senate, while the *ornamenta praetoria* were proposed by Claudius); see Sherwin-White (1966) 439; Pavis D'Escurac (1985) 314; Storchi Marino (1995) 199, 206; Leach (2013) 129. If such was the senate's idea, Pallas evidently did not understand it; otherwise he would have omitted the mention of a financial reward from his tomb inscription.

surprising, however, is that he apparently did not look up any historical work, not even the *A Fine Aufidii Bassi* by Pliny the Elder. A passage from the *Natural History* makes it probable that his uncle included the story concerning the Pallas decree in his lost historical work.[46] In this passage (*HN* 35.201)[47] Pliny the Elder discusses a kind of chalk known as *creta argentaria*, which was used to mark the feet of slaves on sale; this induces him to make a digression on powerful and wicked freedmen in the history of Rome, and he ends the digression thus:

> Quos et nos adeo potiri rerum vidimus, ut praetoria quoque ornamenta decerni a senatu iubente Agrippina Claudi Caesaris videremus tantumque non cum laureatis fascibus remitti illo, unde cretatis pedibus advenissent.
>
> ... persons whom even we have seen risen to such power that we actually beheld the honour of the praetorship awarded to them by decree of the Senate at the bidding of Claudius Caesar's wife Agrippina, and all but sent back with the rods of offices wreathed in laurels to the places from which they came to Rome with their feet whitened with white earth! (*HN* 35.201, trans. Rackham, Loeb)[48]

Pallas is not named, but the mention of the *ornamenta praetoria* must refer to him (no other freedman is known to have been granted this distinction).[49] The detail about Agrippina actually forcing the senate to vote for the insignia is important and it should be connected with the fact that it was Pallas who, after the fall of Messalina, successfully backed the candidacy of Agrippina as Claudius' fourth wife.

But even if Pliny the Elder did not speak of the decree in his history, the event obviously figured in other historical narratives available to his nephew. This may be concluded from Tacitus who, writing his *Annals* 12 some ten years or so after Pliny's *Epistles* 8, discusses the matter in detail

---

[46] As the title of Pliny the Elder's lost history indicates, he began his narrative at the point where his predecessor Aufidius Bassus had ended. Unfortunately, we do not know the finishing-point of Aufidius' history (it seems that the early thirties were still covered) and the first datable fragment of Pliny's work refers to AD 55. However, it is quite likely that Pliny covered (at least) the last years of Claudius, perhaps starting his narrative in about AD 50. See Levick (2013) 532.

[47] See Storchi Marino (1995) 188–92.

[48] Pliny exaggerates for rhetorical effect, because the bestowal of the *ornamenta praetoria* did not amount to the conferment of praetorian rank. But he has good reason to be outraged in view of the fact that no *ornamenta* (*quaestoria, praetoria* or *consularia*) were normally granted to ex-slaves. For such distinctions, see Rémy (1976).

[49] For his role in overthrowing Messalina, Narcissus received only the *ornamenta quaestoria* (Tac. *Ann.* 11.38.4); cf. Oost (1958) 132. Pliny the Elder names Pallas, along with Narcissus and Callistus, in his survey of very rich people (*HN* 33.134). Interestingly, to describe their influence he uses the phrase *rerum potiri* which also appears in the passage quoted above (*HN* 35.201).

and at least some pieces of information he furnishes must have also been used by his predecessors (such as Cluvius Rufus and perhaps Fabius Rusticus). Here is one of the first items from his narrative of AD 52:

> Inter quae refert ad patres de poena feminarum quae servis coniungerentur; statuiturque, ut ignaro domino ad id prolapsae in servitute, sin consensisset, pro libertis haberentur. Pallanti, quem repertorem eius relationis ediderat Caesar, praetoria insignia et centies quinquagies sestertium censuit consul designatus Barea Soranus. Additum a Scipione Cornelio grates publice agendas, quod regibus Arcadiae ortus veterrimam nobilitatem usui publico postponeret seque inter ministros principis haberi sineret. Adseveravit Claudius contentum honore Pallantem intra priorem paupertatem subsistere. Et fixum est <in aere> publico senatus consultum, quo libertinus sestertii ter milies possessor antiquae parsimoniae laudibus cumulabatur.

> During these proceedings he proposed to the senate a penalty on women who united themselves sexually with slaves, and it was decided that those who had thus demeaned themselves without the knowledge of the slave's master should be reduced to slavery; if with his consent, should be ranked as freedwomen. To Pallas who, as the emperor declared, was the author of this proposal, were offered on the motion of Barea Soranus, consul-elect, the insignia of the praetorship and fifteen million sesterces. Scipio Cornelius added that Pallas deserved public thanks for subordinating his ancient nobility as a descendant from the kings of Arcadia to the welfare of the state and allowing himself to be numbered among the emperor's servants. Claudius assured them that Pallas, satisfied with the honour only, would limit himself to his former poverty. And a decree of the senate was publicly inscribed on a bronze tablet, heaping the praises of ancient frugality on a freedman who possessed three hundred million sesterces. (*Ann.* 12.53, trans. Church and Brodribb modified)[50]

If Pliny had also known the pieces of information adduced by Tacitus, they would have provided him with additional rhetorical weapons to be deployed against the subservient senators of the Claudian era. First of all, the stated reason for honouring Pallas would surely have aroused Pliny's interest, namely his proposal concerning the punishment of freeborn women entering into sexual relations with slaves. The irony of this situation is evident, especially if we consider Pallas' depiction elsewhere in the *Annals* as Agrippina's lover (consequently, Agrippina should have been reduced to servile status, since the liaison was certainly formed *ignaro*

---

[50] For the Tacitus passage, see Seif (1973) 214–15; Mehl (1974) 148–52; Hausmann (2009) 379–82.

domino).[51] Also the details of the senatorial proceedings might have been helpful for Pliny – both the fact that it was a later victim of Nero, the brave Stoic-minded senator Barea Soranus who, in his official role as *consul designatus*, put forward the motion[52] and that the formal vote of thanks to the freedman was proposed by someone named Cornelius Scipio. Furthermore, Claudius' statement about the wish of Pallas to remain 'within his earlier poverty' (it is highly likely that Tacitus closely follows the original wording here[53]) would have been a welcome target for Pliny's fulmination. But the final point in Tacitus is already there in Pliny, also as his last item (or the last straw):[54] the public form of commemoration of Pallas. It is perhaps not preposterous to suppose that Tacitus' interest in the Pallas episode of AD 52 (as evidenced by the detailed treatment accorded to it) was first stirred by his reading of Pliny's letter and especially of his remarks on perpetuating the memory of Pallas by means of *publica aeternaque monumenta* (14).

In the closing sentences of the letter, Pliny comes back to his own times, to himself and to his addressee:

> Quam iuvat quod in tempora illa non incidi, quorum sic me tamquam illis vixerim pudet! Non dubito similiter affici te. Scio quam sit tibi vivus et ingenuus animus: ideo facilius est ut me, quamquam indignationem quibusdam in locis fortasse ultra epistulae modum extulerim, parum doluisse quam nimis credas.

---

[51] For both Tacitus and Pliny, there was no real difference between a slave and a freedman; see Lavan (2013) 151. For Pallas' liaison with Agrippina, see Tac. *Ann.* 12.25.1, 12.65.2 and 14.2.2.

[52] At Tac. *Ann.* 16.21.1 Barea is presented, together with Thrasea Paetus, as epitomising *virtus ipsa*; cf. Cass. Dio 62.26.1. As *consul designatus*, Barea Soranus spoke first during the debate (see Talbert 1984: 242 for the practice) and, consequently, was expected to put forward an 'official' motion. For this reason it is highly unlikely that his offer of a financial reward to Pallas was not previously arranged with Claudius (see n. 45 above).

[53] Note *contentum honore Pallantem* (*Ann.* 12.53.3) and *cuius honore contentus fuit* in the text of the Pallas inscription. On the other hand, it is possible that *intra priorem paupertatem* is (also) Tacitus' own ironical allusion to Vergil's Arcadian Evander and Pallas (*Aen.* 8.105–6 and 360: two out of only seven attestations of *pauper* in the *Aeneid*).

[54] Pliny places special emphasis on the clause of the *senatus consultum* which refers to its being put on public display. It is quoted verbatim and commented upon at length, and the whole passage (13–16) amounts to one third of the body of the letter containing the discussion of the decree (4–16; precisely 193 words or 32.9 per cent). Note especially *incisa et insculpta sunt publicis aeternisque monumentis praetoria ornamenta Pallantis, sic quasi foedera antiqua, sic quasi sacrae leges* ('the praetorian distinctions of Pallas were chiselled and cut upon a memorial that will last for ages, as though they were ancient treaties or hallowed laws', 14). Cf. Plin. *HN* 34.99 *usus aeris ad perpetuitatem monimentorum iam pridem tralatus est tabulis aereis, in quibus publicae constitutiones inciduntur* ('the employment of bronze was a long time ago applied to securing the perpetuity of monuments, by means of bronze tablets on which records of official enactments are made', trans. Rackham, Loeb). For the significance of the place in which the plaque was displayed (*ad statuam loricatam divi Iulii*, 'near the statue of the divine Julius Caesar in full armour'), see Corbier (1997).

> How happy I am that my life did not fall in those evil times, which make me blush for shame as though I had lived in them! I have not the least doubt that they affect you as they do me. I know how sensitive and honourable your disposition is, and that you will have no difficulty therefore in thinking my resentment to be under rather than over the mark, although in some passages perhaps I have let my indignation run away with me further than I ought to have done in a letter. (8.6.17)

We may now return to the question raised previously, namely whether the story told in this letter ('a cautionary tale' as I called it earlier, set in the rather distant past, with beign ever precisely fixed) is, in Pliny's view, still relevant to his own times. The question is not easy to answer. It may be supposed that Pliny in fact expresses his satisfaction that he was (to use a twentieth-century formula) 'blessed by the grace of late birth'.[55] But was he, really? We have already noted a strong connection between *Epistles* 8.6 and 8.14 – the two longest letters in this book (see n. 33 above). In the second letter, a minor matter of senatorial procedure (which is, ostensibly, Pliny's main concern) is presented in the wider historical perspective of Domitianic Rome. And Pliny uses the first person plural to refer to the experience of his own generation:

> Iidem prospeximus curiam, sed curiam trepidam et elinguem, cum dicere quod velles periculosum, quod nolles miserum esset. ... Eadem mala iam senatores, iam participes malorum multos per annos vidimus tulimusque.

> We, too, attended the senate-house as spectators, but it was a trembling and tongueless body, for to speak your mind was perilous, and to speak against your conscience was a wretched and miserable performance. ... When we became senators we took our place in this lamentable state of affairs, and we witnessed and endured it for many a long year. (8.14.8–9)

Christopher Whitton has recently called attention to the close similarities between *Epistles* 8.14 and Tacitus' *Agricola* – and indeed between Pliny's and Tacitus' perception of the senatorial slavery under Domitian. Interestingly, in this work Tacitus also resorts to the first person plural to describe the plight of his generation (see esp. *Agr.* 2.2 and cf. 45.1–2). Whitton also notes that Pliny's second Pallas letter is followed by a short letter addressed to Tacitus: 'This is one of four occasions when Pliny places a note to Tacitus concerning literary composition immediately after a

---

[55] The formula (in German: 'Gnade der späten Geburt') is usually associated with the German Chancellor Helmut Kohl (b. 1930) who used it during a TV interview in 1983 in connection with his planned state visit to Israel.

substantial letter featuring the tyranny of an earlier principate.'[56] Taking into account this 'Tacitus connection' it may perhaps be relevant that Pliny's first Pallas letter begins with the word *ridebis*, which is also used, in the same grammatical form, at the opening of *Epistles* 1.6, Pliny's first letter addressed to Tacitus (see n. 9 above).

When Pliny was about to publish Books 7 and 8, Tacitus was still working on the *Histories*, probably approaching the second half of the reign of Domitian.[57] Tacitus' Book 4 had already been finished a few years earlier, and Pliny certainly remembered well the speech of Curtius Montanus (*Hist*. 4.42) – especially because it focused on our author's *bête noire*, Marcus Regulus, and, moreover, it seems to be the historian's homage to his friend.[58] Montanus warns the senators that allowing Regulus to go unpunished for his actions under Nero would be to foster *nequitia* ('wickedness')[59] for the future.

> An Neronem extremum dominorum putatis? Idem crediderant qui Tiberio, qui Gaio superstites fuerunt, cum interim intestabilior et saevior exortus est.
>
> Do you think that Nero was the last tyrant? The same had been believed by those who had survived Tiberius and Gaius – but on both occasions even a more wicked and cruel man came to power. (*Hist*. 4.42)

This is obviously a *vaticinium ex eventu*, written from the post-Domitianic vantage point; and it is Pliny himself who remarks that under Domitian, Regulus *non minora flagitia commiserat quam sub Nerone sed tectiora* ('his misdeeds were better concealed during that emperor's reign, but they were as bad as they were in the time of Nero', *Ep*. 1.5.1). Pliny would not say this explicitly, but, after reading Tacitus, he certainly realised that *in tempora illa non incidere* ('to have not lived in those times' (cf. Plin. *Ep*.

---

[56] Whitton (2010) 138. Other letters are 1.6, 7.20 and 9.14. See also Whitton (2012) 356–9. The mention of the Saturnalia at 8.7.1 serves as a link between 8.7 and 8.6; see Morello (2015) 161: 'The Saturnalia scenario, in which the position of slave and master, pupil and *magister*, are temporarily reversed, is relevant also to the situation which Pliny has only just finished outlining in 8.6' (in which letter it is Pallas who is presented as master and the emperor as his slave, see esp. 8.6.12). See also Neger (2021) 255.

[57] If it may be surmised from *Ep*. 7.33 (on which letter see below).

[58] See Martin (1967), who draws attention to the Ciceronian (and thus also Plinian) clausulae of this speech; Whitton (2012) 361. It may be relevant that (according to one hypothesis) Montanus, the recipient of *Ep*. 7.29 and 8.6, might have been a relative of Montanus the Tacitean speaker; see Birley (2000) 73.

[59] This markedly Ciceronian word, prominent especially in the speeches against Verres, is attested in Tacitus only once, in reference to Regulus (*Hist*. 4.42.5; see Martin 1967: 111). Importantly, also Pliny uses *nequitia* in the context of his depiction of Regulus (*Ep*. 2.20.12, cf. 5); see Matthew Mordue's chapter in the present volume.

6.6.17)) was no guarantee against a change for the worse in Roman political life.[60] The servility of senators 'once upon a time' (8.6), just like their miserable experiences under Domitian (8.14), may not necessarily be regarded as a closed chapter of history.[61]

But perhaps the picture, as implied by the arrangement of the letters, is more complicated. From among the nine epistles between 7.29 and 8.6, one in particular stands out, emphatically placed at the end of Book 7 (and almost in the centre of these nine) and addressed to Tacitus (7.33). This is one of those texts in which Pliny engages in a dialogue with Cicero the epistolographer. The letter is modelled on *Ad Familiares* 5.12, that *epistula valde bella* ('a very fine letter', Cic. *Att.* 4.6.4) of 55 BC in which Cicero tried to persuade his addressee, the historian Lucius Lucceius, to put off his current annalistic project and to compose instead a monograph on Cicero's consulate and its aftermath.[62] Pliny's request is more modest: not a monograph, but an account of a senatorial action of his from the last years of Domitian which, Pliny hopes, Tacitus will include into his *Histories*:

> ... iucundum mihi futurum si factum meum, cuius gratia periculo crevit, tuo ingenio tuo testimonio ornaveris.
>
> ... how pleased I shall be, if you will lend your powers of description and the weight of your testimony to setting forth the way I behaved on an occasion when I reaped credit, owing to the dangers to which I exposed myself. (7.33.3)

Apart from the crucial verb *ornaveris* (*ornare* and *ornatus* appear four times in Cic. *Fam.* 5.12, always in reference to Lucceius' would-be depiction of Cicero), there are other signals pointing to Pliny's epistolographic model, notably his remarks on pictorial and literary representations of people or their deeds[63] and on the (possible) tension between narrative embellishment and historical truth. Here, Pliny is much more unassuming than

---

[60] Cf. *Ep.* 4.24.4–6 for Pliny's awareness of the mutability of political fortunes. Note especially *nulli rei fidere* ('never to impose a blind trust in anything').

[61] It has recently been shown by Whitton that the ideas and language of *Ep.* 8.6 are closely mirrored in *Pan.* 54–5, a section of the speech which deals with Trajan's moderation as regards honours voted to him by the senate, set in contrast to the excesses of his predecessors, most notably Domitian; see Whitton (2019) 373–8. The resemblances highlighted by Whitton strengthen the reading of *Ep.* 8.6 as a 'cautionary tale' which does not belong to the distant past alone.

[62] For Cic. *Fam.* 5.12 as Pliny's model in *Ep.* 7.33, see Marchesi (2008) 221–3.

[63] Plin. *Ep.* 7.33.2 *nam si esse nobis curae solet ut facies nostra ab optimo quoque artifice exprimatur, nonne debemus optare, ut operibus nostris similis tui scriptor praedicatorque contingat?* ('For if it is quite an ordinary thing for us to take care to secure the best painter to paint our portrait, ought we not also to be desirous of getting an author and historian of your calibre to describe our deeds?') Cf. Cic. *Fam.* 5.12.7.

Cicero: yes, you will make these actions of mine *notiora clariora maiora* ('more famous, more distinguished, and more noble', 7.33.10), but I am not asking you to transgress the rules of historical objectivity.[64]

The story which Pliny asks Tacitus to include in his *Histories* concerns the aftermath of the trial of Baebius Massa, condemned for extortion in AD 93. Pliny and Herennius Senecio had acted as Massa's accusers. After the trial Pliny joined Senecio in his efforts to protect Massa's confiscated property from embezzlement (by Massa himself, we are to understand). When Massa threatened Senecio with a charge of *impietas*, Pliny's brave intervention saved (for the time being) his associate from peril. There was no need for Pliny to explain to Tacitus (or to his wider audience) the political implications of the episode. Massa was a powerful informer (Tac. *Agr.* 45.1, *Hist.* 4.50.2, Juv. 1.35) and Senecio an important member of an oppositional group which, just a few months later, was crushed by Domitian's minions, and it is probable that Massa, despite his being condemned, played a role in those events (Tac. *Agr.* 2.1, 45.1, Plin. *Ep.* 1.5.3, 3.11.3, 7.19.5, Suet. *Dom.* 10.3–4).[65] As is well-known, Pliny repeatedly portrays himself in his correspondence as a close friend of Senecio's circle and, by consequence, as a potential victim of Domitian.[66] *Ep.* 7.33 should be seen in this context. What is important for our purpose is that this letter stands in marked contrast to *Ep.* 8.14; we are very far from that gloomy picture of senatorial subservience and misery which is evoked in the later text.

If so, the message of the Pallas diptych seems ambivalent. 'The cautionary tale' of the senators voting honours to a freedman may be relevant to Pliny and his senatorial colleagues in the early second-century AD – or to

---

[64] Contrast Pliny *quamquam non exigo ut excedas actae rei modum. Nam nec historia debet egredi veritatem, et honeste factis veritas sufficit* ('although I do not ask of you to go beyond the strict letter of what actually occurred. For history ought never to transgress against truth, and an honourable action wants nothing more than to be faithfully recorded', *Ep.* 7.33.10) with Cicero: *itaque te plane etiam atque etiam rogo, ut et ornes ea vehementius etiam, quam fortasse sentis et in eo leges historiae neglegas* [...] *amorique nostro plusculum etiam, quam concedet veritas, largiare* ('so I repeat – elaborate my activities even against your better judgement, and in the process disregard the laws of historiography [...] let your affection for me take a degree of precedence over the truth', *Fam.* 5.12.3, trans. in Woodman 1988: 71–2). Yet another intertextual signal is perhaps given at the end of the immediately preceding letter (7.32.2) where Pliny quotes Xenophon's *Memorabilia* 2.1.31. The quotation comes from Virtue's speech to Hercules at the Crossroads, and we know from Cic. *Fam.* 5.12.3 that Lucceius used this story in his proem to illustrate his attachment to the demands of historical objectivity. The quotation itself ('the sweetest of all sounds is praise') is obviously relevant to the subject matter of 7.33.

[65] See Rutledge (2001) 202–4.

[66] See e.g. Shelton (1987); Carlon (2009) 18–67; Strunk (2013). For Pliny's 'troublesome' career under Domitian, see Whitton (2015).

their descendants. But Pliny himself, with his splendid performance under Domitian, demonstrated that, as far as his own senatorial activity was concerned, there was no need for 'cautionary tales'. Perhaps there was even no need to express happiness for not being born in the times of Pallas and his 'Caesar'.

A curious feature of *Ep.* 7.33 is that we have here a letter within a letter. After recounting his brave intervention, Pliny mentions that he was praised on that occasion by the future Emperor Nerva:

> Divus Nerva ... missis ad me gravissimis litteris non mihi solum, verum etiam saeculo est gratulatus, cui exemplum (sic enim scripsit) simile antiquis contigisset.
>
> The late Emperor Nerva ... sent me a letter couched in the most complimentary terms, in which he not only congratulated me, but also the age in which I lived, for having had the privilege to witness an example that was worthy of the good old days. Such were the terms he used. (7.33.9)

Thus we have come full circle and are now back on the *via Tiburtina*, looking at the monument of Pallas. The aim of his arrogant inscription, Pliny assures us, was to present the freedman to posterity as a moral example (*ut moderationis exemplum posteris prodere*, 7.29.3; cf. 8.6.15). No: if we are looking for real examples, we should pay heed to the reliable testimony of the Divine Nerva (*exemplum [...] simile antiquis*, 7.33.9). And if we direct our thoughts to posterity, we should not have confidence in monuments in stone, set up by haughty rascals (or even in bronze plaques decreed by the subservient senate). Rather, we should think about a historical work, especially if penned by an author who can immortalise death itself –[67] or, more modestly, about a collection of letters.[68]

---

[67] Cf. Plin. *Ep.* 6.16.1 (the first Vesuvius letter): *video **morti** eius si celebretur a te **immortalem** gloriam esse propositam* ('for I can see that the immortality of his fame is well assured, if you take in hand to write of it' – or rather 'the immortality of his death's fame'). Ironically, Tacitus' account of Pliny the Elder's death is lost, and it is his nephew's letter which immortalised it.

[68] An important discussion of Pliny's Pallas letters (and of the Pallas chapter in Tacitus), McNamara (2021), appeared too late to be considered in this chapter. While a number of his observations, notably on Tac. *Hist.* 4.42 as a literary context of Plin. *Ep.* 8.6, are parallel to those presented above, McNamara's general interpretation goes in a somewhat different direction, emphasising Pliny's intention to distance himself and his audience from the events he describes in *Ep.* 7.29 and 8.6.

CHAPTER 13

Risus et indignatio: *Scoptic Elements in Pliny's Letters**

Margot Neger

1 Introduction

In his treatise on epistolary style, the ancient theorist Demetrius demands that a letter should be a φιλοφρόνησις σύντομος ('a short expression of courtesy') which obeys the laws of friendship (φιλικόν). Letters are seen as a means of keeping friendship alive between individuals.[1] Or, as Julius Victor in his *Ars rhetorica* argues (p. 448 Halm): *iurgari numquam oportet, sed epistolae minime* ('It is never appropriate to quarrel, but least in a letter'). Pliny the Younger's private letters certainly conform to this idea, and there is no letter in his corpus where we find him attacking his addressees in a serious way. On the other hand, there are plenty of letters where Pliny presents himself as openly hostile to other individuals who do not appear as addressees by ridiculing them or expressing his indignation. Several of Pliny's letters include epistolary satires or invectives, for example: in *Ep.* 1.13 on the laziness of people who have been invited to a recitation; in *Ep.* 2.14 on the decline of oratory and on the claqueurs in the Centumviral court; in the cycle on M. Aquilius Regulus (*Ep.* 1.5; 1.20.14; 2.11.22; 2.20; 4.2; 4.7; 6.2); in *Ep.* 7.29 and 8.6 against Pallas; in *Ep.* 6.15 on Iavolenus Priscus; in *Ep.* 4.25 on the behaviour of an anonymous senator. In other letters, Pliny evokes the iambic and satiric tradition in a more playful manner during the correspondence with his addressees. Especially in political, forensic and literary contexts the scoptic and satiric tradition provides the pre-texts for Pliny's epistolary laughter and indignation. Direct quotations from scoptic genres such as iambic poetry, comedy and satire

---

* I am indebted to the Austrian Science Fund (FWF) for the generous funding of a project entitled 'Embedded poems in ancient prose letters' (P 29721-G25); with its focus on literary interactions between epistolography and, mainly, scoptic poetry, the present paper discusses one of the problems investigated in the project. I am also grateful to the anonymous readers for their comments and suggestions.
[1] For *amicitia* in ancient letters see Thraede (1970) 125–46; Germerodt (2015).

are rare in Pliny's letters and where they do appear an aggressive or derisive tone is absent.[2] For example, when Pliny quotes from Catullus' obscene poem 16 (1–2 *pedicabo ego vos et irrumabo* | *Aureli pathice et cinaede Furi*, 'Up yours both, and sucks to the pair of you, queen Aurelius, Furius the faggot')[3] in letter 4.14.5,[4] he only cites the 'innocent' lines 5–8 and only indirectly recalls the tradition of the 'maculate muse'[5] by mentioning *lascivia rerum* ('lascivious topics') and *verba nuda* ('plain language') (4.14.4) as typical elements of scoptic and epigrammatic poetry.

Rather than quoting directly, Pliny evokes scoptic and invective literature in a more indirect way. As scholars have demonstrated, Pliny published his collection of private letters with the aim of providing a positive image of his own character, deeds and social interactions.[6] In those letters where certain individuals are derided or attacked, Pliny and his respective addressees build a kind of performative 'laughing community' (*Lachgemeinschaft*) or, analogically, a 'community of indignation' where laughter or outrage can have an exclusive and an inclusive effect: on the one hand, by sharing these emotions with his addressees, Pliny creates an in-group which adheres to similar ideals and values, while on the other hand the targets of the satire are branded as outsiders.[7] The general reader of the correspondence between Pliny and his addressees becomes a silent witness or, whenever he/she is also stimulated to laugh, a member of these epistolary laughing communities.

Letter 1.1 provides a significant example of the relationship between epistolography and the tradition of blame and envy (1.1.1): the collection opens with the famous words *Frequenter hortatus es, ut epistulas, si quas paulo curatius scripsissem, colligerem publicaremque* ('You have often urged me to collect and publish any letters of mine which were composed with

---

[2] Cf. *Ep.* 1.20.17 (Eup. fr. 94 Kock) and 19 (Ar. *Ach.* 531); 5.3.2 (Ter. *Haut.* 77).
[3] Translations of Catullus by Green (2005).
[4] For this letter in the context of Pliny's reflections on his poetry see Gamberini (1983) 82–121; Hershkowitz (1995); Auhagen (2003); Morello (2007) 174–5; Canobbio (2015); Janka (2015); Neger (2015b); epigrams without scoptic elements are also quoted in *Ep.* 3.21.5 (Mart. 10.20 [19].12–21), 4.27.4 (Sentius Augurinus), 6.10.4 and 9.19.1 (Verginius Rufus) as well as 7.4.6 and 7.9.11 (Pliny's own).
[5] Cf. the title of Henderson (1975); obscene language is generally rare in ancient epistolography; exceptions are the papyrus letter P.Oxy.XLII 3070 (first-century AD; see Gallavotti 1978–79: 366–9), Cic. *Fam.* 9.22 = 189 SB and a letter by Marc Antony quoted in Suet. *Aug.* 69.2.
[6] Cf. Leach (1990); Krasser (1993a); Offermann (1993); Riggsby (1995); Ludolph (1997); Henderson (2002b); Gibson (2003); Morello (2007); Gauly (2008); Carlon (2009); Bradley (2010).
[7] For 'laughing communities' (*Lachgemeinschaften*) and the social effects of laughter cf. Glenn (2003); Röcke and Velten (2005); Rosen (2015).

some care').[8] Scholars have already drawn attention to the various genres and texts which Pliny evokes in *Ep.* 1.1: there are Ovid's letters from exile (*Pont.* 3.9.53–4), Cicero's letters which were famously described as a *historia contexta* ('continuous history') by Cornelius Nepos (*Att.* 16.3), as well as the genres of dialogue[9] and biography,[10] to mention merely the most striking examples.[11] In addition to these genres, the adverb *frequenter* ('frequently') also seems to recall the beginning of Callimachus' prologue to the *Aetia*, which, as scholars now agree, start with πολλάκι (*Aet.* fr. 1.1 Pf. Πολλάκι μοι Τελχῖνες ἐπιτρύζουσιν ἀοιδῇ, 'Often the Telchines mutter against me, against my poetry').[12] Instead of having to defend his literary work against the envy and criticism of detractors whom Callimachus calls the Βασκανίης ὀλοὸν γένος ('pernicious race of envy'),[13] Pliny through an *imitatio e contrario* characterizes his epistolary collection as originating from his friend's encouragement and depicts himself as being at the centre of a 'society of praise'.[14] Following in the footsteps of Callimachus, Pliny too provides a *recusatio* in his first letter by refusing to write ἓν ἄεισμα διηνεκές ('one continuous poem') of historiography (1.1.1 *neque enim historiam componebam*, 'I was not writing history'). Through artful arrangement of his books of letters, Pliny on the one hand follows Callimachean principles but on the other distinguishes himself from the Hellenistic writer by replacing envy and blame with epistolary friendship.

2 Pliny's Epistolary Invectives

While letter 1.1 both evokes and reverses the motif of literary *invidia*, letter 1.5 recalls the tradition of iambic rage (χολή, 'bile').[15] With *Ep.* 1.5 addressed to Voconius Romanus,[16] the cycle on Marcus Aquilius Regulus begins, a series of seven letters which Rhiannon Ash calls a

---

[8] English translations of Pliny are by Radice (1969).
[9] Cf. Tac. *Dial.* 1.1 *saepe ex me requiris*; 1.3 *servato ordine disputationis*; Plut. *Mor.* 629 D σποράδην δ' ἀναγέγραπται καὶ οὐ διακεκριμένως ἀλλ' ὡς ἕκαστον εἰς μνήμην ἦλθεν.
[10] Cf. Nep. *Pelop.* 1 *ne non vitam eius narrare, sed historiam videar scribere*; Plut. *Alex.* 1 οὔτε γὰρ ἱστορίας γράφομεν ἀλλὰ βίους
[11] Cf. Sall. *Cat.* 4.2 *ut quaeque memoria digna*; Ludolph (1997) 99–106; Tzounakas (2007); Marchesi (2008) 20–2 and 249–50; Gibson (2011a).
[12] Cf. Cameron (1995) 339; Barchiesi (2005) 333–6; translations of Callimachus by Harder (2012).
[13] *Aet.* fr. 1.17 Pf. On *invidia* in Pliny's letters cf. Morello (2007) 179–89.
[14] Cf. Fitzgerald (2016) 99.
[15] For the iambic tradition cf. Cavarzere, Aloni and Barchiesi (2001); Johnson (2012); Hawkins (2014).
[16] He is third in the ranking of Pliny's addressees (behind Tacitus and Calpurnius Fabatus) regarding the number of letters he receives (1.5; 3.13; 6.16; 6.33; 8.8; 9.7; 9.28); cf. Whitton (2013a) 66–7.

'drip-feed invective'.[17] Despite his frequent appearance in the letters, we never encounter Regulus as one of Pliny's addressees. Not only does Pliny in *Ep.* 1.5 describe himself as being wrathful (1 *ne sibi irascerer ... irascebar*; 8 *ne mihi irascatur*),[18] he also quotes invectives which were mutually exchanged between Regulus and members of the so-called Stoic opposition against Domitian: some examples of this include the moment when Regulus called Arulenus Rusticus *Stoicorum simiam* ('Stoics' ape') and *Vitelliana cicatrice stigmosum* ('branded with Vitellius' mark')[19] in a book which he recited and published after Rusticus' death (2); Pliny also quotes Mettius Modestus' mockery of Regulus as *omnium bipedum nequissimus* (14 'the vilest of two-legged creatures') in a letter which was read out before Domitian. Modestus' letter, which is embedded in the narrative of Pliny's letter 1.5, can be read as a *mise en abyme* for the whole letter 1.5 or maybe even the whole letter-cycle on Regulus, who is continuously ridiculed and characterized as a negative figure and a sort of 'anti-Pliny'.[20] Moreover, letter 9.13 on Pliny's speech *De Helvidi Ultione* directed against Publicius Certus thematically clinches letter 1.5, as together they establish anger and revenge against *delatores* of Domitian's regime as an important motif which frames the epistolary collection.[21]

Letter 1.5 to Voconius Romanus is followed by a letter to Tacitus (1.6), who is imagined as laughing (1 *ridebis, et licet rideas*, 'I know you will think it a good joke, as indeed you may'). It has already been observed by scholars that Pliny often juxtaposes letters with a political or historical content with letters addressed to Tacitus.[22] If we read letter 1.6 as a self-contained text, this laughter is a friendly laughter which is elicited by Pliny's self-characterization in the letter (1 *ego, ille quem nosti, apros tres ... cepi*, 'your old friend has caught three boars') and demonstrates the close

---

[17] Ash (2013); cf. *Ep.* 1.20.14; 2.11.22; 2.20; 4.2; 4.7; 6.2; Gibson and Morello (2012) 68–73; on Regulus see also Mordue (Chapter 4), Hanaghan (Chapter 7) and Marchesi (Chapter 14) in this volume; for invective in ancient literature cf. Koster (1980) with a short discussion of Pliny on pp. 160–2; Neumann (1998); for Plin. *Ep.* 1.5 see Illias-Zarifopol (1994) 76–116; Ludolph (1997) 142–66; Marchesi (2013) 108–12.

[18] Cf. Hor. *Ars P.* 79 *Archilochum proprio rabies armavit iambo*; Ov. *Rem. am.* 377 *Liber in adversos hostes stringatur iambus*.

[19] Cf. Tac. *Hist.* 3.80-1; in the course of the civil war the praetor Arulenus Rusticus was sent by Vitellius as a legate to the enemies and was wounded by the soldiers of Petilius Cerialis; Sherwin-White (1966) 95.

[20] Hoffer (1999) 55–93; Modestus' letter embedded in *Ep.* 1.5 corresponds with Nerva's letter quoted in *Ep.* 7.33.9 where Pliny, quite in contrast to Regulus, is praised as *exemplum simile antiquis*; see also Pigoń (chapter 12) in this volume.

[21] Cf. Whitton (2013b) 57.

[22] Gibson and Morello (2012) 149–50 and 168; Whitton (2012) 357; for Pliny and Tacitus see also Whitton (Chapter 1) and Gibson (Chapter 2) in this volume.

bond of friendship between Pliny and Tacitus; if we read the letter in the context of the book, however, the juxtaposition with letter 1.5 would incline the reader to interpret *ridebis* and *rideas* as a reaction to the invective against Regulus in letter 1.5 and thus as a kind of iambic or satiric laughter which corresponds to the reaction Pliny expects from his addressee after reading letter 7.29 on Pallas (1 *ridebis, deinde indignaberis, deinde ridebis . . .*, 'You will think it a joke – or an outrage, but a joke after all . . .'). Thus, Tacitus the addressee of individual letters also appears as a reader of letters addressed to other individuals.

The laughter at the beginning of Pliny's letter 1.6 has been understood as an allusion to the end of Tacitus' *Dialogus* where the participants are also imagined as laughing.[23] I suggest that the opening sentence of letter 1.6 also evokes Catullus 56 which is addressed to Cato:

> O rem ridiculam, Cato, et iocosam
> dignamque auribus et tuo cachinno.
> ride, quidquid amas, Cato, Catullum:
> res est ridicula et nimis iocosa.
> deprendi modo pupulum puellae
> trusantem: hunc ego, si placet Dionae,
> protelo rigida mea cecidi.
>
> Cato, such a ridiculous and comic business, *well* worth your notice, sure to get a giggle, Cato: laugh, if you love Catullus! *So* ridiculous, really, too *too* comic – I just caught my girlfriend's little slave boy getting it up for her, and (Venus love me!) split *him*, tandem-fashion, with *my* banger!

Catullus' poem is modelled on a poem by Archilochus addressed to a certain Charilaus to whom the iambicist promises to tell a funny story (fr. 168 W., 2–3 χρῆμά τοι γελοῖον | ἐρέω, 'I shall tell you a funny thing').[24] By alluding to these iambic predecessors in *Ep.* 1.6, Pliny implicitly highlights the iambic potential of his letter 1.5; his target is not a Lycambes or a *pupulus trusans*, but a prominent figure who profited from the regime of tyrants such as Nero and Domitian. The obscenity of Catullus' poem, however, is absent in Pliny's pair of letters – perhaps the characterization of Regulus as δυσκαθαίρετον (15 'hard to come to grips with') evokes Catullus' *deprendi* (v. 5; cf. *cepi* in 1.6.1);[25] moreover, both

---

[23] The *Dialogus* ends with laughter (42.2 *cum adrisissent, discessimus*); Edwards (2008) 42: 'Although Tacitus was himself present at the historical setting of the dialogue, he does not participate in the laughter. Pliny's invitation and permission to laugh seem all the more relevant if viewed in this light'; Marchesi (2008) 118–35.
[24] Cf. Thomson (1997) ad Catull. 56; Holzberg (2002a) 46–7.
[25] For a link between δυσκαθαίρετον in 1.5.15 and *cepi* in 1.6.1 cf. Whitton (2012) 357.

Catullus and Pliny use diminutives (Regulus – *rex* and *pupulus* – *pupus*) for the targets of their scoptic texts. I wonder whether we could also read the phrase *ego ille quem nosti* in *Ep.* 1.6.1 as a reminiscence of Martial's first epigram (1.1.1–2 *hic est **quem** legis **ille** quem requiris | toto **notus** in orbe Martialis*, 'It's him! I, the man you're reading, am the man you're looking for, Martial, famous throughout the world')[26] or Ovid's *sphragis* in the *Tristia* (4.10.1–2 ***ille ego** qui fuerim tenerorum lusor amorum | **quem** legis, ut **noris**, accipe posteritas*, 'That you may know who I was, I that playful poet of tender love whom you read, hear my words, you of the after time'),[27] which serves as Martial's intertext;[28] instead of the epigrammatist's boastful claim of already enjoying fame in his lifetime or Ovid's address to posterity, Pliny addresses Tacitus who in light of these allusions is not only characterized as a close friend, but also a reader of the letters.

In letter 4.7, which Hanaghan's contribution (chapter 7) discusses in more detail, Pliny mocks his antagonist for his excessive and ostentatious grief after the loss of his son and for reciting a book about the boy's life in front of a vast audience and disseminating copies all over Italy (2).[29] At the end of the letter, Pliny asks his addressee Catius Lepidus[30] if the work was also read aloud in his *municipium* and finally remarks that the book *est enim tam ineptus ut risum magis possit exprimere quam gemitum* (7 'so absurd that it is more likely to meet with laughter than tears').[31] Apart from Seneca's discourse on grief which Hanaghan identifies as an important pre-text, the tradition of scoptic epigram might also play a role here. The topic of a father who excessively mourns the death of his son is reminiscent of an epigram by Lucillius who addresses a character named Marcus and begs him to stop lamenting the death of his child in his elegies (*AP* 11.135):

---

[26] Translation by Howell (1980).   [27] Translation by Wheeler (1996).
[28] Cf. Howell (1980) ad loc.
[29] See also Marchesi (chapter 14) in this volume; cf. *Ep.* 4.2.3 *amissum tamen luget insane*; for a father delivering the funeral oration for his son cf. Cic. *QFr.* 3.6.5 *laudavit pater scripto meo*; Trisoglio (1973) I, 436; with its topic letter 4.7 corresponds with *Ep.* 3.10 where Pliny reveals that he composed and recited a work on Spurinna's deceased son Cottius; whereas Pliny's way of honouring the young man is depicted as positive, Regulus with his exaggerated mourning serves as a negative counterpart.
[30] He is otherwise unknown; cf. Sherwin-White (1966) 270.
[31] Quintilian discusses the dangers which are connected with the rhetorical art of *lacrimas movere* ('to arouse tears'): *nihil habet ista res medium, sed aut lacrimas meretur aut risum* (*Inst.* 6.1.45); cf. Trisoglio (1973) I, 438; Tacitus reports in *Ann.* 13.3 that during Nero's funeral oration for Claudius the audience started laughing (*postquam ad providentiam sapientiamque flexit, nemo risui temperare*, 'when he turned to his foresight and wisdom, no one could resist laughing').

Μηκέτι, μηκέτι, Μάρκε, τὸ παιδίον, ἀλλ' ἐμὲ κόπτου
τὸν πολὺ τοῦ παρὰ σοὶ νεκρότερον τεκνίου,
εἰς ἐμὲ νῦν ἐλέγους ποίει πάλιν, εἰς ἐμὲ θρήνους,
δῆμιε, τὸν στιχίνῳ σφαζόμενον θανάτῳ,
τοῦ σοῦ γὰρ πάσχω νεκροῦ χάριν, οἷα πάθοιεν
οἱ καταδείξαντες βιβλία καὶ καλάμους.

No longer, Marcus, no longer lament the boy, but me, who am much more dead than that child of yours. Make elegies, hangman, now for me, make dirges for me who am slain by this versy death. For all for the sake of that dead child of yours I suffer what I would the inventors of books and pens might suffer.[32]

Besides its exaggerated lamentation of the child, Marcus' amateurish poetry also has the potential to kill its audience – the listeners must have been bored to death during the recitation.[33] Pliny, in a similar fashion, derides a fellow orator who wrote and recited a work on the life of a boy. Regulus' book is a *liber luctuosus* (*Ep.* 4.7.6 'a mournful book') in a double sense: it is written on the sad occasion of the boy's premature death, but it can also move listeners and readers to tears because of its poor quality. Pliny, however, is moved to laughter and concludes his letter with a sentence in the manner of an epigrammatic punchline (7): *credas non de puero scriptum, sed a puero* ('you would think it was written *by* a boy rather than about one'). The Neronian poet Lucillius was an important model for Martial[34] whose epigrams were also read and alluded to by Pliny;[35] it is an open question, however, whether Pliny was also familiar with the scoptic poems of Lucillius.[36] The similar ways of mocking a father's excessive lamentation of his child in Pliny's letter 4.7 and *AP* 11.135 encourage the assumption that Lucillius' poems also belonged to the large scope of Pliny's intertexts and inspired the epistolary satire on Regulus.

Besides the subgenre of the poetic ἐπικήδειον ('mourning poem') as mocked in Lucillius' epigram, Pliny also evokes the prose tradition of the ἐπιτάφιος λόγος ('funeral speech') in his epistolary invective: Pliny's

---

[32] Translation by Paton (1916–18).
[33] The expression στιχίνῳ σφαζόμενον θανάτῳ suggests that there were several lines which Marcus composed on his child – either a long poem in elegiacs or a large number of epigrams; for the hapax στιχίνῳ cf. Floridi (2014) ad loc.; Marcus is also mocked in *AP* 11.312 for composing fake epitaphs.
[34] Cf. Burnikel (1980); Holzberg (2002b) 99–109; Nisbet (2003); Fain (2008) 145–8; Neger (2012) 87–92.
[35] Cf. *Ep.* 3.21; on Pliny and Martial cf. Adamik (1976); Lefèvre (1989); Pitcher (1999); Henderson (2001); Marchesi (2013); Tzounakas (2014); Canobbio (2015); Edmunds (2015); Neger (2015b); Mratschek (2018); Marchesi (chapter 14) in this volume.
[36] That Pliny was familiar with Greek epigram becomes evident from *Ep.* 4.3 and 4.18 to Arrius Antoninus, where the epigrams of Callimachus are mentioned.

reflections on Regulus' *vis* and *audacia* are enriched with a quotation from Pericles' famous funeral oration, as narrated by Thucydides in 2.40.3 (3 *sicut* ἀμαθία μὲν θράσος, λογισμὸς δὲ ὄκνον φέρει, *ita recta ingenia debilitat verecundia, perversa confirmat audacia*, '"Ignorance breeds confidence, reflection leads to hesitation" as the saying goes, and so diffidence is the weakness of right-thinking minds, while depravity gains strength from reckless abandon'), in order to support the idea that *perversa ingenia* like Regulus are encouraged by audacity.[37] The epistolographer continues to mock Regulus' physical and mental skills as a speaker (4);[38] nevertheless, Regulus has won a certain reputation as an orator thanks to his *impudentia* and *furor*. In order to underline this attack, Pliny quotes a *bon mot* by Herennius Senecio, who capsized Cato's definition of the orator as *vir bonus dicendi peritus* ('a good man well trained in speaking') to Regulus (5): '*Orator est vir malus dicendi imperitus*' ('This orator is a bad man untrained in speaking').[39] Finally, Pliny also quotes from Demosthenes (*De cor.* 291) when he asks his addressee Catius Lepidus if he also had to read Regulus' *liber luctuosus* in public (6): ἐπάρας *scilicet, ut ait Demosthenes,* τὴν φωνὴν καὶ γεγηθὼς καὶ λαρυγγίζων ('or, to quote Demosthenes, "bawling in a loud and jubilant strain"').[40] The idea that someone is reciting a mournful book in a 'jubilant' voice (γεγηθώς) is an oxymoron and prepares the letter's punchline which jeers that the book would provoke more laughter than moans (7). The original context of the citation from *De Corona* is Demosthenes' invective against Aeschines whom he blames for not having shown his grief appropriately when recounting the defeat of the Athenians at Chaeronea but, instead, jubilantly raised his voice in order to accuse Demosthenes.[41] Pliny's concluding remark about Regulus' book (7 *est enim tam ineptus ut risum magis possit exprimere quam gemitum*, 'for it is

---

[37] The *ingenium* of the Athenians is opposed to the unbalanced character of other people; cf. Hornblower (1991) 306.
[38] Regulus is depicted as the opposite of the orator whose qualities Crassus lists in Cic. *De or.* 1.114–5 and 127–8; Trisoglio (1973) I, 438.
[39] Cf. Sen. *Controv.* 1 praef. 9; Quint. *Inst.* 1 praef. 9; 12.1.1 *sit ergo nobis orator, quem constituimus, is, qui a M. Catone finitur, vir bonus dicendi peritus*; Trisoglio (1973) I, 438.
[40] On Pliny and Demosthenes cf. Tzounakas (2015); see also Mordue (Chapter 4) in this volume.
[41] *De cor.* 291 μάλιστ' ἐθαύμασα πάντων ὅτε τῶν συμβεβηκότων τότε τῇ πόλει μνησθεὶς οὐχ ὡς ἂν εὔνους καὶ δίκαιος πολίτης ἔσχε τὴν γνώμην οὐδ' ἐδάκρυσεν, οὐδ' ἔπαθεν τοιοῦτον οὐδὲν τῇ ψυχῇ, ἀλλ' ἐπάρας τὴν φωνὴν καὶ γεγηθὼς καὶ λαρυγγίζων ᾤετο μὲν ἐμοῦ κατηγορεῖν δηλονότι ... ('what amazed me most was that, when he recounted the disasters that befell our city at that time, his comments were never such as would have been made by an honest and loyal citizen. He shed no tears; he had no emotion of regret in his heart; he vociferated, he exulted, he strained his throat. He evidently supposed himself to be testifying against me ...'; translation by Vince and Vince 1926); cf. Wankel (1976) ad loc.; Yunis (2001) ad loc. and 21–2 on Demosthenes' use of invective in *De Corona*.

so absurd that it is more likely to meet with laughter than tears') picks up the antithesis in Demosthenes' speech between appropriate grief after a defeat and rejoicing in an accusation.

As becomes clear from the letters looked at so far, Pliny's feelings for Regulus hover between *ira* and *risus*. Another character who is the target of an epistolary invective and provokes laughter as well as indignation is Pallas, the *libertus a rationibus* ('bookkeeper') under the Emperor Claudius. Within a short 'epistolary novel' consisting of two pieces (7.29 and 8.6), Pliny narrates how he had recently discovered Pallas' tombstone outside Rome and cites the inscription which refers to the *senatus consultum* of the year AD 52, a decision according to which the freedman was to be honoured with 15 million sesterces and the *insignia praetoris*.[42] In *Ep.* 7.29, Pliny anticipates his addressee's reaction to the inscription with the words *ridebis, deinde indignaberis, deinde ridebis* (1 'You will think it a joke – or an outrage, but a joke after all') at the beginning and concludes the letter with *sed quid indignor? ridere satius* (4 'But it isn't worth my indignation; better to laugh'). Pigoń has already pointed out in his contribution (Chapter 12) that with *risus* and *indignatio* as the appropriate reaction from the reader, Pliny foregrounds the satirical character of his letters on Pallas: we may recall Horace's programme of *ridentem dicere verum* (*Sat.* 1.1.24 'telling the whole truth with a smile') or Juvenal's *indignatio* as an impetus for writing satire (*Sat.* 1.79).[43] Also the adverb *satius* can be read as an etymological marker which recalls the genre of satire in a similar manner as scholars have observed at the end of Horace's satire 1.1 (120 *iam satis est*, 'that is enough').[44] Notwithstanding the conclusion that *risus* might be better than *indignatio*, the tone of indignation dominates letter 7.29 when Pliny calls the honours for Pallas *mimica et inepta* (7.29.3 'a ridiculous farce') which *in hoc caenum, in has sordes abicerentur* (7.29.3 'have been thrown away on such dirt and filth') and, what is more, have been accepted and refused by *ille furcifer* (7.29.3 'that rascal').[45] At the end of letter 8.6, where Pliny deals with the *senatus*

---

[42] For a more detailed analysis of Pliny's treatment of the *senatus consultum* see Pigoń's chapter in this volume.
[43] See also McNamara (2021) 3–4; cf. Braund (1996) 17–18; Holzberg (2009) 65–6; the traditional view that Juvenal's *Satires* postdate the works of Pliny and Martial has recently been challenged by Uden (2015) 219–26 and Kelly (2018) who suggest that Juvenal published his first book already around AD 101 and Martial alludes to this book in epigram 12.18.
[44] See Dufallo (2000).
[45] Pliny's abusive language here is reminiscent of Roman comedy, see Pigoń (Chapter 12) in this volume; Sherwin-White (1966) 439 compares this passage with Juvenal's outburst against the Greeks in Rome in *Sat.* 3.60 ff.

consultum leading to Pallas' distinction in more detail, he explicitly hints at the generic boundaries between a letter and satirical invective (17): *quamquam indignationem quibusdam in locis fortasse ultra epistulae modum extulerim* ('though in some passages I may have let my indignation carry me beyond the bounds of a letter'). Apart from satire and invective, letter 7.29 also plays with the tradition of epigram and inscription: at the beginning of the letter, Pliny presents himself as a travelling reader who discovers an epitaph on his journey and stops to read it. The figure of the travelling reader is frequently addressed in ancient funeral epigrams; he is asked to stop and offer a gesture of compassion to the deceased.[46] In his letter, Pliny inverts this habit by expressing contempt instead of sympathy. Whereas epitaphs usually serve to keep alive the memory of the life and merits of the deceased person, Pallas' epitaph provokes negative thoughts as *admonuit* ('it reminded') Pliny of *mimica et inepta* consisting of improper honours bestowed on a freedman by the senate.

Letters 7.29 and 8.6 not only criticize Pallas but also – more so – the Roman senate under the Emperor Claudius. The senate during Pliny's own lifetime is the target of epistolary indignation in *Ep.* 3.20 and 4.25, another instance of a short epistolary novel embedded into the letter corpus. In letter 4.25, Pliny narrates how during a secret election in the senate, the voting tablets were abused by some anonymous senators who wrote jokes, obscenities and invalid names on their tablets (1 *proximis comitiis in quibusdam tabellis multa iocularia atque etiam foeda dictu, in una vero pro candidatorum nominibus suffragatorum nomina inventa sunt*, 'At the recent election some of the voting-papers were found to have jokes and obscenities scribbled on them, and on one the names of the candidates were replaced by those of their sponsors'). The anger of the senate, who *magnoque clamore ei, qui scripsisset, iratum principem est comprecatus* (2 'clamoured for the wrath of the emperor to be visited on the culprit') mirrors the indignation with which Pliny comments on the incident (3–4): *quid hunc putamus domi facere, qui in tanta re tam serio tempore tam scurriliter ludat, qui denique omnino in senatu dicax et urbanus et bellus est? ... inde ista ludibria scaena et pulpito digna* ('If this man can play such ribald tricks in an important matter on a serious occasion, and thinks the Senate is the place where he can pass for a nimble wit and a fine fellow, what are we to suppose his personal conduct can be? ... The result was

---

[46] Cf. *CEG* 1.28.2 (epitaph for Thrason from the sixth century BC): οἴκτιρον; *CEG* 1.159; *AP* 7.166.6 (δάκρυα χεῖτε); *GVI* 1312; Mart. 6.28.10 on the boy Glaucias: *qui fles talia, nil fleas, viator*, 11.91; Meyer (2005) 65–8; Höschele (2007); Tueller (2008).

that ribaldry fit for nothing but the vulgar stage'). Pliny compares the anonymous senator's behaviour with performances of comic theatre or mime (*scurriliter ludat ... scaena et pulpito digna*)[47] and calls him *dicax, urbanus* and *bellus*. This characterization creates an intertextual link to Catullus' poem 22[48] where the poet Suffenus[49] is mocked for writing poems ten thousand lines long and having thereby foolishly squandered expensive writing materials:

> Suffenus iste, Vare, quem probe nosti,
> homo est venustus et **dicax** et **urbanus**
> idemque longe plurimos facit versus.
> ...
> haec cum legas tu, **bellus** ille et **urbanus**
> Suffenus unus caprimulgus aut fossor
> rursus videtur: tantum abhorret ac mutat.
> **hoc quid putemus esse**? Qui modo **scurra**
> aut si quid hac re scitius videbatur,
> idem infaceto est infacetior rure ...
>
> That chap Suffenus, Varus, whom you know too well, is a delightful fellow, witty, quite urbane, and *so* prolific, number one for churned-out verse ... But when you *read* it, then that same smart urbane man Suffenus seems a country lout, clod, clown, he's so remote from what he was, *so* changed. How explain this? One moment such a smart town wit, or anything still more clever (could that be?), he becomes on hicker than a backwoods hick ...

Suffenus conforms to Neoteric ideals only as long as he does not write poems; if he does, he stops being *dicax, urbanus, bellus* or a *scurra*, but instead shows himself as rustic and duller than the dullest countryside. Whereas in Catullus' poem the terms *dicax, urbanus, bellus* and *scurra* have a positive connotation and are opposed to Suffenus' tedious poems which are lacking *labor et lima*, Pliny uses these terms as negative attributes in characterizing a fellow senator's behaviour. In his letter, Pliny reverses the line of thought in Catullus' poem: Suffenus loses his *urbanitas* while composing poems, whereas the anonymous senator shows too much *urbanitas* in the act of writing jokes at the wrong moment (4 *poposcit tabellas, stilum accepit, demisit caput*, 'This man could ask for a voting-paper, take a pen, and bend his head to write'). By intertextually engaging with Catullus, Pliny highlights the contrast between the Roman senate and the world of the Neoterics, a world into which he plunges himself, but

---

[47] The phrase *scurriliter ludat* seems to allude to Valerius Maximus, where it also refers to the inappropriate behaviour of a senator (7.8.9 *scurrili lusu*); see Whitton (Chapter 1) in this volume.
[48] Cf. Roller (1998) 287.   [49] Cf. Catull. 14.19; on Catull. 22 cf. Watson (1990); Adamik (1995).

under other circumstances: for Pliny, *lusus* and *ineptiae* are legitimate distractions in the realm of *otium*, but not during the serious business of the senate.[50]

Whereas in letter 4.25 Pliny expresses his indignation about a scandalous incident in the senate, letter 6.15 contains a narration of a *faux pas* during a recitation.[51] Pliny gives an account of an extraordinary incident which neither he nor his addressee Voconius Romanus witnessed in person (1 *mirificae rei non interfuisti, ne ego quidem*, 'you have missed an extraordinary incident, and so have I') but about which Pliny had heard only recently (1 *me recens fabula excepit*, 'a current story has come to my ears'). When Passenus Paulus, a compatriot and descendant of Propertius,[52] was about to recite his elegies, he started with the words *'Prisce iubes'* ('"You bid me, Priscus"'), whereupon his friend Iavolenus Priscus, a famous jurist who was invited as an auditor,[53] interjected *'ego vero non iubeo'* ('"Indeed I don't"'). This heckling provoked laughter and jokes among the other members of the audience (2 *cogita, qui risus hominum, qui ioci!*, 'imagine the people's laughter and jokes'). There are at least two individuals who did not participate in this laughing community: Passenus Paulus, whose recitation had been disturbed and who thereafter received *aliquantum frigoris* (4 'a chilly reception'), and Pliny the narrator, who criticizes Iavolenus Priscus' behaviour by questioning his sanity (3 *est omnino Priscus dubiae sanitatis*, 'in general, his mental state is questionable')[54] and calling his act *ridiculum et notabile* (3 'remarkable and absurd') as well as a form of *deliratio* ('madness').[55] But what moved Priscus to interrupt the recitation and why is Pliny upset about this incident? Did Priscus really act out of mental confusion as Pliny wants us to believe? Or did he try to make a deliberate joke about the *topos* of a literary dedication where a patron is addressed with verbs like *iubes*, *petis* and the like?[56] Did the

---

[50] See also *Ep.* 8.6.3 *dicerem urbanos, si senatum deceret urbanitas* ('I would call them witty if wit befitted the Senate'; my translation).
[51] On this letters cf. Laughton (1971); Yardley (1972); Hiltbrunner (1979); Schröder (2001); Beck (2013b); Roller (2018) 201–5.
[52] His poetry is also praised in *Ep.* 9.22; cf. *ILS* 2925; Sherwin-White (1966) 370.
[53] He was head of the Sabinian school, member of Trajan's *consilium* and author of 14 books *Epistulae* on legal problems; *Dig.* 1.2.2.53; Sherwin-White (1966) 370; Trisoglio (1973) I, 618; Eckardt (1978); Harries (2018); Pliny does not mention him in other letters.
[54] Cf. the *ingenium insanum* of Regulus in *Ep.* 4.7.4; Trisoglio (1973) I, 618.
[55] According to Cicero *Sen.* 36, *deliratio* is synonymous with *senilis stultitia* ('senile dullness').
[56] Cf. Mart. 2.6.1 and 6 *i nunc, edere me iube libellos*; 4.17.1 *facere in Lyciscam, Paule, me iubes versus*; 11.42.3 *mella iubes Hyblaea tibi vel Hymettia nasci*; Pliny himself uses this *topos* in *Ep.* 1.1.1 *frequenter hortatus es*; Janson (1964); Yardley (1972); for a discussion of the various opinions in scholarship concerning Priscus' intentions cf. Schröder (2001) 241–2; Beck (2013b) 297–300.

audience laugh *at* Priscus, or *with* him? In any case, Pliny depicts Priscus' behaviour as completely inappropriate, particularly with regard to his status as a lawyer,[57] and as contradicting Pliny's own 'ideal of the recitation event as a cooperative enterprise by like-minded community members to help one another publish the best books possible'.[58] Thus, Priscus' ridiculous act during Passenus Paulus' recitation parallels the inappropriate behaviour of the anonymous senator during the secret election in *Ep.* 4.25 insofar as both individuals are joking at the wrong moment. There is also a connection between Iavolenus Priscus and Regulus through the use of the term *fabula* with which Pliny tags both the narration in 6.15 (1 *recens fabula*) and three short stories in letter 2.20 where Regulus' activities as a shameless legacy hunter are reported (2.20.1 *accipe auream fabulam, fabulas immo*; 9 *sufficiunt duae fabulae?*).[59] In the light of Pliny's emphasis of the ridiculous (*risus ... ridiculum*) in *Ep.* 6.15 it is also possible to understand *fabula* in the sense of a 'comedy'[60] which is staged by Iavolenus Priscus and his antagonist Passenus Paulus, who involuntarily turns from an elegist into a comic figure.[61] To the internal audience of the narration one could add the letter's addressee Voconius Romanus whom Pliny, for the sake of *evidentia*, invites to imagine the laughter and jokes in the lecture room (2 *cogita*).[62] Would he have also laughed at the expense of Passenus Paulus? From another letter written to Romanus we might conclude that he would not have done so: in *Ep.* 8.8, Pliny tells of inscriptions which were dedicated to the god Clitumnus in his shrine and, partially, had the potential to provoke laughter (7): *plura laudabis, non nulla ridebis; quamquam tu vero, quae tua humanitas, nulla ridebis* ('Most of them you will admire, but some will make you laugh – though I know you are really too charitable to laugh at any of them').

Pliny concludes letter 6.15 with the pointed remark *tam sollicite recitaturis providendum est, non solum ut ipsi sint sani, verum etiam ut sanos adhibeant* (4 'this shows how anyone giving a reading must beware of eccentricity either in himself or in the audience he invites'). With the

---

[57] *Ep.* 6.15.3 *interest tamen officiis, adhibetur consiliis atque etiam ius civile publice respondet* ('but he takes part in public functions, is called on for advice, and is also one of the official experts on civil law').
[58] Roller (2018) 203.
[59] Cf. *Ep.* 8.18.11 *habes omnes fabulas urbis; nam sunt omnes fabulae Tullus*; Schröder (2001) 242–3.
[60] Cf. *OLD*, 665 s.v. 6.
[61] For Pliny's letters and comedy see Fögen (2017); the characterisation of the incident as *mirifica res* (6.15.1), on the other hand, evokes the tradition of paradoxography.
[62] For *evidentia* in the rhetorical theory cf. Quint. *Inst.* 9.2.40–3; 6.2.32; 8.3.61–71; Watson (1994) 4774–7; Otto (2009) 108–27; Webb (2009) 87–106.

polyptoton *sani – sanos* Pliny emphasizes the importance of mental sanity for both the reciter and his audience. There also seems to be a play on the double meaning of the adjective *sanus*, which refers to both mental and physical health.[63] If this is the case, Pliny's letter might be read as an answer to or continuation of Martial's sceptic epigrams on various individuals who recite although they have (or maintain to have) a cold:[64] in 4.80, for example, Martial mocks a character named Maron for declaiming despite running a fever (1–2 *Declamas in febre, Maron: hanc esse phrenesin | si nescis, non es sanus, amice Maron*, 'You declaim in a fever, Maron. If you don't know that this is lunacy, you're not sane, friend Maron') and conjectures that this is probably the only way that Maron is able to sweat (4 *si sudare aliter non potes*, 'if you cannot sweat otherwise').[65] Both Pliny and Martial provide a kind of medical or psychological analysis of their targets – the letter writer speaks of Priscus' *deliratio* ('madness') whereas the epigrammatist reproaches Maron's *phrenesis* ('lunacy').[66] In contrast to Maron who is running a fever stands Passenus Paulus who experienced a 'chilly reception' (*aliquantum frigoris*)[67] of his recitation thanks to Priscus' *deliratio*.

It is striking that Voconius Romanus as addressee of letter 6.15 is juxtaposed with Tacitus as addressee of the following letter (6.16), an arrangement which we already encountered in *Ep.* 1.5–6, discussed above. If my suggestion is correct that we have to imagine Tacitus not only as a reader of the letter directed to him but also of the preceding letter 1.5, this could also be the case in the letter sequence 6.15–16: again, a letter which derides a well-known individual is followed by a letter to Tacitus.[68] The words *'Prisce iubes'* which Passenus Paulus uttered at the beginning of his recitation (6.15.2) are paralleled by Pliny's opening of *Ep.* 6.16 with the words *petis, ut* (1 'you ask me') as well as *ais te . . . cupere cognoscere* ('you say that you wish to know') in 6.20.1. But instead of the failed literary

---

[63] Guillemin (1961–64) II, ad loc.; *sanus* can also refer to the orator's style; cf. Plin. *Ep.* 9.26.1; *OLD*, 1689–90 s.v.

[64] Apologies for a sore throat were a standard topos in rhetorical prefaces: Mart. 3.18; 4.41; 4.80; 6.41; cf. Tac. *Dial.* 20.1 *Quis nunc feret oratorem de infirmitate valetudinis suae praefantem?*

[65] Translation of Martial by Shackleton Bailey (1993); for this poem see Moreno Soldevila (2006) 505–8.

[66] Both terms can denote *febrile delirium*: cf. Cels. 2.1.15; *OLD*, 1375 s.v. *phrenesis*; *TLL* V.1, 465 s.v. *deliratio* 2b.

[67] Also Maron's speech is probably to be imagined as *frigida* ('frigid, lame') although he declaims in a fever; cf. *OLD*, 736 s.v. *frigidus* 8b.

[68] For the juxtaposition of Voconius Romanus and Tacitus as addressees cf. *Ep.* 8.7–8; Gibson and Morello (2012) 149–50 and 168; moreover, letter 8.6 with its derision of Pallas and the senate under Claudius precedes *Ep.* 8.7 to Tacitus; cf. Neger (2021) 255.

interaction presented in *Ep.* 6.15, the Vesuvius letters create a positive picture of the literary friendship between Pliny and Tacitus.[69]

Letter 6.15 has as its companion-piece letter 6.17, where a similar story is narrated. Whereas Iavolenus Priscus' *faux pas* during the recitation in *Ep.* 6.15 is said to have provoked laughter (*risus*) and is characterized as ridiculous (*ridiculum*), the incident reported in letter 6.17 aroused Pliny's indignation (1 *indignatiuncula*; 6 *indignationem*).[70] This time it was not a confused person who disturbed the recitation with an inappropriate comment, but the arrogance of some of the invited *amici* who remained completely impassive during the reading of a *liber absolutissimus* (2 'a more than perfect book'). Differently from *Ep.* 6.15 we do not learn the names of the individuals involved. As with the two letters on Pallas (7.29 and 8.6), this pair of letters also contains a climax from *risus* to *indignatio*, thus integrating two modes of satirical writing into an epistolary framework.

3 Joking with the Addressee

Ancient theorists and letter writers distinguish between two functions of epistolary communication: *narrare* and *loqui* or *iocari* ('narrate' and 'chat' or 'joke').[71] From narrative letters where Pliny derides or reproaches individuals such as Regulus, Pallas, Iavolenus Priscus and other anonymous characters, we move to letters where Pliny jokes with his addressees and in this context alludes to the scoptic tradition. *Ep.* 2.2 discusses the topic of proper epistolary exchange; similarly to *Ep.* 1.5, Pliny also shows himself as *irascens*, but this time in a more jocular manner. The target is Pliny's friend Paulinus[72] who has failed to send letters (2.2.1):

> Irascor, nec liquet mihi an debeam, sed irascor. Scis, quam sit amor iniquus interdum ... haec tamen causa magna est, nescio an iusta ... graviter irascor, quod a te tam diu litterae nullae.
>
> I am furious with you, rightly or not I don't know, but it makes no difference. You know very well that love is sometimes unfair ... I have good reason, whether or not it is a just one ... I am very furious: it is so long since I have had a letter from you.

---

[69] Cf. Gibson and Morello (2012) 67; Beck (2013a) 24–5.
[70] The diminutive *indignatiuncula* is a Plinian hapax (cf. *actiunculas* in *Ep.* 9.15.2; *columbulis* in *Ep.* 9.25.3; *metulae* in *Ep.* 5.6.35); Trisoglio (1973) I, 628.
[71] See Thraede (1970) 27–38; Holzberg (2007). [72] For him see Whitton (2013a) 84.

Among this letter's models, Ilaria Marchesi has identified Catullus 38 (6 *irascor tibi*, 'I am angry with you') and 85 (*Odi et amo. Quare id faciam fortasse requiris. | Nescio, sed fieri sentio et excrucior*, 'I hate and I love. You wonder, perhaps, why I'd do that? I have no idea. I just feel it. I am crucified').[73] I would like to suggest another intertext, which may serve as a window-reference here by also recalling Catullus 85 and which may have inspired the doubling (*redditio*) of the verb *irascor* in the first sentence of Pliny's letter:[74] Martial in epigram 1.32 turns the Catullan distich into a satiric poem mocking a character named Sabidius: *Non amo te, Sabidi, nec possum dicere quare: | hoc tantum possum dicere, non amo te* ('I don't like you, Sabidius, but I can't say why: I can only say that I don't like you').[75] By transforming Martial's *non amo te* into *irascor* and the phrase *nec possum dicere quare* into *nec liquet mihi an debeam*, Pliny turns epigrammatic mockery into epistolary complaint. Thus, the letter forms a kind of epigram in prose and varies the motif of *ira* which also appeared in some of Pliny's poems, as he tells us in *Ep.* 4.14.3 (*his iocamur ludimus amamus dolemus querimur* **irascimur**, 'Here are my jokes and witticisms, my loves, sorrows, complaints and vexations').

Another instance where Pliny recalls one of Catullus' scoptic poems within an epistolary context is letter 5.10 to Suetonius. Pliny states that in his *hendecasyllabi* he had announced to their common friends the appearance of a work by Suetonius who was now hesitant over its publication (1–2):

> Libera tandem hendecasyllaborum meorum fidem, qui scripta tua communibus amicis spoponderunt. Adpellantur cotidie, efflagitantur, ac iam periculum est ne cogantur ad exhibendum formulam accipere ... tu tamen meam quoque cunctationem tarditatemque vicisti. Proinde aut rumpe iam moras aut cave ne eosdem istos libellos, quos tibi hendecasyllabi nostri blanditiis elicere non possunt, convicio scazontes extorqueant.

> Do please release my hendecasyllables from their promise – they were guarantors to our friends for the appearance of your work, and every day brings in some new request and demand; so they now run the risk of being served with a writ to produce it ... you outdo even my doubts and hesitations. So bestir yourself, or else beware lest I drag those books out of you by the fury of my scazons, since my hendecasyllables failed to entice them with honeyed words!

---

[73] Marchesi (2008) 90–2.   [74] For the figure of *redditio* or κύκλος cf. Whitton (2013a) 85.
[75] Translation by Howell (1980); cf. Citroni (1975) 109–10; Holzberg (2002b) 97–8.

This letter is rich in intertextual allusions: the images of demand (*efflagitare*) and reproach (*convicium*) recall the epistolary preface to Quintilian's *Institutio Oratoria*: **Efflagitasti cotidiano convicio** *ut libros . . . iam emittere inciperem . . . sed si tantopere* **efflagitantur** *quam tu adfirmas* ('You have been pressing me every day. . . to start publishing the books . . . But if they are called for as urgently as you alledge . . .').[76] Several scholars assume that the *scripta* mentioned in Pliny's letter can be identified with Suetonius' work *De Viris Illustribus*.[77] Tristan Power has drawn attention to verbal links between this letter and the biography of Vergil in the *Vita Suetoniana-Donatiana*, especially the chapter where the Emperor Augustus in a letter containing jocular threats asks for a sample of the yet unfinished *Aeneid* (*VSD* 31 *supplicibus atque etiam minacibus per iocum litteris* **efflagitarat** *. . .*, 'he demanded by pleading and also jokingly threatening letters. . .').[78] A similar kind of letter was also written by Pliny to Suetonius, and besides the character of Augustus in the biographic tradition the epistolographer also recalls Catullus' poem 42 which addresses the poet's *hendecasyllabi*:

> Adeste, hendecasyllabi, quot estis,
> omnes undique, quotquot estis omnes.
> iocum me putat esse moecha turpis
> et negat mihi nostra redditturam
> pugillaria, si pati potestis.
> . . .
> circumsistite eam et reflagitate:
> 'moecha putida, redde codicillos,
> redde, putida moecha, codicillos!'
> . . .
> sed nil proficimus, nihil movetur.
> mutanda est ratio modusque vobis,
> siquid proficere amplius potestis:
> 'pudica et proba, redde codicillos.'
>
> Come, you hendecasyllables, in force now, each last one of you, from every quarter – this vile slut seems under the impression I'm a walking joke, won't give me back my writing tablets – really, can you beat it? . . . Close in round her now, demand in chorus: 'Rotten slut, give back the writing tablets! Give back, rotten slut, the writing tablets!' . . . Still this gets us nowhere, she remains un-moved, you'll need to change your tune and

---

[76] Translation by Russell (2002).
[77] Cf. the discussion in Power (2010); Gibson and Morello (2012) 222; differently Sherwin-White (1966) 338 ad loc.: 'The implication favours a volume of verses, rather than the lost prose work *De Viris Illustribus*. . .'; cf. Wallace-Hadrill (1983) 52–3 and 59; Kaster (1995) xliv.
[78] Power (2010) 153.

method. Try this, then, see if it gets you further: 'Pure chaste maid, give back the writing tablets!'

In his poem, Catullus provides a literary version of the praxis of *flagitatio*, a means of popular justice which aimed at regaining one's property by surrounding the thief and loudly demanding restitution.[79] Pliny in his letter evokes a similar situation with *adpellantur* and *efflagitantur* and also refers to legal measures with the words *ne cogantur ad exhibendum formulam accipere*.[80] Catullus, who summons his *hendecasyllabi* to insult a *moecha putida* so as to provoke her to give back his *codicilli*, finally realizes that the insults remain ineffective and that it is better to change strategy and use flattery instead. Pliny, on the contrary, in his poems first uses flattery in order to elicit Suetonius' *scripta* and then, in the face of his friend's hesitation to publish his work, threatens him with *scazontes* and *convicia*. Similar to *Ep.* 4.14 discussed above, the obscene elements of Catullus' poem are completely absent from Pliny's letter 5.10;[81] again, the scoptic tone of the pre-text is mitigated and adapted to the conventions of epistolary friendship. As has already been discussed above, in letter 4.14, Pliny explicitly renounces *verba nuda* (4 *quae nos refugimus*) both in his letters and his poems, thereby distinguishing himself from poets such as Martial who followed and even surpassed Catullus' *lascivam verborum veritatem* (cf. Mart. 1 *praef.*).[82] Unlike the genres of epigram or iambic poetry, in ancient epistolography the use of obscene language is a very rare phenomenon:[83] according to Suetonius, Marcus Antonius wrote a letter to Octavian which was full of obscene words and thoughts (*Aug.* 69.2 *Quid te mutavit? quod reginam ineo? . . . an refert, ubi et in qua arrigas?*, 'What has changed you? Because I am tupping the queen? . . . Does it matter where or in whom you get a hard on?')[84] Another exception is a letter by Cicero to Paetus (*Fam.* 9.22 = 189 SB) where the Stoics' position on the matter of 'calling a spade a spade' is discussed (1 *placet Stoicis suo quamque rem nomine appellare*, 'the Stoics hold that we should call everything by its proper name').[85] It seems that Paetus in his preceding letter had used the

---

[79] Cf. Fraenkel (1961); Roman (2006) 354.
[80] On the *interdictum exhibitorium* cf. Sherwin-White (1966) 338.   [81] Cf. Roller (1998) 288.
[82] For Martial surpassing Catullus' obscene language see Lorenz (2007).
[83] A papyrus letter from Oxyrhynchus (P.Oxy.XLII 3070) has survived where two male writers, Apion and Epimas, request from the addressee, Epaphroditus, that he may allow them to penetrate him (πυγίσαι); the letter also contains obscene drawings of a ψωλή (penis) and φίκις (anus); see Gallavotti (1978/79).
[84] Translation by Wardle (2014); cf. id. 442–3.
[85] Translations of Cicero by Glynn Williams (1928); cf. Shackleton Bailey (1977) II, 330–4.

word *mentula* which Cicero compares with the obscene meaning of the word *penis* (2 *quod tu in epistula apellas suo nomine, ille tectius 'penem'*, 'what you in your letter call by its own name, he with more reserve calls "penis"'). Cicero himself, though, prefers *Platonis verecundia* ('Plato's modesty') and says to have used *verba tecta* in his letter in order to describe the subject under discussion (5 *ego servo et servabo . . . Platonis verecundiam. Itaque tectis verbis ea ad te scripsi, quae apertissimis agunt Stoici*, 'As for me, I maintain, and ever shall maintain . . . the modest reserve of Plato; so I have used veiled language in writing to you of what the Stoics deal with in the most outspoken way').[86] In his letter 4.14, Pliny on the one hand recalls the metapoetic statements of Catullus and Martial, but on the other he also seems to evoke Cicero's discussion with Paetus about the use of obscene language and to follow Cicero's example by preferring *verecundia* to *verba aperta*.

4 Conclusion

As Alice König argues in her contribution (Chapter 3) on Book 10, Pliny's epistolary intertextuality encompasses a large spectrum of interaction which reaches from allusions to specific texts to the evocation of whole genres and discourses. Pliny's interaction with the tradition of satire and invective throughout *Epistles* Books 1–9 works in a similar way. Pliny conducts an intertextual dialogue with scoptic and satiric pre-texts through both quotations and verbal allusions while, in a broader sense, he picks up motives, topics and rhetorical techniques familiar from scoptic genres such as satire, iambic poetry, epigram, comedy and invective in oratory. Moreover, transformation and context-shifting, two modes of Plinian *imitatio* discussed in Christopher Whitton's contribution (Chapter 1), also play a crucial role when invective and satire are absorbed in the *Epistles*: Pliny transforms the scoptic tone of his pre-texts into a different context of communication by adapting the tradition of scoptic poetry to the conventions of the epistolary genre. Sometimes the scoptic tone of the pre-text is maintained, sometimes attenuated or even transformed into friendly joking with addressees.

---

[86] On words and images which were regarded as obscene in antiquity cf. Adams (1982).

PART VI

Final Thoughts: Discourses of Representation and Reproduction

CHAPTER 14

Pliny's Calpurnia: Filiation, Imitation, Allusion

Ilaria Marchesi

In the following pages, I examine issues of potential or failed reproduction, felicitous or troubled cross-generational representation, and cultural or biological character transmission, as they emerge, interwoven, from the dynamics of literary allusion in Pliny's *Epistles*. My analysis begins with a scrutiny of Pliny's *Ep.* 4.19, a text apparently devoted to the praise of his wife Calpurnia and the perfect education she received from her aunt Hispulla. I read this letter as permeated by the deep tensions surrounding the role which Roman women were asked to assume in actively shaping future generations, a role which they were also asked to renounce for the sake of transmitting their father's and husband's imprint.[1] In Roman society, women were at once expected to represent their fathers, by markedly resembling them in their own physical and moral features, and to reproduce their husbands, by transparently issuing physical and moral replicas of them in their offspring. This social double bind located women at the critical juncture of questions of paternity, projecting them as ideally transparent intergenerational signifiers of masculine characters. In this chapter, I propose to recover in specifically semiotic terms the role of women as bearers of a paternal imprint and vehicle for the transmission of spousal identity, as it illuminates the cultural construction and common understanding of literary practices.

This constellation may be shown to structure both societal and cultural expectations which Pliny supports and to which he adheres in *Ep.* 4.19 and elsewhere in his collection. As an intra-textual survey shows, the letter about Calpurnia's education is not isolated in Pliny's corpus, which contains a significant sample of letters devoted to questions of biological or surrogate paternity, natural or artificial representation, and maternal or paternal

---

[1] On women's societal role in classical culture, see Dixon (1988) esp. 41–70; Rousselle (1992) 297–336; Hallett (1984) 3–34; Hemelrijk (1999) 7–36. There is a common insistence on 'changing social arrangement' (Rousselle, 324 ff.), 'paradox' (Hallett, 6, with reference to Herrmann and Arthur, as well as de Beauvoir and Pomeroy), and 'contradictory position' (Hemelrijk).

reproduction. The letter also resonates with wider cultural concerns, as it may be shown to align closely with a delicate and debated passage in Tacitus' *Dialogus De Oratoribus* (*Dial.* 28), which develops a similarly structured argument. The cultural tension at the core of Pliny's letter also haunts the language of Tacitus' page, in which the role of women in the formation of future orators is at once evasively praised and loathed. Pliny's letter does not only mobilize culturally charged language that has intra-textual antecedents and contains echoes of a wider cultural discourse, but it also may be shown to have an inter-textual dimension, evoking a surprising target of distanced allusion, Martial's *Ep.* 6.38. This epigram is an encomiastic poem which Martial had dedicated to Regulus, Pliny's adversary in the Centumviral court and the sole living target of sceptic epistolary invectives in his collection. The letter-to-epigram inter-textuality is particularly eerie, I argue, not so much for the contrastive treatment which Regulus receives in either collection, but because it ends up transferring to Pliny's wife and potential mother of his children the charged language which Martial deployed for Regulus' wife and child, drawing Pliny's and Martial's texts together in an uncomfortably shared social and cultural space.

Thanks to Martial, I argue, inter-textual co-implications overcome any social, political, or literary distancing which Pliny had carefully established in his text to mark Regulus as a foil for his own literary self-portrait. The fact that Pliny and Regulus would both eventually be childless adds to the eerie quality of the inter-textual relation Martial indirectly mediated. Before and beyond Martial, however, what united Pliny and Regulus and uncannily connected their work was not simply their shared biographical condition, but an active interest which they both took in child-mourning. This connection is the final object of my study, which concludes with a reading of a contrastive micro-cycle of 'orbative' letters Pliny inserts in his collection: *Ep.* 4.2 and 4.7, which I contrast with *Ep.* 2.7 and 3.10, detailing the diverging strategies of iterative and exemplary commemoration which Regulus (independently and frantically) and Spurinna (through Pliny's actions and works) deployed to mourn their dead sons. In this case, too, as memorializing agents caught in a process of cultural reproduction of images, Pliny and Regulus come closer than they perhaps would have wished, so much so that the texts which construct and convey their proximity also apparently conceal it.[2]

---

[2] On Regulus in Pliny, see White (1975); Hoffer (1999) 55–92; Pitcher (1999); Méthy (2007) 142–51 (with bibliography); Lefèvre (2009) 50–60; Gibson and Morello (2012) 68–73; Ash (2013); Marchesi (2018); Moreno Soldevila, Castillo, and Valverde (2019) 521–3. Cf. Hanaghan (Chapter 7), Mordue (Chapter 4), Neger (Chapter 13), and Pigoń (Chapter 12) in this volume. On the orbative letters, cf. most recently Stucchi (2015).

While proceeding mainly as a literary-critical investigation of the way in which Pliny's letters articulate a cultural discourse around reproduction, my argument also attempts to develop a taxonomy of possible interrelations between the texts it analyses from the point of view of the reader-reception and the mechanisms these textual interactions mobilize. Pliny's epistles are remarkably rich in moments of carefully orchestrated literary dialogue with contemporary readership and with their shared cultural tradition. The general reliance on the readers' work, however, does not imply monotony or uni-modality of reading. Quite the contrary: the kind of reader responsibility which Pliny envisions in the fruition of his text is multifaceted, in particular when surrounding moments of potential interconnection within a corpus of quasi-contemporary texts, circulating in arguably similar (if not fully coincidental) readerships. In his strategy of constructing readers, one may distinguish four different models of intertextuality. Before delving into a reading of the select corpus of primary texts which forms the object of this chapter, a corpus in which all texts appear connected to issues of intergenerational transmission and cultural reproduction, I propose to summarize these forms of textual interaction as follows:

1- Form A. Intra-textuality: Texts are structurally connected within authorially controlled macro-texts by elements of prosopography, recurring themes, and position in the overall architecture of the text (being placed at the beginning or end of an individual section, or appearing as co-numerary in a numbered sequence).[3]
2- Form B. Inter-textuality: Texts are allusively connected by elements of language, diction, and style. The signals are at once more precise (that is, the connection relies on mutually marked lexical or syntactic clinchers) and open to interpretation.[4]
3- Form C. Extra-textuality: Texts are connected by their common association with a discursive field and to the definition of which they collaborate independently from one another (but co-dependently).[5]

---

[3] On the weight of intratextual factors in reading composite collections, see Papanghelis, Harrison and Frangoulidis (2018); for Martial, see Fitzgerald (2007), chapter 3 (with bibliography); for Pliny, see Marchesi (2008) 12–52; Gibson and Morello (2012) 234–50; Whitton (2015a); Gibson (2015).
[4] For a standard orientation on the issues of inter-textuality and allusion, see the line Conte (1986) (and Barchiesi (2001)); Farrell (1991); Thomas (1999); Fowler (2000); Edmunds (2001); cf. Hinds (1998).
[5] For an initial exploration of the category of extra-textuality, see Marchesi (2013); for a theoretical framework, see the introductory remarks by Geue and Giusti (2021) 1–16 to the collection *Unspoken Rome*. The term has been recently adopted by Langlands (2018).

284   ILARIA MARCHESI

4. Form D. Alter-textuality: A situation in which lexical or structural elements prompt readers to read, in parallel, texts that are mutually exclusive and, by design, mutually indifferent, either within the same corpus or across related ones.[6]

In practical terms, the intra-textual connection recommends that we read one text *not* without the other, risking semiotic diminution otherwise. The inter-textual connection stipulates that we would do better to read one text *with* the other; or, at least, it suggests that we are worse off when not doing so. The extra-textual dialogic correlation invites a critical observation of the mechanisms that produce cultural consonance, allowing an appreciation of apparently non-marked contextual discursive elements. Finally, alter-textuality, conceived as the mutual dis-implication of textual strains, dictates that we read one text *only in the absence of* the other (as impossible a request as that may sound). These four kinds of intra-, inter-, extra- and alter-textual relations are active, within the sections of Pliny's letters with which this chapter is concerned, in connection with issues of literary as well as biological filiation, reproduction, and allusion. As such, they involve women as literary characters as well as social subjects in their role as intergenerational mediators. What is more, they all appear in relation to the Regulus material.

1 Mothering: Pliny on Hispulla's Calpurnia

One may begin with *Epistle* 4.19, the letter Pliny writes to his wife's aunt to thank her for the flawless education she has imparted to her niece. The letter is devoted to the outline of a transmission of positive features from one generation, Hispulla's, to the next, Calpurnia's own. In the process of generational reproduction, there are seemingly no dangers in sight, but the situation is not without its tensions. The first element of potential tension is in Hispulla's ability to represent the male members of her family, quite literally to take their place in time.

> Cum sis pietatis *exemplum*, fratremque optimum et amantissimum tui pari caritate dilexeris, filiamque eius ut tuam diligas, nec tantum amitae ei

---

[6] Critically, this is a less defined category, and as such it is proposed here tentatively. Alter-textuality is akin to but does not coincide with extra-textuality. In extratextual (interdiscursive) correlations, textual elements emerge as marked in connection with unmarked discursive ones; in altertextual pairings, each connection is marked – as a non-pertinent element, but marked nonetheless.

affectum verum etiam patris amissi *repraesentes*, non dubito maximo tibi gaudio fore cum cognoveris *dignam patre dignam te dignam avo evadere*. (*Ep.* 4.19.1)

> A model of the family virtues yourself, you reciprocated your good brother's great love for you with equal affection, you also love his daughter as though she were your own. You represent for her not only the affection of an aunt but even that of her lost father. Thus, I am sure you will be delighted to learn that she is turning out worthy of her father, worthy of you, and worthy of her grandfather.[7]

Since she was also charged with molding her niece into the woman she has become, her representative function is balanced by a reproductive one. Her role as putative mother (and sisterly surrogate father) of Pliny's wife, one should note, does not make her, strictly speaking, a model for the woman who would become Pliny's Calpurnia. In the emphatic *tricolon* which the epistle deftly constructs to inform her about her niece's general qualities (*dignam patre dignam te dignam avo evadere*), Calpurnia Hispulla is technically made the intermediary of two male generations. Caught between her role as stand-in for Calpurnia's father and grandfather, she is said to represent the first by way of replica, while, we are invited to understand, she reproduces the other with no less faithfulness than her brother did, since she is able to represent their common father by assuming her brother's role in shaping her niece, his daughter, and the former man's granddaughter, respectively. The result of Hispulla's double role as representative and reproducer of her family's past is a new Calpurnia, who is herself an impeccable reproduction of her own ancestry. This flawlessly transmitted identity becomes, in turn, a new model (*exemplum*) of womanly behavior.[8]

Involved in the dynamic of representation of ancestors and reproduction of male family members, both women conform to a traditional societal role, which is presented as an absolute value as much in Pliny as it was, for example, in Catullus or Martial. It is sufficient to glance at their topic statements, and the lexicon of transparency which they produce, to have a sense of the compact cultural constraints that shape the situation Pliny constructs in the epistle. Children are supposed to look like their fathers,

---

[7] All translations are mine.
[8] On Pliny's letter about, and to, his wife, see, most recently, De Pretis (2003); Carlon (2009) 138–95; Shelton (2013) 96–104 and 111–23. See also Gibson (2021), with updated bibliography on Calpurnia's socio-political role in the *Epistles*.

and the ability to reproduce their husbands in their offspring is the quality most praised in women.

Torquatus volo parvulus
matris e gremio suae
porrigens teneras manus
dulce rideat ad patrem
    semihiante labello.
sit suo similis patri
Manlio et facile insciis
noscitetur ab omnibus,
et pudicitiam suae
    matris indicet ore.
        Catull. 61.216–25
	Bis vicine Nepos—nam tu quoque proxima Florae
	    incolis et veteres tu quoque Ficelias—
	est tibi, *quae patria signatur imagine voltus,*
	    testis maternae nata pudicitiae.
	                               Martial 6.27.1–4

My wish is that a little Torquatus, stretching out his tender hands from his mother's lap, smile sweetly for his father, his lips half-opened. May he resemble his father Manlius, and be recognized right away as being his by all who do not know them. Let his features be the sign of his mother's modesty.	Dear Nepos, you who are twice my neighbor, since you also live next to the Temple of Flora and in the ancient Ficeliae, you have a daughter now, whose face is stamped with the features of her father, attesting her mother's modesty . . .

While the normative situation appears untroubled in its first stage, what happens when these children become parents in their turn? In particular, what will happen when Calpurnia produces Pliny's own offspring? The issue is not only theoretical, of course, nor is the question purely speculative. The first case of intra-textuality will help us appreciate the tension at work in this social and cultural situation. Pliny had already mobilized charged language and some associated notions in *Ep.* 3.3 to Corellia Hispulla, where he had taken upon himself the role of indirect educator of Corellia's son.

> Cum patrem tuum gravissimum et sanctissimum virum *suspexerim* magis an *amaverim* dubitem, teque et in memoriam eius et in honorem tuum unice diligam, *cupiam necesse est* atque etiam *quantum in me fuerit enitar, ut filius tuus avo similis exsistat*; equidem malo materno, *quamquam* illi paternus *etiam* clarus spectatusque *contigerit*, pater *quoque* et patruus illustri laude conspicui. Quibus omnibus ita demum similis adolescet, si imbutus honestis artibus fuerit, quas plurimum refert a quo potissimum accipiat. ... Nihil ex hoc viro filius tuus audiet nisi profuturum, nihil discet quod nescisse rectius fuerit, nec minus saepe ab illo quam a te meque admonebitur, *quibus imaginibus oneretur*, quae nomina et quanta sustineat. Proinde faventibus dis trade eum praeceptori, a quo mores primum mox eloquentiam discat, quae male sine moribus discitur. Vale. (*Ep.* 3.3)

Since I am not sure whether I had for your father, who was so wise and righteous, more reverence or love, and I have a special affection for you both in his memory and on account of your worth, I cannot avoid desiring – and also doing all I can – for your son to turn out like his grandfather. I prefer him to be like his maternal grandfather, though he also happens to have had a distinguished and eminent paternal grandfather, and his father and uncle have been well regarded and amply praised. He will grow up to be like them all, provided that he is educated in the liberal arts – and it is very important who first teaches them to him. ... From that man your son will hear nothing from which he will not eventually benefit; he will learn nothing which he would be better off not knowing; he will remind your son, just as much as would you or I, of how weighty are the examples he has to uphold, what and how great are the names he carries. So, under the good auspices of the gods, pass him on to his teacher, from whom he will first acquire good habits, and then eloquence, which is an art that should not be learned without the former. Farewell.

In the context of recommending a teacher for her child, Pliny adopted the same notion of resemblance and imitation that marks the cultural understanding and construction of heredity which he shares with the traditional normative accounts surveyed above.[9] With high-pitched rhetoric, Pliny states (*Ep.* 3.3.1) that he feels a moral compulsion and hence a call to do everything in his power to ensure that Corellia's son will be a faithful reproduction of his grandfather: 'I feel bound to desire and even to do all that lies in my power to help your son to turn out like his grandfather.' The dynamics of reproduction outlined in the text are clear: Corellia's son is desired – and his education is designed to bring him – to resemble his grandfather, i.e. Corellia's father. Having apparently stated the obvious, however, Pliny immediately retreats from the assertion he just made, going on at some length about a potentially alternative and theoretically complementary intergenerational transmission of characters. The boy, Pliny states, has no dearth of conspicuous ancestors on the male side: he has a grandfather, a father and a paternal uncle after whom he could, just as well, be modelled. Actually, this paternal imprint would better align with social expectations, as we have seen. Pliny's carefully contrastive prose (*equidem, quamquam, etiam, quoque*) is the symptom, however, of more than a simple concern for the social etiquette active in the case at hand. Such rhetorical behavior is possibly an indication of wider preoccupations and deeper cultural tensions in his discourse.

---

[9] On Pliny's attitudes and strategies of paternal surrogacy, see Bernstein (2008).

The double bind in which Pliny's text is apparently caught is the same we may glimpse in 4.19, and is of a cultural-anthropological nature. On the one hand, the letter grants Corellia the role of representing her father, Pliny's allegiance to her being a re-proposition into the present of a lost age, with the hiatus in time marked by the opposition of tenses in the letter – *diligam* versus *suspexerim ... amaverim*. Her role as representative is so strong, however, that her husband's input in the generational process which, after all, produced the child for whom we are now trying to locate a suitable teacher, risks being neutralized. She is such a powerfully representative daughter, in other words, that she ends up reproducing her father in her own son as well, thus neutering her husband. On the other hand, and not simply as an afterthought, Pliny rushes in to say that Corellia's child could also go his own father's way, no matter if this imprint would potentially efface the memory of Corellia's father in her husband's son. After all, the child happens to have been granted (*contigerit* is as oblique a verb as it comes) a good lineage on his father's side as well.

The syntax and rhetoric of the passage locate Corellia's role at the centre of a tension between paternal and maternal imprint. She so strongly and faithfully represents her father that Pliny would even condone her nullifying her husband's imprint on their son, thus failing to reproduce him. If her son, however, is just as open to her father's generational and generative influence as Pliny makes him, and if she allows her husband's male lineage to be reproduced in her son, the markings of her own ancestry are in danger of disappearing. While neither outcome is presented as a problem, Pliny's rhetoric attempts to conceal and potentially reveals that both are problematic. If Corellia's function in the mechanisms of representation and reproduction is a difficult one, the recessive quality of her role is just as clearly, constantly, and un-problematically articulated. What seems to be certain, at least for Pliny, is that Corellia's son has a bright future ahead of him, no matter whether he will eventually resemble the paternal or maternal side of his family. After all, the letter insists, it is on a father (either his father's or his mother's father) that he will be modelled and molded.

While we never learn from the letters how Corellia's son turns out and how he deals with the burden of such great models or 'funerary masks' as he is given to bear (*quibus imaginibus oneretur, Ep.* 3.3.6), we may gather a sense of the effects of the role that Calpurnia Hispulla took in shaping her niece from Pliny's own account. In *Epistle* 4.19, the young Calpurnia is at once, as daughter of Calpurnius, the dutiful representation of her own male ancestry and, as wife of the Younger Pliny, the potential vessel for the reproduction of her husband in their future offspring. The same tension at work in 3.3 takes here a different form, but it is triggered by the same object: the difficulty of defining the role of women in the process of intergenerational representation of their ancestors and of reproduction of their husbands, both considered essential social duties. Rather than emerging as an intra-textual syntactic over-determination, however, the cultural conundrum may be shown to take the form of an uneasy inter-textual connection.

2   Mothering, Again: Martial on Regulus' Wife

In the central paragraphs of *Ep.* 4.19, Pliny details the multiple ways in which his wife has paradoxically proven herself the worthy representation of her family of origin, but also potentially of himself.

> Summum est acumen summa frugalitas; amat me, quod castitatis indicium est. *Accedit his studium litterarum, quod ex mei caritate concepit.* Meos libellos habet lectitat ediscit etiam. 3 Qua illa sollicitudine cum videor acturus, quanto cum egi gaudio afficitur! Disponit qui nuntient sibi quem assensum quos clamores excitarim, quem eventum iudicii tulerim. Eadem, si quando recito, in proximo discreta velo sedet, laudesque nostras avidissimis auribus excipit. 4 *Versus quidem meos cantat etiam formatque cithara non artifice aliquo docente*, sed amore qui magister est optimus. (*Ep.* 4.19.2–4)

> She is intelligent and frugal to the utmost degree. She loves me, which is a sign of her modesty. One may add to this that she appreciates learning, something her love for me has incepted. She owns my works, reads them, even learns them by heart. When she sees I am about to speak in court, what anxiety she feels! When I am done with speaking, what joy! She arranges for people to bring her updates on how I am swaying the audience my way, what kind of applause I am raising, what judgement I have eventually secured. Whenever I give a recitation, she attends in person, sitting nearby behind a curtain, and she is most eager to hear what praise we receive. She even sets my verses to music and sings them out, instructed by no other master than love, which is the best teacher of all.

Calpurnia, Pliny says, is not only frugal and clever, but also in love with her husband, and out of this love for him she has conceived a passion for cultural and literary pursuits which matches his own: she works on his books, finds ways to be in his audience, and puts his verses to music. Pliny's initial word choice is important: Calpurnia has *conceived* her love for the liberal arts out of love for him. Of course, *conceiving* is exactly what society would expect from a dutiful wife, and Pliny rejoices that she has indeed conceived something, although the content of her objective genitive is not yet a child.[10]

Pliny's ambivalent and revealing lexical choice is not an isolated signal in the text: further ambiguities may strike readers of Pliny's text who are aware of its context. While Calpurnia's love has so far produced only cultural offspring, and she has turned into a fully compliant sounding board and music box for Pliny's literary exercises, all her activities and potentialities are apparently in alignment with the social expectations projected onto her. The way she enjoys her husband's oratory at home and in the court, however, triggers a series of circumstantial but suggestive connections with the way the fruit of another woman's transparent love for, and apparent devotion to, a Centumviral orator was said to enjoy his father's success. I am referring to Martial's *Epigram* 6.38, my proposed *intertext* for Pliny's 4.19.

> Aspicis ut parvus nec adhuc trieteride plena
>   Regulus *auditum laudet* et ipse *patrem*?
> Maternosque sinus viso genitore relinquat
>   et *patrias laudes* sentiat esse *suas*?
> Iam *clamor centumque viri* densumque corona
>   volgus et infanti *Iulia tecta* placent.
> Acris equi suboles magno *sic pulvere gaudet*,
>   sic vitulus molli proelia fronte cupit.
> Di, servate, precor, matri sua vota patrique,
>   *audiat* ut natum Regulus, illa *duos*.

Can't you see how little Regulus, who has not yet completed his third year, also praises his father when he hears him praised? How he, when he sees his father, forsakes his mother's lap, and feels that his father's praising is his own? He cannot speak yet, but he already likes the applause, and the Centumviral court, and the crowning throng crowding around in the Julian temple. He is like the scion of a prize horse who cherishes the dust in the wide fields, and like the calf who longs for the clashing while his forehead is still tender. Gods, I pray, grant his mother and father their prayers, so that Regulus may hear his son speak, and she both.

Epigram 6.38 immediately offers itself as one of Martial's most distinctive rote exercises in serving the patronage-economy to which he owes his social survival.[11] The matter at hand is simple. The dedicatee is Marcus Aquilius

---

[10] Readers of Pliny's corpus know that Calpurnia's fertility and her miscarriage will recur in 8.10 and 8.11, on which see Shelton (2013) 125–7.

[11] On the dynamics of patronage and their intersections in the Martial-Pliny connection, see in general Henderson (2001) and Nauta (2002). On Regulus in Martial, and his incipiently setting

Regulus, one of Martial's prominent patrons. Regulus happens to have a three-year-old son.[12] As expected in a positive account of felicitous filiation, this young boy takes after his father in all respects. Most distinctively, he shows a strong inclination to claim the socio-political heritage and cultural capital his father has secured for him, eventually duplicating his sire's role as orator in the court. This felicitous filiation will take place when he, as both a representative and a reproduction of his father, will join the elder Regulus in the Centumviral court, the same space of performance which he now enjoys as spectator. In this deftly phrased ring composition, familial relations, in particular those of a father to son, are paramount. Terms *pater* and *patrius*, *mater* and *maternus*, *genitor*, *infans*, and *natus* – to which one may add also *suboles* and *vitulus* in the ennobling, epic-toned, zoological similes in lines 7 and 8 – construct the sense of a propitious paternal lineage linking Regulus father to Regulus son. The mother, however, is present as well. Apparently caught in an initially oppositional dynamic between private and public spheres of their son's life, between *maternus sinus* and *patrias laudes* in lines 3 and 4, the unnamed wife of the elder Regulus never comes between father and son. If she does, it is only as a transparent intermediary, much like Calpurnia Hispulla for Pliny's wife. Original and copy (Regulus the father and *parvus Regulus*) correspond to one another not simply in name. Father and son are transparently linked as the single point into which the mother's wishes become one with those of the wife. As the perfect wife and mother that she is, her role of witnessing her man in the son extends to her witnessing the son as the essence of her man: in producing an alter-Regulus, that is, she acknowledges that the alter-Regulus is a *Regulus idem*.

The similarities to Pliny's letter about Calpurnia's character are as marked as they are disquieting. Several details in the topics which both texts broach, as well as some relevant lexical choices, correspond across the prose-poetry divide. It is perhaps worth re-citing Pliny's text at this point, in particular the initial sections devoted to Calpurnia, this time highlighting the lexical and thematic convergences with Martial's poem:

> Summum est acumen summa frugalitas; *amat me*, quod castitatis indicium est. Accedit his studium litterarum, quod *ex mei caritate* concepit. *Meos libellos* habet lectitat ediscit etiam. 3 Qua illa sollicitudine cum videor

---

star in Books 6 and 7 of the *Epigrams*, see Howell (1980) ad loc. on *Epigram* 1.12; Sullivan (1991) 17 ff.; Williams (2004), on Book 2; Marchesi (2018) 353–60.

[12] For standard dating and other chronological calculations related to the younger Regulus, see Sherwin-White (1966) ad *Ep.* 4.2 (266–7).

acturus, *quanto cum egi gaudio afficitur*! Disponit qui nuntient sibi quem assensum quos *clamores* excitarim, quem eventum iudicii tulerim. Eadem, si quando recito, in proximo discreta velo sedet, *laudesque nostras avidissimis auribus* excipit. 4 *Versus quidem meos* cantat etiam formatque cithara non artifice aliquo docente, sed amore qui magister est optimus. (*Ep.* 4.19.2–4)

The first inter-textual connection is quite simply the identity, in locale, for the vignette sketched in the epigram's first six lines and in paragraph 3 of Pliny's letter: the *Iulia tecta* of the Centumviral court. Actually, topography and lexical choices go hand-in-hand. The same *clamor* attests Regulus' success as it does Pliny's triumphs, reverberating in the *clamores* of Pliny's letter; the same emphasis on hearing is found in both passages, with Calpurnia's *avidissimis auribus* corresponding to the *auditum patrem* of the younger Regulus or the *audiat . . . illa duos* of his mother. Also, the pleasure elicited in enjoying their relatives' performance is present in similar terms: *quanto cum gaudio afficitur* for Calpurnia; *sic pulvere gaudet* for the younger Regulus (here epically morphed into a happy colt). Finally, and perhaps most importantly, the same *laudes,* the attestations of praise which the young Regulus feels belong to him as much as they belong to his father, are offered in the same interpenetrative modality in Calpurnia's case. Just as Regulus' *laudes* were for his son both *patrias* and *suas*, so too does Calpurnia share in the glory of her husband. In Pliny's phrasing, *laudes nostras,* we are not in the presence of a simple *pluralis maiestatis.* Rather, the possessive adjective *nostras* that Pliny applies to the praise he receives is strikingly inclusive. It is also a unique and notable departure from the rest of the paragraph, which is dominated by first-person singular expressions that allow Pliny to take center stage at every turn: *amat me . . . ex mei caritate concepit . . . meos libellos habet . . . versus quidem meos cantat.*

The proximity of Calpurnia's behavior, as reported by Pliny, to what Martial constructs as an appropriately imitative filial relation in the case of the elder and younger Regulus is technically uncanny. Calpurnia's behavior not only constructs her as the future mother of Pliny's children, appropriately embodying her husband's imprint, but also moves her increasingly closer to being his surrogate child. As the letter progresses, oscillating between child-bearing and child-being, Calpurnia is treated as an opaque sign, bearing both the imprint of her family of origin and that of her husband.

It is now time to address the close of the letter, where we find Hispulla at her most assertive, with her formative role seeming to extend from her niece to her niece's husband.

His ex causis in spem certissimam adducor, perpetuam nobis maioremque in dies futuram esse concordiam. Non enim aetatem meam aut corpus, quae paulatim occidunt ac senescunt, sed gloriam diligit. 6 Nec aliud decet *tuis manibus educatam, tuis praeceptis institutam*, quae nihil in contubernio tuo viderit, nisi sanctum honestumque, quae denique amare me ex tua praedicatione consueverit. 7 Nam cum matrem meam parentis loco vererere, *me a pueritia statim formare laudare, talemque qualis nunc uxori meae videor, ominari solebas.* 8 Certatim ergo tibi gratias agimus, ego quod illam mihi, illa quod me sibi dederis, quasi invicem elegeris. (*Ep.* 4.19.5–8)

By these causes I am led to hope with great assurance that our hearts will enjoy a lasting and always increasing harmony, since in me she loves not so much my youth or my body, things that little by little decrease and age, but rather my renown. After all, nothing else would fit someone who has been raised by your hands, educated by your teachings, who never saw anything in your house that was not unimpeachably honest, and who, finally, grew accustomed to loving me from your words. For you held my mother in reverence as would a daughter, and began shaping and praising me already in my boyhood. You always foretold that I would become the man that I am now in the eyes of my wife. My wife and I try and outdo each other in thanking you, I because you have given her to me, and she because you have given me to her, as if you had chosen one for the other.

Such an actively formative role as Hispulla seems to have exerted on Pliny is remarkable and perhaps surprising. Yet the epistle openly details a series of actions that point in this direction: Hispulla was apparently part of the young Pliny's education – or at least of the portrait of the artist as a young man which he now sketches for his readers. While the implications which the epistle's label *parentis loco* may have for the strange sisterhood, which Pliny predicates on Hispulla, are beyond the scope of this argument, and though the combined import of praising and wishing for a good moral outcome for her future relative have a commonplace ring to them (see *Panegyricus* 4.1–2), the weight of the phrase *formare solebas* should give us pause. What the text appears to say is that Hispulla actively made Pliny who he is. Even in the context of a laudatory and idealized text as this epistle, such a strong vindication of activity for a woman is hardly in keeping with the kind of socio-biological transparency that, we noted, was reserved for maternal role-keepers.

Is Pliny parting ways with tradition and socio-cultural expectations? Perhaps.[13] The language which he uses, however, may point in a different –

---

[13] For a rich, albeit perhaps overly optimistic survey of Pliny's inclusive choice of both masculine and feminine ethical models, see Langlands (2014), developing insights by Méthy (2007).

indeed, in the opposite – direction. In its ambivalent lexical force, the verb *formare* applies both to the process of defining a model and the act of copying it out. That is, it indicates as much formation as reproduction. The formative process Hispulla is applying to Pliny, thus, is not so much the shaping of his character, but rather, and more pointedly, the construction of an image of him as a model to be reproduced. Hispulla's education, after all, is not of Pliny but of Pliny's wife; the form she works on is not Pliny himself, but a – mental (to interpose a modern term) – model which she creates for her niece to reproduce: 'Since you treated my mother as your own, from my early childhood you have formed, praised, and foretold that I would be exactly as I now appear in my wife's eyes'. Reorienting our reading in this direction may help us see a further and final connection that extends beyond intertextual connections to interdiscursive pertinence.

The necessary ambiguity and intrinsic tension which this passage conveys, revolving around a woman's formative influence on a man, is possibly of the same kind as the anxious account which Tacitus gives of the (idealized and yet uncanny) process of education for the orators of time past in his *Dialogus De Oratoribus*.[14] We find ourselves at the same juncture of rhetoric, ethics, and inter-generational proceedings as we have been while making our way through Pliny's and Martial's texts. In offering his ethical and social diagnosis for the ills of contemporary oratory, Messalla, the character in the *Dialogue* to whom a regressive laudatory position is entrusted, focuses on the early stages of puericulture, contrasting traditional methods of education with contemporary ones, which he deems a failed pedagogical opportunity. In so doing, he casts the women of ancient households in the same role (and in the same positive light) as Pliny casts Hispulla:

> ... Quis enim ignorat et eloquentiam et ceteras artis descivisse ab illa vetere gloria non inopia hominum, sed desidia iuventutis et neglegentia parentum et inscientia praecipientium et oblivione moris antiqui? ... Nam pridem suus cuique filius, ex casta parente natus, non in cellula emptae nutricis, sed gremio ac sinu matris educabatur, cuius praecipua laus erat tueri domum et

---

[14] On the difficulty of pinpointing individual positions in the dialogue (as well as the overall inclination of the work), see most recently Van den Berg (2014), with essential bibliography. On a possible internal word-play in the dynamics of the *Dialogus*, see the mediating modernist position which Maternus, the 'motherly one', takes in the text. For the *Dialogus*' relevance to the Pliny-Martial connection, see also the reference to Messalla's and Regulus' common mother in Aper's chiding of Messalla's principled classicism at 15.1 *cum oblitus tuae et fratris tui eloquentiae neminem hoc tempore oratorem esse contenderes* (Messalla and Regulus were born of the same mother). On Regulus as orator, see Rutledge (2001) 192–8.

inservire liberis. Eligebatur autem maior aliqua natu propinqua, cuius probatis spectatisque moribus omnis eiusdem familiae suboles committeretur; coram qua neque dicere fas erat quod turpe dictu, neque facere quod inhonestum factu videretur. Ac non studia modo curasque, sed remissiones etiam lususque puerorum sanctitate quadam ac verecundia temperabat. Sic Corneliam Gracchorum, sic Aureliam Caesaris, sic Atiam Augusti [matrem] praefuisse educationibus ac produxisse principes liberos accepimus. Quae disciplina ac severitas eo pertinebat, ut sincera et integra et nullis pravitatibus detorta unius cuiusque natura toto statim pectore arriperet artis honestas, et sive ad rem militarem sive ad iuris scientiam sive ad eloquentiae studium inclinasset, id solum ageret, id universum hauriret. (*Dial.* 28)

... Who does not know that eloquence and all other arts have fallen from their ancient glory, not from lack of practitioners, but from the indolence of the youth *and* the neglect of parents *and* the ignorance of teachers *and* the oblivion of the old customs? ... In the old days, every boy, the child of a chaste mother, was educated, not in the chamber of a slave nurse, but in that mother's bosom and embrace, a mother whose special glory was to protect her home and serve her children. An elderly kinswoman was also chosen, to whose approved and admirable character was entrusted the charge of all the children of that household. In her presence it was unthinkable to use foul language or commit an unseemly act. She would thus curb, with her imposing presence and distinct reserve, not only the studies and activities of the boys, but also their playtime and games. We have reports that the mothers of the Gracchi, of Caesar, of Augustus – Cornelia, Aurelia, and Atia – controlled their children's education and produced sons who rose above the rest. This discipline and strictness had a goal; namely, that their natural characters, pure and intact and not bent by any vice, could seize with full enthusiasm all liberal arts. Whatever their inclination may be, whether to the military life, to the study of the law or to the practice of eloquence, they would concentrate on it alone and drink it in full.

The cultural convergence of Pliny with Tacitus is surely symptomatic. Tacitus' passage appears to attribute the same polemically articulated active role to women in the molding of their offspring as does Pliny to Hispulla. But he, too, dispels the potentially overpowering model of female influence on their offspring by several means. First, he vindicates the emergence of the children's own dispositions as the end result of their education process. Messalla makes abundantly clear that it is the young men's free and self-determined call to become soldiers, jurists, or orators which their mothers' presence serves to guarantee. Secondly, the motherly role of idealized and formative women of the past is for Tacitus at once active and recessive, so much so that the process of rearing and shaping their sons is phrased as an ambiguous action: his lexical choice of *educare* to describe the process is apparently traditional but etymologically revealing. With its prepositional, extractive valence, the verb *e-ducare* may mean that sons are brought up *by* or *from* women – the actor of their upbringing becoming also the site of cultural abjection. Finally, the potential physiological anxiety of the verb Tacitus uses triggers the redoubled nomination of the female body: the education of boys takes place in and by the bosom and embrace of the mother, as common English renderings go, but it also results in their departure from her lap and breast.[15]

A later detail emerging in the next section of the *Dialogus* appears to confirm the anxiety which the reduplication of the tag *sinu ac gremio* manifested. Once it is decidedly and, one may add, safely projected onto the negative polarity of the argument, the focus having shifted from an environment that ensures felicitous preservation of good dispositions in wellborn male offspring to one that facilitates the acquisition of bad habits, a pregnant womb appears as the central object of Tacitus' lexical and metaphorical abjection: *Iam vero propria et peculiaria huius urbis vitia paene in utero matris concipi mihi videntur, histrionalis favor et gladiatorum equorumque studia* (*Dial.* 29). While ambiguously in charge and not in charge of their sons' moral upbringing, in sum, mothers are unambiguously charged with their sons' immoral outcomes. While on the positive end of the spectrum they are subjected to a dispelling through metaphor of their physical presence (their bodies having been caught in the locative-ablative-instrumental movement of education as an ethical affair), on the negative end, they are given a body that becomes the physical point of articulation for a metaphoric materialization of ethical faults.[16]

When it comes to the evocation of women's bodies, the directional force of the metaphors is actually opposed. The first metaphor Tacitus deploys uses women's bodies as a vehicle, the tenor being the literal act of educating the children. In so doing, it forces the bodily presence of the positive, formative women into the sphere of the 'so-to-speak', tendentially and tendentiously effacing it. On the contrary, the second metaphor uses

---

[15] The lexical ambivalence extends to the syntax of the passage, with the ablatives '*gremio ac sinu matris*' being at once *locative* (on account of the contrastive construction '*in cellula* emptae nutricis' appearing right before it), *ablative of motion* (on account of the force of the prefixed preposition *ex* in *educare*), and *ablative of instrument* (maternal bodies being responsible for their physical interposition between child and world).

[16] Surprisingly, given their pre-eminent presence in the education of their sons (*prefuisse ... ac produxisse*), Tacitus' women are made markedly silent. No *verba dicendi* match their alleged authority and their actual formative work, which uncannily turns out to be pre-linguistic, even pre-cultural. On these issues, see Richlin (2003) and Gleason (2008).

women's bodies as its tenor, the vehicle being the act of figuratively conceiving a vice. Thus, it literalizes and imposes the presence of their bodies in the text. Women's bodies are, in sum, strategically effaced on the positive side of educational models and pointedly evoked on the negative side. Their culturally formative action, as well as their own biologically formative one, is at once necessary (when projected as dutifully recessive) and exorcised (when cast as threateningly overpowering).

In conclusion, in *Ep.* 4.19, the semantic and cultural tensions accompanying the verb *formare* appear to resonate with those explored thus far: in the letter, Hispulla is a woman forming a man. Her active role is, however, not exercised on Pliny himself, at least not in the sense which Horace had assigned to the verb in the father/son interaction explored in *Satire* 1.4, where a canonical and socially acceptable father-to-son formative relation was at stake and was unambiguously articulated in the verse: *sic me formabat puerum*. In line with the examples considered above, Hispulla's formative activity should be taken in a mental, rather than physical sense. What is more, and perhaps more precisely, we are to imagine Hispulla forming the image of a man as a model from which copies will eventually be drawn. The space in which that inception of a form is most likely taking place is the woman who will mediate that process of reproduction: this man's wife.

3 Fathering: Pliny on Regulus' (and Spurinna's) Mourning

As is the case in Tacitus and in the texts briefly surveyed above, the formative process which, according to Pliny in *Ep.* 4.19, Hispulla applies to her niece – turning her into a model to be reproduced by forming in her the image of a husband whom she is called to reproduce – is caught between the spheres of physiology, ethics, and art. These are the same cultural fields, the tensions between which we are about to see at work, in the last form of textual interconnection which I propose to explore here: alter-textuality. In continuity with the argument developed thus far, which has brought to the surface moments of categorial and socio-cultural tension in the rhetorical turns of interconnected texts, with this label I propose to isolate and treat from a meta-poetic point of view another, perhaps more radical case of anxiety.[17] I see just such an anxiety at the root

---

[17] For socio-political anxieties in Pliny, the locus classicus is Hoffer (1999), in particular 55–91 (which treat a different intersection of the Regulus-Spurinna interaction). How a discourse on art may accommodate them is the subject of Henderson (2002b).

of Pliny's unabashed disregard of the fact that he and Regulus function, in questions of child loss and child mourning, much more similarly than he would care to admit. In order to do so, we need to follow two interdependent but mutually indifferent strains of texts.

Let us first return to Regulus. Martial's poem gave us the positive version of the father-to-son relation, insisting on the idea (and the ideal) of the resemblance of son to father, and casting the young Regulus as a natural born orator, a Centumviral lawyer in the making. As an accepted datum of paternity mechanisms, survival of the father in the imprint he has left on his child's physical and moral features is certainly also on Pliny's mind in *Epistle* 4.2, in which he examines the effects of the death of Regulus' son on his father.

> Regulus filium amisit, hoc uno malo indignus, quod nescio an malum putet. Erat puer acris ingenii sed ambigui, qui tamen posset recta sectari, si patrem non referret. (*Ep.* 4.2.1)
>
> Regulus has lost his son. This is the only ill which he has not deserved; though, I am not sure he actually thinks this is an ill. The boy was intelligent but with no clear moral inclination: he might have moved toward good aims, provided he did not resemble his father.

When he wishes that Regulus' child *not* resemble his father, the *vir malus dicendi imperitus* of 4.7.5 or the *omnium bipedum nequissimus* of 1.5.14, Pliny is both ironically treating Regulus to a back-handed compliment and endorsing the usual cultural expectation regarding patrilinear reproduction. As we learn from reading further into Pliny's collection, Regulus' eventual childlessness will frustrate the process of hereditary transmission and trigger instead a frantic search for surrogacy in the field of art. Regulus' theatrical mourning and his industrialized reproductive component (statues, paintings, writings) is the object of one of Pliny's rare scoptic epistolary exercises in *Ep.* 4.7.

> Saepe tibi dico inesse vim Regulo. Mirum est quam efficiat in quod incubuit. Placuit ei lugere filium: luget ut nemo. Placuit *statuas* eius et *imagines quam plurimas* facere: *hoc omnibus officinis agit, illum coloribus illum cera illum aere illum argento illum auro ebore marmore effingit.* 2 Ipse vero nuper adhibito ingenti auditorio librum de vita eius recitavit; de vita pueri, recitavit tamen. *Eundem in exemplaria mille transcriptum per totam Italiam provinciasque dimisit.* (*Ep.* 4.7.1–2)
>
> I have often told you how strong Regulus is. It is amazing how he brings to fruition what he starts. He decided he should mourn his child; now he

mourns like no other. He decided he should make as many statues and portraits of him as possible, so now he does so by having all workshops work on it: representing him in colors, him in wax, him in bronze, him in silver, him in gold, ivory, and marble. He himself has assembled a large crowd of listeners and has recited a book about his child's life – the life of a child it was, and yet he recited it. And then he sent throughout Italy and the provinces a thousand copies he has had made of it.

The wish to have someone's memory preserved in statues and paintings or in a book is not such an outlandish notion in itself. Statues and portraits, as well as literary accounts of a life, recited to an audience, published in written form, and disseminated in thousands of copies, each of which is read again to a gathered audience, are all traditionally hallowed activities. They are also all caught in the same dynamics of reproduction, from exemplar to copy or from model to object, which has been in our focus throughout. Consisting in a transference of identitary features, they are, that is, surrogate acts of the generational process of identity transmission which takes place in fathering. When he attacks Regulus' over-productive grief, what Pliny critiques is not the aim of Regulus' mourning strategies, but rather the means of mechanical reproduction to which he resorts, and on which the epistle's rhetoric emphatically and mercilessly insists. This, in their excessive materiality, is what appears to be deemed uncalled for.

Whether verbal or material, in sum, the memorializing works of art which Regulus commissions or produces for his dead son respond to the socially accepted wish to prolong the life of one's own image. Incidentally, that wish is the same that drives Pliny in his efforts to memorialize the child of one of his friends and patrons, Spurinna. In another short cycle of orbative epistles which stretches across the second and third books of his collection, Pliny inserts two letters worthy of note for their uncanny and potentially co-implicating relation to what we have surveyed thus far, *Epistles* 2.7 and 3.10.

All that seemed wrong or out of place in Regulus' case is now presented as perfectly appropriate. The first letter comments in highly eulogistic tones on the Senate's decree to erect a statue for Spurinna's son, Cottius, a remarkably young honoree (*rarum id in iuvene!*, 2.7.3), and yet fully worthy of that distinction (as 2.7.4 is at pains to prove). Notably, Pliny mobilizes all the cultural reproductive vocabulary which the context requires: *Cottius tam clarum specimen indolis erat; exemplo prospectum est ... effigiem.* Complementarily, *Epistle* 3.10 acts as a cover-letter for Pliny's own experiment in the genre of a *Vita* for Spurinna's dead son, a text which he has already presented in a public reading and which is now being submitted to the parents of the honoree for emendation and eventual publication. It is on this second epistle that we may turn our attention now.

> Difficile est huc usque intendere animum in dolore; difficile, sed tamen, ut scalptorem, ut pictorem, qui filii vestri imaginem faceret, admoneretis, quid exprimere quid emendare deberet, *ita me quoque formate regite*, qui non fragilem et caducam, sed immortalem, ut vos putatis, effigiem conor efficere (*Ep.* 3.10.6).

> It is difficult to set your mind on such a matter, when in pain. It is difficult, but I wish you would advise me as you would do a painter or a sculptor charged with producing a portrait of your son, by indicating what I should bring out and what I should correct. Shape and direct my work, as someone who is trying to create a portrait that is not frail and passing, but (as you think) an immortal one.

Here, too, the language of artistic reproduction is explicitly adopted, with Pliny offering himself as the craftsman whom Cottius' parents should guide and form in his making of an *immortalem effigiem* (3.10.6). In 3.10, however, the dynamic of formation which characterizes Pliny's offer has a dark side to it. By casting his activity as biographer to Spurinna and his wife, allegedly with a hope of producing a literary portrait of their son which has a longer life expectancy than any other art form, Pliny also indirectly evokes the frailty of other (artistic, but also biological) forms of generation. The fine line Pliny treads in his argument divides his vindication of art's power to challenge time from his assertion of the implicit but eerie superiority of art over biology. Artistic reproduction may well be assumed to be immortal, but it is potentially tactless to remind the parents of a dead boy of the immortality which art (and not they) may achieve. The negative connotation within the epistle's pairing of biology and art is only potential, of course, and no breach of etiquette ensues from Pliny's rhetoric. To the contrary, Pliny emerges from the whole affair with seemingly unmatched rhetorical and social savoir faire. The apparent felicity of these transactions should not distract, however, from the fact that it is Pliny's ability to devise the appropriate course of action which ensures success of the operation – a success that does not obfuscate the distinctively tense cultural context within which this case of surrogate mourning unfolds.

Pliny, as Tacitus before him, is more at ease in populating the negative side of the ambivalences in his culture, as the character study of Regulus' mourning suggests. By concentrating not on his grief, but on his display of grief, Pliny has the opportunity to mark the differences between the two memorialization enterprises. Proper senatorial honor and Pliny's own mournful work are made to contrast with Regulus' compulsive and dispersive activity. One statue, if endorsed by the appropriate political and institutional body (the Senate, not a disgraced informant of the disgraced emperor), is more effective than a thousand privately sponsored portraits. One single copy of a book, if properly addressed to the right audience (powerful parents, not provincial petty officers), ensures preservation and circulation of one's memory beyond the labors of a copying workshop. But Pliny does not organize his texts along these lines. Quite the contrary. There is no explicit intra-textual syncrisis, no inter-textual redeployment of lexical elements, no appeal to shared discursive categories. These texts, which are in a way about the same *thing*, are alternative versions of it.

Paradoxically, for Pliny's readers to appreciate the absurdity of Regulus' actions and the propriety of Pliny's offer, it is mandatory that they do not consider them at the same time. Pliny's candid inclusion of his own mediated activity as mourner alongside Regulus' exhibition of grief are predicated on the readers' avoidant behavior. Both Regulus and Pliny, in Pliny's own account, are caught in the same act: entrusting the image of a father to material cultural objects dedicated to a dead son. There is something that distinguishes them – that is, the frantic reliance on the materiality of these objects on Regulus' part, contrasted with Pliny's confidence in the political and artistic value of his own work. But is this really enough? The alter-textual relation of these letters appears, in sum, to create a grey area in which readers are at once required to see and not see the connection, and to read as if the interpretive implications emerging from the contextual closeness were at once necessary and necessarily not there. Readers are asked to ignore all the elements that conjure up intra-textual pertinence, lest the unavoidable cultural conflict, on which the discourse they practice relies, becomes precisely that: unavoidable.

4 Conclusion

As the body of this chapter has demonstrated, the four distinct forms of textual interference I outlined at the start have proved often to be co-implicated with one another. Their practical interdependence is not a peculiar feature of my work, to be sure. Several essays in this collection have shown that the practice of critically reading Pliny's *Epistles* involves negotiating inter-, intra-, alter-, and extra-textual connections. Among the contributions devoted to textual and cultural material akin to this chapter, for instance, one may note how Margot Neger's (chapter 13) assessment of Pliny's tone in the anti-Regulus epistles as 'hovering between *ira* and *risus*' depends as much on the intra-textual placement of skoptic material (*Ep.* 1.5 or 6.15) next to letters to Tacitus (*Ep.* 1.6 or 6.16), with a pointed invitation to laugh in *Ep.* 1.6, as it relies on inter-textual connections to, say, Lucillius, Catullus, and Martial, whose texts are taken both as individual targets of allusion and collective representatives of a genre (thus articulating a progression from Form A to Form C via B). Inversely, but still convergently, Matthew Mordue's (Chapter 4) counterpoint reading of *Ep.* 2.20, in which he demonstrates that Pliny's text directly quotes or indirectly evokes the oratorial models of Demosthenes and Cicero, proceeds from inter-textual to intra-textual considerations, firmly establishing the roots of the pessimistic tone commonly detected in later, closing epistles of Book 2 (thus using Form B to lead into Form A). Similarly, Jakub Pigoń's (Chapter 12) insightful revisiting of the discursive patterns of documentation and argumentation recurrent in historiographic writing, patterns to which Pliny's *Ep.* 7.29 and 8.6 adhere in tackling the Senate's outrageous behavior in the Pallas case, suggests how the closely-knit dialogue between Tacitus' *Histories* and Pliny's *Epistles* may speak to a generational anxiety toward a shared past that lingers on (thus providing a neat Form B to Form C progression). Finally, Michael Hanaghan's (Chapter 7) argument on Pliny's apparently diverging meditations regarding his own inconsolable mourning for Corellius Rufus' suicide in *Ep.* 1.12, as compared to Regulus' ostentatious funerary practices for his son's death in *Ep.* 4.12, combines all possible forms of textual interconnection. His chapter nimbly moves from observations about allusive onomastics and culturally charged diction in neighboring letters to establish Pliny's ambivalent attitude toward general Stoic philosophical tenets regarding end-of-life practices, an attitude based on the alternative pointed evocation and silent dismissal of some of Seneca's teachings about mourning, and the redeployment of specific language.

Similar considerations may be extended to the arguments developed in all chapters, which provide brilliant examples of the hermeneutic advantage of having all forms of interference collaborate in our reading. With no exception, they contain acknowledgements that positional factors, such as the emphatic placement or sequencing of epistles, are connected with pointed allusions to recognizably marked language, present in either traditionally hallowed or currently relevant texts, and that the very language which Pliny and his readership found in their cultural library also constituted the discursive fabric of their culture. The dialogic quality of the works collected in this volume, and the collegial atmosphere of the conference where they were first presented, are to be credited for the overall convergence in approach. My own reading of Pliny's *Ep.* 4.19 as a text haunted by questions of paternity follows, in every sense, the work of the other chapters. It, too, insists on the significance of connections with previous items in the collection, such as the maternal/paternal anxiety surrounding the education of Corellia Hispulla's son, as well as of the external links with texts such as Mart. 6.38, established when Pliny unperturbedly transfers to his wife and the potential mother of his children the charged language Martial had deployed for Regulus' wife and child. In both cases, these intra- and inter- textual connections become for Pliny the locus of an anxiety – one entrusted to (or manifested in) the syntax or the lexicon of his text – which he shares with his culture. These relationships, which Pliny either actively establishes or to which he submits, cast a shadow on the micro-cycle of 'orbative' letters in Pliny's corpus, in which he details the diverging strategies of iterative and exemplary commemoration which Regulus and Spurinna deployed to mourn their sons. Here, too, we have noted that the same dynamics of reproduction, the same issues with artistic imitation, the same difficulties with cross-generational representation and replacement are at play, though transferred from the familial and social realm of biological paternity into the sphere of cultural production. Set up by all these signals of interference and armed with a critical awareness of their interconnection, the reader is left with the difficult but rewarding task to resist and, at the same time, to comply with the instructions embedded in the text.

Bibliography

Adamik, T. (1976). 'Pliny and Martial', *AUB(class)* 4: 63–72.
  (1995). 'Catullus' Urbanity: c. 22', *AAntHung* 36: 77–86.
Adams, J.N. (1982). *The Latin Sexual Vocabulary*. London (first edition).
Anderson, W.B. (1936). *Sidonius*, vol. 1: *Poems. Letters 1–2*. Cambridge, MA.
Ando, C. (2015). *Roman Social Imaginaries: Language and Thought in the Contexts of Empire*, Toronto.
André, J.-M. (1975). 'Pensée et philosophie dans des *Lettres* de Pline le Jeune', *REL* 53: 225–47.
  (1979). 'Philosophie und Denken bei Plinius dem Jüngeren', *Acta Philologica Aenipontana* 4: 25–26.
Armisen-Marchetti, M. (1990). 'Pline le Jeune et le sublime', *REL* 68: 88–98.
Ash, R. (2003). '*Aliud enim est epistulam, aliud historiam . . . scribere* (*Ep.* 6.16.22). Pliny the Historian?', in Morello and Gibson (2003): 211–25.
  (2013). 'Drip-feed Invective: Pliny, Self-Fashioning, and the Regulus Letters', in A. Marmodoro and J. Hill (eds.). *The Author's Voice in Classical and Late Antiquity*. Oxford: 207–32.
  (2018). 'Paradoxography and Marvels in Post-Domitianic Literature: "An Extraordinary Affair, Even in the Hearing!"', in König and Whitton (2018b): 126–45.
Aubrion, É. (1975). 'Pline le Jeune et la rhétorique de l'affirmation', *Latomus* 34: 90–130.
  (1989). 'La *Correspondance* de Pline le Jeune: Problèmes et orientations actuelles de la recherche', *ANRW* II 33.1: 304–74.
Audano, S. (2018). 'La statua, la virtù e la memoria del principe: variazioni di un topos tra Cassio Dione (LXXIV [LXXIII] 14, 2a) e Plinio il Giovane (*Pan.* 55)', *Sileno* 44: 1–12.
Augoustakis, A. (2005). '*Nequaquam historia digna*? Plinian Style in *Ep.* 6.20', *CJ* 100: 265–73.
  (2005/06). 'Pliny *Epistulae* 4.13: "Communal Conspiracy" at Comum', *CW* 99: 419–22.
Auhagen, U. (2003). '*Lusus* und *gloria* – Plinius' *hendecasyllabi* (*Ep.* 4,14; 5,3 und 7,4)', in Castagna and Lefèvre (2003): 3–13.

Baeza-Angulo, E. (2015). 'Plinio y Calpurnia, un matrimonio elegíaco', *Euphrosyne* 43: 69–82.
  (2016). 'Deleite y tormento. El amor de Plinio y Calpurnia (*Epist.* 6.7)', *Agora: Estudos Clássicos em Debate* 18: 121–40.
  (2017). 'Plinius exclusus (*Ep.* 7.5)', *Philologus* 161: 292–318.
Bailey, C. (1947). *Lucretius: De rerum natura*, 3 vols. Oxford.
Baier, T. (2003). 'Κτῆμα oder ἀγώνισμα: Plinius über historischen und rhetorischen Stil (*Epist.* 5,8)', in Castagna and Lefèvre (2003): 69–81.
Bakhtin, M. (1934). 'Discourse in the Novel', in Bakhtin (1981): 269-422.
  (1981). *The Dialogic Imagination: Four Essays by M. Bakhtin*. Edited by M. Holquist, translated by C. Emerson and M. Holquist. Austin.
Baldo, G. (2004). *M. Tulli Ciceronis, In C. Verrem actionis secundae liber quartus (De Signis)*. Florence.
Balmaceda, C. (2017). *Virtus Romana: Politics and Morality in the Roman Historians*. Chapel Hill.
Barchiesi, A. (2001). *Speaking Volumes. Narrative and Intertext in Ovid and Other Latin Poets*. London.
  (2005). 'The Search for the Perfect Book: A PS to the New Posidippus', in K. Gutzwiller (ed.). *The New Posidippus: A Hellenistic Poetry Book*. Oxford: 320–42.
Barsby, J. (1999). *Terence: Eunuchus*. Cambridge.
Bartsch, S. (1994). *Actors in the Audience: Theatricality and Doublespeak from Nero to Hadrian*. Cambridge, MA.
Basile, A. (2014). 'Alcune riflessioni sulla rappresentazione letteraria delle ville campane in età flavia', in Devillers (2014): 79–87.
Basore, J.W. (1928–35). *Seneca. Moral Essays*, 3 vols. Cambridge, MA.
Baumann, H. (2018). *Das Epos im Blick. Intertextualität und Rollenkonstruktionen in Martials Epigrammen und Statius' "Silvae"*. Berlin.
Beagon, M. (1992). *Roman Nature. The Thought of Pliny the Elder*. Oxford.
  (2005). *The Elder Pliny on the Human Animal. Natural History Book 7*. Oxford.
Becatti G. (1951). *Arte e Gusto negli Scrittori Latini*. Florence.
Beck, J.-W. (2013a). '*petis, ut tibi ... scribam ...* (Plinius *epist.* 6,16 und 20)', *GFA* 16: 1–28.
  (2013b). '*Pro captu lectoris habent sua fata ...* – Plinius und der Eklat *Epist.* 6,15', *Hermes* 141: 294–308.
  (2016). '*incidi in materiam ...* Plinius und der Delphin (*epist.* 9,33)', *GFA* 19: 61–87.
Behrendt, A. (2013). *Mit Zitaten kommunizieren: Untersuchungen zur Zitierweise in der Korrespondenz des Marcus Tullius Cicero*. Rahden.
Bek, L. (1976). 'Antithesis: A Roman Attitude and its Changes as Reflected in the Concept of Architecture from Vitruvius to Pliny the Younger', in K. Ascani (ed.). *Studia Romana in honorem P. Krarup septuagenarii*. Odense: 154–66.
Béranger, J. (1953). *Recherches sur l'aspect idéologique du principat*. Basel.
Bernstein, N.W. (2008). 'Each Man's Father Served as His Teacher: Constructing Relatedness in Pliny's *Letters*', *ClAnt.* 27: 203–30.

Berry, D.H. (2008). 'Letters from an Advocate: Pliny's "Vesuvius" Narratives (*Epistles* 6.16; 6.20)', in F. Cairns (ed.). *Hellenistic Greek and Augustan Poetry, Flavian and post-Flavian Latin Poetry, Greek and Roman Prose*. Cambridge: 297–313.
Beutel, F. (2000). *Vergangenheit als Politik: Neue Aspekte im Werk des jüngeren Plinius*. Frankfurt am Main.
Billerbeck, M. (1985). 'Aspects of Stoicism in Flavian Epic', *PLLS* 5: 341–56.
Binder, G. (1995). 'Öffentliche Autorenlesungen. Zur Kommunikation zwischen römischen Autoren und ihrem Publikum', in G. Binder and K. Ehlich (eds.). *Kommunikation durch Zeichen und Wort. Stätten und Formen der Kommunikation im Altertum IV*. Trier: 265–332.
Birley, A.R. (2000). *Onomasticon to the Younger Pliny. Letters and Panegyric*. Munich.
Blake, S.H. (2018). 'Pliny and the Social Life of Philosophy', *Phoenix* 72: 338–54.
Bodel, J. (1995). 'Minicia Marcella: Taken Before Her Time', *AJPh* 116: 453–60.
 (2015). 'The Publication of Pliny's Letters', in Marchesi (2015a): 13–108.
Borg, M. (2014). *"Toeing the Line?": Pliny the Younger and the Senatorial Opposition to Domitian*. Dissertation, Sydney.
Borzsák, S. (1966). 'Der weinende Xerxes: Zur Geschichte seines Ruhmes', *Eos* 56: 39–52.
Boyle, A.J. (1994). *Seneca's Troades, Introduction, Text, Translation and Commentary*. Leeds.
Bradley, K. (2010). 'The Exemplary Pliny', in C. Deroux (ed.). *Studies in Latin Literature and Roman History 15*. Brussels: 384–422.
Braund, S.H. (1989). 'City and Country in Roman Satire', in S.H. Braund (ed.). *Satire and Society in Ancient Rome*. Exeter: 23–47.
 (1996). *Juvenal, Satires, Book I*. Cambridge.
Brink, C.O. (1971). *Horace on Poetry: The 'Ars poetica'*. Cambridge.
Bruère, R.T. (1954). 'Tacitus and Pliny's *Panegyricus*', *CPh* 49: 161–79.
Buchner, A. (A. Buchnerus) (1644). *C. Plinii Caecilii Secundi Epistolarum libri X cum notis*. Frankfurt.
Bütler, H.-P. (1970). *Die geistige Welt der jüngeren Plinius. Studien zur Thematik seiner Briefe*. Heidelberg.
Burnikel, W. (1980). *Untersuchungen zur Struktur des Witzepigramms bei Lukillios und Martial*. Wiesbaden.
Butterfield, D.J. (2013). *The Early Textual History of Lucretius' De Rerum Natura*. Cambridge.
Cameron, A. (1993). *The Greek Anthology from Meleager to Planudes*. Oxford.
 (1995). *Callimachus and his Critics*. Princeton.
Cancik, H. (1965). *Untersuchungen zur lyrischen Kunst des P. Papinius Statius*. Hildesheim.
 (1978). 'Tibur Vopisci: Statius *Silv*. 1.3', *Boreas* 1: 116–34.
Canobbio, A. (2015). 'Echi di Marziale nell'epistola 4.14 die Plinio il Giovane', *Prometheus* 41: 189–207.
 (2017). 'Elementi senecani nell'epistola 3.5 di Plinio il Giovane', *Athenaeum* 105: 120–36.

(2019). 'L'epistola 1.10 di Plinio il Giovane. Il filosofo Eufrate tra Seneca e Quintiliano', *Athenaeum* 107: 128–49.

(2020). 'Polarizzazione e *coincidentia oppositorum* nelle ville di Plinio il Giovane', *Athenaeum* 108: 89–113.

Carey, S. (2003). *Pliny's Catalogue of Culture. Art and Empire in the Natural History*. Oxford.

Carlon, J. (2009). *Pliny's Women: Constructing Virtue and Creating Identity in the Roman World*. Cambridge.

(2017). *Selected Letters from Pliny the Younger's Epistulae*. Oxford.

(2018). 'You Can Go Home Again: Pliny the Younger Writes to Comum', *BICS* 61: 56–65.

Cavarzere, A., A. Aloni and A. Barchiesi (eds.) (2001). *Iambic Ideas: Essays on a Poetic Tradition from Archaic Greece to the Late Roman Empire*. Lanham, MD.

Castagna, L. and E. Lefèvre (eds.) (2003). *Plinius der Jüngere und seine Zeit*. Munich.

Chinn, C.M. (2007). 'Before Your Very Eyes: Pliny *Epistulae* 5.6 and the Ancient Theory of Ekphrasis', *CPh* 102: 265–80.

Church, A.J. and W.J. Brodribb (1942). *The Complete Works of Tacitus*. New York.

Citroni, M. (1975). *M. Valerii Martialis Epigrammaton Liber Primus*. Florence.

Citroni Marchetti, S. (1991). *Plinio il Vecchio e la tradizione del moralismo romano*. Pisa.

Coleman, K. (2012). 'Bureaucratic Language in the Correspondence between Pliny and Trajan', *TAPA* 142: 189–238.

Colish, M.L. (1990). *The Stoic Tradition from Antiquity to the Early Middles Ages, 1. Stoicism in Classical Latin Literature*. Leiden.

Collins, H. and R. Evans (2007). *Rethinking Expertise*. Chicago.

(2015). 'Expertise Revisited, Part 1 – Interactional Expertise', *Studies in History and Philosophy of Science* 54: 113–23.

(2016). 'Expertise Revisited, Part 2 – Contributory Expertise', *Studies in History and Philosophy of Science* 56: 103–110.

(2018). 'A Sociological/Philosophical Perspective in Expertise', in K.A. Ericsson and R.R. Hoffman (eds.). *The Cambridge Handbook of Expertise and Expert Performance*. Cambridge: 21–32.

Conte, G.B. (1986). *The Rhetoric of Imitation: Genre and Poetic Memory in Virgil and Other Latin Poets*. Ithaca.

Cook, A.B. (1901). 'Associated Reminiscences', *CR* 15: 338–45.

Cooley, A.E. (2009). *Res Gestae Divi Augusti. Text, Translation, and Commentary*, Cambridge.

Copony, R. (1987). '*Fortes Fortuna iuvat*. Fiktion und Realität im 1. Vesuvbrief des Jüngeren Plinius VI, 16', *GB* 14: 215–28.

Corbier, M. (1997). 'Pallas et la statue de César. Affichage et espace public à Rome', *RN* 152: 11–40.

Cordes, L. (2017). *Kaiser und Tyrann. Die Kodierung und Umkodierung der Herrscherrepräsentation Neros und Domitians*. Berlin.

Courtney, E. (1993). *The Fragmentary Latin Poets*. Oxford.
Cova, P.V. (1966). *La critica letteraria di Plinio il Giovane*. Brescia.
  (1969). 'Problemi della lettera pliniana sulla storia', *Aevum* 43: 177–99.
  (1975). 'Contributo allo studio della lettera pliniana sulla storia', *RCCM* 17: 117–39.
  (1978). *Lo stoico imperfetto: un'immagine minore dell'uomo nella letteratura latina del Principato*. Naples.
  (1997). 'La presenza di Seneca in Plinio il Giovane', *Paideia* 52: 95–107.
  (2001). 'Plinio il Giovane contro Plinius il Vecchio', *BStudLat* 31: 55–67.
Cugusi, P. (1983). *Evoluzione e forme dell'epistolografia latina nella tarda repubblica e nei primi due secoli dell'impero*. Rome.
  (2003). 'Qualche riflessione sulle idee retoriche di Plinio il Giovane: *Epistulae* 1,20 e 9,26', in Castagna and Lefèvre (2003): 95–122.
Culpepper Stroup, S. (2010). *Catullus, Cicero, and a Society of Patrons. The Generation of the Text*. Cambridge.
Cuomo, S. (2016). 'Tacit Knowledge in Vitruvius', *Arethusa* 49: 125–43.
D'Agostino, V. (1962). *Studi sul neostoicismo: Seneca, Plinio il Giovane, Epitteto, Marco Aurelio*. Turin (second edition).
Dahlmann, H. (1980). 'Die Hendekasyllaben des Sentius Augurinus, Plinius *ep.* 4. 27', *Gymnasium* 87: 167–77.
Danesi Marioni, G. (1989). 'Un martirio stoico: Silio Italico, *Pun.* 1.169 sgg.', *Prometheus* 15: 245–53.
Darab, Á. (2012). '*Corinthium aes* versus *electrum:* The Anecdote as an Expression of Roman Identity in Pliny the Elder's *Naturalis Historia*', *Hermes* 140: 149–59.
  (2015). '*Corinthium aes*. Die Entstehung und Metamorphose einer Anekdote', *WS* 128: 1–14.
Davie, J. and R. Cowan (eds.) (2011). *Horace: Satires and Epistles*. Translated by J. Davie, with an Introduction and Notes by R. Cowan. Oxford.
Deane, S.N. (1918). 'Greek in Pliny's Letters', *CW* 12: 41–4 and 50–4.
DeLaine, J. (1995). '"De aquis suis"? The "commentarius" of Frontinus', in C. Nicolet (ed.). *Les littératures techniques dans l'Antiquité romaine: Statut, public et destination, tradition*. Vanoevres-Geneva: 117–45.
Delarue, F. (2014). 'L'eau et l'imaginaire. Les villas des *Silves* de Stace', in Devillers (2014): 89–98.
De Paolis, P. (2000). 'Cicerone nei grammatici tardoantichi e medievali', in *Cicerone nel medioevo. Atti dell'XI Colloquium Tullianum. Cassino-Montecassino, 26–28 aprile 1999*. Rome (= *Ciceroniana* 11, 2000): 36–67.
De Pretis, A. (2003). 'Insincerity, Facts, and Epistolarity: Approaches to Pliny's *Epistles* to Calpurnia', in Morello and Gibson (2003): 127–46.
De Verger, A.R. (1997–98). 'Erotic Language in Pliny, *Ep.* VII 5', *Glotta* 74: 114–6.
Devillers, O. (ed.) (2014). *Neronia 9: La villégiature dans le monde romaine de Tibère à Hadrien. Actes du IXe congrès de la SIEN*. Bordeaux.
  (ed.) (2015a). *Autour de Pline le Jeune: En hommage à Nicole Méthy*. Bordeaux.

(2015b). 'Néron selon Pline le Jeune: Entre Pline l'Ancien, Tacite et Trajan', in Devillers (2015a): 61–71.
Dickey, E. (2002). *Latin Forms of Address. From Plautus to Apuleius*. Oxford.
Dickison, S.K. (1977). 'Claudius: *saturnalicius princeps*', *Latomus* 36: 634–47.
Dinter, M.T. and B. Reitz-Joosse (eds.) (2019). *Special Issue: 'Intermediality and Roman Literature' (Trends in Classics* 11.1). Berlin.
Dix, T.K. (1996). 'Pliny's Library at Comum', *Libraries and Culture* 31: 85–102.
Dix, T.K. and G.W. Houston (2006). 'Public Libraries in the City of Rome from the Augustan Age to the Time of Diocletian', *MÉFRA* 118: 671–717.
Dixon, S. (1988). *The Roman Mother*. Norman, OK.
Dominik, W. (2007). 'Tacitus and Pliny on Oratory', in W. Dominik and J. Hall (eds.). *Companion to Roman Rhetoric*. Malden, MA: 323–38.
  (2010). 'The Reception of Silius Italicus in Modern Scholarship', in A. Augoustakis (ed.). *Brill's Companion to Silius Italicus*. Leiden: 425–47.
Doody, A. (2010). *Pliny's Encyclopedia: The Reception of the Natural History*. Cambridge.
Dufallo, B. (2000). '*Satis/satura*: Reconsidering the "Programmatic Intent" of Horace's *Satires* 1.1', *CW* 93: 579–90.
Dunkle, J.R. (1967). 'The Greek Tyrant and Roman Political Invective of the Late Republic', *TAPA* 98: 151–71.
Dupraz, E. (2020). 'Une allusion à Épicure dans la lettre de Pline le Jeune sur la mort de Silius Italicus?', in B. Sans and C. Vanhalme (eds.). *À l'école de l'Antiquité, Hommages à Ghislaine Viré*. Brussels: 149–53.
Durry, M. (1938). *Pline le Jeune. Panégyrique de Trajan. Préfacé, édité et commenté*. Paris.
Eck, W. (1982). 'Jahres- und Provinzialfasten der senatorischen Statthalter von 69/70 bis 138/139', *Chiron*: 281–362.
  (2001). 'Die grosse Pliniusinschrift aus *Comum*: Funktion und Monument', in G.A. Bertinelli and A. Donati (eds.). *Varia Epigraphica. Atti del Colloquio Internazionale di Epigrafia. Bertinoro, 8–10 giugno 2000*. Faenza: 225–35.
Eckardt, B. (1978). *Iavoleni Epistulae*. Berlin.
Eco, U. (1990). 'A Portrait of the Elder as a Young Pliny', in U. Eco, *The Limits of Interpretation*. Bloomington: 123–36.
Edmunds, L. (2001). *Intertextuality and the Reading of Roman Poetry*. Baltimore.
  (2015). 'Pliny the Younger on his Verse and Martial's Non-Recognition of Pliny as a Poet', *HSPh* 108: 309–60.
Edwards, C. (1993). *The Politics of Immorality in Ancient Rome*. Cambridge.
  (1996). *Writing Rome. Textual Approaches to the City*. Cambridge.
  (1997). 'Self-Scrutiny and Self-Transformation in Seneca's Letters', *G&R* 54: 23–38.
Edwards, R. (2008). 'Hunting for Boars with Pliny and Tacitus', *ClAnt* 27: 35–58.
Egelhaaf-Gaiser, U. (2002). 'Panegyrik, Denkmal und Publikum. Plinius, Brief 8,4 und die Kommemoration der Dakertriumphe im Orts- und Medienwandel', in C. Auffarth and J. Rüpke (eds.). Ἐπιτομὴ τῆς

οἰκουμένης. *Studien zur römischen Religion in Antike und Neuzeit: für Hubert Cancik und Hildegard Cancik-Lindemaier*. Stuttgart: 113–37.
Evelyn-White, H.G. (1914). *Hesiod. The Homeric Hymns and Homerica*. London.
Fain, G.L. (2008). *Writing Epigrams. The Art of Composition in Catullus, Callimachus and Martial*. Brussels.
Fairclough, R.H. and G.P. Goold (1999). *Virgil. Eclogues, Georgics, Aeneid: Books 1–6*. Cambridge, MA (first edition 1916).
Fantham, E. (2014). 'On Tranquility of Mind', in E. Fantham, H.M. Hine, J. Ker and G.D. Williams (trans.). *Seneca: Hardship and Happiness*. Chicago: 177–215.
Farrell, J. (1991). *Vergil's Georgics and the Traditions of Ancient Epic: The Art of Allusion in Literary History*. Oxford.
  (2001). *Latin Language and Latin Culture from Ancient to Modern Times*. Cambridge.
Fear, A. (2011). 'The Roman's Burden', in Gibson and Morello (2011): 21–34.
Ferri, R. (1993). *I dispiaceri di un epicureo. Uno studio sulla poetica oraziana delle Epistole (con un capitolo su Persio)*. Pisa.
Firth J.B. (1900). *The Letters of the Younger Pliny*, 2 vols. London.
Fitzgerald, W. (2007). *Martial: The World of the Epigrams*. Chicago.
  (2016). *Variety: The Life of a Roman Concept*. Chicago.
  (2018). 'Pliny and Martial', in König and Whitton (2018b): 108–25.
  (2021). 'The Slave, Between Absence and Presence', in Geue and Giusti (2021): 239–49.
Floridi, L. (2014). *Lucillio, "Epigrammi": Introduzione, testo critico, traduzione e commento*. Berlin.
Fögen, T. (2000). *Patrii sermonis egestas: Einstellungen lateinischer Autoren zu ihrer Muttersprache: ein Beitrag zum Sprachbewusstsein in der römischen Antike*. Munich.
  (2007). 'Statius' Roman Penelope: Exemplarity, Praise and Gender in *Silvae* 3.5', *Philologus* 151: 256–72.
  (2015). '*Ars moriendi*: Literarische Portraits von Selbsttötung bei Plinius dem Jüngeren und Tacitus', *A&A* 61: 21–56.
  (2017). 'Gattungsvielfalt in den Briefen des Jüngeren Plinius: Episteln im Spannungsfeld von ethischer Unterweisung und literarischer Pluridimensionalität', *Gymnasium* 124: 21–60.
Foss, P.W. (2022). *Pliny and the Eruption of Vesuvius*. London.
Fowler, D. (2000). *Roman Constructions*. Oxford.
Fraenkel, E. (1957). *Horace*. Oxford.
  (1961). 'Two Poems of Catullus', *JRS* 51: 46–53.
Frazel, T.D. (2005). '*Furtum* and the Description of Stolen Objects in Cicero, *In Verrem* 2.4', *AJPh* 126: 363–76.
  (2009). *The Rhetoric of Cicero's In Verrem*. Göttingen.
Freudenburg, K. (1993). *The Walking Muse. Horace on the Theory of Satire*. Princeton.
Gagliardi, D. (1990). 'Il giudizio di Plinio Jr. su Silio Italico', *CCC* 11: 289–93.

Galán Vioque, G. (2002). *Martial, Book VII. A Commentary*. Translated by J.J. Zoltowski. Leiden.
Gale, M. (2000). *Virgil on the Nature of Things: The Georgics, Lucretius, and the Didactic Tradition*. Cambridge.
Gallavotti, C. (1978/79). 'P.Oxy. 3070 e un graffito di Stabia', *MC* 13–14: 363–9.
Galimberti Biffino, G. (2015). '"Scrivere" il corpo o della salute e della malattia nell'epistolario di Plinio il Giovane', in Devillers (2015a): 171–81.
Gamberini, F. (1983). *Stylistic Theory and Practice in the Younger Pliny*. Hildesheim.
Gascou, J. (1984). *Suétone historien*. Rome.
Gasser, F. (1999). *Germana patria. Die Geburtsheimat in den Werken römischer Autoren der späten Republik und der frühen Kaiserzeit*. Stuttgart.
Gatzemeier, S. (2013). *Ut ait Lucretius: die Lukrezrezeption in der lateinischen Prosa bis Laktanz*. Göttingen.
Gauly, B.M. (2008). '*Magis homines iuvat gloria lata quam magna*: das Selbstlob in Plinius' Briefen und seine Funktion', in B.M. Gauly and A.H. Arweiler (eds.). *Machtfragen: zur kulturellen Repräsentation und Konstruktion von Macht in Antike, Mittelalter und Neuzeit*. Stuttgart: 187–204.
Gazich, R. (2003). 'Retorica dell'esemplarità nelle lettere di Plinio', in Castagna and Lefèvre (2003): 123–41.
Genette, G. (1982). *Palimpsestes. La littérature au second degré*, Paris.
Germerodt, F. (2015). *Amicitia in den Briefen des jüngeren Plinius*, Speyer.
Gesner, I.M. (1770). *C. Plinii Caecilii Secundi Epistolarum libri decem [...]*, Lipsiae (second edition by A.W. Ernesti).
Geue, T. (2018). 'Forgetting the Juvenalien in our Midst: Literary Amnesia in the Satires', in König and Whitton (2018b): 366–84.
Geue, T. and E. Giusti (eds.) (2021). *Unspoken Rome: Absence in Latin Literature and its Reception*. Cambridge.
Gibson R. (2003). 'Pliny and the Art of Inoffensive Self-praise', in Morello and Gibson (2003): 235–54.
　(2011a). '<Clarus> Confirmed? Pliny, *Epistles* 1.1 and Sidonius Apollinaris', *CQ* 61: 655–9.
　(2011b). 'Elder and Better: The *Naturalis Historia* and the *Letters* of the Younger Pliny', in Gibson and Morello (2011): 187–205.
　(2013). 'Letters into Autobiography: The Generic Mobility of the Ancient Letter Collection', in Papanghelis, Harrison and Frangoulidis (2013): 387–416.
　(2014a). 'Starting with the Index in Pliny', in L. Jansen (ed.). *The Roman Paratext. Frame, Texts, Readers*. Cambridge: 33–55.
　(2014b). 'Suetonius and the *viri illustres* of Pliny the Younger', in T. Power and R. Gibson (eds.). *Suetonius the Biographer*. Oxford: 199–230.
　(2015). 'Not Dark Yet...: Reading to the End of Pliny's Nine-Book Collection', in Marchesi (2015a): 185–223.
　(2018). 'Pliny and Plutarch's Practical Ethics: A Newly Rediscovered Dialogue', in König and Whitton (2018b): 402–21.
　(2020). *Man of High Empire. The Life of Pliny the Younger*. Oxford.

(2021). 'Calpurnia of Comum and the Ghost of Umbria: Marriage and Regional Identity in the *Epistulae* of Pliny', in L. Galli Millić and A. Stoehr-Monjou (eds.). *Au-delà de l'épithalame. Le marriage dans la literature latine (IIIe s. av. – VIe s. ap. J.-C.)*. Turnhout: 245–66.
(forthcoming). *Pliny. Epistles Book VI*. Cambridge.
Gibson, R. and R. Morello (eds.) (2011). *Pliny the Elder: Themes and Contexts*. Leiden.
Gibson, R. and R. Morello (2012). *Reading the Letters of Pliny the Younger: An Introduction*. Cambridge.
Gibson, R. and C.L. Whitton (eds.) (2016). *The Epistles of Pliny. Oxford Readings in Classical Studies*. Oxford.
Gierig, G.E. (1800–2). *C. Plinii Caecilii Secundi Epistolarum libri decem*, 2 vols. Leipzig.
Gigante, M. (1979). 'Il racconto pliniano dell'eruzione del Vesuvio dell'a. 79', *PP* 34: 321–76 (reprinted as Gigante 1989).
(1989). *Il fungo sul Vesuvio secondo Plinio il Giovane*. Rome.
Gildenhard, I. (2011). *Creative Eloquence: The Construction of Reality in Cicero's Speeches*. Oxford.
Giumlia-Mair, A.R. and P. Craddock (1993). *Das schwarze Gold der Alchimisten: Corinthium aes*. Mainz.
Gleason, M. (2008). *Making Men: Sophists and Self-Presentation in Ancient Rome*. Princeton.
Glenn, P. (2003). *Laughter in Interaction*. Cambridge.
Glynn, W. (1928). *Cicero. Letters to His Friends*, vol. 2: *Books VII–XII*. London.
Gnilka, C. (1973). 'Trauer und Trost in Plinius' Briefen', *SO* 49: 105–25.
Görgemanns, H. (2001). 'Symposion-Literatur', *DNP* 11: 1138–41.
Görler, W. (1979). 'Kaltblütiges Schnarchen. Zum literarischen Hintergrund der Vesuvbriefe des jüngeren Plinius', in G.W. Bowersock, W. Burkert and M.C.J. Putnam (eds.). *Arktouros. Hellenic Studies Presented to Bernard M.W. Knox on the Occasion of his 65th Birthday*. Berlin: 427–33.
Goetzl, J. (1952). '*Variatio* in the Plinian Epistle', *CJ* 47: 265–68 and 299.
Goguey, D. (1982). 'Le paysage dans les *Silves* de Stace: conventions poétiques et observation réaliste', *Latomus* 41: 602–13.
Gowers, E. (ed.) (2012). *Horace, Satires Book I*. Cambridge.
Graver, M. (2007). *Stoicism and Emotion*. Chicago.
(2009). 'The Weeping Wise: Stoic and Epicurean Consolations in Seneca's 99th Epistle', in T. Fögen (ed.). *Tears in the Greco-Roman World*. Berlin: 235–52.
Green, P. (2005). *The Poems of Catullus. A Bilingual Edition*. Berkeley.
Green, R.P.H. (1991). *The Works of Ausonius. Edited with Introduction and Commentary*. Oxford.
Green, S.J. (2014). *Disclosure and Discretion in Roman Astrology*. Oxford.
Greenwood, L.H.G. (1928–35). *Cicero. The Verrine Orations*, 2 vols. Cambridge, MA.
Griffin, M. (1976). *Seneca: A Philosopher in Politics*. Oxford.

(1986a). 'Philosophy, Cato, and Roman Suicide: I', *G&R* 33: 64–77.
(1986b). 'Philosophy, Cato, and Roman Suicide: II', *G&R* 33: 192–202.
(2000). 'Seneca and Pliny', in C. Rowe and M. Schofield (eds.). *The Cambridge History of Greek and Roman Political Thought*. Cambridge: 532–58.
(2007). 'The Younger Pliny's Debt to Moral Philosophy', *HSPh* 103: 451–81.
Grilli, A. (1992). 'Musonio o il sospetto d'un mondo alla rovescia', in *La langue latine, langue de la philosophie. Actes du colloque de Rome (17–19 mai 1990)*. Rome: 173–86.
Gros, P. (1978). 'Vie et mort de l'art hellénistique selon Vitruve et Pline', *REL* 56: 289–313.
Gualandri, I. (2020). 'Sidonius' Intertextuality', in G. Kelly and J. van Waarden (eds.). *The Edinburgh Companion to Sidonius Apollinaris*. Edinburgh: 279–316.
Guérin, C. (2012–13). '*Intempestiua philosophia*? Éloquence déclamatoire et éloquence philosophique au Ier siècle ap. J.-C', *Ítaca. Quaderns Catalans de Cultura Clàssica* 28-29: 21–43.
Guillemin, A.-M. (1929). *Pline et la vie littéraire de son temps*. Paris.
(1953–62). *Pline le Jeune. Lettres I–IX*, 3 vols. Paris (second edition).
(1961–64). *Pline le Jeune: Lettres. Panégyrique de Trajan*, 4 vols. Paris.
Gummere, R.M. (1917–25). *Seneca. Epistles*, 3 vols. Cambridge, MA.
Gunderson, E. (1997). 'Catullus, Pliny, and Love-Letters', *TAPA* 127: 201–31.
Gutzwiller, K. (1998). *Poetic Garlands. Hellenistic Epigrams in Context*. Berkeley.
Haack, M.L. (2002). '*Haruspices* publics et privés: tentative d'une distinction', *REA* 104: 111–33.
Haake, M. (2019). '"How to do things with *senatus consulta*": Die Autorität des Rechtsdokuments und die Stimme des Autors im Briefcorpus des Jüngeren Plinius', in P. Buongiorno and G. Traina (eds.). *Rappresentazione e uso dei senatus consulta nelle fonti letterarie del principato*. Stuttgart: 117–42.
Hagendahl, H. (1947). 'Methods of Citation in Post-Classical Latin Prose', *Eranos* 45: 114–28.
Hallett, J. (1984). *Fathers and Daughters in Roman Society: Women and the Elite Family*. Princeton.
(2002). 'The Vindolanda Letters from Claudia Severa', in L. Churchill, P. Brown and J. Jeffrey (eds.). *Women Writing Latin*, vol. 1. New York: 93–9.
Halm, K. (1863). *Rhetores Latini minores*. Leipzig.
Hammar, I. (2013). *Making Enemies: The Logic of Immorality in Ciceronian Oratory*. Lund.
Hanaghan, M.P. (2017a). 'Latent Criticism of Anthemius and Ricimer in Sidonius Apollinaris' *Epistulae* 1.5', *CQ* 67: 631–49.
(2017b). 'Micro Allusions to Pliny the Younger and Virgil in Sidonius' Programmatic Epistles', *IJCT* 24: 249–61.
(2017c). 'Note de lecture: The Temporality of Seneca's *Epistles*', *Latomus* 76: 203–6.
(2018). 'Pliny's Epistolary Directions', *Arethusa* 51: 137–62.

Harder, A. (2012). *Callimachus: Aetia*, 2 vols. Oxford.
Hardie, A. (1983). *Statius and the Silvae: Poets, Patrons, and Epideixis in the Graeco-Roman World*. Liverpool.
Hardie, P.R. (2009). *Lucretian Receptions: History, the Sublime, Knowledge.* Cambridge.
Harich-Schwarzbauer, H. and J. Hindermann (2010). 'Garten und Villenlandschaft in der römischen Literatur. Sozialer und ästhetischer Diskurs bei Vergil und Plinius dem Jüngeren', in R. Faber and C. Holste (eds.). *Arkadische Kulturlandschaft und Gartenkunst. Eine Tour d'Horizon.* Würzburg: 57–68.
Harries, J.D. (2018). 'Saturninus the Helmsman, Pliny and Friends: Legal and Literary Letter Collections', in König and Whitton (2018b): 260–79.
Harrison, S.J. (2007). *Generic Enrichment in Vergil and Horace.* Oxford.
  (2013). 'Introduction', in Papanghelis, Harrison and Frangoulidis (2013): 1–19.
Harrison, S.J., S. Frangoulidis and T.D. Papanghelis (eds.) (2018). *Intratextuality and Latin Literature*. Berlin.
Hartelius, J.E. (2011). *The Rhetoric of Expertise*. Lanham, MD.
Hartmann, E. (2012). 'Die Kunst der edlen Selbstdarstellung. Plinius der Jüngere als Kunstkenner und Euerget', in T. Fuhrer and A.B. Renger (eds.). *Performanz von Wissen. Strategien der Wissensvermittlung in der Vormoderne*. Heidelberg: 109–27.
Hausmann, M. (2009). *Die Lesererlenkung durch Tacitus in den Tiberius- und Claudiusbüchern der "Annalen"*. Berlin.
Hawkins, T. (2014). *Iambic Poetics in the Roman Empire*. Cambridge.
Hawthorn, J.R. (1962). 'The Senate after Sulla', *G&R* 9: 53–60.
Haywood, R.M. (1952). 'The Strange Death of the Elder Pliny', *CW* 46: 1–3.
Hemelrijk, E.A. (1999). *Matrona Docta: Educated Women in the Roman Élite from Cornelia to Julia Domna*. London.
Henderson, J. (1975). *The Maculate Muse. Obscene Language in Attic Comedy.* New Haven.
Henderson, J.G. (1993). 'Be Alert (Your Country Needs Lerts): Horace, *Satires* 1.9', *PCPS* 39: 67–93.
  (2001). 'On Pliny on Martial on Pliny on Anon … (*Epistles* 3.21/*Epigrams* 10.19)', *Ramus* 30: 56–87.
  (2002a). 'Knowing Someone Through Their Books: Pliny on Uncle Pliny (*Epistles* 3.5)', *CPh* 97: 256–84.
  (2002b). *Pliny's Statue: The Letters, Self-portraiture, and Classical Art*. Exeter.
  (2011). 'The Nature of Man: Pliny, *Historia Naturalis* as Cosmogram', *MD* 66: 139–71.
Hershkowitz, D. (1995). 'Pliny the Poet', *G&R* 42: 168–81.
Higham, T.F. (1960). 'Nature Note: Dolphin-Riders. Ancient Stories Vindicated', *G&R* 7: 82–6.
Hiltbrunner, O. (1979). '*Prisce, iubes…*', *Zeitschrift der Savigny-Stiftung für Rechtsgeschichte (Romanist. Abt.)* 96: 31–42.
Hindermann, J. (2009). 'Orte der Inspiration in Plinius' *Epistulae*', *MH* 66: 223–31.

(2010). '*similis excluso a vacuo limine recedo* – Plinius' Inszenierung seiner Ehe als elegisches Liebesverhältnis', in M. Formisano and T. Fuhrer (eds.). *Gender-Studies in den Altertumswissenschaften: Gender-Inszenierungen in der antiken Literatur*. Trier: 45–63.

(2011a). 'Verliebte Delphine, schwimmende Inseln und versiegende Quellen beim älteren und jüngeren Plinius: *mirabilia* und ihre Erzählpotenz (*epp.* 4,30; 8,20; 9,33)', *Gymnasium* 118: 345–54.

(2011b). 'Zoophilie in Zoologie und Roman: Sex und Liebe zwischen Mensch und Tier bei Plutarch, Plinius dem Älteren, Aelian und Apuleius', *Dictynna* 8 (en ligne).

(2014). 'Beispielhafte männliche Trauer in Plinius' *Epistulae*. Zum Normdiskurs römischer Konsolation', in S. Plotke and A. Ziem (eds.). *Sprache der Trauer. Verbalisierung einer Emotion in historischer Perspektive*. Heidelberg: 285–304.

Hinds, S. (1998). *Allusion and Intertext: Dynamics of Appropriation in Roman Poetry*. Cambridge.

(2001). 'Cinna, Statius, and "Immanent Literary History" in the Cultural Economy', in E.A. Schmidt (ed.), *L'histoire littéraire immanente dans la poésie latine*. Geneva: 221–57.

Höschele, R. (2007). 'The Traveling Reader: Journeys through Ancient Epigram Books', *TAPA* 137: 333–69.

(2010). *Die blütenlesende Muse. Poetik und Textualität antiker Epigrammsammlungen*. Tübingen.

Hoffer, S.E. (1999). *The Anxieties of Pliny the Younger*. Atlanta.

(2006). 'Divine Comedy? Accession Propaganda in Pliny, *Epistles* 10.1-2 and the *Panegyric*', *JRS* 96: 73–87.

Holford-Strevens, L. (2001). 'Getting Away with Murder: The Literary and Forensic Fortune of Two Roman *exempla*', *IJCT* 7: 489–514.

Holzberg, N. (2002a). *Catull. Der Dichter und sein erotisches Werk*. Munich.

(2002b). *Martial und das antike Epigramm*. Darmstadt.

(2007). '*Narrare* und *iocari*. Lateinische Briefe von Cicero bis in die frühe Neuzeit als Literatur', in R. Kussl (ed.). *Antike Welt und Literatur. Einblicke, Analysen und Vermittlung im Unterricht*. Speyer: 101–14.

(2009). *Horaz. Dichter und Werk*. Munich.

Hornblower, S. (1991). *A Commentary on Thucydides*, vol. 1: *Books 1–2*. Oxford.

Howe, N. (1985). 'In Defense of the Encyclopedic Mode: On Pliny's Preface to the *Natural History*', *Latomus* 46: 561–76.

Howell, P. (1980). *A Commentary on Book One of the Epigrams of Martial*. London.

Hünemörder, C. (1997). 'Delphin', *DNP* 3: 400–1.

Hutchinson, G. (2013). 'Genre and Super-Genre', in Papanghelis, Harrison and Frangoulidis (2013): 19–34.

Illias-Zarifopol, C. (1994). *Portrait of a Pragmatic Hero: Narrative Strategies of Self-Presentation in Pliny's Letters*. Dissertation, Indiana University.

Isager, J. (1998). *Pliny on Art and Society. The Elder Pliny's Chapters on the History of Art*. Odense.
Jacquier, J. (2019). 'Leere Räume – die Kunst der Beschreibung in Plinius' *epistula* 5, 6', in M. Citroni, M. Labate and G. Rosati (eds.). *Luoghi dell'abitare, immaginazione letteraria e identità romana. Da Augusto ai Flavi*. Pisa: 289–300.
Jaeger, M. (2002). 'Cicero and Archimedes' Tomb', *JRS* 92: 49–61.
Janka, M. (2015). 'Plinius und die Poesie. Von der Freizeitdichtung zur Literaturtheorie', *Gymnasium* 122: 597–618.
Janson, T. (1964). *Latin Prose Prefaces. Studies in Literary Conventions*. Stockholm.
Jensen, K.B. (2016). 'Intermediality', in K.B. Jensen and R.T. Craig (eds.). *The International Encyclopaedia of Communication Theory and Philosophy*. Chichester. (https://doi.org/10.1002/9781118766804.wbiect170).
Johnson, T.S. (2012). *Horace's Iambic Criticism*. Leiden.
Johnson, W.A. (2010). *Readers and Reading Culture in the High Roman Empire: A Study of Elite Communities*. Oxford.
Jones, N.F. (2001). 'Pliny the Younger's Vesuvius *Letters* (6.16 and 6.20)', *CW* 95: 31–48.
Joseph, T.A. (2012). *Tacitus the Epic Successor. Virgil, Lucan, and the Narrative of Civil War in the Histories*. Leiden.
Kaster, R.A. (1995). *C. Suetonius Tranquillius, de Grammaticis et Rhetoribus*. Oxford.
  (1997). 'The Shame of the Romans', *TAPA* 127: 1–19.
  (2005). *Emotion, Restraint, and Community in Ancient Rome*. Oxford.
Keeline, T. (2013). 'The Literary and Stylistic Qualities of a Plinian Letter: A Commentary on *Ep*. 7.9', *HSPh* 107: 229–64.
  (2018). 'Model or Anti-model?: Pliny on Uncle Pliny', *TAPA* 148: 173–203.
Kelly, G. (2018). 'From Martial to Juvenal (*Epigrams* 12.18)', in König and Whitton (2018b): 160–79.
Kenney, E.J. (1970). '*Doctus Lucretius*', *Mnemosyne* 23: 366–92.
Ker, J. (2004). 'Nocturnal Writers in Imperial Rome: The Culture of *Lucubratio*', *CPh* 99: 209–42.
King, J.E. (1927). *Cicero. Tusculan Disputations*. Cambridge, MA.
Klodt, C. (2012). '*Patrem mira similitudine exscripserat*. Plinius' Nachruf auf eine perfekte Tochter (*epist*. 5, 16)', *Gymnasium* 119: 23–61.
Kochin, M.S. (2002). 'Time and Judgement in Demosthenes' *De Corona*', *Philosophy and Rhetoric* 35: 77–89.
Köhler, H. (1995). *C. Sollius Apollinaris Sidonius, Briefe Buch I. Einleitung-Text-Übersetzung-Kommentar*. Heidelberg.
König, A. (2007). 'Knowledge and Power in Frontinus' *On Aqueducts*', in J. König and T. Whitmarsh (eds.). *Ordering Knowledge in the Roman Empire*. Cambridge: 177–205.
  (2013). 'Frontinus' Cameo Role in Tacitus' *Agricola*', *CQ* 63: 361–76.

(2020). 'Tactical Interactions: Dialogues between Greece and Rome in the Military Manuals of Aelian and Arrian', in König, Langlands and Uden (2020): 134–56.
König, A., R. Langlands and J. Uden (eds.) (2020). *Literature and Culture in the Roman Empire, 96–235 CE: Cross-cultural Interactions*. Cambridge.
König, A. and C. Whitton (2018a). 'Introduction', in König and Whitton (2018b): 1–34.
  (eds.) (2018b). *Roman Literature under Nerva, Trajan and Hadrian: Literary Interactions, AD 96–138*. Cambridge.
König, J. and G. Woolf (eds.) (2017). *Authority and Expertise in Ancient Scientific Culture*. Cambridge.
König, R. (1973). *C. Plinius Secundus d.Ä. Naturkunde. Lateinisch-Deutsch, Buch 1. Herausgegeben und übersetzt, in Zusammenarbeit mit Gerhard Winkler*. Munich.
Koster, S. (1980). *Die Invektive in der griechischen und römischen Literatur*. Meisenheim am Glan.
Krasser, H. (1993a). '*Claros colere viros* oder über engagierte Bewunderung. Zum Selbstverständnis des jüngeren Plinius', *Philologus* 137: 62–71.
  (1993b). '*extremos pudeat rediisse* – Plinius im Wettstreit mit der Vergangenheit. Zu Vergilzitaten beim jüngeren Plinius', *A&A* 39: 144–54.
  (1993c). 'Laszives Vergnügen oder philosophisches Gespräch? Zum Text von Plinius *Epist.* 5,3,2', *Hermes* 121: 254–8.
Krieckhaus, A. (2006). *Senatorische Familien und ihre patriae (1./2. Jahrhundert n. Chr.)*. Hamburg.
Kroll, W. (1924). *Studien zum Verständnis der römischen Literatur*. Stuttgart.
Kubiak, D.P. (2010). 'An Erotic Epigram of Cicero?', in C. Deroux (ed.). *Studies in Latin Literature and Roman History 15*. Brussels: 110–29.
La Bua, G. (2019). *Cicero and Roman Education. The Reception of the Speeches and Ancient Scholarship*. Cambridge.
Laguna, G. (1996). 'Philosophical Topics in Statius' *Silvae*: Sources and Aims', in F. Delarue, S. Georgacopoulou, P. Laurens et al. (eds.). *Epicedion: Hommage à P. Papinius Statius 96–1996*. Poitiers: 247–59.
Langlands, R. (2014). 'Pliny's *Role Models of Both Sexes*: Gender and Exemplarity in the *Letters*', *EuGeStA* 4: 214–37.
  (2018). 'Extratextuality: Literary Interactions with Oral Culture and Exemplary Ethics', in König and Whitton (2018b): 330–46.
Laughton, E. (1971). '*Prisce iubes*', *CR* 21: 171–2.
Laurenti, R. (1989). 'Musonio, maestro di Epitteto', in W. Haase (ed.). *Philosophie, Wissenschaften, Technik (ANRW 36.3)*. Berlin: 2105–47.
Lavan, M. (2013). *Slaves to Rome: Paradigms of Empire in Roman Culture*. Cambridge.
  (2018). 'Pliny *Epistles* 10 and Imperial Correspondence: The Empire of Letters', in König and Whitton (2018b): 280–301.
Lazzeretti, A. (2006). *M. Tulli Ciceronis, In C. Verrem actionis secundae liber quartus (De Signis). Commento archeologico*. Pisa.

Leach, E.W. (1990). 'The Politics of Self-Representation: Pliny's *Letters* and Roman Portrait Sculpture', *ClAnt* 9: 14–39.
  (2003). '*Otium* as *luxuria*: Economy of Status in the Younger Pliny's *Letters*', in Morello and Gibson (2003): 147–65.
  (2013). 'Pliny's Epistolary Re-inscription: Writing the Tombs of Verginius Rufus and Pallas the Claudian Secretary *a rationibus*', *SyllClass* 24: 125–44.
Leary, T.L. (1996). *The Apophoreta. Martial Book 14*. London.
Lefèvre, E. (1988). 'Plinius-Studien IV: Die Naturauffassung in den Beschreibungen der Quelle am *Lacus Larius* (4,30), des *Clitumnus* (8,8) und des *Lacus Vadimo* (8,20)', *Gymnasium* 95: 236–69.
  (1989). 'Plinius-Studien V: Vom Römertum zum Ästhetizismus. Die Würdigungen des älteren Plinius (3,5), Silius Italicus (3,7) und Martial (3,21)', *Gymnasium* 96: 113–28.
  (1996a). 'Plinius-Studien VI: Der grosse und der kleine Plinius. Die Vesuv-Briefe (6,16; 6,20)', *Gymnasium* 103: 193–215.
  (1996b). 'Plinius-Studien VII, Cicero das unerreichbare Vorbild (1,2; 3,15; 4,8; 7,4; 9,2)', *Gymnasium* 103: 333–53.
  (2009). *Vom Römertum zum Ästhetizismus: Studien zu den Briefen des jüngeren Plinius*. Berlin.
Lehmann-Hartleben, K. (1936). *Plinio il Giovane. Lettere scelte con commento archeologico*. Florence (reprinted with an introduction by P. Zanker and up-to-date bibliography by A. Anguissola. Pisa 2007).
Leigh, M. (2013). *From Polypragmon to Curiosus: Ancient Concepts of Curious and Meddlesome Behaviour*. Oxford.
Levick, B.M. (1975). 'Mercy and Moderation on the Coinage of Tiberius', in B.M. Levick (ed.). *The Ancient Historian and His Material. Essays in Honour of C.E. Stevens*. Westmead: 123–37.
  (2013). 'C. Plinius Secundus', in T.J. Cornell (ed.). *The Fragments of the Roman Historians*, vol. 1. Oxford: 525–34.
Lewis, J.D. (1879). *The Letters of the Younger Pliny*. London.
Lillge, F. (1918). 'Die literarische Form der Briefe Plinius des Jüngeren über den Ausbruch des Vesuvius', *Sokrates* 6: 209–34 and 273–97.
Long, O. (1901). *On the Usage of quotiens and quotienscumque in Different Periods of Latin*. Baltimore.
Lorenz, S. (2007). 'Catullus and Martial', in M.B. Skinner (ed.). *A Companion to Catullus*. Malden, MA: 418–38.
Ludolph, M. (1997). *Epistolographie und Selbstdarstellung. Untersuchungen zu den 'Paradebriefen' Plinius des Jüngeren*. Tübingen.
Lutz, C.E. (1947). 'Musonius Rufus "The Roman Socrates"', *YClS* 10: 3–150.
Lyne, R. (2016). *Memory and Intertextuality in Renaissance Literature*. Cambridge.
Lyne, R.O.A.M. (1994). 'Vergil's *Aeneid*: Subversion by Intertextuality: Catullus 66.39–40 and Other Examples', *G&R* 41: 187–204.
McAlindon, D. (1956). 'Dolphin Stories and P.I.R.', *Orpheus* 3: 166.

McDermott, W.C. and A.E. Orentzel (1977). 'Silius Italicus and Domitian', *AJPh* 98: 24–34.
McDonnell, M. (2006). *Roman Manliness: 'Virtus' and the Roman Republic.* Cambridge.
MacDowell, D.M. (2009). *Demosthenes the Orator.* Oxford.
McNamara, J. (2021). 'Pliny, Tacitus and the Monuments of Pallas', *CQ* FirstView articles, 1–22, doi: http://10.1017/S0009838821000203 (accessed on 6/5/2021).
Malamud, M. (2007). 'A Spectacular Feast: *Silvae* 4.2', *Arethusa* 40: 223–44.
Malaspina, E. (2019). 'Euphratès, Artémidore et ceux *qui sapientiae studium habitu corporis praeferunt* (*Ep.*, I, 22, 6): la place de la philosophie dans la culture de Pline', in S. Aubert-Baillot, C. Guérin and S. Morlet (eds.). *La philosophie des non-philosophes dans l'Empire romain du Ier au IIIe siècle.* Paris: 121–56.
Malherbe, A.J. (1988). *Ancient Epistolary Theorists*, Atlanta.
Manuwald, G. (2003). 'Eine "Schule" für Novum Comum (*Epist.* 4.13): Aspekte der liberalitas des Plinius', in Castagna and Lefèvre (2003): 203–17.
(2015). *Cicero.* London.
Marchesi, I. (2008). *The Art of Pliny's Letters: A Poetics of Allusion in the Private Correspondence.* Cambridge.
(2013). 'Silenced Intertext: Pliny on Martial on Pliny (on Regulus)', *AJPh* 134: 101–18.
(ed.) (2015a). *Pliny the Book-maker: Betting on Posterity in the Epistles.* Oxford.
(2015b). 'Uncluttered Spaces, Unlittered Texts: Pliny's Villas as Editorial Places', in Marchesi (2015a): 223–51.
(2018). 'The Regulus Connection: Displacing Lucan between Martial and Pliny', in König and Whitton (2018b): 349–65.
Marshall, A. (2009). 'Statius and the *Veteres*: *Silvae* 1.3 and the Homeric House of Alcinous', *Scholia* 18: 78–88.
Martelli, F. (2009). 'Plumbing Helicon: Poetic Property and the Material World of Statius' *Silvae*', *MD* 62: 145–77.
Martin, G. (2009). *Divine Talk: Religious Argumentation in Demosthenes.* Oxford.
Martin, R.H. (1967). 'The Speech of Curtius Montanus: Tacitus, *Histories* IV, 42', *JRS* 57: 109–14.
Mastrorosa, I.G. (2010). 'La pratica dell'oratoria giudiziaria nell'alto impero: Quintiliano e Plinio il Giovane', in P. Galand-Hallyn, F. Hallyn, C. Lévy et al. (eds.). *Quintilien: ancien et moderne études réunies. Latinitates, 3.* Turnhout: 125–52.
Matier, K.O. (1981). 'Prejudice and the *Punica*: Silius Italicus – A Reassessment', *AClass* 24: 141–51.
(1988). 'Prejudice and the *Punica* Again: Silius Italicus and his Critics', *Akroterion* 33: 14–21.
(1989). *Silius Italicus at Bay: Pliny, Prejudice and the Punica.* Durban-Westville.
(1990). 'Stoic Philosophy in Silius Italicus', *Akroterion* 35: 68–72.

May, J.M. (1988). *Trials of Character: The Eloquence of Ciceronian Ethos*. Chapel Hill.
Mayer, R. (2003). 'Pliny and *Gloria Dicendi*', in Morello and Gibson (2003): 227–34.
Mayor, J. (1880). *Pliny's Letters Book III*. London.
Mazurek, T. (1997). 'Self-parody and the Law in Horace's *Satires* 1.9', *CJ* 93: 1–17.
Mehl, A. (1974). *Tacitus über Kaiser Claudius. Die Ereignisse am Hof.* Munich.
Merwald, G. (1964). *Die Buchkomposition des jüngeren Plinius (Epistulae I–IX)*. Erlangen.
Mesk, J. (1911) 'Zur Quellenanalyse des Plinianischen Panegyricus', *WS* 33: 71–100.
Méthy, N. (2003). '*Ad exemplar antiquitatis*: les grandes figures du passé dans la correspondance de Pline le Jeune', *REL* 81: 200–14.
  (2004). 'Lettre d'art et vie sociale: les citations dans la correspondance de Pline le Jeune', in L. Nadjo and E. Gavoille (eds.). *Epistulae antiquae III*. Leuven: 463–76.
  (2007). *Les lettres de Pline le Jeune: une représentation de l'homme*. Paris.
Meyer, D. (2005). *Inszeniertes Lesevergnügen. Das inschriftliche Epigramm und seine Rezeption bei Kallimachos*. Stuttgart.
Millar, F. (2004). 'Trajan: Government by Correspondence', in H.M. Cotton and G.M. Rògers (eds.). *Rome, the Greek World and the East*, vol. 2. Chapel Hill: 23–46.
Miller, C.L. (1966). 'The Younger Pliny's Dolphin Story (*Epistulae* IX 33): An Analysis', *CW* 60: 6–8.
Mindt, N. (2013). *Martials 'epigrammatischer Kanon'*. Munich.
Minos, C. (C. Minois or Mignault) (1598). *Cai Plinii Secundi Epistolae [. . .]*, 2 vols. Paris.
Montgomery, H.C. (1966). 'The Fabulous Dolphin', *CJ* 61: 311–14.
Morello, R. (2003). 'Pliny and the Art of Saying Nothing', in Morello and Gibson (2003): 187–209.
  (2007). 'Confidence, *Inuidia*, and Pliny's Epistolary Curriculum', in Morello and Morrison (2007): 169–89.
  (2011). 'Pliny and the Encyclopaedic Addressee', in Gibson and Morello (2011): 147–65.
  (2015). 'Pliny Book 8. Two Viewpoints and the Pedestrian Reader', in Marchesi (2015a): 144–84.
  (2018). 'Traditional *exempla* and Nerva's New Modernity: Making Fabricius Take the Cash', in König and Whitton (2018b): 302–29.
Morello, R. and R. Gibson (eds.) (2003). *Re-imagining Pliny the Younger* (= *Arethusa* 36.2). Baltimore.
Morello, R. and A.D. Morrison (eds.) (2007). *Ancient Letters: Classical and Late Antique Epistolography*. Oxford.
Moreno Soldevila, R. (2006). *Martial, Book IV: A Commentary*. Leiden.
Moreno Soldevila, R., A.M. Castillo and J.F. Valverde (eds.) (2019). *A Prosopography of Martial's Epigrams*. Berlin.

Morzadec, F. (2009). *Les Images du Monde. Structure, écriture, et esthétique du paysage dans les oeuvres de Stace et Silius Italicus.* Brussels.

Mratschek, S. (2003). '*Illa nostra Italia*. Plinius und die "Wiedergeburt" der Literatur in der Transpadana', in Castagna and Lefèvre (2003): 219–41.

 (2018). 'Images of Domitius Apollinaris in Pliny and Martial: Intertextual Discourses as Aspects of Self-Definition and Differentiation', in König and Whitton (2018b): 208–32.

Murphy, T. (2004). *Pliny the Elder's Natural History. The Empire in the Encyclopedia.* Oxford.

Murray, O. (1965). 'The "Quinquennium Neronis" and the Stoics', *Historia* 14: 41–61.

Myers, K.S. (2000). '*Miranda Fides*: Poet and Patrons in Paradoxographical Landscapes in Statius' *Silvae*', *MD* 44: 103–38.

 (2005). '*Docta Otia*: Garden Ownership and Configurations of Leisure in Statius and Pliny the Younger', *Arethusa* 38: 103–29.

Mynors, R.A.B. (1963). *C. Plini Caecili Secundi Epistularum libri decem.* Oxford (with corrected reprint, 1968).

 (1990). *Virgil: Georgics. Edited with Commentary.* Oxford.

Naas, V. (2002). *Le projet encyclopédique de Pline l'Ancien.* Rome.

 (2011). 'Imperialism, *Mirabilia* and Knowledge: Some Paradoxes in the Naturalis Historia', in Gibson and Morello (2011): 57–70.

Nauta, R.R. (2002). *Poetry for Patrons: Literary Communication in the Age of Domitian.* Leiden.

Neger, M. (2012). *Martials Dichtergedichte. Das Epigramm als Medium der poetischen Selbstreflexion.* Tübingen.

 (2015a). '*Neque enim vereor, ne iactantior videar...*: Plinius und der kaiserzeitliche Diskurs über das Selbstlob', *Gymnasium* 122: 315–38.

 (2015b). 'Pliny's Martial and Martial's Pliny: The Intertextual Dialogue between the *Letters* and the *Epigrams*', in Devillers (2015a): 131–44.

 (2016). '*Satius est enim otiosum esse quam nihil agere*: Die Inszenierung von Mußezeit und Mußeräumen im Briefkorpus des Jüngeren Plinius', in F.C. Eickhoff (ed.). *Muße und Rekursitivät in der antiken Briefliteratur. Mit einem Ausblick in andere Gattungen.* Tübingen: 133–60.

 (2018). 'Telling Tales of Wonder: *Mirabilia* in the *Letters* of Pliny the Younger', in M. Gerolemou (ed.). *Recognizing Miracles in Antiquity and Beyond.* Berlin: 179–203.

 (2019). '*Laudabo digne non satis tamen Baias*: Martial's Epigrammatic Campania', in A. Augoustakis and J. Littlewood (eds.). *Campania in the Flavian Poetic Imagination.* Oxford: 83–98.

 (2021). *Epistolare Narrationen. Studien zur Erzähltechnik des jüngeren Plinius.* Tübingen.

Netz, R. (2020). *Scale, Space and Canon in Ancient Literary Culture.* Cambridge.

Neudecker, R. (2004). 'Aspekte öffentlicher Bibliotheken in der Kaiserzeit', in B. Borg (ed.). *Paideia: the World of the Second Sophistic.* Berlin: 293–313.

Neuhausen, K.A. (1968). '*Plinius proximus Tacito.* Bemerkungen zu einem Topos der römischen Literaturkritik', *RhM* 111: 333–57.

Neumann, U. (1998). 'Invektive', *HWRh* 4, 549–61.
Newlands, C. (2002). *Statius' Silvae and the Poetics of Empire*. Cambridge.
  (2010). 'The Eruption of Vesuvius in the *Epistles* of Statius and Pliny', in J.F. Miller and A. Woodman (eds.). *Latin Historiography and Poetry in the Early Empire: Generic Interactions*. Leiden: 105–21.
  (2011). *Statius Silvae Book II. Edited with Commentary*. Cambridge.
  (2013). 'Architectural Ecphrasis in Roman Poetry', in Papanghelis, Harrison and Frangoulidis (2013): 55–78.
Nikitinski, O. (1998). 'Plinius der Ältere: Seine Enzyklopädie und ihre Leser', in W. Kullmann, J. Althoff and M. Asper (eds.). *Gattungen wissenschaftlicher Literatur in der Antike*. Tübingen: 341–60.
Nisbet, G. (2003). *Greek Epigram in the Roman Empire: Martial's Forgotten Rivals*. Oxford.
Nisbet, R.G.M. and M. Hubbard (1978). *A Commentary on Horace: Odes, Book II*. Oxford.
Nisbet, R.G.M. and N. Rudd (2004). *A Commentary on Horace: Odes, Book III*. Oxford.
Noreña, C.F. (2007). 'The Social Economy of Pliny's Correspondence with Trajan', *AJPh* 128: 239–77.
Önnerfors, A. (1976). 'Traumerzählung und Traumtheorie beim Älteren Plinius', *RhM* 119: 352–65.
Offermann, H. (1993). 'Offenheit oder Maskierung: Plinius', *Anregung* 39: 83–92, 162–71.
Oliensis, E. (1995). 'Life After Publication: Horace, *Epistles* 1.20', *Arethusa* 28: 209–26.
Onorato, M. (2020). '*Velut de quodam speculo formatum*: l'intertestualità sidoniana tra teoria e prassi', in A. Di Stefano and M. Onorato (eds.). *Lo specchio del modello. Orizzonti intertestuali e Fortleben di Sidonio Apollinare*. Naples: 13–53.
Oost, S.I. (1958). 'The Career of M. Antonius Pallas', *AJPh* 79: 113–39.
O'Rourke, D. and A. Pelttari (forthcoming). 'Intertextuality', in R. Gibson and C. Whitton (eds.). *The Cambridge Critical Guide to Latin Literature*. Cambridge.
O'Sullivan, T.M. (2011). *Walking in Roman Culture*. Cambridge.
Otto, N. (2009). *Enargeia. Untersuchungen zur Charakteristik alexandrinischer Dichtung*. Stuttgart.
Pagán, V. (2010). 'The Power of the Epistolary Preface from Statius to Pliny', *CQ* 60: 194–201.
Page, S. (2015). *Der ideale Aristokrat. Plinius der Jüngere und das Sozialprofil der Senatoren in der Kaiserzeit*. Heidelberg.
Papanghelis, T.D., S.J. Harrison and S. Frangoulidis (eds.) (2013). *Generic Interfaces in Latin Literature*. Berlin.
Paton, W.R. (1916–18). *The Greek Anthology*, 5 vols. London.
Pausch, D. (2004). *Biographie und Bildungskultur. Personendarstellungen bei Plinius dem Jüngeren, Gellius und Sueton*. Berlin.

Pavis D'Escurac, H. (1985). 'Pline le Jeune et l'affranchi Pallas', *Index* 13: 313–25.
Pavlovskis, Z. (1973). *Man in an Artificial Landscape: The Marvels of Civilization in Imperial Roman Literature*. Leiden.
Peachin, M. (2004). *Frontinus and the Curae of the Curator Aquarum*. Stuttgart.
Pecere, O. (1990). 'I meccanismi della tradizione testuale', in G. Cavallo, P. Fedeli and A. Giardina (eds.). *Lo spazio letterario di Roma antica*, vol. 3: *La ricezione del testo*. Rome: 297–386.
Pepe, L. (1958). 'Petronio conosce l'epistolario di Plinio', *GIF* 11: 289–94.
Peterson, W. (1970). *Tacitus. Dialogus*. Revised by M. Winterbottom. Cambridge, MA.
Pflips, H. (1973). *Ciceronachahmung und Ciceroferne des jüngeren Plinius. Ein Kommentar zu den Briefen des Plinius über Repetundenprozesse (epist. 2,11; 2,12; 3,9; 4,9; 5,20; 6,13; 7,6)*. Dissertation, Münster.
Picone, G. (1978). *L'eloquenza di Plinio: teoria e prassi*. Palermo.
Pitcher, R.A. (1999). 'The Hole in the Hypothesis: Pliny and Martial Reconsidered', *Mnemosyne* 52: 554–61.
Pittà, A. (2015). *M. Terenzio Varrone, de vita populi Romani. Introduzione e commento*. Pisa.
Porter, R. and G.S. Rousseau (1998). *Gout: The Patrician Malady*. Yale.
Potter, D.S. (1999). *Literary Texts and the Roman Historian*. London.
Power, T. (2010). 'Pliny, Letters 5.10 and the Literary Career of Suetonius', *JRS* 100: 140–62.
  (2014). 'Calvus' Poetry in Suetonius and Pliny, Letters 5.3', *Athenaeum* 102: 543–5.
Price, J.J. (2014). 'A Curious Case: Pliny Does Not Write History (*Ep.* 5.8)', *SCI* 33: 171–89.
Quadlbauer, F. (1958). 'Die *genera dicendi* bei Plinius d. J.', *WS* 71: 56–111.
Rabinovitch, M. (1947). *Der Delphin in Sage und Mythos der Griechen*. Dornach.
Rackham, H. (1952). *Pliny. Natural History*, vol. 9: *Books 33–35*. Cambridge, MA.
Radice, B. (1969). *Pliny: Letters and Panegyricus*, 2 vols. Cambridge, MA.
Radicke, J. (2003). 'Der öffentliche Privatbrief als "kommunizierte Kommunikation" (Plin. *Epist.* 4,28)', in Castagna and Lefèvre (2003): 23–34.
Ratti, S. (2015). 'Relire le *Satyricon*: Pline le Jeune et les chrétiens, cibles du roman secret d'un affranchi cultivé', *Anabases* 22: 99–145.
Rawson, E. (1985). *Intellectual Life in the Late Roman Republic*. London.
Rémy, B. (1976). 'Ornati et ornamenta quaestoria, praetoria et consularia sous le haut empire romain', *REA* 78–79: 160–98.
Richlin, A. (2003). 'Gender and Rhetoric: Producing Manhood in the Schools', in M. Golden and P. Toohey (eds.). *Sex and Difference in Ancient Rome*. Edinburgh: 74–90.
Rieks, R. (1967). *Homo, humanus, humanitas: Zur Humanität in der lateinischen Literatur des ersten nachchristlichen Jahrhunderts*. Munich.

Riffaterre, M. (1978). *Semiotics of Poetry*. Bloomington.
Riggsby, A.M. (1995). 'Pliny on Cicero and Oratory: Self-Fashioning in the Public Eye', *AJPh* 116: 123–35.
Rimell, V. (2008). *Martial's Rome. Empire and the Ideology of Epigram*. Cambridge.
Roberts, C.H. and T.C. Skeat (1983). *The Birth of the Codex*. London.
Rocca-Serra, G. (1990). '*Imitatio Alexandri* et stoïcisme: Manilius et Silius Italicus', in J.-M. Croisille (ed.). *Neronia IV. Alejandro Magno, modelo de los emperadores romanos. Actes du IVe Colloque international de la SIEN*. Brussels: 379–87.
Rocchi, S. (2015). 'Plinius, Brief 8,17: Eine Überschwemmung des Tiber und des Aniene. Text, Textkritik und Intertextualität', *Gymnasium* 122: 389–402.
  (2021). 'Corinthian Bronzes and Vases from Pliny the Elder to Pliny the Younger (in the Light of a Passage by Cicero)', in A. Anguissola and A. Grüner (eds.). *The Nature of Art. Pliny the Elder on Materials*. Leiden: 217–23.
Rocchi, S. and C. Mussini (eds.) (2017). *Imagines Antiquitatis. Representations, Concepts, Receptions of the Past in Roman Antiquity and the Early Italian Renaissance*. Berlin.
Röcke, W. and H.R. Velten (eds.) (2005). *Lachgemeinschaften: Kulturelle Inszenierungen und soziale Wirkungen von Gelächter im Mittelalter und in der frühen Neuzeit*. Berlin.
Rogers, R.S. (1931). 'Quinti Veranii, Pater et Filius', *CPh* 26: 172–7.
Rolfe, J.C. (1997–98). *Suetonius. Lives of the Caesars. Lives of Illustrious Men*, 2 vols. Cambridge, MA (first edition 1914).
Roller, M.B. (1998). 'Pliny's Catullus: The Politics of Literary Appropriation', *TAPA* 128: 265–304.
  (2001). *Constructing Autocracy: Aristocrats and Emperors in Julio-Claudian Rome*. Princeton.
  (2018). 'Amicable and Hostile Exchange in the Culture of Recitation', in König and Whitton (2018b): 183–207.
Roman, L. (2006). 'A History of Lost Tablets', *ClAnt* 25: 351–88.
Rosen, R. (2015). 'Laughter', in P. Destrée and P. Murray (eds.). *A Companion to Ancient Aesthetics*. Chichester: 455–71.
Ross, D.O. (1975). *Backgrounds to Augustan Poetry. Gallus, Elegy and Rome*. Cambridge.
Rossiter, J.J. (2003). 'A Shady Business: Building for the Seasons at Pliny's Villas', *Mouseion* 3: 355–62.
Roth, U. (2016). 'Liberating the *Cena*', *CQ* 66: 614–34.
Rouse, R.H. and M.D. Reeve (1983). 'Cicero / Speeches', in L.D. Reynolds (ed.). *Texts and Transmission. A Survey of the Latin Classics*. Oxford: 54–98.
Rouse, W.H.D. (1924). *Lucretius. On the Nature of Things*. Revised by M.F. Smith. Cambridge, MA.
Rousselle, A. (1992). 'Body Politics in Ancient Rome', in P. Schmitt Pantel (ed.). *A History of Women: From Ancient Goddesses to Christian Saints*. Cambridge, MA: 297–336.

Russell, D. (2002). *Quintilian. The Orator's Education*, 5 vols. Cambridge, MA.
Rutledge, S.H. (2001). *Imperial Inquisitions: Prosecutors and Informants from Tiberius to Domitian.* London.
  (2010). 'Oratory and Politics in the Empire', in W. Dominik and J. Hall (eds.). *A Companion to Roman Rhetoric.* Oxford: 109–21.
Salles, C. (1981). '*Assem para et accipe auream fabulam*: Quelques remarques sur la littérature populaire et le répertoire des conteurs publics dans le monde romain', *Latomus* 40: 3–20.
Saylor, C. (1972). 'The Emperor as *Insula*: Pliny *Epist.* 6.31', *CPh* 67: 47–51.
  (1982). 'Overlooking Lake Vadimon: Pliny on Tourism (*Epist.* 8.20)', *CPh* 77: 139–44.
Sblendorio Cugusi, M.T. (1982). *M. Porci Catonis orationum reliquiae [...].* Turin.
  (2001). *Opere di Marco Porcio Catone Censore*, vol. 1. Turin.
Scarcia, R. (1985). '*Ad tantas opes processit*. Note a Plinio il Giovane', *Index* 13: 289–312.
Schanz, M. and C. Hosius (1935). *Geschichte der römischen Litteratur bis zum Gesetzgebungswerk des Kaisers Justinian. Zweiter Teil: Die römische Litteratur in der Zeit der Monarchie bis auf Hadrian.* Munich (fourth edition).
Scheffer, J. (I. Schefferus) (1675). 'In C. Plinium Caecilium Secundum notae', in I. Schefferus. *Lectionum academicarum liber.* Hamburg: 59–109.
Schenk, P. (1999). 'Formen von Intertextualität im Briefkorpus des jüngeren Plinius', *Philologus* 143: 114–34.
Schlegel, C.M. (2005). *Satire and the Threat of Speech. Horace's Satires, Book 1.* Madison, WI.
Schmeling, G. (2011). *A Commentary on the Satyrica of Petronius.* Oxford.
Schönberger, O. (1990). 'Die Vesuv-Briefe des jüngeren Plinius (VI 16 und 20)', *Gymnasium* 97: 526–48.
Schröder, B.J. (2001). 'Literaturkritik oder Fauxpas? – Zu Plin. *epist.* 6, 15', *Gymnasium* 108: 241–7.
Schubert, C. (2015). 'Nepos als Biograph: der Tod des Atticus', *RhM* 158: 260–303.
Schuster, M. (1958). *Plinius Minor*, Lipsiae.
Schwartz, J. (1969). 'Le fantôme de l'Académie', in J. Bibauw (ed.). *Hommages à M. Renard*, vol. 1. Brussels: 671–6.
Schwerdtner, K. (2015). *Plinius und seine Klassiker: Studien zur literarischen Zitation in den Pliniusbriefen.* Berlin.
Seider, R. (1979). 'Beiträge zur Geschichte und Paläographie der antiken Cicerohandschriften', *Bibliothek und Wissenschaft* 13: 101–49.
Seif, K.P. (1973). *Die Claudiusbücher in den Annalen des Tacitus.* Dissertation, Mainz.
Setaioli, A. (2016). 'Ancora sul *maximus poetarum* (Sen. *brev.* 2.2)', in B. Pieri and D. Pellacani (eds.). *Si verba tenerem: Studi sulla poesia latina in frammenti.* Berlin: 149–56.
Shackleton Bailey, D.R. (1977). *Cicero: Epistulae ad Familiares*, 2 vols. Cambridge.

(1993). *Martial, Epigrams*, 3 vols. Cambridge, MA.
(2001). *Cicero. Letters to Friends*, 3 vols. Cambridge, MA.
(2003). *Statius. Silvae, Thebaid, Achilleid*, 3 vols. Cambridge, MA.
Shannon, K.E. (2013). 'Authenticating the Marvellous: *Mirabilia* in Pliny the Younger, Tacitus, and Suetonius', *Working Papers in Nervan, Trajanic and Hadrianic Literature* 1.9 (6/6/13): 1–26.
Shelton, J.-A. (1987). 'Pliny's Letter 3.11: Rhetoric and Autobiography', *C&M* 38: 121–39.
(2013) *The Women of Pliny's Letters*. Abingdon.
Sherwin-White, A.N. (1962). 'Trajan's Replies to Pliny: Authorship and Necessity', *JRS* 52: 114–25.
(1966). *The Letters of Pliny. A Historical and Social Commentary*. Oxford (with corrected reprint, 1985, 1998).
Sinclair, B.W. (1980). *Valerius Maximus and the Evolution of Silver Latin*, Dissertation, University of Cincinatti.
Spahlinger, L. (2005). *Tulliana simplicitas. Zur Form und Funktion des Zitats in den philosophischen Dialogen Ciceros*. Göttingen.
Stadter, P.A. (2006). 'Pliny and the Ideology of Empire: The Correspondence with Trajan', *Prometheus* 32: 61–76.
Stärk, E. (1995). *Kampanien als geistige Landschaft. Interpretationen zum antiken Bild des Golfs von Neapel*. Munich.
Stebbins, E. (1929). *The Dolphin in the Literature and Art of Greece and Rome*. Menasha, WI.
Steel, C.E.W. (2001). *Cicero, Rhetoric, and Empire*. Oxford.
(2014). 'The Roman Senate and the Post-Sullan *Res Publica*', *Historia* 63: 323–39.
Stefani, G. (2011). 'Das Datum des Vesuvausbruchs 79 n. Chr.', in H. Meller and J.-A. Dickmann (eds.). *Pompeji – Nola – Herculaneum: Katastrophen am Vesuv*. Munich: 81–4.
Stevens, B. (2009). 'Pliny and the Dolphin – or a Story about Storytelling', *Arethusa* 42: 161–79.
Stoffel, C. (2017). '*otium Campanum* – Silius im Ruhestand (Plin. *epist.* 3,7), Hannibal in Capua (Sil. 11)', *Hermes* 145: 375–85.
Storchi Marino, A. (1995). 'Tra fonti documentarie e letteratura: il caso di Pallante da *insolens* a *sublimatus*', in S. Cerasuolo (ed.). *Mathesis e philia. Studi in onore di Marcello Gigante*. Naples: 187–214.
Strunk, T.E. (2012). 'Pliny the Pessimist', *G&R* 59: 178–92.
(2013). 'Domitian's Lightning Bolts and Close Shaves in Pliny', *CJ* 109: 88–113.
Stucchi, S. (2015). 'Lutto, dolore e *dignitas* in Plinio il Giovane', in Devillers (2015a): 183–96.
Sullivan, J.P. (1991). *Martial: The Unexpected Classic. A Literary and Historical Study*. Cambridge.
Summerson Carr, E. (2010). 'Enactments of Expertise', *Annual Review of Anthropology* 39: 17–32.

Sutton, E.W. and H. Rackham (1942). *Cicero, De oratore*, 2 vols. Cambridge, MA.
Syme, R. (1991). *Roman Papers VII*, ed. A.R. Birley. Oxford.
Talbert, R.J.A. (1984). *The Senate of Imperial Rome*. Princeton.
Tamás, Á. (2020). 'The Art of Framing. Pliny the Younger, *Epistles* 4.27', in P. Hegyi (ed.). *Tradition and Innovation in Literature. From Antiquity to the Present*. Budapest: 29–44.
Tarrant, R.J. (2012). *Virgil. Aeneid Book XII*. Cambridge.
Tempest, K. (2011). *Politics and Persuasion in Ancient Rome*. London.
Thomas, R. (1988). *Virgil: Georgics. Edited with Commentary*, 2 vols. Cambridge.
 (1999) *Reading Virgil and his Texts: Studies in Intertextuality*. Ann Arbor
Thomson, D.F.S. (1997). *Catullus, Edited with a Textual and Interpretative Commentary*. Toronto.
Thorsteinsson, R. (2003). *Paul's Interlocutor in Romans 2. Function and Identity in the Context of Ancient Epistolography*. Stockholm (reprint: 2015, Eugene, OR).
Thraede, K. (1970). *Grundzüge griechisch-römischer Brieftopik*. Munich.
Tischer, U. (2010). 'Aspekte des Zitats. Überlegungen zur Anwendung eines modernen Konzepts auf antike lateinische Texte', in U. Tischer and A. Binternagel (eds.). *Fremde Rede – Eigene Rede. Zitieren und verwandte Strategien in antiker Prosa*, Frankfurt am Main: 93–109.
 (2018). *Zitat und Markierung. Signalisieren und Erfassen von Zitaten in römischer Prosa*. Habilitation treatise, Univ. Potsdam.
 (2019). 'Quotations in Roman Prose as Intermedial Phenomena', in Dinter and Reitz-Joosse (2019): 34–50.
Torelli, M. (2017). 'The Etruscan Legacy', in A. Naso (ed.). *Etruscology*, vol. 1. Berlin: 685–720.
Traub, H.W. (1955). 'Pliny's Treatment of History in Epistolary Form', *TAPA* 86: 213–32.
Trinacty, C.V. (2020). 'Answering the *Natural Questions*: Pliny's *Ep.* 4.30 and *Ep.* 8.20', *CJ* 116: 82–99.
Trisoglio, F. (1972). *La personalità di Plinio il Giovane nei suoi rapporti con la politica, la società e la letteratura*. Turin.
 (1973). *Opere di Plinio Cecilio Secondo*, 2 vols. Turin.
Tueller, M.A. (2008). *Look Who's Talking: Innovations in Voice and Identity in Hellenistic Epigram*. Leuven.
Tyrrell, R.Y. and L.C. Purser (1918). *The Correspondence of M. Tullius Cicero*, vol. 4. Dublin (second edition).
Tzounakas, S. (2007). '*Neque enim historiam componebam*: Pliny's First Epistle and his Attitude towards Historiography', *MH* 64: 42–54.
 (2011). 'Seneca's Presence in Pliny's *Epistle* 1.12', *Philologus* 155: 346–60.
 (2012). 'Pliny and his Elegies in Icaria', *CQ* 62: 301–6.
 (2014). 'Martial's Pliny as Quoted by Pliny', *C&M* 64: 247–68.
 (2015). 'Pliny as the Roman Demosthenes', in Devillers (2015a): 207–18.
Uden, J. (2015). *The Invisible Satirist. Juvenal and Second-Century Rome*. Oxford.

Urban, R. (1979). 'Tacitus und die *Res gestae divi Augusti*. Die Auseinandersetzung des Historikers mit der offiziellen Darstellung', *Gymnasium* 86: 59–74.
Ussani, V. (1971). 'Leggendo Plinio il Giovane, II. Oratio – historia', *RCCM* 13: 70–135.
Van Buren, A.W. (1905). 'Note on Pliny, *Epp.* III. 6, IX. 39', *CR* 19: 446–7.
Van Dam, H.-J. (1984). *Publius Papinius Statius Silvae Book II: A Commentary*. Leiden.
Van den Berg, C. (2014). 'Intratext, Declamation and Dramatic Argument in Tacitus' *Dialogus de oratoribus*', *CQ* 64: 298–315.
Van der Blom, H. (2010). *Cicero's Role Models: The Political Strategy of a Newcomer*. Oxford.
Van Hooff, A.J.L. (1990). *From Autothanasia to Suicide: Self-killing in Classical Antiquity*. London.
Vasaly, A. (2009). 'Domestic Politics and the First Action of the *Verrines*', *ClAnt* 28: 101–37.
Venini, P. (1952). 'Le parole Greche nell'epistolario di Plinio', *RIL* 85: 259–69.
Vessey, D.W.T.C. (1971). 'Thoughts on Tacitus' Portrayal of Claudius', *AJPh* 92: 385–409.
  (1974). 'Pliny, Martial and Silius Italicus', *Hermes* 102: 109–16.
Vince, C.A. and J.H. Vince (1926). *Demosthenes, Orations 18–19: De Corona, De Falsa Legatione*. Cambridge, MA.
von Baumhauer, M.M. (1842). Περὶ τῆς εὐλόγου ἐξαγωγῆς. *Veterum philosophorum praecipue Stoicorum doctrina de morte voluntaria*. Dissertation, Trier.
Wallace-Hadrill, A. (1983). *Suetonius: The Scholar and his Caesars*. London.
  (1990). 'Pliny the Elder and Man's Unnatural History', *G&R* 37: 80–96.
Walsh, P.G. (ed.) (2006). *Pliny the Younger: Complete Letters. Translated with an Introduction and Notes*. Oxford.
Wankel, H. (1976). *Demosthenes, Rede für Ktesiphon über den Kranz*, 2 vols. Heidelberg.
Wardle, D. (2014). *Suetonius: Life of Augustus*. Oxford.
Watson, G. (1994). 'The Concept of "Phantasia" from the Late Hellenistic Period to Early Neoplatonism', *ANRW* II.36.7: 4765–810.
Watson, L. (1990). 'Rustic Suffenus (Catullus 22) and Literary Rusticity', *PLLS* 6: 13–33.
Webb, R. (2009). *Ekphrasis, Imagination and Persuasion in Ancient Rhetorical Theory and Practice*, Farnham.
Weilbach, C. (2020). *Wie Laien und Fachleute über Medizinisches sprechen. Ein Vergleich medizinischer Äußerungen in Briefen und Fachtexten aus der Zeit der späten römischen Republik bis in die frühe Kaiserzeit*, Heidelberg.
Welch, T.S. (2001). '*Est locus uni cuique suus*: City and Status in Horace's *Satires* 1.8 and 1.9', *ClAnt* 20: 165–92.
Wenskus, O. (1993). 'Zitatzwang als Motiv für Codewechsel in der lateinischen Prosa', *Glotta* 71: 205–16.
Wheeler, L.A. (1996). *Ovid: Tristia, Ex Ponto*. Cambridge, MA.

White, P. (1975). 'The Friends of Martial, Statius, and Pliny, and the Dispersal of Patronage', *HSPh* 79: 265–300.
Whitton, C.L. (2010). 'Pliny, *Epistles* 8.14: Senate, Slavery and the *Agricola*', *JRS* 100: 118–39.
  (2012). '"Let us Tread our Path Together": Tacitus and the Younger Pliny', in V.E. Pagán (ed.). *A Companion to Tacitus*. Malden, MA: 345–68.
  (2013a). *Pliny the Younger. Epistles Book 2*. Cambridge.
  (2013b). 'Trapdoors: The Falsity of Closure in Pliny's *Epistles*', in F. Grewing, B. Acosta-Hughes and A. Kirichenko (eds.). *The Door Ajar: False Closure in Greek and Roman Literature and Art*. Heidelberg: 43–61.
  (2014). 'Minerva on the Surrey Downs: Reading Pliny (and Horace) with John Toland', *CCJ* 60: 127–57.
  (2015a). 'Grand Designs: Unrolling *Epistles* 2', in Marchesi (2015a): 109–43.
  (2015b). 'Pliny on the Precipice (*Ep.*, 9.26)', in Devillers (2015a): 219–37.
  (2015c). 'Pliny's Progress: On a Troublesome Domitianic Career', *Chiron* 45: 1–22.
  (2018). 'Quintilian, Pliny, Tacitus', in König and Whitton (2018b): 37–62.
  (2019). *The Arts of Imitation in Latin Prose. Pliny's Epistles / Quintilian in Brief*. Cambridge.
  (forthcoming). *Tacitus Revoiced. Reading the Histories with Pliny the Younger*.
Whitton, C.L. and R.K. Gibson (2016). 'Readers and Readings of Pliny's *Epistles*', in Gibson and Whitton (2016): 1–48.
Williams, C.A. (2004). *Martial's Epigrams Book Two*. Oxford.
  (2013). 'When a Dolphin Loves a Boy: Some Graeco-Roman and Native American Love Stories', *ClAnt* 32: 200–42.
Williams, G.D. (2003). *Seneca, De Otio; De Brevitate Vitae*. Cambridge.
  (2014). '*On the Shortness of Life*', in E. Fantham, H.M. Hine, J. Ker and G.D. Williams (trans.). *Seneca: Hardship and Happiness*. Chicago: 105–39.
Williams, K.F. (2006). 'Pliny and the Murder of Larcius Macedo', *CJ* 104: 409–24.
Williams, W. (1990). *Pliny: Correspondence with Trajan from Bithynia (Epistles X); Translated, with Introduction and Commentary*. Warminster.
Wills, J. (1996). *Repetition in Latin Poetry: Figures of Allusion*. Oxford.
Wilson, M. (1997). 'The Subjugation of Grief in Seneca's *Epistles*', in S.M. Braund and C. Gill (eds.). *The Passions in Roman Thought and Literature*. Cambridge: 48–67.
Winniczuk, L. (1975). 'The Ending Phrases in Pliny's "Letters" (Contribution to the Epistolography)', *Eos* 63: 319–28.
Winsbury, R. (2014). *Pliny the Younger: A Life in Roman Letters*. London.
Winterbottom, M. (1974). *The Elder Seneca*, 2 vols. Cambridge, MA.
Wolff, É. (2003). *Pline le Jeune ou Le refus du pessimisme: Essai sur sa correspondance*. Rennes.
Wolpert, A. (2003). 'Addresses to the Jury in the Attic Orators', *AJPh* 124: 537–55.

Woodman, A.J. (1988). *Rhetoric in Classical Historiography. Four Studies*. Oxford.
  (1998). 'Review of D.S. Potter, *Literary Text and the Roman Historian*', *Histos* 2: 308–16.
  (2012). 'Pliny on Writing History: *Epistles* 5.8', in A.J. Woodman (ed.). *From Poetry to History: Selected Papers*. Oxford: 223–42.
  (2014). *Tacitus. Agricola*. With C.S. Kraus. Cambridge.
Woodman, A.J. and R.H. Martin (1996). *The Annals of Tacitus. Book 3*. Cambridge.
Woolf, G. (1998). *Becoming Roman: The Origins of Provincial Civilization in Gaul*. Cambridge.
  (2006). 'Pliny's Province', in T. Bekker-Nielsen (ed.). *Rome and the Black Sea Region: Domination, Romanisation, Resistance*. Åarhus: 93–108 (= in Gibson and Whitton 2016: 442–60).
  (2015). 'Pliny/Trajan and the Poetics of Empire', *CPh* 110: 132–51.
Wooten, C.W. (1979). 'Unnoticed Medical Language in Demosthenes', *Hermes* 107: 157–60.
Worthington, I. (2013). *Demosthenes of Athens and the Fall of Classical Greece*. Oxford.
Wray, D. (2007). 'Wood: Statius' *Silvae* and the Poetics of Genius', *Arethusa* 40: 127–43.
Yardley, J.C. (1972). '*Prisce iubes* again', *CR* 22: 314–15.
Yunis, H. (2001). *Demosthenes: De Corona*. Cambridge.
Zeiner, N. (2005). *Nothing Ordinary Here: Statius as Creator of Distinction in the Silvae*. London.
Zerbini, L. (2006). 'Il piacere di vivere in villa: testimonianze letterarie', in J. Ortalli (ed.). *Vivere in villa: le qualità delle residenze agresti in età romana*. Florence: 11–18.

General Subject Index

Achilles (shield of), 199, 201, 211–12
acta senatus, 250
addressees, *See also* under individual names
  distribution of (in Book 6), 48–9
  as interlocutors, 1
  joking with, 25, 225, 273–7
  personal interest of, 23, 146, 165
Aeneas, 10, 52, 190
  shield of, 199, 201, 211–12
aerarium Saturni, 76, 126, 220–1, 249, 250
Aeschines, 5, 65, 103–5, 110, 266
Agricola, 45, 75
Agrippina, 251, 252
Alexandrian footnote, 9, 10, 151
Alsium, 10, 50, 56
alter-textuality, 9, 25, 180, 284, 297
Anaxagoras, 32
anecdotes, 4, 5, 10, 40, 41
Annius Severus, 128
anthology, 16
antiquarian writing, 25, 244, 249
Aper, 61–2, 64, 124
Aratus, 199, 212
Archilochus, 263
Archimedes' tomb (verses on), 244
Aristotle, 11, 175
Arrianus Maturus, 2
Arrius Antoninus, 18, 30–5, 41, 265
Artemidorus, 183
Arulenus Rusticus, 262
Asinius Pollio, 19, 65
Athens, 31, 37, 103, 104, 105, 110
  plague of 430 BC, 36–7, 42
Augustus, 120, 246, 275
  Augustan period, 5, 6, 7, 56, 134
  autobiography, 246

Baebius Massa, 125, 257
Baetica, 2
Barea Soranus, 253

biography, 11, 13, 112, 183, 245, 261, 275, 282, 299–300
  autobiography, 219–20, 224, 246
  biographical de-concretisation, 220, 221, 225, 239
Bithynia-Pontus, 69, 72, 81–2, 85, 88, 93, 95

Caelius, 65
Calestrius Tiro, 151
Callimachus (and his poetics), 18, 65, 192, 261, 265
  Aetia, 192, 261
Calpurnia, 25, 49, 50, 54, 113, 139, 144, 281, 284–6, 288–9, 290–2
Calpurnia Hispulla, 281, 284–9, 291, 292–7
Calpurnius Fabatus, 49, 50, 136, 139
Calpurnius Piso, Lucius, 169–70
Calvisius Rufus, 108
Calvus, 2, 16, 17, 65
Campania, 50, 169, 182, 183
Caninius Rufus, 2, 3, 4, 23, 24, 133, 167, 178, 181–2, 183, 187–99
Cassius Longinus, 20, 175, 176
Catius Lepidus, 264, 266
Cato the Censor, 116, 117
  definition of the orator, 266
  oration against Quintus Sulpicius, 116
Cato the Younger, 263
Catullus, 13, 16–19, 21, 22, 25, 47, 54, 55, 64, 138, 223, 260, 263–4, 269–70, 274–7, 285, 302
cena (dinner), 4, 135
Centum Cellae, 50, 56
Centumviral court, 5, 49, 57, 61, 62, 63, 64, 259, 282, 290, 291, 292, 298
Cicero, 2, 17, 20, 21, 22, 23, 26, 34, 41, 42, 46, 47, 55, 64, 65, 138, 150, 151, 166, 175–81, 184, 193, 227, 231, 244, 245, 261, 276–7, 302
  De finibus, 20
  De officiis, 184

331

Cicero (cont.)
  De oratore, 11
  Epistulae ad familiares, 23, 166, 256–7
  Orator, 30–3
  as Pliny's epistolary predecessor, 13, 149, 165
  rhetorical treatises, 29, 31
  Tusculanae disputationes, 11
  In Verrem, 22, 99–115, 116–26
  quotation of, 124–5
Claudius, 5, 25, 245, 246, 250, 251, 252, 253, 267, 268
Clitumnus (god), 6, 271
Clitumnus (river), 55
clusters of references, 21, 22, 48, 57, 170
cognition, 31, 37
collectors and collections, 120, 121, 123, 173–4, 175
comedy, 11, 13, 198, 223, 229, 230, 232, 245, 259, 267, 269, 271, 277
  palliata, 230, 245
  servus callidus, 245
Como (lake), 55, 56, 136, 187
Comum, 2, 3, 24, 50, 108, 122, 129, 136, 139–40, 181, 196
  Comum inscription, 220
  moral power of, 139, 146
  public library in, 2, 3
consolation, 7, 23, 43, 150–2, 159, 162–3, 169, 302
Corellia Hispulla, 286–9, 303
Corellius Rufus, 23, 139, 150–5, 158, 162, 302
Corinthian bronzes and vases, 6, 18, 22, 117–28
Cornelius Nepos, 3, 19, 261
curiosity, 141, 227–33, 240
Curtius Montanus, 255

Dacian wars, 48, 72, 197
delatores, 101, 112, 126, 155, 162, 180, 257, 262, 301
Demetrius, 11, 224, 259
Demosthenes, 2, 30–1, 41, 65, 110–11, 112, 114, 139, 302
  Against Meidias, 109
  On the Crown, 5, 22, 99–106, 266–7
dialogue (genre), 261
didactic poetry, 7, 23, 24, 166, 177–8, 208, 209, 211–12, 214
Dido, 39, 56
documents (verbatim quotation of), 244, 249, 253
dolphin, 4, 129, 133–6, 137, 143, 197–8, 242–3
Domitian, 2, 4, 49, 75–7, 126, 153, 162, 220, 254, 255–6, 257–8, 262, 263
  death of, 4, 72, 152–3, 220, 221, 239

ekphrasis, 24, 199, 200–1, 209, 211–12
  as a figure of praise, 24, 201, 209, 214–15
elegy, 7, 11, 13, 54, 264, 270, 271
encyclopaedic writing, 22, 93, 94, 95, 135, 138, 139, 140
Ennius, 195
epic poetry, 2, 7, 11, 13, 17, 26, 39, 48, 51, 166, 180, 182, 197, 200, 212
epicedium, 198, 265, *See also* epitaph
Epictetus, 155, 163
Epicurus
  Epicurean philosophy, 18, 20, 157, 166, 175–6, 206, 207, 213
  portraits of, 18
epigram, 7, 13–18, 26, 30, 70, 260, 264, 268, 272, 274, 276, 277, 282
epigraphy, 24, 25, 194, 199, 244, 246, 247, *See also* inscription
epistolography
  ancient epistolary theory, 1, 11, 259, 273
  generic flexibility and interactivity of, 12, 26
  generic mobility of, 8
  as a humble genre, 13, 26
  immanent theory of, 12
  as 'super-genre', 7, 12, 26, 101
epitaph, 6, 16, 183, 195, 247, 265, 268, *See also* epicedium
Esquiline, 232, 237, 238, 239
Euphrates, 4, 183, 222
exemplarity, *exempla*-tradition, 13, 23, 30, 36, 41–2, 43, 46, 48, 49, 56, 57, 59, 64, 123, 138, 226, 246, 258, 299
extra-textuality, 9, 283, 284, 301

Frontinus, 21, 81
  as *curator aquarum*, 79, 88
  De aquis, 22, 70, 78–80, 86–95
Fuscus Salinator, 61

genres
  catalogues of, 11–12
  'crossing of genres', 12
  generic enrichment, 6–7, 101
  generic ventriloquisation, 93

Hadrian, 9
Hellenistic era, 12, 65, 261
Herennius Senecio, 257, 266
Herennius Severus, 3, 18, 19
Herodotus, 41, 168, 244
Hesiod, 23, 65, 166, 177–8, 206, 208
heteroglossia, 22, 69–71, 83, 85, 91, 93
Hippo Diarrhytus, 4, 133
Hippocrates, 175

General Subject Index

historiography, 7, 12, 13, 26, 48, 51, 55, 65, 90, 132, 139, 142, 182, 245, 248–9, 251, 252, 255, 256–7, 258, 261, 302
Homer, 65, 199, 201
   Odyssey, 39, 200–1
   quotations from, 2
Horace, 11, 21, 23–4, 187–8, 191–9, 203, 214, 221–40, 243, 267, 297
   Epistles, 52
   'parade odes', 228
   Sabine farm, 227
   sermo, 24, 233
Hortensius, 102, 106, 107
hybridity, 22, 71
hypertext, 11
hypotext, 10, 13

iambic poetry, 11, 25, 259, 261, 263, 276, 277
Iavolenus Priscus, 259, 270–2, 273
imitation, 17, 24, 29–46, 53, 124, 130, 180, 205, 277, 287, 292, 303
   and *exemplum*, 160
   imitatio e contrario, 261
   limits of, 19
   nature imitating art, 139
immortality, 2, 142, 165, 178, 183, 187, 193, 195, 196, 199, 247, 258, 300
indignation, 12, 25, 241, 243, 245, 247, 248, 249, 259–60, 267–73
informers, *See delatores*
inscription, 6, 127–8, 220, 268, 271, *See also* epigraphy
   the Pallas inscription, 244–9, 258, 267
interdiscursivity, 5–13, 22, 26, 68, 71, 74, 80, 83, 85, 93, 294
intermediality, 20, 24, 122
intratextuality, 25, 72, 158, 165, 167, 190, 198, 281, 282, 283, 284, 286, 289, 301, 302
invective, 2, 24, 25, 26, 70, 259–68, 277, 282
invidia, 180, 261

Julius Florus, 191
Julius Victor, 11, 259
Juvenal, 12, 102, 106, 223, 234, 236, 243, 267

Lacus Vadimonis, *See* Vadimon (lake)
laughter, 25, 243, 259, 260, 262–71, 273, 302
law (Roman) and legal discourse, 7, 70, 77, 79, 82, 84–5, 92, 94, 95, 107, 113, 144–5, 194, 199, 222, 233, 234, 276
Lex Aurelia, 107
libraries, 2, 3, 19, 20, 170
   cultural library, 302
   epistolary library, 23, 170
   literary criticism, 7, 11, 26

Livy, 5, 29, 51, 52, 54, 131, 248
locus amoenus, 24, 189
Lucan, 52
Lucceius, Lucius, 256
Lucceius, addresse of Seneca's *Letters*, 149
Lucillius (epigrammatist), 264–5, 302
Lucretius, 20, 21, 23–4, 29, 30–9, 42, 46, 51, 52, 54, 56, 184, 201–15
   quotation of, 213, 215
lucubratio, 23, 129, 142–6
luxuria, 7, 22, 116–23, 182, 203, 211, 214, 238
lyric poetry, 7, 21, 23

Maecenas, 233, 237–8, 239
   horti Maecenatis, 237, 238, 239, 240
Maecilius Nepos, 18–19
Maecilius or Metilius Nepos, 5
Marius Priscus, 77, 101, 126
Martial, 6, 10, 11, 13, 17, 21, 25–6, 75, 123, 167, 178–80, 223, 234, 236, 238–9, 264, 265, 272, 274, 276, 277, 282, 285, 290–2, 294, 298, 302, 303
Maternus, 58, 59, 63, 64
Messalla, 58, 59, 62, 64, 65, 294, 295
metafiction, 24, 239–40
metaliterary meaning, 41, 45, 81, 95, 171, 191, 192, 277, 297
metaphor, 192, 194, 238, 296–7
   comes-metaphor, 18
   as intertextual marker, 10
   metaphor of the *liber fugitivus*, 196
   return-to-life metaphor, 75
   ship-of-state metaphor, 74
Metrodorus, 157
Mettius Modestus, 262
mime, 245, 269
mimiambs, 30
Minicia Marcella, 43, 158
Minicius Fundanus, 3, 45, 160, 184, 225–6, 228, 229
mirabilia, 22, 129–41, 146, 197, 244
Montanus (identity uncertain), 241, 247, 255
monumentum, 24, 194–6, 199, 247
   funerary monument, 194
moralising and moral values, 22, 99, 105, 109, 116, 118, 119–20, 121, 139, 140, 146, 180, 184, 192, 202–6, 214, 258, 281, 287, 293, 296, 298
Musonius Rufus, 152, 154, 155, 162, 184

Naples (bay of), 50, 53, 54, 56, 167, 200, 212

nature
  art-nature contrast, 212–13
  control over, 7, 24, 201–4, 211, 214
  natural science, 13, See also Pliny the Elder
  and Roman moralising, 139, 202–6, 208, 209, 211
negotium, 24, 130, 146, 187, 196, 219, 220, 221–2, 231
Nero, 5, 52, 120, 149, 155, 162, 164, 166, 168, 177, 180, 253, 255, 263, 265
Nerva, 9, 72, 73, 74, 75, 76, 79, 89, 220, 222, 223, 224, 225, 258
novel, 7, 135
  epistolary novel, 267, 268
numerological parallelism, 24, 191, 224, 227–8, See also paratextuality

obscenity, 260, 263, 268, 276–7
Octavius Rufus, 2, 16, 195
orality, 2, 3–4, 15–16, 20, 65
oratory, 5, 7, 12, 13, 21, 22, 26, 30–1, 48, 49, 57–66, 99–115, 124–6, 178–81, 191, 259, 265–7, 277, 282, 290–2, 294, 295, 298, 302, See also rhetoric
ornamenta praetoria, 250, 251
otium, 3, 23, 24, 130, 146, 173, 174, 181, 182, 187, 190, 196, 219, 220, 221–7, 228, 229, 230–1, 236, 237, 238–9, 240, 270
Ovid, 10, 11, 39, 52, 54, 149, 191, 261, 264
  Metamorphoses, 52, 195

Pallas (freedman), 6, 25, 241–58, 259, 263, 267–8, 273, 302
paradoxography, 4, 7, 25, 26, 139, 242, 243, 244, 271
paratextuality, 228, 240
Passenus Paulus, 270–2
performativity, 65–6, 260
personification, 20, 189, 192, 196, 208
Petronius, 21, 52–4, 55, 193
philosophy, 7, 13, 19–20, 23, 32, 33, 42, 43–4, 149–84, 191, 225, 231, 302
  expulsion of the philosophers from Rome, 4
Plato, 11
  discussion of μίμησις, 19, 20
  middle Platonism, 184
Plautus, 198, 223, 230, 245
  Menaechmi, 223
Pliny the Elder, 18, 49, 51–4, 168, 235–6
  A fine Aufidii Bassi, 251
  Natural history, 21, 22–3, 94–5, 116, 118–21, 129–46, 197, 251
  as a Stoic sage, 132
Pliny the Younger
  attitude towards the Greeks, 139
  as biographer of Spurinna's dead son, 299–300
  De Helvidi ultione, 103, 109, 262
  eclecticism (intertextual), 21, 42
  length of individual letters, 12, 200–1, 247
  letters as a polyphonic work, 1
  mix of public and private in the letters, 3, 74, 76, 80
  opportunistic approach to genres, 21, 23, 149, 165, 184
  and optimism, 49–50, 75, 95, 99, 113, 114
  'orbative letters', 282, 299, 303
  pairs of letters, 25, 50, 54, 78, 84, 85, 89, 241, 263, 273
  Panegyricus, 6, 65, 73–4, 77, 78, 95, 126
  'parade letters', 2, 228
  and pessimism, 22, 48, 50, 63, 72, 99–100, 102, 105, 110, 112–15, 302
  as *praefectus*, 222, 223
    aerarii militaris, 220
    aerarii Saturni, 220
  Pro Attia Viriola, 62
  proemial sequence, 187
  reworking of the letters in view of publication, 128
  ring composition, See Pliny the Younger: symmetry in the *Epistles*
  senate (Pliny's presentation of), 25, 77–9, 80, 110, 248–58, 268–70, 299, 301, 302
  symmetry in the *Epistles*, 49, 81, 92, 243, 291
  use of Greek words, 105, 166, 175, 177
  varietas and variety, 21, 26, 46, 71, 103, 114, 139, 164, 165, 221, 236
Plutarch, 102, 184, 225
poetae novi, 192, 269–70
poetology, 38, 192
Pollius Felix, 200, 201–4, 206–9, 212, 214–15
Pompeius Falco, 15, 16, 17
Pompeius Saturninus, 2
Priam, 56
Propertius, 270
prosimetrum, 16
proverbs, 11, 131
Publicius Certus, 220, 262

Quintilian, 5, 11, 20, 21, 22, 29, 33, 43, 47–8, 55, 57–66, 102, 170, 184, 191, 275
  as optimist, 48, 60–1, 64
quotation, 2, 5, 6, 7, 9–10, 11, 13, 16, 17, 34–5, 51, 63, 102, 103, 108, 124, 157, 191, 213, 215, 231, 238, 249, 259–60, 262, 266, 277, 302

recitation, 3, 6, 16, 18, 112, 259, 262, 264, 265, 266, 270, 271, 272, 273, 299
Regulus, 2, 4, 22, 23, 25, 26, 48, 49, 57, 59, 77, 99–115, 150, 155–62, 180, 184, 241, 255, 259, 261–7, 271, 273, 282, 284, 289–92, 297–303

biography of his son, 112
compared to tyrant, 106
as *delator, See delatores*
rhetoric, 4, 5, 31, 48, 61, 65, 67–8, 73, 74, 75–6, 93, 101, 103, 124–5, 179, 180–1, 184, 190, 192, 196, 225, 226, 228, 243, 250, 252, 277, 287–8, 294, 297, 299, 300, *See also* Cicero: rhetorical treatises, *See also* oratory
rhetorical education, 3
rhetorical question, 40, 102
risus, See laughter
Rome's moral decline, *See* nature and Roman moralising
Rosianus Geminus, 35, 40

Sallust, 29, 54
  Bellum Catilinae, 51
satire, 7, 12, 21, 24, 25, 221–40, 243–4, 259–60, 263, 265, 267–8, 273, 274, 277
sceptic writing, 21, 25, 259–77, 282, 298
senatus consulta, 6, 93, 249, 250, 253, 267
Seneca the Elder, 10, 29
Seneca the Younger, 10, 21, 23, 54, 164–75, 181, 182–3, 184, 198, 203, 214, 227, 234, 264, 302
  consolatory philosophy, 149–63
  Natural questions, 52
  as Pliny's epistolary predecessor, 13, 149, 165
Sentius Augurinus, 13–18
Septicius Clarus, 2
Servilius Vatia, 182–3
Servius Sulpicius, 65
Sibyl, 190
Sicily, 106, 107
  Sicilians, 108, 125
Sidonius Apollinaris, 8, 145
Silius Italicus, 10, 13, 17, 23, 123, 164–84, 198–9
Socrates, 39–42
Sosius Senecio, 151, 184
Stabiae, 53, 54
Statius, 13
  Silvae, 6, 13, 21, 23
    villa poems, 24, 200–15
Stoicism, 23, 132, 149–63, 166–75, 253, 276–7, 302
  Stoic opposition, 2, 101, 112, 162, 184, 262
studia, 2, 3, 4, 130–1, 143, 171, 177, 181, 182, 183, 187, 190, 191, 196
Suetonius, 244, 274–6
  De viris illustribus, 183, 275
  Vita Suetoniana-Donatiana, 275
suicide, 23, 56, 150–5, 162, 167, 168, 302
Sulla, Publius, 175–7
Sullan proscriptions, 166

Tacitus, 2, 3, 13, 21, 22, 47, 48, 49, 55, 64, 132, 142, 241, 254–6, 262–3, 264, 272–3, 295–7, 300, 302
  Agricola, 21, 29, 43–6, 51, 52, 68, 75, 78, 246, 254
  Annals, 245, 251–3
  Dialogus, 29, 48, 57–64, 124, 227, 263, 282, 294
  Histories, 255–7, 302
  as pessimist, 48, 57, 61, 64
technical discourse, 7, 21, 22, 26, 70, 80–2, 90, 91, 92, 93
Terence, 198, 245
  Eunuchus, 229–30
Theophrastus, 223, 230
Thucydides, 266
  quotation of, 266
Tiber, 56
Tiberius, 120
Tibur, 200, 201, 242, 258
Titius Aristo, 4
Titus, 94, 95, 140
Titus Catius, 3, 18, 19, 20
Trajan, 1, 3, 9, 48, 49–50, 56, 64, 67–95, 99, 112–13, 114, 115, 126, 127, 197, 220, 221, 223, 250
Transpadana, 55, 139, 146
Treasury of Saturn, *See aerarium Saturni*
Troy, 51, 56
Tullia, 43
Tuscany, 4, 24, 200, 210, 211

Ummidius Quadratus, 61, 62

Vadimon (lake), 55, 136–7
Valerius Maximus, 21, 29, 39–42, 46, 168, 269
Varro, 117, 244
Verania, 99, 110–11, 155
Vergil, 11, 17, 21, 22, 23–4, 39, 47, 48, 51, 55, 64, 179–80, 190–1, 192, 198, 199, 200, 201, 275
  Aeneid, 52, 54, 55–7, 212
    quotation of, 51–2, 63
  Georgics, 201, 204–6, 208–12, 214–15
    and toil, 206, 208, 209, 210, 211, 214
Vergilius Romanus, 198
Verginius Rufus, 6, 10, 16, 49, 56, 130, 139, 247
Verres, 22, 102, 106–10, 118–26, 255
  compared to tyrant, 106
versus minuti, 16
Vespasian, 120
Vestricius Spurinna, 18, 22, 117–18, 121, 123, 139, 143, 168, 282
  and his dead son Cottius, 299–300, 303
Vesuvius, 5, 47, 50–4, 63, 129, 130–2, 135, 241, 273

Vibius Severus, 19, 20
villas, 7, 24, 56, 167, 176, 235, 237
   Caninius' villa in Comum, 2, 3, 24, 187–99
   Pliny's villas, 24, 200–15, 222, 231
      Laurentine villa, 3, 55, 56, 200, 219, 223, 225, 235, 238, 239
      as Mouseion, 236–9
      Tuscan villa, 4, 50, 200, 201, 203, 209

Pollius' villa, 200, 201, 202, 207, 209
Vatia's villa, 182–3
Vopiscus' villa, 200
Voconius Romanus, 261, 262, 270, 271, 272
Vopiscus, 200, 201, 215

Xerxes, 41, 168

Index Locorum

Archilochus
  fr. 168 W., 2–3: 263
Arrian
  The Discourses of Epictetus
    2.19.24–5: 163
Augustus
  Res gestae divi Augusti
    8.5: 246

Callimachus
  Aetia
    fr. 1.1 Pf.: 261
Cato the Censor
  Oration against Quintus Sulpicius
    orat. fr. 181 Sbl.: 116
Catullus
  1: 19
  10: 223
  16: 16, 260
  22: 18, 269–70
  38: 274
  42: 275–6
  56: 263–4
  61.216–25: 286
  85: 274
Cicero
  De oratore
    2.257: 11
  Epistulae ad Atticum
    4.6.4: 256
    16.3: 261
  Epistulae ad familiares
    5.12: 256
    9.22: 276–7
    15.16.1: 20
    15.19: 175–7
  Orator
    23: 30–1
  Tusculan disputations
    2.26: 11
    5.64–6: 244
  In Verrem
    2.1.58: 107
    2.1.121: 124
    2.2.52: 125
    2.3.7: 102
    2.3.60: 125
    2.3.228: 125
    2.4.5: 124–5
    2.4.49: 22
    2.4.95: 125
    2.4.97–8: 120–1
    2.4.98: 22, 123
    2.5.184: 22
Corpus Inscriptionum Latinarum
  VI 36787: 127
  VI 8686: 127

Demetrius
  De elocutione
    223: 224
    232: 11
Demosthenes
  De corona
    69: 105
    142: 102
    158–9: 104
    291: 266–7

Frontinus
  De aquis
    1: 79, 89
    1–2: 86–7, 88
    2: 90
    4–22: 87
    16: 87–8
    64–86: 88
    88: 91

Frontinus (cont.)
  88–93: 91

Hesiod
  Works and days
    11–13: 178
    20–6: 177–8
Horace
  Epistles
    1.3.28: 191
    1.20: 196
  Odes
    1.1–8: 228
    2.14: 24
    2.14.21–8: 193
    3.30: 24, 194–6
    3.30.1: 187
  Satires
    1.1.24: 243, 267
    1.1.120: 267
    1.4: 297
    1.6: 237
    1.9: 24–5, 221, 224, 227–40
    2.6: 227, 235, 237

Jerome
  Epistles
    53.1: 5
Julius Victor
  Ars rhetorica
    p. 448 Halm: 259
    p. 448.14–16 Halm: 11
Juvenal
  Satires
    1.79: 243, 267

Livy
  Ab urbe condita
    praef. 1: 248
Lucillius
  AP 11.135: 264–5
Lucretius
  De rerum natura
    1.830–3: 32–4
    1.936–41: 38–9
    2.59: 207
    2.61: 207
    4.11–16: 38–9
    4.30: 20
    4.63–4: 20
    4.69: 20
    4.96–7: 20
    5.1361–2: 204–5, 207, 213
    5.1361–78: 24
    5.1362: 210
    5.1367–9: 213
    5.1367–78: 204–5
    5.1368: 207
    5.1368–9: 209
    5.1369: 207
    5.1370: 210
    5.1370–1: 207
    5.1371: 209, 210
    5.1372: 207
    5.1372–3: 210
    5.1374: 210
    5.1376–7: 210
    6.1172–3: 37
    6.1174–7: 37
    6.1178: 37
    6.1178–9: 36–8

Martial
  Epigrams
    1. *praef.*: 276
    1.1.1–2: 264
    1.2: 18
    1.32: 274
    4.80: 272
    6.27.1–4: 286
    6.38: 25–6, 282, 290–2, 303
    7.63: 17, 179, 180
    10.20[19]: 15, 238
    10.20[19].16–17: 123
    10.78.15–16: 17
    11.48: 179, 180
    14.11: 11–12
    14.183–96: 170
Musonius Rufus
  fr. 29: 155

Ovid
  Ars amatoria
    1.453: 191
  Epistulae ex Ponto
    3.9.53–4: 261
  Remedia amoris
    371–88: 11
  Tristia
    1.3: 52
    4.10.1–2: 264

Petronius
  Satyricon
    115.6: 52–4
Plato
  Republic
    394b–c: 11
    596e–602c: 19

Index Locorum

Plautus
  Menaechmi
    453: 223
Pliny the Elder
  Natural history
    praef. 18: 142–3
    praef. 33: 94–5
    2.209: 137
    2.227–33: 136
    9.26: 133–6
    33.148: 116
    33.149–50: 116
    34.6–7: 22, 118–20
    34.48: 18, 22, 118–20
    34.84: 120
    35.5: 18
    35.201: 251
Pliny the Younger
  Epistles
    1.1: 2, 12, 187, 228, 260–1
    1.1–3: 2
    1.1–8: 2, 228
    1.2: 2, 103, 187
    1.2.2: 190
    1.3: 2, 3, 23–4, 167, 181–3, 187–99
    1.5: 2, 261–4, 272, 273, 302
    1.5.1: 4, 220, 255
    1.5.2: 112
    1.5.3: 180
    1.5.12: 109
    1.5.14: 298
    1.5.15: 101
    1.5–6: 25, 272
    1.6: 2, 255, 262–4, 272, 302
    1.7: 2
    1.8: 2–3
    1.9: 3, 24–5, 219–40
    1.10: 4, 220–3, 239
    1.12: 23, 150–5, 158, 162–3, 302
    1.13: 4
    1.13.3: 5
    1.20: 50, 55, 124–5
    1.20.14–15: 4
    2.2: 25, 273–4
    2.3: 5
    2.7: 282, 299
    2.8: 167, 181, 196
    2.10: 16, 195–6
    2.11: 77, 125–6
    2.11.22: 101
    2.14.1: 63
    2.14.10–11: 5
    2.17: 24, 200
    2.17.8: 3
    2.20: 99–115, 161, 271, 302
    2.20.5–6: 155–6
    3.1: 22, 117–18, 121, 123, 143, 168
    3.3: 286–9
    3.4: 125–6
    3.5: 129, 132, 142–3, 168
    3.5.15–16: 235–6
    3.6: 22, 121–3, 127–8
    3.6.5: 6
    3.7: 10, 23, 123, 164–84, 197, 198–9
    3.9: 125, 126
    3.10: 282, 299–300
    3.11: 4–5
    3.13: 74
    3.18: 6, 74
    3.20: 268
    3.21: 15, 16, 238–9
    3.21.1: 167
    3.21.5: 123, 178–9
    4.2: 23, 112, 150, 156–61, 282, 298
    4.3: 30–5, 42, 45
    4.7: 112, 150, 158–9, 161, 162, 264–7, 282, 298–9
    4.7.5: 298
    4.8: 79
    4.9: 125–6
    4.12: 302
    4.13: 3
    4.14: 16, 260, 276–7
    4.14.3: 274
    4.15: 225
    4.18.1: 34–5
    4.19: 25–6, 281–2, 284–97, 303
    4.25: 18, 25, 113, 268–70, 271
    4.26: 18–19
    4.26–8: 13–20
    4.27: 13–19
    4.28: 3, 18, 19–20
    4.30: 129, 136–8
    5.3: 4
    5.6: 24, 50, 200, 201, 209–14
    5.6.6: 4
    5.6.7–11: 203–4
    5.6.13: 203–4
    5.6.41–4: 200–1
    5.6.46: 201
    5.10: 25, 274–6
    5.16: 43–6, 158, 160, 162, 225
    6.2: 49, 57–9, 112–13, 160, 161
    6.4: 48, 54
    6.6: 225
    6.7: 48, 54
    6.8: 54, 125
    6.9: 49
    6.10: 6, 10, 16, 49, 56
    6.11: 49, 57, 59–61, 62

Pliny the Younger (cont.)
  6.15: 270–3, 302
  6.16: 49, 51, 56, 129, 130–2, 136, 142, 241, 272–3, 302
  6.16.7: 142
  6.16.18–21: 53
  6.17: 273
  6.20: 5, 47, 49, 51–5, 56, 129, 131, 241
  6.20.1: 272
  6.21: 54, 61–2, 197
  6.24.4: 56
  6.25: 50
  6.29: 62
  6.31: 56
  6.33: 49, 57, 62–4, 113
  6.33.1: 10
  7.1: 35–42
  7.3.3: 236
  7.4: 11, 16
  7.5: 49
  7.9: 16, 50–1, 55
  7.12: 225
  7.18: 197
  7.25: 197
  7.26.4: 42
  7.29: 6, 25, 241, 242–8, 256, 258, 263, 267–8, 273, 302
  7.33: 125, 256–8
  8.4: 197
  8.4.1: 197
  8.6: 6, 12, 25, 241, 247–56, 258, 267–8, 273, 302
  8.8: 271
  8.8.7: 6
  8.14: 78, 247, 254, 256, 257
  8.20: 23, 129, 136–8, 139
  8.20.1–2: 141
  9.6: 236
  9.13: 262
  9.13.2: 4
  9.13.26: 12
  9.19: 6, 16, 79
  9.33: 4, 129, 133–6, 197–8, 242–3
  9.38: 197
  9.40: 144–5
  10.1: 73–4, 80–1
  10.1–3b: 72–80
  10.1–14: 71, 72, 80, 83
  10.2: 74–6
  10.3a: 76–8, 79
  10.3b: 77–8
  10.13: 80–1
  10.13–14: 85
  10.14: 81
  10.15: 81
  10.15–18: 81
  10.17: 81
  10.17a: 81–2, 84
  10.17a–37: 83–4
  10.17b: 83–4
  10.18: 84
  10.19–22: 84
  10.20: 84
  10.22: 84
  10.23: 84
  10.24: 84
  10.27–30: 84–5
  10.30: 84–5
  10.31: 84–5
  10.32: 84–5
  10.35–6: 85
  10.37: 85–9, 90, 91
  10.38: 89–90
  10.41: 90, 91
  10.56: 94–5
  10.61: 90
  10.62: 90
  10.81.7: 3
  10.90: 91–2
  10.91: 82, 91–2
  Panegyricus
    1: 73
    1–2: 73
    2–3: 74
    4.1–2: 293
    6: 74
    9–10: 73
    10: 73
    76–7: 77

Quintilian
  Institutio oratoria
    praef.: 275
    4.2.44: 57–8
    6.2.7: 191
    10.1.38–131: 64–5
    10.1.122: 60
    10.1.124: 20
    10.2.10: 60

Seneca the Elder
  Suasoriae
    3.7: 11
Seneca the Younger
  De brevitate vitae
    1.1–2: 175
    2.2: 175
    2.4: 174

3.4: 170
7.2: 174
7.6: 174
7.10: 171–2
10.2: 170
10.4: 173
12.2: 173
12.6: 172
12.6–7: 172
12.7: 173
13: 173
14.1: 171
14.2: 171
17.2: 168
De ira
  1.18.3–6: 169–70
De tranquillitate animi
  2.13: 169
  9.4–7: 173
Epistulae morales
  2.3–4: 170
  55: 182–3
  85: 150
  98: 23, 150, 153–4
  99: 23, 150, 156–61
Statius
 Silvae
  1.3: 24, 200
  1.3.2: 213
  1.3.7–8: 213
  1.3.15–17: 213
  1.3.17: 214
  1.3.20–2: 213
  1.3.22–3: 201
  1.3.61: 204
  1.3.81–2: 200
  2.2: 24, 200, 201, 206–9
  2.2.29: 201
  2.2.52: 208, 209, 214
  2.2.52–3: 207, 209, 212
  2.2.52–61: 202–3
  2.2.53: 208, 209
  2.2.55: 204
  2.2.56: 204, 208
  2.2.57: 204, 208
  2.2.58: 207
  2.2.61: 204
  2.2.72–82: 200
  2.2.138–9: 206–7
Suetonius
 Augustus
  69.2: 276

Tacitus
 Agricola
  1.1: 246
  2.2: 254
  3: 75–6
  44–5: 75
  45.1–2: 254
  46.1–4: 43–6
 Annals
  12.53: 251–3
 Dialogus de oratoribus
  2: 124
  7.1: 61
  7.3: 60
  15.1: 61–2
  20.1: 124
  28: 282, 294–6
  28.2: 58–9
  29: 296–7
  38.1: 58–9
  38.2: 63–4
 Histories
  4.42: 255
Terence
 Eunuchus
  553–61: 229–30
Theophrastus
 Characters
  5: 230
  7: 230
  13: 230
  23: 230
Thucydides
 Histories
  2.40.3: 266
Valerius Maximus
 Facta et dicta memorabilia
  7.2.*ext*.1: 39–42
Varro
 De vita populi Romani
  fr. 41 P.: 117
Vergil
 Aeneid
  1.364: 56
  2.3: 10
  6.129–31: 190–1
  6.149–235: 51–2
 Georgics
  1.60–1: 208
  1.60–3: 206
  1.60–70: 24, 205–6
  1.61: 209

Vergil (cont.)
   1.65: 211
   1.65–6: 211
   1.68: 211
   1.69: 208, 211
   3.163–4: 208
Vita Suetoniana-Donatiana
   31: 275

Printed in the United States
by Baker & Taylor Publisher Services